SSAT* & ISEE†

For Private and Independent School Admissions

2010 Edition

OTHER KAPLAN BOOKS

Catholic High School Entrance Exams: COOP, HSPT, TACHS, 2010 Edition

Essay Writing for High School Students: A Step-by-Step Guide

Sharp Math

Sharp Vocab

Sharp Writing

Sharp Grammar

SSAT* & ISEE†

For Private and Independent School Admissions

2010 Edition

by Joanna Cohen, Ed.M.; Darcy L. Galane, J.D.;
and the Staff of Kaplan Publishing

 PUBLISHING

New York

© 2009 by Kaplan, Inc

Published by Kaplan Publishing, a division of Kaplan, Inc.
1 Liberty Plaza, 24th Floor
New York, NY 10006

Printed in the United States of America

10 9 8 7 6 5 4 3 2 1

ISBN: 978-1-4195-5066-9

Kaplan Publishing books are available at special quantity discounts to use for sales promotions, employee premiums, or educational purposes. Please email our Special Sales Department to order or for more information at kaplanpublishing@kaplan.com, or write to Kaplan Publishing, 1 Liberty Plaza, 24th Floor, New York, NY 10006.

Table of Contents

About the Authors ix

Available Online xi

A Note to Parents xiii

A Note to Students: Getting Started xv

PART 1: SSAT WORKSHOP
Chapter 1: Inside the SSAT 3

    The SSAT Exam 3

    Scoring 3

    How to Register 4

Chapter 2: SSAT Specific Verbal Workout: Analogies 5

    The Format 5

    Kaplan Three-Step Method for Analogies 6

    Strong Bridges and Weak Bridges 8

    Six Classic Bridges 9

    Predicting on Three-Term Analogies 10

    Backsolving 11

    Guessing 12

    Practice Questions 14

    Practice Question Answers 16

PART 2: ISEE WORKSHOP
Chapter 3: Inside the ISEE 19

    The ISEE Exam 19

    How to Register 20

    How the ISEE Differs from the SSAT 20

Chapter 4: ISEE Specific Verbal Workout: Sentence Completions 21

    The Format 21

    Kaplan Four-Step Method for Sentence Completions 22

    Picking Up On Clues 24

    Tackling Hard Questions 25

    Practice Questions 28

    Practice Question Answers 29

Chapter 5: ISEE Specific Math Workout: Quantitative Comparisons 31

The Format 31

Kaplan's Five Strategies for QCs 32

Practice Questions 40

Practice Question Answers 41

PART 3: COMMON CONTENT FOR THE SSAT AND ISEE

Chapter 6: SSAT/ISEE Mastery 45

Using the Test Structure to Your Advantage 45

Approaching SSAT/ISEE Questions 47

Managing Stress 49

Chapter 7: Synonyms 51

The Format 51

Kaplan Three-Step Method for Synonyms 52

Avoiding Pitfalls 53

Vocabulary Techniques 54

Practice Questions 58

Practice Question Answers 60

Chapter 8: Critical Reading 61

Reading Strategies 61

SSAT/ISEE Reading Is Different from Everyday Reading!!! 62

Kaplan Four-Step Method for Critical Reading 63

Critical Reading Skills in Action 65

Practice Questions 72

Practice Question Answers 73

Chapter 9: The Essay 75

Introduction to the Essay 75

Kaplan Four-Step Method for Writing 76

Pacing 78

Brainstorming in Action 78

Show, Don't Tell 80

Just the Facts 80

Practice Essay 81

Chapter 10: Introduction to SSAT/ISEE Math 85

How to Approach SSAT/ISEE Math 85

Word Problems 89

Percent Increase/Decrease Problems 90

A Word About Calculators 92

Chapter 11: Arithmetic 93

   Definitions 93

   The Order of Operations 97

   Rules for Divisibility 98

   Fractions and Decimals 98

   Common Percent Equivalencies 101

   Exponents and Roots 102

   Powers of Ten and Scientific Notation 103

   Percents 105

   Average, Median, and Mode 106

   Ratios, Proportions, and Rates 106

   Probability 107

   Strange Symbolism and Terminology 108

   Practice Questions 109

   Practice Question Answers 115

Chapter 12: Algebra 121

   Algebra Concepts 121

   Working with Equations 125

   Working with Inequalities 127

   Practice Questions 128

   Practice Question Answers 131

Chapter 13: Geometry 135

   Lines and Angles 135

   Triangles 137

   Quadrilaterals 142

   Circles 143

   Coordinate Geometry 144

   Practice Questions 148

   Practice Question Answers 157

Chapter 14: Word Problems 163

   Translation 163

   Symbolism Word Problems 164

   Word Problems with Formulas 165

   Backdoor Strategies 165

   Roman Numeral Word Problems 167

   Practice Questions 169

   Practice Question Answers 173

Chapter 15: Managing Your Stress 177

The Week Before the Test 177

The Days Just Before the Test 177

The Night Before the Test 178

The Morning of the Test 179

During the Test 179

After the Test 180

PART 4: SSAT PRACTICE TESTS AND EXPLANATIONS

Chapter 16: SSAT Practice Test 1: Upper-Level 183

Answer Explanations 221

Chapter 17: SSAT Practice Test 2: Upper-Level 237

Answer Explanations 273

Chapter 18: SSAT Practice Test 3: Lower-Level 291

Answer Explanations 323

Chapter 19: Scoring Your SSAT Practice Test 339

PART 5: ISEE PRACTICE TESTS AND EXPLANATIONS

Chapter 20: ISEE Practice Test 1: Upper- and Middle-Level 345

Answer Explanations 378

Chapter 21: ISEE Practice Test 2: Upper- and Middle-Level 395

Answer Explanations 430

Chapter 22: ISEE Practice Test 3: Lower-Level 451

Answer Explanations 483

Chapter 23: Scoring Your ISEE Practice Test 495

PART 6: LEARNING RESOURCES

Chapter 24: Vocabulary Reference 499

Root List 499

Vocabulary List 510

Chapter 25: Math Reference 557

Chapter 26: Writing Skills 571

ABOUT THE AUTHORS

Joanna Cohen received her B.S. in Human Development and Family Studies from Cornell University and her Ed.M. from Harvard University. As an educator, she has taught, conducted research, and written educational materials for students and teachers. Until recently, Ms. Cohen was manager of Kaplan's Pre-College Curriculum.

Darcy L. Galane is the Associate Director of Pre-College Curriculum at Kaplan's Corporate Office. She received a B.A. from UCLA and began teaching SAT and LSAT classes for Kaplan while earning her J.D. at the University of Connecticut School of Law. Having taught and written curriculum for most of Kaplan's courses, Ms. Galane has helped thousands of students to raise their scores on standardized tests.

AVAILABLE ONLINE

FOR ANY TEST CHANGES OR LATE-BREAKING DEVELOPMENTS

kaptest.com/publishing

The material in this book is up-to-date at the time of publication. However, the test makers may have instituted changes in the test after this book was published. Be sure to carefully read the materials you receive when you register for the test. If there are any important late-breaking developments—or any changes or corrections to the Kaplan test preparation materials in this book—we will post that information online at **kaptest.com/publishing**.

FEEDBACK AND COMMENTS

kaplansurveys.com/books

What did you think of this book? We'd welcome your comments and suggestions and invite you to fill out our online survey form at **kaplansurveys.com/books**. Your feedback is extremely helpful as we continue to develop high-quality resources to meet your needs.

A NOTE TO PARENTS

Congratulations! By purchasing this book, you have taken the first step toward helping your son or daughter prepare for the SSAT or ISEE and then go on to private school. Each school has a different requirement policy for admissions exams, so check with your schools of interest to find out which test your child should take. These days, many schools accept either test.

HOW CAN I HELP MY CHILD PREPARE FOR THE EXAM?

This book covers all levels of the SSAT and ISEE: Upper, Middle, and Lower. If your son or daughter is applying to private school at the high-school level, chances are that he or she already studies well alone. Check on his or her progress regularly as the test date nears.

If your child is at the Middle- or Lower-level, you may have to get more involved. Sit down together and write out a study plan. To start, your child should take a practice exam as a diagnostic under timed conditions.

Then, once you have identified the areas that need focus, set up specific study activities.

WHAT DO THE SCORES MEAN?

Scores are designed to measure a student's potential performance in private school—not to measure intelligence.

Each level of the test encompasses more than one grade level, but students are graded only against others in their own grade.

WHAT SHOULD I KNOW ABOUT TEST DAY?

A few things you will want to know about Test Day:

- On the answer sheet during the test, your child must remember to mark his or her current grade level, not the grade he or she will be entering next year.

- No calculators, cell phones, alarm watches, or books will be permitted in the test room.

- Testing normally begins at 9:00 A.M., so students should arrive at the test center by 8:15–8:30 A.M.

- It is possible to get a good score even if some questions are left blank. Many students leave a few questions unanswered.

A NOTE TO STUDENTS: GETTING STARTED

In your hands, you have the best test prep available for the SSAT and ISEE, the admissions tests for private and independent schools. This book covers *all levels* of these tests (grades 4–11):

SSAT

- *Upper-level* (for students currently in grades 8–11)
- *Lower-level* (for students currently in grades 5–7)

ISEE

- *Upper-level* (for students currently in grades 8–11)
- *Middle-level* (for students currently in grades 6 and 7)
- *Lower-level* (for students currently in grades 4 and 5)

Since this book covers all levels of the SSAT and ISEE, you will understandably find certain questions too difficult. While you should try your best to solve all of the questions, do not be discouraged if you cannot. Other students in your age group will find these hard to solve as well, and keeping in mind that your test will be scored in relation to the other students your age, this should help relieve some pressure.

Not every topic covered in this book appears on every test level. Quantitative Comparisons, for instance, do not appear on the Lower-level ISEE, though they do appear on the Upper- and Middle-levels. (They do not appear at all on the SSAT.) At the beginning of each chapter, there is a note indicating what level or test applies to that topic. Keep an eye out for these notes to guide you in your preparation, and skip those chapters that are not relevant.

Ideally, you should take a couple of months to work through this book. That gives you enough time before test day to absorb the strategies thoroughly and often enough so that they become second nature. Do just two or three chapters a week, and let the material sink in slowly.

If you don't have a few months for review, however, don't freak: By working through a chapter or two every day, you can finish this book in a couple of weeks.

Here's how you should approach the review:

1. Read through each chapter completely, learning from the examples and trying the practice questions. Don't just read them: Work through them first as much as you can, before reading the explanation.

2. Read the stress management section in chapter six to set the stage for your training and testing success.

3. Take the practice tests for your level under strictly timed conditions. Score your test, find out where you need help, and then review the appropriate chapters.

4. Give yourself a day of rest right before the real exam.

Don't hesitate to take some time off from your SSAT/ISEE preparation when you need to.

Q. It's two days before the SSAT/ISEE and I'm clueless. What I do?

A. First of all, don't panic. If you have only a day or two to prepare, then you won't be able to prepare thoroughly. But that doesn't mean you should give up. There's a lot you can do. First and foremost, get familiar with the test. And if you don't do anything else, take a full-length practice test under reasonably test-like conditions. When you have finished that, check your answers to see what you didn't get right.

Q: The test is tomorrow. Should I stay up all night studying geometry formulas?

A: The best thing to do now is to stay calm. Read the "Managing Stress Before the Test" chapter at the end of this book to find out the best way to survive—and thrive—on Test Day.

Q: I don't feel confident. Should I just guess?

A: That depends on whether you're taking the SSAT or the ISEE. The SSAT does penalize you for wrong answers (one-quarter of a point), so you want to be careful, but that doesn't mean you should never guess. If you can rule out at least one answer choice, preferably two, you should guess, because you have better odds at guessing correctly. Also, on questions that appear early in a section, more obvious answers will tend to be correct, so you can guess more confidently on those questions. If you're taking the ISEE, you should ALWAYS guess, since there's no wrong-answer penalty.

Q: What's the most important thing I can do to get ready quickly?

In addition to basic math and verbal skills, the SSAT/ISEE mainly tests your ability to take the test. So the most important thing you can do is to familiarize yourself with the directions, the question types, the answer grid, and the overall structure. Read everything carefully—many mistakes are the result of simply not reading thoroughly.

Q. So it's okay to panic, right?

A. No! No matter how prepared you are for the test, stress will hurt your performance, and it's really no fun. Stay confident, and don't cram. So...breathe, stay calm, and remember, it's just a test.

| Part One |

SSAT WORKSHOP

CHAPTER 1:   INSIDE THE SSAT

THE SSAT EXAM

The SSAT has two tests, one for upper-level students and one for lower-level students.

- Upper level (for students currently in grades 8–11)
- Lower level (for students currently in grades 5–7)

Following is a breakdown of the tests. Both levels of the test have the same format.

	Lower-Level	Upper-Level
Math I	25 questions	25 questions (30 min)
Verbal	60 questions	60 questions (30 min)
Reading	40 questions	40 questions (40 min)
Math II	25 questions	25 questions (30 min)
Essay*	one writing prompt (25 min)	

* The essay will not be scored, nor will it be included with your home report, but it will be sent to the schools to which you are applying.

- All questions have five answer choices, (A) through (E).
- You are not permitted to use calculators, dictionaries, or rulers.
- Bring your own pencils and erasers; they will not be provided.

SCORING

The first thing you might notice with respect to grades is that students from other class years are taking the same test as you. Not to worry! You are graded according to your age. In other words, if you're in 9th grade, you aren't expected to get as many questions right as someone in 11th grade, even though you take the same test. One note of caution: You are scored according to the grade level you report on the answer sheet on Test Day. Be sure to indicate your current grade level, not the grade for which you are applying.

Given this fact, you can expect to see questions on the test that may be too hard for you. But just remember, you don't need to get every question right to get a great score.

Your score report will include:

Scaled scores for Verbal, Math, and Reading, in addition to a total scaled score. The scale for the upper-level test is 500–800 (V/Q/R), 1,500–2,400 (Total). For the lower-level test the scale is 440–710 (V/Q/R), 1,320–2,130 (Total).

Percentile ranks for each category, comparing your scores to those of others who have taken the SSAT in the past three years.

Regarding points for each question, each correct answer earns one point. For every wrong answer, one fourth of a point is deducted, though for questions left blank, nothing is deducted.

Scores are mailed to you and your school two to three weeks after you take the test. Make sure you test early enough in the year so that schools will receive your scores by application deadlines.

If you feel that you have not tested well after you depart from the test, you have the option of canceling your score. To do so, you must send your request to SSAT by mail, fax, or email (info@ssat.org). This request must be received no later than the Tuesday immediately following the test date. In that case, canceled scores will not be sent to any of your designated score recipients.

HOW TO REGISTER

The SSAT is given eight times per academic year: October, November, December, January, February, March, April, and June. You may register online, by fax, or by mail. For more information, go to the official test site at ssat.org.

Phone: (609) 683-4440
Email: info@ssat.org
Fax: 800-442-7728 or (609) 683-4507
Mail: SSAT Registration
          CN 5339
          Princeton, NJ 08543

CHAPTER 2: SSAT SPECIFIC VERBAL WORKOUT: ANALOGIES

Analogies appear only **on the SSAT.** If you are not taking the SSAT, you should skip this section.

Analogies may seem frightening because they look pretty weird at first glance. You'll feel better about them as soon as you realize that you speak and think in analogies all the time. Any time you say "my sister is like a slug," you're drawing an analogy between your sister and slugs—perhaps your sister is as gross as a slug, or maybe she's as slow as a slug getting out of bed in the morning. That may not be the kind of relationship that will appear on your test, but the thinking is the same.

Once you get familiar with their format, you'll find that Analogy questions are pretty straightforward, and very predictable. In fact, prepping often gains you more points on Analogies than on any other Verbal question type. With practice, you can even learn to get them right when you don't know all of the vocabulary words involved.

THE FORMAT

The instructions will tell you to select the pair of words that is *related in the same way* as the two words in the beginning of the question. Those two words are called the *stem words*.

1. Flake is to snow as

   (A) storm is to hail.
   (B) drop is to rain.
   (C) field is to wheat.
   (D) stack is to hay.
   (E) cloud is to fog.

In this example, the answer is (B). A flake is a small unit of snow, just as a drop is a small unit of rain.

Did you get the right answer? If so, how did you determine the right answer? Did you just *feel* that one choice was right, or did you try to figure out how the words in the stem were related, then go through the choices one by one? The Kaplan Three-Step Method will help you handle any Analogy question, even the toughest ones, because you'll be approaching every question systematically, rather than just using instincts. Let's see how it works.

KAPLAN THREE-STEP METHOD FOR ANALOGIES

Step 1. Build a bridge.

Step 2. Plug in the answer choices.

Step 3. Adjust your bridge if necessary.

What does it mean to "build a bridge"? A suspension bridge? A steel bridge? No, we're not spanning oceans here; we're bubbling ovals on a piece of paper. Wait a minute and it will all make sense. A bridge expresses the relationship between the words in the stem pair, and building a bridge helps you zone in on the correct answer quickly, and helps you avoid wrong-answer traps. Let's take a closer look to see how it works.

STEP 1: BUILD A BRIDGE

In every Analogy question, there's a strong, definite connection between the two stem words. Your task is to identify this relationship, and then to look for a similar relationship among the answer pairs.

What's a strong, definite relationship?

- The words *library* and *book* have a strong, definite connection. A library is defined as a place where books are kept. *Library is to book as* could be a question stem.

- The words *library* and *child* do not have a strong, definite connection. A child may or may not have anything to do with a library. *Library is to child* would never be a question stem.

In our original example, a good bridge would be "A flake is a small unit of snow." A bridge is a short sentence that relates the two words in the stem, and every pair of stem words will have a strong bridge that links them.

STEP 2: PLUG IN THE ANSWER CHOICES

You figured out how the words *flake* and *snow* are related. Now you need to determine which answer choice relates words in the same way. Don't just rely on your feeling about the words unless you don't know the vocabulary (more on that later). Go through the choices systematically, building bridges between each word pair as you go. Here's how it would work:

Format | **3-Step Method** | Strong & Weak Bridges | Six Classic Bridges | Predicting Answers

If a *flake* is a small unit of *snow*, then . . .

(A) A *storm* is a small unit of *hail*?

(B) A *drop* is a small unit of *rain*?

(C) A *field* is a small unit of *wheat*?

(D) A *stack* is a small unit of *hay*?

(E) A *cloud* is a small unit of *fog*?

Going through the choices, you can see that only one of them makes sense, (B). At this point, you would be done.

STEP 3: ADJUST YOUR BRIDGE IF NECESSARY

If your bridge is very specific, you won't need to go to step 3, but sometimes you will. For example, if you had the question:

Fish is to gill as

(A) oyster is to shell.

(B) penguin is to wing.

(C) whale is to spout.

(D) mammal is to lung.

(E) dolphin is to flipper.

Let's say you made the bridge "A fish has a gill." Then you went to the choices and plugged in that bridge:

(A) An oyster has a shell.

(B) A penguin has a wing.

(C) A whale has a spout.

(D) A mammal has a lung.

(E) A dolphin has a flipper.

Every choice fits! In this case, the bridge was too general, so you'll need to adjust your bridge.

What would a good adjustment be? Try to articulate to yourself the most specific relationship between the words, because the more specific your bridge is, the fewer choices will match it. A good bridge for this pair might be: A *fish uses a gill to breathe*. Now try plugging the bridge into the answer choices.

(A) An oyster uses a shell to breathe?

(B) A penguin uses a wing to breathe?

(C) A whale uses a spout to breathe?

(D) A mammal uses a lung to breathe?

(E) A dolphin uses a flipper to breathe?

Format | **3-Step Method** | Strong & Weak Bridges | Six Classic Bridges | Predicting Answers

It should now be easier to see the correct answer, (D), A mammal uses a lung to breathe.

STRONG BRIDGES AND WEAK BRIDGES

Just to make sure you have your strong and weak bridges straight, try the following exercise. For each phrase, decide whether there is a strong relationship or a weak one.

1. dog is to canine   _____

2. dog is to friendly   _____

3. dog is to kennel   _____

4. dog is to mammal   _____

5. dog is to cat   _____

6. dog is to paw   _____

7. dog is to puppy   _____

8. dog is to hound   _____

9. dog is to bark   _____

10. dog is to biscuit   _____

ANSWERS TO STRONG/WEAK BRIDGES

1. strong	6. strong
2. weak	7. strong
3. strong	8. strong
4. strong	9. strong
5. weak	10. weak

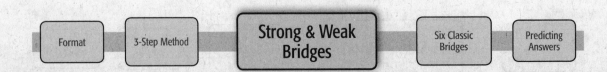

Format | 3-Step Method | **Strong & Weak Bridges** | Six Classic Bridges | Predicting Answers

SIX CLASSIC BRIDGES

There are some bridges that appear on the SSAT/ISEE over and over again. We call these *Classic Bridges* because no matter what other bridges come and go, these tend to stick around. By getting to know these bridges, you'll be able to identify them quickly, saving yourself a lot of time as you go through Analogy questions.

BRIDGE TYPE 1: CHARACTER

One word characterizes the other.
Quarrelsome is to argue [Someone quarrelsome tends to argue.]

BRIDGE TYPE 2: LACK

One word describes what someone or something is *not*.
Coward is to bravery [A coward lacks bravery.]

BRIDGE TYPE 3: FUNCTION

One word names an object; the other word defines its function.
Scissors is to cut [Scissors are used to cut.]

BRIDGE TYPE 4: DEGREE

One word is a greater or lesser degree of the other word.
Deafening is to loud [Something deafening is extremely loud.]

BRIDGE TYPE 5: EXAMPLE

One word is an example of the other word.
Measles is to disease [Measles are a type of disease.]

BRIDGE TYPE 6: GROUP

One word is made up of several of the other word.
Forest is to trees [A forest is made up of many trees.]

> ### I AM, BY DEFINITION, CONFUSED
>
> " When making a bridge, a good rule of thumb is to relate the words in such a way that you'd be able to insert the phrase *by definition* and the relationship would hold true. A poodle, by definition, is a type of dog. However, a poodle does not, by definition, have a collar. If you can't use *by definition* in the sentence that relates the stem words, your bridge isn't strong and it needs to be reworked. "

PREDICTING ON THREE-TERM ANALOGIES

Some analogies will have three terms in the stem and only one word in each answer choice. For example:

Delight is to grin as dismay is to

(A) frown.
(B) smile.
(C) shrug.
(D) stare.
(E) giggle.

Three-term analogies aren't very different from two-term analogies. The key difference is that you need to predict your answer *before* you look at the answer choices. Otherwise, the choices won't make much sense to you! Here's how it works.

First, make your bridge:

A grin shows delight and a —— shows dismay.

Now predict your answer. What might show *dismay*? *Tears,* perhaps, or a *frown.* Look at the answer choices. At this point, it should be easier than a two-term analogy, because you already have one of the two words in the answer.

Does a *frown* show dismay?
Does a *smile* show dismay?
Does a *shrug* show dismay?
Does a *stare* show dismay?
Does a *giggle* show dismay?

As you'll see, (A) is the answer: A frown shows dismay. That makes a lot of sense. Can you see how much harder this would have been if you hadn't gone through the steps of building a bridge and predicting the answer? You would likely be staring blankly at five words. Always predict your answer on three-term analogies, and you'll whiz through them in no time.

Practice your skills of prediction on these stems:

1. Thicket is to bush as grove is to ——.

2. Mason is to brick as carpenter is to ——.

3. Enthusiast is to apathy as miser is to ——.

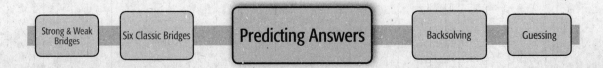

Strong & Weak Bridges   Six Classic Bridges   **Predicting Answers**   Backsolving   Guessing

Now let's see how well you did on predicting:

1. Thicket is to bush as grove is to *tree*.

2. Mason is to brick as carpenter is to *wood*.

3. Enthusiast is to apathy as miser is to *generosity*.

Even with your arsenal of tools, you may run into Analogy questions where you don't know what to do. Perhaps you won't know what a word in the question stem means, or how the words relate to one another. What should you do?

There are a few strategies that will really up your chances of getting the question right, even if you're stuck. How cool is THAT?

WHAT TO DO IF YOU'RE STUCK

" • Backsolving

• Educated guessing

• Remembering context

• Using Word Charge "

BACKSOLVING

What is backsolving? It may sound like an obscure form of chiropractic medicine, but it's actually just a nifty way of approaching Analogies when you can't answer them directly. So how does it work?

Basically, you skip right past the question stem and head straight for the answer choices. You may be wondering, "How you can figure out the answer without knowing what the question is asking?" Well, you can't necessarily figure out the *answer* right away, but you can start to eliminate *clearly* wrong answer choices, leaving fewer options to choose from. When you rule out choices that you know can't be right, the odds are better that you'll pick the right choice from what's left.

Screwdriver is to tool as

(A) animal is to plant.
(B) garden is to bed.
(C) fertilizer is to soil.
(D) tree is to leaf.
(E) rose is to flower.

Even if you didn't know that a screwdriver is a type of tool, what could you rule out? Well, in (A), there's no logical connection between animal and plant, except that they're both living things. Choice (B), garden is to bed, also sounds somewhat off. You could make the argument that a garden has a bed, but does it have to? What about a hanging garden, or a rock garden? You could rule out (B) as having a weak bridge.

BOTH ARE . . . WRONG!

" Watch out for the *Both Are* trap, seen in choice (A) in the screwdriver example: Both *animal* and *plant* are part of a larger group, but there's no connection, by definition, between the words themselves. Bread and bananas are both types of food, but what exactly is their relationship? Bananas aren't a type of bread, a lack of bread, or a function of bread. Watch out for this trap, particularly on harder Analogy questions. "

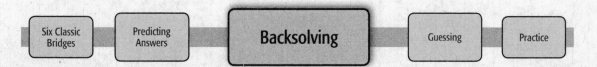

By eliminating even one illogical answer choice, you'll narrow down your choices and have a better chance of getting the question right. Always keep your eye out for *Both Are* traps and *Weak Bridges* as you work through the Analogy section, and you'll rack up lots of points on even the toughest questions.

GUESSING

What if you reach the point where: You can't figure out the bridge for the stem words, you can't rule out wrong answer choices, and you want to cry? Well, first of all, don't cry. It's a waste of time and it makes it difficult to read the questions. You have a few options.

TECHNIQUE 1: MAKE AN EDUCATED GUESS

You know the Six Classic Bridges. You know they show up often on Analogy questions. So even if you don't know the exact definition of one (or both!) words, you could make an educated guess about the bridge. For example, say you saw the stem:

Word is to philologist as

(A) ——————
(B) ——————
(C) ——————
(D) ——————
(E) ——————

What might the bridge be? Well, a *philologist* sounds like a type of person (since it ends in -ologist), and a *word* is a thing, so maybe a philologist does something with words. Philologist is a tricky word, but you could make a great guess by saying that a philologist studies words, which is exactly right!

TECHNIQUE 2: REMEMBER THE CONTEXT

Sometimes a word sounds familiar, but you can't remember why. If that happens, try to think of a place where you may have heard it before. Putting words into context makes it easier to determine their meaning. For example,

Vote is to suffrage as

(A) ——————
(B) ——————
(C) ——————
(D) ——————
(E) ——————

What does *suffrage* mean? Have you heard of the suffrage movement? Or the suffragists? Think about the word *suffrage* in the context of *voting*. What could the words have to do with each other? Well, suffrage is the right to vote, and the movement to give women the right to vote at the beginning of the 20th century was commonly known as the Suffrage Movement. Just looking at the word *suffrage* in isolation might have left you scratching your head, but putting it in context with the concept of voting could get you back on track and help you zone in on the right answer.

TECHNIQUE 3: USE WORD CHARGE

Some words give you the feeling that they're either positive or negative. Use this sense to help you figure out the bridge between words in the stem when you don't actually know what one of them means—or both!

Decide whether the following words are positive or negative:

1. Cruel (+, –) is to clemency (+, –) as
2. Boorish (+, –) is to polite (+, –) as
3. Animated (+, –) is to ecstatic (+, –) as
4. Annoyed (+, –) is to enraged (+, –) as

So how does Word Charge help you find the right answer? Once you determine the charge of the words in the stem pair, you can look for words in the answer choices that have the same charge relationship. When both words in the stem are either positive or negative, both words in the correct answer choice will have the same charge, too, though it may be the opposite charge from the words in the stem. If one stem word is positive and the other is negative, chances are that the right answer will have the same relationship.

So, what charge does each word above have?

1. (–, +)
2. (–, +)
3. (+, +)
4. (–, –)

PRACTICE QUESTIONS

1. Circumference is to circle as

    (A) diameter is to sphere.
    (B) height is to width.
    (C) side is to hexagon.
    (D) perimeter is to square.
    (E) round is to oval.

2. Write is to paper as paint is to

    (A) board.
    (B) canvas.
    (C) brush.
    (D) palette.
    (E) can.

3. Collar is to shirt as

    (A) toe is to shoe.
    (B) cuff is to trousers.
    (C) waist is to belt.
    (D) hat is to head.
    (E) zipper is to button.

4. Hysteria is to control as

    (A) joke is to laughter.
    (B) feeling is to emotion.
    (C) absurdity is to sense.
    (D) calm is to serenity.
    (E) passion is to insanity.

5. Square is to cube as

    (A) dot is to point.
    (B) angle is to triangle.
    (C) rectangle is to parallelogram.
    (D) hexagon is to octagon.
    (E) circle is to sphere.

6. Shark is to aquatic as

    (A) world is to hungry.
    (B) camel is to terrestrial.
    (C) bird is to winged.
    (D) bat is to blind.
    (E) pig is to hairless.

7. Admonish is to mild as castigate is to

    (A) tepid.
    (B) sweet.
    (C) unbeatable.
    (D) uncertain.
    (E) harsh.

8. Abrupt is to gradual as

    (A) corrupt is to virtuous.
    (B) stirring is to sudden.
    (C) sneaky is to criminal.
    (D) remarkable is to alarming.
    (E) conspicuous is to extreme.

9. Stanza is to poem as

    (A) rhythm is to beat.
    (B) verse is to word.
    (C) movement is to symphony.
    (D) play is to theater.
    (E) column is to journal.

10. Violin is to string as

    (A) harp is to angelic.
    (B) drum is to stick.
    (C) score is to music.
    (D) oboe is to reed.
    (E) bass is to large.

11. Canter is to horse as

(A) hop is to rabbit.
(B) halt is to pony.
(C) hunt is to lion.
(D) beg is to dog.
(E) chew is to cow.

12. Baseball is to game as

(A) hurricane is to storm.
(B) overcast is to cloud.
(C) stadium is to sport.
(D) wind is to tornado.
(E) conflict is to violence.

13. Rigid is to bend as

(A) tremulous is to sway.
(B) incomprehensive is to think.
(C) immortal is to die.
(D) lazy is to perspire.
(E) stiff is to divide.

14. Canine is to wolf as feline is to

(A) panther.
(B) pig.
(C) monkey.
(D) rat.
(E) vulture.

15. Rind is to melon as

(A) skin is to mammal.
(B) armor is to shield.
(C) shell is to claw.
(D) peel is to core.
(E) pod is to vine.

16. Mile is to length as

(A) acre is to land.
(B) inch is to foot.
(C) kilometer is to race.
(D) yard is to fabric.
(E) fathom is to depth.

17. Truthful is to dishonest as arid is to

(A) sublime.
(B) aloof.
(C) innocent.
(D) moist.
(E) clear.

18. Tarnish is to silver as

(A) streak is to glass.
(B) dirt is to car.
(C) rust is to iron.
(D) dull is to wax.
(E) dust is to wood.

19. Delay is to hasten as

(A) misunderstand is to dislike.
(B) undermine is to improve.
(C) sink is to descend.
(D) remove is to indict.
(E) facilitate is to impede.

20. Think is to daydream as walk is to

(A) stagger.
(B) crawl.
(C) meander.
(D) run.
(E) prance.

Predicting Answers   Backsolving   Guessing   **Practice**   Answers

PRACTICE QUESTION ANSWERS

1.	D	11.	A
2.	B	12.	A
3.	B	13.	C
4.	C	14.	A
5.	E	15.	A
6.	B	16.	E
7.	E	17.	D
8.	A	18.	C
9.	C	19.	E
10.	D	20.	C

| Part Two |

ISEE WORKSHOP

CHAPTER 3: INSIDE THE ISEE

THE ISEE EXAM

The ISEE has three tests: Upper-level, Middle-level, and Lower-level.

* Upper-level   (for students currently in grades 8–11)
* Middle-level   (for students currently in grades 6 or 7)
* Lower-level   (for students currently in grades 4 or 5)

Following is a breakdown of the tests.

	Lower-Level	Middle-Level	Upper-Level
Math I	35 questions (35 min)	35 questions (35 min)	35 questions (35 min)
Verbal	40 questions (25 min)	40 questions (20 min)	40 questions (20 min)
Reading	36 questions (40 min)	40 questions (40 min)	40 questions (40 min)
Math II	35 questions (40 min)	45 questions (40 min)	45 questions (40 min)
Essay*	one writing prompt (30 min)		

* The essay will not be scored, nor will it be included with your home report, but it will be sent to the schools to which you are applying.

- All questions have four answer choices, (A) through (D).
- You are not permitted to use calculators, dictionaries, or rulers.
- You must bring your own pencils and erasers, as well as black or blue pens for your essay.

SCORING

Scores on the ISEE work similarly to the SSAT, in that you will be compared against in national and local averages. Your score report for the ISEE will include test scores and diagnostic information. It will also indicate whether your scores are at the expected level given your performance on the Verbal and Quantitative Reasoning sections.

ISEE Exam   Scoring   How to Register   ISEE vs. SSAT

Like the SSAT, you are not expected to answer every question. Your test performance is compared only to others in your grade. Unlike the SSAT, you are not penalized for wrong answers. You will be graded only on the number of correct answers you get.

HOW TO REGISTER

ISEE accepts registration by mail, phone, fax, or online. For more information, go to the official site at www.erbtest.org.

Phone: 800-446-0320
Fax: (919) 682-5775
Mail: ISEE Operations
          423 Morris Street
          Durham, NC 27701
Email: ISEE@erbtest.org

HOW THE ISEE DIFFERS FROM THE SSAT

- On the ISEE, the Verbal section contains Synonym and Sentence Completion questions. On the SSAT, the Verbal section contains Synonym and Analogy Questions.

- On the ISEE, there are Quantitative Comparisons in the Math section (Upper and Middle levels only).

- On the ISEE, there is no penalty for a wrong answer. That means it is always in your favor to guess if you're not sure of the answer.

- On the ISEE, there are four answer choices, (A) through (D). On the SSAT, there are five answer choices, (A) through (E).

CHAPTER 4: ISEE SPECIFIC VERBAL WORKOUT: SENTENCE COMPLETIONS

Sentence Completions appear **on every level of the ISEE.**

THE FORMAT

Of the 40 questions in the Verbal Ability section, 20 are Sentence Completions. They're arranged in order of increasing difficulty.

Sentence Completions are "fill-in-the-blank" questions. Each question will have one or two blanks, and you must select the best fit from the four choices provided.

These are probably the easiest of all the Verbal question types. Unlike Analogies, they give you some context in which to think about vocabulary words, and unlike Critical Reading, they only require you to focus on a single sentence at a time.

The directions will look something like this:

Select the word(s) that best fits the meaning of each sentence.

EXAMPLE

Although the tomato looked sweet and ———, it tasted more like a very sour, dried out old sponge.

(A) arid
(B) juicy
(C) enormous
(D) cloying

A contrast is presented between the way the tomato looked and the way it tasted. It tasted sour and had the texture of dry sponge. Since we were previously told that it looked *sweet* (the opposite of *sour*), we can infer that we need to find the opposite of *dry*. Therefore the tomato must have looked juicy, so (B) is the answer.

KAPLAN FOUR-STEP METHOD FOR SENTENCE COMPLETIONS

Step 1: Read the sentence carefully, looking for clues.

Step 2: Predict the answer.

Step 3: Pick the best match.

Step 4: Plug in your selection.

Let's take a closer look at each step.

1. READ THE SENTENCE CAREFULLY, LOOKING FOR CLUES

Think carefully about the sentence before looking at the answer choices. What does the sentence mean? Are there any clue words?

2. PREDICT THE ANSWER

Take a look at the following examples:

"They say that M&M's do not melt in your hands, but last summer . . ."

"Despite the fact that it was 50 degrees below zero, we were . . ."

"I am so hungry I could . . ."

You could probably fill in the rest of these sentences using words similar to the speaker's own. It's often easy to see the direction in which a sentence is going; that's because the structure and the tone of a sentence can clue you in to its meaning.

Your job for the ISEE Sentence Completion questions is to fill in the missing piece. One way to do this is to anticipate the answer before looking at the answer choices. Clue words and sentence structure (construction and punctuation) can help you determine where a sentence is headed.

Making an exact prediction isn't necessary. If you can even identify the missing word as just positive or negative, that will often be sufficient.

3. PICK THE BEST MATCH

Make sure to scan every choice before deciding.

4. PLUG IN YOUR SELECTION

Only one of the four possible answer choices will make sense. If you've gone through the four steps and more than one choice still seems possible, though, don't dwell on it. Try to eliminate at least one choice, guess and move on. Remember, on the ISEE, a wrong answer will not affect your score.

Using some examples, let's see how the four-step method works.

EXAMPLE

Most North American marsupials are ——; at night they forage for food and during the day they sleep.

(A) fastidious

(B) amiable

(C) monolithic

(D) nocturnal

Read the sentence carefully, looking for clues. The semicolon (;) is a big clue. It tells you that the first part of the sentence follows the direction of second first part. In other words, you're looking for a word that means nighttime activity and daytime rest.

Predict which word should go into the blank.

Compare the answer choices with your prediction. Pick the best match. (A) *fastidious*, has nothing to do with being active at night. Neither does (B), *amiable*, or for that matter (C) *monolithic*. (D) *nocturnal*, however, means to be active at night, so that seems correct.

Check your choice by plugging it into the sentence. Try it out: "Most North American marsupials are nocturnal; at night they forage for food and during the day they sleep." Sounds pretty good. Finally, scan the other choices to make sure that (D) is indeed the best choice. No other choice works in the sentence, so (D) is right.

EXAMPLE

Juniper skated with such ——, that no one could —— her talent any longer.

(A) speed . . ascertain

(B) melancholy . . deny

(C) agility . . question

(D) grace . . affirm

Read the sentence carefully, looking for clue words. A major clue here is *such … that*. You know that Juniper's skating ability, whether good or bad, has led to everybody agreeing about her talent. So whatever words go into the two blanks, they must agree.

Format   4-Step Method   Picking Up Clues   Tackling Hard Questions   Practice

Predict the words that go into the blanks, making sure that whatever goes in the second blank supports the meaning of the first. If Juniper skated well, no one would deny that she has a lot of talent. If she skated terribly, everyone would agree that she had no talent. Don't let the negative structure of the second part of the sentence fool you: It's written as "no one could ——," as opposed to "everyone could ——." Make some predictions about the two missing pieces.

Compare your predictions with each answer choice, and pick the best fit. Which two words, when in context, will agree and support each other?

In (A), *speed* and *ascertain* don't make much sense together. In (B), *melancholy* and *deny* don't support one another. It doesn't make sense that "no one could *deny* her talent" because she skated sadly, or with *melancholy*. In (C), *agility* and *question* do fit together well. Juniper skates with *agility,* so who could question her ability? In (D), *grace* and *affirm,* initially seem to support one another. But remember the negative in the second part of the sentence: " . . . *no one* could —— her talent." It's illogical to say that she skated with such *grace* that "no one could *affirm* her talent." (C) must be the answer.

PICKING UP ON CLUES

In order to do well on Sentence Completions, you need to be able to show how a sentence fits together. Clue words will help you do that. The more clues you can find, the clearer the sentence will become. The clearer the sentence, the better your prediction.

What are clue words? There are a variety of clue words. Some will indicate **cause-and-effect,** others a **contrast,** and some others will **define the missing word.**

EXAMPLES

- Clues that indicate cause-and-effect:

  <u>Because</u> he was so scared of the dark, we were —— to find him sleeping without a night light.

  <u>As a result</u> of her constant lying, Sheila was —— to trust anyone else.

- Clues that indicate contrast:

  Rita is funny and light-hearted; her twin, Wendy, <u>however</u> is —— and ——.

  <u>Following</u> the wonderful news, Harry's visage changed <u>from</u> an expression of —— to one of ——.

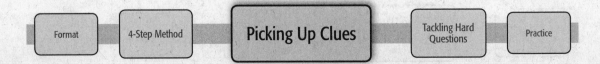

- Clues that define the missing word:

  A <u>loud and tiresome child</u>, he acted particularly —— during the long car trip.

  <u>Smart and witty</u>, Roger was the most —— student in the class.

EXAMPLES

Fiona's bedroom still looks like a ——, despite her efforts to keep it tidy.

In this last example, whatever goes into the blank must complete the contrast implied by the word *despite*. You know then, that it must describe the *opposite of tidy*. *Mess* or *sty* would be good predictions.

BE CAREFUL

A single word can change the meaning of the entire sentence, so make sure to read the sentence carefully.

TACKLING HARD QUESTIONS

Sentence Completions will get increasingly harder as you go through them, so the last few will be the most difficult. If you get stuck, here are a few tips to help you through:

- Avoid tricky wrong answers.
- Take apart tough sentences.
- Work around tough vocabulary.

AVOIDING TRICKY WRONG ANSWERS

Toward the end of a set, keep your eyes open for tricky answer choices. Avoid:

- Opposites of the correct answer.
- Words that may sound right because they are tough.
- Questions with two missing pieces, where one word sounds right but the other doesn't.

The following would be the 12th question out of a 15-problem set.

EXAMPLE

At first the house seemed frightening with all its cobwebs and creaking shutters, but we soon realized that it was quite ——.

(A) benign
(B) deceptive
(C) affluent
(D) haunted

Read this sentence carefully or you may get tricked. If you read it too quickly, it may sound like "The house was really scary with all of those cobwebs and creaking shutters, and we soon realized … it was!" So, you would pick (D) *haunted,* or maybe (B) *deceptive,* when in fact the correct answer is (A) *benign.*

PICK UP THE CLUES

There are two major clue words here, and you should have picked them up right away. The first one, At first, indicates that the author perceived something to be one way *at first*—but after taking a second look, realized it was different. That leads us to the second clue word, *but.* Just as we predicted, the author thought the house was creepy at first, *but* then felt differently. We know, therefore, that the word in the blank must be the *opposite,* or at least not the same, as *creepy,* or *haunted.*

DON'T PICK AN ANSWER JUST BECAUSE IT SOUNDS HARD

Affluent means wealthy. You might be tempted to choose it because it looks or sounds impressive. But it's thrown in there to trick you. Don't choose a word without good reason.

Let's look at a two-blank sentence. The following example is the 15th of a 15-problem set.

EXAMPLE

Screaming and laughing, the students were — by their —— experience on the white-water raft.

(A) amused .. tepid

(B) irritated .. continued

(C) exhilarated .. first

(D) frightened .. secure

LOOK AT ALL THE CHOICES

Check out the first blank first. Sometimes you can eliminate one or more answer choices right away if some possibilities don't fit. *Irritated* and/or *frightened* students do not scream and laugh. So, eliminate (B) and (D).

Now check the second blank. A *tepid* (or half-hearted) experience wouldn't make a bunch of students scream and laugh, either, so (A) is out. Only (C) fits both of the blanks: The students would laugh and scream of exhilaration on their first whitewater rafting experience.

TAKING APART TOUGH SENTENCES

Look at the following example, the last question in a 15-question set.

> ## TWO-BLANK SENTENCES
>
> " Sentences with two blanks can be easier than those with one blank.
> - Try the easier blank first.
> - Save time by eliminating all choices that won't work for that blank. "

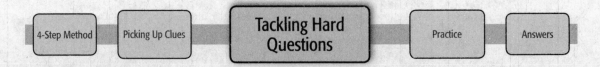

EXAMPLE

The ——— agreement had never been written down but was understood and upheld by the governments of both countries.

(A) tacit

(B) public

(C) distinguished

(D) illegal

What if you were stumped. What if you had no idea which word to pick? Try this method:

Tacit—hmmm, sounds familiar.

Public—nope. It doesn't sound right in this context.

Distinguished—if it was so distinguished, why was it never written down?

Illegal—nope. Do governments uphold illegal agreements? That doesn't sound right.

Choice (A) sounds the best. As it turns out, it's also correct. Tacit agreements are unspoken or silent ones; they're not expressed or declared openly, but implied.

Let's try a complex sentence with two blanks. Remember the rules:

- Try the easier blank first.

- Save time by eliminating all choices that won't work for that blank.

EXAMPLE

The old ——— hated parties and refused to ——— in the festivities.

(A) actor .. direct

(B) curmudgeon .. partake

(C) mediator .. take

(D) surgeon .. place

Well, the easier of the two blanks here is the first one, but it's impossible to rule out any choices, because an actor, a curmudgeon (especially), a mediator, and a surgeon all have the potential of hating parties.

Try the second blank, and see what can be ruled out. (A) doesn't make any sense; what does *direct* in the festivities mean? It's nonsensical. (B) *partake* makes sense. (C) take in the festivities doesn't sound right, and neither does (D) *place* in the festivities. That leaves (B) as the best and only fit. A *curmudgeon* is, by definition, an ornery or grumpy person, so it makes sense that he wouldn't want to *partake* in the festivities.

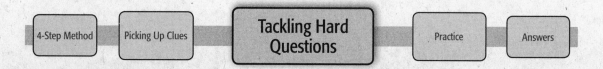

4-Step Method   Picking Up Clues   **Tackling Hard Questions**   Practice   Answers

PRACTICE QUESTIONS

1. The firm employed many lackadaisical employees, who had a(n) —— approach to their work.

   (A) creative
   (B) independent
   (C) unproductive
   (D) discontented

2. Due to —— weather, the school closed and —— all classes.

   (A) cold . . continued
   (B) severe . . cancelled
   (C) humid . . relieved
   (D) frosty . . alleviated

3. Many paleontologists believe that modern birds and crocodiles are the —— of the ancient dinosaurs.

   (A) descendants
   (B) ancestors
   (C) neologisms
   (D) reptiles

4. Her eyes were wide with —— as the ship —— with gold, jewels, and precious metals sailed into port.

   (A) amazement . . arrived
   (B) reason . . purged
   (C) wonder . . laden
   (D) purpose . . meandered

5. It was Mt. Vesuvius that erupted and —— the city of Pompeii in the year 79 A.D.

   (A) desiccated
   (B) decimated
   (C) erected
   (D) detected

6. The determined young cadet —— every character trait that the ideal soldier should have.

   (A) embodied
   (B) created
   (C) secluded
   (D) vaporized

PRACTICE QUESTION ANSWERS

1. C

Lackadaisical means showing a lack of interest or spirit, listless or languid. If the firm employed lackadaisical workers, these workers probably had an *unproductive* approach to their work.

2. B

If you tried each of the choices in the first blank, you'd see that they all fit. As for the second blank, only one choice makes sense: Because of *severe* weather, all classes were *cancelled*.

3. A

This question is filled with elements that the test makers hope to fool you with. Both the answer choices and the question itself contain difficult vocabulary, i.e., *neologisms* and *paleontologists*. In addition, the antonym for the correct answer is thrown in as a curve ball. However, the only choice that makes sense is (A) *descendants*. Many paleontologists believe that birds and crocodiles are *descended* from dinosaurs.

4. C

Her eyes could well have been wide with *amazement, reason, wonder,* and *purpose* as the ship sailed in. But the only choice that makes sense when you try to fill in the second blank is that "her eyes were wide with *wonder* as the ship *laden* with gold, jewels, and precious metals sailed into port." The other combinations just don't make sense.

5. B

It's possible to infer from the information in the sentence that Mt. Vesuvius is a volcano. Regular hills and mountains don't erupt, only volcanoes do. And volcanoes don't erect cities, nor do they *detect* or *desiccate* cities. Indeed, volcanoes are very dangerous because they have the potential to *decimate* cities.

6. A

To *embody* means to *personify*. (A) is the only choice that works here. The cadet doesn't *create* the characters of an ideal soldier, nor does he *seclude* or for that matter *vaporize* those character traits.

4-Step Method | Picking Up Clues | Tackling Hard Questions | Practice | **Answers**

CHAPTER 5: ISEE SPECIFIC MATH WORKOUT: QUANTITATIVE COMPARISONS

Quantitative Comparisons, or QCs, appear **on only the Upper- and Middle-level ISEE**. If you are not taking one of those tests, you may skip this section.

THE FORMAT

Of the 35 math questions in the Quantitative Ability section, 15 are QCs. In a QC, instead of solving for a particular value, you need to compare two quantities. You'll see two mathematical expressions; one in Column A, the other in Column B. Your job is to compare them.

Some questions include additional information about one or both quantities. This information is centered, unboxed, and essential to making the comparison.

The directions will look something like this:

In questions 1–10, note the given information, if any, and then compare the quantity in Column A to the quantity in Column B. Next to the number of each question write

(A) if the quantity in Column A is greater.

(B) if the quantity in Column B is greater.

(C) if the two quantities are equal.

(D) if the relationship cannot be determined from the information given.

THREE RULES FOR CHOICE (D)

Choice (D) is the only choice that represents a relationship that cannot be determined. (A), (B), and (C) all mean that a definite relationship can be found between the quantities in Columns A and B.

There are three things to remember about choice (D):

Rule 1: (D) is rarely correct for the first few QC questions.

Rule 2: (D) is never correct if the two columns contain only numbers.

Rule 3: (D) is correct if there's more than one possible relationship between the two columns.

EXAMPLE

Column A	Column B
$3x$	$2x$

(A) If the quantity in Column A is greater
(B) If the quantity in Column B is greater
(C) If the two quantities are equal
(D) If the relationship cannot be determined from the information given

If x is a positive number, then Column A is larger. If x is equal to zero, then the quantities in Columns A and B are equal. If x is a negative number, then Column B is larger.

There is more than one possible relationship between Columns A and B here, so according to rule 3, (D) is the correct choice. As soon as you realize that there is *more than one* possible relationship, choose (D) and move on.

KAPLAN'S FIVE STRATEGIES FOR QCS

The following is a list of five strategies that will help you to make quick comparisons. The key is to *compare* the values rather than *calculate* them.

Strategy 1:   Compare piece by piece.

Strategy 2:   Make one column look like the other.

Strategy 3:   Do the same thing to both columns.

Strategy 4:   Pick numbers.

Strategy 5:   Avoid QC traps.

Let's look at each strategy in detail.

STRATEGY 1: COMPARE PIECE BY PIECE

This applies to QCs that compare two sums or two products.

EXAMPLE

Column A	Column B

$$a > b > c > d$$

$a + c$	$b + d$

We're given four variables, or "pieces," in the above example, as well as the relationship between these pieces. We're told that a is greater than all of the other pieces, while c is greater than only d, etc. The next step is to compare the value of each piece in each column. If every piece in one column is greater than the corresponding piece in the other column, and if addition is the only mathematical operation involved, the column with the greater individual values *(a > b*, and *c > d)* will have the greater total value *(a + c > b + d)*.

In other words, we knew from the information given that $a > b$, and $c > d$. Therefore, the first term in Column A, *a*, is greater than its corresponding term in Column B, *b*. Likewise, the second term in Column A, *c*, is greater than *d*, its corresponding term in Column B. Since each individual "piece" in Column A is greater than its corresponding "piece" in Column B, the total value of Column A must be greater. The answer is (A).

STRATEGY 2: MAKE ONE COLUMN LOOK LIKE THE OTHER

Use this strategy when the quantities in the two columns look so different that a direct comparison would be impossible.

If the quantities in Column A and B are expressed differently, or if one looks more complicated than the other, try to make a direct comparison easier by changing one column to look more like the other.

Let's try an example in which the quantities in Column A and Column B are expressed differently.

EXAMPLE

Column A	Column B

$2(x + 1)$	$2x + 2$

In the example above, it's difficult to make a direct comparison as the quantities are written. However, if you get rid of the parentheses in Column A so that the quantity more closely resembles that in Column B, you should see right away that a comparison can be made. So, if you get rid of the parentheses in Column A, you'll end up with $2x + 2$ in both columns. Therefore, the columns are equal in value, and the answer is (C).

This strategy is also useful when one column looks more complicated than the other.

EXAMPLE

Column A   Column B

$$\frac{2\sqrt{3}}{\sqrt{6}}$$ $$\sqrt{2}$$

Try simplifying Column A, since it is the more complicated looking quantity of the two.

1) $\dfrac{2\sqrt{3}}{\sqrt{6}} = \dfrac{2\sqrt{3}}{\sqrt{2}\sqrt{3}}$

2) $\dfrac{2\sqrt{3}}{\sqrt{2}\sqrt{3}} = \dfrac{2}{\sqrt{2}}$

3) $\dfrac{2}{\sqrt{2}} = \dfrac{2}{\sqrt{2}} \times \dfrac{\sqrt{2}}{\sqrt{2}} = \dfrac{2\sqrt{2}}{2}$

4) $\dfrac{2\sqrt{2}}{2} = \sqrt{2}$

By simplifying Column A, we are able to make a direct and easy comparison between the two columns. Column A, when simplified, is equivalent to $\sqrt{2}$, which is the quantity in Column B. Therefore, (C) is the correct answer.

STRATEGY 3: DO THE SAME THING TO BOTH COLUMNS

By adding or subtracting the same amount from both columns, you can often unclutter a comparison, and make it more apparent. You can also multiply or divide both columns by the same positive number. This keeps the relationship between the columns the same. If the quantities in both columns are positive, you can square both columns. This keeps the relationship between the columns the same.

Changing the values, and not just the appearances of the quantities in both columns is often helpful in tackling QC questions. Set up the problem as an inequality, with the two columns as opposing sides of the inequality.

To change the values of the columns, add or subtract the same amount from both columns and multiply or divide by a positive number without changing the absolute

KAPLAN EXCLUSIVE TIPS

"Do not multiply or divide both QC columns by a negative number."

| Format | 5 Strategies | Practice | Answers |

relationship. But **be careful.** Remember that the direction of an inequality sign will be reversed if you multiply or divide by a negative number. Since this reversal will alter the relationship between the two columns, avoid multiplying or dividing by a negative number. You can also square the quantities in both columns when both columns are positive. But **be careful.** Do not square both columns unless you know for certain that both columns are positive.

You can only square both columns when both are positive. Remember these two things when squaring the quantities in both columns: (1) the direction of an inequality sign can be reversed if one or both quantities are negative, and (2) the inequality sign can be changed to an equals sign if one quantity is positive and the other quantity is negative, with one quantity being the negative of the other. For example, $4 > -5$, yet $4^2 < (-5)^2$, since $16 < 25$. $2 > -2$, yet $2^2 = (-2)^2$, since $2^2 = (-2)^2 = 4$.

In the QC below what could you do to both columns?

EXAMPLE

Column A	Column B

$$x > y > 0$$

$\dfrac{2y + x}{2}$	$y + x$

Try multiplying both columns by 2 to get rid of that fraction in Column A. You're left with $2y + x$ in Column A and $2y + 2x$ in Column B. We know that $2y = 2y$. But what about the relationship between x and $2x$? The centered information tells us that $x > 0$, therefore, $2x > x$, and Column B is greater than Column A. Choice (B) is the right answer.

In the next QC, what could you do to both columns?

EXAMPLE

Column A	Column B

$\dfrac{1}{4} + \dfrac{1}{5} - \dfrac{1}{3}$	$\dfrac{1}{2} - \dfrac{1}{3} + \dfrac{1}{20}$

Try adding $\dfrac{1}{3}$ to both sides. If you do this, you'll be left with $\dfrac{1}{4} + \dfrac{1}{5}$ in Column A and $\dfrac{1}{2} + \dfrac{1}{20}$ in Column B. Now treat this QC like a standard fraction problem. To find

> **KAPLAN EXCLUSIVE TIPS**
>
> " When you plug in negative numbers and fractions, remember the following:
>
> - When you square a positive fraction less than one, the result is a smaller fraction than the original.
>
> - When you square a negative number, the result is a positive number.
>
> - When you square 0 and 1, they remain the same. "

Format   **5 Strategies**   Practice   Answers

the sums in each column, you must find the lowest common denominator. You're left with $\frac{9}{20}$ in Column A and $\frac{11}{20}$ in Column B. Column B is greater than Column A, so the answer is (B).

STRATEGY 4: PICK NUMBERS

Substitute numbers into those abstract algebra QCs . Try using a positive, a negative, and zero.

If a QC involves variables, pick numbers to clarify the relationship. Here's what to do:

- Pick numbers that are easy to work with.

- Plug in the numbers and calculate the values. What's the relationship between the columns?

- Pick a different number for each variable and recalculate.

Column A	Column B
	$x > 0$
x	$\frac{1}{x}$

Try choosing a relatively easy number like 1. Plug it in and calculate. If you have calculated correctly, you'll find that Columns A and B are equal, $1 = \frac{1}{1}$. Remember to try another number. Let's try $x = \frac{1}{2}$. If we plug in $\frac{1}{2}$ and recalculate, Column A is now equal to $\frac{1}{2}$, and Column B is equal to 2. The relationship is not the same as before. Therefore, the answer is (D).

PICK DIFFERENT KINDS OF NUMBERS

Never assume that all variables represent positive integers. Unless you're told otherwise, as in the case above, variables can be positive or negative, they can be zero or fractions. Because different kinds of numbers behave differently, you should always choose a different kind of number the second time around. In the example above, we knew that x wasn't a negative number, nor was it zero, so we tried a fraction, and discovered that the relationship between the columns did not remain the same.

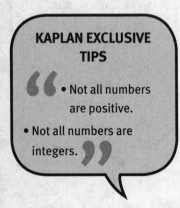

KAPLAN EXCLUSIVE
TIPS

- Not all numbers are positive.
- Not all numbers are integers.

In the next three examples, we'll choose different kinds of numbers, and observe the results. Remember that if there's more than one possible relationship between the two columns, the answer is (D).

EXAMPLE

Column A	Column B
x	$-x$

If $x = 1$, Column A = 1 and Column B = –1.
In this case, Column A is greater

If $x = -1$, Column A = –1 and Column B = 1.
In this case, Column B is greater.

EXAMPLE

Column A	Column B
	$x > 0$
x	$\dfrac{1}{x}$

If $x = 2$, Column A = 2 and Column B = $\dfrac{1}{2}$.
In this case, Column A is greater.

If $x = \dfrac{1}{2}$, Column A = $\dfrac{1}{2}$ and Column B = 2.
In this case, Column B is greater.

EXAMPLE

Column A	Column B
x	x^2

If $x = \dfrac{1}{2}$, Column A = $\dfrac{1}{2}$ and Column B = $\dfrac{1}{4}$.
In this case, Column A is greater.

If $x = 2$, Column A = 2 and Column B = 4.
In this case, Column B is greater.

STRATEGY 5: AVOID QC TRAPS!

Keep your eyes open for those trick questions designed to fool you into the obvious, but wrong answer. Questions are arranged in order of increasing difficulty, so chances are, you're likely to see traps toward the end of the set.

| Format | **5 Strategies** | Practice | Answers |

To avoid these nasty traps, always be on your toes. Never assume anything. Be particularly careful towards the end of a QC set.

- **Don't Be Tricked by Misleading Information**

EXAMPLE

Column A	Column B

Frank weighs more
than Hector.

Frank's height in meters	Hector's height in meters

The test makers are hoping that you'll make some faulty logic, and think "If Frank is heavier, he must be taller." But that's not necessarily so. The answer in this case would be (D). If you keep your eyes open for these kinds of things, you'll spot them immediately.

- **Don't Assume**

EXAMPLE

Column A	Column B

$$1 + x^2 = 10$$

x	3

A common mistake on QC questions is to assume that variables represent positive integers. We already dealt with these kinds of problems in the Picking Numbers strategy. Remember that positive and negative numbers, as well as fractions and zeros, behave differently.

In the example above, the test makers are hoping you'll assume that $x = 3$, since the square of 3 = 9. But x could also be equal to –3. Because x could be 3 or –3, (D) is the correct answer.

- **Don't Fall for Look-alikes**

EXAMPLE

Column A	Column B
$\sqrt{4} + \sqrt{4}$	$\sqrt{8}$

Now, 4 + 4 = 8, *but* $\sqrt{4} + \sqrt{4} > \sqrt{8}$! Don't forget the rules of radicals. The test makers are counting on you to rush and look for the obvious choice, (C), that the two quantities are equal. Don't let them fool you. If a > 0 and b > 0, then $\sqrt{a+b} \uparrow \sqrt{a} + \sqrt{b}$.

Remember the convention that if x is positive, $\sqrt{x}$ means the positive square root. So $\sqrt{4} + \sqrt{4} = 2 + 2 = 4$. Now we have 4 in Column A and $\sqrt{8}$ in Column B. Since $\sqrt{8} < \sqrt{9}$ and $\sqrt{9} = 3$, $\sqrt{8} < 3 < 4$. Thus, $4 > \sqrt{8}$ and Column A is greater. Because 4 and $\sqrt{8}$ are both positive, you could also show that $4 > \sqrt{8}$ by squaring both 4 and $\sqrt{8}$. $4^2 = 16$ and $(\sqrt{8})^2 = 8$. $16 > 8$, so $4 > \sqrt{8}$. Choice (A) is correct.

PRACTICE QUESTIONS

Directions: In questions 1–9, note the given information, if any, and then compare the quantity in Column A to the quantity in Column B. Next to the number of each question write

A if the quantity in Column A is greater.

B if the quantity in Column B is greater.

C if the two quantities are equal.

D if the relationship cannot be determined from the information given.

<u>Column A</u>   <u>Column B</u>   <u>Column A</u>   <u>Column B</u>

x is an even integer.

1. | The average of 106, 117, 123, and 195 | The average of 110, 118, 124, and 196 |

5. | x^2 | x^3 |

$$2x - 6 = 2x + 3x$$

6. | $\dfrac{6 + \sqrt{3}}{2}$ | $\dfrac{3 + \sqrt{6}}{\sqrt{4}}$ |

2. | x^2 | 4 |

7. | $6 + 10$ | $\sqrt{16} + \sqrt{36}$ |

$x > 0$
$y > 0$

8. | 25% of 65 | $65 \times \sqrt{\dfrac{1}{4}}$ |

3. | $x - y$ | $y - x$ |

$a > b > c > d$

$x \uparrow 0$

9. | $a^2 + c$ | $b^2 + d$ |

4. | $\dfrac{x + 2}{3}$ | $x + 5$ |

PRACTICE QUESTION ANSWERS

1. B

The corresponding numbers in Column B are greater than those in Column A. Therefore, the average in Column B must be greater.

2. C

Solve for x in the centered equation. First, subtract $2x$ from both sides. This will leave you with $-6 = 3x$. Divide both sides by 3. Now, $x = -2$. Plug in -2 for x to find the value of x^2 in Column A. Then $x^2 = (-2)^2 = 4$. The quantities in both columns are equal.

3. D

From the centered information, you know only that the variables x and y must be positive. So plug in some positive integers. If $x = 5$ and $y = 3$, then Column A is $x - y = 5 - 3 = 2$ and Column B is $y - x = 3 - 5 = -2$. In this case, Column A is greater. Now plug in some different numbers. Notice that you have not been given any information about the relationship between x and y. If you were to switch the values that you used on the first try, so that now $x = 3$ and $y = 5$, then Column A is $x - y = 3 - 5 = -2$ and Column B is $y - x = 5 - 3 = 2$. Column B is greater. Since more than one relationship between the columns is possible, choice (D) is correct.

4. D

This problem appears to be an obvious candidate for the pick-a-number strategy. But be careful with the numbers you choose. Let's plug in 2 for x. Column A is $\frac{2+2}{3}$, or $\frac{4}{3}$, and Column B is $2 + 5$, or 7. Column B is greater. Your next likely step would be to switch your plug-in number from a positive to a negative. Here's where the test makers trick

you if you aren't careful. By letting $x = -2$, you find that Column A is $\frac{-2+2}{3}$, or 0, while Column B is $-2 + 5$, or 3. Once again, Column B is greater. But what happens if you plug in a negative number considerably further away from 0 ? If $x = -100$, then Column A is $\frac{-100+2}{3} = \frac{-98}{3}$, or $-32\frac{2}{3}$, and Column B is $-100 + 5$, or -95. In this case, Column A is greater. More than one relationship between the columns is possible.

5. D

The centered information is actually not very helpful in this QC. This is another pick-a-number type of problem. Let's begin by plugging in a positive value for x that is consistent with the centered information. Let $x = 2$. So Column A is $2^2 = 2 \times 2$, or 4, and Column B is $2^3 = 2 \times 2 \times 2$, or 8. In this case, Column B is greater. Now pick a negative value for x that is consistent with the centered information. Let $x = -2$. Now, Column A is $(-2)^2 = (-2) \times (-2) = 4$ and Column B is $(-2)^3 = (-2) \times (-2) \times (-2) = -8$. Column A is greater. Since more than one relationship between the columns is possible, (D) is correct.

6. A

While it is true that every positive number has two square roots—a positive and a negative square root—the convention with the symbol $\sqrt{}$ is that if x is positive, $\sqrt{x}$ means the positive square root of x. 16 has the two square roots 4 and -4 , while $\sqrt{16}$ means the positive square root of 16, which is 4. Thus, $\sqrt{16} = 4$.

First notice that the denominator $\sqrt{4}$ of Column B is equal to 2. So we're comparing $\dfrac{6+\sqrt{3}}{2}$ in Column A with $\dfrac{3+\sqrt{6}}{2}$ in Column B. Now try doing the same thing to both columns. Multiplying both columns by 2 leaves us with $6 + \sqrt{3}$ for Column A and $3 + \sqrt{6}$ for Column B. Next, subtracting 3 from both columns leaves us with $3 + \sqrt{3}$ for Column A and $\sqrt{6}$ for Column B. Now $3 = \sqrt{9}$ and $\sqrt{9}$ is greater than $\sqrt{6}$. So 3 is greater than $\sqrt{6}$. Surely $3 + \sqrt{3}$ (which is what we now have for Column A) is greater than 3. Also, 3 is greater than $\sqrt{6}$, with $\sqrt{6}$ being what we have for Column B. So $3 + \sqrt{3}$ for Column A must be greater than $\sqrt{6}$ for Column B. Choice (A) is correct.

7. A

Just as we saw in the previous question, if x is positive, $\sqrt{x}$ means the positive square root of x. In Column A, $6 + 10 = 16$. In Column B we have $\sqrt{16} + \sqrt{36}$. By convention, $\sqrt{16} = 4$ and $\sqrt{36} = 6$. So $\sqrt{16} + \sqrt{36} = 4 + 6 = 10$. Column A is greater.

8. B

Change one of the columns so you can make a direct comparison. A percentage can be written as a fraction and vice-versa. It's generally easier to work with fractions, so convert 25% in Column A to a fraction. The fractional equivalent of 25% is $\dfrac{1}{4}$. You convert a percent to a fraction (or decimal) by dividing the percent by 100%, so $25\% = \dfrac{25\%}{100\%} = \dfrac{25}{100} = \dfrac{1}{4}$.

Therefore, Column A is $\dfrac{1}{4}$ of 65, or $\dfrac{65}{4}$. Column B is $65 \times \sqrt{\dfrac{1}{4}}$. Let's first simplify $\sqrt{\dfrac{1}{4}} \cdot \sqrt{\dfrac{1}{4}} = \dfrac{\sqrt{1}}{\sqrt{4}} = \dfrac{1}{2}$. So Column B is $65 \times \dfrac{1}{2}$, or $\dfrac{65}{2}$. Since $\dfrac{65}{2}$ is greater than $\dfrac{65}{4}$, Column B is greater.

9. D

Since the variables could be positive or negative, pick different kinds of numbers for the variables to see if different relationships between the columns are possible. Remember that the values you pick must be consistent with the centered information, which is that $a > b > c > d$.

If $a = 4$, $b = 3$, $c = 2$, and $d = 1$, then the value of Column A is $a^2 + c = 4^2 + 2 = 16 + 2 = 18$ and the value of Column B is $b^2 + d = 3^2 + 1 = 9 + 1 = 10$. Column A is greater. If you pick only positive numbers, then it will always be true that $a^2 + c > b^2 + d$. You could fall for the trap here of thinking that $a^2 + c$ is always greater than $b^2 + d$ if you don't let some or all of the variables be negative. Let $a = -1$, $b = -2$, $c = -3$, and $d = -4$. These values are consistent with the centered information. This time the value of Column A is $a^2 + c = (-1)^2 + (-3) = 1 - 3 = -2$ and the value of Column B is $b^2 + d = (-2)^2 + (-4) = 4 - 4 = 0$. So in this case Column B is greater. More than one relationship between the columns is possible.

Part Three

COMMON CONTENT FOR THE SSAT AND ISEE

CHAPTER 6: SSAT/ISEE MASTERY

Every year, close to 100,000 students take either the SSAT or ISEE for admission to nearly 2,000 independent (private) schools. Although the components of the two tests are remarkably similar, there are some critical differences.

To get a great score on a private school admissions test, you need to to know some key things that have nothing to do with vocabulary words or isosceles triangles. Namely, you need to know how to be a good test taker.

- You need to have a basic understanding of the nature of the test.
- You need to hone your math and verbal skills.
- You need to develop strategies and test-taking techniques.

Having a solid grasp of the content on the test is obviously important. You can't do well if you don't know the material. But it's also just as important to know how the test is set up, what kinds of questions it has, and what kinds of traps it commonly sets. If you don't know these things, you will be at a severe disadvantage on test day.

USING THE TEST STRUCTURE TO YOUR ADVANTAGE

Whether you're taking the SSAT (Secondary School Admission Test) or the ISEE (Independent School Entrance Exam), you'll notice pretty quickly that it is very different from the tests you're used to taking in school. On a school test, you're often told to show your work, to spend more time on tough questions (since they're worth more points), and to work thoroughly, even if it means taking extra time.

None of these things applies in the world of standardized testing. On your private school admissions test, it won't matter how you answer a question; it only matters what your final answer is.

Test Structure   Approaching Questions   Managing Stress

Also, all questions are worth the same number of points, so it's always to your advantage to answer easier questions first, to get them out of the way.

The SSAT and ISEE are each given to students in a range of grades, so if you're in 8th grade, for example, you're not expected to get as many questions right as someone in 11th grade (for the Upper-level test). Keep that in mind as you take the test so you won't get discouraged if you find a lot of questions that you can't answer!

To succeed in this unique testing environment, you need to know some fundamentals. Both the SSAT and ISEE have some quirks about them, so read carefully.

Because the format and directions of the SSAT and ISEE remain relatively unchanged from year to year, you can learn the setup in advance. Then on Test Day, all you'll have to worry about will be answering each question, not learning how a Synonym question works.

One of the easiest and most useful things you can do to boost your performance is to learn and understand the directions before Test Day. Since the instructions are always exactly the same, there's no reason to waste your time on the day of the test reading them. Get them straight in your head beforehand, while you go through this book, and you'll be able to skip them during the test.

SKIPPING AROUND

You're allowed to skip around as much as you'd like within each section of the SSAT/ISEE. High scorers know this and use it to their advantage. They move through the test efficiently, quickly marking and leaving questions they can't answer immediately, racking up points on questions they do know, then coming back to the tough ones later. They don't dwell on any questions, even a hard one, until they've tried every question at least once.

When you see questions that look tough, circle them in your test booklet and skip them for later. Gather points on other questions first. On a second look, some tricky-looking questions can turn out to be much easier than they initially looked. And remember, if you're on the younger side of the testing group within your level, expect to see several questions that you won't be able to answer. The test is intentionally set up this way, so don't let it discourage you.

GUESSING—KNOW YOUR TEST

When should you guess? That's a question we hear from students all the time. It depends which test you're taking. Read the information below and follow the instructions for your test. Guessing is one of the few areas in which the SSAT and ISEE operate differently, so read carefully!

SSAT: There is a wrong-answer penalty. For each answer you get right, you get one point. For each answer you get wrong, 1/4 of a point is deducted from your total score. Does this mean you shouldn't guess? No, not at all. What it means is that you need to be smart about it. Essentially, if

Test Structure   Approaching Questions   Managing Stress you can eliminate one—preferably two—answer choices, it's to your advantage to guess, because you've tipped the odds of guessing correctly in your favor. If you can't eliminate anything, however, you're better off leaving the question blank.

ISEE: There is no wrong-answer penalty. That means you should answer every single question on the test, even if you have no idea what it's asking you. The ISEE calculates your score simply by adding up your right answers, so you might as well fill in all those ovals completely. You never know what you might get right by luck!

GRIDDING—THE ANSWER GRID HAS NO HEART

Misgridding. It sounds so basic, but it happens all the time: When time is short, it's easy to get confused going back and forth between your test booklet and your answer grid. If you know the answer, but misgrid, you won't get any points, so be careful. Don't let it happen to you. Here are some tips to help you avoid making mistakes on the answer grid:

CIRCLE THE QUESTIONS YOU SKIP

Put a big circle in your test booklet around any question numbers you skip. When you go back, these questions will be easy to locate. Also, if you accidentally skip a box on the grid, you can check your grid against your booklet to see where you went wrong.

ALWAYS CIRCLE THE ANSWERS YOU CHOOSE

Circling your answers in the test booklet as you work on each question makes it easier to check your grid against your booklet.

GRID FIVE OR MORE ANSWERS AT ONCE

Don't transfer your answers to the grid after every question. Do it after every five questions, or at the end of each reading passage. That way, you won't keep breaking your concentration. You'll save time and you'll gain accuracy.

Be careful at the end of a section, when time may be running out. You don't want to have your answers in the test booklet and not be able to transfer them to your answer grid because you have run out of time. Make sure to transfer your answers after every five questions or so.

APPROACHING SSAT/ISEE QUESTIONS

Apart from knowing the setup of the SSAT or ISEE, you need to have a system for attacking the questions. You wouldn't travel around a foreign city without a map and

> **KAPLAN EXCLUSIVE TIPS**
>
> " On the SSAT, guess only if you can eliminate at least one or two answer choices.
>
> On the ISEE, always guess, even if you can't eliminate *anything*. "

> **CIRCLE BEFORE YOU SKIP**
>
> " One common test disaster is filling in all of the questions with the right answers—in the wrong spots. Every time you skip a question, *circle it* in your test book. Make sure that you skip it on the answer grid, too. "

Test Structure | **Approaching Questions** | Managing Stress you shouldn't approach your private-school admissions test without a plan, either. Once you know the basics about how each test is set up, you can approach each section a little more strategically. We recommend the following method for approaching test questions systematically.

THINK ABOUT THE QUESTION BEFORE YOU LOOK AT THE ANSWER

The people who make the tests love to put distracters among the answer choices. Distracters are answer choices that look like the right answer, but aren't. If you jump right into the answer choices without thinking first about what you're looking for, you're more likely to fall for one of these traps.

USE BACKDOOR STRATEGIES IF NECESSARY

There are usually a number of ways to get to the right answer on an SSAT/ISEE question. Most of the questions are multiple choice. That means the answer is right in front of you—you just have to find it. But if you can't figure out the answer in a straightforward way, try other techniques. We'll talk about specific Kaplan methods such as backsolving, picking numbers, and eliminating wrong answers in later chapters.

PACE YOURSELF

The SSAT/ISEE gives you a lot of questions in a short period of time. In order to get through an entire section, you can't spend too much time on any one question. Keep moving through the test at a good speed; if you run into a hard question, circle it, skip it, and go back later if there's time.

Typically, the questions get harder as you move through a problem set. Ideally, you can work through the easy problems at a brisk, steady clip, and use a little more of your time for the harder ones that come at the end of the set.

One caution: Don't completely rush through the easy problems just to save time for the harder ones. These early problems are points in your pocket, and you don't want to work through them in such haste that you end up making careless mistakes.

LOCATE QUICK POINTS IF YOU'RE RUNNING OUT OF TIME

Some questions can be done quickly; for instance, some reading questions will ask you to identify the meaning of a particular word in the passage. These can be done at the last minute, even if you haven't read the passage. When you start to run out of time, locate and answer any of the quick points that remain.

When you take the SSAT/ISEE, you have one clear objective in mind: to score as many points as you can. It's that simple. The rest of this book will help you do that.

MANAGING STRESS

The countdown has begun. Your date with the test is looming on the horizon. Anxiety is on the rise. The butterflies in your stomach have gone ballistic. Your thinking is getting cloudy. Maybe you think you won't be ready. Maybe you already know your stuff, but you're going into panic mode anyway. Don't freak! It's possible to tame that anxiety and stress—*before* and *during* the test.

Remember, a little stress is good. Anxiety is a motivation to study. The adrenaline that gets pumped into your bloodstream when you're stressed helps you stay alert and think more clearly. But if you feel that the tension is so great that it's preventing you from using your study time effectively, here are some things you can do to get it under control.

TAKE CONTROL

Lack of control is a prime cause of stress. Research shows that if you don't have a sense of control over what's happening in your life, you can easily end up feeling helpless and hopeless. Try to identify the sources of the stress you feel. Which sources can you do something about? Can you find ways to reduce the stress you're feeling about any of these sources?

FOCUS ON YOUR STRENGTHS

Make a list of areas of strength you have that will help you do well on the test. We all have strengths, and recognizing your own is like having reserves of solid gold at Fort Knox. You'll be able to draw on your reserves as you need them, helping you solve difficult questions, maintain confidence, and keep test stress and anxiety at a distance. And every time you recognize a new area of strength, solve a challenging problem, or score well on a practice test, you'll increase your reserves.

IMAGINE YOURSELF SUCCEEDING

Close your eyes and imagine yourself in a relaxing situation. Breathe easily and naturally. Now, think of a real-life situation in which you scored well on a test or did well on an assignment. Focus on this success. Now turn your thoughts to the SSAT/ISEE, and keep your thoughts and feelings in line with that successful experience. Don't make comparisons between them; just imagine yourself taking the upcoming test with the same feelings of confidence and relaxed control.

SET REALISTIC GOALS

Facing your problem areas gives you some distinct advantages. What do you want to accomplish in the time remaining? Make a list of realistic goals. You can't help feeling more confident when you know you're actively improving your chances of earning a higher test score.

Test Structure · Approaching Questions · **Managing Stress**

MASTER YOUR PHYSICAL WELL-BEING

How well you do on Test Day doesn't only have to do with how prepared you are. It also has to do with what kind of condition you are in physically.

EXERCISE YOUR FRUSTRATIONS AWAY

Whether it's jogging, biking, pushups, or a pickup basketball game, physical exercise will stimulate your mind and body, and improve your ability to think and concentrate. A surprising number of students fall out of the habit of regular exercise, ironically because they're spending so much time prepping for exams. A little physical exertion will help to keep your mind and body in sync and sleep better at night.

AVOID DRUGS

Using drugs (prescription or recreational) specifically to prepare for and take a big test is definitely self-defeating. (And if they're illegal drugs, you may end up with a bigger problem than the SSAT/ISEE on your hands.) Mild stimulants, such as coffee or cola can sometimes help as you study, since they keep you alert. On the down side, too much of these can also lead to agitation, restlessness, and insomnia. It all depends on your tolerance for caffeine.

EAT WELL

Good nutrition will help you focus and think clearly. Eat plenty of fruits and vegetables, low-fat protein such as fish, skinless poultry, beans, and legumes, and whole grains such as brown rice, whole wheat bread, and pastas. Don't eat a lot of sugar and high-fat snacks, or salty foods.

KEEP BREATHING

Conscious attention to breathing is an excellent way to manage stress while you're taking the test. Most of the people who get into trouble during tests take shallow breaths: They breathe using only their upper chests and shoulder muscles, and may even hold their breath for long periods of time. Conversely, those test takers who breathe deeply in a slow, relaxed manner are likely to be in better control during the session.

STRETCH

If you find yourself getting spaced out or burned out as you study or take the test, stop for a brief moment and stretch. Flex your feet and arms. Even though you'll be pausing on the test for a moment, it's a moment well spent. Stretching will help to refresh you and refocus your thoughts.

CHAPTER 7: SYNONYMS

Synonyms appear on all levels of the SSAT & ISEE. At its most basic level, a synonym is a word that is similar in meaning to another defined word. *Fast* is a synonym for *quick*. OK, that makes sense. Unfortunately, if Synonyms were that easy on the SSAT/ISEE, the tests wouldn't tell admissions officers very much.

THE FORMAT

The synonyms you'll see on your actual test will be much trickier than the example above, but they'll all follow the same logic. You'll see a word in capital letters (we call this the *stem word*), and it will be followed by five other words (four on the ISEE). One of them will be the synonym to the given word, and the others will not.

EXAMPLE

AUTHENTIC:

(A) genuine
(B) valuable
(C) ancient
(D) damaged
(E) historical

Which of these words means AUTHENTIC? Maybe you "just knew" that the answer was (A) *genuine,* and maybe you didn't. Either way, you need a method that will work for you on both the easy and the hard Synonym questions. What you need is the . . .

Format   3-Step Method   Avoiding Pitfalls   Vocab Techniques   Practice

KAPLAN THREE-STEP METHOD FOR SYNONYMS

Step 1. Define the stem word.

Step 2. Find the answer choice that best fits your definition.

Step 3. If no choice fits, think of other definitions for the stem word and go through the choices again.

Let's take another look at the example above, using the Three-Step Method.

STEP 1: DEFINE THE STEM WORD

What does *authentic* mean? Something authentic is something *real,* such as an authentic signature, rather than a forgery. Your definition might be something like this: Something authentic can be *proven* to be what it *claims* to be.

STEP 2: FIND THE ANSWER CHOICE THAT BEST FITS YOUR DEFINITION

Go through the answer choices one by one to see which one fits best. Your options are: *genuine, valuable, ancient, damaged,* and *historical.* Something AUTHENTIC could be worth a lot or not much at all, old or new, in good shape or bad, or even recent or historical. The only word that really means the same thing as AUTHENTIC is (A) genuine.

STEP 3: IF NO CHOICE FITS, THINK OF OTHER DEFINITIONS FOR THE STEM WORD AND GO THROUGH THE CHOICES AGAIN

In this instance, one choice fits, but take a look at the following example:

EXAMPLE

GRAVE:

(A) regrettable

(B) unpleasant

(C) serious

(D) careful

(E) lengthy

Say you defined GRAVE as *a burial location.* You looked at the choices, and didn't see any words like *tomb* or *coffin.* What to do? Move to step 3, and go back to the stem word, thinking about other definitions. Have you ever heard of a "grave situation"? GRAVE can also mean *serious* or *solemn,* and you can see that (C) serious, now fits the bill perfectly. If none of the answer choices seem to work with your definition, there may be a secondary definition you haven't yet considered.

> ## WALK THE WALK
>
> " What if WALK were your stem word. What part of speech is it? It could be the *act of* walking (a verb), or *to take* a walk (the noun). Just look at the answer choices. They'll always be the same part of speech as the stem word. So you'll always know whether to WAVE to Mom or ride the WAVE . . . though she'd probably prefer you do both at once! "

Format | **3-Step Method** | Avoiding Pitfalls | Vocab Techniques | Practice

AVOIDING PITFALLS

OK, so we lied just a little bit. The Three-Step Method should always be the basis for tackling every question, but there are a few other things you need to know to perform your best on Synonyms. Fortunately, there are only two big pitfalls to watch out for.

PITFALL 1: RUNNING OUT OF TIME

Pace yourself. You have a limited amount of time, so make sure you use it wisely. Never waste time on a question you don't know—circle it and come back to it later. Synonyms get harder as they go, so move through the early questions quickly, leaving more time for the tougher ones at the end.

PITFALL 2: CHOOSING TEMPTING WRONG ANSWERS

The test makers choose their wrong answer choices very carefully. Sometimes that means throwing in answers that will tempt you, but that aren't right. Be a savvy test taker; don't fall for these distracters!

What kinds of wrong answers are we talking about here? There are two types of wrong answers to watch out for: answers that are *almost right,* and answers that *sound like the stem word.* Let's illustrate both types to make it concrete.

EXAMPLE

REPUTE:

(A) renewal
(B) renown
(C) priority
(D) mutability
(E) reaction

FAVOR:

(A) award
(B) recognize
(C) respect
(D) improve
(E) prefer

In the first example, choices (A), (B), and (E) might be tempting, because they all start with the prefix *re-,* just like the stem word, REPUTE. It's important that you examine all the answer choices, because otherwise you might choose (A) and never get to the correct answer, (B).

> **ARDUOUS, OR JUST HARD?**
>
> "One other trap to watch out for is answer choices that sound hard. Particularly if the stem word is pretty tough, you might be tempted to pick an answer choice that sounds similarly difficult. Often, the correct answer is straightforward. When you see a tough word, keep your cool, and ask yourself, is this arduous, or just hard?"

In the second example, you might look at the word FAVOR and think, oh, that's something positive. It's something you do for someone else. It sounds a lot like choice (A), award. Maybe you pick (A) and move on. If you do that, you would fall for a trap. The correct answer is (E) prefer, since FAVOR is being used as a verb, and to FAVOR someone or something is to like it better than something else, in other words, to prefer it. Like in the first example, if you don't read through all of the choices, you might be tricked into choosing a wrong answer.

At this point, you have a great set of tools for answering most Synonym questions. You know how to approach them and you know some traps to avoid. But what happens if you look at the word in capitals and you don't know what it means? Should you just give up and move on, fill out the rest of your test in crayon, or start waving your arms around, saying "They're after us!"? Well, probably not.

VOCABULARY TECHNIQUES

There are several things you can do to figure out the meaning of a tough vocabulary word and, thus, to answer a hard Synonym question. Here are four techniques that will help you when you don't know a stem word.

Technique 1.	Look for familiar roots and prefixes.
Technique 2.	Use your knowledge of foreign languages.
Technique 3.	Remember the context.
Technique 4.	Use Word Charge.

Let's examine each technique more closely.

TECHNIQUE 1: LOOK FOR FAMILIAR ROOTS AND PREFIXES

Remember how we told you in the "Mastery" chapter to start working on your vocabulary skills? Well, having a good grasp of how words are put together will help you tremendously on Synonyms, particularly when you don't know a vocabulary word. If you can break a word into pieces that you do understand, you'll be able to answer questions that you might have thought too difficult to tackle.

Look at the words below. Circle any prefixes or roots that you know.

- BENEVOLENCE
- INSOMNIA
- INSCRIBE
- CONSPIRE
- VERITY

3-Step Method   Avoiding Pitfalls   **Vocab Techniques**   Practice   Answers

BENE means *good*; SOMN has to do with *sleep*; SCRIB has to do with *writing*; CON means doing something *together*; and VER has to do with *truth*.

TECHNIQUE 2: USE YOUR KNOWLEDGE OF FOREIGN LANGUAGES

Do you study a foreign language? If so, it can help you decode lots of vocabulary words on the SSAT/ISEE, particularly if it's one of the Romance languages (French, Spanish, Italian, Rumanian, Portuguese). Look at the example words below. Do you recognize any foreign language words in them?

- FACILITATE
- DORMANT
- EXPLICATE

Facile means *easy* in French and Italian; *dormir* means *to sleep* in French and Spanish; and *expliquer* means *to explain* in French.

TECHNIQUE 3: REMEMBER THE CONTEXT

Sometimes a word might look strange sitting on the page by itself, but if you think about it, you realize you've heard it before in other phrases. If you can put the word into context, such as in a cliché, you're well on your way to deciphering its meaning.

EXAMPLE

GNARLED:
(A) fruitful
(B) dead
(C) twisted
(D) flowering
(E) drooping

What kind of a plant have you heard described as gnarled? *Trees* are often described as gnarled, particularly old ones. They are knotty and twisted, the kind you think would appear in fairy tales.

3-Step Method | Avoiding Pitfalls | **Vocab Techniques** | Practice | Answers

EXAMPLE

ALLEGATION:

(A) evidence

(B) accusation

(C) conservation

(D) foundation

(E) fabrication

What does "making an allegation" mean? "*Making an allegation*" is accusing someone *of* committing a crime, a phrase you might have seen on the news or on a police-related TV *show*.

EXAMPLE

LAURELS:

(A) vine

(B) honor

(C) lavender

(D) cushion

(E) work

Have you heard the phrase "*Don't rest on your laurels*"? What do you think it might mean? The phrase "*Don't rest on your laurels*" originated in ancient Greece, where heroes were given wreaths of laurel branches to signify their accomplishments. Telling someone to not rest on his laurels is the same thing as telling him to not get too comfortable or smug, living off the success of his accomplishment, rather than striving for improvement.

TECHNIQUE 4: USE WORD CHARGE

Even if you know nothing about the word, have never seen it before, don't recognize any prefixes or roots, and can't think of any word in any language that it sounds like, you can still make a stab at a Synonym question. One useful strategy when you're stumped is Word Charge.

What do we mean by Word Charge? Are some words electric? Do they spend too much money on credit cards? No, and no. Word charge refers to the *sense* that a word gives you as to whether it's a positive word or a negative one.

VILIFY: This sounds like *villain*, a word most people would say is bad.

GLORIFY: This sounds like *glorious*, a word most people would say is good.

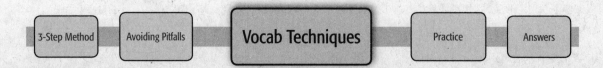

3-Step Method | Avoiding Pitfalls | **Vocab Techniques** | Practice | Answers

Let's say that VILIFY has a negative charge (–) and GLORIFY has a positive charge (+). On all Synonym questions, the correct answer will have *the same charge as the stem word*, so use your instincts about word charge to help you when you're stuck on a tough word.

Decide whether each of the following words has a positive (+) or negative (–) charge.

AUSPICIOUS   _____

MALADY   _____

NOXIOUS   _____

AMIABLE   _____

BOORISH   _____

MELANCHOLY_____

HUMANE   _____

Often words that sound harsh have a negative meaning, while smooth-sounding words tend to have positive meanings. If *cantankerous* sounds negative to you, you would be right. It means "difficult to handle."

You can also use prefixes and roots to help determine a word's charge. *Mal*, *de*, *dis*, *un*, *in*, *im*, *a*, and *mis* often indicate a negative, while *pro*, *ben*, and *magn* are often positives.

Not all words sound positive; some sound neutral. But if you can define the charge, you can probably eliminate some answer choices on that basis alone.

Now let's see how you did on identifying the charge of the words listed above.

Auspicious (+) means favorable; a *malady* (–) means an illness; *noxious* (–) means harmful; *amiable* (+) means agreeable; *boorish* (–) means rude; *melancholy* (–) means sadness; and *humane* (+) means kind.

PRACTICE MAKES PERFECT

Now that you've been through all of the techniques to succeed on Synonym questions, it's time for some practice. Work through the following 20 questions, using the Kaplan Three-Step Method, avoiding pitfalls, and employing vocabulary techniques when you get stuck.

PRACTICE QUESTIONS

1. DISMAL:

   (A) bleak
   (B) crowded
   (C) comfortable
   (D) temporary
   (E) typical

2. HUMID:

   (A) damp
   (B) windy
   (C) hot
   (D) stormy
   (E) hazy

3. DEPORT:

   (A) punish
   (B) banish
   (C) censor
   (D) jail
   (E) praise

4. PEDDLE:

   (A) assemble
   (B) steal
   (C) edit
   (D) deliver
   (E) sell

5. TERMINATE:

   (A) extend
   (B) renew
   (C) end
   (D) sell
   (E) finalize

6. DEARTH:

   (A) explosion
   (B) increase
   (C) shortage
   (D) change
   (E) surplus

7. OBSCURE:

   (A) tragic
   (B) dark
   (C) obligatory
   (D) ignored
   (E) legendary

8. MOURN:

   (A) inaugurate
   (B) celebrate
   (C) greet
   (D) oppose
   (E) grieve

9. RECLUSE:

   (A) artist
   (B) beggar
   (C) lunatic
   (D) scavenger
   (E) hermit

10. HOMAGE:

   (A) youth
   (B) wreath
   (C) respect
   (D) affection
   (E) household

3-Step Method | Avoiding Pitfalls | Vocab Techniques | **Practice** | Answers

11. HERBIVOROUS:

    (A) huge
    (B) warm-blooded
    (C) endangered
    (D) plant-eating
    (E) intelligent

12. SYNOPSIS:

    (A) summary
    (B) satire
    (C) paragraph
    (D) update
    (E) rebuttal

13. WANTON:

    (A) fantastic
    (B) repeated
    (C) lustful
    (D) careful
    (E) needy

14. IMPERIOUS:

    (A) royal
    (B) friendly
    (C) gusty
    (D) arrogant
    (E) insightful

15. HALLOW:

    (A) revere
    (B) dig
    (C) inhabit
    (D) discover
    (E) release

16. BLISS:

    (A) ecstasy
    (B) escape
    (C) prayer
    (D) terror
    (E) fun

17. INDECENT:

    (A) centralized
    (B) immortal
    (C) improper
    (D) incessant
    (E) recent

18. TANGIBLE:

    (A) unrelated
    (B) glib
    (C) touchable
    (D) tanned
    (E) incapable

19. FEROCITY:

    (A) hardness
    (B) humility
    (C) narrowness
    (D) scarcity
    (E) fierceness

20. TENACIOUS:

    (A) tender
    (B) determined
    (C) temporary
    (D) talkative
    (E) discouraged

3-Step Method | Avoiding Pitfalls | Vocab Techniques | **Practice** | Answers

PRACTICE QUESTION ANSWERS

1. A
2. A
3. B
4. E
5. C
6. C
7. B
8. E
9. E
10. C

11. D
12. A
13. C
14. D
15. A
16. A
17. C
18. C
19. E
20. B

CHAPTER 8: CRITICAL READING

Critical Reading questions appear on all levels of the SSAT & ISEE. The Reading section presents you with seven or eight passages and questions that follow. The passages will be in the form of serious articles, stories, and poems. For each passage, you'll be asked about the main idea and details presented. You'll only get points for answering questions correctly, not for reading the text thoroughly, so keep your attention on reading as quickly as possible and answering as many questions as you can.

However, remember that if you are in the lower grade within your level, you DON'T need to answer all of the questions—in fact, you don't even need to read all of the passages. You can get a great score even if you don't answer all the questions, so don't sweat it.

READING STRATEGIES

On the one hand, it's a good thing that you're inherently prepared for this section because you already know how to read. On the other hand, your previous reading experience has the potential to get you into a bit of trouble on this section of the test. Reading habits that may serve you well in school can get in the way on the test.

There are three traps that students commonly fall into on the test.

> **Trap 1:** Reading too slowly.
>
> **Trap 2:** Continually rereading things you do not understand.
>
> **Trap 3:** Spending more time on the passages than on the questions.

It is a mistake to approach the reading passages with the intention of understanding them thoroughly. You need to focus on answering the questions, not on getting to know the text.

> **READ, DON'T LEARN**
>
> " On the SSAT/ISEE, you'll have to read quickly and efficiently. Your goal is not to learn the information presented, or even to think about it very much. Rather, you need to figure out the main point and where to look for any details you might be asked about. "

Strategies — SSAT/ISEE Reading Different — 4-Step Method — Critical Skills in Action — Practice

SSAT/ISEE READING IS DIFFERENT FROM EVERYDAY READING!!!

So that wasn't exactly subtle. It's an important point. You already know how to read, but the way that you read normally may not help you maximize your points on the test. There are three main skills you'll need to employ to ace the Reading section:

1. **Summarize:** You'll need to be able to sum up what the passage is all about.

2. **Research:** You'll need to be able to find facts, figures, and names in the passage.

3. **Make Inferences:** You'll need to be able to piece together information that isn't directly stated.

How can you make sure you do all of these very official-sounding things? Here are some solid strategies:

1. LOOK FOR THE BIG IDEA

Don't read as if you're memorizing everything. Aim to pick up just the gist of the passage—the author's main idea.

2. PAY ATTENTION TO LANGUAGE

The author's choice of words can tell you everything about his or her point of view, attitude and style.

3. BE A CRITICAL READER

As you read, ask yourself critical questions: "What's the author's main point? What message is the author trying to get across?"

4. MAKE IT SIMPLE

Despite the fancy language, Reading passages are usually about pretty simple topics. Don't get bogged down by technical language; translate the author's ideas into your *own words*.

5. KEEP MOVING

Aim to spend no more than one minute reading each passage; remember, just reading the passage won't score you points.

6. DON'T SWEAT THE DETAILS

Don't waste time reading and rereading parts you don't understand. Move swiftly through the passage to answer the questions, which is what really counts.

You've probably realized by now that Kaplan has a multistep method for all the question types on the SSAT/ISEE. It's in your best interest to approach the test as a whole and the individual sections systematically. If you approach every passage the same way, you'll work your way through the Reading section efficiently.

KAPLAN FOUR-STEP METHOD FOR CRITICAL READING

Step 1. Read the passage.

Step 2. Decode the question.

Step 3. Research the details.

Step 4. Predict the answer and check the answer choices.

Like the other multistep methods, the Kaplan Four-Step Method for Critical Reading requires you to do most of your work before you attempt to answer the questions. It's very tempting to read the questions and immediately jump to the answer choices. Don't do this. The work you do up front will not only save you time in the long run, it will increase your chances of avoiding the tempting wrong answers.

STEP 1: READ THE PASSAGE

The first thing to do is to read the passage. This shouldn't come as a big surprise. And although you don't want to memorize or dissect the passage, you **do** need to read it. If you try to answer the questions without doing so, you're likely to make mistakes. Although you'll learn more about *how* to read the passages later, keep in mind that the main things you want to look for are the **Big Idea,** and the **Paragraph topics.** Additionally, you'll want to note where the passage seems to be going.

For example, if you saw the following passage (which, admittedly, is a little shorter than the average SSAT/ISEE passage), these are some of the thing you might want to note . . .

The first detective stories, written by Edgar Allen Poe and Sir Arthur Conan Doyle, emerged in the mid-nineteenth century, at a time when there was an
Line enormous public interest in scientific progress. The
(5) newspapers of the day continually publicized the latest scientific discoveries, and scientists were acclaimed as the heroes of the age. Poe and Conan Doyle shared this fascination with the step-by-step, logical approach used by scientists in their experiments, and instilled
(10) their detective heroes with outstanding powers of scientific reasoning.

The character of Sherlock Holmes, for example, illustrates Conan Doyle's admiration for the scientific mind. In each case that Holmes investigates, he is able
(15) to use the most insubstantial evidence to track down his opponent. Using only his restless eye and ingenious reasoning powers, Holmes pieces together the identity of the villain from such unremarkable details as the type of cigar ashes left at the crime scene,

This passage is basically about detective stories . . . and science.

Holmes is an <u>example</u> of a detective hero with a brilliant scientific mind . . .

← Poe and Conan Doyle seem to be important.

← Comparison between Holmes and Darwin.

(20)   or the kind of ink used in a handwritten letter. In fact,
          Holmes' painstaking attention to detail often reminds
          the reader of Charles Darwin's On the Origin of the
          Species, published some twenty years earlier.

Again, you'll spend more time later learning how to read the passage. The point here is that the first thing you want to do is read through the entire passage noting the major themes and a few details.

STEP 2: DECODE THE QUESTION

Several questions will follow the passage. And *before* you can answer each question, you'll have to figure out exactly what's being asked. You need to make the question make sense to you.

> Which of the following is implied by the statement that Holmes was able to identify the villain based on "unremarkable details"?
>
> (A) Holmes's enemies left no traces at the crime scene.
> (B) The character of Holmes was based on Charles Darwin.
> (C) Few real detectives would have been capable of solving Holmes's cases.
> (D) Holmes was particularly brilliant in powers of detection.
> (E) Criminal investigation often involves tedious, time-consuming tasks.

STEP 3: RESEARCH THE DETAILS

This does *not* mean that you should start rereading the passage from the beginning to find the reference to "unremarkable details." Focus your research. Where does the author mention Holmes? You should have noted when you read the passage that the author discusses Holmes in the second paragraph. So scan that paragraph for the reference to "unremarkable details." (Hint: the reference can be found in line 18.)

Additionally, don't answer questions based on your memory. Go back and do the research. In other words, if you can answer questions based on your memory, you have spent too much time on the passage.

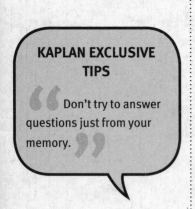

KAPLAN EXCLUSIVE TIPS

Don't try to answer questions just from your memory.

STEP 4: PREDICT THE ANSWER AND CHECK THE ANSWER CHOICES

When you find the detail in the passage, think about the *purpose* that it serves. Why does the author mention the "unremarkable details"? If you read the lines surrounding the phrase, you'll see that the author talks about how amazing it is that Holmes can solve mysteries based on such little evidence. Therefore, the *reason* the author mentions "unremarkable details" is to show how impressive Holmes is. Now scan your answer choices.

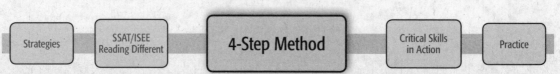

Strategies | SSAT/ISEE Reading Different | **4-Step Method** | Critical Skills in Action | Practice

(A) Holmes's enemies left no traces at the crime scene.

(B) The character of Holmes was based on Charles Darwin.

(C) Few real detectives would have been capable of solving Holmes's cases.

(D) Holmes was particularly brilliant in powers of detection.

(E) Criminal investigation often involves tedious, time-consuming tasks.

Answer (D) should leap out at you.

CRITICAL READING SKILLS IN ACTION

Remember earlier in the lesson when we discussed the three key critical reading skills: summarizing, researching, and making inferences? Let's look at how these skills can help you not only to read the passage, but also to answer the questions.

SUMMARIZING

For the purposes of the SSAT/ISEE, *summarizing* means capturing in a single phrase what the *entire* passage is about. Most passages will be followed by a question that deals with the passage as a whole. Wrong answers will include choices that cover only one paragraph or some other subset of the passage. You'll need to recognize the answer choice that deals with the passage as a whole. If you've thought about the Big Picture ahead of time, you're more likely to home in on the correct answer.

    The four brightest moons of Jupiter were the first objects in the solar system discovered with the use of the telescope. Their proven existence played a central
Line role in Galileo's famous argument in support of the
(5) Copernican model of the solar system, in which the planets are described as revolving around the Sun.
    For several hundred years after their discovery by Galileo in 1610, scientific understanding of these moons increased fairly slowly. Observers on earth
(10) succeeded in measuring their approximate diameters, their relative densities, and eventually some of their light-reflecting characteristics. However, the spectacular close-up photographs sent back by the 1979 Voyager missions forever changed our
(15) impressions of these bodies.

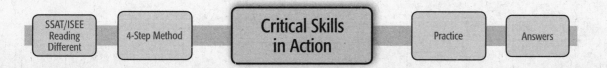

EXAMPLE

Which of the following best tells what this passage is about?

(A) Galileo's invention of the telescope

(B) The discovery of the Galilean moons

(C) Scientific knowledge about Jupiter's four brightest moons

(D) The Copernican model of the solar system

(E) The early history of astronomy

There is only one answer choice here that sums up the contents of both paragraphs. (B) is just a detail. (A) cannot be correct because Galileo's telescope is not even mentioned. (D) is mentioned only in the first paragraph and is a distortion of the author's point. (E) is too broad in scope.

Only (C) summarizes the entire passage. The passage deals with scientific knowledge about Jupiter's four brightest moons. The four moons are the first thing mentioned in the first paragraph, and the rest of the first paragraph discusses the role they played for Galileo. The second paragraph deals with how the moons were perceived by scientists throughout history. In sum, both paragraphs deal with scientific knowledge about these moons.

RESEARCHING

Researching essentially means knowing *where* to look for the details. Generally, if you note your paragraph topics, you should be in pretty good shape to find the details. Once you know where to look, just scan for key phrases found in the question.

A human body can survive without water for several days and without food for as much as several weeks. If breathing stops for as little as three to six
Line minutes, however, death is likely. All animals require a
(5) constant supply of oxygen to the body tissues, and especially to the heart or brain. In the human body, the respiratory system performs this function, by delivering air containing oxygen to the blood.

Breathing is the most urgent human bodily function.

But respiration in large animals possessing lungs
(10) involves more than just breathing. It is a complex process that delivers oxygen to internal tissues while eliminating waste carbon dioxide produced by cells. More specifically, respiration involves two processes known as bulk flow and diffusion. Oxygen and carbon
(15) dioxide are moved in bulk through the respiratory and circulatory systems; gaseous diffusion occurs at different points across thin tissue membranes.

Respiration in large animals is a complex process.

SSAT/ISEE Reading Different — 4-Step Method — **Critical Skills in Action** — Practice — Answers

Take a look at the previous passage and paragraph topics. The paragraph topics are very general; they just note the gist of the paragraphs. If you saw the following questions, would you know where to find the answers?

EXAMPLE

Which bodily function, according to the passage, is least essential to the survival of the average human being?

(A) eating

(B) drinking

(C) breathing

(D) blood circulation

(E) the oxygen supply

The first paragraph deals with bodily functions. Lines 2–3 note that food is most expendable.

EXAMPLE

Which part of an animal's body is responsible for producing waste carbon dioxide?

(A) The internal tissues

(B) The circulatory systems

(C) The tissue membranes

(D) The bloodstream

(E) The cells

The second paragraph deals with the complex details of respiration. Carbon dioxide is mentioned in lines 14–15.

MAKING INFERENCES

Making an inference means looking for something that is strongly implied, but not stated explicitly. In other words, making an inference means *reading between the lines*. What did the author *almost* say, but not say exactly?

Inferences will not stray too far from the language of the text. Wrong answers on Inference questions will often fall beyond the subject matter of the passage.

Children have an amazing talent for learning
vocabulary. Between the ages of one and seventeen,
the average person learns the meaning of about 80,000
Line words—about 14 per day. Dictionaries and traditional
(5) classroom vocabulary lessons only account for part of
this spectacular knowledge growth. More influential
are individuals' reading habits and their interaction
with people whose vocabularies are larger than their
own. Reading shows students how words are used in
(10) sentences. Conversation offers several extra benefits
that make vocabulary learning engaging—it supplies
visual information, offers frequent repetition of new
words, and gives students the chance to ask questions.

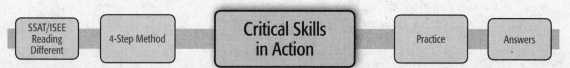

EXAMPLE

When is a child most receptive to learning the meaning of new words?

(A) When the child reaches high school age

(B) When the child is talking to other students

(C) When the child is assigned vocabulary exercises

(D) When the child is regularly told that he or she needs to improve

(E) When vocabulary learning is made interesting

This short passage discusses how children learn vocabulary. The question asks when children are *most* receptive to learning new words. No sentence in the passage states that "Children are *most* receptive to learning new words . . ." However, in lines 6–8, the author mentions that reading and conversation are particularly helpful. Lines 10–13 note how conversation makes vocabulary engaging. This is consistent with (E). There is nothing in the passage to suggest that children learn more at high school age, (A). (B) might be tempting, but it is too specific: There's no reason to believe that talking to students is more helpful than talking to anyone else. (C) contradicts the passage and (D) is never mentioned at all.

At this point, you have a lot of tools to help you read passages and approach questions. It's a good idea to have a solid understanding of what the questions are, what types of questions you'll see, and how to best approach each one. There are three basic question types in the Reading Section: **Main Idea, Detail,** and **Inference** questions.

Since you can't exactly deal with questions unless you have an accompanying passage, take three or four minutes to read the following passage. As usual, mark it up. Read it with the goal of answering questions afterwards.

The first truly American art movement was formed by a group of landscape painters that emerged in the early nineteenth century called the Hudson River
Line School. The first works in this style were created by
(5) Thomas Cole, Thomas Doughty, and Asher Durand, a trio of painters who worked during the 1820s in the Hudson River Valley and surrounding locations. Heavily influenced by European Romanticism, these painters set out to convey the remoteness and splendor
(10) of the American wilderness. The strongly nationalistic tone of their paintings caught the spirit of the times, and within a generation the movement had mushroomed to include landscape painters from all over the United States. Canvases celebrating such typically American
(15) scenes as Niagara Falls, Boston Harbor, and the expansion of the railroad into rural Pennsylvania were greeted with enormous popular acclaim.

One factor contributing to the success of the Hudson River School was the rapid growth of
(20) American nationalism in the early nineteenth century. The War of 1812 had given the United States a new sense of pride in its identity, and as the nation continued to grow, there was a desire to compete with Europe on both economic and cultural grounds. The vast
(25) panoramas of the Hudson River School fitted the bill perfectly by providing a new movement in art that was unmistakably American in origin. The Hudson River School also arrived at a time when writers in the United
(30) States were turning their attention to the wilderness as a unique aspect of their nationality. The Hudson River

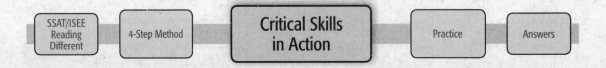

School profited from this nostalgia because they effectively represented the continent the way it used to be. The view that the American character was formed (35) by the frontier experience was widely held, and many writers were concerned about the future of a country that was becoming increasingly urbanized.

In keeping with this nationalistic spirit, even the painting style of the Hudson River School exhibited a (40) strong sense of American identity. Although many of the artists studied in Europe, their paintings show a desire to be free of European artistic rules. Regarding the natural landscape as a direct manifestation of God, the Hudson River School painters attempted to record (45) what they saw as accurately as possible. Unlike European painters who brought to their canvases the styles and techniques of centuries, they sought neither to embellish nor to idealize their scenes, portraying nature with the care and attention to detail of (50) naturalists.

Hopefully, you understood that this passage was about why the Hudson River School became so successful. You should have also noted that the second paragraph addresses how American nationalism contributed to the success of the Hudson River School and the third paragraph discusses how nationalist sentiment was evident in the Hudson River School painting style.

Main Idea Questions

A **Main Idea** question asks you to summarize the topic of the passage.

EXAMPLE

Which of the following best tells what this passage is about?

(A) The history of American landscape painting
(B) Why an art movement caught the public imagination
(C) How European painters influenced the Hudson River School
(D) Why writers began to romanticize the American wilderness
(E) The origins of nationalism in the United States

> Main Idea questions are pretty easy to recognize. They will always ask something general about the passage.
>
> Look for the answer choice that summarizes the entire passage. Rule out choices that are too broad or too narrow.

Do you see which one of these answers describes the entire passage without being too broad or too narrow?

(A) is too broad, as is (E). The passage is not about all American landscape painting; it's about the Hudson River School. Nationalism in the United States is much larger than the role of nationalism in a particular art movement. (C) and (D) are too narrow. European painters did influence the Hudson River School painters, but that wasn't the point of the whole passage. Similarly, writers are mentioned in paragraph 2, but the passage is about an art movement. Only (B) captures the essence of the passage—it's about an art movement that caught the public imagination.

Detail Questions

Detail questions are straightforward—all you've got to do is locate the relevant information in the passage. The key strategy is to **research** the details by relating facts, figures and names in the question to a *specific* paragraph.

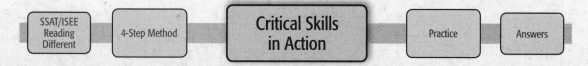

EXAMPLE

Which of the following is not mentioned as one of the reasons for the success of the Hudson River School?

(A) American nationalism increased after the War of 1812.

(B) Americans were nostalgic about the frontier.

(C) Writers began to focus on the wilderness.

(D) The United States wanted to compete with Europe.

(E) City-dwellers became concerned about environmental pollution.

> Note how the Detail question asks about what is specifically mentioned—or not mentioned.
>
> Scan the passage words or phrases in the answer choices. When you find the references, cross out the answer choices that do appear in the passage. The one left over will be the correct answer.

Four of the five answer choices are mentioned explicitly in the passage. (A) is mentioned in lines 19–20. (B) appears in line 32. (C) shows up in line 30. (D) is mentioned in line 23. Only (E) does not appear in the passage.

INFERENCE QUESTIONS

An **Inference** question, like a **Detail** question, asks you to find relevant information in the passage. But once you've located the details, you have to go one step further: you have to figure out the underlying point of a particular phrase or example. Use your inference skills to figure out the author's point. The answer will not be stated, but it will be *strongly implied*.

EXAMPLE

Which of the following best describes what is suggested by the statement that the Hudson River School paintings "fitted the bill perfectly" (line 25)?

(A) The paintings depicted famous battle scenes.

(B) The paintings were very successful commercially.

(C) The paintings reflected a new pride in the United States.

(D) The paintings were favorably received in Europe.

(E) The paintings were accurate in their portrayal of nature.

> "Suggested" is a classic Inference clue. If something is "suggested," it is not stated outright.
>
> Read the lines surrounding the quote. Summarize the author's point in your mind before you check the answer choices.

First, read the lines surrounding the quote to put the quote in context. Paragraph 2 talks about American pride; that's why Hudson River School paintings "fitted the bill." Hudson River School paintings were about America. (C) summarizes the point nicely. Note how this question revolves around the interplay between main idea and details. This detail strengthens the topic of the paragraph, the growing sense of nationalism in America. (A) superficially relates to the War of 1812, but doesn't answer the question. (B), (D), and (E) are way off base.

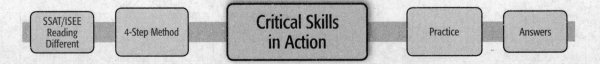

A REMINDER ABOUT TIMING

Plan to spend approximately three minutes reading the passage and roughly a minute to a minute and a half on each question. When you first start practicing, you'll probably find yourself spending more time than that on the passages. That's OK. However, you need to pay attention to your timing and cut the time down to around three minutes. If you don't, it will hurt you in the long run.

> ### A WORD ABOUT SCIENCE PASSAGES
>
> " At least one reading passage may deal with a scientific or technical topic. You will NOT be tested on any outside science knowledge, so do not answer the questions based on anything other than the information contained in the passage. "

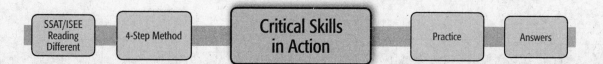

SSAT/ISEE Reading Different | 4-Step Method | **Critical Skills in Action** | Practice | Answers

PRACTICE QUESTIONS

Almost everyone enjoys hearing some kind of live music. But few of us realize the complex process that goes into designing the acoustics of concert and
Line lecture halls. In the design of any building where
(5) audibility of sound is a major consideration, architects have to carefully match the space and materials they use to the intended purpose of the venue. One problem is that the intensity of sound may build too quickly in an enclosed space. Another problem is that only part
(10) of the sound we hear in any large room or auditorium comes directly from the source. Much of it reaches us a fraction of a second later after it has been reflected off the walls, ceiling, and floor as reverberated sound. How much each room reverberates depends upon both
(15) its size, and the ability of its contents to absorb sound. Too little reverberation can make music sound thin and weak; too much can blur the listener's sense of where one note stops and the next begins.

Consequently the most important factor
(20) in acoustic design is the time it takes for these reverberations to die down altogether, called the reverberation time.

1. Which of the following is the main topic of this passage?

   (A) The challenges of an architect's job
   (B) The differences between speech and music
   (C) The experience of hearing live music
   (D) The role of reverberation in acoustic design
   (E) The construction of large buildings

2. The passage suggests that the "complex process" of acoustic design (line 2) is

   (A) not widely appreciated by the public.
   (B) really a matter of listener sensitivity.
   (C) wholly dependent on the choice of construction materials.
   (D) an engineer's problem, not an architect's.
   (E) most difficult in concert hall construction.

3. According to the passage, audibility of sound is influenced by which of the following factors?

   I. The type of materials used to construct a building
   II. The reflection of sound off a room's ceiling or walls
   III. The size and purpose of a particular room or space

   (A) I only
   (B) II only
   (C) I and II only
   (D) II and III only
   (E) I, II and III

4. According to the passage, too little reverberation in a concert hall can result in

   (A) a rapid increase in the volume of sound.
   (B) the blurring of details in a piece of music.
   (C) a quiet and insubstantial quality of sound.
   (D) confusion among a listening audience.
   (E) an inaccurate estimate of its reverberation time.

5. Which of the following does the author regard as the most significant consideration in the design of a concert hall?

   (A) An appreciation for music
   (B) An understanding of reverberation time
   (C) The choice of building materials
   (D) The purpose of the venue
   (E) The audience capacity

PRACTICE QUESTION ANSWERS

This passage is a discussion of the challenge of proper acoustic design of concert and lecture halls. The author pays special attention to the problem of fine-tuning reverberated sound, which is the sound that comes to the listener after it has been reflected off the walls, ceiling, and floor.

1. D

Lines 14–21 focus on reverberation, which the author describes as the "most important factor in acoustic design" at the end of the passage.

2. A

Choice (A) is the correct answer because the author says that "few of us realize the complex process that goes into designing the acoustics of concert and lecture halls."

3. E

All three options are mentioned in the passage as factors that affect the acoustics of a building, so (E) is the right answer.

4. C

According to the passage, too little reverberation can make sound thin and weak.

5. B

The final sentence of the passage says that the important factor in acoustic design is the reverberation time, which makes (B) correct.

CHAPTER 9:   THE ESSAY

Both the SSAT and ISEE require an essay (all levels), though neither one is graded. So why do you need to write it? Well, the essay is a great way for schools to see how you express yourself, particularly how well you present and argue your opinions. The rest of the test tells them how well you perform on a series of standard tasks, but the essay is the one part of the exam where you get to shine through. Schools look closely at your essay, so think of it as part of your application and take it seriously.

So, what do you need to know to write an essay that will stand out? Really, only a few key things. First and most important, answer the question. No other aspect about your essay will matter if you don't answer the question. Second, write clearly and logically. And finally, proofread your essay before you finish. Even if you think you have been very careful, you'll undoubtedly find things that you'll want to fix or change.

INTRODUCTION TO THE ESSAY

There are five important things to know about the Essay:

1. You'll need to organize your thoughts quickly (you'll have 25 minutes on the SSAT and 30 minutes on the ISEE to write a complete essay).
2. Your essay is limited to two pages.
3. Essay topics will be easy to grasp.
4. What you say is more important than using perfect grammar.
5. Your essay will not be graded.

What's Wrong with This Picture?

Writing a good essay means following a few key rules about writing. Take a look at the following paragraph and think about what's wrong with it. Use the space below to jot down the problems you notice.

Intro Essay   4-Step Method   Pacing   Brainstorming   Show, Don't Tell

Sample Topic: <u>No good deed goes unpunished.</u>

> It always bothers me when people talk about punishment. It's not fair. I mean, there are some kids out there who do really *good* things, even though people don't notice them. In my opinion, everyone spends too much time talking about whether or not there is enough punishment in the world. We should really be talking about more important things like the environment . . .

PLEASE JUST ANSWER THE QUESTION, MA'AM.

"" The Golden Rule of essay writing is to answer the question. That means you need to decide whether you agree or disagree with the statement, think of a few reasons why, and lay them out for the reader. You don't need to be very creative; all you need to do is stick to the topic and write clearly. Before you write a word, though, decide what your opinion is. ""

COMMON PITFALLS IN ESSAY WRITING

What's wrong with the paragraph you just read? The biggest problem with it is that it fails to answer the question. Granted, you're only seeing the beginning of the essay, but you can tell from the way it ends that the author is about to go off on a tangent about the environment instead of discussing the topic. Remember, *always* answer the question.

What else is wrong with the sample paragraph? You might have noticed that it sounds very casual, almost like a conversation. Phrases such as "I mean" and "In my opinion" give the essay a tone that's too familiar and too emotional. While you always want to present your opinion, you should do it in a detached, formal way, like a newspaper article. Try to avoid "I" statements in your essay writing.

How can you avoid making these types of mistakes? How can you make sure you don't get sidetracked while you write, arguing rather than defending, or being redundant? Kaplan has an easy method that you should follow when you write your essay. By following each and every step, you'll be guaranteed to create an organized, clear essay.

KAPLAN FOUR-STEP METHOD FOR WRITING

Step 1. Brainstorm

Step 2. Make an outline

Step 3. Write your essay

Step 4. Proofread

Intro Essay | **4-Step Method** | Pacing | Brainstorming | Show, Don't Tell

This might sound pretty general, a lot like the essays you've written for school. In fact, the essay is the part of the test that most closely resembles the work you do in school. However, the essay follows a much more specific format than other essays, and you don't have a lot of time to do it, so it's very important that you follow all four steps. Let's break them down.

STEP 1: BRAINSTORM

When you start to brainstorm for ideas, ask yourself, "Do I agree or disagree with the topic?" With the sample topic <u>No good deed goes unpunished</u>, your thinking might go like this: I believe that people are rewarded for good deeds, not punished. Okay, what examples can I use to support this point of view?

It's important that you're clear in your head about what your stance is *before* you start to organize your essay. Once you start to put your examples together, you don't want to have to go back and figure out what you're trying to show. It doesn't matter what position you take, as long as you support it well. So don't stress too much about what you really think—just choose a position that will be easy for you to argue.

STEP 2: MAKE AN OUTLINE

Once you've decided your opinion, the next step is to write an outline. Come up with three examples to support your opinion. Your examples should serve to argue why your opinion is right, so make sure they all support the point of view that you're presenting.

Next, decide the best order in which to present your examples. Is there a logical order to lay out your ideas? How do you want to start your essay? How do you want to end it? Make some notes on your scratch paper so when you start to write, you can glance at them to keep you on track and writing quickly.

STEP 3: WRITE YOUR ESSAY

Now you have to write the essay. Follow your outline carefully, but be flexible. Maybe you'll think of another great idea midway through your writing. Should you ignore it, or should you substitute it for the third example you had planned to include? If you think it's better than what you originally came up with, go ahead and write about it instead. Just make sure that any deviation you make from your outline is in fact an improvement over the original idea.

> **WHAT WAS I THINKING?**
>
> " Even if you're feeling rushed, don't skip the Outlining step. Planning your essay will make the entire writing process easier and faster, and will ensure that your writing is well organized. Remember, wear a watch on test day so you can keep a handle on your pacing. "

Intro Essay | **4-Step Method** | Pacing | Brainstorming | Show, Don't Tell

STEP 4: PROOFREAD

Wrap up your writing five minutes before the end of your allotted time. Give your essay a good read-through, making sure you haven't made any spelling mistakes, written run-on sentences, or forgotten to capitalize a proper name. You won't be able to make any huge changes at this point—after all, you only have five minutes left—but you do want to make sure that you haven't made any egregious errors.

PACING

How much time should you spend on each step? Use your watch and this guideline as you write. You want to give yourself sufficient time for each step, because planning and proofreading will make your essay much stronger. Use the following guidelines for timing:

	SSAT	ISEE
Outlining/ Planning	5 minutes	5 minutes
Writing	15 minutes	20 minutes
Proofreading	5 minutes	5 minutes
Total time:	25 minutes	30 minutes

BRAINSTORMING IN ACTION

When you get to the essay section, the last thing you want to happen is a *brain freeze*. You know the feeling: You look at the page, you see the words, your brain doesn't register, you stare into space . . . you can't think of a thing to write about.

How do you avoid such a situation? One of the best ways to make sure your brain is in gear and ready to brainstorm on the spot is to practice doing it. Take a look at the statements below. For each one, decide what position you would take and think of three examples you would present in support of your opinion. Give yourself about five minutes to do each one.

Remember, for each topic, ask yourself the following two questions:

- Do you agree or disagree?
- What examples could you use to support your opinion?

Sample Topic 1: Free speech on the Internet should be protected at all costs.

_____

_____

_____

_____

_____

_____

_____

Sample Topic 2: We learn more from our mistakes than our successes.

_____

_____

_____

_____

_____

_____

_____

Sample Topic 3: Thanks to technological advances, the world is getting smaller every day.

_____

_____

_____

_____

_____

_____

_____

| 4-Step Method | Pacing | **Brainstorming** | Show, Don't Tell | Just the Facts |

SHOW, DON'T TELL

You've probably heard the saying that good writing *shows* rather than *tells*. What does that mean, and what do examples have to do with it?

Take the statement "You can't teach an old dog new tricks." Say you wanted to disagree with it. You could explain why you believe the statement isn't true, what you think about teaching and age, and so forth. Or, you could use examples that *illustrate* the same point. You could discuss the fact that retired people now use the Internet on a regular basis. The fact that people generally considered *old* by society are adapting to a new technology in large numbers serves to show that you can, in fact, teach an old dog new tricks.

What makes a good example? A good example illustrates the point you want to make. In addition, it comes from the world at large, rather than from your personal life. While it may be true that your grandmother e-mails you, it's more powerful to say that many retirees use the Internet every day.

If you're not doing so already, try reading the newspaper on a regular basis. Not only will you know more about what's going on in the world and be ready with great examples for your essays, you'll also improve your vocabulary, which will improve your performance on all of the Verbal sections of your test.

JUST THE FACTS

Aside from answering the question with supporting examples, what do you need to do as you write your essay?

- Develop and organize your ideas.
- Use three paragraphs.
- Use appropriate examples.
- Write in standard English.
- Stick to the topic.
- Use proper spelling, grammar, and punctuation.

> **READING TIPS**
>
> " When you read the newspaper, look at the Editorial page. You'll see how writers argue their opinions on a variety of topics and what kinds of examples they use. And you might learn something interesting in the process, too. "

PRACTICE ESSAY

Work through this topic as though it were the real thing. Brainstorm your ideas, make an outline, write, and proofread. Time yourself (25 minutes if you're taking the SSAT and 30 minutes if you're taking the ISEE).

Essay Topic: <u>Voting is such an important responsibility that all citizens should be required to vote in every election.</u>

Step 1. Brainstorm.

Brainstorm in the space provided below. Do you agree or disagree? What examples might you use to support your argument? (Remember, give yourself only a few minutes to do this!)

_____

_____

_____

_____

_____

_____

Step 2. Make an Outline.

Write your outline here. Keep your essay to three paragraphs. Paragraph 1 gives your introduction and an example. Paragraph 2 gives another example, and paragraph 3 gives your final example and your conclusion.

Paragraph 1

_____

_____

Paragraph 2

_____

_____

Pacing   Brainstorming   Show, Don't Tell   Just the Facts   **Practice Essay**

Paragraph 3

_____

_____

Step 3. Write your Essay.

Write your essay below. Give yourself 15 minutes if you're taking the SSAT and 20 minutes if you're taking the ISEE.

_____

_____

_____

_____

_____

_____

_____

_____

_____

_____

_____

_____

_____

_____

_____

_____

_____

_____

_____

_____

_____

_____

_____

_____

_____

_____

_____

_____

_____

Step 4. Proofread.

Go back to your essay and read through it again. Does it make sense? Have you made any spelling or grammar errors? Fix them. Get used to making corrections clearly on your page, since that's how you will do it the day of the test.

CHAPTER 10: INTRODUCTION TO SSAT/ISEE MATH

Before we dive into the actual math, let's take a step back and think about how to approach math problems in general. You've done math before. You've most likely already been exposed to most of the math concepts you'll see on your private-school admissions test. This begs the question as to why you need to approach SSAT/ISEE math differently than you approach any other math.

The answer is that it's not that you have to do the math *differently*, it's just that you have to do it *deliberately*. You'll be under a lot of time pressure when you take your test, so you need to use your time well.

HOW TO APPROACH SSAT/ISEE MATH

Ultimately, the best way to take control of your testing experience is to approach every math question the same way. This doesn't mean you'll *solve* every problem the same way, it means that you'll use the same process to *decide* how to solve, or even whether to solve, each problem.

READ THROUGH THE QUESTION

Okay, this may seem a little too obvious. Of course, you're going to read the question. How else can you solve the problem? In reality, this isn't quite as obvious as it seems. The point here is that you need to read the entire question carefully before you start solving. When you don't do that, it's incredibly easy to make careless mistakes. Consider the following problem:

EXAMPLE

For what positive value of x does $\dfrac{4}{3} = \dfrac{x^2}{27}$?

(A) 3
(B) 6
(C) 12
(D) 18
(E) 36

How to Approach   Word Problems   % Increase/ Decrease   Calculators

It's crucial that you pay close attention to precisely what the question is asking. The question contains a classic trap that's very easy to fall into if you don't read it carefully. Did you notice how easy it would be to solve for x^2 instead of x? Yes, this would be careless, but it's easy to be careless when you're working quickly.

There are other reasons to read the whole question before you start solving the problem. One is that you may save yourself some work. If you start to answer too quickly, you may assume that a problem is more difficult than it actually is. Or you might assume that it is *less* difficult than it actually is and skip a necessary step or two.

Another reason to read carefully before answering is that you probably shouldn't solve every question on your first pass. Taking control of your test experience means deciding which questions to answer, which to save for later, and which to skip (unless you're taking the ISEE, in which case you should NEVER skip a question).

DECIDE WHETHER TO DO THE QUESTION OR SKIP IT FOR NOW

Each time you approach a new math problem you have the option of answering it immediately or putting it aside. You have to make a decision each time about how to best use your time. You have three options.

1. **If you can solve the question relatively quickly and efficiently, do it! This is the best option.**

2. **If you think you can solve it but that it will take you a long time, circle the number in your test booklet and go back to it later.**
    Remember that when you go back to the problems you have skipped the first time, you'll want to try your best to fill in an answer. Don't underestimate your ability to eliminate wrong answers even when you don't know how to solve. Every time you rule out a wrong answer choice, you increase your chances of guessing correctly.

3. **If you have no idea what to do, skip the question and circle it. Save your time for the questions you can do.**

EXAMPLE

Tamika, Becky, and Kym were investors in a new restaurant. Tamika and Becky each invested one half as much as Kym invested. If the total investment made was $5,200, how much did Kym invest?

(A) $900
(B) $1,300
(C) $1,800
(D) $2,100
(E) $2,600

How to Approach   Word Problems   % Increase/Decrease   Calculators

Different test takers will have different reactions to this question. Some students may quickly see the algebra—or the backdoor method for solving this problem—and do the math. Others may see a word problem and run screaming from the room. This approach is not recommended. However, if you know that you habitually have difficulty with algebra word problems, you may choose to save this problem for later or make an educated guess.

Here's the algebra, by the way. Kym, Tamika, and Becky contributed a total of $5,200. You can represent this algebraically as $K + T + B = \$5,200$. Since Tamika and Becky each contributed half as much as Kym, you can represent these relationships as follows:

$$T = \frac{1}{2}K$$
$$B = \frac{1}{2}K$$

Now, substitute variables so that you can solve the equation.

$$K + T + B = 5,200$$

$$K + \frac{1}{2}K + \frac{1}{2}K = 5,200$$
$$2K = 5,200$$

$$K = 2,600 \text{ (E)}$$

If you choose to tackle the problem, look for the fastest method.

EXAMPLE

Jenna is now x years old and Amy is 3 years younger than Jenna. In terms of x, how old will Amy be in 4 years?

(A) $x - 1$

(B) x

(C) $x + 1$

(D) $x + 4$

(E) $2x + 1$

Here is the algebraic solution. If Jenna is x years old, then Amy is $x - 3$ years old, since Amy is 3 years younger than Jenna. So, in 4 years, Amy will be $(x - 3) + 4$, or $x + 1$.

Here is the picking numbers solution. Suppose that $x = 10$. Then Jenna is now 10 years old. Amy is now 7 years old because Amy is 3 years younger than Jenna. In 4 years, Amy will be 11. Now plug 10 for x into all of the answer choices and see which one equals 11. You can eliminate any answer choice that does not equal 11. Since only (C), $x + 1$, equals 11, it must be correct.

How to Approach | Word Problems | % Increase/ Decrease | Calculators

With the method of picking numbers, it sometimes happens that more than one answer choice gives you the correct result for the particular number or numbers that you choose. When that happens, go back and pick another number(s) to eliminate the remaining incorrect answer choices.

The lesson here is that you have to know your own strengths. Again, in case you missed the point, *know your strengths and use them to your advantage.*

Some people *see* algebra. Others have a harder time with it. The same is true for geometry, word problems, etc. There's often more than one way to solve a question. The *best* method is the method that will get you the correct answer accurately and quickly.

Remember, only guess on the SSAT if you can eliminate at least one answer choice. But on the ISEE, don't leave any answers blank. Since there's no penalty for wrong answers, there is no harm in guessing. Of course, the fact that random guessing won't hurt you does not mean that you shouldn't be strategic about guessing. Remember, every answer choice you rule out increases your odds of guessing correctly.

HELPFUL HINT

When you skip a question, circle it in your test booklet so that it will be easy to spot if you have time to go back.

EXAMPLE

What is the greatest common factor of 95 and 114?

(A) 1
(B) 5
(C) 6
(D) 19
(E) 38

If you couldn't remember how to find the greatest common factor or were running out of time on the test and wanted to save your time for other questions, you should be able to eliminate at least one answer choice pretty easily. Do you see which one?

Since all multiples of 5 end in 5 or zero, 5 cannot be a factor of 114. Therefore, (B) must be incorrect. Eliminate it and then guess.

PICK NUMBERS

Sometimes a math problem can appear more difficult than it actually is because it's general or abstract. You can make it more concrete—and easier—by temporarily substituting numbers for the variables. This "picking numbers" strategy can help make the math easier.

How to Approach

Word Problems | % Increase/Decrease | Calculators

EXAMPLE

$3a(2b + 2) =$

(A) $2b + 3a$

(B) $5ab + 2b$

(C) $5ab + 2a + 1$

(D) $6ab + 2a$

(E) $6ab + 6a$

The algebra in this question is pretty straightforward. According to the distributive property, $3a(2b + 2) = (3a)(2b) + (3a)(2) = 6ab + 6a$ or choice (E). Most test takers will probably do the algebra to solve the question.

However, if you have trouble with algebra or simply find that it takes you a long time, you can approach the problem another way. Pick simple numbers for a and b and plug them into the expression $3a(2b + 2)$. If $a = 2$ and $b = 3$, then $3a(2b + 2) = (3)(2)[2(3) + 2] = 6(6 + 2) = 48$. Now you know that if $a = 2$ and $b = 3$, the expression equals 48.

Once you know this, simply plug 2 in for a and 3 in for b in each of the answer choices. Any answer choice that does not equal 48 can be eliminated. Since only (E) equals 48, (E) is the answer.

(A) $2b + 3a = 2(3) + 3(2) = 12$

(B) $5ab + 2b = 5(2)(3) + 2(3) = 36$

(C) $5ab + 2a + 1 = 5(2)(3) + 2(2) + 1 = 35$

(D) $6ab + 2a = 6(2)(3) + 2(2) = 40$

(E) $6ab + 6a = 6(2)(3) + 6(2) = 48$

If two or more answer choices had come out to 48, you would have had to do a little more work. You would have had to pick new numbers for a and b, come up with a new value and then plug those numbers into the answer choices that came out the same the first time.

In other words, if (B) and (E) had both equaled 48, you could have made $a = 3$ and $b = 4$, discovered that the expression $3a(2b + 2)$ equals 90, and then plugged 3 and 4 into only choices (B) and (E) to determine which one equaled 90.

WORD PROBLEMS

Picking numbers can be extremely helpful when the answer choices to a word problem contain variables. Remember this problem?

How to Approach   **Word Problems**   % Increase/Decrease   Calculators

EXAMPLE

Jenna is now x years old and Amy is 3 years younger than Jenna. In terms of x, how old will Amy be in 4 years?

(A) $x - 1$

(B) x

(C) $x + 1$

(D) $x + 4$

(E) $2x + 1$

As you saw earlier, there's more than one way to solve this problem. Some test takers will find it easier to solve this question by working with algebraic expressions. Others may feel that this will slow them down. Picking a number for x may be faster and easier.

If you say that $x = 10$, then Jenna is 10 years old and Amy is 7, since she's three years younger. In four years, Amy will be 11. Once you have this value, plug in 10 for x in each of the answer choices to see which ones equal 11. Those answer choices that don't equal 11 can be eliminated.

(A) $10 - 1 = 9$

(B) 10

(C) $10 + 1 = 11$

(D) $10 + 4 = 14$

(E) $2(10) + 1 = 21$

Only (C) equals 11, so (C) must be correct.

PERCENT INCREASE/DECREASE PROBLEMS

If you see a problem that deals with percents, picking 100 is the easiest and quickest way to solve.

EXAMPLE

If the price of a stock decreases by 20 percent, and then by an additional 25 percent, by what percent has the price decreased from its original value?

(A) 40%

(B) 45%

(C) 50%

(D) 55%

(E) 60%

How to Approach | Word Problems | **% Increase/ Decrease** | Calculators

Make the original price of the stock $100. The initial 20 percent decrease brings the price down to $80. (Twenty percent of 100 is 20.) Twenty-five percent of 80 or one-quarter of $80 is $20, so the stock price is decreased by an additional $20, bringing the final price down to $60. Since the price dropped from $100 to $60, the total decrease is $40 or 40 percent of the original price. (A) is the correct answer.

You may have been able to solve this problem by setting up algebraic equations, but picking 100 is easier and faster here.

BACKSOLVE

Backsolving is another tool to help you get a math answer more quickly. What this means is that you can work backward from the answer choices. Backsolving will work only if your answer choices are all numbers (and they don't include variables.)

Here's how it works. When answer choices are numbers—i.e., not variables—you can expect them to be arranged from *small to large* or *large to small*. The test maker does not get creative with the order of the answer choices. What you do is to start with the *middle* answer choice and plug it directly into the problem. If it works, you're set. If it doesn't, you can usually determine whether to try a larger or smaller answer choice. Look at the following problem and explanation.

EXAMPLE

Three consecutive multiples of 20 have a sum of 300. What is the greatest of these numbers?

(A)   60
(B)   80
(C)   100
(D)   120
(E)   140

Begin with the middle answer choice. If 100 is the greatest of the three numbers, the three numbers must be 100, 80, and 60. 100 + 80 + 60 = 240. The correct three numbers will add up to 300, so the greatest of these numbers must be greater than 100. Try answer (D). If 120 is the greatest, the three numbers must be 120, 100, and 80. 120 + 100 + 80 = 300. Answer (D) is correct.

It's worth noting that if (D) had also given you a sum less than 300, you would not have to check choice (E). Think about it. If the numbers are arranged from small to large and the second largest number gives you an answer that is too small, you know that the largest number has to be correct.

> **SPEED TIP**
>
> " Always start with the middle answer choice when backsolving. If it's too small, move to the bigger ones. "

| How to Approach | Word Problems | % Increase/ Decrease | Calculators |

A WORD ABOUT CALCULATORS

This is an easy one. You *cannot* use a calculator on the SSAT or ISEE. Leave your calculator home. End of story.

The rest of the Math chapters in this book deal with Math Content review. Some of this will be familiar; some may be less familiar. Take a look at all of it, but spend more time with the subjects that are less familiar. Even if you don't need to review a particular subject, make sure you do the practice set. There's no harm in practicing extra problems.

CHAPTER 11: ARITHMETIC

On the SSAT/ISEE, **arithmetic** means more than addition and subtraction. **Arithmetic** is the umbrella term for a wide range of math concepts, including **number properties, factors, divisibility, fractions, decimals, exponents, radicals, percents, averages, ratios, proportions, rates,** and **probability.** These concepts are summarized in your Math Reference at the end of the book. This section will go over these important concepts and give you a chance to practice problems dealing with these subjects.

DEFINITIONS

Number Type	Definition	Examples
Integers	*Whole numbers including 0 and their opposites (negative whole numbers)*	$-900, -3, 0, 1, 54$
Fractions	*A **fraction** is a number that is written in the form $\frac{A}{B}$ where A is the numerator and B is the denominator.*	$-\frac{5}{6}, -\frac{3}{17}, \frac{1}{2}, \frac{899}{901}$
Improper fractions	*An **improper fraction** is a fraction whose value is greater than 1 (or less than −1).*	$-\frac{65}{64}, \frac{9}{8}, \frac{57}{10}$
Mixed numbers	*An improper fraction can be converted into a **mixed number**. A mixed number has an integer part and a fraction part.*	$-1\frac{1}{64}, 1\frac{1}{8}, 5\frac{7}{10}$
Positive/Negative	*Numbers greater than 0 are **positive numbers**; numbers less than 0 are **negative**. 0 is neither positive nor negative.*	Positive: $\frac{7}{8}, 1, 5, 900$ Negative: $-64, -40, -11, -\frac{6}{13}$

Number Type	Definition	Examples
Even/Odd	An **even number** is an integer that is a multiple of 2. Even numbers end in 0, 2, 4, 6, or 8. An **odd number** is an integer that is not a multiple of 2. Odd numbers end in 1, 3, 5, 7, or 9.	Even numbers: −8, −2, 0, 4, 12, 188 Odd numbers: −17, −1, 3, 9, 457
Prime number	A **prime number** is an integer greater than 1 that has exactly two factors: 1 and itself. 2 is the only even prime number.	2, 3, 5, 7, 11, 59, 83
Composite number	A **composite number** is an integer greater than 1 that has more than two factors.	12, 35, 84
Consecutive numbers	Numbers that follow one after another, in order, without skipping any.	Consecutive integers: 3, 4, 5, 6 Consecutive even integers: 2, 4, 6, 8, 10 Consecutive multiples of 9: 9, 18, 27, 36
Factor	A positive integer that divides evenly into a given number with no remainder.	The complete list of factors of 12: 1, 2, 3, 4, 6, 12
Multiple	A number that a given number will divide into with no remainder.	Some multiples of 12: 0, 12, 24, 60

ODDS AND EVENS

There are a few things to remember when you're dealing with odd and even numbers:

Even ± Even = Even

Even ± Odd = Odd

Odd ± Odd = Even

Even × Even = Even

Even × Odd = Even

Odd × Odd = Odd

POSITIVES AND NEGATIVES

You will not see many problems that focus specifically on positives and negatives, but you must know the basics because these concepts will show up as part of harder problems.

Definitions | Order of Operations | Divisibility Rules | Fractions & Decimals | Common % Equivalencies

To **add** any two integers with the **same sign,** keep the sign and add the integers.

EXAMPLES:

$$(-3) + (-8) = -11$$
$$9 + 12 = 21$$

To **add** any two integers with **opposite signs,** keep the sign of the integer further from zero, then subtract the integers, ignoring the signs.

EXAMPLES:

$$3 + (-8) = -(8 - 3)$$
$$= -5$$
$$-9 + 12 = +(12 - 9)$$
$$= 3$$

REMEMBER

Negative ×
or ÷ Negative = Positive

Positive × or ÷ Negative =
Negative

To **subtract** two integers, change the subtraction sign to addition, then change the sign of the number being subtracted to its opposite.

EXAMPLES:

$$(3) - (-8) = 3 + (+8)$$
$$= 11$$
$$-9 - 12 = -9 + (-12)$$
$$= -21$$

Multiplying and **dividing** positives and negatives is like all other multiplication and division, with one catch. To figure out whether your answer is positive or negative, count the number of negatives you had to start. If you had an odd number of negatives, the answer is negative. If you had an even number of negatives, the answer is positive.

$$6 \times (-4) = -24 \text{ (1 negative} \rightarrow \text{negative product)}$$
$$(-6) \times (-4) = 24 \text{ (2 negatives} \rightarrow \text{positive product)}$$
$$(-1) \times (-6) \times (-4) = -24 \text{ (3 negatives} \rightarrow \text{negative product)}$$

Similarly,

$$-24 \div 6 = -4 \text{ (1 negative} \rightarrow \text{negative quotient)}$$
$$-24 \div (-4) = 6 \text{ (2 negatives} \rightarrow \text{positive quotient)}$$

Definitions | Order of Operations | Divisibility Rules | Fractions & Decimals | Common % Equivalencies

ABSOLUTE VALUE

To find the **absolute value** of a number, simply find the number's distance from zero on a number line. Because distance cannot be negative, the absolute value of a number will always be greater than or equal to zero.

$$|4| = 4*$$
$$|-4| = 4**$$

*because 4 is four units from zero

**because –4 is four units from zero

When absolute value expressions contain different arithmetic operations, perform the operation inside the bars first and then find the absolute value of the result.

$$|-6 + 4| = |-2|$$
$$= 2$$
$$|(-6) \times 4| = |-24|$$
$$= 24$$

FACTORS AND MULTIPLES

To find the **prime factorization** of a number, keep factoring it until you are left with only prime numbers. To find the prime factorization of 168:

$$168 = 4 \times 42$$
$$= 4 \times 6 \times 7$$
$$= 2 \times 2 \times 2 \times 3 \times 7$$

To find the **greatest common factor (GCF)** of two integers, break down both integers into their prime factorizations and multiply all prime factors they have in common. If you're looking for the GCF of 40 and 130, first identify the prime factors of each integer.

$$40 = 4 \times 10$$
$$= 2 \times 2 \times 2 \times 5$$
$$140 = 10 \times 14$$
$$= 2 \times 5 \times 2 \times 7$$
$$= 2 \times 2 \times 5 \times 7$$

Next, see what prime factors the two numbers have in common and then multiply these common factors. Both integers share two 2's and one 5, so the GCF is $2 \times 2 \times 5$ or 20.

If you need to find a **common multiple** of two integers, you can always multiply them. However, you can use prime factors to find the **least common multiple (LCM)**. To do this, multiply all of the prime factors of each integer the most amount of times as they appear. This may sound confusing, but it becomes pretty clear once it's demonstrated. Take a look at the example to see how it works.

Common multiple

of 20 and 16: $20 \times 16 = 320$

Three hundred twenty is a common multiple of 20 and 16, but it is not the least common multiple.

LCM of 20 and 16:
$$20 = 2 \times 2 \times 5$$
$$16 = 2 \times 2 \times 2 \times 2$$
$$= 2 \times 2 \times 2 \times 2 \times 5 = 80$$

Note that there are four factors of 2 in the LCM because there were four factors of 2 in 16, and that's the largest number of 2s present in either number.

THE ORDER OF OPERATIONS

There is a specific order in which arithmetic operations must be performed.

1. Parentheses (Simplify all operations inside parentheses first.)

2. Exponents (Simplify any exponential expressions.)

3. Multiplication and Division (Perform all multiplications and divisions as they occur in the problem from left to right.)

4. Addition and Subtraction (Perform all additions and subtractions as they occur in the problem from left to right.)

An easy way to help you remember this order is to use the mnemonic "Please Excuse My Dear Aunt Sally" (or **PEMDAS**). This phrase uses the first letter of each operation in the order in which it is to be performed.

$$(3 + 5)^2 - 7 + 4 = (8)^2 - 7 + 4$$
$$= 64 - 7 + 4$$
$$= 57 + 4$$
$$= 61$$

Definitions | **Order of Operations** | Divisibility Rules | Fractions & Decimals | Common % Equivalencies

RULES FOR DIVISIBILITY

If you've forgotten—or never learned—divisibility rules, spend a little time with this chart. Even if you remember the rules, take a moment to refresh your recollection. Remember, there are no easy divisibility rules for 7 and 8.

Divisible by	The Rule	EXAMPLES: 558
2	The last digit is even	a multiple of 2 because 8 is even
3	The sum of the digits is a multiple of 3	a multiple of 3 because 5 + 5 + 8 = 18, which is a multiple of 3
4	The last 2 digits comprise a 2-digit multiple of 4	NOT a multiple of 4 because 58 is not a multiple of 4
5	The last digit is 5 or 0	NOT a multiple of 5 because it doesn't end in 5 or 0
6	The last digit is even AND the sum of the digits is a multiple of 3	a multiple of 6 because it's a multiple of both 2 and 3
9	The sum of the digits is a multiple of 9	a multiple of 9 because 5 + 5 + 8 = 18, which is a multiple of 9
10	The last digit is 0	not a multiple of 10 because it doesn't end in 0

Hint: To test for 2, 4, 5, or 10, look at the last digit or two. To test for 3 or 9, add all the digits.

FRACTIONS AND DECIMALS

Generally, there are seven operations you should feel comfortable performing with fractions. They are:

- simplifying fractions
- converting a fraction to one with a different denominator
- adding fractions
- subtracting fractions
- multiplying fractions
- dividing fractions
- comparing fractions

Order of Operations | **Divisibility Rules** | Fractions & Decimals | Common % Equivalencies | Exponents & Roots

To **simplify a fraction,** find the GCF of the numerator and denominator of the fraction, then divide both numerator and denominator by this quantity:

EXAMPLES: Simplify $\dfrac{18}{30}$

The GCF of 18 and 30 is 6, so divide both 18 and 30 by 6:

$$\frac{18}{30} = \frac{18 \div 6}{30 \div 6}$$

$$= \frac{3}{5}$$

To **convert a fraction to one with a different denominator,** multiply both numerator and denominator by the same quantity:

EXAMPLES: Convert $\dfrac{3}{7}$ into a fraction with a denominator of 28.

Since $7 \times 4 = 28$, multiply the 3 and the 7 each by 4:

$$\frac{3}{7} = \frac{3 \times 4}{7 \times 4}$$

$$= \frac{12}{28}$$

To **add and subtract fractions with the same denominator,** keep the denominator the same, and add or subtract the numerators. Simplify the result if possible.

EXAMPLES: Add

$$0.4 = \frac{4}{10}$$

$$= \frac{2}{5}$$

To **add and subtract fractions with the different denominators,** find the least common multiple (LCM) of the denominators, convert the fractions so they have this denominator, then add or subtract and simplify.

EXAMPLES: Subtract

$$\frac{7}{8} - \frac{5}{12} = \frac{21}{24} - \frac{10}{24}$$

$$= \frac{11}{24}$$

To **multiply fractions,** multiply the numerators and multiply the denominators, then simplify the result. It is also possible to simplify the fractions before multiplying by canceling like factors from the numerators and denominators of the fractions:

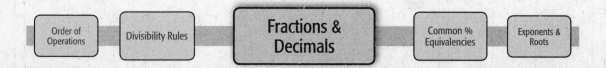

Order of Operations   Divisibility Rules   **Fractions & Decimals**   Common % Equivalencies   Exponents & Roots

EXAMPLES: Multiply

$$\frac{11}{12} \times \frac{9}{22} = \frac{99}{264}$$

$$= \frac{99 \div 3}{264 \div 3} \text{ OR } \frac{\overset{1}{\cancel{11}}}{\underset{4}{\cancel{12}}} \times \frac{\overset{3}{\cancel{9}}}{\underset{2}{\cancel{22}}} = \frac{3}{8}$$

$$= \frac{33 \div 11}{88 \div 11}$$

$$= \frac{3}{8}$$

To **divide fractions,** multiply the dividend (the first fraction) by the reciprocal of the divisor (the second fraction):

EXAMPLES: Divide

$$\frac{8}{15} \div \frac{2}{3} = \frac{\overset{4}{\cancel{8}}}{\underset{5}{\cancel{15}}} \times \frac{\overset{1}{\cancel{3}}}{\underset{1}{\cancel{2}}}$$

$$= \frac{4}{5}$$

To **compare fractions,** convert both fractions to the same denominator and compare the numerators OR, find the cross-products and compare as follows:

EXAMPLES: Which is larger, $\frac{3}{4}$ or $\frac{10}{13}$?

Find the cross-products by multiplying the numerator of the first fraction by the denominator of the second, then multiplying the denominator of the first by the numerator of the second:

$$
\begin{array}{cc}
3 \times 13 & 4 \times 10 \\
39 & 40
\end{array}
$$

Because 39 is less than 40, the first fraction is less than the second. The second fraction is the larger fraction.

To **convert a fraction to a decimal**, divide the denominator into the numerator.

To convert $\frac{8}{25}$ to a decimal, divide 25 into 8.00.

$$
\begin{array}{r}
.32 \\
25\overline{)8.00} \\
-7\,5 \\
\hline
50 \\
-50 \\
\hline
0
\end{array}
$$

| Order of Operations | Divisibility Rules | Fractions & Decimals | Common % Equivalencies | Exponents & Roots |

To **convert a decimal to a fraction,** use the place value of the digits in the decimal. Recall that beginning at the decimal point, the first place to the right is the tenths place, followed by the hundredths place, the thousandths place, the ten-thousandths place, the hundred-thousandths place, etc.

EXAMPLES:

Convert the decimal 0.4 into a fraction.

Because the last decimal place is the tenths place, the decimal is four tenths, so the fraction is as well:

$$0.4 = \frac{4}{10}$$
$$= \frac{2}{5}$$

Convert the decimal 0.825 into a fraction.

Because the last decimal place is the thousandths place, the decimal is eight hundred twenty-five thousandths, so the fraction is as well:

$$0.825 = \frac{825}{1,000}$$
$$= \frac{165}{200}$$
$$= \frac{33}{40}$$

KAPLAN EXCLUSIVE TIPS

"To change a fraction to a percent, multiply by 100%."

COMMON PERCENT EQUIVALENCIES

Familiarity with the relationships among percents, decimals, and fractions can save you time on test day. Don't worry about memorizing the following chart. Simply use it to refresh your recollection of relationships you already know (e.g., $50\% = 0.50 = \frac{1}{2}$) and to familiarize yourself with some that you might not already know. To convert a decimal to a percent, multiply by 100 and add a % sign. To convert a percent to a decimal, divide by 100% (drop the percent sign and move the decimal point two spaces to the left).

KAPLAN EXCLUSIVE TIPS

"A handy shortcut: x % of y = y % of x."

Fraction	Decimal	Percent
$\frac{1}{20}$	0.05	5%
$\frac{1}{10}$	0.10	10%
$\frac{1}{8}$	0.125	12.5%

Fraction	Decimal	Percent
$\frac{1}{6}$	$0.16\overline{6}$	$16\frac{2}{3}\%$
$\frac{1}{5}$	0.20	20%
$\frac{1}{4}$	0.25	25%
$\frac{1}{3}$	$0.33\overline{3}$	$33\frac{1}{3}\%$
$\frac{3}{8}$	0.375	37.5%
$\frac{2}{5}$	0.40	40%
$\frac{1}{2}$	0.50	50%
$\frac{3}{5}$	0.60	60%
$\frac{2}{3}$	$0.66\overline{6}$	$66\frac{2}{3}\%$
$\frac{3}{4}$	0.75	75%
$\frac{4}{5}$	0.80	80%
$\frac{5}{6}$	$0.83\overline{3}$	$83\frac{1}{3}\%$
$\frac{7}{8}$	0.875	87.5%

EXPONENTS AND ROOTS

Exponents are the small raised numbers written to the right of a variable or number. They indicate the number of times that variable or number is to be used as a factor. On the SSAT/ISEE, you'll usually deal with numbers or variables that are squared, but you could see a few other concepts involving exponents.

EXAMPLES:

$$2^3 = 2 \times 2 \times 2$$
$$= 8$$
$$-3^2 = -(3 \times 3)$$
$$= -9$$
$$3(-2)^2 = 3[(-2)(-2)]$$
$$= 3(4)$$
$$= 12$$

Fractions & Decimals | Common % Equivalencies | **Exponents & Roots** | Scientific Notation | Percents

A **square root** of a nonnegative number is a number that, when multiplied by itself, produces the given quantity. The radical sign $\sqrt{\ }$ is used to represent the positive square root of a number, so $\sqrt{25} = 5$, since $5 \times 5 = 25$.

To **add** or **subtract** radicals, make sure the numbers under the radical sign are the same. If they are, you can add or subtract the coefficients outside the radical signs.

$$2\sqrt{2} + 3\sqrt{2} = 5\sqrt{2}$$

$\sqrt{2} + \sqrt{3}$ cannot be combined because the quantities beneath the radical signs are not the same.

To **simplify** a radical, factor out the perfect square factor(s) from under the radical, simplify them, and put the result in front of the radical sign.

$$\sqrt{32} = \sqrt{16 \times 2} = \sqrt{16}\sqrt{2} = 4\sqrt{2}$$

To **multiply** or **divide** radicals, multiply (or divide) the coefficients outside the radical. Then, multiply (or divide) the numbers inside the radicals.

$$\sqrt{x} \times \sqrt{y} = \sqrt{xy}$$
$$3\sqrt{2} \times 4\sqrt{5} = 12\sqrt{10}$$
$$\frac{\sqrt{x}}{\sqrt{y}} = \sqrt{\frac{x}{y}}$$
$$\frac{12\sqrt{10}}{3\sqrt{2}} = 4\sqrt{5}$$

To **take the square root of a fraction,** break the fraction into two separate roots and take the square root of the numerator and the denominator.

$$\sqrt{\frac{16}{25}} = \sqrt{\frac{16}{25}} = \frac{4}{5}$$

POWERS OF TEN AND SCIENTIFIC NOTATION

The exponent of a power of 10 indicates how many zeros the number would contain if it were written out. $10^4 = 10,000$ (4 zeros) since the product of 4 factors of 10 is equal to 10,000.

When multiplying a number by a power of 10, move the decimal point to the right the same number of places as the number of zeros in that power of 10.

$0.0123 \times 10^4 = 123$ (four places to the right)

When dividing by a power of 10, move the decimal point to the left.

$43.21 \div 10^3 = 0.04321$ (three places to the left)

Multiplying by a power with a negative exponent is the same as dividing by a power with a positive exponent. Therefore, when you multiply by a number with a positive exponent, move the decimal to the right. When you multiply by a number with a negative exponent, move the decimal to the left.

$$28.5 \times 10^{-2} = 28.5 \div 10^2$$
$$= 0.285$$
$$.36 \div 10^{-4} = .36 \times 10^4$$
$$= 3,600$$

Scientific notation is commonly used in science and mathematics as a shorthand method for writing very large or very small numbers. A number is in scientific notation if it is in the form $a \times 10^n$ where $1'' a < 10$ and n is an integer.

To write a number in **standard notation from scientific notation,** simply move the decimal point in the number to the right if the exponent on 10 is a positive number and to the left if the exponent is negative.

EXAMPLES:

$4.23 \times 10^6 = 4,230,000$ The decimal point moved to the right 6 places.
$9.6 \times 10^{-2} = 0.096$ The decimal point moved to the left 2 places.

To write a number in **scientific notation from standard notation,** find the decimal point in the number. If there is no decimal point, put one at the end of the number. Now move the decimal point to the right or to the left until the resulting quantity is a number between one and 10. The number of places the decimal point moved indicates the exponent to be placed on the 10. The direction indicates the sign of the exponent; if the decimal point was moved to the left, the exponent will be positive, if the decimal point was moved to the right, the exponent will be negative.

EXAMPLES:

$82,000,000,000 = 8.2 \times 10^{10}$ The decimal point moved from the end of 82,000,000,000 to the left 10 places.

$0.00004138 = 4.138 \times 10^{-5}$ The decimal point moved from the front of 0.00004138 to the right 5 places.

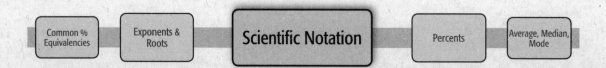

PERCENTS

The key to solving most fractions and percents word problems is to identify the part and the whole. Usually you'll find the **part** associated with the verb *is/are* and the **whole** associated with the word *of.* In the sentence, "Half of the boys are blonds," the whole is the boys ("*of* the boys"), and the part is the blonds ("*are* blonds").

Whether you need to find the part, the whole, or the percent, use the same formula:

Part = Percent × Whole

OR

Percent = $\dfrac{\text{Part}}{\text{Whole}}$

Let's look at some examples.

EXAMPLES: What is 12% of 25?   **Setup:** Part = 0.12 × 25
                                                   Part = 3

EXAMPLES: 15 is 3% of what number?   **Setup:** $\dfrac{15}{0.03} = \dfrac{0.03 \times \text{Whole}}{0.03}$
                                                   500 = Whole

EXAMPLES: 45 is what percent of 9?   **Setup:** $\dfrac{45}{9} = \dfrac{\text{Percent} \times 9}{9}$
                                                   5 = Percent

Move decimal point 2 places to the right to convert to a percent: 5.00 = 500%.

To increase or decrease a number by a given percent, **take that percent of the original number and add it to or subtract it from the original number.** To increase 25 by 60%, first find 60% of 25.

25 × 0.6 = 15

Then, add the result to the original number:

25 + 15 = 40

To decrease 25 by 60%, subtract the 15:

25 − 15 = 10

To find the **original whole before a percent increase or decrease,** set up an equation. Think of a 15% increase over x as $1.15x$, since it's really 115% of x.

EXAMPLES: A country's population after a 5% increase was 59,346. What was the population *before* the increase?

Setup: $\dfrac{1.05x}{1.05} = \dfrac{59,346}{1.05}$

$x = 56,520$

To determine the combined effect of multiple percent increases and/or decreases, **start with 100 and see what happens.**

EXAMPLES: A price went up 10% one year, and the new price went up 20% the next year. What was the combined percent increase?

Setup: First year: 100 + (10% of 100) = 110

Second year: 110 + (20% of 110) = 132

Combined increase = 32%

AVERAGE, MEDIAN, AND MODE

The *average* of a group of terms is the sum of the terms divided by the number of terms.

The average of 15, 18, 15, 32, and 20 is $\dfrac{15 + 18 + 15 + 32 + 20}{5} = \dfrac{100}{5} = 20$

The *median* is the value of the middle term, with the terms arranged in increasing or decreasing order. Suppose you want to find the median of the terms 15, 18, 15, 32, and 20. First, put the terms in order from small to large. 15, 15, 18, 20, 32. Then, identify the middle term. The middle term is 18. If there is an even number of terms, the median becomes the average of the two middle terms with the terms arranged in order.

The *mode* is the value of the term that occurs most. Of the terms 15, 18, 15, 32, and 20, the number 15 occurs twice, so it is the mode. If every number occurs only once, there is no mode. If more than one number occurs the most, then both numbers would be the modes.

RATIOS, PROPORTIONS, AND RATES

Ratios can be expressed in two forms. The first form is $\dfrac{a}{b}$.

If you have 15 dogs and 5 cats, the ratio of dogs to cats is $\dfrac{15}{5}$. (The ratio of cats to dogs is $\dfrac{5}{15}$.) Like any other fraction, this ratio can be simplified. $\dfrac{15}{5}$ can be simplified to $\dfrac{3}{1}$. In other words, for every three dogs, there is one cat.

The second form is *a:b.*

The ratio of dogs to cats is 15:5 or 3:1. The ratio of cats to dogs is 5:15 or 1:3.

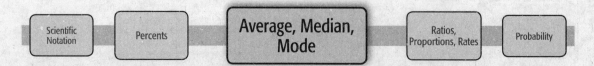

Pay attention to what ratio is specified in the problem. Remember that the ratio of dogs to cats is different from the ratio of cats to dogs.

A *proportion* is a statement that two ratios are equal. To solve a proportion, cross-multiply and solve for the variable.

$$\frac{x}{6} \diagup\!\!\!\!\times \frac{2}{3}$$

$$3x = 12$$

$$x = 4$$

A *rate* is a ratio that compares quantities measured in different units. The most common example is *miles per hour*. Use the following formula for such problems:

Distance = Rate × Time

Remember that although not all rates are speeds, this formula can be adapted to any rate.

PROBABILITY

An *event* is a collection or set of possible outcomes. Suppose that a die with faces numbered 1, 2, 3, 4, 5, and 6 is rolled. All the possible outcomes are 1, 2, 3, 4, 5, and 6. Let *A* be the event that a 1, 3, or 5 is rolled. The event *A* is made up of the outcomes 1, 3, and 5. Thus *A* can also be described by saying that the number rolled is odd. A possible outcome is the elementary building block from which events are made up.

Of course, it is possible for an event to consist of a single possible outcome. For example, suppose that *B* = {4}, that is, the event *B* is the result that a 4 is rolled. An event consisting of a single possible outcome is called an elementary event. Thus, *B*, which is {4}, is an elementary event.

To find the *probability* that an event will occur, use the formula

$$\text{Probability} = \frac{\text{Number of desirable outcomes}}{\text{Number of possible outcomes}}$$

EXAMPLES:

If 12 books are on a shelf and 9 of them are mysteries, what is the probability of picking a mystery?

$\frac{9}{12} = \frac{3}{4}$. This probability can also be expressed as 0.75 or 75%.

> **KAPLAN EXCLUSIVE TIPS**
>
> " Probability is a part-to-whole ratio and can therefore never be greater than one. "

Average, Median, Mode | Ratios, Proportions, Rates | **Probability** | Symbols and Terms | Practice

To find the probability that two *events* will occur, find the probability that the first event occurs and multiply this by the probability that the second event occurs—given that the first event occurs.

EXAMPLES:

If there are 12 books on a shelf and 9 of them are mysteries, what is the probability of picking a mystery first and a non-mystery second if exactly two books are selected?

Probability of picking a mystery: $\dfrac{9}{12} = \dfrac{3}{4}$

Probability of picking a non-mystery: $\dfrac{3}{11}$

(Originally there were 9 mysteries and 3 non-mysteries. After the mystery is selected, there are 8 mysteries and 3 non-mysteries, i.e., 11 books remaining.)

Probability of picking both books: $\dfrac{3}{4} \times \dfrac{3}{11} = \dfrac{9}{44}$

STRANGE SYMBOLISM AND TERMINOLOGY

Some questions will be confusing because you're unfamiliar with the math concept being tested. Others will seem confusing because the math has literally been made up just for the purposes of the test. The test makers make up math symbols and terminology to test your ability to deal with unfamiliar concepts.

These problems aren't as hard as they seem. When you see a strange symbol, the question stem will *always* indicate what the symbol means. And if you see strange terminology, it will *always* be defined. The problems are essentially about following directions, so don't panic when you see them. All you have to do is slow down, read the problem and follow the directions.

EXAMPLES:

If $x <<\!<>\!>> y = \sqrt{x + y}$, what is $9 <<\!<>\!>> 16$?

All you have to do here is to substitute 9 and 16 into the defining equation:

$$\sqrt{9 + 16} = \sqrt{25} = 5.$$

To "chomp" a number, take the sum of the digits of that number and divide this value by the number of digits.

EXAMPLES:

What value do you get when you "chomp" 43,805?

$$4 + 3 + 8 + 0 + 5 = 20$$

$$20 \div 5 = 4$$

Ratios, Proportions, Rates | Probability | **Symbols and Terms** | Practice | Answers

PRACTICE QUESTIONS

1. Which of the following is not even?

   (A) 330
   (B) 436
   (C) 752
   (D) 861
   (E) 974

2. What is the least prime number greater than 50?

   (A) 51
   (B) 53
   (C) 55
   (D) 57
   (E) 59

3. Which of the following is a multiple of 2?

   (A) 271
   (B) 357
   (C) 463
   (D) 599
   (E) 756

4. $\dfrac{15 \times 7 \times 3}{9 \times 5 \times 2} =$

   (A) $\dfrac{2}{7}$

   (B) $\dfrac{3}{5}$

   (C) $3\dfrac{1}{2}$

   (D) 7

   (E) $7\dfrac{1}{2}$

5. What is the least common multiple of 18 and 24?

   (A) 6
   (B) 54
   (C) 72
   (D) 96
   (E) 432

6. Which of the following is a multiple of 3?

   (A) 115
   (B) 370
   (C) 465
   (D) 589
   (E) 890

7. $-6(3 - 4 \times 3) =$

   (A) -66
   (B) -54
   (C) -12
   (D) 18
   (E) 54

8. Which of the following is a multiple of 10?

   (A) 10,005
   (B) 10,030
   (C) 10,101
   (D) 100,005
   (E) 101,101

9. Which of the following is a multiple of both 5 and 2?

   (A) 2,203
   (B) 2,342
   (C) 1,005
   (D) 7,790
   (E) 9,821

10. Which of the following is a multiple of both 3 and 10?

    (A) 103
    (B) 130
    (C) 210
    (D) 310
    (E) 460

11. Which of the following is a multiple of 2, 3, and 5?

    (A) 165
    (B) 235
    (C) 350
    (D) 420
    (E) 532

12. Which of the following is an even multiple of both 3 and 5?

    (A) 135
    (B) 155
    (C) 250
    (D) 350
    (E) 390

13. Professor Jones bought a large carton of books. She gave 3 books to each student in her class and there were no books left over. Which of the following could be the number of books she distributed?

    (A) 133
    (B) 143
    (C) 252
    (D) 271
    (E) 332

14. Two teams are having a contest. The prize is a box of candy that the members of the winning team will divide evenly. If team *A* wins, each player will get exactly 3 pieces of candy and if team *B* wins, each player will get exactly 5 pieces. Which of the following could be the number of pieces of candy in the box?

    (A) 153
    (B) 325
    (C) 333
    (D) 425
    (E) 555

15. Three consecutive multiples of 4 have a sum of 60. What is the greatest of these numbers?

    (A) 8
    (B) 12
    (C) 16
    (D) 20
    (E) 24

16. Sheila cuts a 60 foot wire cable in equal strips of $\frac{4}{5}$ of a foot each. How many strips does she make?

    (A) 48
    (B) 51
    (C) 60
    (D) 70
    (E) 75

17. Which of the following is NOT odd?

    (A) 349
    (B) 537
    (C) 735
    (D) 841
    (E) 918

Ratios, Proportions, Rates   Probability   Symbols and Terms   Practice   Answers

18. Which of the following can be the sum of two negative numbers?

    (A) 4
    (B) 2
    (C) 1
    (D) 0
    (E) −1

19. Which of the following is NOT a prime number?

    (A) 2
    (B) 7
    (C) 17
    (D) 87
    (E) 101

20. All of the following can be the product of a negative integer and positive integer EXCEPT

    (A) 1
    (B) −1
    (C) −2
    (D) −4
    (E) −6

21. Susie and Dennis are training for a marathon. On Monday, they both run 3.2 miles. On Tuesday, Susie runs $5\frac{1}{5}$ miles and Dennis runs 3.6 miles. On Wednesday, Susie runs 4.8 miles and Dennis runs $2\frac{2}{5}$ miles. During those 3 days, how many more miles does Susie run than Dennis?

    (A) 4.8
    (B) 4.0
    (C) 3.2
    (D) 3.0
    (E) 2.4

22. Which number is a multiple of 60?

    (A) 213
    (B) 350
    (C) 540
    (D) 666
    (E) 1,060

23. Two odd integers and one even integer are multiplied together. Which of the following could be their product?

    (A) 1.5
    (B) 3
    (C) 6
    (D) 7.2
    (E) 15

24. If the number 9,899,399 is increased by 2,082, the result will be

    (A) 9,902,481
    (B) 9,901,481
    (C) 9,901,471
    (D) 9,891,481
    (E) 901,481

25. What is the sum of five consecutive integers if the middle one is 13?

    (A) 55
    (B) 60
    (C) 65
    (D) 70
    (E) 75

Ratios, Proportions, Rates   Probability   Symbols and Terms   **Practice**   Answers

26. $\dfrac{4x^5}{2x^2} =$

(A) $2x^2$

(B) $2x^3$

(C) $2x^4$

(D) $4x^2$

(E) $4x^3$

27. $-2^3 (1-2)^3 + (-2)^3 =$

(A) -12

(B) -4

(C) 0

(D) 4

(E) 12

28. n is an odd integer and $10 < n < 19$. What is the mean of all possible values of n?

(A) 13

(B) 13.5

(C) 14

(D) 14.5

(E) 15.5

29. $a \Delta b = \dfrac{3a}{b}$. What is $\dfrac{14}{32} \Delta 1\dfrac{3}{4}$?

(A) $\dfrac{1}{4}$

(B) $\dfrac{1}{3}$

(C) $\dfrac{1}{2}$

(D) $\dfrac{3}{4}$

(E) $\dfrac{49}{64}$

30. Jon works 4.5 hours a day, 3 days each week after school. He is paid $4.25 per hour. How much is his weekly pay (rounded to the next highest cent)?

(A) $12.75

(B) $13.50

(C) $19.13

(D) $54.00

(E) $57.38

31. Zim buys a calculator that is marked 30% off. If he pays $35, what was the original price?

(A) $24.50

(B) $45.50

(C) $47.00

(D) $50.00

(E) $62.50

32. A museum records 16 visitors to an exhibit on Monday, 21 on Tuesday, 20 on Wednesday, 17 on Thursday, 19 on Friday, 21 on Saturday, and 17 on Sunday, what is the median number of visitors for the week?

(A) 18.5

(B) 18.75

(C) 19

(D) 19.5

(E) 19.75

33. A bag contains 8 white, 4 red, 7 green, and 5 blue marbles. Eight marbles are withdrawn randomly. How many of the withdrawn marbles were white if the chance of drawing a white marble is now $\frac{1}{4}$?

   (A) 0
   (B) 3
   (C) 4
   (D) 5
   (E) 6

34. $\sqrt{1,500} =$

   (A) $10 + \sqrt{15}$
   (B) $10\sqrt{15}$
   (C) 25
   (D) $100 + \sqrt{15}$
   (E) $10\sqrt{150}$

35. $2(3 \times 2)^2 - 27(6 \div 2) + 3^2 =$

   (A) 72
   (B) 9
   (C) 3
   (D) 0
   (E) −24

36. Which of the following numbers is closest to the product 48.9×21.2?

   (A) 10,000
   (B) 8,000
   (C) 1,000
   (D) 100
   (E) 70

37. $|16 - 25| + \sqrt{25 - 16} =$

   (A) −12
   (B) −6
   (C) 0
   (D) 6
   (E) 12

38. Which of the following is 81,455 rounded to the nearest 100?

   (A) 81,000
   (B) 81,400
   (C) 81,500
   (D) 82,000
   (E) 90,000

39. If 35% of x is 7, what is x% of 35?

   (A) 7
   (B) 20
   (C) 28
   (D) 35
   (E) 42

40. A number is considered "blue" if the sum of its digits is equal to the product of its digits. Which of the following numbers is "blue"?

    (A) 111
    (B) 220
    (C) 321
    (D) 422
    (E) 521

To "fix" a number, you must perform the following four steps:

Step 1: Raise the number to the 3rd power.

Step 2: Divide the result by 2.

Step 3: Take the absolute value of the result of Step 2.

Step 4: Round off this result to the nearest whole number.

41. When you "fix" −3, you get

    (A) −13
    (B) 4
    (C) 5
    (D) 13
    (E) 14

42. When D is divided by 15 the result is 6 with a remainder of 2. What is the remainder when D is divided by 6?

    (A) 0
    (B) 1
    (C) 2
    (D) 3
    (E) 4

43. For any two numbers a and b, $a ? b = (a + b)(a − b)$. For example, $10 ? 5 = (10 + 5)(10 − 5) = (15)(5) = 75$. The value of $7 ? 5$ is

    (A) 2
    (B) 12
    (C) 24
    (D) 36
    (E) 48

44. What is the greatest integer less than $\frac{71}{6}$?

    (A) 9
    (B) 10
    (C) 11
    (D) 12
    (E) 13

45. Which of the following is NOT less than 0.25?

    (A) $\frac{2}{9}$
    (B) $\frac{3}{14}$
    (C) $\frac{16}{64}$
    (D) $\frac{19}{80}$
    (E) $\frac{4}{17}$

46. If the average of 5 consecutive odd numbers is 11, then the largest number is

    (A) 17
    (B) 15
    (C) 13
    (D) 11
    (E) 9

PRACTICE QUESTION ANSWERS

1. D

The way to tell if an integer is even is to look at the last digit to the right—the ones' digit. If that digit is divisible by 2, or is 0, the number is even. Looking at the choices, only (D) ends in a number that isn't divisible by 2, so only it is not even.

2. B

A prime number is an integer greater than 1 that is divisible by only two different positive integers, itself and 1. Of the choices, only (B), 53 and (E), 59 are prime. You want the least prime number greater than 50, so (B) is correct. Using the divisibility rules would quickly show you that 51 and 57 are divisible by 3, while 55 is divisible by 5.

3. E

If the ones digit of a number is even (0, 2, 4, 6, or 8), the number is even. The only choice whose last digit is even is (E), 756.

4. C

Before you do the multiplication, see which common factors in the numerator and denominator can be canceled. Canceling a 3 from the 3 in the numerator and the 9 in the denominator leaves $\frac{15 \times 7 \times 1}{3 \times 5 \times 2}$. Canceling a 5 from the 15 in the numerator and the 5 in the denominator leaves $\frac{3 \times 7 \times 1}{3 \times 1 \times 2}$. Canceling the 3 in the numerator and the 3 in the denominator leaves $\frac{7 \times 1}{1 \times 2} = \frac{7}{2} = 3\frac{1}{2}$, (C).

5. C

The least common multiple (LCM) of two integers is the product of their prime factors, each raised to the highest power with which it appears. The prime factorization of 18 is $2 \cdot 3^2$ and that of 24 is $2^3 \cdot 3$. So their LCM is $2^3 \cdot 3^2 = 8 \cdot 9 = 72$. You could also find their LCM by checking out the multiples of the larger integer until you find the one that's also a multiple of the smaller. Check out the multiples of 24: 24? No. 48? No. 72? Yes, $72 = 4 \times 18$.

6. C

If a number is divisible by 3, the sum of its digits will be divisible by 3. Checking the answer choices, only (C), 465 works, since $4 + 6 + 5 = 15$, which is divisible by 3.

7. E

According to PEMDAS, start in the parentheses. As per PEMDAS, perform multiplication before subtraction: $-6(3 - 12)$. After the subtraction: $-6(-9)$. Since a negative times a negative is a positive, the answer is 54, (E).

8. B

If a number is divisible by 10, its last digit will be a 0. Only G fits this criterion.

9. D

If a number is divisible by both 5 and 2, then it must also be divisible by $5 \cdot 2$ or 10. Since a number divisible by 10 must have a 0 as its last digit, (D) is correct.

10. C

For a number to be divisible by 3 and 10, it must satisfy the divisibility rules of both: its last digit must be 0 (which automatically eliminates (A), and the sum of its digits must be divisible by 3. Checking the rest of the answer choices, only (C) is also divisible by 3, since $2 + 1 + 0 = 3$.

Ratios, Proportions, Rates   Probability   Symbols and Terms   Practice   **Answers**

11. D

For a number to be a multiple of both 2 and 5 it must also be a multiple of 2 • 5 = 10. This means it must have a 0 as its last digit, which eliminates all but (C) and (D). To be a multiple of 3, the number's digits must sum to a multiple of 3. (D) is the only of the remaining two choices that fits this requirement, since 4 + 2 + 0 = 6.

12. E

Since an even number is divisible by 2, the question is asking for a number that is divisible by 2, 3, and 5. If the number is divisible by 2 and 5, it must also be divisible by 10, so its last digit must be 0. To be a multiple of 3, its digits must sum to a multiple of 3. Eliminate (A) and (B) since they don't end in 0. Of the remaining choices, only (E) is a multiple of 3, since 3 + 9 + 0 = 12.

13. C

If Professor Jones was able to distribute all the books in groups of 3 without any left over, the number of books she started with was divisible by 3. Whichever choice is divisible by 3 must therefore be correct. For a number to be divisible by 3, the sum of its digits must also be divisible by 3. Only (C) fits this requirement: 2 + 5 + 2 = 9.

14. E

The problems tells you that the number of pieces of candy in the box can be evenly divided by 3 and 5. So the correct answer is the choice that has a 0 or 5 as its last digit, and the sum of whose digits is divisible by 3. Eliminate (A) and (C) since they don't end in either 0 or 5. Of the remaining choices, only (E) is also divisible by 3, since 5 + 5 + 5 = 15.

15. E

Use the answer choices to help find the solution. When backsolving, start with the middle choice, since it will help you determine if the correct answer needs to be greater or less than it. In this case the middle choice is 16. The sum of 16 and 2 numbers that are each smaller than 16 has to be less than 3 • 16 or 48, so it is obviously too small. Therefore, (A) and (B) must also be too small and you can eliminate all three. Try (D), 20. Again, 20 plus two numbers smaller than 20 will be less than 3 • 20 or 60, so it's not correct. The only choice remaining is (E), 24, so it must be correct. To prove it, 24 plus the two preceding consecutive multiples of 4, which are 16 and 20, do indeed sum to 60: 16 + 20 + 24 = 60.

16. E

When you're asked how many strips $\frac{4}{5}$ of a foot long can be cut from a 60 foot piece of wire, you're being asked how many times $\frac{4}{5}$ goes into 60, or what is $60 \div \frac{4}{5}$. Before you even do the division, you can eliminate some unreasonable answer choices. Since $\frac{4}{5}$ is less than 1, $\frac{4}{5}$ must go into 60 more than 60 times. Eliminate (A), (B), and (C) because they're all less than or equal to 60. Dividing by a fraction is the same as multiplying by its reciprocal, so $60 \div \frac{4}{5} = 60 \cdot \frac{5}{4} = 75$.

17. E

If a number is odd, its last digit must be odd. (E) ends in an even digit, so it is not odd.

18. E

The sum of two negative numbers is always negative. (E) is the only negative choice, so it must be correct. If you're wondering how two negative numbers can add up to –1, remember, "number"

Ratios, Proportions, Rates | Probability | Symbols and Terms | Practice | **Answers**

doesn't necessarily mean "integer." It can also mean "fraction." For example, $\left(-\dfrac{1}{4}\right) + \left(-\dfrac{3}{4}\right) = -1$. Always read the questions carefully to see what types of numbers are involved.

19. D

A prime number has only two different positive factors, 1 and itself. Two, 7, and 17 are obviously prime, so eliminate them. Use the divisibility rules to check out the two remaining choices. Both end in an odd number, so neither is divisible by 2. But the digits of 87 sum to 15 which is a multiple of 3, so 87 is divisible by 3 and is therefore not prime.

20. A

The product of a positive integer and a negative integer is always negative. (A) is positive, so it couldn't be the product of a negative and a positive.

21. B

The simplest way to solve this problem is to convert the numbers so that they're all decimals or all fractions: $5\dfrac{1}{5} = 5\dfrac{2}{10} = 5.2$; $2\dfrac{2}{5} = 2\dfrac{4}{10} = 2.4$. Now you can more easily compare the distances. On Monday, they ran the same number of miles. On Tuesday, Susie ran 5.2 miles and Dennis ran 3.6 miles. The difference between the two amounts is 5.2 − 3.6, or 1.6, so on Tuesday Susie ran 1.6 more miles than Dennis did. On Wednesday, Susie ran 4.8 miles and Dennis ran 2.4. 4.8 − 2.4 = 2.4, so on Wednesday Susie ran 2.4 miles more than Dennis. The total difference for the three days is 1.6 + 2.4 = 4.0 more miles.

22. C

A number that is a multiple of 60 must be a multiple of every factor of 60. The factors of 60 are 1, 2, 3, 4, 5, 6, 10, 12, 15, 20, 30, and 60. (A) and (D) are not multiples of 10. (B) and (E) are not multiples of 3. The answer is 540, (C).

23. C

The product of three integers must be an integer, so eliminate (A) and (D). A product of integers that has at least one even factor is even, so the product of two odd integers and one even integer must be even. The only even choice is 6, (C).

24. B

This question is simply asking for the sum of 9,899,399 and 2,082, which is 9,901,481, (B).

25. C

If the middle of five consecutive integers is 13, the first two are 11 and 12 and the last two are 14 and 15. So the sum is 11 + 12 + 13 + 14 + 15 = 65. You could get to this answer more quickly if you knew that the middle term in a group of consecutive numbers is equal to the average of the group of numbers. In other words, the average of these five integers is 13, so their sum would be 13 • 5 = 65.

26. B

Simplify the expression by first simplifying the fraction $\dfrac{4}{2}$ which equals 2. Then, to divide the exponential expressions with the same base, subtract the exponents:

$$\frac{x^5}{x^2} = x^{5-2}$$
$$= x^3$$

So $\dfrac{x^5}{x^2} = 2x^3$.

27. C

A negative number raised to an odd power is negative. Using PEMDAS,

$$-2^3(1-2)^3 + (-2)^3$$
$$= -2^3(-1)^3 + (-2)^3$$
$$= -8(-1) + (-8)$$
$$= 8 + (-8)$$
$$= 8 - 8$$
$$= 0$$

28. C

The mean (or average) is the sum of the terms divided by the number of terms. The numbers included are 11, 13, 15, and 17. Note that 19 is not in the set, since n is less than 19. The average is $\frac{11+13+15+17}{4} = \frac{56}{4} = 14$. The average is an even number although the numbers in the set are all odd.

29. D

Stay calm, and simply substitute the number on the left for a and the number on the right for b in the formula given for the strange symbol. First convert b to an improper fraction: $\frac{7}{4}$. So the numerator is 3 times $\frac{14}{32}$, or (simplifying the fraction) 3 times $\frac{7}{16}$, or $\frac{21}{16}$. Dividing by $\frac{7}{4}$ is the same as multiplying by $\frac{4}{7}$. So we have $\frac{21}{16} \times \frac{4}{7}$ or $\frac{3}{4} \times \frac{1}{1} = \frac{3}{4}$.

30. E

Multiply the number of hours per day, times the number of days, times the rate per hour. Wrong answer (A) results if you skip the first factor, 4.5. Wrong answer (B) results if you skip the third factor, 4.25. Wrong answer (C) results if you skip the second factor, 3.

31. D

Let's say the original price is x dollars. The price paid is 70 percent of the original price (100% minus 30%). So, $0.7x = 35$, $70x = 3,500$, $x = 50$.

32. C

The numbers for the week are: 16, 21, 20, 17, 19, 21, 17. Listing them in ascending order, we have: 16, 17, 17, 19, 20, 21, 21. There are an odd number of numbers, so the median is the number in the middle of the set: 19.

33. C

By adding the 8 white, 4 red, 7 green, and 5 blue marbles, we have a total of 24 marbles. If 8 are withdrawn, 16 remain in the bag. If the chance of drawing a white marble is now one-fourth, 4 white marbles remain in the bag, so 8 – 4, or 4 must have been drawn out.

34. B

To simplify the square root of a large number, break the number down into two or more factors, and write the number as the product of the square roots of those factors. This is especially useful when one of the factors is a perfect square. In this case, break 1,500 down into two factors. $1,500 = 15 \cdot 100$, and 100 is a perfect square. So $1,500 = \sqrt{100 \cdot 15} = \sqrt{100} \cdot \sqrt{15} = 10\sqrt{15}$.

35. D

This is a basic arithmetic problem and if you remember PEMDAS, it will be a breeze. PEMDAS tells you the order in which you need to do the different calculations: parentheses, exponents, multiplication and division, addition and subtraction. Take the expression and solve the parts in that order:

$$2(3 \times 2)^2 - 27(6 \div 2) + 3^2$$
$$= 2(6)^2 - 27(3) + 3^2$$
$$= 2(36) - 27(3) + 9$$
$$= 72 - 81 + 9$$
$$= -9 + 9$$
$$= 0$$

36. C

Obviously, one way to solve this one would be to do the calculation. But this is really a test to see if you understand how to approximate a calculation by rounding off numbers. You could round off both numbers to the nearest whole number, but that wouldn't make the calculation much easier. And besides, the answer choices you're choosing between are pretty far apart, so you can probably round both numbers to the nearest ten. 48.9 is close to 50, so round it up to 50. And 21.2 is close to 20, so round it down to 20. Now the multiplication is 50 • 20 or 1,000, choice (C).

37. E

In terms of order of operations, treat absolute value bars and roots just like parentheses: simplify them first. In this case, first find the value of $16 - 25$: $16 - 25 = -9$. The absolute value of a number is its distance from zero on the number line. Now -9 is 9 units from zero so

$$|16 - 25| = |-9|$$
$$= 9$$

Now, simplify $\sqrt{25 - 16}$. $25 - 16 = 9$, so $\sqrt{25 - 16} = \sqrt{9}$. Because the radical sign is being

used, simplify $\sqrt{9}$ by finding only the positive square root of 9, which is 3. The problem becomes $9 + 3$ which is 12, (E).

38. C

You're being asked whether 81,455 is closest to 81,400 or 81,500. Logically, because 81,455 is greater than 81,450 (the halfway point between 81,400 and 81,500), it is closer to 81,500. Formally, to round a number to the nearest hundred, consider the tens digit. If the tens digit is 5 or greater, round the hundreds digit up 1. If the tens digit is 4 or smaller, keep the same hundreds digit. Here the tens digit is 5, so round the hundreds digit up 1 from 4 to 5. To the nearest 100, 81,455 is 81,500, (C).

39. A

This problem is a snap if you remember that $a\%$ of $b = b\%$ of a. In this case, 35% of $x = x\%$ of 35, so $x\%$ of 35 is 7.

If you didn't remember that $a\%$ of $b = b\%$ of a, you could also have solved the question by solving the statement that 35% of x is 7 for x and then found $x\%$ of 35. Percent • Whole = Part, so

$$\frac{35}{100}x = 7$$
$$35x = 700$$
$$x = 20$$

So $x\%$ of 35 is 20% of 35, which is 7, (A).

40. C

In this type of problem you're given a rule or definition you've never heard before and then asked a question involving that new rule. In this example, you're given a definition of the term blue: a number is blue if the sum of its digits is equal to the product

Ratios, Proportions, Rates | Probability | Symbols and Terms | Practice | **Answers**

of its digits. To solve, simply try each answer until you find the one that fits the definition of blue. Only (C) is blue, because $3 + 2 + 1 = 3 \cdot 2 \cdot 1 = 6$.

41. E

This is another invented rule question. This time all you have to do is follow directions. To "fix" –3, you first raise it to the 3rd power: $(-3)^3 = -27$. Then divide this result by 2: $-27 \div 2 = -13.5$. Next take the absolute value of –13.5, which is just 13.5. Finally, round off this result to the nearest integer: 13.5 rounds up to 14, (E).

42. C

One way to do this problem is to realize that the remainder would have to be the same whether D were divided by 15 or 6, since $D = 15 \times 6 + 2$. In other words, D is 2 more than a multiple of both 15 and 6, hence, the remainder of 2 regardless of whether D is divided by 15 or 6.

Otherwise, find the actual value of D by calculating:

$$D = 15 \times 6 + 2$$
$$= 90 + 2$$
$$= 92$$

Now divide D by 6 to find the remainder: $92 \div 6 = 15$, with a remainder of 2. (C) is correct.

43. C

This is another follow the instructions problem. Just replace a with 7 and b with 5. So 7? 5 = (7 + 5) (7 – 5) = (12)(2), or 24, (C).

44. C

$\frac{71}{6} = 11\frac{5}{6}$, so the greatest integer less than $\frac{71}{6}$ is 11.

45. C

$0.25 = \frac{1}{4}$, so just find which choice is NOT less than $\frac{1}{4}$. (C), $\frac{16}{64}$, reduces to $\frac{1}{4}$ so it is equal to, not less than, 0.25.

46. B

The average of an odd number of consecutive numbers is equal to the middle term. Since 11 is the average of these five consecutive odd numbers, 11 is the third and middle term. So the five numbers are 7, 9, 11, 13, and 15. The largest number is 15.

CHAPTER 12: ALGEBRA

Algebra questions **appear only on the SSAT and the Upper-level ISEE.** If you are taking the Middle or Lower-level ISEE, you may skip this section.

Algebra problems will appear in two forms on the SSAT/ISEE: as regular math problems and as word problems. Word problems will be dealt with in another section. This section will give you a chance to review the basic algebra concepts that you'll see on the test. The Word Problems section will build on these concepts and introduce word problem-specific skills.

ALGEBRA CONCEPTS

VOCABULARY

In that algebra consists of the same basic operations as arithmetic, it can best be defined as abstract arithmetic. The difference is that letters, called *variables,* are often substituted for numbers. Before we discuss algebraic topics, let's review some important definitions:

A *variable* is a letter (usually lower case) used to represent a numerical value that is unknown. The value of the variable may differ in any particular problem.

A *constant* is a value that does not change its value regardless of the problem. Constants are typically numbers.

A *term* is a variable, a constant, or the product of a constant and one or more variables. The variables may be raised to exponents. A term containing only a number is called a *constant term* because it contains no variable factors.

The *coefficient* of a term is understood to be the numerical factor of that term. If no numerical factor is present, the coefficient is understood to be 1 (or −1).

Concepts   Equations   Inequalities   Practice   Answer

EXAMPLES:

Term	Variable(s)	Coefficient	Constant(s)
$5x$	x	5	5
$-3yz$	y, z	-3	-3
12			12

Like terms are terms that contain exactly the same variables raised to exactly the same exponents. Like terms can be added and subtracted by combining the numerical coefficients and keeping the variable portion of the terms.

Examples:	Can be simplified to:
$7x + 5x$	$12x$
$3xy - 2 - xy$	$2xy - 2$
$8a^2b + 5ab^2 - 4a^{2b}$	$4a^{2b} + 5ab^2$ (this expression cannot be simplified further because the exponents on the variables a and b are not the same.)

In algebra you work with expressions and equations. An algebraic *expression* contains one or more terms separated by addition and subtraction signs.

EXAMPLES:

$$4x^3 + 12x^2 + 7x + 8$$
$$18a^3b^4 + 14a^2b^5 + 12a + 56$$

An algebraic *equation* is a statement that two expressions are equal. An equal sign, =, is used to indicate that the two expressions are equal.

EXAMPLES:

$$5x + 10 = 4x + 26$$
$$x^2 + 5x + 12 = 3y + 4$$

A *polynomial* is an algebraic expression that is the sum of two or more terms. If a polynomial has two terms, it is called a *binomial*. If it has three terms it is called a trinomial. If an expression only has one term, it is called a *monomial*.

FOR ALGEBRAIC EXPRESSIONS

" Make sure you combine only 'like terms.' "

EXAMPLES:

$16x^3 - 10x^2$	binomial, polynomial
$-3a^3b^4 + 4a + 6$	trinomial, polynomial
$13p^6k^9$	monomial

Concepts   Equations   Inequalities   Practice   Answer

SUBSTITUTION

If a problem gives you the value for a variable, just substitute the value into the expression
and solve. Make sure that you follow the correct order of operations and are careful with your
calculations.

> If $x = 15$ and $y = 10$, what is the value of $4x(x - y)$?
> Substitute 15 for x and 10 for y.

> $4(15)(15 - 10) =$

Then evaluate.

> $(60)(5) = 300$

SIMPLIFYING POLYNOMIAL EXPRESSIONS

To simplify a polynomial expression, remove all grouping symbols (parentheses) using distribution,
simplify each term so that each variable appears no more than once in any one term, then combine
like terms.

EXAMPLES:

$$6(3b - 4) = 18b - 24$$

$$-3(4x + 1) + 2 = -12x - 3 + 2$$
$$= -12x - 1$$

$$(2b)^3 - 5b^2(3b) = 8b^3 - 15b^3$$
$$= -7b^3$$

$$3a + 2b - 8a = 3a - 8a + 2b$$
$$= -5a + 2b \text{ or } 2b - 5a$$

$$(4w + 9h) - (3w - 4h) = 4w + 9h - 3w + 4h$$
$$= 4w - 3w + 9h + 4h$$
$$= w + 13h$$

FACTORING POLYNOMIAL EXPRESSIONS

The main factoring method you need to master for the test is factoring using the greatest common
factor (GCF) of an algebraic expression. The GCF of an expression consists of the largest
numerical factor and the largest number of variable factors that can be factored out of all terms in
the expression.

Concepts   Equations   Inequalities   Practice   Answer

To find the GCF of an expression, first make sure that the expression is simplified. Second, find the largest factor common to all coefficients in the expression (it is possible to have a numerical GCF of one). Finally, identify the variable factors common to all terms in the expression. The GCF will contain these factors raised to the lowest exponent given on the variable in any one term.

To write an expression in factored form, use the distributive property to write the GCF followed by the polynomial factor in parentheses.

EXAMPLES:

$$7y^3 + 14y^2 - 21y = 7y(y^2 + 2y - 3)$$
$$12ab^3 - 15a^2b^2 = 3ab^2(4b - 5a)$$

In the first example, $7y$ is the GCF of the expression. In the second example, $3ab^2$ is the GCF of the expression.

MULTIPLYING AND DIVIDING MONOMIALS AND BINOMIALS

To **add** or **subtract** terms consisting of a coefficient (the number in front of the variable) multiplied by a power (a power is a base raised to an exponent), both the base and the exponent *must* be the same. As long as the bases and the exponents are the same, you can add the coefficients.

$$x^2 + x^2 = 2x^2$$

$$3x^4 - 2x^4 = x^4$$

$x^2 + x^3$ cannot be combined.

$x^2 + y^2$ cannot be combined.

To **multiply** terms consisting of coefficients multiplied by powers having the same base, multiply the coefficients and add the exponents.

$$2x^5 \times 8x^7 = (2 \times 8)(x^{5+7}) = 16x^{12}$$

To **divide** terms consisting of coefficients multiplied by powers having the same base, divide the coefficients and subtract the exponents.

$$6x^7 \div 2x^5 = (6 \div 2)(x^{7-5}) = 3x^2$$

To **raise a power to an exponent,** multiply the exponents.

$$(x^2)^4 = x^{2 \times 4} = x^8$$

KAPLAN EXCLUSIVE TIPS

To multiply powers with the same base, add exponents. To raise a power to an exponent, multiply exponents.

Concepts | Equations | Inequalities | Practice | Answer

When you multiply monomials, multiply the coefficients of each term. (In other words, multiply the numbers that come before the variables.) Then, multiply the variables. Exponents of like variables should be added, while those of different variables should be multiplied.

$$(6a)(4b) = (6 \times 4)(a \times b) = 24ab$$
$$(6a)(4ab) = (6 \times 4)(a \times a \times b) =$$
$$= (6 \times 4)(a^{1+1} \times b)$$
$$= 24\,a^2 b$$

When you divide monomials, divide the coefficient of the numerator by the coefficient of the denominator. When the same variable appears in both the numerator and the denominator, subtract from the exponent of that variable in the numerator the exponent of that variable in the denominator.

$$24a \div 3b = \frac{24a}{3b} = \frac{8a}{b}$$
$$40x^2 y^5 \div 5xy^2 z^4 = \frac{40x^2 y^5}{5xy^5 z^4} = \frac{8x^{2-1} y^{5-2}}{z^4} = \frac{8x^1 y^3}{z^4} = \frac{8xy^3}{z^4}.$$

Remember that $x^1 = x$.

Use the FOIL method to **multiply binomials.** FOIL stands for <u>F</u>irst <u>O</u>uter <u>I</u>nner <u>L</u>ast.

$$(y + 1)(y + 2) = (y \times y) + (y \times 2) + (1 \times y) + (1 \times 2)$$
$$= y^2 + 2y + y + 2$$
$$= y^2 + 3y + 2$$

WORKING WITH EQUATIONS

The key to **solving equations** is to do the same thing to both sides of the equation until you have your variable isolated on one side of the equation and all of the numbers on the other side.

$$12a + 8 = 23 - 3a$$

First, subtract 8 from each side so that the left side of the equation has only a variable term.

$$12a + 8 - 8 = 23 - 3a - 8$$
$$12a = 15 - 3a$$

Then, add $3a$ to each side so that the right side of the equation has only numbers.

$$12a + 3a = 15 - 3a + 3a$$
$$15a = 15$$

Finally, divide both sides by 15 to isolate the variable.

$$\frac{15a}{15} = \frac{15}{15}$$
$$a = 1$$

Sometimes you're given an equation with two variables and asked to **solve for one variable in terms of the other.** This means that you must isolate the variable for which you are solving on one side of the equation and put everything else on the other side. In other words, when you're done, you'll have x (or whatever the variable is) on one side of the equation and an expression on the other side.

Solve $7x + 2y = 3x + 10y - 16$ for x in terms of y.

Since you want to isolate x on one side of the equation, begin by subtracting $2y$ from both sides.

$$7x + 2y - 2y = 3x + 10y - 16 - 2y$$
$$7x = 3x + 8y - 16$$

Then, subtract $3x$ from both sides to get all the x's on one side of the equation.

$$7x - 3x = 3x + 8y - 16 - 3x$$
$$4x = 8y - 16$$

Finally, divide both sides by 4 to isolate x.

$$\frac{4x}{4} = \frac{8y - 16}{4}$$
$$x = 2y - 4$$

PICKING NUMBERS

Picking numbers is a useful strategy for avoiding tedious calculations. Instead of solving the equation and figuring out which answer choice matches your answer, you plug choices back into the equation until one fits.

Some typical questions that can be solved by picking numbers are:

- Age stated in terms of variables
- Remainder problems
- Percentages or fractions of variables
- Even/odd variables calculations
- Questions with algebraic expressions as answers

WORKING WITH INEQUALITIES

Solving inequalities is very similar to solving equations with two important differences:

1. When **multiplying or dividing both sides of an inequality by a negative number, the direction of the inequality must change.**

2. The **solution of an inequality** will be a **range of values for the variable,** rather than just one value.

When solving the inequality $-5a < 10$, for instance, it is correct to divide both sides of the inequality by -5. Because -5 is a negative number, the solution, after simplifying, would be $a > -2$, not $a < -2$.

If this is confusing, consider the rules for multiplying signed numbers. If -5 multiplied by some value must be less than 10, any positive number will do. That's because -5 multiplied by a positive number yields a negative number and ALL negative numbers are less than 10. In addition, some negative numbers like -1 and $-1/2$ will also work; though when multiplied by -5 they yield positive results, the positive product is less than 10. Once -5 is multiplied by -2 and numbers smaller, however, the product becomes too large.

EXAMPLES:

$$4a + 6 > 2a + 10$$
$$4a - 2a > 10 - 6$$
$$2a > 4$$
$$a > 2$$

$$5(g - 6) \le 6g + 18$$
$$5g - 30 \le 6g + 18$$
$$5g - 6g \le 18 + 30$$
$$-g \le 48$$
$$g \ge -48$$

PRACTICE QUESTIONS

1. What is the value of $a(b-1) + \dfrac{bc}{2}$ if $a = 3$, $b = 6$, and $c = 5$?

   (A) 0
   (B) 15
   (C) 30
   (D) 45
   (E) 60

2. If $\dfrac{c}{d} = 3$ and $d = 1$, then $3c + d =$

   (A) 3
   (B) 4
   (C) 6
   (D) 7
   (E) 10

3. What is the value of x in the equation $5x - 7 = y$, if $y = 8$?

   (A) −1
   (B) 1
   (C) 2
   (D) 3
   (E) 70

4. What is the value of $x(y-2) + xz$, if $x = 2$, $y = 5$, and $z = 7$?

   (A) 12
   (B) 20
   (C) 22
   (D) 28
   (E) 32

5. If $x = \sqrt{3}$, $y = 2$, and $z = \dfrac{1}{2}$, then $x^2 - 5yz + y^2 =$

   (A) 1
   (B) 2
   (C) 4
   (D) 7
   (E) 8

6. If $x + y = 7$, what is the value of $2x + 2y - 2$?

   (A) 5
   (B) 9
   (C) 12
   (D) 14
   (E) 16

7. What is the value of a in the equation $3a - 6 = b$, if $b = 18$?

   (A) 4
   (B) 6
   (C) 8
   (D) 10
   (E) 18

8. If $\dfrac{x}{y} = \dfrac{2}{5}$ and $x = 10$, $y =$

   (A) 4
   (B) 10
   (C) 15
   (D) 20
   (E) 25

9. $-5n(3m - 2) =$

   (A) $-15mn + 10n$
   (B) $15mn - 10n$
   (C) $-8mn + 7n$
   (D) $8mn + 7n$
   (E) $-2mn - 7n$

Concepts | Equations | Inequalities | **Practice** | Answer

10. What is the value of $(a + b)^2$, when $a = -1$ and $b = 3$?

   (A) 2
   (B) 4
   (C) 8
   (D) 10
   (E) 16

11. If $s - t = 5$, what is the value of $3s - 3t + 3$?

   (A) 2
   (B) 8
   (C) 11
   (D) 12
   (E) 18

12. $(3d - 7) - (5 - 2d) =$

   (A) $d - 12$
   (B) $5d - 2$
   (C) $5d + 12$
   (D) $5d - 12$
   (E) $8d + 5$

13. What is the value of $xyz + y(z - x) + 2x$ if $x = -2, y = 3$ and $z = 1$?

   (A) −13
   (B) −7
   (C) −1
   (D) 7
   (E) 19

14. If $3x + 7 = 14$, then $x =$

   (A) −14
   (B) 0
   (C) $\dfrac{7}{3}$
   (D) 3
   (E) 7

15. If x is an integer, which of the following expressions is always even?

   (A) $2x + 1$
   (B) $3x + 2$
   (C) $4x + 3$
   (D) $5x + 4$
   (E) $6x + 2$

16. If $4z - 3 = -19$, then $z =$

   (A) −16
   (B) $-5\dfrac{1}{2}$
   (C) −4
   (D) 0
   (E) 4

17. If $3ab = 6$, what is the value of a in terms of b?

   (A) 2
   (B) $\dfrac{2}{b}$
   (C) $\dfrac{2}{b^2}$
   (D) $2b$
   (E) $2b^2$

18. If x and y are integers, in which equation must x be negative?

   (A) $xy = -1$
   (B) $xy^2 = -1$
   (C) $x^2y = -1$
   (D) $x^2y^2 = 1$
   (E) $xy^2 = 1$

19. If n is an odd number, which of the following expressions is always odd?

   (A) $2n + 4$
   (B) $3n + 2$
   (C) $3n + 5$
   (D) $5n + 5$
   (E) $5n + 7$

Concepts   Equations   Inequalities   **Practice**   Answer

20. If $5p + 12 = 17 - 4\left(\dfrac{p}{2}+1\right)$, what is the value of p?

    (A) $\dfrac{1}{7}$

    (B) $\dfrac{1}{3}$

    (C) $\dfrac{6}{7}$

    (D) $1\dfrac{2}{7}$

    (E) 2

21. If $\dfrac{2x}{5y} = 6$, what is the value of y, in terms of x?

    (A) $\dfrac{x}{15}$

    (B) $\dfrac{x}{2}$

    (C) $\dfrac{15}{x}$

    (D) $15x$

    (E) $\dfrac{30}{x}$

22. If x is an odd integer and y is an even integer, which of the following expressions MUST be odd?

    (A) $2x + y$

    (B) $2(x + y)$

    (C) $x^2 + y^2$

    (D) $xy + y$

    (E) $2x + y^2$

23. If $100 \div x = 10n$, then which of the following is equal to nx?

    (A) 10

    (B) $10x$

    (C) 100

    (D) $10xn$

    (E) 1,000

24. For what value of y is $4(y-1) = 2(y + 2)$?

    (A) 0

    (B) 2

    (C) 4

    (D) 6

    (E) 8

25. $\dfrac{3}{4} + x = 8.3$

    What is the value of x in the equation above?

    (A) 4.9

    (B) 6.75

    (C) 7.55

    (D) 8

    (E) 9.05

26. If $2(a + m) = 5m - 3 + a$, what is the value of a, in terms of m?

    (A) $\dfrac{3m}{2}$

    (B) 3

    (C) $5m$

    (D) $4m + 33$

    (E) $3m - 3$

PRACTICE QUESTION ANSWERS

1. C

Substitute $a = 3$, $b = 6$, and $c = 5$.

$$3(6 - 1) + \frac{6 \times 5}{2} = 3(5) + \frac{30}{2}$$
$$= 15 + 15$$
$$= 30$$

2. E

Since we're told the value of d, we can substitute it into the equation $\frac{c}{d} = 3$ to find the value of c. We are told that $d = 1$, so $\frac{c}{d} = 3$ can be rewritten as $\frac{c}{1} = 3$. Since $\frac{c}{1}$ is the same as c, we can rewrite the equation again as $c = 3$. Now we can substitute the values of c and d into the expression $3c + d$ to get $3(3) + 1 = 10$.

3. D

We are told that $y = 8$, so first we'll substitute 8 for y, and then we can solve for x.

$$5x - 7 = y$$
$$5x - 7 =$$

Now we can add 7 to both sides:

$$5x - 7 + 7 = 8 + 7$$
$$5x = 15$$

Next we divide both sides by 5:

$$\frac{5x}{5} = \frac{15}{5}$$
$$x = 3$$

4. B

Here we have three values to substitute. Remember, xz means x times z. After we substitute the values of x, y, and z, we will do the operations in PEMDAS order—parentheses, exponents, multiplication and division, addition and subtraction.

$$x(y - 2) + xz = 2(5 - 2) + 2 \times 7$$
$$= 2(3) + 2 \times 7$$
$$= 6 + 14$$
$$= 20$$

5. B

This is another "plug in" question. Remember, $5yz$ means $5 \times y \times z$. First we will replace x, y, and z with the values given. Then we will carry out the indicated operations using PEMDAS.

$$x^2 - 5yz + y^2 = (\sqrt{3})^2 - 5 \times 2 \times \frac{1}{2} + 2^2$$
$$= 3 - 5 \times 2 \times + 4$$
$$= 3 - 5 + 4$$
$$= -2 + 4$$
$$= 2$$

6. C

If you look carefully at the expression $2x + 2y - 2$, you should see some similarity to $x + y = 7$. If we ignore the -2 for a moment, $2x + 2y$ is really just twice $x + y$. If it helps to make it clearer, we can factor out the 2, making $2x + 2y$ into $2(x + y)$. Since $x + y = 7$, $2(x + y)$ must equal $2(7)$, or 14. If we replace $2x + 2y$ with 14, the expression $2x + 2y - 2$ becomes $14 - 2$, which equals 12, (C)

7. C

This question is solved the same way as question 3.

Plug in 18 for b in the equation:

$$3a - 6 = 18$$

Isolate a on one side of the equation:

$$3a = 18 + 6$$

$$3a = 24$$

Divide both sides by 3 to find the value of a: $a = 8$

Concepts   Equations   Inequalities   Practice   **Answers**

8. E

Substitute 10 for x in the equation:

$$\frac{10}{y} = \frac{2}{5}$$

Cross multiply:

$$(10)(5) = (2)(y)$$

$$50 = 2y$$

Divide both sides by 2 to find the value of y:

$$\frac{50}{2} = \frac{2y}{2}$$

$$25 = y$$

9. A

Distribute $-5n$ to each term within the parentheses:

$$-5n(3m - 2) = (-5n)(3m) + (-5n)(-2)$$

Multiply through:

$$= -15mn + 10n$$

Note that $(-5n)(-2) = +10n$, because a negative 3 a negative yields a positive.

10. B

Plug $a = -1$ and $b = 3$ into the expression:

$$(-1 + 3)^2 = (2)^2 = 4$$

11. E

The expression can be rewritten as $3(s - t) + 3$.

Plug in 5 for $s - t$:

$$3(5) + 3 = 15 + 3$$

$$= 18$$

12. D

Perform the operations: $3d - 7 - 5 - (-2d)$. Combine like terms:

$$3d - (-2d) - 7 - 5$$

$$5d - 12$$

$3d$ minus $-2d$ equals $+5d$, because subtraction is equivalent to "addition of the opposite." $3d - (-2d)$ becomes $3d + (+2d)$ which is equal to $5d$.

13. C

Plug in $x = -2$, $y = 3$, and $z = 1$:

$$(-2)(3)(1) + 3[(1 - (-2)] + 2(-2)$$

$$= -6 + 3(3) - 4$$

$$= -6 + 9 - 4$$

$$= 3 - 4$$

$$= -1$$

14. C

We have to rearrange the equation until the x is alone on one side of the equal sign. You must do the same thing to the both sides of the equation. First we will take away the 7:

$$3x + 7 = 14$$

$$3x + 7 - 7 = 14 - 7$$

$$3x = 7$$

$$\frac{3x}{3} = \frac{7}{3}$$

$$x = \frac{7}{3}$$

15. E

Notice that the question asks which expression is always even. (E), $6x + 2$, is correct because the product of an even number and any integer is even, so $6x$ is even because 6 is even. When two even numbers are added, their sum is also even, so $6x + 2$ is even. (A) and (C) are always odd regardless of what integer is substituted for x. (B) and (D) are even only when x is even.

16. C

We must rearrange the equation until the z is alone on one side of the equal sign. Anything we do to one

Concepts   Equations   ·Inequalities   Practice   **Answers**

side of the equation we must also do to the other side. First we'll add 3 to both sides:

$$4z - 3 = -19$$

$$4z - 3 + 3 = -19 + 3$$

$$4z = -16$$

Next we'll divide both sides by 4:

$$\frac{4z}{4} = -\frac{16}{4}$$

$$z = -4$$

17. B

Rearrange the equation until the variable a is alone on one side of the equal sign.

$$3ab = 6$$

$$\frac{3ab}{3} = \frac{6}{3}$$

$$ab = 2$$

$$\frac{ab}{b} = \frac{2}{b}$$

$$a = \frac{2}{b}$$

18. B

Try each answer choice until you find the correct one.

(A) $xy = -1$. If the product of two integers is negative, then one of the two integers must be negative. In this case x could be negative, but it's possible that y is negative and x is positive. We're looking for an equation where x will always have to be negative.

(B) $xy^2 = -1$. The exponent here applies only to the y, not to the x. The square of any non-zero number is positive, so whatever y is, y^2 must be positive. (We know that y isn't zero; if it were, then the product xy^2 would also be zero.) Since y^2 is positive and the product of y^2 and x is negative, x must be negative. (B) is the answer.

19. B

We're told that n is odd, so we don't have to check to see what happens if n is even. We do have to try each answer to see which one represents an odd number. Let's say $n = 3$ and replace all the n's with 3's.

(A) $2n + 4$. $2(3) + 4 = 6 + 4 = 10$. 10 is even.

(B) $3n + 2$. $3(3) + 2 = 9 + 2 = 11$. 11 is odd, so (B) is the answer.

20. A

This equation takes a few more steps than the previous ones, but it follows the same rules.

First we multiply using the distributive law:

$$5p + 12 = 17 - 4\left(\frac{p}{2} + 1\right)$$

$$5p + 12 = 17 + (-4)\left(\frac{p}{2}\right) + (-4)(1)$$

$$5p + 12 = 17 + \left(-\frac{4p}{2}\right) + (-4)$$

is equal to $2p$, so $5p + 12 = 17 - 2p - 4$

Combine the integers on the right side:

$$5p + 12 = 13 - 2p$$

We can add $2p$ to each side to get all the ps on one side:

$$5p + 2p + 12 = 13 - 2p + 2p$$

$$7p + 12 = 13$$

Now we will subtract 12 from both sides:

$$7p + 12 - 12 = 13 - 12$$

$$7p = 1$$

And lastly, we divide both sides by 7:

$$\frac{7p}{7} = \frac{1}{7}$$

$$p = \frac{1}{7}$$

Concepts | Equations | Inequalities | Practice | **Answers**

21. A

We want to rearrange the equation until y is alone on one side of the equal sign. There's more than one way to do this, but here's one way:

$$\frac{2x}{5y} = 6$$

$$(5y)\frac{2x}{5y} = 6(5y)$$

$$2x = 30y$$

$$\frac{2x}{30} = y$$

$$\frac{x}{15} = y$$

22. C

This is another "try each answer" problem. We know that x is odd and y is even. Let's say that $x = 3$ and $y = 4$.

(A) $2x + y$. $2(3) + 4 = 6 + 4 = 10$. 10 is even, so this isn't correct.

(B) $2(x + y)$. $2(3 + 4) = 2(3 + 4) = 2(7) = 14$. 14 is even.

(C) $x^2 + y^2$. $32 + 42 = 9 + 16 = 25$. 25 is odd, so (C) is correct.

23. A

This problem looks harder than it really is. If

$$100 \div x = 10n \text{ then}$$

$$(10n)(x) = 100 \text{ or}$$

$$10nx = 100$$

$$nx = 10, \text{ (A)}$$

24. C

Multiply through and solve for y by isolating it on one side of the equation:

$$4(y - 1) = 2(y + 2)$$

$$4y - 4 = 2y + 4$$

$$2y - 4 = 4$$

$$2y = .8$$

$$\frac{2y}{2} = \frac{8}{2}$$

$$y = 4$$

25. C

Isolate x on one side of the equation:

$$\frac{3}{4} + x = 8.3$$

$$\frac{3}{4} + x - \frac{3}{4} = 8.3 - \frac{3}{4}$$

$$x = 8.3 - \frac{3}{4}$$

$\frac{3}{4}$ can be rewritten as 0.75, so subtracting 0.75 from 8.3 gives you 7.55.

26. E

Multiply through and find a in terms of m by isolating a on one side of the equation:

$$2(a + m) = 5m - 3 + a$$

$$2a + 2m = 5m - 3 + a$$

$$2a = 3m - 3 + a$$

$$a = 3m - 3$$

Concepts   Equations   Inequalities   Practice   **Answers**

CHAPTER 13: GEOMETRY

Geometry questions **appear only on the SSAT and the Upper-level ISEE.** If you are taking the Middle or Lower-level ISEE, you may skip this section.

Like the rest of the math you'll see on your private-school admissions test, the geometry will range from straightforward to difficult and tricky. You can count on seeing questions that test your knowledge of lines and angles, triangles, circles, and other assorted geometric figures. And a little coordinate geometry will show up, too. And finally, diagramless geometry can also show up in the form of word problems.

The most helpful thing you can do is review geometry content and practice a whole lot. If you're concerned about your math readiness, spend more time with the subjects that are less familiar to you. Make certain that you do all of the problems in the practice set even if you feel comfortable with the example questions presented.

It's important to know that unless otherwise indicated, *figures are drawn to scale.* That means you can usually eyeball the measurements of a figure.

LINES AND ANGLES

LINE SEGMENTS

Some of the most basic geometry problems deal with line segments. A **line segment** is a piece of a line, and it has an exact measurable length. A question might give you a segment divided into several pieces, provide the measurements of some of these pieces, and ask you for the measurement of a remaining piece.

Lines & Angles Triangles Quadrilaterals Circles Coordinate Geometry

If $PR = 12$ and $QR = 4$, $PQ =$

$PQ = PR - QR$

$PQ = 12 - 4$

$PQ = 8$

The point exactly in the middle of a line segment, halfway between the endpoints, is called the **midpoint** of the line segment. To bisect means to cut in half, so the midpoint of a line segment bisects that line segment.

M is the midpoint of AB, so $AM = MB$.

ANGLES

A **right angle** measures 90 degrees and is usually indicated in a diagram by a little box. The figure above is a right angle. Lines that intersect to form right angles are said to be **perpendicular.**

Angles that form a straight line add up to 180 degrees. In the figure above, **$a + b = 180$.**

Lines & Angles   Triangles   Quadrilaterals   Circles   Coordinate Geometry

When two lines intersect, **adjacent angles are supplementary,** meaning they add up to 180 degrees. In the previous figure, $a + b = 180$.

Angles around a point add up to 360 degrees. In the figure above, $a + b + c + d + e = 360$.

When lines intersect, angles across the vertex from each other are called **vertical angles** and **are equal to each other.** Above, $a = c$ and $b = d$.

PARALLEL LINES

When parallel lines are crossed by a transversal:

- Corresponding angles are equal (for example, $a = e$).
- Alternate interior angles are equal ($d = f$).
- Same side interior angles are supplementary ($c + f = 180$).
- All four acute angles are equal, as are all four obtuse angles.

TRIANGLES

There are a few basic rules with respect to triangles in general.

The three interior angles of any triangle add up to 180°. In the previous figure, $x + 50 + 100 = 180$, so $x = 30$.

An exterior angle equals the sum of the remote interior angles. In the figure above, the exterior angle labeled $y°$ equals the sum of the remote interior angles: $y = 40 + 95 = 135$.

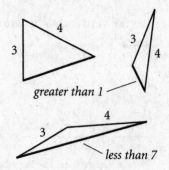

The length of one side of a triangle must be greater than the positive difference and less than the sum of the lengths of the other two sides. If it is given that the length of one side is 3 and the length of another side is 4, then the length of the third side must be greater than $4 - 3 = 1$ and less than $4 + 3 = 7$.

TRIANGLES—PERIMETER AND AREA

The **perimeter** of a triangle is the sum of the lengths of its sides.

The perimeter of the triangle in the figure above is: $3 + 4 + 6 = 13$

The **area** of a triangle is one-half base times height. The height is the perpendicular distance between the side that's chosen as the base and the opposite vertex. In this triangle, 4 is the height when the 7 is chosen as the base.

$$\text{Area} = \frac{1}{2}bh = \frac{1}{2}(7)(4) = 14$$

SIMILAR TRIANGLES

Similar triangles have the same shape: **corresponding angles are equal and corresponding sides are proportional.**

These triangles are similar because they have the same angles. The 3 corresponds to the 4 and the 6 corresponds to the s.

$$\frac{3}{4} = \frac{6}{s}$$
$$3s = 24$$
$$s = 8$$

SPECIAL TRIANGLES

Special triangles are the isosceles, equilateral, and right triangles.

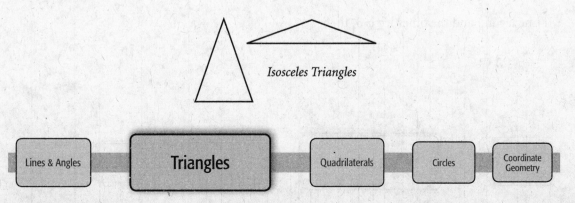

Isosceles Triangles

Lines & Angles   Triangles   Quadrilaterals   Circles   Coordinate Geometry

An isosceles triangle is a triangle that has two equal sides. Not only are two sides equal, but the angles opposite the equal sides, called base angles, are also equal.

Equilateral Triangles

Equilateral triangles are triangles in which all three sides are equal. Since all the sides are equal, all the angles are also equal. All three angles in an equilateral triangle measure 60 degrees, regardless of the lengths of the sides.

Right Triangles

A right triangle is a triangle with a right angle. Every right triangle has exactly two acute angles. The sides opposite the acute angles are called the legs. The side opposite the right angle is called the hypotenuse. Since it's opposite the largest angle, the hypotenuse is the longest side of a right triangle.

RIGHT TRIANGLES

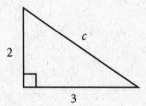

PYTHAGOREAN THEOREM:

The Pythagorean theorem is as follows:

$$(\text{leg}_1)^2 + (\text{leg}_2)^2 = (\text{hypotenuse})^2 \text{ or } a^2 + b^2 = c^2$$

If one leg is 2 and the other leg is 3, then:

$$2^2 + 3^2 = c^2$$
$$c^2 = 4 + 9$$
$$c = \sqrt{13}$$

Lines & Angles   **Triangles**   Quadrilaterals   Circles   Coordinate Geometry

PYTHAGOREAN "TRIPLETS"

If a right triangle's leg-to-leg ratio is 3:4, or if the leg-to-hypotenuse ratio is 3:5 or 4:5, it's a 3-4-5 triangle and you don't need to use the Pythagorean theorem to find the third side. Just figure out what multiple of 3-4-5 it is. In this right triangle, one leg is 30 and the hypotenuse is 50. This is 10 times 3-4-5. The other leg is 40.

If a right triangle's leg-to-leg ratio is 5:12, or if the leg-to-hypotenuse ratio is 5:13 or 12:13, then it's a **5-12-13 triangle** and you don't need to use the Pythagorean theorem to find the third side. Just figure out what multiple of 5-12-13 it is. Here one leg is 36 and the hypotenuse is 39. This is 3 times 5-12-13. The other leg is 15.

SIDE–ANGLE RATIOS

The sides of a 30-60-90 triangle are in a ratio of $x : x\sqrt{3} : 2x$. You don't need to use the Pythagorean theorem. If the hypotenuse is 6, then the shorter leg is half that, or 3; and then the longer leg is equal to the short leg times $\sqrt{3}$, or $3\sqrt{3}$.

The sides of a 45-45-90 triangle are in a ratio of $x : x : x\sqrt{2}$. If one leg is 3, then the other leg is also 3, and the hypotenuse is equal to a leg multiplied by $\sqrt{2}$, or $3\sqrt{2}$.

Lines & Angles   **Triangles**   Quadrilaterals   Circles   Coordinate Geometry

QUADRILATERALS

The **perimeter** of a polygon is the sum of the lengths of its sides. The perimeter of the quadrilateral in the figure above is: $5 + 8 + 3 + 7 = 23$

A **rectangle** is a parallelogram containing four right angles. Opposite sides are equal. The formula for the area of a rectangle is:

   Area = (length)(width)

In the figure above, ℓ = length and w = width, so area = ℓw. Perimeter = $2(\ell + w)$

A **square** is a rectangle with four equal sides. The formula for the area of a square is:

   Area = (side)^2

In the figure above, s = the length of a side, so area = s^2. Perimeter = $4s$.

Lines & Angles   Triangles   **Quadrilaterals**   Circles   Coordinate Geometry

A **parallelogram** is a quadrilateral with two sets of parallel sides. Opposite sides are equal, as are opposite angles. The formula for the area of a parallelogram is:

Area = (base)(height)

In the diagram above, h = height and b = base, so area = bh

A **trapezoid** is a quadrilateral with one pair of parallel sides. The formula for the area of a trapezoid is:

Area = $\frac{1}{2}$ (sum of the lengths of the parallel sides)(height)

In the figure above, the area of the trapezoid is $\frac{1}{2}(4 + 9)(5) = 32.5$

If two polygons are similar, then corresponding angles are equal and corresponding sides are in proportion.

The two rectangles above are similar because all the angles are right angles, and each side of the larger rectangle is $1\frac{1}{2}$ times the corresponding side of the smaller.

CIRCLES

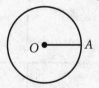

A **circle** is a figure each point of which is an equal distance from its center. In the diagram, O is the center of the circle.

Triangles · Quadrilaterals · **Circles** · Coordinate Geometry · Practice

The **radius** of a circle is the straight line distance from its center to any point on the circle. All radii of one circle have equal lengths. In the previous figure, OA is a radius of circle O.

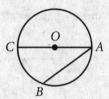

A **chord** is a line segment that connects any two points on a circle. Segments AB and AC are both chords. The largest chord that may be drawn in a circle will be a diameter of that circle.

A **diameter** of a circle is a chord that passes through the circle's center. All diameters are the same length and are equal to twice the radius. In the figure above, AC is a diameter of circle O.

$$AC = 6$$

The **circumference** of a circle is the distance around it. It is equal to πd, or $2\pi r$. In this example: Circumference $= \pi d = 6\pi$

The **area** of a circle equals π times the square of the radius, or πr^2. In this example, since AC is the diameter, $r = \dfrac{6}{2} = 3$, and area $= \pi r^2 = \pi(3^2) = 9\pi$

COORDINATE GEOMETRY

WHAT'S π ?

" π is an infinite and nonrepeating decimal, but all you need to remember is that it's approximately 3.14. "

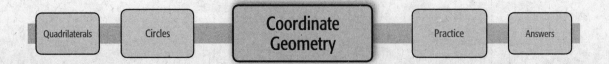

Quadrilaterals | Circles | **Coordinate Geometry** | Practice | Answers

The previous diagram represents the **coordinate axes**—the perpendicular "number lines" in the coordinate plane. The horizontal line is called the **x-axis.** The vertical line is called the **Y-axis.** In a coordinate plane, the point O at which the two axes intersect is called the **origin.**

The pair of numbers, written inside parentheses, which specifies the location of a point in the coordinate plane, are called **coordinates.** The first number is the **x-coordinate** and the second number is the **y-coordinate.** The **origin** is the zero point on both axes, with coordinates (0, 0).

Starting at the origin:

to the right: *x* is positive
to the left: *x* is negative
up: *y* is positive
down: *y* is negative

The two axes divide the coordinate plane into four quadrants. When you know what quadrant a point lies in, you know the signs of its coordinates. A point in the upper left quadrant, for example, has a negative x-coordinate and a positive y-coordinate.

PLOTTING POINTS

If you were asked to graph the point (2, –3) you would start at the origin, count 2 units to the right and 3 down. To graph (–4, 5) you would start at the origin, go 4 units to the left and 5 units up.

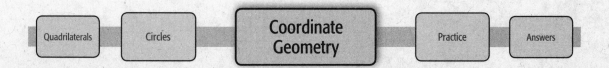

Quadrilaterals   Circles   **Coordinate Geometry**   Practice   Answers

SLOPE OF A LINE

To use two points to find the slope of a line, use the following formula:

$$\text{Slope} = \frac{\text{change in } y}{\text{change in } x} \text{ or slope} = \frac{\Delta y}{\Delta x} \text{ or } \frac{y_2 - y_1}{x_2 - x_1}.$$

The slope of a line that contains the points $A(4, 6)$ and $B(0, -3)$

$$\frac{y_2 - y_1}{x_2 - x_1} = \frac{-3 - 6}{0 - 4} = \frac{-9}{-4} = \frac{9}{4}$$

To use an equation of a line to find the slope, put the equation into the slope-intercept form:

$y = mx + b$ where the slope is m.

To find the slope of the equation $5x + 3y = 6$, rearrange it:

$5x + 3y = 6$

$3y = -5x + 6$ Subtract $5x$ from both sides of the equation.

$y = -\frac{5}{3}x + 2$ Isolate y by dividing by 3.

The slope is $-\frac{5}{3}$.

FIGURING LENGTHS

To find the length of a line segment **parallel to the x-axis** in the coordinate plane, its length is the absolute value of the difference of its x-coordinates.

To find the length of a line segment **parallel to the y-axis** in the coordinate plane, its length is the absolute value of the difference of its y-coordinates.

In the figure above, the length of AB is $|7 - 1| = 6$. The length of CD is $|0 - (-4)| = 4$.

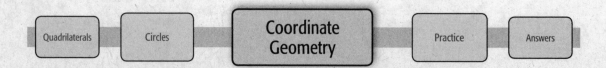

Quadrilaterals · Circles · **Coordinate Geometry** · Practice · Answers

RETRACING A GEOMETRIC FIGURE

Some geometry questions ask you to determine whether a figure can be drawn without lifting the pencil. There's a simple rule for determining this: In any given figure, if exactly zero or two points have an odd number of intersecting line segments and/or curves, it can be drawn without lifting the pencil or retracing.

KAPLAN EXCLUSIVE TIPS

"Length is always positive."

The figure above has two points that have three intersecting lines (an odd number), so it can be drawn without lifting your pencil.

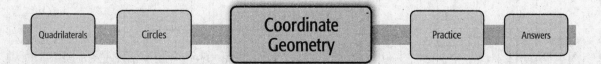

Quadrilaterals · Circles · **Coordinate Geometry** · Practice · Answers

PRACTICE QUESTIONS

1. In the figure above, segments AB, BC, CD, and AC are all equal. What is the value of x?

   (A) 30
   (B) 45
   (C) 60
   (D) 90
   (E) 120

2. If the measure of angle ABC is 145°, what is the value of x?

   (A) 39
   (B) 45
   (C) 52
   (D) 55
   (E) 62

3. If the perimeter of a square is 32 meters, what is the area of the square, in square meters?

   (A) 16
   (B) 32
   (C) 48
   (D) 56
   (E) 64

4. In triangle XYZ the measure of angle Y is twice the measure of angle X, and the measure of Z is three times the measure of angle X. What is the degree measure of angle Y?

   (A) 15
   (B) 30
   (C) 45
   (D) 60
   (E) 90

5. The perimeter of triangle ABC is 24. If AB = 9 and BC = 7, then AC =

   (A) 6
   (B) 8
   (C) 10
   (D) 15
   (E) 17

6. If the perimeter of an equilateral triangle is 150, what is the length of one of its sides?

   (A) 35
   (B) 35
   (C) 50
   (D) 75
   (E) 100

7. In triangle *RST*, if *RS* = *RT*, what is the degree measure of angle *S*?

   (A) 40
   (B) 55
   (C) 70
   (D) 110
   (E) It cannot be determined from the information given.

8. In triangle *XYZ*, what is the degree measure of angle *YXZ*?

   (A) 18
   (B) 36
   (C) 54
   (D) 72
   (E) 90

9. If the perimeter of triangle *ABC* is 18, what is the length of *AC*?

   (A) 2
   (B) 4
   (C) 5
   (D) 6
   (E) 8

10. What is the area, in square units, of a square that has the same perimeter as the rectangle above?

    (A) 25
    (B) 36
    (C) 49
    (D) 64
    (E) 81

11. What is the value of *a* in the figure above?

    (A) 20
    (B) 40
    (C) 60
    (D) 80
    (E) 140

12. In the figure above, what is the value of *n*?

(A)   30

(B)   60

(C)   45

(D)   90

(E)   135

13. In the figure above, what is the value of *x* − *y*?

(A)   30

(B)   45

(C)   75

(D)   105

(E)   150

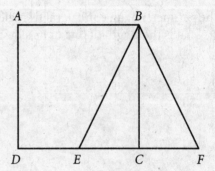

14. A square and a triangle are drawn together as shown above. The perimeter of the square is 64 and *DC* = *EF*. What is the area of triangle *BEF*?

(A)   32

(B)   64

(C)   128

(D)   256

(E)   It cannot be determined from the information given.

15. If line *p* is parallel to line *q*, what is the value of *x* + *y* ?

(A)   90

(B)   110

(C)   125

(D)   180

(E)   250

$2\sqrt{2}$

16. What is the area of the square above?

(A) 4
(B) 8
(C) $4\sqrt{2}$
(D) 16
(E) 24

17. What is the area of the frame in the figure above if the inside picture has a length of 8 and a width of 4?

(A) 4
(B) 8
(C) 16
(D) 24
(E) 48

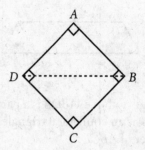

18. In the figure above, ABCD is a square and the area of triangle ABD is 8. What is the area of square ABCD?

(A) 2
(B) 4
(C) 8
(D) 16
(E) 64

Note: Figure not drawn to scale.

19. In the figure above, ABFG and CDEF are rectangles, CD bisects BF, and EF has a length of 2. What is the area of the entire figure?

(A) 4
(B) 16
(C) 32
(D) 36
(E) 72

20. In the figure above, *ABDE* is a parallelogram
    and *BCD* is an equilateral triangle. What is the
    perimeter of *ABCE*?

    (A) 12
    (B) 16
    (C) 24
    (D) 32
    (E) 36

21. In the figure above, what is the perimeter of
    ABCDEF?

    (A) 14
    (B) 24
    (C) 28
    (D) 38
    (E) 40

22. If the shaded regions are 4 rectangles, what is
    the area of the unshaded region?

    (A) 9
    (B) 12
    (C) 16
    (D) 19
    (E) 20

Note: Figure not drawn to scale.

23. In the figure above, *AB* is twice the length of
    BC, *BC* = *CD* and *DE* is triple the length of
    CD. If *AE* = 49, what is the length of *BD*?

    (A) 14
    (B) 21
    (C) 28
    (D) 30
    (E) 35

8 inches

24. In the figure above, circle P is inscribed in a square with sides of length 8 inches. What is the area of the circle?

   (A) 4π square inches

   (B) 16 square inches

   (C) 8π square inches

   (D) 16π square inches

   (E) 32π square inches

25. What is the radius of a circle whose circumference is 36π?

   (A) 3

   (B) 6

   (C) 8

   (D) 18

   (E) 36

26. If the perimeter of the square is 36, what is the circumference of the circle?

   (A) 6π

   (B) 9π

   (C) 12π

   (D) 15π

   (E) 18π

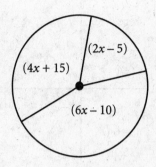

27. In the figure above, what is the value of x?

   (A) 15

   (B) 30

   (C) 55

   (D) 70

   (E) 135

28. In the figure above, a square is graphed on the coordinate plane. If the coordinates of one corner are $(-2, 0)$, what is the area of the square?

   (A) $\dfrac{1}{4}$

   (B) 1

   (C) 2

   (D) 4

   (E) 16

29. Points (a, b) and (c, d) are graphed in the coordinate plane as shown above. Which of the following statements must be true?

(A) $bd > ac$

(B) $c > ad$

(C) $b > acd$

(D) $bc > ad$

(E) It cannot be determined from the information given.

30. What is the distance from the point $(0, 6)$ to the point $(0, 8)$ in a standard coordinate plane?

(A) 2

(B) 7

(C) 10

(D) 12

(E) 14

31. Circle O above has its center at the origin. If point P lies on circle O, what is the area of circle O?

(A) 4π

(B) 8π

(C) 10π

(D) 12π

(E) 16π

32. In the figure above, right triangle ABC is inscribed in circle P, with AC passing through center P. If $AB = 6$, and $BC = 8$, what is the area of the circle?

(A) 10π

(B) 14π

(C) 25π

(D) 49π

(E) 100π

33. In the figure above, a circle is inscribed within a square. If the area of the circle is 25π, what is the perimeter of the shaded region?

(A) 40 + 5π

(B) 40 + 10π

(C) 100 + 10π

(D) 100 + 25π

(E) 40 + 50π

34. What is the slope of the line that contains points $(3, -5)$ and $(-1, 7)$?

(A) -3

(B) $-\dfrac{1}{3}$

(C) $-\dfrac{1}{4}$

(D) $\dfrac{1}{3}$

(E) 3

35. If the circumference of a circle is 16≠, what is its area?

(A)   8π

(B) 16π

(C) 32π

(D) 64π

(E) 256π

36. What is the area of the square above with diagonals of length 6?

(A) 9

(B) 12

(C) $9\sqrt{2}$

(D) 15

(E) 18

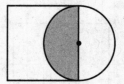

37. A square and a circle are drawn as shown above. The area of the square is 64. What is the area of the shaded region?

(A) 4π

(B) 8π

(C) 16π

(D) 32π

(E) It cannot be determined from the information given.

38. What is the area of the polygon above if each corner of the polygon is a right angle?

    (A) 40

    (B) 62

    (C) 68

    (D) 74

    (E) 80

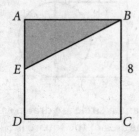

39. *ABCD* is a square. If *E* is the midpoint of *AD*, what is the area of the shaded region?

    (A) 8

    (B) 12

    (C) 16

    (D) 24

    (E) 32

40. Circle *A* has radius $r + 1$. Circle *B* has radius $r + 2$. What is the positive difference between the circumference of circle *B* and the circumference of circle *A*?

    (A) 1

    (B) 2π

    (C) $2\pi + 3$

    (D) $2\pi r + 3$

    (E) $2\pi(2r + 3)$

41. Erica has 8 squares of felt, each with area 16. For a certain craft project she cuts the largest circle possible from each square of felt. What is the combined area of the excess felt left over after cutting out all the circles?

    (A) $4(4 - \pi)$

    (B) $8(4 - \pi)$

    (C) $8(\pi - 2)$

    (D) $32(4 - \pi)$

    (E) $8(16 - \pi)$

42. In the figure above, points *A*, *B*, and *C* lie on the circumference of the circle centered at *O*. If $\angle OAB$ measures 50° and $\angle BCO$ measures 60°, what is the degree measure of $\angle AOC$?

    (A) 110

    (B) 125

    (C) 140

    (D) 250

    (E) It cannot be determined from the information given.

Quadrilaterals   Circles   Coordinate Geometry   **Practice**   Answers

PRACTICE QUESTION ANSWERS

1. E

Since $AB = BC = AC$, triangle ABC is equilateral. Therefore, all of its angles are 60°. Since angle BCD or x is supplementary to angle BCA, a 60° angle, the value of x is $180 - 60$ or 120.

2. C

Since the degree measure of angle ABC is 145, $45 + 48 + x = 145$, $93 + x = 145$, and $x = 52$.

3. E

A square has four equal sides, so its perimeter is equal to $4s$, where s is the length of a side of the square. Its perimeter is 32, so its side length is $32 \div 4 = 8$. The area of a square is equal to s^2, so the area of the square is 8^2 or 64.

4. D

In any triangle, the measures of the three interior angles sum to 180°, so $X + Y + Z = 180$. Since the measure of angle Y is twice the measure of angle X, $Y = 2X$. Similarly, $Z = 3X$. So $X + 2X + 3X = 180$, $6X = 180$ and $X = 30$. Since $Y = 2X$, the degree measure of angle Y is $2 \cdot 30 = 60$.

5. B

The perimeter of a triangle is the sum of the lengths of its sides, in this case, $AB + BC + AC$. The perimeter of triangle ABC is 24, so plugging in the given values, $9 + 7 + AC = 24$, $16 + AC = 24$, and $AC = 8$.

6. C

In an equilateral triangle, all three sides have equal length. The perimeter of a triangle is equal to the sum of the lengths of its three sides. Since all three sides are equal, each side must be $\frac{1}{3}$ of 150, or 50.

7. B

Since RS and RT are equal, the angles opposite them must be equal. Therefore, angle T = angle S. Since the three angles of a triangle sum to 180, $70 +$ angle $S +$ angle $T = 180$ and angle $S +$ angle $T = 110$. Since the two angles, S and T, are equal, each must be half of 110, or 55.

8. C

The three interior angles of a triangle add up to 180 degrees, so $2x + 3x + 5x = 180$, $10x = 180$ degrees and $x = 18$. So angle YXZ has a degree measure of $3x = 3(18) = 54$.

9. E

The perimeter of triangle ABC is 18, so $AB + BC + AC = 18$. Plugging in the algebraic expressions given for the length of each side, you get:

$$(3a - 1) + (2a + 1) + (5a - 2) = 18$$
$$10a - 2 = 18$$
$$10a = 20$$
$$a = 2$$

The length of AC is given as $5a - 2$, so $AC = 5(2) - 2 = 8$.

10. C

The perimeter of a rectangle is $2(\ell + w)$, where ℓ represents its length and w its width. The perimeter of this rectangle is $2(9 + 5) = 28$. A square has four equal sides, so a square with a perimeter of 28 has sides of length 7. The area of a square is equal to the length of a side squared, so the area of a square with a perimeter of 28 is 7^2 or 49.

11. B

An exterior angle of a triangle equals the sum of the two remote interior angles. So $7x = 4x + 60$, $3x = 60$, and $x = 20$. So the angle marked $7x°$ has a degree measure of $7(20) = 140$. The angle marked $a°$ is supplementary to this angle, so its measure is $180 - 140 = 40$.

12. C

We are given a right angle, so that is 90°. A straight angle contains 180°, so $2n + 90 = 180$, $2n = 90$, and $n = 45$.

13. B

Since $AC = CB$, the angles opposite these sides are equal as well. So angle CAB = angle CBA, and $x = 75$. The three interior angles of a triangle sum to 180 degrees, so $2(75) + y = 180$ and $y = 30$. The question asks for the value of $x - y$, or $75 - 30 = 45$.

14. C

The area of a triangle is equal to $\frac{1}{2}bh$. In triangle BEF, the height is BC and the base is EF. The square's perimeter is 64, so each of its sides is a fourth of 64, or 16. Therefore $BC = 16$. The question also states that $DC = EF$, so $EF = 16$ as well. Plugging into the formula, the area of triangle BEF is $\frac{1}{2}(16 \times 16) = 128$.

15. D

When parallel lines are crossed by a transversal, all acute angles formed are equal, and all acute angles are supplementary to all obtuse angles. So in this diagram, the obtuse angle measuring $y°$ is supplementary to the acute angle measuring $x°$, so $x + y = 180$.

16. B

The area of a square is equal to the square of one of its sides. In this case, the square has a side length of $2\sqrt{2}$, so its area is $(2\sqrt{2})^2$ or $2 \times 2 \times \sqrt{2} \times \sqrt{2}$ or $4 \times 2 = 8$.

17. E

To find the area of the frame, find the area of the frame and picture combined (the outer rectangle) and subtract from it the area of the picture (the inner rectangle). The outer rectangle has area $10 \times 8 = 80$, the inner rectangle has area $8 \times 4 = 32$, so the area of the frame is $80 - 32 = 48$.

18. D

Diagonal BD divides square $ABCD$ into two identical triangles. If the area of triangle ABD is 8, the area of the square must be twice this, or 16.

19. D

The area of the entire figure is equal to the area of rectangle $ABFG$ plus the area of rectangle $CDEF$. The area of $ABFG$ is $8 \cdot 4 = 32$. So the area of the entire figure must be greater than 32, and at this point you can eliminate (A), (B), and (C). Since BF has length 4, and C bisects BF, CF has length 2. The question states that EF has length 2, so $CDEF$ is actually a square, and its area is 2^2 or 4. So the area of the entire figure is $32 + 4 = 36$, choice (D).

20. E

The perimeter of $ABCE$ is equal to $AB + BC + CD + DE + EA$. Since triangle BCD is equilateral, $BC = CD = BD = 4$. Because $ABDE$ is a parallelogram, $AB = DE = 12$ and $BD = EA = 4$. Therefore the perimeter of $ABCE$ is $12 + 4 + 4 + 12 + 4 = 36$, choice (E).

21. E

Simply add the six sides of the L-shaped figure. Four of them are labeled, and you can use these to figure out the remaining two. The length of side EF must be equivalent to the sum of sides AB and CD, so $4 + 6 = 10$ and $EF = 10$. The length of side BC is equivalent to the difference between sides AF

and *DE*, so 10 − 4 = 6 and *BC* = 6. Therefore, the perimeter is 10 + 10 + 4 + 6 + 6 + 4 = 40.

22. A

Each of the shaded rectangles has a side of length 3 opposite the side contributing to the interior unshaded region. So the interior region, a square, has an area of 3^2, or 9.

23. A

Let *BC* = *x*. *AB* has twice the length of *BC*, so it is 2*x*. *BC* = *CD*, so *CD* = *x*. *DE* is three times the length of *CD*, or 3*x*. Since *AE* = 49, 2*x* + *x* + *x* + 3*x* = 49, 7*x* = 49, and *x* = 7. *BD* is composed of segments *BC* and *CD*, so its length is 7 + 7 = 14.

24. D

Since circle *P* is inscribed within the square, its diameter is equal in length to a side of the square. Since the circle's diameter is 8, its radius is half this, or 4. Area of a circle = πr^2, where *r* is the radius, so the area of circle *P* is $\pi(4)^2$ = 16π square inches.

25. D

Circumference of a circle = 2π*r*, where *r* is the radius of the circle. So a circle with a circumference of 36π has a radius of $\frac{36\pi}{2\pi}$ = 18.

26. B

The perimeter of the square is 36, and since all four sides are equal, one side has length 9. Since the circle is inscribed in the square, its diameter is equal in length to a side of the square, or 9. Circumference is π*d*, where *d* represents the diameter, so the circumference of the circle is 9π.

27. B

A circle contains 360°, so:

$$(4x + 15) + (2x - 5) + (6x - 10) = 360$$
$$4x + 2x + 6x + 15 - 5 - 10 = 360$$
$$12x = 360$$
$$x = 30$$

28. D

The area of a square is equal to the square of the length of one of its sides. Since one vertex (corner) of the square lies on the origin at (0, 0) and another vertex lies on the point (−2, 0), the length of a side of the square is the distance from the origin to the point (−2, 0). This can be found by calculating the absolute value of the difference between the *x*-coordinates of the points, namely |−2 − 0| = |−2| = 2. Therefore, the area of the square is 2^2 = 4.

29. C

While there's no way to determine the numerical values of *a*, *b*, *c*, or *d*, from their positions on the coordinate plane, you do know that *a* is negative, *b* is positive, *c* is negative, and *d* is negative. Bearing in mind that a negative times a negative is a positive, consider each answer choice. (C) is indeed true: *b*, which is positive, is greater than the product *acd*, which is negative.

30. A

The points (0, 6) and (0, 8) have the same *x*-coordinate. That means that the segment that connects them is parallel to the *y*-axis and that all you have to do to figure out the distance is subtract the *y*-coordinate and find the absolute value of the difference. |8 − 6| = 2, so the distance between the points is 2.

Quadrilaterals · Circles · Coordinate Geometry · Practice · **Answers**

31. E

OP is the radius of the circle. Since O has coordinates $(0, 0)$, the length of OP is $|4 - 0| = |4| = 4$. The area of a circle is πr^2 where r is the radius, so the area of circle O is $\pi(4)^2 = 16\pi$.

32. C

Right triangle ABC has legs of 6 and 8, so the legs are in a ratio of 3:4 and the triangle is a multiple of the 3-4-5 right triangle. Since the $3 \times 2 = 6$ and $4 \times 2 = 8$, double the hypotenuse length of 5 and the hypotenuse of triangle ABC equals 10. Notice that the hypotenuse is also the diameter of the circle. To find the area of the circle, we need its radius. Radius is half the diameter, so the radius of circle P is 5. The area of a circle is πr^2 where r is the radius, so the area of circle P is $\pi(5)^2 = 25\pi$.

33. B

The area of a circle is πr^2 where r is the radius, and since the area of the circle is 25π, its radius is 5. Circumference is equal to $2\pi r$, or $2\pi(5) = 10\pi$. Only (B) and (C) contain 10π, so you can eliminate (A), (D), and (E). Since the circle is inscribed within the square, its diameter is equal to a side of the square. The diameter of the circle is $2r$ or 10, so a side of the square is 10 and its perimeter is $4(10) = 40$. Therefore the perimeter of the shaded region is $40 + 1\pi$, choice (B).

34. A

Slope of a line is defined by the formula $\dfrac{y_2 - y_1}{x_2 - x_1}$, where (x_1, y_1) and (x_2, y_2) represent two points on the line. Substitute the given coordinates into the formula (it doesn't matter which you designate as point 1 or point 2):

$$\text{slope} = \frac{y_2 - y_1}{x_2 - x_1} = \frac{7 - (-5)}{-1 - 3}$$

$$= \frac{12}{-4}$$

$$= -3$$

35. D

The circumference of a circle is $2\pi r$, where r is the radius, so a circle whose circumference is 16π has a radius of $\dfrac{16\pi}{2\pi} = 8$. The area of a circle is πr^2, so in this case the area is $\pi(8)^2 = 64\pi$, (D).

36. E

Since all sides of a square are equal, notice that the diagonal of the square is also the hypotenuse of an isosceles right triangle. Use this information to determine the length of a side of the square, marked s in the figure. The ratio of the sides in such a triangle is $1:x:x\sqrt{2}$. Since $x\sqrt{2}$ represents the hypotenuse, which is equal to 6, solve the equation $x\sqrt{2} = \dfrac{6}{\sqrt{2}}$. Divide by $\sqrt{2}$ to get $x = \dfrac{6}{\sqrt{2}}$. So the length of a side of the square is $\dfrac{6}{\sqrt{2}}$. The area of a square is therefore $\left(\dfrac{6}{\sqrt{2}}\right)^2 = \dfrac{36}{2} = 18$.

37. B

The shaded region represents one half the area of the circle. Find the length of the radius to determine this area. Notice that the diameter of the circle is equal to a side of the square. Since the area of the square is 64, it has a side length of 8 (because $8^2 = 64$). So the diameter of the circle is 8, and its radius is 4. The area of the circle is πr^2, or $\pi(4)^2 = 16\pi$. This isn't the answer though; the shaded region is only half the circle, so its area is 8π.

38. B

Think of the figure as a rectangle with two rectangular bites taken out of it. Sketch in lines to make one large rectangle (see diagram below):

Now find the area of the large rectangle, and subtract the areas of the two rectangular pieces that weren't in the original figure. The area of a rectangle is length times width. Since the length of the large rectangle is 10, and its width is 8, its area is $10 \times 8 = 80$. The rectangular bite taken out of the top right corner has dimensions 6 and 2, so its area is 6×2 or 12. The bite taken out of the bottom has dimensions 2 and 3, so its area is $2 \times 3 = 6$. To find the area of the polygon, subtract the areas of the two bites from the area of the large rectangle: $80 - (12 + 6) = 80 - 18 = 62$, (B).

39. C

Since *ABCD* is a square, all four sides have the same length, and the corners meet at right angles. The area you're looking for is that of a triangle, and since all corners of the square are right angles, angle *EAB* is a right angle, which makes triangle *EAB* a right triangle. The area of a right triangle is $\frac{1}{2}(\text{leg}_1)(\text{leg}_2)$. The diagram shows that *BC* has length 8, so *AB* = *AD* = 8. Point *E* is the midpoint of *AD*, so *AE* is 4.

Now that you have the lengths of both legs, you can substitute into the formula: $\frac{1}{2}(AB)(AE) = \frac{1}{2}(8)(4) = 16$, (C).

40. B

The circumference of a circle is equal to $2\pi r$, where r is the radius. The circumference of circle *A* is $2\pi(r + 1) = 2\pi r + 2\pi$. The circumference of circle *B* is $2\pi(r + 2) = 2\pi r + 4\pi$. So the positive difference between the two circumferences is simply 2π.

41. D

A square with area 16 has sides of length 4. Therefore the largest circle that could possibly be cut from such a square would have a diameter of 4.

Such a circle would have a radius of 2, making its area $\pi(2)^2 = 4\pi$. So the amount of felt left after cutting such a circle from one of the squares of felt would be $16 - 4\pi$, or $4(4 - \pi)$. There are 8 such squares, so the total area of the left over felt is $8 \times 4(4 - \pi) = 32(4 - \pi)$, (D).

42. C

The key to solving this problem is to draw in *OB*:

Because *OA*, *OB*, and *OC* are all radii of the same circle, triangle *AOB* and triangle *BOC* are both isosceles triangles, each therefore having equal base angles:

Using the fact that the 3 interior angles of a triangle add up to 180°, you can figure out that the vertex angles measure 80° and 60° as shown:

Angle *AOC* measures 80 + 60 = 140, (C).

CHAPTER 14: WORD PROBLEMS

Word Problems. Two simple words that evoke more fear and loathing than most other math concepts and question types combined.

When the subject of word problems arises, you might envision the following nightmare:

> Two trains are loaded with equal amounts of rock salt and ball bearings. Train *A* leaves Frogboro at 10:00 A.M. carrying 62 passengers. Train *B* leaves Toadville at 11:30 A.M. carrying 104 passengers. If Train *A* is traveling at a speed of 85 mph and makes four stops, and Train *B* is traveling at an average speed of 86 mph and makes three stops, and the trains both arrive at Lizard Hollow at 4:30 P.M., what is the average weight of the passengers on Train *B*?

The good news is that you won't see anything this ugly. SSAT/ISEE word problems are pretty straightforward. Generally, all you have to do is translate the prose to math and solve.

The bad news is that you can expect to see a lot of word problems on your test. Keep in mind that, while word problems are generally algebra problems, they can contain other math concepts.

TRANSLATION

Many word problems seem tricky because it's hard to figure out what they're asking. It can be difficult to translate English into math. The following table lists some common words and phrases that turn up in word problems, along with their mathematical translations.

Translation — Symbolism — Formulas — Backdoor Strategies — Roman Numerals

When you see:	Think:
sum, plus, more than, added to, combined total	+
minus, less than, difference between, decreased by	−
is, was, equals, is equivalent to, is the same as, adds up to	=
times, product, multiplied by, of, twice, double, triple	×
divided by, over, quotient, per, out of, into	÷
what, how much, how many, a number	x, n, etc.

Now, try translating the following phrases from English to math.

English   **Math**

1. y is 5 more than x _____

2. r equals half of s _____

3. x is twice as great as y   _____

4. 2 less than m is equal to n _____

5. the product of a and b is 3 more than their sum   _____

Now let's look at how you did:

1. $y = x + 5$

2. $r = \dfrac{1}{2}s$ or $2r = s$

3. $x = 2y$

4. $n = m - 2$

5. $ab = (a + b) + 3$

TRANSLATE THE STORY

❝ In some questions, the translation will be embedded within a "story." Don't be put off by the details of the scenario—it's the numbers that matter. Focus on the math and translate. ❞

SYMBOLISM WORD PROBLEMS

Word problems, by definition, require you to translate English to math. But some word problems contain an extra level of translation. *Symbolism* word problems are like any other word problem; just translate the English and the symbols into math and then solve.

Assume that the notation □ (w, x, y, z) means "Divide the sum of w and x by y and multiply the result by z." What is the value of

□ $(10, 4, 7, 8)$ + □ $(2, 6, 4, 5)$?

First, translate the English/symbols into math.

□ (w, x, y, z) means $\dfrac{w + x}{y} \times z$

KAPLAN EXCLUSIVE TIPS

❝ If you see a symbol you've never seen before, it's usually a safe bet that the test maker just made it up! ❞

Translation · **Symbolism** · Formulas · Backdoor Strategies · Roman Numerals

Next, substitute the given values into the expression.

$$\square\,(10, 4, 7, 8) + \square\,(2, 6, 4, 5) = \left(\frac{10+4}{7}\times 8\right)+\left(\frac{2+6}{4}\times 5\right)$$

$$= 16 + 10$$

$$= 26$$

WORD PROBLEMS WITH FORMULAS

Some of the more difficult word problems may involve translations with mathematical formulas. For example, you might see questions dealing with averages, rates, or areas of geometric figures. Since the SSAT/ISEE does *not* provide formulas for you, you'll have to know these going in.

EXAMPLE

If a truck travels at 50 miles per hour for $6\frac{1}{2}$ hours, how far will the truck travel?

(A) 600 miles

(B) 425 miles

(C) 325 miles

(D) 300 miles

(E) 500 miles

To answer this question, you need to remember that Distance = Rate × Time. Once you note the formula, you can just plug in the numbers.

$D = 50 \times 6.5$

$D = 325$ miles, (C).

BACKDOOR STRATEGIES

Word problems are extraordinarily susceptible to backdoor strategies. Here's a quick recap of Kaplan's **Picking Numbers** and **Backsolving** Strategies.

PICKING NUMBERS

Step 1. Pick simple, easy to use numbers for each variable.

Step 2. Solve the problem using the numbers you pick.

Step 3. Substitute your numbers into each answer choice. The choice that gives you the same numerical solution you arrived at in step 2 is correct.

A few things to remember are:

- You can pick numbers only when the answer choices contain variables.

- Pick easy numbers rather than realistic ones. Keep the numbers small and manageable.

- You have to try all the answer choices. If more than one works, pick another set of numbers.

- Don't pick the same number for more than one variable.

- When picking a number for a remainder problem, add the remainder to the number you're dividing by.

- Always pick 100 for percent questions.

EXAMPLE

The average of four numbers is n. If three of the numbers are $n + 3$, $n + 5$, and $n - 2$, what is the value of the fourth number?

(A) $n - 6$

(B) $n - 4$

(C) n

(D) $n + 2$

(E) $n + 4$

Pick an easy number for n, such as 10. If the average of four numbers is 10, the sum of the four numbers is 40 ($4 \times 10 = 40$). If three of the numbers are $n + 3$, $n + 5$, and $n - 2$, then those three numbers are $10 + 3$, $10 + 5$ and $10 - 2$ or 13, 15, and 8. $13 + 15 + 8 = 36$. The sum of the four numbers must equal 40, so the remaining number is 4. If you plug 10 in for n in each of the answer choices, only (A) gives you 4.

BACKSOLVING

- You can backsolve when the answer choices are only numbers.

- Always start with the middle answer choice, (C).

- If the middle answer choice is not correct, you can usually eliminate two more choices simply by determining whether the value you're looking for must be higher or lower.

EXAMPLE

Mike has *n* Hawaiian shirts and Adam has 3 times as many Hawaiian shirts. If Adam gives Mike six Hawaiian shirts, both boys would have an equal number of Hawaiian shirts. How many Hawaiian shirts does Mike have?

(A) 3

(B) 6

(C) 9

(D) 15

(E) 18

Start with the middle answer choice, 9. If Mike has 9 shirts, then Adam has three times as many, or 27. If Adam gives Mike 6 shirts, Adam now has 21 and Mike has 15. This is not equal, so (C) is not correct. Since Adam was left with too many shirts when Mike had 9, Mike must have fewer than 9. Try (B). If Mike has 6 shirts, then Adam has 18. If Adam gives Mike 6, then they both have 12 shirts. Bingo.

ROMAN NUMERAL WORD PROBLEMS

You might see a Roman numeral problem on your test. If you do, keep a few things in mind. Keeping with the problem style, let's lay them out in Roman numerals . . .

I. You don't have to work with the statements in the order they are given. Deal with them in whatever order is easiest for you.

II. If you find a statement that is true, eliminate all of the choices that *don't* include it.

III. If you find a statement that is false, eliminate all of the choices that *do* include it.

EXAMPLE

If the product of the positive numbers *x* and *y* is 20 and *x* is less than 4, which of the following must be true?

 I. *y* is greater than 5.

 II. The sum of *x* and *y* is greater than 10.

 III. Twice the product of *x* and *y* is equal to 40.

(A) I only

(B) II only

(C) I and III only

(D) II and III only

(E) I, II, and III

We're told that $xy = 20$ and $x < 4$. Now let's look at the statements. Statement I says that $y > 5$. Since $xy = 20$, $y = \dfrac{20}{x}$. When $x = 4$, $y = 5$. If we replace x with a smaller number than 4 in $\dfrac{20}{x}$, then $\dfrac{20}{x}$, which is y, will be greater than 5. Statement I must be true. Statement I must be part of the correct answer. Eliminate choices (B) and (D). Statement II says that $x + y > 10$. Try picking some values such that $xy = 20$ and $x < 4$. If $x = 3$, then $y = \dfrac{20}{x} = \dfrac{20}{3} = 6\dfrac{2}{3}$. The sum of x and y is not greater than 10. Statement II does not have to be true. It will not be part of the correct answer. Eliminate (E). Statement III says that $2(xy) = 40$, or $2xy = 40$. The question stem says that $xy = 20$. Multiplying both sides of the equation $xy = 20$ by 2, we have that $2(xy) = 2(20)$, or $2xy = 40$. Statement III must be true. (C) is correct.

Now it's time to put all of your skills into play with some practice questions. Remember to translate the English to math, don't get intimidated, and keep your cool. Off you go!

PRACTICE QUESTIONS

1. During a sale, a bookstore sold $\frac{1}{2}$ of all its books in stock. On the following day, the bookstore sold 4,000 more books. Now, only $\frac{1}{10}$ of the books in stock before the sale are remaining in the store. How many books were in stock before the sale?

   (A) 8,000
   (B) 10,000
   (C) 12,000
   (D) 15,000
   (E) 20,000

2. Brad bought a radio on sale at a 20% discount from its regular price of $118. If there is an 8% sales tax that is calculated on the sale price, how much did Brad pay for the radio?

   (A) $23.60
   (B) $86.85
   (C) $94.40
   (D) $101.95
   (E) $127.44

3. Sheila charges $5 per haircut during the week. On Saturday, she charges $7.50. If Sheila has 6 customers each day of the week except Sunday, how much money does she earn in five weekdays and Saturday?

   (A) $150
   (B) $175
   (C) $180
   (D) $195
   (E) $210

4. The original price of a television decreases by 20 percent. By what percent must the discounted price increase to reach its original value?

   (A) 15%
   (B) 20%
   (C) 25%
   (D) 30%
   (E) 40%

5. Ed has 100 dollars more than Robert. After Ed spends 20 dollars on groceries, Ed has five times as much money as Robert. How much money does Robert have?

   (A) $20
   (B) $30
   (C) $40
   (D) $50
   (E) $120

6. A worker earns $15 an hour for the first 40 hours he works each week, and one and a half times this much for every hour over 40 hours. If he earned $667.50 for one week's work, how many hours did he work?

   (A) 40
   (B) 41
   (C) 42
   (D) 43
   (E) 44

Formulas | Backdoor Strategies | Roman Numerals | Practice | Answers

7. Liza has 40 less than three times the number of books that Janice has. If *B* is equal to the number of books that Janice has, which of the following expressions shows the total number of books that Liza and Janice have together?

   (A) $3B - 40$

   (B) $3B + 40$

   (C) $4B - 40$

   (D) $4B$

   (E) $4B + 40$

8. If $a \cdot b = \dfrac{ab}{a-b}$, which of the following does $3 \cdot 2$ equal?

   (A) $2 \cdot 3$

   (B) $6 \cdot 1$

   (C) $6 \cdot 2$

   (D) $6 \cdot 3$

   (E) $8 \cdot 4$

9. If William divides the amount of money he has by 5, and he adds $8, the result will be $20. If *X* is equal to the number of dollars that William has, which of the following equations shows this relationship?

   (A) $(X \div 8) + 5 = 20$

   (B) $(X \div 5) + 8 = 20$

   (C) $(X + 8) \div 5 = 20$

   (D) $(X + 5) \div 8 = 20$

   (E) $8(X + 5) = 20$

10. If a six-sided pencil with a trademark on one of its sides is rolled on a table, what is the probability that the side with the trademark is not touching the surface of the table when the pencil stops?

   (A) $\dfrac{1}{6}$

   (B) $\dfrac{1}{3}$

   (C) $\dfrac{1}{2}$

   (D) $\dfrac{2}{3}$

   (E) $\dfrac{5}{6}$

11. Yesterday, a store sold 8 times as many hats as it sold coats. It also sold 3 times as many sweaters as it sold coats. What could be the total number of hats, sweaters, and coats that were sold?

   (A) 16

   (B) 21

   (C) 25

   (D) 36

   (E) 54

12. Five hundred eighty seven people are travelling by bus for a field trip. If each bus seats 48 people and all the buses are filled to capacity except one, how many people sit in the unfilled bus?

   (A) 37

   (B) 36

   (C) 12

   (D) 11

   (E) 7

Formulas | Backdoor Strategies | Roman Numerals | Practice | Answers

13. Rose has finished $\frac{5}{6}$ of her novel after one week of reading. If she reads an additional tenth of the novel during the next two days, what part of the novel will she have read?

(A) $\frac{1}{10}$

(B) $\frac{7}{15}$

(C) $\frac{4}{5}$

(D) $\frac{14}{15}$

(E) $\frac{29}{30}$

14. A farmer has $4\frac{2}{3}$ acres of land for growing corn, and $2\frac{1}{2}$ times as many acres for growing wheat. How many acres does she have for wheat?

(A) $2\frac{2}{3}$

(B) $4\frac{1}{2}$

(C) $8\frac{1}{6}$

(D) $10\frac{1}{2}$

(E) $11\frac{2}{3}$

15. Joyce baked 42 biscuits for her 12 guests. If six biscuits remain uneaten, what is the average number of biscuits that the guests ate?

(A) 2

(B) 3

(C) 4

(D) 6

(E) 12

16. The average weight of Jake, Ken, and Larry is 60 kilograms. If Jake and Ken both weigh 50 kilograms, how much, in kilograms, does Larry weigh?

(A) 40

(B) 50

(C) 60

(D) 70

(E) 80

17. If 3 added to 4 times a number is 11, the number must be

(A) 1

(B) 2

(C) 3

(D) 4

(E) 5

18. The sum of 8 and a certain number is equal to 20 minus the same number. What is the number?

(A) 2

(B) 4

(C) 6

(D) 10

(E) 14

19. Liz worked 3 hours less than twice as many hours as Rachel did. If W is the number of hours Rachel worked, which of the following expressions shows the total number of hours worked by Liz and Rachel together?

(A) $2W - 3$

(B) $2W + 3$

(C) $3W - 3$

(D) $3W + 3$

(E) $4W - 2$

Formulas   Backdoor Strategies   Roman Numerals   **Practice**   Answers

20. The area of a circle is πr^2 where r is the radius. If the circumference of a circle is $h\pi$, what is the area of the circle, in terms of h ?

    (A) $h^2 r^2$

    (B) $\dfrac{\pi h^2}{4}$

    (C) $\dfrac{\pi h^2}{2}$

    (D) πh^2

    (E) $4\pi h^2$

21. If $m \neq 0$, $m \neq 1$, and $m \ddagger = \dfrac{m}{m^2 - m}$, what is the value of $(6\ddagger) - ((-5)\ddagger)$?

    (A) $\dfrac{1}{30}$

    (B) $\dfrac{1}{20}$

    (C) $\dfrac{1}{4}$

    (D) $\dfrac{11}{30}$

    (E) $\dfrac{9}{20}$

22. Five less than 3 times a certain number is equal to twice the original number plus 7. What is the original number?

    (A) 2

    (B) $2\dfrac{2}{5}$

    (C) 6

    (D) 11

    (E) 12

23. The volume of a sphere is $\dfrac{4}{3}\pi r^3$ where r is the radius. What is the volume of a sphere with a radius of 3 in terms of π ?

    (A) 4π

    (B) 8π

    (C) 16π

    (D) 36π

    (E) 72π

PRACTICE QUESTION ANSWERS

1. B

Call the original number of books in stock N. On the first day of the sale, $\frac{1}{2}$ of all the books in stock were sold. So on the first day of the sale, $\frac{1}{2}N$ books were sold. After the first day of the sale, $N - \frac{1}{2}N$ books remained. On the next day, 4,000 more books were sold. So after two days of the sale, $N - \frac{1}{2}N - 4,000$ books remained. We are told that after two days of the sale, $\frac{1}{10}$ of the books in stock before the sale remained in the store. So the number of books that remained in the store after two days of the sale was $\frac{1}{10}N$. Thus $N - \frac{1}{2}N - 4,000 = \frac{1}{10}N$. Solve for N.

$$N - \frac{1}{2}N - 4,000 = \frac{1}{10}N$$

$$\frac{1}{2}N - 4,000 = \frac{1}{10}N$$

$$\frac{1}{2}N - \frac{1}{10}N = 4,000$$

$$\frac{5}{10}N - \frac{1}{10}N = 4,000$$

$$\frac{4}{10}N = 4,000$$

$$\frac{2}{5}N = 4,000$$

$$N = 4,000\left(\frac{5}{2}\right)$$

$$= 2,000(5)$$

$$= 10,000$$

2. D

This problem needs to be done in several steps. First find out the sale price of the radio. The discount was 20%, so the sale price was 80% of the original price.

Percent × Whole = Part

80% × $118 = Sale Price

0.80 × $118 = Sale Price

$94.40 = Sale Price

Now figure out how much tax Brad paid. The tax was 8% of the sale price.

Percent × Whole = Part

8% × $94.40 = Tax

0.08 × $94.40 = Tax

$7.5520 = Tax

$7.55 = Tax

Now just add the tax to the sale price.

$94.40 + 7.55 = $101.95

3. D

Each weekday Sheila earns: $5 × 6 haircuts = $30. Each Saturday Sheila earns $7.50 × 6 haircuts = $45. In five weekdays she earns 5 × $30 = $150. In one Saturday she earns $45. So in five weekdays plus one Saturday she earns $150 + $45, or $195.

4. C

It is important to note that while the value of the television decreases and increases by the same dollar amount, it doesn't increase and decrease by the same percent. Let's pick $100 for the price of the television. If the price decreases by 20%, then since 20% of $100 is $20, the price decreases by $20. The new price is $100 − $20, or $80. For the new price to reach the original price ($100), it must be increased by $20. Twenty dollars is $\frac{1}{4}$ of 80, or 25% of $80. The new price must be increased by 25%, choice (C).

5. A

Translate to get two equations. Let E be the amount Ed has and R be the amount Robert has. "Ed has $100 more than Robert" becomes $E = R + 100$. "Ed spends $20" means he'll have $20 less, or $E - 20$. "Five times as much as Robert" becomes $5R$. Therefore, $E - 20 = 5R$. Substitute $R + 100$ for E in the second equation and solve for R:

$$(R + 100) - 20 = 5R$$
$$R + 80 = 5R$$
$$80 = 4R$$
$$20 = R, \text{ so Robert has } \$20$$

6. D

Run the answer choices through the information in the stem to see which one gives a total of $667.50. Since the answer choices are in numerical order, start with the middle choice, (C). If he works for 42 hours, he earns $15 per hour for the first 40 hours, or $600, and he earns $1\frac{1}{2}$ times his normal rate for the two extra hours. So, $\frac{3}{2}$ times $15 is $22.50 per hour, and since he worked 2 hours at that rate, he made an additional $45. The total is $645, which isn't enough. So (C) is too small, as are (A) and (B). Now try (D). He still earns $600 for the first 40 hours, but now you have to multiply the overtime rate, $22.50, by 3, which gives you $67.50. The total is $667.50, which means that (D) is correct.

Another way to approach the question is to see that for the first 40 hours, the worker earns $15 an hour. 40 hours × $15 an hour = $600. For any additional

hours, he earns one and a half times $15. So, 1.5 × $15 = $22.50 per hour. If he earned $667.50 in one week, $600 was earned in the first 40 hours and the remaining $67.50 was earned working additional hours. To find out how many additional hours the worker worked , divide the amount earned ($67.50) by the amount earned per hour ($22.50). And $67.50 ÷ $22.50 = 3. So 40 hours + 3 additional hours equals 43 hours.

7. C

This is a simple translation problem. You're told that Janice has B books. Liza has 40 less than three times the number of books Janice has, which you can translate as $L = 3B - 40$. The total number they have together equals $B + (3B - 40)$, or $4B - 40$.

8. D

Substitute the given values. Then try the values in each answer choice until you find the one that produces the same result. Substituting 3 and 2 yields $\frac{(3)(2)}{3 - 2} = \frac{6}{1} = 6$. So you're looking for the answer choice that produces a result of 6. Only (D) does: $\frac{(6)(3)}{6 - 3} = \frac{18}{3} = 6$.

9. B

This problem asks you to translate from English sentences into math.

The amount of money William has is X.
This amount divided by 5: $(X \div 5)$.
Add 8 dollars: $(X \div 5) + 8$.
The result is 20 dollars: $(X \div 5) + 8 = 20$, choice (B). Since division comes before addition in the order of operations, the parentheses aren't really necessary.

10. E

The probability of an event happening is the ratio of the number of desired outcomes, to the number of possible outcomes or

$$\text{Probability} = \frac{\text{Number of desired outcomes}}{\text{Number of possible outcomes}}$$

One side of the pencil has the trademark on it, and the other 5 sides are blank. When any one of the 5 blank sides is touching the surface of the table, the marked side cannot be touching the table. So there are 5 different ways for the pencil to lie on the table without the marked side touching the surface. The total number of possible sides for the pencil to lie on is 6. The probability that the trademark will not be touching the surface of the table when the pencil stops rolling is $\frac{5}{6}$, choice (E).

11. D

Let x be the number of coats that the store sold yesterday. Keep in mind that x must be an integer. The store sold 8 times the number of hats as coats yesterday. So the store sold $8x$ hats. The store sold 3 times the number of sweaters as coats yesterday. So the store sold $3x$ sweaters. The total number of hats, sweaters, and coats that the store sold was $8x + 3x 1 x = 12x$. Since x is an integer, $12x$ must be a multiple of 12. Only (D), 36, is a multiple of 12 $(36 = 3 \times 12)$.

12. D

There are 587 people traveling and each bus holds 48 people. Therefore, $587 \div 48 = 12$ with a remainder of 11. So 12 buses are full and 11 people remain to ride in the unfilled bus.

13. D

Rose read $\frac{5}{6}$ of the novel and plans to read another $\frac{1}{10}$, which will result in her having read $\frac{5}{6} + \frac{1}{10}$ of the novel. Add these two fractions, using 30 as the common denominator: $\frac{5}{6} + \frac{1}{10} = \frac{25}{30} + \frac{3}{30} = \frac{28}{30} = \frac{14}{15}$

14. E

The farmer has $4\frac{2}{3} \times 2\frac{1}{2}$ acres for growing wheat. Change these mixed numbers to fractions in order to multiply: $\frac{\overset{7}{\cancel{14}}}{3} \times \frac{5}{\underset{1}{\cancel{2}}} = \frac{35}{3} = 11$ acres.

15. B

If 6 biscuits remain, $42 - 6 = 36$ were eaten by the 12 guests.

$\text{Average} = \dfrac{\text{Sum of the terms}}{\text{Number of the terms}}$, so the average number of biscuits eaten by the guests is $\frac{36}{12} = 3$.

16. E

$\text{Average} = \dfrac{\text{Sum of the terms}}{\text{Number of the terms}}$, so

$60 = \dfrac{\text{Total weight}}{3}$

$60 \times 3 = \text{Total weight}$

$180 = \text{Total weight}$

Jake and Ken each weigh 50 kilograms, so $50 + 50 +$ Larry's weight $= 180$ kilograms. Doing the math, Larry must weigh 80 kilograms.

17. B

Let the number be x. Translating gives you $3 + 4x = 11$. Therefore, $4x = 8$ and $x = 2$.

18. C

Translate from English to math. The sum of 8 and b is simply $8 + b$. The question states that this is equal to 20 minus the same number, or $20 - b$. So your equation is $8 + b = 20 - b$, and you can solve for b:

$$8 + b = 20 - b$$
$$8 + 2b = 20$$
$$2b = 12$$
$$b = 6$$

19. C

Rachel worked W hours, and Liz worked 3 hours less than twice as many hours as Rachel, or $2W - 3$. Add these expressions to find the total number of hours worked by Liz and Rachel together:

$$W + 2W - 3 = 3W - 3$$

20. B

Circumference of a circle is π times diameter, so a circumference of $h\pi$ means a diameter of h. The radius is half the diameter, or $\frac{h}{2}$. Substitute $\frac{h}{2}$ into the area formula:

$$\pi\left(\frac{h}{2}\right)^2 = \pi\left(\frac{h^2}{4}\right) = \frac{h^2\pi}{4}$$

21. D

Substitute into the expression that defines the symbol ‡:

$$(6‡) - (-5)‡ = \frac{6}{6^2 - 6} - \frac{-5}{(-5)^2 - (-5)}$$
$$= \frac{6}{36 - 6} - \frac{-5}{25 + 5}$$
$$= \frac{6}{30} - \frac{-5}{30}$$
$$= \frac{6}{30} + \frac{5}{30}$$
$$= \frac{11}{30}$$

At two points in your calculation it is crucial to remember that subtracting a negative is the same as adding a positive.

22. E

Call the unknown number x. Five less than 3 times the number, or $3x - 5$, equals twice the original number plus 7, or $2x + 7$. So $3x - 5 = 2x + 7$. Solve for x:

$$3x - 5 = 2x + 7$$
$$x - 5 = 7$$
$$x = 12$$

23. D

Substitute the value of $r = 3$ into the formula and simplify:

$$\text{volume} = \frac{4}{3}\pi(3)^3$$
$$= \frac{4}{3}\pi(27)$$
$$= 36$$

Formulas | Backdoor Strategies | Roman Numerals | Practice | **Answers**

CHAPTER 15: MANAGING YOUR STRESS

Is it starting to feel like your whole life is a build-up to the SSAT/ISEE? You really want to go to a certain school and you know your parents want you to as well. You have worried about the test for months, and spent at least a few hours in solid preparation for it. As the test gets closer, you may find your anxiety is on the rise. Don't worry. After the preparation you've received from this book, you're in good shape for the test.

To calm any pretest jitters you may have, this chapter leads you through a sane itinerary for the last week.

THE WEEK BEFORE THE TEST

- Focus on strategy and backup plans.

- Practice strategies you had the best success rate with.

- Decide and know **exactly** how you're going to approach each section and question type.

- Sit down and do practice problems in the Question Bank or complete extra drills you might have skipped the first time through.

- Practice waking up early and eating breakfast so that you'll be alert in the morning on Test Day.

THE DAYS JUST BEFORE THE TEST

- The best test takers do less and less as the test approaches. Taper off your study schedule and take it easy. Give yourself time off, especially the evening before the exam. By that time, if you've studied well, everything you need to know is firmly stored in your memory bank.

- Positive self-talk can be extremely liberating and invigorating, especially as the test looms closer. Tell yourself things such as "I will do well" rather than "I hope things go well";

Week Before   Days Just Before   Night Before   Morning of   During the Test

"I can" rather than "I cannot." Replace any negative thoughts with affirming statements that boost your self-esteem.

- Get your act together sooner rather than later. Have everything (including choice of clothing) laid out in advance. Most important, make sure you know where the test will be held and the easiest, quickest way to get there. You'll have great peace of mind by knowing that all the little details—gas in the car, directions, etcetera—are set before the day of the test.

- Go to the test site a few days in advance, particularly if you are especially anxious. If at all possible, find out what room your part of the alphabet is assigned to, and try to sit there (by yourself) for a while. Better yet, bring some practice material and do at least a section or two.

- Forego any practice on the day before the test. It's in your best interest to marshal your physical and psychological resources for 24 hours or so. Even race horses are kept in the paddock and treated like princes the day before a race. Keep the upcoming test out of your consciousness; go to a movie, take a pleasant hike, or just relax. Don't eat junk food or tons of sugar. And, of course, get plenty of rest the night before—just don't go to bed too early. It's hard to fall asleep earlier than you're used to, and you don't want to lie there worrying about the test.

THE NIGHT BEFORE THE TEST

Don't study. Get together the following items:

- Your admission/registration ticket
- Photo ID
- A watch (choose one that is easy to read)
- Slightly dull No. 2 pencils (so they fill in the ovals faster)
- Pencil sharpener
- Erasers
- Clothes you'll wear (Dress in layers! The climate at the test location may vary, as may your body temperature. Make sure you can warm up or cool down easily.)
- Snacks (easy to open or partially unwrapped)
- Money
- Packet of tissues

Relax the night before the test. Read a good book, take a bubble bath, watch TV. Get a good night's sleep. Go to bed at a reasonable hour and leave yourself extra time in the morning.

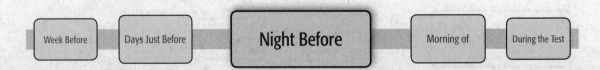

THE MORNING OF THE TEST

Eat breakfast. Make it something substantial and nutritious, but don't deviate too much from your everyday pattern.

Dress in layers so that you can adjust to the temperature of the test room.

Read something to warm up your brain with a newspaper or a magazine before the test starts.

Be sure to get there early. Leave enough time to allow for traffic, mass transit delays, your dad getting lost en route, and any other snag that could slow you down.

DURING THE TEST

Don't be shaken. If you find your confidence slipping, remind yourself how well you've prepared. You know the structure of the test; you know the instructions; you've studied for every question type.

The biggest stress monster will be the test itself. Fear not; there are methods of quelling your stress during the test.

- Keep moving forward instead of getting bogged down in a difficult question. You don't have to get everything right to achieve a fine score. So, don't linger out of desperation on a question that is going nowhere even after you've spent considerable time on it. The best test takers skip difficult material temporarily in search of the easier stuff. They mark the ones that require extra time and thought.

- Don't be thrown if other test takers seem to be working more busily and furiously than you are. Don't mistake the other people's sheer activity as signs of progress and higher scores.

- *Keep breathing!* Weak test takers tend to share one major trait: They don't breathe properly as the test proceeds. They might hold their breath without realizing it, or breathe erratically or arrhythmically. Improper breathing hurts confidence and accuracy. Just as important, it interferes with clear thinking.

Some quick isometrics during the test—especially if concentration is wandering or energy is waning—can help. Try this: Put your palms together and press intensely for a few seconds. Concentrate on the tension you feel through your palms, wrists, forearms, and up into your biceps and shoulders. Then, quickly release the pressure. Feel the difference as you let go. Focus on the warm relaxation that floods through the muscles.

THE NIGHT BEFORE THE TEST, DO NOT

- try to copy the dictionary onto your fingernails.

- stay up all night watching all the *Friday the 13th* movies.

- eat a large double anchovy and pepper pizza with a case of chocolate soda.

- send away for brochures for clown school.

- start making flashcards.

- tattoo yourself.

Days Just Before | Night Before | Morning of | **During the Test** | After the Test

Now you're ready to return to the task.

- Here's another isometric that will relieve tension in both your neck and eye muscles. Slowly rotate your head from side to side, turning your head and eyes to look as far back over each shoulder as you can. Feel the muscles stretch on one side of your neck as they contract on the other. Repeat five times in each direction.

With what you've just learned here, you're armed and ready to do battle with the test. This book and your studies will give you the information you'll need to answer the questions. It's all firmly planted in your mind. You also know how to deal with any excess tension that might come along, both when you're studying for and taking the exam. You've experienced everything you need to tame your test anxiety and stress. You're going to get a great score.

Even if something goes really wrong, don't panic. If the test booklet is defective—two pages are stuck together or the ink has run—try to stay calm. Raise your hand, tell the proctor you need a new book. If you accidentally misgrid your answer page or put the answers in the wrong section, again don't panic. The proctor might be able to arrange for you to regrid your test after it's over, when it won't cost you any time.

AFTER THE TEST

Once the test is over, put it out of your mind. Start thinking about more interesting things. You might walk out of the SSAT/ISEE thinking that you blew it. You probably didn't. You tend to remember the questions that stumped you, not the many that you knew.

| Part Four |

SSAT PRACTICE TESTS AND EXPLANATIONS

SSAT TEST OVERVIEW

TOTAL TIME

Approximately two and a half hours.

QUESTIONS

Aside from the essay, all questions are multiple-choice in format, with all answer choices labeled (A)–(E).

CONTENT

The SSAT tests Math and Verbal skills. There are two Math sections, two Verbal sections, and one unscored Essay.

PACING

You are not expected to complete all items on the SSAT. This is particularly true if you are at the low end of the age range of test takers for your level. The best approach to pacing is to work as quickly as you can without losing accuracy. Further, if a question is giving you difficulty, circle it and move on. You can always come back to it later, but you shouldn't waste time on a question that is stumping you when you could be gaining valuable points elsewhere.

GUESSING

You receive 1 point for each question answered correctly. For those questions you answer incorrectly, you lose one quarter of a point. As a result, guess *only* when you can do so intelligently. In other words, don't guess wildly, but *do* guess if you can eliminate at least one answer choice as clearly wrong.

CHAPTER 16: SSAT PRACTICE TEST ONE: UPPER-LEVEL

HOW TO TAKE THIS PRACTICE TEST

Before taking this practice test, find a quiet room where you can work uninterrupted for two and a half hours. Make sure you have a comfortable desk and several No. 2 pencils.

Use the answer sheet provided to record your answers. (You can cut it out or photocopy it.)

Once you start this practice test, don't stop until you've finished. Remember—you can review any questions within a section, but you may not go backward or forward a section.

You'll find an answer key and explanations following the test. Scoring information is in chapter 19.

Good luck.

SSAT Practice Test One: Upper-Level Answer Sheet

Remove (or photocopy) the answer sheet and use it to complete the practice test.

Start with number 1 for each section. If a section has fewer questions than answer spaces, leave the extra spaces blank.

SECTION 1

1 (A)(B)(C)(D)(E)	13 (A)(B)(C)(D)(E)	25 (A)(B)(C)(D)(E)	37 (A)(B)(C)(D)(E)	49 (A)(B)(C)(D)(E)
2 (A)(B)(C)(D)(E)	14 (A)(B)(C)(D)(E)	26 (A)(B)(C)(D)(E)	38 (A)(B)(C)(D)(E)	50 (A)(B)(C)(D)(E)
3 (A)(B)(C)(D)(E)	15 (A)(B)(C)(D)(E)	27 (A)(B)(C)(D)(E)	39 (A)(B)(C)(D)(E)	51 (A)(B)(C)(D)(E)
4 (A)(B)(C)(D)(E)	16 (A)(B)(C)(D)(E)	28 (A)(B)(C)(D)(E)	40 (A)(B)(C)(D)(E)	52 (A)(B)(C)(D)(E)
5 (A)(B)(C)(D)(E)	17 (A)(B)(C)(D)(E)	29 (A)(B)(C)(D)(E)	41 (A)(B)(C)(D)(E)	53 (A)(B)(C)(D)(E)
6 (A)(B)(C)(D)(E)	18 (A)(B)(C)(D)(E)	30 (A)(B)(C)(D)(E)	42 (A)(B)(C)(D)(E)	54 (A)(B)(C)(D)(E)
7 (A)(B)(C)(D)(E)	19 (A)(B)(C)(D)(E)	31 (A)(B)(C)(D)(E)	43 (A)(B)(C)(D)(E)	55 (A)(B)(C)(D)(E)
8 (A)(B)(C)(D)(E)	20 (A)(B)(C)(D)(E)	32 (A)(B)(C)(D)(E)	44 (A)(B)(C)(D)(E)	56 (A)(B)(C)(D)(E)
9 (A)(B)(C)(D)(E)	21 (A)(B)(C)(D)(E)	33 (A)(B)(C)(D)(E)	45 (A)(B)(C)(D)(E)	57 (A)(B)(C)(D)(E)
10 (A)(B)(C)(D)(E)	22 (A)(B)(C)(D)(E)	34 (A)(B)(C)(D)(E)	46 (A)(B)(C)(D)(E)	58 (A)(B)(C)(D)(E)
11 (A)(B)(C)(D)(E)	23 (A)(B)(C)(D)(E)	35 (A)(B)(C)(D)(E)	47 (A)(B)(C)(D)(E)	59 (A)(B)(C)(D)(E)
12 (A)(B)(C)(D)(E)	24 (A)(B)(C)(D)(E)	36 (A)(B)(C)(D)(E)	48 (A)(B)(C)(D)(E)	60 (A)(B)(C)(D)(E)

right in section 1

wrong in section 1

SECTION 2

1 (A)(B)(C)(D)(E)	6 (A)(B)(C)(D)(E)	11 (A)(B)(C)(D)(E)	16 (A)(B)(C)(D)(E)	21 (A)(B)(C)(D)(E)
2 (A)(B)(C)(D)(E)	7 (A)(B)(C)(D)(E)	12 (A)(B)(C)(D)(E)	17 (A)(B)(C)(D)(E)	22 (A)(B)(C)(D)(E)
3 (A)(B)(C)(D)(E)	8 (A)(B)(C)(D)(E)	13 (A)(B)(C)(D)(E)	18 (A)(B)(C)(D)(E)	23 (A)(B)(C)(D)(E)
4 (A)(B)(C)(D)(E)	9 (A)(B)(C)(D)(E)	14 (A)(B)(C)(D)(E)	19 (A)(B)(C)(D)(E)	24 (A)(B)(C)(D)(E)
5 (A)(B)(C)(D)(E)	10 (A)(B)(C)(D)(E)	15 (A)(B)(C)(D)(E)	20 (A)(B)(C)(D)(E)	25 (A)(B)(C)(D)(E)

right in section 2

wrong in section 2

SECTION 3

1 (A)(B)(C)(D)(E)	9 (A)(B)(C)(D)(E)	17 (A)(B)(C)(D)(E)	25 (A)(B)(C)(D)(E)	33 (A)(B)(C)(D)(E)
2 (A)(B)(C)(D)(E)	10 (A)(B)(C)(D)(E)	18 (A)(B)(C)(D)(E)	26 (A)(B)(C)(D)(E)	34 (A)(B)(C)(D)(E)
3 (A)(B)(C)(D)(E)	11 (A)(B)(C)(D)(E)	19 (A)(B)(C)(D)(E)	27 (A)(B)(C)(D)(E)	35 (A)(B)(C)(D)(E)
4 (A)(B)(C)(D)(E)	12 (A)(B)(C)(D)(E)	20 (A)(B)(C)(D)(E)	28 (A)(B)(C)(D)(E)	36 (A)(B)(C)(D)(E)
5 (A)(B)(C)(D)(E)	13 (A)(B)(C)(D)(E)	21 (A)(B)(C)(D)(E)	29 (A)(B)(C)(D)(E)	37 (A)(B)(C)(D)(E)
6 (A)(B)(C)(D)(E)	14 (A)(B)(C)(D)(E)	22 (A)(B)(C)(D)(E)	30 (A)(B)(C)(D)(E)	38 (A)(B)(C)(D)(E)
7 (A)(B)(C)(D)(E)	15 (A)(B)(C)(D)(E)	23 (A)(B)(C)(D)(E)	31 (A)(B)(C)(D)(E)	39 (A)(B)(C)(D)(E)
8 (A)(B)(C)(D)(E)	16 (A)(B)(C)(D)(E)	24 (A)(B)(C)(D)(E)	32 (A)(B)(C)(D)(E)	40 (A)(B)(C)(D)(E)

right in section 3

wrong in section 3

SECTION 4

1 (A)(B)(C)(D)(E)	6 (A)(B)(C)(D)(E)	11 (A)(B)(C)(D)(E)	16 (A)(B)(C)(D)(E)	21 (A)(B)(C)(D)(E)
2 (A)(B)(C)(D)(E)	7 (A)(B)(C)(D)(E)	12 (A)(B)(C)(D)(E)	17 (A)(B)(C)(D)(E)	22 (A)(B)(C)(D)(E)
3 (A)(B)(C)(D)(E)	8 (A)(B)(C)(D)(E)	13 (A)(B)(C)(D)(E)	18 (A)(B)(C)(D)(E)	23 (A)(B)(C)(D)(E)
4 (A)(B)(C)(D)(E)	9 (A)(B)(C)(D)(E)	14 (A)(B)(C)(D)(E)	19 (A)(B)(C)(D)(E)	24 (A)(B)(C)(D)(E)
5 (A)(B)(C)(D)(E)	10 (A)(B)(C)(D)(E)	15 (A)(B)(C)(D)(E)	20 (A)(B)(C)(D)(E)	25 (A)(B)(C)(D)(E)

right in section 4

wrong in section 4

SECTION 1

Time—25 Minutes
60 Questions

This section consists of two different types of questions. There are directions for each type.

Each of the following questions consists of one word followed by five words or phrases. You are to select the one word or phrase whose meaning is closest to the word in capital letters.

---

1. PLEAD:

   (A) strike
   (B) cry
   (C) tease
   (D) beg
   (E) try

2. PROWL:

   (A) growl
   (B) sneak
   (C) scrub
   (D) leave
   (E) fight

3. VESSEL:

   (A) blood
   (B) decoration
   (C) car
   (D) account
   (E) container

4. APPROVE:

   (A) withhold information
   (B) regard innocently
   (C) watch attentively
   (D) judge favorably
   (E) consider carefully

5. SEEP:

   (A) ooze
   (B) gurgle
   (C) liquefy
   (D) stick
   (E) fall

6. VEX:

   (A) scribble
   (B) locate
   (C) scream
   (D) play
   (E) irritate

7. DOZE:

   (A) graze
   (B) sleep
   (C) refresh
   (D) bore
   (E) ignore

8. BOUNTY:

   (A) outside border
   (B) new harvest
   (C) woven basket
   (D) upper limit
   (E) generous gift

GO ON TO THE NEXT PAGE

9. COARSE:

(A) sifted
(B) sticky
(C) unpopular
(D) difficult
(E) rough

10. MEEK:

(A) submissive
(B) old
(C) tiny
(D) worried
(E) quick

11. SATURATE:

(A) anger
(B) measure
(C) soak
(D) boil
(E) pour

12. GENTEEL:

(A) timid
(B) loud
(C) stupid
(D) harmless
(E) refined

13. WINSOME:

(A) athletic
(B) charming
(C) critical
(D) small
(E) shy

14. REPROACH:

(A) retreat
(B) blame
(C) insist
(D) complain
(E) whine

15. DEMONSTRATE:

(A) object
(B) show
(C) require
(D) renew
(E) imply

16. CAMOUFLAGE:

(A) jewelry
(B) outfit
(C) disguise
(D) outlook
(E) helmet

17. AGHAST:

(A) shocked
(B) swollen
(C) irritated
(D) nasty
(E) rude

18. RECOLLECT:

(A) invent
(B) remove
(C) discover
(D) reject
(E) remember

GO ON TO THE NEXT PAGE

19. INITIATE:

    (A) gather
    (B) try
    (C) start
    (D) command
    (E) celebrate

20. SUFFOCATE:

    (A) give instruction
    (B) pull out
    (C) make willing
    (D) surround completely
    (E) deprive of air

21. PREVAIL:

    (A) triumph
    (B) predict
    (C) entrust
    (D) cover
    (E) enlighten

22. PRANCE:

    (A) boast
    (B) lead
    (C) strut
    (D) pry
    (E) sing

23. PROFOUND:

    (A) stubborn
    (B) unfounded
    (C) perplexing
    (D) absurd
    (E) deep

24. LIMBER:

    (A) supple
    (B) wooden
    (C) skinny
    (D) sober
    (E) sociable

25. TERMINATE:

    (A) extend
    (B) renew
    (C) finalize
    (D) sell
    (E) end

26. CONTEMPLATE:

    (A) ponder
    (B) reject
    (C) founder
    (D) dominate
    (E) deserve

27. CAPRICE:

    (A) idea
    (B) mistake
    (C) whim
    (D) decision
    (E) guess

28. ADAGE:

    (A) permission
    (B) disdain
    (C) humor
    (D) prevention
    (E) proverb

GO ON TO THE NEXT PAGE

29. DIN:

(A) outline
(B) clamor
(C) improvement
(D) demonstration
(E) pressure

30. EXPUNGE:

(A) erase
(B) handle
(C) label
(D) assault
(E) keep

The following questions ask you to find relationships between words. For each question, select the choice that best completes the meaning of the sentence.

31. Pilot is to airplane as

(A) team is to players
(B) horse is to cart
(C) captain is to ship
(D) passenger is to train
(E) army is to country

32. Snake is to python as dog is to

(A) terrier
(B) canine
(C) pet
(D) mammal
(E) quadruped

33. Mayor is to city as

(A) governor is to state
(B) member is to union
(C) board is to district
(D) secretary is to committee
(E) citizen is to legislature

34. Paper is to novel as

(A) person is to poll
(B) paint is to brush
(C) canvas is to portrait
(D) back is to chair
(E) color is to palette

35. Refined is to vulgar as

(A) calm is to placid
(B) submissive is to recalcitrant
(C) happy is to ecstatic
(D) helpful is to victorious
(E) tranquil is to forgivable

36. Whip is to lash as

(A) stick is to throw
(B) shoe is to walk
(C) saddle is to sit
(D) food is to eat
(E) club is to beat

37. Migrate is to swallow as

(A) hibernate is to ground hog
(B) pet is to dog
(C) reproduce is to fish
(D) sting is to bee
(E) pounce is to cat

GO ON TO THE NEXT PAGE

38. Weather is to meteorologist as vegetation is to

(A) driver
(B) artist
(C) oceanographer
(D) hunter
(E) botanist

39. Track is to horse racing as

(A) circus is to elephant
(B) court is to tennis
(C) net is to basketball
(D) goal is to football
(E) air is to bird

40. Director is to actor as coach is to

(A) executive
(B) player
(C) chorus
(D) airplane
(E) officer

41. Dessert is to meal as

(A) finale is to performance
(B) lunch is to breakfast
(C) fork is to spoon
(D) plate is to table
(E) ocean is to river

42. Confirm is to deny as

(A) accept is to reject
(B) assert is to proclaim
(C) contend is to imply
(D) pull is to tug
(E) simplify is to organize

43. Tower is to airport as lighthouse is to

(A) museum
(B) jet
(C) park
(D) farm
(E) shoreline

44. Fidelity is to unfaithfulness as

(A) loyalty is to honor
(B) friendship is to gossip
(C) honesty is to deceit
(D) laziness is to slothfulness
(E) intelligence is to unconcern

45. Widespread is to limited as

(A) encompassed is to surrounded
(B) enlarged is to big
(C) broad is to narrow
(D) unusual is to strange
(E) provincial is to international

46. Saw is to carpenter as plow is to

(A) banker
(B) surveyor
(C) farmer
(D) physician
(E) steelworker

47. Sword is to fence as glove is to

(A) box
(B) soccer
(C) hockey
(D) baseball
(E) golf

GO ON TO THE NEXT PAGE

48. Encourage is to demand as

 (A) insinuate is to hint
 (B) fire is to dismiss
 (C) suggest is to order
 (D) motivate is to undermine
 (E) condemn is to reprimand

49. Grin is to delight as

 (A) anxiety is to confusion
 (B) frown is to dismay
 (C) perspiration is to exhaustion
 (D) laugh is to happiness
 (E) resignation is to uncertainty

50. Mysterious is to understandable as

 (A) unknown is to indefinable
 (B) doubtful is to incredulous
 (C) skillful is to swift
 (D) clouded is to warm
 (E) obscure is to clear

51. Injury is to heal as malfunction is to

 (A) repair
 (B) bandage
 (C) misinterpret
 (D) throw
 (E) disassemble

52. Jog is to sprint as trot is to

 (A) ramble
 (B) gallop
 (C) roam
 (D) saunter
 (E) soar

53. Bone is to body as

 (A) floor is to house
 (B) motor is to boat
 (C) driver is to car
 (D) knob is to door
 (E) beam is to building

54. Amorphous is to shape as odorless is to

 (A) appearance
 (B) weight
 (C) worth
 (D) scent
 (E) anger

55. Vain is to humble as

 (A) anxious is to boisterous
 (B) cantankerous is to thoughtless
 (C) judicious is to lenient
 (D) authoritative is to discursive
 (E) extroverted is to shy

56. Test is to study as

 (A) job is to apply
 (B) train is to practice
 (C) play is to rehearse
 (D) office is to employ
 (E) income is to work

57. Smile is to frown as cheer is to

 (A) jeer
 (B) wince
 (C) laugh
 (D) extricate
 (E) leap

GO ON TO THE NEXT PAGE

58. Banana is to peel as

    (A) egg is to crack
    (B) carrot is to uproot
    (C) apple is to core
    (D) bread is to slice
    (E) corn is to husk

59. Touch is to tactile as

    (A) sound is to noise
    (B) smell is to olfactory
    (C) mouth is to oral
    (D) eye is to visual
    (E) taste is to sense

60. Articulateness is to speech as

    (A) etiquette is to society
    (B) music is to note
    (C) ballet is to form
    (D) legibility is to handwriting
    (E) painting is to palette

IF YOU FINISH BEFORE TIME IS CALLED, YOU MAY CHECK YOUR WORK ON THIS SECTION ONLY. DO NOT TURN TO ANY OTHER SECTION IN THE TEST.

STOP

SECTION 2

Time—25 Minutes

25 Questions

In this section, there are five possible answers after each problem. Choose which one is best. You may use the blank space at the right of the page for scratch work.

Note: Figures provided with the problems are drawn with the greatest possible accuracy, UNLESS stated "Not Drawn to Scale."

1. Each member of a club sold the same number of raffle tickets. If the club sold a total of 120 tickets, which of the following CANNOT be the number of tickets sold by each member?

   (A) 2

   (B) 8

   (C) 10

   (D) 12

   (E) 16

USE THIS SPACE FOR FIGURING.

2. According to the graph in Figure 1, about how many students are art majors?

   (A) 200

   (B) 225

   (C) 280

   (D) 300

   (E) 360

MAJORS OF 900 STUDENTS

Figure 1

3. Sean arrives home 14 minutes before midnight and his sister gets home 25 minutes later. When does Sean's sister arrive home?

   (A) 11 minutes before midnight

   (B) 11 minutes after midnight

   (C) 14 minutes after midnight

   (D) 25 minutes after midnight

   (E) 39 minutes after midnight

4. Which of the following is closest to 0.52 ¥ 78 ?

(A) $\frac{1}{5}$ of 70

(B) $\frac{1}{5}$ of 80

(C) $\frac{2}{5}$ of 70

(D) $\frac{1}{2}$ of 70

(E) $\frac{1}{2}$ of 80

USE THIS SPACE FOR FIGURING.

GO ON TO THE NEXT PAGE

Questions 5-6 refer to the graph in Figure 2.

5. Brian's summer savings is greater than James's summer savings by how many dollars?

   (A)   3
   (B)   4
   (C) 100
   (D) 150
   (E) 200

6. The amount of money saved by Andy is how many times the amount of money saved by James?

   (A)   3
   (B)   4
   (C)   6
   (D 300
   (E) 400

7. How many students are in a class if 30 percent of the class is equal to 30 students?

   (A)   10
   (B)   90
   (C) 100
   (D) 900
   (E) It cannot be determined from the information given.

8. Each of the following is less than 2 EXCEPT

   (A) $\dfrac{15}{8}$

   (B) $\dfrac{45}{22}$

   (C) $\dfrac{99}{50}$

   (D) $\dfrac{180}{100}$

   (E) $\dfrac{701}{400}$

USE THIS SPACE FOR FIGURING.

SUMMER SAVINGS

= $50

James:

Brian:

Andy:

Figure 2

GO ON TO THE NEXT PAGE

9. The sides and angles of triangles *ABC*, *BDE*, *BCE*, and *CEF* in Figure 3 are all equal. Which of the following is the longest path from *A* to *F*?

   (A) $A - C - B - D - F$
   (B) $A - B - E - C - F$
   (C) $A - B - C - E - F$
   (D) $A - C - E - F$
   (E) $A - B - D - F$

USE THIS SPACE FOR FIGURING.

Figure 3

10. Which of the following is closest to 80.08?

    (A) 80
    (B) 80.01
    (C) 80.1
    (D) 81
    (E) 90

11. If $\frac{1}{3}$ of a number is less than 12, then the number is always

    (A) less than 36
    (B) equal to 4
    (C) greater than 4
    (D) equal to 36
    (E) greater than 36

12. In a basketball game, Team *A* scored 39 points and Team *B* scored more points than Team *A*. If Team *B* has 5 players, the average score of the players on Team *B* must have been at least how many points?

    (A) 1
    (B) 5
    (C) 6
    (D) 8
    (E) 12

GO ON TO THE NEXT PAGE

13. In the triangle shown in Figure 4, what is the value of *a* ?

    (A) 4
    (B) 6
    (C) 8
    (D) 9
    (E) It cannot be determined from the information given.

USE THIS SPACE FOR FIGURING.

Figure 4

14. A man bought a piece of land for 40 thousand dollars. Then he spent 2 million dollars to build a house on it. The cost of the house is how many times the cost of the land?

    (A)   5
    (B) 20
    (C) 50
    (D) 200
    (E) 500

15. If $(x - y) + 2 = 6$ and *y* is less than 3, which of the following CANNOT be the value of *x* ?

    (A) −3
    (B) 0
    (C) $1\frac{1}{2}$
    (D) 4
    (E) 8

16. In Figure 5, the distance from *A* to *D* is 55 and the distance from *A* to *B* is equal to the distance from *C* to *D*. If the distance from A to B is twice the distance from *B* to *C*, how far apart are *B* and *D* ?

    (A) 11
    (B) 30
    (C) 33
    (D) 44
    (E) 45

Figure 5

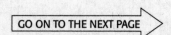
GO ON TO THE NEXT PAGE

17. A book is placed on a flat table surface, as shown in Figure 6. Which of the following best shows all of the points where the book touches the table?

    (A)

    (B) ⬬

    (C) ▱

    (D) ◯

    (E) ◼

USE THIS SPACE FOR FIGURING.

Figure 6

18. Which of the following can be expressed as $(J + 2) \times 3$ where J is a whole number?

    (A) 40
    (B) 52
    (C) 65
    (D) 74
    (E) 81

19. If $a - 7 = 3b + 4$, what does $a + 5$ equal?

    (A) $b - 1$
    (B) $4b - 1$
    (C) $3b + 9$
    (D) $3b + 16$
    (E) It cannot be determined from the information given.

20. According to a census report for Country A, 21.5 out of every 100 families live in rural areas. Based on this report, how many of the 2 million families in Country A live in rural areas?

    (A) 430,000
    (B) 215,000
    (C) 43,000
    (D) 4,300
    (E) 430

GO ON TO THE NEXT PAGE

21. Bob is x years old and Jerry is 7 years older. In terms of x, what was the sum of their ages, in years, 5 years ago?

    (A) $2x + 3$
    (B) $2x + 2$
    (C) $2x - 3$
    (D) $x - 3$
    (E) $x - 10$

USE THIS SPACE FOR FIGURING.

22. A game show contestant answered exactly 20 percent of the questions correctly. Of the first 15 questions, he answered 4 correctly. If he answered only one of the remaining questions correctly, which of the following must be true?

    I.   There were a total of 20 questions.
    II. He answered 10 percent of the remaining questions correctly.
    III. He didn't answer 9 of the remaining questions correctly.

    (A) I only
    (B) II only
    (C) I and II only
    (D) II and III only
    (E) I, II, and III

23. If C is the product of consecutive integers A and B, then C must be

    (A) greater than $A + B$
    (B) a negative integer
    (C) a positive integer
    (D) an even integer
    (E) an odd integer

GO ON TO THE NEXT PAGE

24. A 20 percent discount is offered on all sweaters at Store *S*. If a cotton sweater is on sale for $48.00 and a wool sweater is on sale for $64.00, what was the difference in price of the sweaters before the discount?

   (A) $16.00

   (B) $19.20

   (C) $20.00

   (D) $24.00

   (E) $32.00

25. The maximum load that a railway car can carry is $17\frac{1}{3}$ tons of freight. If a train has 36 railway cars, and each of these carries $\frac{5}{9}$ of a ton less than its maximum load, how many tons of freight is the train carrying?

   (A) 604

   (B) $612\frac{7}{9}$

   (C) $640\frac{5}{9}$

   (D) 648

   (E) 660

USE THIS SPACE FOR FIGURING.

IF YOU FINISH BEFORE TIME IS CALLED, YOU MAY CHECK YOUR WORK ON THIS SECTION ONLY. DO NOT TURN TO ANY OTHER SECTION IN THE TEST.

SECTION 3

Time—25 Minutes
40 Questions

Read each passage carefully and then answer the questions about it. For each question, decide on the basis of the passage which one of the choices best answers the question.

Line
(5)

(10)

(15)

(20)

Typical lemurs are primates with bodies similar to those of monkeys but with pointed muzzles and large eyes; most have long, bushy tails. Their fur is woolly and may be colored red, gray, brown, or black. The name of the lemur stems from the Latin *lemures,* the Roman name for vampire-like ghosts of the dead, which these large-eyed creatures were thought to resemble. Found only off the east coast of Africa on the island of Madagascar and neighboring islands, lemurs spend some time on the ground but most often are in the trees, building nests high in the branches. Besides leaves, lemurs eat eggs, fruit, insects, and small animals. They are active throughout the day and night and are reputed to be gentle, friendly creatures. Besides typical lemurs, the lemur family includes avahi, aye-aye, loris, and galogo. However, contrary to popular belief, the so-called flying lemur is not even a primate, much less a true lemur; it is, in fact, a member of an altogether different order of mammals known as *Dermoptera.*

1. The style of the passage is most like that found in a

   (A) biology textbook.
   (B) novel about Madagascar.
   (C) zoologist's diary.
   (D) tourist's guidebook.
   (E) personal letter.

2. Which of the following would be the best title for this passage?

   (A) The Lemur: Friend or Foe?
   (B) Madagascar's Loneliest Hunters
   (C) Facts About Lemurs
   (D) African Vampires
   (E) The Diet of the Lemur

3. According to the passage, all of the following are true about lemurs EXCEPT

   (A) they spend much of their time in trees.
   (B) most have long, bushy tails.
   (C) the flying lemur is not a true lemur.
   (D) they eat only fruits and leaves.
   (E) the body of the lemur resembles the body of the monkey.

4. The passage suggests that

   (A) the typical lemur is a member of an order of mammals known as *Dermoptera.*
   (B) flying lemurs are only active during the night.
   (C) the lemur is not an aggressive animal.
   (D) lemurs spend most of their time on the ground.
   (E) flying lemurs can only be found on Madagascar and neighboring islands.

Eleanor Roosevelt was the niece of the 26th president of the United States, Theodore Roosevelt, and the wife of the 33rd president, Franklin D.
Line Roosevelt. It would be doing her a great injustice,
(5) however, to describe her only in terms of her relationship to men in powerful and important positions. She was, in her own right, an important figure in twentieth-century American history who strongly supported a variety of social causes and
(10) simply used her political position to further these causes.

A dedicated worker for humanitarian causes before her marriage, and prior to her husband's election to the presidency, she simply expanded
(15) her role when she became the First Lady. She took a more powerful voice on behalf of a broad range of social issues, which included employment of youths and civil rights for women and blacks. She conducted press conferences, had her own radio
(20) program, and wrote a nationally syndicated column in a daily newspaper. After her husband died, she served as the United States' delegate to the United Nations and played a role in the drafting of the UN Declaration of Human Rights.
(25) In short, she clearly proved to be an important and influential figure, above and beyond her political connections.

5. All of the following are true about Eleanor Roosevelt EXCEPT

(A) she was the First Lady of the United States.

(B) she served as the United States' delegate to the United Nations.

(C) she was a dedicated supporter of many social causes.

(D) she began to work for humanitarian causes only after her marriage.

(E) she had her own radio program.

6. When discussing Eleanor Roosevelt, the author's tone in this passage could best be described as

(A) critical.

(B) admiring.

(C) bitter.

(D) serene.

(E) neutral.

7. The passage is mainly about

(A) the success of the Roosevelt family.

(B) Eleanor Roosevelt's background and accomplishments.

(C) the various social causes that Eleanor Roosevelt supported.

(D) Eleanor Roosevelt's role in the United Nations.

(E) important figures in twentieth-century American history.

8. The author of the passage describes Eleanor Roosevelt's accomplishments in order to show that

(A) she should have been elected to the presidency.

(B) she could have done more with her life if she had used her political connections to a greater extent.

(C) her greatest achievement was marrying a man who later became president.

(D) she was more successful than either her uncle or husband in gaining public support.

(E) she deserves recognition beyond her family and marital connections.

GO ON TO THE NEXT PAGE

Before a joint session of Congress in January 1918, President Woodrow Wilson outlined his plan for a post–World War I peace settlement. Known as
Line the Fourteen Points, Wilson's plan is best
(5) remembered for its first point, which declared that international diplomacy should be conducted in the open and that quiet, unpublicized diplomacy should be made illegal. Wilson believed that public diplomacy would end the threat of war by
(10) preventing immoral national leaders from secretly plotting aggressive actions against others.

Although Wilson was a highly intelligent and well-meaning man, he lacked insight into the complexities of international politics. Contrary to
(15) Wilson's belief, war rarely results from the behind-the-scenes plotting of unscrupulous national leaders. Rather, war usually stems from unresolved disagreements among nations—disagreements over territory, access to resources,
(20) and so forth. Even if quiet diplomacy could be eliminated, these disagreements would still remain, as would the threat of war.

9. The second paragraph of this passage is primarily about

(A) a post–World War I peace settlement.

(B) diplomacy's role in international politics.

(C) disagreements among nations.

(D) the actual causes of war.

(E) the first point in Wilson's Fourteen Points.

10. The attitude of the writer toward the subject is

(A) calculating.

(B) suspicious.

(C) opinionated.

(D) cheerful.

(E) apologetic.

11. The author would most likely agree that war between country A and country B would result from which of the following situations?

(A) A dispute over ownership of a piece of land bordering both countries

(B) An agreement by a leader in country A to tax imports from a third country

(C) The capture of a spy from country A in country B

(D) An unpublicized agreement by country A to sell weapons to country B

(E) A secret alliance made between country A and another country

12. Why does the author say that open diplomacy would not prevent war?

(A) Quiet diplomacy will always be a part of international relations.

(B) War breaks out because immoral rulers make decisions in secret.

(C) Open diplomacy is not a solution to the problems which lead to war.

(D) Disagreements over territory and resources rarely lead to conflict.

(E) International relations are too complex to be conducted in the public eye.

13. Which of the following is the author most likely to discuss next?

(A) Wilson's domestic policies in the post-World War I period

(B) The impact of import taxes on foreign trade relations

(C) An example of a war that resulted from a territorial or resource dispute

(D) The events leading up to World War I

(E) Other examples of Wilson's intelligence

GO ON TO THE NEXT PAGE

Live thy Life,
      Young and old,
Like yon oak,
Line   Bright in spring,
(5) Living gold;

Summer-rich
      Then: and then
Autumn-changed,
Soberer-hued
(10)   Gold again.

All his leaves
      Fall'n at length,
Look, he stands,
Trunk and bough,
(15)   Naked strength.

"The Oak," by Alfred, Lord Tennyson.

14. In this poem, the seasons represent different

(A) kinds of trees.
(B) times of day.
(C) stages of life.
(D) styles of dress.
(E) periods of history.

15. The "he" mentioned in line 13 refers to

(A) the poet.
(B) life.
(C) the oak.
(D) autumn.
(E) the reader.

16. What does "Gold again" in line 10 signify?

(A) The arrival of autumn
(B) The richness of summer
(C) The increased wealth of the narrator
(D) The color of oak trees
(E) The revival of the past

17. During which season is the oak referred to as "Living gold"?

(A) Spring
(B) Summer
(C) Autumn
(D) Winter
(E) This description does not refer to a season.

18. With which of the following statements about life would the speaker be most likely to agree?

(A) People should live every period of their lives to the fullest.
(B) It is important to try to accomplish something during one's lifetime.
(C) Life is too short to spend time doing unpleasant things.
(D) The seasons are unpredictable.
(E) Trees are an integral part of the enjoyment of life.

GO ON TO THE NEXT PAGE

Tea is consumed by more people and in greater amounts than any other beverage in the world, with the exception of water. The tea plant, from whose
Line leaves tea is made, is native to India, China,
(5) and Japan and was first cultivated for use by the Chinese in prehistoric times. The plant, which is characterized as an evergreen, can reach a height of about thirty feet but is usually pruned down to three or four feet for cultivation. It has dark green
(10) leaves and cream-colored, fragrant blossoms.

Cultivation of the tea plant requires a great deal of effort. The plant must grow in a warm, wet climate, in a carefully protected, well-drained area. Its leaves must be picked by hand. (Cultivation in
(15) North America has been attempted, but was found to be impractical because of a shortage of cheap labor.) Today, the plant is cultivated in the lands to which it is native, as well as in Sri Lanka, Indonesia, Taiwan, and South America.
(20) Tea was probably first used as a vegetable relish and for medicinal purposes. In the 1400's Chinese and Japanese Buddhists developed a semi-religious ceremony surrounding tea-drinking. It was not until after 1700, however, that it was first imported
(25) into Europe. Today, the United Kingdom imports more tea than does any other nation— almost one third of the world's production. The United States is also a large importer, but Americans have seemed to prefer coffee ever since
(30) the famous Boston Tea Party in 1773.

19. This passage is mainly about

   (A) the tea plant.
   (B) the uses of the tea plant.
   (C) tea-drinking throughout history.
   (D) the tea trade.
   (E) the cultivation of the tea plant.

20. According to the passage, the tea plant

   (A) was first cultivated in Japan in prehistoric times.
   (B) requires well-drained soil to grow properly.
   (C) is the largest import of the United Kingdom.
   (D) has odorless flowers.
   (E) is native to South America.

21. Why is a large supply of cheap labor important for the cultivation of tea?

   (A) Since the tea plant can reach a height of thirty feet, several workers are required to harvest each plant.
   (B) Since tea is exported all over the world, a lot of people are needed to handle the trade complications that arise.
   (C) Since tea has been around since prehistoric times, many workers are employed to protect it and ensure that it doesn't die out.
   (D) Since England and China are far away from each other, many workers are required to coordinate tea shipments and deliveries.
   (E) Since the tea plant is hand picked, many laborers are needed at harvest time.

22. The style in the passage is most like that found in a

   (A) newspaper article.
   (B) passage in an encyclopedia.
   (C) cookbook.
   (D) journal entry.
   (E) history textbook.

GO ON TO THE NEXT PAGE

23. Which of the following is the author most likely to discuss next?

    (A) The details and aftermath of the Boston Tea Party

    (B) Other major imports of the United Kingdom and United States

    (C) Current trends in tea consumption

    (D) Other examples of plants that have a medicinal value

    (E) A description of what China was like in prehistoric times

24. The purpose of the second paragraph is to

    (A) describe the role of tea in religious ceremonies.

    (B) explain why Americans prefer coffee.

    (C) discuss historical uses of tea.

    (D) describe the cultivation of tea.

    (E) question the importance of tea.

There were moments of waiting. The youth
thought of the village street at home before the
arrival of the circus parade on a day in the spring.
Line He remembered how he had stood, a small thrillful
(5) boy, prepared to follow the band in its faded
chariot. He saw the yellow road, the lines of
expectant people, and the sober houses. He
particularly remembered an old fellow who used to
sit upon a cracker box in front of the store and
(10) pretend to despise such exhibitions. A thousand
details of color and form surged in his mind.
    Someone cried, "Here they come!" There was
rustling and muttering among the men.
    They displayed a feverish desire to have every
(15) possible cartridge ready to their hands. The boxes
were pulled around into various positions, and
adjusted with great care.
    The tall soldier, having prepared his rifle,
produced a red handkerchief of some kind. He was
(20) engaged in knitting it about his throat with

exquisite attention to its position, when the cry
was repeated up and down the line in a muffled
roar of sound.
    "Here they come! Here they come!" Gun locks
(25) clicked.
    Across the smoke-infested fields came a brown
swarm of running men who were giving shrill
yells. They came on, stooping and swinging their
rifles at all angles. A flag, tilted forward, sped near
(30) the front.

25. In the first paragraph, the youth is primarily concerned with

    (A) reliving a fond childhood memory.

    (B) describing a turning point in his life.

    (C) preparing for the upcoming battle.

    (D) planning his day at the circus.

    (E) watching a soldier tie a handkerchief.

26. What is meant by the exclamation "Here they come!" in line 12?

    (A) A band in a chariot is approaching.

    (B) The circus is coming to town.

    (C) The enemy soldiers are advancing.

    (D) A group of men selling handkerchiefs is on its way.

    (E) The youth's family is arriving to save him.

27. The tone of the passage undergoes a change from the first to the second paragraph that can best be described as a movement from

    (A) anger to amusement.

    (B) reminiscence to anticipation.

    (C) informality to formality.

    (D) reluctance to fear.

    (E) respect to indifference.

GO ON TO THE NEXT PAGE →

28. According to the passage, all of the following are ways the soldiers prepare for battle EXCEPT

(A) gathering cartridges.

(B) positioning ammunition.

(C) priming their guns.

(D) tying handkerchiefs.

(E) saddling horses.

29. Why are the men in the last paragraph carrying a flag?

(A) It is going to be raised in the youth's village.

(B) It needs to be protected from gunfire.

(C) It is going to be burned in a public demonstration.

(D) It represents the side they are fighting for.

(E) It has been damaged and needs to be mended.

Acupuncture is a type of medical therapy that has been part of Chinese medicine since ancient times. It involves the insertion of thin,
Line solid needles into specific sites on the body's
(5) surface. The belief is that the application of a needle at one particular point produces a specific response at a second point. It is based on the ancient Chinese philosophy that human beings are miniature versions of the universe and that the
(10) forces that control nature also control health. These forces are divided between two main principles called the yin and the yang, which have an opposite but complementary effect on each other. For example, one force keeps the body's
(15) temperature from rising too high and the other keeps it from dropping too low. When they are in balance, the body maintains a constant, normal state. Disease occurs when these forces get out of balance.

(20)   Although acupuncture had been used in Western countries during many periods, it was not until the 1970s that it gained widespread interest, when it was determined that it could be used to control pain during surgery. The mechanism for its
(25) effectiveness is still a mystery, but it has become a very popular technique in many countries in the treatment of various diseases and medical problems.

30. Which of the following is true about acupuncture?

I. Although originally only a part of Chinese medicine, it is now practiced in many Western countries.

II. It has been used to control pain during surgery since ancient times.

III. The mechanism for its effectiveness was discovered during the 1970s.

(A) I only

(B) I and II only

(C) I and III only

(D) II and III only

(E) I, II, and III

31. This passage is primarily about

(A) various diseases that are particularly common among the Chinese.

(B) the meaning and use of the yin and the yang.

(C) different types of medical therapies and their relative effectiveness.

(D) the historical and philosophical background to acupuncture.

(E) modern uses of acupuncture both in China and in Western countries.

GO ON TO THE NEXT PAGE

32. According to the passage, acupuncture is based on

   (A) the idea that the human body is a model of the universe and is therefore controlled by the forces of nature.

   (B) a firm belief in the Chinese gods known as the yin and the yang.

   (C) an ancient Chinese religious ceremony that involves the insertion of needles into the body.

   (D) a philosophy of health and disease that originated in China but has been totally changed by Western countries.

   (E) the ideas of an astronomer who was attempting to study the universe in ancient times.

33. According to the passage, the yin and the yang are principles that represent

   (A) high and low extremes of temperature.

   (B) states of health and disease.

   (C) similar treatments for different diseases.

   (D) competing, balancing forces within the body.

   (E) the ideas of comfort and pain.

34. The author includes the example of the yin and the yang controlling the extremes of body temperature in order to

   (A) back up her claim that the forces within the body mirror the forces of the universe.

   (B) clarify how these forces have a complementary effect on each other.

   (C) provide proof that acupuncture is an effective medical therapy.

   (D) suggest a possible explanation for why people sometimes run high fevers.

   (E) highlight a feature of the body that acupuncture has not yet been shown to influence.

The painter Georgia O'Keeffe was born in Wisconsin in 1887, and grew up on her family's farm. At seventeen she left for Chicago and New *Line* York but she never lost her bond with the land.
(5) Like most painters, O'Keeffe painted the things that were most important to her, and she became famous for her simplified paintings of nature. During a visit to New Mexico in 1929, O'Keeffe was moved by the desert's stark beauty, and she
(10) began to paint many of its images. From about 1930 until her death in 1986, her true home was in the western desert, and bleached bones, barren hills, and colorful flowers were her characteristic subjects.
(15) O'Keeffe is widely considered to have been a pioneering American modernist painter. While most early modern American artists were strongly influenced by European art, O'Keeffe's position was more independent.
(20) Almost from the beginning, her work was more identifiably American—in its simplified and idealized treatment of color, light, space, and natural forms. Her paintings are generally considered "semiabstract," because, while they
(25) often depict recognizable images and objects, they don't present those images in a very detailed or realistic way. Rather, the colors and shapes in her paintings are often so reduced and simplified that they begin to take on a life of their own,
(30) independent from the real-life objects they are taken from.

35. According to the passage, all of the following strongly influenced O'Keeffe's paintings EXCEPT

   (A) her rural upbringing.

   (B) her life in the West.

   (C) the work of artists in other countries.

   (D) the appearance of the natural landscape.

   (E) animal and plant forms.

GO ON TO THE NEXT PAGE

36. O'Keeffe's relationship to nature is most similar to

    (A) a photographer's relationship to a model.
    (B) a writer's relationship to a publisher.
    (C) a student's relationship to a part-time job.
    (D) a sculptor's relationship to an art dealer.
    (E) a carpenter's relationship to a hammer.

37. O'Keeffe's paintings have been called "semiabstract" because they

    (A) involve a carefully realistic use of color and light.
    (B) depict common, everyday things.
    (C) show recognizable scenes from nature.
    (D) depict familiar things in an unrealistic way.
    (E) refer directly to real-life activities.

38. According to the passage, O'Keeffe is considered an artistic pioneer because

    (A) her work became influential in Europe.
    (B) she painted the American Southwest.
    (C) her paintings had a definite American style.
    (D) she painted things that were familiar to her.
    (E) her work was very abstract.

39. The passage's main point about O'Keeffe is that she

    (A) was the best painter of her generation.
    (B) was a distinctive modern American painter.
    (C) liked to paint only what was familiar to her.
    (D) never developed fully enough as an abstract artist.
    (E) used colors and shapes that are too reduced and simple.

40. It can be inferred from the passage that modern European art of the time

    (A) did not depict images of the desert.
    (B) was extremely abstract.
    (C) did not portray natural shapes in a simple, idealistic manner.
    (D) was not influenced by rural landscapes.
    (E) approached colors in a semiabstract manner.

IF YOU FINISH BEFORE TIME IS CALLED, YOU MAY CHECK YOUR WORK ON THIS SECTION ONLY. DO NOT TURN TO ANY OTHER SECTION IN THE TEST.   STOP

SECTION 4

Time—25 Minutes
25 Questions

In this section, there are five possible answers after each problem. Choose which one is best. You may use the blank space at the right of the page for scratch work.

Note: Figures provided with the problems are drawn with the greatest possible accuracy, UNLESS stated "Not Drawn to Scale."

1. The crown in Figure 1 is made up of toothpicks that each have the same length. If each toothpick is 2 meters long and each side is equal to one toothpick, what is the perimeter of the crown in meters?

   (A) 5
   (B) 7
   (C) 10
   (D) 12
   (E) 14

USE THIS SPACE FOR FIGURING.

Figure 1

2. D is an odd number between 4 and 11. If D is also between 7 and 18, what is the value of D?

   (A) 5
   (B) 7
   (C) 8
   (D) 9
   (E) 11

3. Gary has a collection of 16 different operas and his roommate Paul has a collection of 18 different operas. If Paul and Gary have 4 operas common to both record collections, how many different operas do they have between them?

   (A) 18
   (B) 30
   (C) 34
   (D) 36
   (E) 38

GO ON TO THE NEXT PAGE

USE THIS SPACE FOR FIGURING.

4. If $\frac{1}{9}G = 18$, then $\frac{1}{3}G =$

(A)   6

(B)   9

(C) 36

(D) 54

(E) 63

5. A model sailboat floating on the water is
attached to a string 1 meter long, as shown in
Figure 2. If the string is tied to a post on the
dock, which of the following best shows the
area of water on which the sailboat can float?

Figure 2

(A)   (B)   (C)

(D)   (E)

6. At a party, there are exactly 4 times as many
adults as children. Which of the following could
be the total number of people at this party?

(A) 14

(B) 16

(C) 21

(D) 25

(E) 29

7. Using a pair of scissors, which of the
following can be made from a 20 cm by 28 cm
rectangular sheet of paper by 1 straight cut?

   I. Triangle

   II. Square

   III. Rectangle

(A) I only

(B) II only

(C) III only

(D) I and II only

(E) I, II, and III

GO ON TO THE NEXT PAGE

8. According to the graph in Figure 3, the average number of students taking the swimming class during the four months of March through June was

    (A) 50
    (B) 55
    (C) 60
    (D) 65
    (E) 70

Questions 9–11 refer to the following definition.

For all real numbers n and r, $n \clubsuit r = (n-1) - \dfrac{n}{r}$.

EXAMPLE: $5 \clubsuit 3 = (5-1) - \dfrac{5}{3} = 4 - \dfrac{5}{3} = 2\dfrac{1}{3}$.

9. What is the value of $4 \clubsuit 2$?

    (A) 1
    (B) 2
    (C) 6
    (D) 8
    (E) 16

10. If $Q \clubsuit 2 = 4$, then $Q =$

    (A) 10
    (B) 8
    (C) 6
    (D) 4
    (E) 2

USE THIS SPACE FOR FIGURING.

NUMBER OF STUDENTS TAKING
SWIMMING CLASS

Figure 3

GO ON TO THE NEXT PAGE

11. If $n \neq 0$ and $r \neq 0$, which of the following must be true?

 I. $n \clubsuit 1 = -1$
 II. $1 \clubsuit n = 0$
 III. $n \clubsuit n = r \clubsuit r$

 (A) I only
 (B) II only
 (C) I and II only
 (D) II and III only
 (E) I, II, and III

USE THIS SPACE FOR FIGURING.

---

12. Robert wants to leave a 15 percent tip for a dinner that costs $20.95. Which of the following is closest to the amount of tip he should leave?

 (A) $2.70
 (B) $3.00
 (C) $3.15
 (D) $3.50
 (E) $3.75

13. Juan studied from 4:00 P.M. to 6:00 P.M. and finished one-third of his assignments. He is taking a break and wants to finish his homework by 10:30 P.M. If he plans to continue working at the same rate, what is the latest that he can return to his studies?

 (A) 6:30 P.M.
 (B) 7:00 P.M.
 (C) 7:30 P.M.
 (D) 8:00 P.M.
 (E) 8:30 P.M.

GO ON TO THE NEXT PAGE

14. Mrs. Brown and her *z* children each ate 2 peaches. What's the total number of peaches they ate?

    (A) $z + 1$

    (B) $z + 2$

    (C) $2z$

    (D) $2z + 1$

    (E) $2z + 2$

USE THIS SPACE FOR FIGURING.

15. Which figure can be drawn WITHOUT lifting the pencil or retracing?

    (A)   (B)   (C)

    (D)   (E)

16. If 0.59 is about $\dfrac{N}{5}$, then *N* is closest to which of the following?

    (A)   0.3

    (B)   1

    (C)   2

    (D)   3

    (E)   30

17. If the largest of 7 consecutive integers is 25, what is the average of the 7 integers?

    (A) 24

    (B) 22

    (C) 21

    (D) 20

    (E) 16

GO ON TO THE NEXT PAGE

18. The price of a box of raisins increased from $0.93 to $1.08. The increase in price is closest to what percent?

    (A) 1%

    (B) 14%

    (C) 15%

    (D) 16%

    (E) 20%

USE THIS SPACE FOR FIGURING.

$$21\overline{)Q} \quad \begin{array}{c} 15 \end{array}$$

$$15\overline{)S} \quad \begin{array}{c} 21 \text{ remainder } 8 \end{array}$$

19. In the division problems shown above, $S - Q =$

    (A) 6

    (B) 8

    (C) 15

    (D) 18

    (E) 21

20. What is the least number of square tiles with side 6 cm needed to cover a rectangular floor 72 cm long and 48 cm wide?

    (A) 14

    (B) 72

    (C) 96

    (D) 144

    (E) 192

21. It takes Craig 5 minutes to type n pages. At this rate, how many minutes will it take him to type 20 pages?

   (A) $\dfrac{n}{100}$

   (B) $\dfrac{4}{n}$

   (C) $\dfrac{100}{n}$

   (D) $4n$

   (E) $100n$

USE THIS SPACE FOR FIGURING.

$$\frac{n}{5} = \frac{20}{x}$$

22. The width of a rectangular swimming pool is one quarter of its length. If the length is 60 meters, what is the perimeter of the pool?

   (A) 60 m
   (B) 120 m
   (C) 150 m
   (D) 180 m
   (E) 240 m

$60 \times \frac{1}{4} = 15$

$60 \times 2 + 15 \times 2$

23. The price of a dress at a department store decreases by 20 percent every month it is not sold. After 3 months, the current price of the unsold dress is approximately what percent of the original price?

   (A) 40%
   (B) 50%
   (C) 60%
   (D) 70%
   (E) 80%

$$\begin{array}{r} 100 \\ -20 \\ \hline 80 \\ -20 \\ \hline 60 \\ -20 \\ \hline 40 \end{array}$$

24. If p is a positive integer and n is a negative integer, which of the following is greatest?

    (A) $\dfrac{p}{n}$

    (B) $\dfrac{n}{p}$

    (C) $\dfrac{1}{p-n}$

    (D) $\dfrac{1}{n-p}$

    (E) It cannot be determined from the information given.

25. In a yoga school, $\dfrac{1}{9}$ of the men and $\dfrac{1}{3}$ of the women are vegetarians, and twice as many men as women are vegetarians. If there are 84 people in the yoga school, how many men are vegetarians?

    (A) 4
    (B) 8
    (C) 12
    (D) 27
    (E) 72

SECTION 5

Time—25 Minutes

> Write an essay on the following prompt on the paper provided. Your essay should NOT exceed two pages and must be written in ink. Erasing is not allowed.

Prompt: <u>Capital punishment serves no purpose and should be ended.</u>

Do you agree or disagree with this statement? Use examples from history, literature, or your own personal experience to support your point of view.

_____

_____

_____

_____

_____

_____

_____

_____

_____

_____

_____

_____

_____

_____

_____

_____

_____

_____

_____

_____

_____

_____

_____

_____

_____

_____

_____

_____

_____

_____

_____

_____

_____

_____

_____

_____

_____

_____

_____

_____

_____

_____

_____

_____

_____

_____

IF YOU FINISH BEFORE TIME IS CALLED, YOU MAY CHECK YOUR WORK ON
THIS SECTION ONLY. DO NOT TURN TO ANY OTHER SECTION IN THE TEST.

ANSWER EXPLANATIONS

SECTION 1: VERBAL

SYNONYMS

1. D

To plead is to appeal earnestly or desperately—to beg.

2. B

To prowl is to move around secretly, stealthily—in other words, to sneak.

3. E

A vessel, such as a bowl or glass, is a container for holding something.

4. D

To approve means to judge favorably.

5. A

To seep means to flow through little cracks, or to ooze.

6. E

To vex means to anger, or irritate.

7. B

To doze is to sleep lightly. You might doze because someone bores you, but the two words are not synonymous.

8. E

A bounty is a reward or gift.

9. E

Something coarse is harsh or rough.

10. A

Meek means mild-mannered or submissive.

11. C

To saturate is to wet something thoroughly or soak it. You saturate a sponge in water, for example.

12. E

Genteel describes something elegant, aristocratic, or refined.

13. B

Winsome means pleasing or charming, such as a winsome smile.

14. B

To reproach means to express disapproval or disappointment in someone. (D) is tempting, but you can complain without blaming anything specific.

15. B

To demonstrate means to explain clearly or show.

16. C

A camouflage is a disguise or a concealment. An outfit, (B), may or may not be a camouflage.

17. A

Aghast is an adjective that means to be struck with amazement or horror—in other words, to be shocked.

18. E

To recollect means to remember.

19. C

To initiate means to begin or start.

20. E

To suffocate is to choke or deprive of air.

21. A

To prevail means to win, overcome, or triumph.

22. C

To prance is to walk in a cocky way or to strut. The closest wrong answer choice, in attitude at least, is (A), but boasting is not a way of walking.

23. E

Profound means deep-seated or intense. A parent has a profound love for his child.

24. A

Limber means flexible, lithe, nimble, or supple. (B), wooden, is a good antonym for limber.

25. E

To terminate means to finish or bring to an end.

26. A

To contemplate means to think about or ponder.

27. C

A caprice is a sudden fancy or whim. (A) is tempting, but not all ideas are whims or caprices.

28. E

An adage is a common saying or proverb.

29. B

A din is a loud, confused mixture of noises—in other words, a clamor.

30. A

To expunge is to get rid of, obliterate, erase.

ANALOGIES

31. C

A pilot directs a plane as a captain directs a ship.

32. A

One breed of snake is a python. One breed of dog is a terrier. The relationships in the other answer choices are in wrong order as compared to the stem words. In other words, a python is a subset of the snake family, and that same relationship is not reflected in (B)–(E). Quadruped, by the way, means four-legged.

33. A

A mayor is the highest official in a city. A governor is the highest official in a state. The suggested bridge easily eliminates (B), (C), and (E). With (D), a secretary is not usually the highest official on a committee—the chairperson is.

34. C

Paper is the material a novel is written on. Similarly, canvas is the material a portrait is painted on.

35. B

Refined is the opposite of vulgar. In (B), submissive is the opposite of recalcitrant, which means stubbornly defiant. (A) represents synonyms, not opposites. Ecstatic in (C) is an extreme state of happiness. And the word pairs in (D) and (E) have no obvious relationship to each other.

36. E

You use a whip to lash someone. You use a club to beat someone. As for (A), you may throw a stick at someone, but the more common association with stick is that it's used to hit or beat someone, and that is not what is listed here.

37. A

Migrate is a seasonal, adaptive action taken by a swallow (a kind of bird). In the winter, swallows migrate. In the winter, groundhogs hibernate (hide and sleep). Petting is something a person does to a dog, so (B) is incorrect, and (C), (D), and (E) are not specifically done in the winter—even though they all are things these animals do.

38. E

Flip the words: a meteorologist studies weather. Similarly, a botanist studies plants or vegetation.

39. B

Again, flip the pairs: horse racing is done, or played, on a track. Tennis is played on a court.

40. B

A director tells an actor what to do, the way a coach tells a player what to do.

41. A

The relationship here is one of order or sequence. A dessert is eaten at the end of a meal. A finale is played at the end of a performance. Lunch is eaten after breakfast, but it's a different meal, not part of the same one, so the bridge doesn't fit.

42. A

The words in the stem are opposites. The only pair of opposites among the choices is in (A): accept is the opposite of reject, as confirm is the opposite of deny.

43. E

A tower is the tall structure that enables planes to navigate safely at an airport. A lighthouse is the tall structure that enables ships to navigate safely at the shoreline.

44. C

Fidelity is the opposite or absence of unfaithfulness. Honesty is the opposite or absence of deceit. The words in (A) and (D) are synonyms, and there's no clear relationship between the words in (B) and (E).

45. C

If something is widespread, it's not limited. If something is broad, it's not narrow. The words in (A) are synonyms, as are the words in (B) and (D). (E) is a little tough: international seems to suggest sophisticated, which is the opposite of provincial, but the words are in the opposite order as those presented in the stem.

46. C

A saw is a tool used by a carpenter. A plow is a tool used by a farmer. No other occupation listed here requires the use of a plow.

47. A

A sword is used against an opponent in fencing, as a glove is used in boxing.

48. C

Here the relationship is one of degree, with the second word being much stronger than the first. You can encourage or suggest that someone do something, and they may or may not do it. But if you demand or order them to do it, then they must. The words in (A) and (B) are synonyms, and the words in (D) are opposites. Condemn in (E) is stronger than to reprimand, not the other way around, so the order is wrong.

49. B

A grin is a facial expression showing delight. A frown is a facial expression showing dismay. (Dismay is a mixture of fear and discouragement.) A laugh in

(D) expresses happiness, but it isn't precisely a facial expression.

50. E

Something mysterious is not understandable. Something obscure is not clear.

51. A

When an injury heals, it disappears. When a malfunction is repaired, it disappears. In both cases, the thing that heals or is repaired gets better, which is why (E) is not quite right.

52. B

A jog is a slow run; a sprint is a fast run. A trot is, a slow run for a horse, while a gallop is a fast run. (C) means to wander about—not at a great speed, while (D) means to stroll. (E) means flying, not running.

53. E

A bone is one part of the structural system of the body—the system that holds it up. Similarly, a beam—a long piece of timber or steel—is one part of the structural system that holds up a building. (A) may be tempting, but floors don't generally connect to other floors the way beams and bones do.

54. D

Amorphous means "without shape." So amorphous is to shape as odorless is to odor, or scent.

55. E

Another relationship of opposites. A vain person is, by definition, not humble. Similarly, an extroverted or outgoing person is, by definition, not shy. (A) may be tempting since boisterous means noisy, exuberant. But anxious people aren't by definition quiet; one may be anxious and act boisterously, by talking too much out of nervousness, for example.

Cantankerous in (B) means bad-tempered, quarrelsome, and discursive in (D) means to talk in a rambling way.

56. C

You study for a test the way you rehearse for a play. One is preparation for the other. (A) seems close, but apply is not quite "preparation" for a job.

57. A

You smile when you're happy and frown when you're sad or angry. You cheer to signal your approval and jeer your disapproval of a sports team, for example. Wince, in (B), means to express pain.

58. E

To peel a banana is to pull off its outer covering. To husk an ear of corn is to pull off its outer covering (also called a husk).

59. B

Tactile refers to anything perceptible through the sense of touch, just as olfactory refers to anything perceptible through the sense of smell. If they had been correct, (D) would have read, "sight is to visual," and (C), "taste is to oral."

60. D

Articulateness is the quality of speaking or writing in a clear manner. Similarly, legibility is handwriting that's clear.

SECTION 2: MATH

1. E

We need an answer here which is not a factor of 120. In other words, a number which will not evenly divide into 120. Only (E), 16, is not a factor of 120.

2. B

Recall that all figures on the SSAT are always drawn to scale unless stated otherwise. Extending the vertical line segment boundary of the art slice upward and extending the horizontal line segment boundary of the art slice to the right shows that the art slice is about 25% of the pie. Twenty-five percent or $\frac{1}{4}$ of 900 (the total number of students) is 225 art students.

3. B

Sean's sister must arrive (25 − 14) or 11 minutes after midnight because it takes 14 minutes to reach midnight and 11 more minutes to add up to 25 minutes.

4. E

The key here is to make what you are given look like the answer choices. No calculation is needed here. Round off 0.52 to 0.5 or $\frac{1}{2}$ and round 78 to 80.

5. E

Careful! The question asks for dollars. Each sack of money = $50 as is noted in the table. Brian has 4 more sacks than James, so the amount more than James that Brian saved is 4 times $50 which equals $200.

6. B

We must determine how much was saved by Andy and how much was saved by James and compare the two. Andy saved 8 sacks which is 8 times $50 or $400 and James saved 2 sacks which is 2 times $50 or $100. Thus, Andy's $400 is 4 times James's $100.

7. C

Using the formula Part = Percent × Whole, 30 = 30% × N (total number of students). We need to isolate the total number of students (N). Thirty percent = $\frac{30}{100}$ so the equation can be written as $30 = \frac{30}{100} \times N$. Now multiply both sides of this equation by $\frac{100}{30}$; the N is now by itself once $\frac{30}{100}$ and $\frac{100}{30}$ cancel out to 1. Multiplying $30 \times \frac{100}{30}$ gives a value of 100 for N.

8. B

Because of the word *except*, we need to determine which fraction is not less than 2. So we are looking for a fraction which is greater than or equal to 2. In order to determine this, make all of the fractions improper: With (A), $\frac{15}{8} = 1\frac{7}{8}$ The only fraction where the denominator can be divided into the numerator with a result of at least 2 is (B): $\frac{45}{22} = 2\frac{1}{22}$

9. A

We are told all the sides are equal, thus set each segment = 1 and add. With (A), $A - C - B - D - F = 1$ (A to C) + 1 (C to B) + 1 (B to D) + 2 (D to E and then E to F) = 5. (B) counts to 4, hence cross it out. (C) counts to 4 also so cross it out. (D) counts to 3 and (E) counts to 4. The longest path is 5, so (A) is correct.

10. C

Scan the answer choices. (A), 80, is 80.08 − 80 = 0.08 away from 80.08. (B), 80.01, is 80.08 − 80.01 = 0.07 away from 80.08. (C), 80.1, is 80.1 − 80.08 = 0.02 away from 80.08. (D), 81, is 0.92 away from 80.08 and (E), 90, is more than 9 away from 80.08. The question asks for the choice closest to 80.08, and thus (C), 80.1, is correct.

11. A

Call the number N. Write an inequality using the information given. Remember, "of" means multiply. $\frac{1}{3} \times N < 12$. We need to isolate N, our unknown value. Multiplying both sides by the reciprocal of $\frac{1}{3}$ which is 3 produces a result of $N < 12 \times 3$, and thus $N < 36$. (A) is correct.

12. D

The minimum number of points Team B could have scored is one more than Team A or 40. Using the aver-age formula, Average $= \dfrac{\text{Sum of the terms}}{\text{Number of terms}}$ we can plug in our given information: Average $= \dfrac{40 \text{ points}}{5 \text{ players}}$. Thus the average score of the players on Team B must have been at least 8 points per player.

13. B

The sum of the 3 interior angles of any triangle is 180 degrees. Figure 4 indicates that two of the angles have degree measures of 90 and 45. So the degree measure of the third angle is $180 - 90 - 45 = 45$. So this is a 45–45–90 triangle. In any triangle, the sides opposite two equal angles must be equal. Hence, $a = 6$.

14. C

Here, we need to divide 40,000 into 2,000,000: $\dfrac{2,000,000}{40,000}$. Simply cancel out 4 zeros from the bottom and 4 zeros from the top. We now have $\dfrac{200}{4}$ which equals 50.

15. E

The question states that y is less than 3, and we want the value which x cannot equal, so let's solve the equation for x in terms of y and see if we can conclude something about x. The equation is $(x - y) + 2 = 6$. First subtract 2 from both sides. Then $(x - y) = 6 - 2$, or $(x - y) = 4$. The parentheses are not needed, so $x - y = 4$. Adding y to both sides, we have that $x = y + 4$. Since y is less than 3, $y + 4$ must less than 7. Now $x = y + 4$, so x must be less than 7. Now look for a choice which is not less than 7. Only (E), 8, is not less than 7. So x cannot be 8 and (E) is correct.

16. C

Segment $AD = 55$. Because the length of AB is 2 times the length of BC, let $BC = x$ and let $AB = 2x$. Since $AB = CD$, let $CD = 2x$ also. The total length of $AD = AB + BC + CD = 2x + x + 2x = 5x = 55$. Hence, $x = 11$ and $BD = BC + CD = x + 2x = 3x = 3 \times 11 = 33$.

17. E

The question asks for all the points. (A) is incorrect because it only includes the rectangular boundary of the set of all the points that touch the table; it does not include the points inside this rectangle which also touch the surface of the table. (E) indicates all the points and is correct.

18. E

The question is not asking for a value of J. Indeed, J could be any whole number. The question is asking for the answer choice which can be written in the form $(J + 2) \times 3$, where J is a whole number. Since 3 is a factor of $(J + 2) \times 3$, the choice we're looking for must be a multiple of 3. A whole number is a multiple of 3 if and only if the sum of its digits is a multiple of 3. Looking at the answer choices, only the sum if the digits of (E), 81, is a multiple of 3. That is, the sum of the digits of 81 is $8 + 1 = 9$, which is a multiple of 3. So (E) is correct.

19. D

Using the information given, isolate a: $a = 3b + 4 + 7 = 3b + 11$. Thus, $a = 3b + 11$. Next add 5 to both sides of this equation: $a + 5 = 3b + 11 + 5 = 3b + 16$.

20. A

They give us 21.5 out of 100 which is easily translated into 21.5%. Hence, 21.5% of (multiplication) 2,000,000 is $\frac{21.5}{100} \times 2,000,000$. Cancel out two zeros from the 100 in the denominator and from the 2,000,000 in the numerator to get $21.5 \times 20,000 = 430,000$.

21. C

Translate from English into math. Let Bob's current age $= x$ and let Jerry's current age $= x + 7$. To find their ages 5 years ago, subtract 5 years from each current age: 5 years ago Bob was $x - 5$ and Jerry was $x + 7 - 5 = x + 2$. The sum of Bob and Jerry's ages 5 years ago was: $x - 5 + x + 2 = 2x - 3$.

22. D

The contestant answered a total of 5 questions correctly. Using our percent formula, Percent × Whole = Part, 20% × total number of questions = 5. Multiply both sides of the equation by $\frac{100}{20}$, (the reciprocal of 20%) and the total number of questions = 25. Thus, statement I is incorrect so eliminate (A), (C) and (E). For statement II, there were $25 - 15 = 10$ questions remaining and 1 of these 10 questions was answered correctly. So he answered $\frac{1}{10}$, or 10% of the remaining questions correctly, so statement II is true. (Also, both remaining answer choices, (B) and (D), contain this Roman numeral.) Finally, statement

III is true because 1 of the remaining 10 was answered correctly so 9 of these 10 were not answered correctly. Eliminate choice (B). (D) remains and is correct.

23. D

This problem is perfect for our Picking Numbers strategy. $C = A \times B$. Pick two consecutive numbers for A and B such as 2 and 3. Their product is 6 and positive. However, if we selected 1 and 0, the product would be 0 which is neither positive nor negative. Because the integers are consecutive, one of the integers must be even, or a multiple of 2, and hence the product of any two consecutive integers must be even. (D) is correct.

24. C

Be careful here. The question asks for the difference before the discount. The sweaters were sold for 100% – 20% of their old price. Using our percent formula, Part = Percent × Whole, we have that $48 = 80\% \times$ old price. Convert 80% to $\frac{80}{100}$ and multiply both sides by $\frac{100}{80}$. We now have $\frac{100}{80} \times 48 =$ old price. Canceling yields $60. Use the percent formula for the wool sweater and you have the equation $64 = 80\% \times$ old price. You'll find that its original price was $80. The difference is $80 – $60 = $20.

25. A

The maximum load that a car can carry is $17\frac{1}{3}$ tons. If each car carries the maximum load minus $\frac{5}{9}$ of a ton then each car carries $17\frac{1}{3} - \frac{5}{9} = \frac{52}{3} - \frac{5}{9} = \frac{52}{3} \times \frac{3}{3} - \frac{5}{9} = \frac{156-5}{9} = \frac{151}{9}$ tons. Next multiply this amount carried in each car by 36 cars and we get $\frac{151}{9} \times 36$ tons. Cancel the 9 into the 36 and we get $151 \text{¥} 4 = 604$.

SECTION 3: READING COMPREHENSION

LEMURS PASSAGE

This fact-based passage introduces us to the lemur, a monkey-like animal that lives chiefly in Madagascar. We're given various information about lemurs: their physical characteristics, the origin of their name, where they're found, and soon.

1. A

The author's style is straightforward and informative, like the style of a biology textbook. A zoologist's diary would more likely be in the first-person ("June 20: saw two lemurs in a jungle in Southern Madagascar."), and a tourist's guidebook would go into less scientific detail and would place lemurs in a specific location ("Be sure to check out the lemurs in Avahi National Park.").

2. C

Summarize the passage in your own mind. You might have come up with something like, "Things to Know About Lemurs." (C) restates this idea. The passage doesn't mention whether lemurs hunt alone or in groups, (B) is incorrect, and the rest of the answer choices focus on details.

3. D

You're looking for the detail that's false. The author states that lemurs eat "leaves . . . eggs, fruit, insects, and small animals," so (D) must be incorrect.

4. C

In the second half of the paragraph, the author states that lemurs "are reputed to be gentle, friendly creatures." If they're "gentle" and "friendly," you can infer that they're not very aggressive. (A) is contradicted in the final sentence of the passage. (B) and (D) are refuted when the author says that lemurs "are active throughout the day and night" and are "most often are in the trees." We don't know enough about the flying lemur to infer that it can only be found in and around Madagascar, so (E) is incorrect.

ROOSEVELT PASSAGE

This history passage deals with Eleanor Roosevelt, niece of one American president and wife to another. The author says "it would be an injustice" to reduce her to an historical footnote, because she accomplished many things in her own right.

5. D

Paragraph 2 states that Eleanor Roosevelt worked for humanitarian causes "before her marriage," so (D) is the false detail here.

6. B

The author calls Eleanor Roosevelt "in her own right, an important figure," "dedicated" and "influential." Strongly positive words such as this signal that (B) sums up the author's opinion of Roosevelt. (A) and (C) are too negative, and (D) and (E) too neutral.

7. B

The text is about the life and achievements of Eleanor Roosevelt. Other Roosevelts, (A), are only mentioned briefly, and (C) and (D) are too narrow. (E) doesn't even mention Eleanor Roosevelt and is way too broad.

8. E

According to paragraph 1, it would be unjust to say that Eleanor Roosevelt was only related or married to famous, powerful men. To the author, she was, "in her own right, an important figure in . . . American history" who used her position to further various social causes. (A) and (B) speculate on what Roosevelt could or might have done, while (C) takes the opposite view of the author.

Woodrow Wilson Passage

This historical passage focuses on President Woodrow Wilson and his post-World War I peace settlement—specifically, on the Fourteen-Point Plan, which called for the abolition of secret diplomacy. Wilson considered open negotiations vital for peace, but in paragraph 2 the author disagrees, arguing that Wilson's view was too simplistic.

9. D

The first and second sentences of each paragraph usually reveal the paragraph's topic. In this case, it's the second sentence: Wilson was wrong—war stems not from secret deals by national leaders, but from "unresolved disagreements among nations." (A) and (E) summarize the topic of paragraph 1, not paragraph 2. (B) is too general; the paragraph mainly discusses why one form of diplomacy usually fails to avert wars. Not all disagreements among nations lead to war, so (C) is also too broad.

10. C

We're told that Wilson called for an end to secret negotiations as a way to end war, and then that Wilson was wrong, that "he lacked insight into the complexities of international politics." Clearly, the author disagrees with Wilson. (A) is tempting, given the author's "realpolitik" attitude, but she isn't being

Machiavellian, she's simply stating why Wilson's idea was wrong. (B) and (D) are too emotional, and (E) is wrong because the author doesn't apologize for criticizing Wilson.

11. A

The scenario in (A) is the closest parallel to the author's thinking. As the next-to-last sentence of the passage puts it, "war usually stems from unresolved disagreements among nations . . . over territory . . . " (B)'s scenario is an economic trade agreement involving a third country—not very likely to lead to war. The other answer choices involve secret deals or covert activity of the kind that Wilson—not the author—thought would lead to war.

12. C

Look at the last two sentences of the text. According to the author, open diplomacy can't solve the kinds of problems that lead to war. (A)'s assertion that quiet diplomacy will always be with us doesn't explain why open diplomacy won't prevent war.

13. C

To imagine where the author might go next, retrace the steps of the argument: 1) Wilson offered a peace proposal that argued for open diplomacy, which he thought would end wars; 2) Wilson failed to grasp that secret diplomacy is not the cause of most wars, which occur because of unresolved disputes among nations over such things as territory and resources. Having disagreed with Wilson, it's most likely that the author will try to illustrate this last point, by giving an example of a war that occurred because of a territorial or resource dispute. (A), (D) and (E) suggest that the author will return to the subjects of President Wilson or World War I, but the text moves beyond Wilson to discuss the cause of war.

POETRY PASSAGE

You are sure to see one poem on the SSAT. When you do, be alert for tone and the use of metaphor. Here, an oak tree is used as a metaphor—for living our lives as an oak tree does, in accordance with nature and the change of seasons. The first three lines of the poem generate its central metaphor: "Live thy life, young and old, like yon oak..." ("Yon" is short for "yonder," meaning "that oak over there.") In other words, "live your life, at all ages, like that oak tree does."

14. C

You're asked to infer the poem's central metaphor. What do the seasons represent? The successive stages of life, (C): spring is youth, summer is maturity, autumn is middle age, and winter is old age.

15. C

Who is the "he" of line 13? The entire stanza provides clues: "he" has lost his leaves, "he" stands, "trunk and bough, naked strength." "He," then, is the oak tree.

16. A

The second stanza shows the oak tree in summer and in autumn; "gold again" refers to the seasonally-changed color of the oak tree's leaves, so (A) is best here. (B), (C), and (E) are pretty easily eliminated, and (D) isn't right because the arrival of autumn signals a change in foliage—and the quoted phrase refers to the latter, not the former.

17. A

An easy detail question. The oak is referred to as "living gold" in line 5 of the poem; the previous line says, "bright in spring."

18. A

This question basically asks for the statement that mirrors the poem's Big Idea, which is that we should be like the oak tree, living each season of our lives as well as we can. (A) restates this best. (B) is wrong because its "something" can apparently be accomplished at any point in one's life; what about the other "seasons"? (C) makes little sense, and (D) contradicts the poem. (E) dispenses with the poem's central metaphor altogether; it's not that a good life includes the enjoyment of trees, it's that a good life is lived as a tree lives its life.

TEA PASSAGE

This passage is about tea—the plant, and the history of its cultivation and uses. Paragraph 1 describes its universal appeal, its origin, and its description and look. Paragraph 2 describes the difficulties of cultivating tea, and where the plant is currently grown. The final paragraph summarizes tea's history, from ancient times to today.

19. A

The choice that best sums up the passage is (A). The other answer choices touch on only one aspect of the text.

20. B

(A) is wrong because tea was first cultivated in China. (C) distorts lines 25–27: the author states that the UK is the world's largest importer of tea, not that tea is the UK's largest import.

21. E

The phrase "cheap labor" in the question stem is also found in paragraph 2, which states that, since tea leaves "must be picked by hand," cultivation in North America "was found to be impractical because of a shortage of cheap labor." In other words, tea cultivation requires a supply of cheap labor because the leaves must be hand-picked. (A) contradicts paragraph 1, which says that tea plants are "usually pruned down" to "three or four feet for cultivation." (B) and (C) are never mentioned, and (E) incorrectly reduces the world's cultivation and consumption of tea to two countries, England and China.

22. B

The author's style is informative, offering an encyclopedic summary of the cultivation and uses of tea.

23. C

Since paragraph 3 summarizes the historic uses of tea, beginning with ancient times and ending with consumption today, it's likely that the author will continue to discuss current consumption trends. (A) temptingly mentions the last detail in the passage, but the Boston Tea Party is really only a footnote, a lighthearted explanation of why consumption of tea in the United States today lags behind that of coffee.

24. D

Paragraph 2 describes the difficulties of cultivating tea and where it is currently cultivated.

FICTION PASSAGE

This passage reflects the thoughts going through a soldier's mind in the final moments before battle. Notice how the two lines of dialogue toward the end of the passage increase the tension of the imminent attack. Be alert for shifts of tone and perspective, and the use of metaphor.

25. A

After the teaser in the opening sentence (moments of waiting for what?), the first paragraph details the youth's childhood memory of the circus in town, (A). The circus arrival couldn't be called a turning point in his life—it was simply a fond memory—so (B) is incorrect. (D) is incorrect because he wasn't planning his day at the circus, he was simply enjoying the day as a spectator. Neither (C) nor (E) are discussed in the first paragraph, so they are wrong as well.

26. C

This question is a little tricky. The text jumps from one "scene" to another. That is, the quoted exclamation breaks us away from the youth's daydream of the circus and into the reality of his current situation. A fellow soldier has shouted that the enemy is approaching, (C), and we are jolted into the reality of the situation. (A) and (B) wrongly assume that the exclamation is part of the youth's memory, and (D) and (E) are completely unwarranted inferences.

27. B

As we have just seen in the previous question, the youth reminisces in paragraph one. As we jump to the next paragraph and to the reality of the battle, the men prepare with anticipation. No other answer choice fits.

28. E

An easy detail question. Horses are never mentioned here; all the soldiers are on foot.

29. D

Why do soldiers carry a flag? In the same way flags are raised on ships in the ocean, raising a flag on land is meant to represent one's side or country. (A) is tempting, but true only if the enemy wins. (B) makes no sense, since the flag is carried at the front of a charging line of soldiers.

ACUPUNCTURE PASSAGE

This modified science passage discusses acupuncture, an ancient Chinese form of medical therapy. There's very little science in the passage. Instead, the author describes the thinking behind acupuncture and gives a brief history of its use in Western countries.

30. A

A Roman Numeral question. The only true statement, according to the passage, is statement I: Acupuncture was first practiced in China, but is now practiced in many Western countries as well. Statement II is false: According to the first sentence of paragraph 2, acupuncture was not used to control pain during surgery until the 1970s. And the final sentence of the passage disputes statement III: The mechanism for its effectiveness "is still a mystery."

31. D

The author tells us what acupuncture involves, what ancient Chinese philosophy it's based on, and how it recently spread to the West. The passage is primarily about the historical and philosophical background of acupuncture, (D). (A) is not mentioned, and (B) focuses too narrowly on the first paragraph. (C) is too general.

32. A

Paragraph one states that acupuncture is based on the ancient Chinese belief that "human beings are miniature versions of the universe" and that the same forces control nature and health. Yin and yang are not Chinese gods, (B), they're principles. And contrary to (D), Western countries have not "totally changed" the Chinese philosophy of health and disease. They may have ignored it or failed to understand it, but they did not change it.

33. D

Yin and yang have "an opposite but complementary effect on each other. . . . When they are in balance, the body maintains a constant, normal [i.e., healthy] state." (A) names an example of how the two principles operate, not what they represent. (B) wrongly states that one principle is healthy and the other unhealthy, but it's a balance of both that maintains health, and an imbalance that results in sickness.

34. B

When yin and yang are in balance, the body is healthy, but when they're out of balance, disease occurs. These two forces work together, or complement, each other. The claim in (A) was made by ancient Chinese philosophy, and there is no actual proof in the passage for (C). The author does not mention any part of the body that isn't influenced by acupuncture, so (E) is incorrect.

O'KEEFFE PASSAGE

The final passage is about the American painter Georgia O'Keeffe—her life, her fame, and the subjects of her paintings. The opening sentence of paragraph 2 sums up the main point: O'Keeffe is "widely considered to have been a pioneering American modernist painter."

35. C

(C) is contradicted by paragraph 2, which states that O'Keeffe was "more independent" than most other early modern American artists, who were "strongly influenced by European art." The other choices can be found in the passage as influences on O'Keeffe.

36. A

O'Keeffe was the artist, and nature was her favorite subject. Do this one like an analogy. The relationship of artist to subject is repeated in (A): the model *is* the photographer's subject. Similarly, nature is O'Keeffe's subject.

37. D

Why are the paintings "semi-abstract" (line 24)? (B) and (C) are only half the answer: It was her treatment of these objects and scenes—the way she painted them—that made them "semi-abstract."

38. C

According to paragraph 2, O'Keeffe was unlike her contemporary American painters—"independent," not influenced by European art. Her work was "identifiably American," which makes (C) correct. (B) and (D) are factually true, but they're not the reason why she's considered a pioneer. And (E) is wrong since O'Keeffe's work was considered "semi-abstract," not very abstract.

39. B

The main point is summed up in the opening sentence of paragraph 2. The author never claims that O'Keeffe was the best painter of her generation, (A), or that she didn't develop a fully abstract style, (D), or even that her colors and shapes were too simple, (E). (C) is plausible (though we never learn that O'Keeffe painted only familiar subjects), but it's not the main point.

40. C

We're told that European art strongly influenced most American artists of O'Keeffe's time. Unlike European art, however, O'Keeffe's paintings offered a "simplified and idealized treatment of color, light, space, and natural forms." Since European art was different from O'Keeffe's art, we can infer that it did not portray natural shapes in a simple, idealistic way, making (C) correct. No other answer choice can be inferred.

SECTION 4: MATH

1. E

The perimeter of a polygon is the sum of the lengths of its sides. Label each of the sides with a value of 2 and add.

2. D

(C) can be immediately eliminated because it is an even integer and we are looking for an odd. Since D is an odd integer between 4 and 11, D must be one of the integers 5, 7, or 9. Since D is also between 7 and 18, D must be one of the integers 9, 11, 13, 15, or 17. The only choice which meets both requirements is (D), 9. (D) is correct. Notice that (E), 11, is not between 4 and 11.

3. B

Gary and Paul have a total of 16 + 18 = 34 operas put together. This number is equal to the number of operas that only Gary has plus the number of operas that only Paul has plus twice the number of operas that they both have in common. The number that they have in common was counted twice. It was counted once in the number of operas that Gary has and once in the number of operas that Paul has. Since the number of operas that they have in common should only be counted once, subtract the 4 they have in common from 34 and our result is 30 different operas.

4. D

Solve for G by multiplying both sides by the reciprocal of $\frac{1}{9}$: $G = 18 \times \frac{9}{1} = 162$. Substitute 162 for G into the expression $\frac{1}{3} G$ and you will get $\frac{1}{3} G = \frac{1}{3} \times 162 = 54$.

5. A

The boat can swing out and around as far as the line extends or the wind can push it anywhere within this semicircle. If you chose (B), you assumed the boat could float onto the dock. You want the choice indicating all the points of the semicircle shaded, which is (A).

6. D

Let x = the number of children. Hence, $4x$ = the number of adults. The total number of people is then $x + 4x = 5x$. The key to solving this is keeping in mind that x must be an integer. It is because of this that $5x$ must be a multiple of 5. Therefore the answer must be a multiple of 5. (D), 25, is correct.

7. E

Draw a figure! With a diagonal cut, triangles can be created. By cutting to decrease the length 28 of the rectangle by 8 with a cut parallel to the sides of length 20, a square can be created, and cutting anywhere parallel to any side of the original rectangle, a rectangle with new dimensions can be created.

8. D

We must note how many students were in the class each month. March = 40, April = 60, May = 80, and June = 80. Use the formula:

$$\text{Average} = \frac{\text{Sum of the terms}}{\text{Number of terms}}.$$ Here, the average is

$$\frac{40 + 60 + 80 + 80}{4} = \frac{260}{4} = 65.$$

9. A

The value of n is 4 and the value of r is 2. Simply substitute these values into the equation which defines the symbol: $4 \clubsuit 2 = (4 - 1) - \frac{4}{2} = 3 - \frac{4}{2} = 3 - 2 = 1$, (A).

10. A

Here, you are given $n = Q$ and $r = 2$. Use the equation given in the definition to set $Q \clubsuit 2$ equal to 4 and solve for Q: $(Q - 1) - \frac{Q}{2} = 4$. First, eliminate the denominator by multiplying both sides by 2: $2(Q - 1) - Q = 8$. Then, distribute the 2 through the parentheses: $2Q - 2 - Q = 8$. Third, isolate the Q: $Q = 10$, (A).

11. A

In statement I, $n = n$ and $r = 1$. So $n \clubsuit 1 = (n - 1) - \frac{n}{1} = n - 1 - n = -1$. So $n \clubsuit 1 = -1$ and statement I is true. Eliminate (B) and (D). Statement II: $n = 1$ and $r = n$. According to the definition, $1 \clubsuit n = (1 - 1) - \frac{1}{n} = -\frac{1}{n}$, and $-\frac{1}{n}$ is not equal to 0. Thus $1 \clubsuit n$ is not equal to 0, so eliminate (C) and (E). The answer must be (A). There is no need to go any further but for argument's sake, $n \clubsuit n = (n - 1) 2 \frac{n}{n} = n - 1 - 1 = n - 2$ and $r \clubsuit r = (r - 1) - \frac{r}{r} = r - 1 - 1 = r - 2$. So $n \clubsuit n = n - 2$ and $r \clubsuit r = r - 2$. Since nothing in the question indicates that n must equal r, n could very well not be equal to r and statement III does not have to be true.

12. C

Using our percent formula, Part = Percent × Whole. Here, tip = 15% of $20.95 = 15% \times \$20.95$. Round the $20.95 to $21.00 and evaluate: $\frac{15}{100} \times 21 = \frac{3}{20} \times 21 = \frac{63}{20} = 3 \frac{3}{20} = \$3.15$.

13. A

Break down the problem into steps. Juan finishes one-third of his homework in 2 hours, thus he has two-thirds still left to do. If it takes 2 hours to do one-third, it must take 4 hours to do two-thirds (twice as much). Finally, subtract 4 hours from 10:30 P.M. and we are left with 6:30 P.M.

14. E

Mrs. Brown ate 2 peaches plus each child ate 2 peaches. She has z children so 2 for each of z children and 2 for Mrs. Brown = $2z + 2$.

15. D

You'll recall the rule for geometry questions that ask about drawing figures in one fluid motion without lifting the pencil. In any given figure, if exactly zero or two points have an odd number of intersecting line segments and/or curves, it can be drawn without lifting the pencil or retracing. (A), (B), (C), and (E) are incorrect because they all have four points at which three line segments intersect. Four points is too many. (D) is the answer because it has two points that have three (an odd number) intersecting lines.

16. D

Round 0.59 to 0.6. Now, $0.6 = \dfrac{N}{5}$. Isolate the N by multiplying both sides by 5. Then $N = 3$ (Be careful in placing the decimal point).

17. B

The consecutive integers must be 19, 20, 21, 22, 23, 24, and 25. The average of an odd number of equally spaced numbers is always the middle one. Consecutive integers are an instance of equally spaced numbers. The answer is 22.

18. D

The percent increase can be found using this formula: $\dfrac{\text{new price} - \text{old price}}{\text{old price}} \times 100\%$. Here, the percent increase is $\dfrac{1.08 - 0.93}{0.93} \times 100\% = \dfrac{0.15}{0.93} \times 100\% = \dfrac{15}{93} \times 100\% = \dfrac{5}{31} \times 100\% \approx 16\%$.

19. B

To find Q, use the first division problem. $Q = 15 \times 21 = 315$. To find S, use the second division problem. Then $S = 21 \times 15 + 8$. We already know that $15 \times 21 = 315$, so add 8 to the value 315 of Q to get 323. Finally, $S - Q = 323 - 315 = 8$. Notice that this is also the remainder of the second division problem.

20. C

The area of the floor is found by multiplying 72×48. Dividing this result by the area of a single tile, which is 6×6, gives us the number of tiles needed. In the fraction $\dfrac{72 \times 48}{6 \times 6}$ cancel the 6's leaving $12 \times 8 = 96$.

21. C

Set up a ratio here. n pages is to 5 minutes as 20 pages is to how many minutes? Call x is the number of minutes it will take to type 20 pages. Then $\dfrac{n}{5} = \dfrac{20}{x}$. Cross-multiplying we get: $xn = 100$. Finally, isolate the x by dividing each side by n: $x = \dfrac{100}{n}$, choice (C).

22. C

Draw a figure. The length is 60 and the width is $\dfrac{1}{4}$ of 60 or $\dfrac{1}{4} \times 60 = 15$. The perimeter is simply the sum of the lengths of all the sides: $60 + 60 + 15 + 15 = 150$ meters.

23. B

Pick 100 when dealing with percent problems. If the dress was $100 the first month, the second month it costs 80% of 100 or $80, and the third month it costs 80% of 80, which is $64. After 3 months it costs 80% of $64, which is about $51. So, after 3 months, the cost of it is about 50% of the original price.

24. C

Picking numbers is your best option here. If $p = 4$ and $n = -2$, then the results are: (A), -2; (B), $-\frac{1}{2}$; (C), $\frac{1}{6}$; (D), $-\frac{1}{6}$. The greatest value is thus $\frac{1}{6}$, making (C) the correct choice. This question can also be solved by realizing that for any positive integer p and any negative integer n, (A), (B), and (D) will be negative, while (C) will be positive.

25. B

This is a challenging problem. Call the number of men in the school m and the number of women in the school w. The first sentence can be translated into $\frac{1}{9} m = 2\left(\frac{1}{3} w\right)$. We also know that $m + w = 84$. Solving the equation for w in terms of m gives us $w = \frac{3}{2} \times \frac{1}{9} m = \frac{3}{18} m = \frac{1}{6} m$. Substituting $\frac{1}{6} m$ for w in the equation $m + w = 84$ gives us $m + \frac{1}{6} m = 84$. Then, $\frac{7}{6} m = 84$. Multiplying both sides by $\frac{6}{7}$, which is the reciprocal of $\frac{7}{6}$, we find that $m = 84 \times \frac{6}{7} = 12 \times 6 = 72$. Hence, there are 72 men in the school, and $\frac{1}{9}$ of these 72 men, or 8 men, are vegetarians.

CHAPTER 17: SSAT PRACTICE TEST 2: UPPER-LEVEL

HOW TO TAKE THIS PRACTICE TEST

Before taking this practice test, find a quiet room where you can work uninterrupted for two and a half hours. Make sure you have a comfortable desk and several No. 2 pencils.

Use the answer sheet provided to record your answers. (You can cut it out or photocopy it.)

Once you start this practice test, don't stop until you've finished. Remember—you can review any questions within a section, but you may not go backward or forward a section.

You'll find an answer key and explanations following the test. Scoring information can be found in chapter 19.

Good luck.

SSAT Practice Test Two: Upper-Level Answer Sheet

Remove (or photocopy) this answer sheet and use it to complete the practice test.

Start with number 1 for each section. If a section has fewer questions than answer spaces, leave the extra spaces blank.

SECTION 1

1 Ⓐ Ⓑ Ⓒ Ⓓ Ⓔ   6 Ⓐ Ⓑ Ⓒ Ⓓ Ⓔ   11 Ⓐ Ⓑ Ⓒ Ⓓ Ⓔ   16 Ⓐ Ⓑ Ⓒ Ⓓ Ⓔ   21 Ⓐ Ⓑ Ⓒ Ⓓ Ⓔ
2 Ⓐ Ⓑ Ⓒ Ⓓ Ⓔ   7 Ⓐ Ⓑ Ⓒ Ⓓ Ⓔ   12 Ⓐ Ⓑ Ⓒ Ⓓ Ⓔ   17 Ⓐ Ⓑ Ⓒ Ⓓ Ⓔ   22 Ⓐ Ⓑ Ⓒ Ⓓ Ⓔ
3 Ⓐ Ⓑ Ⓒ Ⓓ Ⓔ   8 Ⓐ Ⓑ Ⓒ Ⓓ Ⓔ   13 Ⓐ Ⓑ Ⓒ Ⓓ Ⓔ   18 Ⓐ Ⓑ Ⓒ Ⓓ Ⓔ   23 Ⓐ Ⓑ Ⓒ Ⓓ Ⓔ
4 Ⓐ Ⓑ Ⓒ Ⓓ Ⓔ   9 Ⓐ Ⓑ Ⓒ Ⓓ Ⓔ   14 Ⓐ Ⓑ Ⓒ Ⓓ Ⓔ   19 Ⓐ Ⓑ Ⓒ Ⓓ Ⓔ   24 Ⓐ Ⓑ Ⓒ Ⓓ Ⓔ
5 Ⓐ Ⓑ Ⓒ Ⓓ Ⓔ   10 Ⓐ Ⓑ Ⓒ Ⓓ Ⓔ   15 Ⓐ Ⓑ Ⓒ Ⓓ Ⓔ   20 Ⓐ Ⓑ Ⓒ Ⓓ Ⓔ   25 Ⓐ Ⓑ Ⓒ Ⓓ Ⓔ

right in section 1

wrong in section 1

SECTION 2

1 Ⓐ Ⓑ Ⓒ Ⓓ Ⓔ   9 Ⓐ Ⓑ Ⓒ Ⓓ Ⓔ   17 Ⓐ Ⓑ Ⓒ Ⓓ Ⓔ   25 Ⓐ Ⓑ Ⓒ Ⓓ Ⓔ   33 Ⓐ Ⓑ Ⓒ Ⓓ Ⓔ
2 Ⓐ Ⓑ Ⓒ Ⓓ Ⓔ   10 Ⓐ Ⓑ Ⓒ Ⓓ Ⓔ   18 Ⓐ Ⓑ Ⓒ Ⓓ Ⓔ   26 Ⓐ Ⓑ Ⓒ Ⓓ Ⓔ   34 Ⓐ Ⓑ Ⓒ Ⓓ Ⓔ
3 Ⓐ Ⓑ Ⓒ Ⓓ Ⓔ   11 Ⓐ Ⓑ Ⓒ Ⓓ Ⓔ   19 Ⓐ Ⓑ Ⓒ Ⓓ Ⓔ   27 Ⓐ Ⓑ Ⓒ Ⓓ Ⓔ   35 Ⓐ Ⓑ Ⓒ Ⓓ Ⓔ
4 Ⓐ Ⓑ Ⓒ Ⓓ Ⓔ   12 Ⓐ Ⓑ Ⓒ Ⓓ Ⓔ   20 Ⓐ Ⓑ Ⓒ Ⓓ Ⓔ   28 Ⓐ Ⓑ Ⓒ Ⓓ Ⓔ   36 Ⓐ Ⓑ Ⓒ Ⓓ Ⓔ
5 Ⓐ Ⓑ Ⓒ Ⓓ Ⓔ   13 Ⓐ Ⓑ Ⓒ Ⓓ Ⓔ   21 Ⓐ Ⓑ Ⓒ Ⓓ Ⓔ   29 Ⓐ Ⓑ Ⓒ Ⓓ Ⓔ   37 Ⓐ Ⓑ Ⓒ Ⓓ Ⓔ
6 Ⓐ Ⓑ Ⓒ Ⓓ Ⓔ   14 Ⓐ Ⓑ Ⓒ Ⓓ Ⓔ   22 Ⓐ Ⓑ Ⓒ Ⓓ Ⓔ   30 Ⓐ Ⓑ Ⓒ Ⓓ Ⓔ   38 Ⓐ Ⓑ Ⓒ Ⓓ Ⓔ
7 Ⓐ Ⓑ Ⓒ Ⓓ Ⓔ   15 Ⓐ Ⓑ Ⓒ Ⓓ Ⓔ   23 Ⓐ Ⓑ Ⓒ Ⓓ Ⓔ   31 Ⓐ Ⓑ Ⓒ Ⓓ Ⓔ   39 Ⓐ Ⓑ Ⓒ Ⓓ Ⓔ
8 Ⓐ Ⓑ Ⓒ Ⓓ Ⓔ   16 Ⓐ Ⓑ Ⓒ Ⓓ Ⓔ   24 Ⓐ Ⓑ Ⓒ Ⓓ Ⓔ   32 Ⓐ Ⓑ Ⓒ Ⓓ Ⓔ   40 Ⓐ Ⓑ Ⓒ Ⓓ Ⓔ

right in section 2

wrong in section 2

SECTION 3

1 Ⓐ Ⓑ Ⓒ Ⓓ Ⓔ   6 Ⓐ Ⓑ Ⓒ Ⓓ Ⓔ   11 Ⓐ Ⓑ Ⓒ Ⓓ Ⓔ   16 Ⓐ Ⓑ Ⓒ Ⓓ Ⓔ   21 Ⓐ Ⓑ Ⓒ Ⓓ Ⓔ
2 Ⓐ Ⓑ Ⓒ Ⓓ Ⓔ   7 Ⓐ Ⓑ Ⓒ Ⓓ Ⓔ   12 Ⓐ Ⓑ Ⓒ Ⓓ Ⓔ   17 Ⓐ Ⓑ Ⓒ Ⓓ Ⓔ   22 Ⓐ Ⓑ Ⓒ Ⓓ Ⓔ
3 Ⓐ Ⓑ Ⓒ Ⓓ Ⓔ   8 Ⓐ Ⓑ Ⓒ Ⓓ Ⓔ   13 Ⓐ Ⓑ Ⓒ Ⓓ Ⓔ   18 Ⓐ Ⓑ Ⓒ Ⓓ Ⓔ   23 Ⓐ Ⓑ Ⓒ Ⓓ Ⓔ
4 Ⓐ Ⓑ Ⓒ Ⓓ Ⓔ   9 Ⓐ Ⓑ Ⓒ Ⓓ Ⓔ   14 Ⓐ Ⓑ Ⓒ Ⓓ Ⓔ   19 Ⓐ Ⓑ Ⓒ Ⓓ Ⓔ   24 Ⓐ Ⓑ Ⓒ Ⓓ Ⓔ
5 Ⓐ Ⓑ Ⓒ Ⓓ Ⓔ   10 Ⓐ Ⓑ Ⓒ Ⓓ Ⓔ   15 Ⓐ Ⓑ Ⓒ Ⓓ Ⓔ   20 Ⓐ Ⓑ Ⓒ Ⓓ Ⓔ   25 Ⓐ Ⓑ Ⓒ Ⓓ Ⓔ

right in section 3

wrong in section 3

SECTION 4

1 Ⓐ Ⓑ Ⓒ Ⓓ Ⓔ   13 Ⓐ Ⓑ Ⓒ Ⓓ Ⓔ   25 Ⓐ Ⓑ Ⓒ Ⓓ Ⓔ   37 Ⓐ Ⓑ Ⓒ Ⓓ Ⓔ   49 Ⓐ Ⓑ Ⓒ Ⓓ Ⓔ
2 Ⓐ Ⓑ Ⓒ Ⓓ Ⓔ   14 Ⓐ Ⓑ Ⓒ Ⓓ Ⓔ   26 Ⓐ Ⓑ Ⓒ Ⓓ Ⓔ   38 Ⓐ Ⓑ Ⓒ Ⓓ Ⓔ   50 Ⓐ Ⓑ Ⓒ Ⓓ Ⓔ
3 Ⓐ Ⓑ Ⓒ Ⓓ Ⓔ   15 Ⓐ Ⓑ Ⓒ Ⓓ Ⓔ   27 Ⓐ Ⓑ Ⓒ Ⓓ Ⓔ   39 Ⓐ Ⓑ Ⓒ Ⓓ Ⓔ   51 Ⓐ Ⓑ Ⓒ Ⓓ Ⓔ
4 Ⓐ Ⓑ Ⓒ Ⓓ Ⓔ   16 Ⓐ Ⓑ Ⓒ Ⓓ Ⓔ   28 Ⓐ Ⓑ Ⓒ Ⓓ Ⓔ   40 Ⓐ Ⓑ Ⓒ Ⓓ Ⓔ   52 Ⓐ Ⓑ Ⓒ Ⓓ Ⓔ
5 Ⓐ Ⓑ Ⓒ Ⓓ Ⓔ   17 Ⓐ Ⓑ Ⓒ Ⓓ Ⓔ   29 Ⓐ Ⓑ Ⓒ Ⓓ Ⓔ   41 Ⓐ Ⓑ Ⓒ Ⓓ Ⓔ   53 Ⓐ Ⓑ Ⓒ Ⓓ Ⓔ
6 Ⓐ Ⓑ Ⓒ Ⓓ Ⓔ   18 Ⓐ Ⓑ Ⓒ Ⓓ Ⓔ   30 Ⓐ Ⓑ Ⓒ Ⓓ Ⓔ   42 Ⓐ Ⓑ Ⓒ Ⓓ Ⓔ   54 Ⓐ Ⓑ Ⓒ Ⓓ Ⓔ
7 Ⓐ Ⓑ Ⓒ Ⓓ Ⓔ   19 Ⓐ Ⓑ Ⓒ Ⓓ Ⓔ   31 Ⓐ Ⓑ Ⓒ Ⓓ Ⓔ   43 Ⓐ Ⓑ Ⓒ Ⓓ Ⓔ   55 Ⓐ Ⓑ Ⓒ Ⓓ Ⓔ
8 Ⓐ Ⓑ Ⓒ Ⓓ Ⓔ   20 Ⓐ Ⓑ Ⓒ Ⓓ Ⓔ   32 Ⓐ Ⓑ Ⓒ Ⓓ Ⓔ   44 Ⓐ Ⓑ Ⓒ Ⓓ Ⓔ   56 Ⓐ Ⓑ Ⓒ Ⓓ Ⓔ
9 Ⓐ Ⓑ Ⓒ Ⓓ Ⓔ   21 Ⓐ Ⓑ Ⓒ Ⓓ Ⓔ   33 Ⓐ Ⓑ Ⓒ Ⓓ Ⓔ   45 Ⓐ Ⓑ Ⓒ Ⓓ Ⓔ   57 Ⓐ Ⓑ Ⓒ Ⓓ Ⓔ
10 Ⓐ Ⓑ Ⓒ Ⓓ Ⓔ   22 Ⓐ Ⓑ Ⓒ Ⓓ Ⓔ   34 Ⓐ Ⓑ Ⓒ Ⓓ Ⓔ   46 Ⓐ Ⓑ Ⓒ Ⓓ Ⓔ   58 Ⓐ Ⓑ Ⓒ Ⓓ Ⓔ
11 Ⓐ Ⓑ Ⓒ Ⓓ Ⓔ   23 Ⓐ Ⓑ Ⓒ Ⓓ Ⓔ   35 Ⓐ Ⓑ Ⓒ Ⓓ Ⓔ   47 Ⓐ Ⓑ Ⓒ Ⓓ Ⓔ   59 Ⓐ Ⓑ Ⓒ Ⓓ Ⓔ
12 Ⓐ Ⓑ Ⓒ Ⓓ Ⓔ   24 Ⓐ Ⓑ Ⓒ Ⓓ Ⓔ   36 Ⓐ Ⓑ Ⓒ Ⓓ Ⓔ   48 Ⓐ Ⓑ Ⓒ Ⓓ Ⓔ   60 Ⓐ Ⓑ Ⓒ Ⓓ Ⓔ

right in section 4

wrong in section 4

SECTION 1

Time—25 Minutes
25 Questions

In this section, there are five possible answers after each problem. Choose which one is best. You may use the blank space at the right of the page for scratch work.

Note: Figures provided with the problems are drawn with the greatest possible accuracy, UNLESS stated "Not Drawn to Scale."

1. The polygon in Figure 1 has a perimeter of 30. If each side of the polygon has the same length, what is the length of one side?

    (A) 3
    (B) 4
    (C) 5
    (D) 6
    (E) 7

USE THIS SPACE FOR FIGURING.

Figure 1

2. Mr. Stuart sold peppermint candy to 25 customers and caramel candy to 17 customers. If 4 of these customers bought both types of candy, how many bought only caramel candy?

    (A) 29
    (B) 25
    (C) 21
    (D) 17
    (E) 13

3. In a bag of 24 balloons, there is an equal number of balloons of each color. Which of the following CANNOT be the number of different colors in the bag?

    (A) 2
    (B) 3
    (C) 4
    (D) 5
    (E) 6

GO ON TO THE NEXT PAGE

4. Which of the following is a whole number less than 13 and also a whole number between 11 and 18?

   (A) 11
   (B) 12
   (C) 12.5
   (D) 13
   (E) 14

USE THIS SPACE FOR FIGURING.

5. According to the graph in Figure 2, Susan spent about how many hours watching movies?

   (A) 2
   (B) 3
   (C) 4
   (D) 6
   (E) 9

HOW SUSAN SPENT 12 HOURS
WATCHING TV

Figure 2

6. If $\frac{1}{2}R = 16$, then $\frac{3}{4}R =$

   (A) 24
   (B) 20
   (C) 16
   (D) 12
   (E) 8

7. Which of the following is closest to $\frac{1}{4}$ of 59?

   (A) 0.26×50
   (B) 0.41×50
   (C) 0.26×60
   (D) 0.41×60
   (E) 41×60

GO ON TO THE NEXT PAGE

8. According to the graph in Figure 3, the average sales of Company M from 1983 to 1987 was

   (A) $250,000
   (B) $260,000
   (C) $265,000
   (D) $270,000
   (E) $275,000

Questions 9–10 refer to the following definition.

For all real numbers u and v, $u \oslash v = u - \left(1 - \dfrac{1}{v}\right)$.

(Example: $3 \oslash 2 = 3 - \left(1 - \dfrac{1}{2}\right) = 3 - \dfrac{1}{2} = 2\dfrac{1}{2}$.)

9. Which of the following is equal to $5 \oslash 5$?

   (A) 0
   (B) 1
   (C) $4\dfrac{1}{5}$
   (D) $4\dfrac{4}{5}$
   (E) 25

10. If $a \oslash 3 = 4\dfrac{1}{3}$, then $a =$

   (A) $\dfrac{2}{3}$
   (B) 3
   (C) 4
   (D) $4\dfrac{2}{3}$
   (E) 5

USE THIS SPACE FOR FIGURING.

SALES OF COMPANY M: 1983–1987

Figure 3

GO ON TO THE NEXT PAGE

11. Twenty percent of 64 is equal to 5 percent of what number?

    (A) 16

    (B) 20

    (C) 64

    (D) 128

    (E) 256

USE THIS SPACE FOR FIGURING.

12. During the 4 fishing trips that Rich and Andy made, Rich caught a total of 35 fish. If Andy caught more fish than Rich, Andy must have caught an average of a least how many fish per trip?

    (A) $8\frac{3}{4}$

    (B) 9

    (C) 36

    (D) 140

    (E) 144

13. Jeff, Todd, and Lee were hired by their father to work on the yard, and each was paid at the same hourly rate. Jeff worked 4 hours, Todd worked 6 hours, and Lee worked 8 hours. If the 3 boys together earned $27, how much did Lee earn?

    (A) $8   (B) $12   (C) $15   (D) $16   (E) $27

14. Johnny picked apples from 9:00 A.M. to 11:30 A.M. and gathered 200 apples. He wants to pick a total of at least 600 apples before 7:15 P.M. If he plans to pick apples at the same rate, what is the latest time that he can start picking apples again?

    (A) 1:15 P.M.

    (B) 1:45 P.M.

    (C) 2:15 P.M.

    (D) 2:45 P.M.

    (E) 3:15 P.M.

GO ON TO THE NEXT PAGE

15. If 0.88 equals $8W$, what is the value of W?

    (A) 0.11
    (B) 0.9
    (C) 1.1
    (D) 9
    (E) 11

USE THIS SPACE FOR FIGURING.

16. In the triangle shown in Figure 4, what is the value of r ?

    (A) 50
    (B) 60
    (C) 70
    (D) 80
    (E) It cannot be determined from the information given.

Figure 4

17. A company's income increased from 9 thousand dollars in 1958 to 4.5 million dollars in 1988. Its income in 1988 was how many times its income in 1958?

    (A)   200
    (B)   500
    (C)   2,000
    (D)   5,000
    (E) 20,000

18. Which of the following can be expressed as $(5 \times R) + 2$, where R is a whole number?

    (A) 25
    (B) 33
    (C) 47
    (D) 56
    (E) 68

GO ON TO THE NEXT PAGE

19. Which of the following can be drawn without lifting the pencil or retracing?

USE THIS SPACE FOR FIGURING.

(A)

(B)

(C)

(D)

(E)

20. If the population of Country X increased by 10 percent each year over a 2-year period, what was the total percent increase in the population over the entire period?

   (A) 2%
   (B) 10%
   (C) 11%
   (D) 20%
   (E) 21%

21. If $z = y + 2$, what does $2z + 1$ equal?

   (A) $y + 3$
   (B) $2y + 3$
   (C) $2y + 5$
   (D) $2y + 6$
   (E) It cannot be determined from the information given.

GO ON TO THE NEXT PAGE

22. If x is greater than 0 but less than 1, and y is greater than x, which of the following is the LEAST?

   (A) $\dfrac{y}{x}$

   (B) $\dfrac{x}{y}$

   (C) xy

   (D) $\dfrac{1}{x-y}$

   (E) It cannot be determined from the information given.

USE THIS SPACE FOR FIGURING.

23. In a restaurant, there are x tables that can each seat 6 people and there are y tables that can each seat 5 people. What is the maximum number of people that may be seated?

   (A) $5x + 6y$

   (B) $6x + 5y$

   (C) $11x + 11y$

   (D) $11xy$

   (E) $30xy$

24. Mrs. Smith bought 3 square pieces of fabric. A side of the largest piece is 3 times as long as a side of the middle one, and a side of the middle one is 3 times as long as a side of the smallest one. The area of the largest piece is how many times the area of the smallest piece?

   (A) 112

   (B) 81

   (C) 27

   (D)   9

   (E)   3

GO ON TO THE NEXT PAGE

25. Mr. Dali's car uses $\frac{3}{4}$ gallons of gas each time he drives to work. If his gas tank holds exactly 9 gallons of gas, how many tanks of gas does he need to make 18 trips to work?

(A) $1\frac{1}{2}$

(B) $2\frac{1}{2}$

(C) 4

(D) 6

(E) 9

USE THIS SPACE FOR FIGURING.

IF YOU FINISH BEFORE TIME IS CALLED, YOU MAY CHECK YOUR WORK ON THIS SECTION ONLY. DO NOT TURN TO ANY OTHER SECTION IN THE TEST.

STOP

SECTION 2
Time—25 Minutes
40 Questions

Read each passage carefully and then answer the questions about it. For each question, decide on the basis of the passage which one of the choices best answers the question.

Scott Joplin composed approximately 60 works during his lifetime, including 41 piano pieces called "rags," many songs, and marches, and an *Line* opera entitled Treemonisha. His most significant
(5) creative contribution was to the development of ragtime, a type of instrumental music marked by its distinctive, choppy rhythm. Joplin's rhythmic diversity was very important to the development of ragtime as a genre, a unique musical form. In
(10) 1899, his "Maple Leaf Rag" became the most popular piano rag of the time and he was dubbed the "King of Ragtime." Despite all of those accomplishments, he was not considered a serious composer during his lifetime. It was not until 59
(15) years after his death that he was properly recognized: In 1976, he was awarded the Pulitzer Prize for music, at last receiving the praise he deserved.

1. The term "rag," as it is used in the passage refers to

    (A) a specific piece of operatic music.

    (B) a genre of dance music.

    (C) a piece of piano music known for its unique rhythm.

    (D) a kind of instrumental music played by marching bands.

    (E) a style of songs invented by Joplin.

2. This passage deals primarily with

    (A) the fact that Joplin was not taken seriously during his lifetime.

    (B) the history and development of ragtime music.

    (C) the diversity of styles in which Joplin composed.

    (D) how Joplin came to win the Pulitzer Prize.

    (E) Joplin's contributions to and accomplishments in the world of music.

3. According to the passage, Joplin died in

    (A) 1899.

    (B) 1917.

    (C) 1941.

    (D) 1959.

    (E) 1976.

4. When discussing Scott Joplin, the author's tone in this passage could best be described as

    (A) indifferent.

    (B) amused.

    (C) envious.

    (D) resentful.

    (E) appreciative.

GO ON TO THE NEXT PAGE

5. It can be inferred from the passage that a genre is

(A) a particular type of ragtime music.

(B) a distinct category or style.

(C) a term that Joplin coined when he created ragtime.

(D) a rhythmic style characteristic of Joplin's period.

(E) an early form of "rag".

John Podgers was broad, sturdy, short, and a very hard eater, as men of his figure often are. Being a hard sleeper likewise, he divided his time *Line* pretty equally between these two recreations, (5) always falling asleep when he had done eating, and always taking another turn at the feeding trough when he had done sleeping, by which means he grew more obese and more drowsy every day of his life. Indeed, it used to be currently reported that (10) when he strolled up and down the sunny side of the street before dinner (as he never failed to do in fair weather), he enjoyed his soundest nap; but many people held this to be a fiction, as he had several times been seen to look after fat oxen on (15) market days, and had even been heard, by persons of good credit and reputation, to chuckle at the sight, and say to himself with great glee, 'Live beef, live beef!'

It was upon this evidence that the wisest (20) people in Windsor (beginning with the local authorities, of course) held that John Podgers was a man of strong, sound sense, not what is called smart, perhaps, and might be of a rather lazy turn, but still a man of solid parts and one who meant (25) much more than he cared to show.

6. John Podgers is described as being all of the following EXCEPT

(A) intelligent.

(B) stocky.

(C) lazy.

(D) sensible.

(E) solid.

7. The author of the passage is primarily concerned with

(A) explaining why people think John Podgers is smarter than he lets on.

(B) questioning why John Podgers comments on the oxen in the marketplace.

(C) discussing John Podgers's reasons for eating so much.

(D) providing the details of John Podgers's daily stroll up the street.

(E) describing John Podgers's physical and mental qualities.

8. John Podgers spent the majority of his time doing which of the following pairs of things?

(A) Drinking and eating

(B) Strolling and resting

(C) Chuckling and walking

(D) Eating and sleeping

(E) Napping and thinking

9. The tone of the writer toward the subject is

(A) cautious.

(B) formal.

(C) respectful.

(D) angry.

(E) humorous.

Thousands of species of birds exist today, and nearly every species has its own special courtship procedures and "identification checks." *Line* Identification checks are important, because if (5) birds of different species mate, any offspring will usually be sterile or badly adapted to their surroundings.

GO ON TO THE NEXT PAGE ⟩

Plumage often plays a key role in both identification and courtship. In breeding season,
(10) male birds often acquire distinctive plumage which they use to attract females who will, in turn, only respond to males with the correct markings. In some species, the females are more brightly colored, and the courtship roles are
(15) reversed. Distinctive behavioral changes can also be important aspects of courtship and breeding activity. Aggressiveness between males, and sometimes between females, is quite common. Some birds, like whooping cranes and trumpeter
(20) swans, perform wonderfully elaborate courtship dances in which both sexes are enthusiastic participants.

Bird sounds are often a very central part of identification and courtship behavior between
(25) individuals in a given species. When a female migrates in the spring to her breeding region, she often encounters numerous birds of different species. By its singing, the male of a species both identifies itself and communicates to females of
(30) that species that it is in breeding condition. This information allows a female to predict a male's response to her approach. Later, after mating has taken place, the note patterns of a particular male's song enable a nesting female to continue to
(35) identify her own partner.

10. The author implies that a bird engages in identification and courtship procedures mainly in order to

(A) find a better nesting spot.

(B) find the most colorful partner it can.

(C) attract a mate of its own species.

(D) increase its control over its nesting partner.

(E) try to dominate the bird population of a given area.

11. According to the passage, a feature of the male song bird is its ability to

I. attract a female of its own species.

II. intimidate rival males.

III. communicate its identity to its mate.

(A) I only

(B) III only

(C) I and II only

(D) I and III only

(E) I, II, and III

12. The author uses the whooping crane as an example of a bird that

(A) seldom participates in courtship procedures.

(B) acquires a distinctive breeding plumage.

(C) behaves in an unusual and noteworthy way during courtship.

(D) reverses the normal male and female courtship roles.

(E) displays unusual aggressiveness while courting.

13. According to the passage, matings between birds of different species

(A) are quite common.

(B) produce more sturdy offspring.

(C) may help to establish a permanent new species.

(D) do not usually result in healthy offspring.

(E) have never happened.

GO ON TO THE NEXT PAGE

14. The passage is primarily about

   (A) causes of aggression between male birds.
   (B) several courtship and identification methods used by birds.
   (C) the breeding season of birds.
   (D) the role of bird sounds in courtship identification.
   (E) why birds migrate to particular breeding regions.

   More than 1,500 Native American languages have thus far been discovered by linguists. Edward Sapir, a pioneer in the field of Native American
Line linguistics, grouped these languages into six
 (5) "families" more than three-quarters of a century ago.
    Ever since that time, the classification of Native American languages has been a source of controversy. A small group of linguists has recently
(10) argued that all Native American languages fit into three linguistic families. These scholars believe that similarities and differences among words and sounds leave no doubt about the validity of their classification scheme. The vast majority of
(15) linguists, however, reject both the methods and conclusions of these scholars, arguing that linguistic science has not yet advanced far enough to be able to group Native American languages into a few families. According to these scholars,
(20) Native American languages have diverged to such an extent over the centuries that it may never be possible to group them in distinct language families.

15. This passage is primarily about

   (A) the classification of Native American languages.
   (B) the six families of Native American languages.
   (C) scholars' views about language.
   (D) the similarities and differences between words of Native American languages.
   (E) linguistic debates about how to group languages.

16. The scholars who believe that Native American languages can be classified into three families apparently believe that

   (A) these languages have diverged significantly over the last 75 years.
   (B) languages can be classified according to the degree of similarities and differences between words.
   (C) linguistic science has not advanced far enough to safely classify languages so narrowly.
   (D) languages are all related by their common origins.
   (E) distinct language families have their own peculiar grammatical rules.

17. The style of the passage is most like that found in a

   (A) personal letter written by a linguistics student.
   (B) textbook about linguistics.
   (C) novel about Native American tribes.
   (D) diary of a linguist.
   (E) biography of Edward Sapir.

GO ON TO THE NEXT PAGE

18. It can be inferred that the classification of Native American languages has been a source of controversy because

    (A) scholars do not agree on the method for classifying languages.

    (B) languages have split in several directions.

    (C) linguistics is a very new field.

    (D) there is not enough known about Native American vocabulary.

    (E) Native Americans dislike such classifications.

19. Which of the following questions is answered by the passage?

    (A) Did Edward Sapir study languages other than Native American languages?

    (B) How many languages are in a typical linguistic family?

    (C) How many Native American languages are yet to discovered?

    (D) In what ways have Native American languages changed over time?

    (E) Into how many families did Edward Sapir classify Native American languages?

Hope is the thing with feathers
That perches in the soul,
And sings the tune without the words
And never stops at all,
Line
(5) And sweetest in the gale is heard;
And sore must be the storm
That could abash[1] the little bird
That kept so many warm.

I've heard it in the chillest land,
(10) And on the strangest sea;
Yet, never, in extremity,
It asked a crumb of me.

[1]discourage
"Hope" by Emily Dickinson

20. In this poem, hope is compared to

    (A) a gale.

    (B) a sea.

    (C) a storm.

    (D) a bird.

    (E) a song.

21. What is the poet saying in the last stanza of the poem?

    (A) It is terrible to imagine a world without hope and we must therefore do everything possible to preserve our hopes.

    (B) The bird continues to sing through all conditions.

    (C) Hope can be found anywhere and never asks anything in return for its loyalty.

    (D) The bird is very hungry because it is constantly singing and never takes any time to eat.

    (E) The potential for hope is always present but it takes a great effort to make it a reality.

22. The lines "the little bird/That kept so many warm" in the second stanza refer to the fact that

    (A) the feathers of birds have traditionally provided protection against the cold.

    (B) hope has comforted a great many people over the years.

    (C) the bird provided protection before it was destroyed in a storm.

    (D) hope has often proven useless in the face of real problems.

    (E) hope is a good last resort when faced with a difficult situation.

GO ON TO THE NEXT PAGE ➡

23. The attitude of the speaker in this poem can best be described as

(A) angry.

(B) unconcerned.

(C) respectful.

(D) nervous.

(E) grateful.

Although recycling has taken place in various forms for some time, today we are being asked to regard recycling as not only an important, but even
Line a necessary measure.
(5)　Recycling, in its broadest sense, refers to the remaking of waste products and other used materials for practical purposes. For example, an old soda bottle can be returned, washed, and used as a bottle again, or it can be ground down and its
(10)　glass can be employed for another useful purpose. Since fixing up old things is often cheaper than making brand new ones, this saves money. More importantly, it saves resources and reduces the amount of waste produced.
(15)　Businesses have been performing large-scale recycling for some time, based primarily on the goal of saving money. However, the amount of residential waste, that is, the waste produced at home, has been steadily increasing, and the role of the individual in
(20)　the recycling campaign has been seriously underemphasized. Although it is true that we, as individuals, cannot reduce the overall amount of waste significantly or save large amounts of money and resources on our own, taken collectively, we can
(25)　have an important impact. Our increased efforts toward recycling can have a dramatic effect on the future availability of resources and the condition of the environment. It is our duty to ourselves and to our fellow human beings to pitch in and help protect
(30)　what remains of it.

24. According to the passage, which of the following is true?

   I. Recycling increases the amount of waste produced.

   II. Re-using waste products can be very economical.

   III. The amount of waste produced in the home has been continuously growing.

(A) II only

(B) I and II only

(C) I and III only

(D) II and III only

(E) I, II, and III

25. The author would most likely agree that

(A) recycling is a good idea for big businesses but, on an individual level, it makes very little difference.

(B) although businesses recycle to save money, individuals are motivated to recycle by a desire to serve the general good of society.

(C) recycling is extremely important and everyone has a responsibility to contribute to the overall effort to preserve our environment.

(D) although our natural resources are limited, we only live once and we shouldn't concentrate on conservation to such a degree that it interferes with our enjoyment of life.

(E) recycling is a very expensive process and should be left to the owners of big businesses.

GO ON TO THE NEXT PAGE

26. All of the following are examples of recycling EXCEPT

    (A) turning old newspapers into cardboard.

    (B) melting down scraps of metal and recasting them.

    (C) washing out empty soda bottles and using them as vases.

    (D) selling a piece of jewelry and using the money to buy a car.

    (E) crushing old cans and reusing the aluminum to make new ones.

27. The tone of this passage is

    (A) insistent.

    (B) relaxed.

    (C) formal.

    (D) amused.

    (E) disinterested.

28. Which of the following is the author most likely to discuss next?

    (A) The current problem of toxic waste disposal

    (B) The negative side to recycling and the many problems that can develop when it is done too much

    (C) Different ways that an old bottle can be either reused or remade into an entirely different object

    (D) Other important differences between the way businesses and residences are run

    (E) Examples of ways in which people can recycle their own waste and help out on an individual basis

29. What can be said about the author based on lines 15–17?

    (A) She is only interested in the economic aspects of recycling.

    (B) She believes that businesses are motivated to recycle primarily for monetary gain.

    (C) She knows little about the possible financial savings of recycling.

    (D) She is more concerned with the environmental benefits of recycling than the economic rewards.

    (E) She values recycling even though it results in the production of greater amounts of waste.

Most of us who live in relatively mild climates rarely view bad weather as more than an inconvenience, but in certain, less fortunate parts
Line of the world, a change in weather can have
 (5) disastrous consequences for an entire society. Weather fluctuations along the northwest coast of South America, for instance, can periodically have a dramatic effect on the area's fishing villages. Under normal circumstances, the cold, steadily
(10) flowing waters of the Humboldt Current bring nutrients up from the sea floor along the coast, providing a dependable food supply for fish and squid. For centuries, the fishing villages have depended on this rich ocean harvest for food and
(15) trade. Occasionally, however, global weather patterns cause the current to fail, setting off a deadly chain reaction. Without nutrients, the fish and squid die, depriving the villagers of their livelihood. This destructive weather phenomenon,
(20) called "El Niño" (The Christ Child) because it occurs at Christmastime, has sometimes forced entire villages to disband and move elsewhere merely to avoid starvation.

GO ON TO THE NEXT PAGE →

30. According to the passage, the Humboldt Current flows

(A) only at Christmastime.

(B) without fail.

(C) east to west.

(D) along the northwest coast of South America.

(E) through warm water.

31. This passage is mainly about

(A) how the economy of South American villages depends exclusively on fishing.

(B) the importance of fish and squid in the food chain.

(C) the advantages of living in a mild climate.

(D) the undependable nature of the Humboldt Current.

(E) how changes in weather patterns can have a dramatic effect on the way people live.

32. According to the passage, all of the following are true EXCEPT

(A) the actions of the Humboldt Current help provide nutrients for fish and squid.

(B) the Humboldt Current affects the survival of fishing on the northwest coast of South America.

(C) the warm waters of the Humboldt Current affect the climate of nearby land masses.

(D) the failure of the Humboldt Current can set off a deadly chain reaction.

(E) the Humboldt Current sometimes fails as a result of global weather patterns.

33. Which of the following would be the best title for this passage?

(A) An Example of Weather's Social Impact

(B) Fishing Villages of South America

(C) El Niño: A Christmas Occurrence

(D) Fish and Squid: A Rich Ocean Harvest

(E) The Impact of Fishing to Coastal Villages

34. The author's attitude toward the villagers along the northwest coast of South America can best be described as

(A) sympathetic.

(B) unconcerned.

(C) condescending.

(D) angry.

(E) emotional.

35. Which of the following is an example of a chain reaction?

(A) Forest fires kill off thousands of acres of land, destroying valuable resources.

(B) When temperatures start to fall, many birds fly south to spend winter in warm climates.

(C) Earthquakes cause extensive damage to property and often result in the loss of human life.

(D) Global warming causes glaciers to melt, resulting in rising water levels, which reduce the amount of habitable land.

(E) The moon revolves around the Earth and the Earth revolves around the sun.

GO ON TO THE NEXT PAGE

World War II left much of Western Europe deeply scarred in many ways. Economically, it was devastated. In early 1948, as the Cold War
Line developed between the United States and the
(5) Soviet Union and political tensions rose, U.S. policymakers decided that substantial financial assistance would be required to maintain a state of political stability. This conclusion led the Secretary of State, George C. Marshall, to
(10) announce a proposal: the European countries were advised to draw up a unified plan for reconstruction, to be funded by the United States.

This European Recovery Program, also known as the Marshall Plan, provided economic and
(15) technical assistance to 16 countries. Between 1948 and 1952, participating countries received a combined total of 12 billion dollars in U.S. aid. In the end, the program was seen as a great success; it revived the economies of Western Europe and set
(20) them on a course for future growth.

36. Which of the following would be the best title for this passage?

(A) The Aftermath of World War II
(B) The Marshall Plan: A Program for European Reconstruction
(C) The Economic Destruction of Europe
(D) George C. Marshall: The Man Behind the Plan
(E) Western European Recovery

37. The tone of the author toward the Marshall Plan is

(A) objective.
(B) excited.
(C) insistent.
(D) anxious.
(E) unfavorable.

38. All of the following are true about the Marshall Plan EXCEPT

(A) it provided economic assistance to 16 countries.
(B) it went into action in 1948.
(C) it supplied economic aid for a period spanning four years.
(D) it gave each of the participating countries 12 billion dollars.
(E) it was considered a great long-term success.

39. The passage suggests that the driving force behind the Marshall Plan was

(A) a formal request for aid by European leaders.
(B) fear of economic repercussions for the U.S. economy.
(C) George C. Marshall's desire to improve his political career and public image.
(D) a joint U.S.-Soviet agreement to assist the countries of Western Europe.
(E) the increase in tension between the United States and the Soviet Union.

40. Which of the following would the author be most likely to discuss next?

(A) Developments in the Cold War during and after the years of the Marshall Plan
(B) The events leading up to Western Europe's economic collapse
(C) The detailed effects of the Marshall Plan on specific countries
(D) Other successful economic recovery programs employed throughout history
(E) How George C. Marshall became the U.S. Secretary of State

IF YOU FINISH BEFORE TIME IS CALLED, YOU MAY CHECK YOUR WORK ON THIS SECTION ONLY. DO NOT TURN TO ANY OTHER SECTION IN THE TEST.   STOP

SECTION 3

Time—25 Minutes

25 Questions

In this section, there are five possible answers after each question. Choose which one is best. You may use the blank space at the right of the page for scratch work.

Note: Figures are drawn with the greatest possible accuracy, UNLESS stated "Not Drawn to Scale."

1. Justine bought a comic book at $5 above the cover price. A year later she sold the book for $9 less than she paid. At what price did Justine sell the book?

    (A) $14 below the cover price
    (B) $4 below the cover price
    (C) The cover price
    (D) $4 above the cover price
    (E) $14 above the cover price

USE THIS SPACE FOR FIGURING.

Questions 2–3 refer to the graph in Figure 1.

2. How many fewer boxes of cereal were sold in February than in March?

    (A) 2
    (B) 3
    (C) 20
    (D) 40
    (E) 60

CEREAL SALES AT STORE X

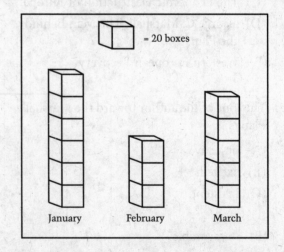

Figure 1

3. The number of boxes sold in January was how many times the number of boxes sold in February?

    (A) 2
    (B) $2\frac{1}{2}$
    (C) 3
    (D) 40
    (E) 60

GO ON TO THE NEXT PAGE

4. Team *A* has 4 times as many losses as it had ties in a season. If Team *A* won none of its games, which could be the total number of games it played that season?

   (A) 12
   (B) 15
   (C) 18
   (D) 21
   (E) 26

USE THIS SPACE FOR FIGURING.

5. Figure 2 contains rectangles and a triangle. How many different rectangles are there in Figure 2?

   (A) 5
   (B) 7
   (C) 9
   (D) 10
   (E) 12

Figure 2

6. Which of the following is NOT less than $\frac{1}{4}$?

   (A) $\frac{2}{9}$

   (B) $\frac{3}{14}$

   (C) $\frac{14}{64}$

   (D) $\frac{19}{70}$

   (E) $\frac{27}{125}$

7. In Figure 3, the sides of triangles *ABC* and *FGH*, and of squares *BCFE* and *CDGF*, are all equal in length. Which of the following is the longest path from *A* to *H* ?

   (A) $A - B - C - F - H$

   (B) $A - B - E - F - H$

   (C) $A - C - D - G - H$

   (D) $A - B - E - G - H$

   (E) $A - C - F - G - H$

8. If $5\frac{1}{3} \times (14 - x) = 0$, then what does *x* equal?

   (A) 0

   (B) 1

   (C) $5\frac{1}{3}$

   (D) 14

   (E) It cannot be determined from the information given.

9. Which of the following is closest to 1.18?

   (A) 12

   (B) 2.2

   (C) 1.9

   (D) 1.1

   (E) 1

10. If *X* is greater than 15, then $\frac{1}{3}$ of *X* must always be

    (A) less than 5

    (B) equal to 5

    (C) greater than 5

    (D) equal to 45

    (E) less than 45

USE THIS SPACE FOR FIGURING.

Figure 3

GO ON TO THE NEXT PAGE

11. Of the following, 35 percent of $26.95 is closest to

   (A) $7.00
   (B) $9.45
   (C) $10.50
   (D) $11.15
   (E) $12.25

12. If a factory can make 600 nails every 3 minutes, how long would it take to make 27,000 nails?

   (A) 45 minutes
   (B) 1 hour
   (C) 1 hour, 45 minutes
   (D) 2 hours, 15 minutes
   (E) 3 hours, 15 minutes

13. Sally has x dollars and receives $100 for her birthday. She then buys a bicycle that costs $125. How many dollars does Sally have remaining?

   (A) $x + 125$
   (B) $x + 100$
   (C) $x + 25$
   (D) $x - 25$
   (E) $x - 100$

14. If $\dfrac{A+B}{3} = 4$ and A is greater than 1, which of the following could NOT be the value of B?

   (A) −3
   (B) 0
   (C) 1
   (D) 2
   (E) 12

USE THIS SPACE FOR FIGURING.

GO ON TO THE NEXT PAGE

15. The average of five numbers is 10. If two of the five numbers are removed, the average of the remaining three numbers is 9. What is the sum of the two numbers that were removed?

    (A) 17
    (B) 18
    (C) 21
    (D) 22
    (E) 23

USE THIS SPACE FOR FIGURING.

16. The bottom of the shopping bag shown in Figure 4 is placed flat on a table. Except for the handles, this shopping bag is constructed with rectangular pieces of paper. Which of the following diagrams best represents all the points where the shopping bag touches the table?

    (A)   (B)   (C)

    (D)   (E)

Figure 4

17. The number of students in a certain school is expected to increase from 1,086 students in 1990 to 1,448 students in 1991. What is the expected increase to the nearest percent?

    (A) 20%
    (B) 33%
    (C) 37%
    (D) 40%
    (E) 45%

GO ON TO THE NEXT PAGE

18. In Figure 5, the distance between *W* and *Y* is
    three times the distance between *W* and *X*,
    and the distance between *X* and *Z* is twice the
    distance between *X* and *Y*. If the distance from
    W to *X* is 2, how far apart are *W* and *Z*?

    (A) 10
    (B) 12
    (C) 14
    (D) 16
    (E) 18

19. A fence surrounds a rectangular field whose
    length is 3 times its width. If 240 meters of the
    fence is used to surround the field, what is the
    width of the field?

    (A) 30 m
    (B) 40 m
    (C) 60 m
    (D) 80 m
    (E) 90 m

20. Ms. Kirschner receives $50 for every $900 she
    collects from stock sales. How much does she
    receive if she collects $18,000 from stock sales?

    (A) $100
    (B) $180
    (C) $1,000
    (D) $1,200
    (E) $1,800

USE THIS SPACE FOR FIGURING.

Figure 5

GO ON TO THE NEXT PAGE

21. What is the greatest number of rectangles 4 centimeters wide and 6 centimeters long that can be cut from a square piece of paper with a side of 24 centimeters?

    (A)   2
    (B) 10
    (C) 24
    (D 36
    (E) 48

22. R is the sum of consecutive integers S and T. If S and T are negative, which of the following is always true?

    (A) $R = -4$
    (B) $R = -1$
    (C) R is less than either S or T.
    (D) R is greater than either S or T.
    (E) $R + S + T$ is positive.

23. Initially, Greg had a total of 60 records and cassettes in his music collection. He then sold $\frac{1}{8}$ of his cassettes and $\frac{1}{2}$ of his records. If the number of records he sold is twice the number of cassettes he sold, how many records did he sell?

    (A)   4
    (B)   5
    (C)   8
    (D) 10
    (E) 20

USE THIS SPACE FOR FIGURING.

GO ON TO THE NEXT PAGE

24. Mary saved exactly 60 percent of the total
allowance she received in the last two weeks,
and spent the rest. If she received $20 for
allowance each week and spent $12 of her first
week's allowance, which of the following must
be true?

   I. She saved a total of $24.

   II. She spent $6 of her second week's
      allowance.

   III. She saved 80 percent of her second
       week's allowance.

(A) None

(B) I only

(C) II only

(D) I and III only

(E) I, II, and III

25. Paul and Bill each received a raise of
20 percent. If Paul now earns $4.50 per hour
while Bill earns $5.40 per hour, Bill earned
how much more per hour than Paul before
their raises?

(A) $0.70

(B) $0.73

(C) $0.75

(D) $0.80

(E) $0.90

USE THIS SPACE FOR FIGURING.

IF YOU FINISH BEFORE TIME IS CALLED, YOU MAY CHECK YOUR WORK ON
THIS SECTION ONLY. DO NOT TURN TO ANY OTHER SECTION IN THE TEST.

SECTION 4
Time—25 Minutes
60 Questions

This section consists of two different types of questions. There are directions and a sample question for each type.

Each of the following questions consists of one word followed by five words or phrases. You are to select the one word or phrase whose meaning is closest to the word in capital letters.

1. HARSH:

   (A) cold
   (B) angry
   (C) poor
   (D) useless
   (E) severe

2. INDICATE:

   (A) meet with
   (B) look at
   (C) help with
   (D) point out
   (E) search for

3. BLEAK:

   (A) unknown
   (B) quiet
   (C) cheerless
   (D) trembling
   (E) timid

4. SECURE:

   (A) unseen
   (B) aware
   (C) secret
   (D) safe
   (E) knotty

5. ALIEN:

   (A) strange
   (B) futile
   (C) valuable
   (D) brutal
   (E) unclear

6. CHRONIC:

   (A) persistent
   (B) difficult
   (C) doubtful
   (D) legal
   (E) elaborate

7. QUENCH:

   (A) complete
   (B) compare
   (C) demean
   (D) satisfy
   (E) withdraw

8. SEVERE:

   (A) frozen
   (B) extreme
   (C) long
   (D) limited
   (E) essential

GO ON TO THE NEXT PAGE

9. RANSACK:

    (A) search thoroughly

    (B) act quickly

    (C) cover completely

    (D) make secure

    (E) denounce publicly

10. SUMMIT:

    (A) plateau

    (B) landscape

    (C) slope

    (D) island

    (E) peak

11. TUMULT:

    (A) annoyance

    (B) commotion

    (C) insignificance

    (D) disagreement

    (E) blockage

12. RETARD:

    (A) turn around

    (B) push apart

    (C) slow down

    (D) change position

    (E) see through

13. ANTIDOTE:

    (A) fantasy

    (B) remedy

    (C) substitute

    (D) award

    (E) decoration

14. SOLITARY:

    (A) mindful

    (B) careless

    (C) friendly

    (D) alone

    (E) troubled

15. CAMOUFLAGE:

    (A) obstacle

    (B) range

    (C) emergency

    (D) disguise

    (E) amount

16. EXPEL:

    (A) finish off

    (B) teach

    (C) question

    (D) scold

    (E) cast out

17. LUNGE:

    (A) pursue

    (B) turn

    (C) thrust

    (D) restore

    (E) startle

18. BREVITY:

    (A) ambition

    (B) consistency

    (C) conflict

    (D) imagination

    (E) shortness

GO ON TO THE NEXT PAGE

19. MARVEL:

   (A) discard
   (B) usurp
   (C) confuse
   (D) point
   (E) wonder

20. CANDOR:

   (A) majesty
   (B) daring
   (C) honesty
   (D) perception
   (E) fatigue

21. CONVENE:

   (A) clarify
   (B) serve
   (C) assemble
   (D) elect
   (E) dignify

22. CATASTROPHE:

   (A) illusion
   (B) disaster
   (C) indication
   (D) warning
   (E) estimate

23. GREGARIOUS:

   (A) sloppy
   (B) sociable
   (C) happy
   (D) intelligent
   (E) talented

24. DEXTERITY:

   (A) secrecy
   (B) equality
   (C) reserve
   (D) nimbleness
   (E) determination

25. IMMINENT:

   (A) intense
   (B) impressive
   (C) proper
   (D) observable
   (E) forthcoming

26. ANIMOSITY:

   (A) doubt
   (B) hatred
   (C) sadness
   (D) illness
   (E) guilt

27. AMEND:

   (A) create
   (B) address
   (C) observe
   (D) exclude
   (E) improve

28. DESPONDENT:

   (A) depressed
   (B) unintended
   (C) artificial
   (D) literary
   (E) unconcerned

GO ON TO THE NEXT PAGE

29. UNFLINCHING:

   (A) uncommitted
   (B) distinct
   (C) uncompromising
   (D) transitory
   (E) invalid

30. REPUDIATE:

   (A) renounce
   (B) impede
   (C) provoke
   (D) divert
   (E) submit

**The following questions ask you to find
relationships between words. For each
question, select the choice that best completes
the meaning of the sentence.**

31. Sun is to solar as

   (A) earth is to terrestrial
   (B) pond is to marine
   (C) ground is to subterranean
   (D) tower is to architectural
   (E) planet is to lunar

32. Botany is to plants as meteorology is to

   (A) weather
   (B) flora
   (C) health
   (D) language
   (E) style

33. Hammer is to nail as

   (A) axe is to wood
   (B) lathe is to molding
   (C) chisel is to marble
   (D) nut is to bolt
   (E) screwdriver is to screw

34. Bone is to mammal as girder is to

   (A) skyscraper
   (B) steel
   (C) rivet
   (D) crane
   (E) concrete

35. Human is to primate as

   (A) kangaroo is to vegetarian
   (B) snake is to reptile
   (C) disease is to bacterium
   (D) bird is to amphibian
   (E) dog is to pet

36. Tremor is to earthquake as

   (A) eye is to hurricane
   (B) desert is to sandstorm
   (C) faucet is to deluge
   (D) wind is to tornado
   (E) flood is to river

GO ON TO THE NEXT PAGE

37. Amusing is to uproarious as

  (A) silly is to serious
  (B) dead is to immortal
  (C) interesting is to mesmerizing
  (D) humorous is to dull
  (E) worthless is to valuable

38. Fickle is to steadfastness as tempestuous is to

  (A) worthlessness
  (B) openness
  (C) inspiration
  (D) peacefulness
  (E) ire

39. School is to fish as

  (A) fin is to shark
  (B) library is to student
  (C) flock is to bird
  (D) leg is to frog
  (E) college is to mascot

40. Cartographer is to map as chef is to

  (A) flower
  (B) silverware
  (C) table
  (D) meal
  (E) ingredient

41. Throne is to monarch as

  (A) miter is to pope
  (B) bench is to judge
  (C) lobby is to doorman
  (D) armchair is to general
  (E) ship is to captain

42. Canal is to river as

  (A) boat is to driftwood
  (B) puddle is to lake
  (C) hammer is to mallet
  (D) mine is to cavern
  (E) telephone is to computer

43. Milk is to sour as bread is to

  (A) bent
  (B) stale
  (C) folded
  (D) baked
  (E) hot

44. Ore is to mine as

  (A) apple is to peel
  (B) water is to purify
  (C) batter is to stir
  (D) grain is to plow
  (E) oil is to drill

45. Weight is to scale as

  (A) distance is to speedometer
  (B) number is to slide rule
  (C) length is to thermometer
  (D) reading is to gauge
  (E) altitude is to altimeter

46. Porcupine is to quill as

  (A) bat is to wing
  (B) horse is to tail
  (C) skunk is to odor
  (D) oyster is to pearl
  (E) tiger is to stripe

GO ON TO THE NEXT PAGE

47. Jar is to contain as pillar is to

 (A) stand
 (B) ascend
 (C) prepare
 (D) support
 (E) swing

48. Irrigate is to dry as

 (A) soften is to uneven
 (B) smooth is to coarse
 (C) purify is to distasteful
 (D) depend is to supportive
 (E) ferment is to salty

49. Electricity is to wire as

 (A) sound is to radio
 (B) water is to aqueduct
 (C) music is to instrument
 (D) light is to bulb
 (E) river is to bank

50. Contempt is to sneer as

 (A) shame is to shrug
 (B) anger is to laugh
 (C) enjoyment is to groan
 (D) agreement is to grimace
 (E) displeasure is to frown

51. Building is to foundation as plant is to

 (A) pane
 (B) grotto
 (C) primer
 (D) floor
 (E) root

52. Nose is to olfactory as ear is to

 (A) beautiful
 (B) edible
 (C) auditory
 (D) raspy
 (E) allergic

53. Irk is to soothing as support is to

 (A) conciliating
 (B) elevating
 (C) undermining
 (D) irritating
 (E) vilifying

54. Illegible is to read as

 (A) invisible is to see
 (B) illegal is to act
 (C) broken is to fix
 (D) irreparable is to break
 (E) intense is to strain

55. Tact is to diplomat as

 (A) parsimony is to philanthropist
 (B) agility is to gymnast
 (C) vulnerability is to victim
 (D) training is to physician
 (E) bias is to judge

GO ON TO THE NEXT PAGE

56. Ravenous is to hunger as

    (A) pliable is to obstinacy
    (B) agitated is to placidity
    (C) concerned is to apathy
    (D) smart is to tenacity
    (E) furious is to indignation

57. Amplify is to sound as bolster is to

    (A) smell
    (B) courage
    (C) insomnia
    (D) light
    (E) silence

58. Auditorium is to lecture as

    (A) theater is to concert
    (B) attic is to storage
    (C) temple is to religion
    (D) cafeteria is to food
    (E) target is to arrow

59. Philanthropic is to benevolence as

    (A) smooth is to surface
    (B) ostentatious is to reserve
    (C) miserly is to stinginess
    (D) devout is to malice
    (E) realistic is to plan

60. Spurious is to authenticity as

    (A) lavish is to expense
    (B) abject is to subjectivity
    (C) affluent is to character
    (D) laughable is to seriousness
    (E) totalitarian is to completeness

IF YOU FINISH BEFORE TIME IS CALLED, YOU MAY CHECK YOUR WORK ON
THIS SECTION ONLY. DO NOT TURN TO ANY OTHER SECTION IN THE TEST.   STOP

SECTION 5
Time—25 Minutes

Write an essay on the following prompt on the paper provided. Your essay should NOT exceed two pages and must be written in ink. Erasing is not allowed.

Prompt: <u>Tougher restrictions should be imposed on buying handguns.</u>

Do you agree or disagree with this statement? Use examples from history, literature, or your own personal experience to support your point of view.

_____

_____

_____

_____

_____

_____

_____

_____

_____

_____

_____

_____

_____

_____

_____

_____

GO ON TO THE NEXT PAGE

_____

_____

_____

_____

_____

_____

_____

_____

_____

_____

_____

_____

_____

_____

_____

_____

_____

_____

_____

IF YOU FINISH BEFORE TIME IS CALLED, YOU MAY CHECK YOUR WORK ON
THIS SECTION ONLY. DO NOT TURN TO ANY OTHER SECTION IN THE TEST.

ANSWERS AND EXPLANATIONS

SECTION 1: MATH

1. D

With a perimeter of 30 and 5 sides of equal length, the length of one side is $\frac{30}{5}$, or 6.

2. E

There were a total of 17 customers who bought caramel candy. Subtract from these the 4 who bought both and you are left with the 13 who bought only caramel.

3. D

Only factors of 24 (numbers that can be divided evenly into 24) can be the number of different colors in the bag. Since 5 is not a factor of 24, (D), 5, is the correct choice.

4. B

Since the whole number is less than 13 and also between 11 and 18, it must be between 11 and 13. We can immediately eliminate (C) because we need a whole number. (D) and (E) are out, too, because 13 and 14 are not "less than 13." And (A) is wrong because 11 is not "between 11 and 18." Therefore, the number must be 12, choice (B).

5. A

Movies take up 60 degrees of 360 degrees, one-sixth of the pie chart. So Susan spent about one-sixth of 12, or 2 hours, watching movies.

6. A

To solve for R, multiply both sides of the equation by 2, hence $R = 32$. Plug 32 for R into the expression $\frac{3}{4}R$, and you find that $\frac{3}{4}R = \frac{3}{4} \times 32 = 24$.

7. C

The fraction $\frac{1}{4}$ has a decimal value of 0.25; thus (B), (D), and (E) can be eliminated. Fifty nine rounded to the nearest ten is 60; indeed, 59 is much closer to 60 than to 50, so (C) is correct.

8. B

There is no calculation necessary on this problem. Three of the five points lie on the horizontal $260,000 line and the only other two points are the identical distance above and below the line, thus $260,000 is the correct answer.

9. C

This problem calls for substitution. $u = 5$ and $v = 5$. Plugging these values in yields $5 \oslash 5 = 5 - (1 - \frac{1}{5}) = 5 - \frac{4}{5} = 4\frac{1}{5}$; (C) is correct.

10. E

This problem calls for substitution. $u = a$, $v = 3$, and $a \oslash 3 = 4\frac{1}{3}$. Using the definition for the left side of this equation, which is $a \oslash 3$, we have $a - (1 - \frac{1}{3}) = 4\frac{1}{3}$; then $a - \frac{2}{3} = 4\frac{1}{3}$ and $a = 5$.

11. E

Call the unknown number x and translate the information in the question into math. Remember that "of" means "times." Twenty percent of 64 means $\frac{20}{100}(64)$ and 5% of x means $\frac{5}{100}x$. Then 20% of 64 is equal to 5% of x means that $\frac{20}{100}(64) = \frac{5}{100}x$. Reducing $\frac{5}{100}$ and $\frac{5}{100}$ yields $\frac{1}{5}(64) = \frac{1}{20}x$. Isolate the x by multiplying both sides by 20. Then $x = \frac{1}{5}(64) \times 20 = \frac{64}{5} \times 20 = 64 \times 4 = 256$.

12. B

The minimum number of fish Andy could have caught was 36 or 1 more than Rich caught. Use the average formula, Average = $\dfrac{\text{Sum of the terms}}{\text{Number of terms}}$. Sum of the terms = 36 and number of terms (or number of fishing trips) = 4. Hence, Andy must have caught an average of at least $\dfrac{36}{4}$ = 9 fish per trip.

13. B

We need to set up an equation here. We know all the boys earned the same amount per hour, so: 4 × Rate + 6 × Rate + 8 × Rate = 27. Thus, 18 × Rate = 27 and the Rate = $\dfrac{27}{18}$ = $1.50 per hour. Lee worked 8 hours so Lee earned 8 × $1.50 = $12.

14. C

Johnny has already picked 200 apples in 2.5 hours. He must pick an additional 600 – 200 = 400 apples. Call the number of additional hours that Johnny must spend picking apples x. To find x, set up a ratio and solve for x: $\dfrac{200 \text{ apples}}{2.5 \text{ hours}} = \dfrac{400 \text{ apples}}{x \text{ hours}}$. Since the numerator of the fraction on the right is equal to twice the numerator of the fraction on the left, the denominator of the fraction on the right must also be equal to twice the denominator of the fraction on the left. So $x = 2 \times 2.5 = 5$. Since Johnny must work an additional 5 hours, the latest time that he can begin picking apples again is 5 hours earlier than 7:15 PM. So 2:15 p.m. is the latest that Johnny can start picking apples again.

15. A

Set up an equation: $8W = 0.88$. Isolate the W by dividing each side by 8. $W = \dfrac{0.88}{8} = 0.11$.

16. D

Figure 4 indicates that the legs of two sides of the triangle are equal and thus the triangle is isosceles. Angles which are opposite equal sides must be equal. Thus, each of the two base angles is 50 degrees, and we know that the sum of the three interior angles of any triangle is 180 degrees, so $r = 180 - 50 - 50 = 80$.

17. B

To determine how many times the income of 1958 was in 1988, divide the 1988 income by the 1958 income. Then the number we are seeking is $\dfrac{4,500,000}{9,000}$. Dividing the numerator and the denominator by 1,000, we have that this number is $\dfrac{4,500}{9} = 500$.

18. C

The correct answer choice, when 2 is subtracted from it, must be a multiple of 5. A number is a multiple of 5 only if its one's digit is a 5 or a 0. Looking at the choices, 25 – 2 = 23 is not a multiple of 5, so eliminate choice (A). 33 – 2 = 31 is not a multiple of 5, so eliminate (B). 47 – 2 = 45, which is a multiple of 5. So (C) is correct.

19. C

Recall Kaplan's strategy: A figure can be drawn without lifting the pencil or retracing if there are exactly 0 or 2 points where an odd number of lines intersect. (C) has no points where an odd number of lines intersect, hence this is the correct answer.

20. E

Pick 100 as the initial population of Country X. The increase for the first year was $\dfrac{10}{100}$ of 100 = 10 and the total at the end of the first year was 100 + 10 or 110 people. The increase for the second year was $\dfrac{10}{100}$ of 110 = 11 and the total at the end of the second year was 110 + 11 or 121 people. The population increased from 100 to 121 over the two-year period. The increase in the population was 121 − 100 = 21. Hence the percent increase in the population over the entire two-year period was $\frac{21}{100}$ or 21%.

21. C

The value of z is given to us in terms of y; we need to multiply this value by 2 and add 1. Hence, $2z + 1 = 2(y + 2) + 1 = 2y + 4 + 1 = 2y + 5$, (C).

22. D

Picking numbers for x and y is a foolproof method for solving this problem. Pick a positive fraction for x which is less than 1, such as $\frac{1}{2}$. Then pick a positive value for y which is greater than x, which in this case means that the y that we pick must also be greater than $\frac{1}{2}$. Remember, the question says that y is greater than x and the numbers you pick must always be consistent with the question stem. So let's pick 1 for y. So we're letting x be $\frac{1}{2}$ and y be 1. With these values, (A) is 2, (B) and (C) are both $\frac{1}{2}$, and (D) is −2. Further examining (D), we see that the denominator, $x − y$, has a larger positive number y subtracted from a smaller positive number x. So $x − y$ will always be negative. Therefore $\frac{1}{x − y}$ will also always be negative.

23. B

If 6 people can sit at each of x tables and 5 people can sit at each of y tables, then the maximum number of people that may be seated is $6x + 5y$.

24. B

Draw 3 squares: big, bigger, and biggest. Let the side of the middle fabric piece be 9. The side of the largest fabric piece must be three times this, or 27. Likewise, the side of the smallest square piece must be 3. The area of the largest piece is 27 × 27 = 729 and the area of the smallest piece is 9. Now determine the number of times that 9 goes into 729: $\frac{729}{9} = 81$.

25. A

Begin by determining how many gallons of gas it takes to make the 18 trips: $\frac{3}{4} \times 18 = \frac{27}{2} = 13.5$ gallons. If there are 9 gallons in a tank, Mr. Dali will need $\frac{13.5}{9} = 1.5$ tanks of gas.

SECTION 2: READING COMPREHENSION

SCOTT JOPLIN PASSAGE

First up is a brief history passage about Scott Joplin, a composer best known for his ragtime music. Don't try to absorb all the details even in a brief passage like this. Just get a feel for the big idea, which is that Joplin was instrumental in developing the ragtime genre, but wasn't recognized as a serious composer until almost 60 years after his death.

1. C

Line 2 notes that Joplin composed 41 piano pieces known as "rags," the only time the word is used in the passage. (C), then, must be correct. (E) is tempting, but the genre or style of songs Joplin invented is described as "ragtime," not "rag." (A)'s "operatic" is wrong; Joplin's Treemonisha was his only opera. (B) and (D) fail because ragtime is never described as "dance" music, or as played by marching bands.

2. E

Only (E) has the proper scope here. (A) and
(B) focus too narrowly on details. It was Joplin's
"rhythmic diversity," not his stylistic diversity (C),
that distinguished his composing. The passage
doesn't say how Joplin finally won the Pulitzer (D).

3. B

An easy detail question, unless the math threw you.
The passage states that Joplin received the Pulitzer in
1976, "59 years after his death." Subtract 59 from 76
and you get 17, so Joplin died in 1917, choice (B).

4. E

The author discusses Joplin's "significant creative
contribution" to music, his great popularity, and
how he "at last" received "the praise he deserved."
Thus, (E)'s "appreciative" best sums up the author's
tone toward Joplin.

5. B

The passage states that Joplin was instrumental in
developing ragtime "as a genre, a unique musical
form." Therefore, (B) is the correct inference: a
genre is a distinct category or style. While ragtime
is an example of a musical genre, a genre is not an
example of a particular type of ragtime (A). There's
no evidence that Joplin coined the term "genre" (C).

JOHN PODGERS PASSAGE

Next up is a fiction passage describing a man named
John Podgers, "hard eater" and "hard sleeper," a man
who "grew more obese and more drowsy every day
of his life." Now the author never actually says,
"I'm making fun of this man," but hopefully, you
sensed a humorous tone throughout the passage.
This dry, "deadpan" humor comes out of the
discrepancy between Podgers and the style in which

he's described. They don't match. Podgers is lazy
and a compulsive eater, but he's described in a style
more befitting a hero, someone other people watch,
admire and talk about.

6. A

Podgers is never described as intelligent (A). The
author describes Podgers as "broad, sturdy, and
short," in other words, stocky (B). The people of
Windsor describe him as "of a rather lazy turn" (C),
of "good strong sense" (D), and "of solid parts (E),
but "not what is called smart."

7. E

A quick comparison of the verbs in the answer
choices hints strongly at (E), since the passage is
composed of one descriptive sentence after another.
(A) refers to the opinion of Podgers held by the
"wisest people in Windsor," but the author doesn't
explain why they hold this opinion. Similarly,
Podgers's comments on the oxen (B) and his reasons
for eating so much (C) are not explained; they're just
reported. And his daily stroll (D) is just one detail in
the descriptive portrait of Podgers, so (E) is in fact
correct.

8. D

As the second sentence of the passage states, Podgers
spends all his time either eating or sleeping (D).
(A) leaves out Podgers's sleeping, (B) leaves out his
eating. (C) names things Podgers is described as
doing only at one point in the passage, and (E)'s
"thinking" is something Podgers rarely does.

9. E

The writer depicts a man who is always either
eating or sleeping, yet who is well thought of by the
"smartest" people in his town. The writer's tone,

then, is humorous. (B) and (C) may tempt, but their very similarity should make you suspicious of picking either one. Both fail to catch on that the author is making fun of Podgers while describing him in a superficially formal and respectful style.

BIRD COURTSHIP PASSAGE

Next up is a science passage, about the courtship procedures and "identification checks" used by birds during courtship and mating. Paragraph 1 introduces the topic; paragraph 2 details the roles of plumage and aggressive behavior, and paragraph 3 the role of sounds, in the birds' courting and mating rituals.

10. C

This Inference question is answered in the opening paragraph. The author states that the bird's identification and courtship procedures are important "because if birds of different species mate, any offspring" will be sterile and have a low chance for survival. Thus, the procedures are important because they help a bird find a mate of its own species. (B) focuses too narrowly on a detail from paragraph 2.

11. D

The answer lies in paragraph 3, which states that a male's singing tells females of its species that "it is in breeding condition," I, and, after mating, enables the nesting female "to continue to identify" her partner, III. The passage does not mention that male birds use sound to intimidate male rivals, II, so I and III only are correct.

12. C

This Detail question focuses on the last sentence of paragraph 2. There we learn that whooping cranes

"perform wonderfully elaborate courtship dances." So the whooping crane's an example of a bird that behaves in an unusual, noteworthy way during courtship, and (C) is correct. (B), (D) and (E) incorrectly mention other details from paragraph 2—plumage, reversed roles, and aggressiveness.

13. D

The answer here is taken from the same sentence—the last of paragraph 1—that answered question 10. If birds of different species mate, "any offspring will usually be sterile or badly adapted to their surroundings." This point is restated in (D). (B) is the opposite of the correct choice. The frequency of interspecies mating (A) is not mentioned in the passage, but it must happen occasionally, contrary to (E), or the author wouldn't warn against its dangers. The idea of a new species evolving (C) is not discussed.

14. B

This time the big idea question comes at the end of the set. The passage is about the various courtship behaviors and "identification checks" used by birds, which makes (B) correct. (A) and (E) raise issues not debated in the passage. (C) and (D) focus too narrowly on details.

NATIVE AMERICAN PASSAGE

Next up is a brief passage about the 1,500 Native American languages that have been discovered by linguists. The big idea here is simple: a pioneering linguist originally divided these 1,500 languages into six main groups; a recent group of scholars thinks they can all be divided into three broader groups, but other scholars disagree with this new theory.

15. A

(A) is the most specific and accurate, and it's correct here. (B) leaves out the recent debate over the revised classification of Native American languages into three groups. (C) and (E) are too broad; they could be talking about any group of languages, not just Native American languages. And (D) focuses too narrowly on a detail from paragraph 2.

16. B

According to paragraph 2, scholars believe Native American languages can be classified into only three families because of "similarities and differences among words and sounds." (B) can be inferred from this statement. (A) distorts a detail from paragraph 1. (C) is the argument of those who think Native American languages can't be classified into three families. (D) is too broad, and (E) is beyond the scope of the passage.

17. B

Where would you be likely to come upon this passage? In a discussion of Native American languages, or a linguistics textbook (B). (A), (C), and (D) are wrong because there's nothing either personal or fictional in the text; it's just a series of factual statements. And while Sapir (E) pioneered the field of Native American linguistics, the passage doesn't contain any significant biographical information about his life.

18. A

Why is classifying Native American languages controversial? Those who group them into three families have "no doubt about the validity" of their theory. But "the vast majority of linguists" argue that "linguistic science has not yet advanced far enough" to group 1500 languages into only three families.

So the controversy exists because scholars do not yet agree on how to classify languages, and (A) is correct. (B) is a point argued by linguists who think Native American languages might never be properly grouped into families, but it's not the source of the controversy. We don't know when the field of linguistics was founded, but even though it hasn't "advanced far enough" it is not a "very new" field, as (C) suggests. There's no evidence for (D) or (E).

19. E

Paragraph 1 states that Sapir classified Native American languages into six families. None of the other questions is answered in the passage.

POETRY PASSAGE

Next up is a famous poem by Emily Dickinson. The first stanza creates a metaphor of hope as a bird that lives inside us and never stops singing. The second stanza says that the bird of hope sings even in bad weather, i.e., bad times. And in the final stanza, the poet claims that, while she has heard the bird of hope singing in distant places, "it never asked a crumb of me."

20. D

Hope is "the thing with feathers" in stanza 1, and "the little bird" in stanza 2, so (D) is correct. (A), (B), and (C) are trials and dangers that the bird/hope faces; (E) is what the bird sings.

21. C

Paraphrase the final stanza: "I've heard the bird of hope in far-off places, and it never asked me for anything." This points to (C) as correct. (A) is wrong because the poem says nothing about a world without hope, or preserving hope at all costs. (B) summarizes the second stanza, not the third.

(D) takes the poem literally to the point of absurdity; the "crumb" line doesn't mean that the bird is always hungry, but rather that it gives its song of hope freely. And (E) fails because, according to the poet, hope is always present; no great effort is required to make it so.

22. B

Remember you're dealing with metaphor. This poem isn't about a bird; it's comparing hope to a bird that never stops singing. The statement that it "kept so many warm" means that hope has given comfort to a lot of people, and (B) is correct. (A) and (C) take the poem literally. (D) is pessimistic where the poet is optimistic about hope, and (E) implies that hope *only* works in the worst of situations. But the poet is saying that hope is helpful even in the worst of situations.

23. E

The poet likens hope to a bird that, thankfully, is always there to help people, never asking anything in return. Her tone is one of gratitude, making choice (E) correct. (C) is the closest wrong choice, but "respectful" is too formal, too distancing. Hope in this poem isn't a great person or awesome display of nature, it's a little bird "that perches in the soul."

RECYCLING PASSAGE

The next passage is about recycling, the remaking of waste products and materials for practical purposes. In paragraph 1, we learn that recycling is now considered a necessity, that it saves money and resources and reduces waste. In paragraph 2, the author focuses on residential recycling—what we as private citizens can do to reduce waste.

24. D

Statement I is false: recycling "reduces the amount of waste produced" (lines 14–15). This eliminates (B), (C), and (E). Since statement II is included in both of the remaining answer choices, it must be true, and it is: we're told twice that recycling can save money. Statement III, then, is the crucial one. And it's true: lines 19–20 state that "the amount of...waste produced at home has been steadily increasing." So only Statements II and III are true, and choice (D) is correct.

25. C

(A) is easily eliminated: the author thinks the individual's role in recycling "has been seriously underemphasized." The first half of (B) is correct: businesses do recycle to save money. But the second half is wrong: the author doesn't think individuals are motivated to recycle by a sense of the greater good; but the author does think that we should be so motivated. This point is restated in correct choice (C). As for (D) and E, (D) says we shouldn't recycle, which the author would certainly disagree with, and (E) claims that recycling is only the responsibility of businesses, which goes against the thrust of paragraph 2.

26. D

You're looking for the choice that is not an example of recycling, which the author defines at lines 5–7 as "the remaking of waste products and other used materials for practical purposes." Using this definition, (A), (B), and (E) are easily checked off as examples of recycling. (C) involves a second use for empty soda bottles, as does the author's example in lines 8–11. This leaves (D): selling jewelry to buy a car is not recycling, because the jewelry is not a waste product that's being remade.

27. A

The author argues that recycling is "important...even necessary," that "it is our duty to ourselves and to our fellow human beings." These and similar signals throughout the passage reveal the author's tone as insistent, (A). By the same token, (B), (D), and (E) are easy to eliminate. (C) may be tempting since the author tells us that the future of humanity is at stake, but (A) remains the best choice, because more than being formal, the author is trying to motivate us, to get us to do something (recycle).

28. E

Paragraph 2 argued that individuals can and must learn to recycle their waste products. You can predict, then, that the author will go on to suggest one or more ways in which individuals can pitch in to help the recycling effort, a point restated in (E). There's no evidence to suggest (A) or (B). (C) wrongly suggests the author will return to a detail from paragraph (D). And (D) doesn't even mention recycling.

29. B

In lines 15–17, the author states that businesses recycle "based primarily on the goal of saving money." So you can infer that the author believes that businesses recycle primarily for financial gain, (B). (A) is wrong because the economics of recycling are of greatest interest to businesses, not to the author. Nor can it be inferred from the passage that the author's knowledge of the financial aspects of recycling (C) is limited. And while (D) is probably true, it can't be inferred from lines 15–17.

EL NIÑO PASSAGE

The passage begins with a statement that, although bad weather is usually only an "inconvenience" for us, it can have "disastrous consequences" for communities in other parts of the world. The remainder of the passage describes an example of this disastrous bad weather: El Niño, a change in the Humboldt current (an ocean current, not an air current) that disrupts marine life and can thereby threaten villagers on the northwest coast of South America with starvation.

30. D

The Humboldt Current flows off the northwest coast of South America, making (D) correct. Each of the other choices contradicts the passage. El Niño occurs only at Christmastime (A), not the Humboldt Current, which otherwise flows all year long. The Humboldt Current does fail (B) when El Niño occurs. The passage does not state the directional flow of the Humboldt Current (C), but does state that it is a cold-water current, not a hot-water current (E).

31. E

The bulk of the passage concerns what happens when the Humboldt Current fails, which makes (D) very tempting, but the Big Idea of the passage is really stated in the first sentence: changes in weather patterns can dramatically affect the way people live, making (E) correct here. Remember, the Humboldt Current–El Niño information is there only to back up this claim by the author. (A), (B), and (C) focus on details, and should have been easier to eliminate.

32. C

Here you're looking for the one choice that isn't true. Only (C) is not confirmed in the passage. As we noted in question 30, (E), the Humboldt Current carries cold water, not warm; the passage also never states that the current affects "the climate of nearby land masses."

33. A

If you got question 31 correct, you probably answered this one too. This passage is not about El Niño; the El Niño is discussed in order to prove the author's larger point: that bad weather can harm communities. This means that (A), not (C), is the correct answer.

34. A

We're told that bad weather can have a "dramatic effect" on these villages, "depriving" them "of their livelihood." The author's attitude toward the villagers, then, is—what? Not condescending (C), angry (D), or emotional (E). And though the author doesn't express undue alarm, you wouldn't say she was simply unconcerned about the villagers, as (B) has it. No, the author's attitude is best described as sympathetic, (A). The villagers occasionally have this awful problem, and the author expresses concern about it.

35. D

The "chain reaction" described in the passage is as follows: the current fails, stopping the flow of nutrients to the fish and squid, which die, thereby harming the villagers. A chain reaction then, is not a pair but a series of causally-linked occurrences. (A), (B), and (C), concern only a pair—not a chain—of occurrences. The best example of a chain reaction in the choices is therefore (D), where global warming leads to melted glaciers, which leads to higher water levels and then less available land for people. (E) gives two phenomena which occur at the same time.

MARSHALL PLAN PASSAGE

The final passage is a history passage about the Marshall Plan, an American scheme to help rebuild Europe after World War II. Paragraph 1 sets the scene, explaining that the United States was worried

that Europe's economic devastation needed to be cured in order to keep it from falling under the domination of the Soviet Union. Paragraph 2 explains that in 1948, U.S. Secretary of State George Marshall instituted the Marshall Plan, which distributed 12 billion dollars among 16 different European countries over the next four years.

36. B

The answer will probably mention the Marshall Plan and how it helped Europe; (B) fits this bill nicely. (A) and (E) are way too broad. (C) describes what happened during World War II that made the Marshall Plan so necessary, but says nothing about the Plan itself. (D) suggests that the passage is about Marshall himself, when the author actually tells you nothing more than Marshall's name and job— Secretary of State.

37. A

The author's tone is not noticeably positive (B) or negative (E). It betrays no personal feelings such as insistence (C) or anxiety (D). Instead, it's objective.

38. D

This is a relatively easy detail question, for careful readers. Paragraph 2 states that the Marshall Plan doled out "a combined total of $12 billion" to the 16 "participating countries." So each country did not get $12 billion. All of the other statements are substantiated in the passage.

39. E

What was the driving force behind the Marshall Plan? Early in paragraph 1, we learn that post–World War II Western Europe was economically devastated, and that when tensions between the United States and the Soviet Union escalated, U.S. policymakers felt that "substantial financial assistance" was needed in Western Europe "to maintain a state of political stability." This points to (E). None of the other choices draws a correct inference from the passage.

40. C

The first paragraph describes the post-war economic and political problems that the Marshall Plan was intended to solve, and paragraph 2 describes, in general terms, how much money was distributed and how well the plan worked. You can infer, then, that the author will go on to talk about specifics—how the Plan's money was put to work in some or all of the 16 participating countries. (A) wrongly sees the Cold War, not the Marshall Plan, as the focus of the passage. (B) goes back in time, to events before the Marshall Plan was ever dreamed up. Other economic recovery plans are never mentioned, and (E) is also unwarranted.

SECTION 3: MATH

1. B

Begin with $5 + cover price – $9 and simplify it. This can be simplified to cover price – $4, which means $4 below the cover price. (B) is correct.

2. D

Note here that each cube = 20 boxes. February has two cubes less than March, hence 2(20) = 40 boxes less.

3. A

In January, 6 cubes were sold and in February, 3 cubes were sold. Thus, in January, the number of boxes sold was $\frac{6}{3}$ = 2 times the number of boxes sold in February. It is not necessary to perform

the calculation using the fact that 20 boxes are represented by each cube.

4. B

Let x = the number of ties for Team A; keep in mind that x is an integer here. Thus, Team A had $4x$ losses. Adding the losses and ties (there were no wins), the number of games the team played was $x + 4x = 5x$. Thus, the correct answer choice must be a multiple of 5 (because x is an integer). Only (B), 15, is a multiple of 5.

5. E

In order to make the discussion simpler, the five rectangles which are in the figure to begin with have been labeled.

Systematically count the different rectangles in the figure. There are the 5 rectangles in the figure to begin with, which we will call basic rectangles. Next, let's count the number of rectangles that are made up of 2 basic rectangles. Rectangles made up of 2 basic rectangles can be formed from basic rectangles A and B, C and D, D and E, A and C, and B and D. There are 5 rectangles made up of 2 basic rectangles. Next, let's count the number of rectangles that can be made up of 3 basic rectangles. There is just one such rectangle. This is the rectangle which is made up of the 3 basic rectangles at the bottom, rectangles C, D, and E. Next, let's count the number of rectangles which can be made up of 4 basic rectangles. There is just one such rectangle. This is the rectangle which is made up of basic rectangles A, B, C, and D. There are no other rectangles which can be made up of basic rectangles. There is a total of $5 + 5 + 1 + 1 = 12$ different rectangles in the figure.

6. D

We are looking for the fraction that is NOT less than $\frac{1}{4}$, that is, a fraction that is greater than or equal to $\frac{1}{4}$. (D) is correct because $\frac{1}{4} = \frac{19}{19 \times 4} = \frac{19}{76}$ is less than $\frac{19}{70}$ because $\frac{19}{70}$ has a smaller denominator. Looking at the other choices, since $\frac{2}{8} = \frac{1}{4}$, $\frac{2}{9}$ must be less than $\frac{1}{4}$ (since 9 is a greater denominator). Since $\frac{3}{12} = \frac{1}{4}$, $\frac{3}{14}$ must be less than $\frac{1}{4}$ (due to the greater denominator 14). Reducing $\frac{14}{64}$, we get $\frac{7}{32}$ and since $\frac{8}{32} = \frac{1}{4}$, $\frac{14}{64} = \frac{7}{32}$ is less than $\frac{1}{4}$. Since $\frac{1}{4} = \frac{27}{27 \times 4} = \frac{27}{108}$, then $\frac{27}{125}$ is less than $\frac{27}{108} = \frac{1}{4}$.

7. D

Begin by labeling each side 1. Using the answer choices, count the lengths of 1 in the path: (A) = 4, (B) = 4, (C) = 4, (D) = 5, and (E) = 4. (D) is the longest path.

8. D

No long calculation is needed here. In order for a product of numbers to equal 0, at least one of the numbers must equal zero. Since $5\frac{1}{3}$ is not 0, the other factor, $14 - x$, must equal 0. So $14 - x = 0$, and $x = 14$.

9. D

Since 1.18 has 2 places after the decimal point, write each answer choice with 2 places after the decimal point. (A) and (B) are more than 1.00 away from

1.18. (C), 1.90, is more than 0.7 away from 1.18, (D), 1.10, is 0.08 away from 1.18, and (E), 1.00, is 0.18 away from 1.18.

10. C

Write out the given inequality: $X > 15$. Next multiply both sides by $\frac{1}{3}$ (or divide both sides by 3). We now have $\frac{1}{3}X > \frac{15}{3}$ and $\frac{1}{3}X > 5$, (C).

11. B

Round $26.95 to 27.00. Then we have $\frac{35}{100} \times 27 = ?$. Canceling yields $\frac{7}{20} \times 27 = \frac{189}{20} = 9.45$.

12. D

Let T be the number of minutes. Set up a ratio: $\frac{600}{3} = \frac{27,000}{T}$. Reduce $\frac{600}{3}$ to $\frac{200}{1}$. Then $\frac{200}{1} = \frac{27,000}{T}$. Next cross multiply: $200T = 27,000$. Divide both sides by 100: $2T = 270$, and thus $T = 135$. Put this into the time format of hours and minutes by dividing 135 minutes by 60 minutes per hour and we have $2\frac{1}{4}$ hours, which is 2 hours and 15 minutes.

13. D

Translate what is stated in the question step by step. To begin with, Sally has x dollars. After she receives 100 dollars she has $x + 100$ dollars. She spends 125 dollars so she has $(x + 100) - 125$ dollars left. Now simplify $(x + 100) - 125$. $(x + 100) - 125 = x + 100 - 125 = x - 25$. Sally has $x - 25$ dollars left, so (D) is correct.

14. E

Begin by multiplying both sides by 3 to eliminate the denominator. Then $A + B = 12$. If A is greater than 1, then B must be less than 11, thus (E), 12, could not be the value of B.

15. E

Use the average formula, which is Average = $\dfrac{\text{Sum of the terms}}{\text{Number of terms}}$. Call X the sum of all 5 numbers. Then $\dfrac{X}{5} = 10$, so $X = 50$. Call Y the sum of the 3 remaining numbers. Then $\dfrac{Y}{3} = 9$, so $Y = 27$.

Subtracting from the sum of all 5 numbers the sum of the three numbers that remain leaves the sum of the 2 numbers that were removed. So the sum of the 2 numbers that were removed is $X - Y = 50 - 27 = 23$.

16. B

The bottom surface of the bag is a rectangle and all points are inside the rectangle so choice (A) can be eliminated. (B) is correct.

17. B

The formula for percent increase is Percent Increase = $\dfrac{\text{New Value} - \text{Old Value}}{\text{Old Value}} \times 100\%$.

Here, $\dfrac{1,448 - 1,086}{1,086} \times 100\% = \dfrac{362}{1,086}. \times 100\% = \dfrac{1}{3} \times 100\% = 33\dfrac{1}{3}\%$, so (B) is the best choice.

18. A

Let the length of WX be represented by a. Then the length of WY is $3a$. The length of XY must be $3a - a = 2a$. Then, the length of XZ must be $2 \times 2a = 4a$. So $WZ = WX + XZ = a + 4a = 5a = 5(2) = 10$.

19. A

Draw a rectangle. Label its width w and its length $3w$. The perimeter is 240, thus $3w + w + 3w + w = 240$, so $8w = 240$ and $w = 30$.

20. C

The phrase "for every" indicates a ratio is needed. Call the amount she receives from the $18,000 collection x. Here set up $\dfrac{50}{900} = \dfrac{x}{18,000}$. After cancellation on the left we have $\dfrac{1}{18} = \dfrac{x}{18,000}$. Cross-multiply and get $18x = 18,000$. Solve for x by dividing each side by 18 and $x = 1,000$.

21. C

We need to find out how many 4×6 rectangles fit into a square with a side of 24. Use our area formula $A = L \times W$: $\dfrac{24 \times 24}{4 \times 6} = 24$.

22. C

Pick numbers. Let $S = -2$ and $T = -3$. Thus we have $R = -5$. Taking this value for R through our choices, only (C) fits.

23. D

Call the number of records Greg has r and the number of cassettes he has c. Our first equation is: $r + c = 60$. The second equation is $\dfrac{1}{2}r = 2(\dfrac{1}{8}c)$. So $\dfrac{1}{2}r = \dfrac{1}{4}c$ and $c = 4 \times \dfrac{1}{2}r = 2r$. Now, substitute $2r$ for c in the first equation, $r + c = 60$. Then $r + 2r = 60$, $3r = 60$, and $r = \dfrac{60}{3} = 20$. The problem asks how many records he sold, which is $\dfrac{1}{2}(20) = 10$.

24. D

Mary received $20 each week for 2 weeks and saved 60% of this or $\dfrac{60}{100}(\$40) = \$24$. Since she saved only $8 the first week, she must have saved $16 the second week. Looking at the roman numeral statements, I is true so eliminate (A) and (C). Looking at statement II, $20 − $16 = $4 was spent during the second week, not $6, so it is not true. Eliminate (E). Finally in III, the percent of the second week's allowance that she saved was $\frac{16}{20} \times 100\% = \frac{4}{5} \times 100\% = 80\%$, so statement III is true. (D) is correct.

25. C

First work with Paul: original wage + 20% of his original wage = $4.50. Convert this into the equation: $x + 0.20x = 4.50$, then $1.2x = 4.50$ and $x = \$3.75$. Set up a similar equation for Bill: $y + 0.20y = 5.40$ and $1.2y = 5.40$, so $y = \$4.50$. Hence, $4.50 - $3.75 = $0.75.

SECTION 4: VERBAL

SYNONYMS

1. E

Harsh means rough or overly demanding—in other words, severe, (E). A harsh penalty, for example. One can be angry, (B), without being harsh; these words are not synonyms.

2. D

Indicate means to show, state, or point out.

3. C

Bleak means desolate and barren, or cheerless, (C). "We camped out in a bleak wilderness."

4. D

Secure means free from danger, or safe.

5. A

Alien means foreign, or strange.

6. A

Chronic means frequently occurring, habitual, or persistent, (A), as in a "chronic cough."

7. D

To quench a thirst means to slake or satisfy it, (D).

8. B

Severe, as we saw in question 1, means harsh, overly demanding, or extreme, (B). Severe cold leaves you frozen, (A), but severe and frozen are not synonyms. Don't just think associatively; look for the word that's closest in meaning to the stem word.

9. A

When thieves ransack an apartment, they turn it upside down looking for things to steal. In other words, to ransack is to search thoroughly, (A).

10. E

The summit is the top of something, as in the summit of a mountain peak, which makes (E) correct.

11. B

A tumult is a loud noise, an uproar or commotion, (B).

12. C

To retard means to delay the progress of, to hold back or slow down, (C).

13. B

An antidote is a cure or remedy (B), such as an antidote for poison.

14. D

Solitary is the state of being secluded, or alone, (D).

15. D

To conceal means to hide, or disguise, (D). The closest wrong choice is E, which means to overthrow, or corrupt.

16. E

To expel means to drive out, to reject, or to cast out, (E).

17. C

To lunge is to make a sudden forward stride or leap. A lunge—especially with a weapon—is also called a thrust, (C). To pursue, (A), means to chase, to follow with the intent of overtaking. Pursuit may begin with a lunge, but the two verbs are not synonyms. In similar fashion, a lunge may involve a turn, (B), or startle someone, (E), but these words are not synonyms of lunge, either.

18. E

Brevity is the quality of being brief, which means of short duration—so shortness, (E), is correct.

19. E

To marvel is to feel surprise, amazed curiosity, or wonder, (E).

20. C

Candor is truthfulness, or honesty, (C). To be daring, (B), is to be bold, but not necessarily honest.

21. C

To convene is to meet, or to assemble, (C). The closest wrong choices, (B) and (D), are actions associated with meetings that are convened, but they're not synonyms.

22. B

A catastrophe is a great misfortune, a terrible occurrence, or a disaster, (B).

23. B

Gregarious means talkative, outgoing, or sociable, (B).

24. D

Dexterity is mental or physical skill and quickness. The best synonym here is nimbleness, (D).

25. E

To say that something is imminent means that it's about to happen, that it is forthcoming, (E).

26. B

Animosity is hostility, ill-will, resentment. The best synonym here is hatred, (B).

27. E

To amend means to change, alter, or improve, (E).

28. A

Someone who feels despondent is very sad, or depressed, (A).

29. C

Unflinching means not flinching or shrinking from; it's the quality of being steadfast. The best synonym here is uncompromising, (C). (A) and (D) are near-antonyms for unflinching.

30. A

To repudiate means to cast off, disown, or refuse to have anything to do with. The choice with the closest meaning to repudiate is renounce, (A). To impede, (B), is to slow or interfere with someone's progress.

ANALOGIES

31. A

Anything having to do with the sun is solar. In the same way, anything having to do with the earth is terrestrial, (A). Marine refers to a sea or ocean, not to a pond. Subterranean refers to what is below the ground, not to the ground itself. You might suspect (E), but lunar refers to anything having to do with the moon, not planets.

32. A

Botany is the study of plants. Similarly, meteorology is the study of weather, (A). Flora is the generic word for plant life or vegetation.

33. E

You use a hammer to *put in* a nail. In the same way, you use a screwdriver to *put in* a screw, (E). You use an axe to chop wood, a lathe to smooth or shape molding; a chisel to chip marble, and a nut to secure a bolt.

34. A

A bone is part of the structural system that supports a mammal. A girder is part of the structural system that supports a skyscraper, (A). The other choices are also part of the structural system that supports a skyscraper, not the skyscraper itself.

35. B

A primate is an order of mammals that includes monkeys, apes, and humans. So a human is one species of the primate order, just as a snake is one species of the order of reptiles. Vegetarians are not an order in the same way as primates and reptiles. A disease is not necessarily bacterial in nature. Birds are mammals, not amphibians; amphibians are a class in the animal kingdom that includes frogs and toads.

36. D

A tremor is a quivering motion of the earth. A powerful tremor may be an earthquake. In the same way, wind is a motion of the air, and a powerful wind may be a tornado, (D). The analogy isn't exact here, but it's better than the other choices. An eye is the calm center of a hurricane (A); a powerful desert is not a sandstorm (B). A faucet is a manmade object through which water flows; a deluge (C) is a great flood. And a powerful flood (E) is not a river.

37. C

Something tremendously amusing is uproarious; similarly, something tremendously interesting is hypnotic, fascinating, or mesmerizing, (C).

38. D

Being fickle, or inconstant, is the opposite of steadfastness. In the same way, being tempestuous, or stormy, is the opposite of peacefulness, (D). Ire, (E), means anger.

39. C

A group of fish is called a school, just as a group of birds is called a flock.

40. D

A cartographer is a designer of maps, just as a chef is a designer of meals.

41. B

A throne is the official chair for a monarch, just as a bench is the official chair for a judge, (B). A miter is the headdress worn by bishops.

42. D

A canal is a manmade river, just as a mine is a manmade cavern, (D). It's stretching things to call a boat a manmade piece of driftwood, (A), even though both float.

43. B

When milk goes bad it gets sour; when bread goes bad it gets stale, (B).

44. E

Ore is mined to bring it up out of the earth, just as oil is drilled to bring it up out of the earth, (E). Grain is plowed, (D), but it's not found buried in the earth.

45. E

Weight is measured on a scale, just as altitude is measured on an altimeter. Speed, not distance, is measured on a speedometer (A). (B) is a little tricky: Numbers are measured on a slide rule, but only special kinds of numbers called logarithms.

46. C

A porcupine protects itself with quills. In a similar fashion, a skunk protects itself with odor.

47. D

The purpose of a jar is to contain, just as the purpose of a pillar is to support, (D).

48. B

Irrigate means to flush with liquid. So you irrigate something dry, just as you smooth something that's coarse, (B). (A) and (C) are tempting, but not as good. You soften something that's hard, not uneven. And you purify something that's impure, or tainted.

To ferment something is to create a state of chemical agitation in it; this has nothing to do with saltiness.

49. B

Electricity flows through a wire, just as water flows through an aqueduct. Sound is broadcast from a radio, choice (A), which is not the same thing. (C) and (D) have similar problems; in each case the music or light is emitted from the object, it doesn't flow through it. And in (E), a river is contained by its bank.

50. E

You can express contempt with a sneer. In the same way, you express displeasure with a frown, (E). Each of the other actions is inappropriately matched to its emotion.

51. E

The base of a building is its foundation. The base of a plant is its root, (E). If you chose (A), (C), or (D), you were probably confusing the vegetative meaning of "plant" with, say, a manufacturing plant. A grotto is a cave.

52. C

Olfactory refers to anything having to do with the sense of smell. So our bridge could be, the nose is the organ of the olfactory sense. Similarly, the ear is the organ of the sense of hearing or auditory sense, (C).

53. C

Irk means to annoy, disgust or irritate. So the relationship here is of opposites: something that irks is not soothing. In the same way, something that supports is not weakening or undermining, (C). Irritating, (D), is second-best here; it would go better with soothing than with support.

54. A

Something illegible is impossible to read, just as something invisible is impossible to see, (A). Something broken is not by definition impossible to fix.

55. B

Tact is sensitivity, skill at doing or saying the right thing with people. So tact is a necessary quality for a diplomat. In the same way, agility is a necessary quality for a gymnast, which makes (B) correct. Parsimony, (A), or stinginess, is a quality a philanthropist had better not have, since a philanthropist is someone who gives generous amounts of money to charity. Similarly, a judge, (E), should be unbiased, not biased, which means having a declared preference for one side or the other. Victims may be vulnerable, (C), but you wouldn't ordinarily say that vulnerability is a necessary quality for being a victim. And training in (D) is too vague; it's not a quality specific to the practice of medicine.

56. E

Ravenous means extremely hungry. So to be ravenous is to be in an extreme state of hunger. In the same way, to be furious is to be in an extreme state of indignation, (E). None of the other choices has a first word that's an extreme version of the second word. Pliable, (A), means flexible, while obstinacy is stubbornness, so these words are opposites. The same is true for (B) and (C). Tenacity, (D), is stubborn persistence; being smart is not being in an extreme state of tenacity.

57. B

To amplify sound is to make it stronger or louder. To bolster something means to strengthen it. In the same way, then, to bolster courage is to make it stronger. Getting the right answer here depends a little on knowing common usage. You can't bolster a smell, (A), insomnia or sleeplessness, (C), or light or silence, (D), (E).

58. A

Reverse the order of the stem pair: you attend a lecture in an auditorium. In the same way, you attend a concert in a theatre, (A). This bridge clearly doesn't work on (B), (D), or (E). You attend religious services, not religion itself, in a temple, (C).

59. C

Philanthropic means generous, giving; benevolence is the quality of generosity. So our bridge might be, a philanthropic act is evidence of benevolence. In the same way, a miserly act is evidence of stinginess, (C). Ostentatious, (B), means showy or extravagant.

60. D

Spurious is simply a fancy word meaning fake. So we've got a relationship of opposites here: something spurious has no authenticity. Similarly, something laughable has no seriousness, (D). Lavish, (A), means extravagantly expensive. Abject means miserable; subjectivity may or may not be miserable, (B). There's no obvious bridge between the words in (C), and in (E), "totalitarian" refers to an imposing system of government, so it is not the opposite of "completeness."

CHAPTER 18: SSAT PRACTICE TEST 3: LOWER-LEVEL

HOW TO TAKE THIS PRACTICE TEST

Before taking this practice test, find a quiet room where you can work uninterrupted for two and a half hours. Make sure you have a comfortable desk and several No. 2 pencils.

Use the answer sheet provided to record your answers. (You can cut it out or photocopy it.)

Once you start this practice test, don't stop until you've finished. Remember—you can review any questions within a section, but you may not go backward or forward a section.

You'll find an answer key, and explanations following the test. Scoring information can be found in chapter 19.

Good luck.

ISEE Practice Test Three: Lower-Level Answer Sheet

Remove (or photocopy) the answer sheet and use it to complete the practice test.

Start with number 1 for each section. If a section has fewer questions than answer spaces, leave the extra spaces blank.

SECTION 1

1 (A) (B) (C) (D) (E) 6 (A) (B) (C) (D) (E) 11 (A) (B) (C) (D) (E) 16 (A) (B) (C) (D) (E) 21 (A) (B) (C) (D) (E)
2 (A) (B) (C) (D) (E) 7 (A) (B) (C) (D) (E) 12 (A) (B) (C) (D) (E) 17 (A) (B) (C) (D) (E) 22 (A) (B) (C) (D) (E)
3 (A) (B) (C) (D) (E) 8 (A) (B) (C) (D) (E) 13 (A) (B) (C) (D) (E) 18 (A) (B) (C) (D) (E) 23 (A) (B) (C) (D) (E)
4 (A) (B) (C) (D) (E) 9 (A) (B) (C) (D) (E) 14 (A) (B) (C) (D) (E) 19 (A) (B) (C) (D) (E) 24 (A) (B) (C) (D) (E)
5 (A) (B) (C) (D) (E) 10 (A) (B) (C) (D) (E) 15 (A) (B) (C) (D) (E) 20 (A) (B) (C) (D) (E) 25 (A) (B) (C) (D) (E)

right in section 1

wrong in section 1

SECTION 2

1 (A) (B) (C) (D) (E) 9 (A) (B) (C) (D) (E) 17 (A) (B) (C) (D) (E) 25 (A) (B) (C) (D) (E) 33 (A) (B) (C) (D) (E)
2 (A) (B) (C) (D) (E) 10 (A) (B) (C) (D) (E) 18 (A) (B) (C) (D) (E) 26 (A) (B) (C) (D) (E) 34 (A) (B) (C) (D) (E)
3 (A) (B) (C) (D) (E) 11 (A) (B) (C) (D) (E) 19 (A) (B) (C) (D) (E) 27 (A) (B) (C) (D) (E) 35 (A) (B) (C) (D) (E)
4 (A) (B) (C) (D) (E) 12 (A) (B) (C) (D) (E) 20 (A) (B) (C) (D) (E) 28 (A) (B) (C) (D) (E) 36 (A) (B) (C) (D) (E)
5 (A) (B) (C) (D) (E) 13 (A) (B) (C) (D) (E) 21 (A) (B) (C) (D) (E) 29 (A) (B) (C) (D) (E) 37 (A) (B) (C) (D) (E)
6 (A) (B) (C) (D) (E) 14 (A) (B) (C) (D) (E) 22 (A) (B) (C) (D) (E) 30 (A) (B) (C) (D) (E) 38 (A) (B) (C) (D) (E)
7 (A) (B) (C) (D) (E) 15 (A) (B) (C) (D) (E) 23 (A) (B) (C) (D) (E) 31 (A) (B) (C) (D) (E) 39 (A) (B) (C) (D) (E)
8 (A) (B) (C) (D) (E) 16 (A) (B) (C) (D) (E) 24 (A) (B) (C) (D) (E) 32 (A) (B) (C) (D) (E) 40 (A) (B) (C) (D) (E)

right in section 2

wrong in section 2

SECTION 3

1 (A) (B) (C) (D) (E) 6 (A) (B) (C) (D) (E) 11 (A) (B) (C) (D) (E) 16 (A) (B) (C) (D) (E) 21 (A) (B) (C) (D) (E)
2 (A) (B) (C) (D) (E) 7 (A) (B) (C) (D) (E) 12 (A) (B) (C) (D) (E) 17 (A) (B) (C) (D) (E) 22 (A) (B) (C) (D) (E)
3 (A) (B) (C) (D) (E) 8 (A) (B) (C) (D) (E) 13 (A) (B) (C) (D) (E) 18 (A) (B) (C) (D) (E) 23 (A) (B) (C) (D) (E)
4 (A) (B) (C) (D) (E) 9 (A) (B) (C) (D) (E) 14 (A) (B) (C) (D) (E) 19 (A) (B) (C) (D) (E) 24 (A) (B) (C) (D) (E)
5 (A) (B) (C) (D) (E) 10 (A) (B) (C) (D) (E) 15 (A) (B) (C) (D) (E) 20 (A) (B) (C) (D) (E) 25 (A) (B) (C) (D) (E)

right in section 3

wrong in section 3

SECTION 4

1 (A) (B) (C) (D) (E) 13 (A) (B) (C) (D) (E) 25 (A) (B) (C) (D) (E) 37 (A) (B) (C) (D) (E) 49 (A) (B) (C) (D) (E)
2 (A) (B) (C) (D) (E) 14 (A) (B) (C) (D) (E) 26 (A) (B) (C) (D) (E) 38 (A) (B) (C) (D) (E) 50 (A) (B) (C) (D) (E)
3 (A) (B) (C) (D) (E) 15 (A) (B) (C) (D) (E) 27 (A) (B) (C) (D) (E) 39 (A) (B) (C) (D) (E) 51 (A) (B) (C) (D) (E)
4 (A) (B) (C) (D) (E) 16 (A) (B) (C) (D) (E) 28 (A) (B) (C) (D) (E) 40 (A) (B) (C) (D) (E) 52 (A) (B) (C) (D) (E)
5 (A) (B) (C) (D) (E) 17 (A) (B) (C) (D) (E) 29 (A) (B) (C) (D) (E) 41 (A) (B) (C) (D) (E) 53 (A) (B) (C) (D) (E)
6 (A) (B) (C) (D) (E) 18 (A) (B) (C) (D) (E) 30 (A) (B) (C) (D) (E) 42 (A) (B) (C) (D) (E) 54 (A) (B) (C) (D) (E)
7 (A) (B) (C) (D) (E) 19 (A) (B) (C) (D) (E) 31 (A) (B) (C) (D) (E) 43 (A) (B) (C) (D) (E) 55 (A) (B) (C) (D) (E)
8 (A) (B) (C) (D) (E) 20 (A) (B) (C) (D) (E) 32 (A) (B) (C) (D) (E) 44 (A) (B) (C) (D) (E) 56 (A) (B) (C) (D) (E)
9 (A) (B) (C) (D) (E) 21 (A) (B) (C) (D) (E) 33 (A) (B) (C) (D) (E) 45 (A) (B) (C) (D) (E) 57 (A) (B) (C) (D) (E)
10 (A) (B) (C) (D) (E) 22 (A) (B) (C) (D) (E) 34 (A) (B) (C) (D) (E) 46 (A) (B) (C) (D) (E) 58 (A) (B) (C) (D) (E)
11 (A) (B) (C) (D) (E) 23 (A) (B) (C) (D) (E) 35 (A) (B) (C) (D) (E) 47 (A) (B) (C) (D) (E) 59 (A) (B) (C) (D) (E)
12 (A) (B) (C) (D) (E) 24 (A) (B) (C) (D) (E) 36 (A) (B) (C) (D) (E) 48 (A) (B) (C) (D) (E) 60 (A) (B) (C) (D) (E)

right in section 4

wrong in section 4

SECTION 1

Time—25 Minutes
25 Questions

> In this section, there are five possible answers after each question. Choose which one is best. You may use the blank space at the right of the page for scratch work.
>
> **Note:** Figures are drawn with the greatest possible accuracy, UNLESS stated "Not Drawn to Scale."

1. Which of the following shapes can be folded to create a cube with no overlapping flaps?

   (A)

   (B)

   (C)

   (D)

   (E)

USE THIS SPACE FOR FIGURING.

2. Of the following, 20 percent of $19.95 is closest to

   (A) $1.95
   (B) $2.00
   (C) $4.00
   (D) $5.00
   (E) $20.00

GO ON TO THE NEXT PAGE

USE THIS SPACE FOR FIGURING.

3. Dividing 93 by 5 leaves a remainder of

(A) 18
(B) 5
(C) 4
(D) 3
(E) 2

4. If $7,000 + \square - 500 = 9,500$, then $\square =$

(A) 200
(B) 300
(C) 2,000
(D) 2,500
(E) 3,000

5. The width of a rectangle is one third of its length. If the length is 12, what is its perimeter?

(A) 3
(B) 4
(C) 16
(D) 24
(E) 32

6. What is the value of a in Figure 1?

(A) 30
(B) 60
(C) 90
(D) 120
(E) It cannot be determined from the information given.

Figure 1

7. Of the following, which number is the greatest?

(A) 0.08
(B) 0.7899
(C) 0.7923
(D) 0.792
(E) 0.79

GO ON TO THE NEXT PAGE

8. "When 4 is added to three times a number
    N, the result is 36." Which of the following
    equations represents this statement?

    (A) $4N + 3 = 36$

    (B) $36 + 4N = 3$

    (C) $36N + 3 = 4$

    (D) $3N + 4 = 36$

    (E) $36 - 4N = 3$

9. If $N + 5$ is an odd, whole number, then *N*
    could be which of the following?

    (A) 5

    (B) 3

    (C) $\dfrac{1}{2}$

    (D) 0

    (E) −7

10. A bull is tied to a seven-foot leash in the center
    of a square pen, as shown in Figure 2. If a side
    of the pen is 14 feet in length, which figure
    best shows the shape and size of the area in
    which the bull can move?

    (A)

    (B)

    (C)

    (D)

    (E)

USE THIS SPACE FOR FIGURING.

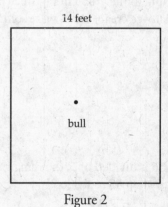

Figure 2

GO ON TO THE NEXT PAGE

11. $\dfrac{7}{8} - \dfrac{5}{8} =$

USE THIS SPACE FOR FIGURING.

    (A) 0.58

    (B) 0.5

    (C) 0.375

    (D) 0.25

    (E) 0.125

12. At sunset the temperature was 20 degrees. By midnight, it had dropped another 32 degrees. What was the temperature at midnight?

    (A) 12 degrees below zero

    (B) 6 degrees below zero

    (C) 0 degrees

    (D) 12 degrees above zero

    (E) 20 degrees above zero

13. According to the graph in Figure 3, how many chocolate ice cream cones were sold?

    (A) 25

    (B) 30

    (C) 50

    (D) 75

    (E) 100

Flavors of 300
Ice Cream Cones Served

Figure 3

14. When 36 is divided by 5, the remainder is the same as when 65 is divided by

    (A) 10

    (B) 9

    (C) 8

    (D) 7

    (E) 6

GO ON TO THE NEXT PAGE

15. According to the graph in Figure 4, what is the average number of 911 calls made from Monday through Thursday, inclusive?

    (A)   500
    (B)   750
    (C)   875
    (D) 1,000
    (E) 1,125

Questions 16–18 refer to the following definition.

For all real numbers y and z, let $y @ z = y \times z - 2$.

16. $3 @ 7 =$

    (A) 15
    (B) 19
    (C) 21
    (D) 25
    (E) 27

17. If $y @ 4 = 6$, then y must equal

    (A)   1
    (B)   2
    (C)   4
    (D)   6
    (E) 12

18. If $y = \dfrac{1}{4}$, what value of z will $y @ z$ equal 0?

    (A) –4
    (B)   4
    (C)   6
    (D)   8
    (E) 10

USE THIS SPACE FOR FIGURING.

911 Emergency Calls

Figure 4

GO ON TO THE NEXT PAGE

19. A class of 25 girls and 15 boys built a haunted house for the Halloween carnival. If $\frac{1}{5}$ of the girls and $\frac{2}{3}$ of the boys participated, what fraction of the total class participated?

    (A) $\frac{1}{5}$

    (B) $\frac{3}{8}$

    (C) $\frac{3}{7}$

    (D) $\frac{3}{5}$

    (E) $\frac{13}{15}$

20. The ratio of 7 to 4 is equal to the ratio of 28 to what number?

    (A) 7

    (B) 8

    (C) 12

    (D) 14

    (E) 16

21. Which figure CANNOT be drawn without lifting the pencil or retracing?

    (A)

    (B)

    (C)

    (D)

    (E)

USE THIS SPACE FOR FIGURING.

GO ON TO THE NEXT PAGE

22. Sparkly stickers are $0.50 and smelly stickers are $0.60. If Jill buys 5 sparkly stickers and 8 smelly stickers, what is her change from $10? (Stickers are not taxable.)

    (A) $1.20
    (B) $2.00
    (C) $2.70
    (D) $3.00
    (E) $7.30

23. Greg read from 5:00 P.M. to 5:45 P.M and finished one-third of his book. He wants to finish reading his book by 11:00 P.M. If he plans to read at the same rate, what is the latest time he can start reading again?

    (A) 7:15 P.M.
    (B) 8:00 P.M.
    (C) 8:45 P.M.
    (D) 9:30 P.M.
    (E) 10:15 P.M.

24. The map in Figure 5 shows all the paths that connect X and Y, and all distances are expressed in miles. How many paths are there from X to Y measuring exactly seven miles?

    (A) 2
    (B) 3
    (C) 4
    (D) 5
    (E) 6

25. A palindrome is a number that is unchanged when the order of its digits is reversed. For example, 232 is a palindrome. Which of the following is one more than a palindrome?

    (A) 7,336
    (B)   373
    (C) 8,337
    (D) 7,338
    (E) 8,338

USE THIS SPACE FOR FIGURING.

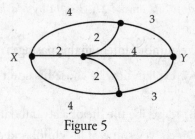

Figure 5

SECTION 2
Time—25 Minutes
40 Questions

Read each passage carefully and then answer the questions about it. For each question, decide on the basis of the passage which one of the choices best answers the question.

When I was a boy, there was but one permanent ambition among my comrades in our village on the west bank of the Mississippi River. That was, to be
Line a steamboat-man. We had transient ambitions of
(5) other sorts, but they were only transient. When a circus came and went, it left us all burning to become clowns; the first minstrel show that came to our section left us all suffering to try that kind of life; now and then we had a hope that if we loved
(10) and were good, God would permit us to be pirates. These ambitions faded out, each in its turn; but the ambition to be a steamboat-man always remained.

From Life on the Mississippi by Mark Twain

1. The author's intent in this passage is to

   (A) explain how he chose his adult profession.
   (B) describe the life of a steamboat-man.
   (C) convey some of his childhood aspirations.
   (D) compare the merits of several different occupations.
   (E) present a social history of the Mississippi.

2. According to the passage, the author considered all of the following as possible careers EXCEPT

   (A) steamboat-man.
   (B) clown.
   (C) minstrel.
   (D) writer.
   (E) pirate.

3. As it is used in line 5, the word "transient" means

   (A) appealing.
   (B) relative.
   (C) short-lived.
   (D) disastrous.
   (E) equal.

4. The author most likely uses the phrase "all burning to become clowns" in order to

   (A) provide an example of the boys' fleeting ambitions.
   (B) illustrate the lack of cultural life in Mississippi.
   (C) encourage his readers to follow similar career paths.
   (D) clarify why the boys all wanted to be steamboat-men.
   (E) show the kind of people that traveled on steamboats.

5. Which of the following best describes the effect of the phrase "if we loved and were good, God would permit us to be pirates"?

   (A) Pathos
   (B) Humor
   (C) Exaggeration
   (D) Mockery
   (E) Rhyme

GO ON TO THE NEXT PAGE

6. The attitude of the author toward the subject is

   (A) nostalgic.
   (B) regretful.
   (C) optimistic.
   (D) cynical.
   (E) somber.

     Alchemy is the name given to the attempt
to change lead, copper, and other metals into
silver or gold. Today, alchemy is regarded as a
Line pseudoscience. Its associations with astrology and
(5) the occult suggest primitive superstition to the
modern mind, and the alchemist is generally
portrayed by historians as a charlatan obsessed
with dreams of impossible wealth. For many
centuries, however, alchemy was a highly
(10) respected art. In the search for the elusive secret to
making gold, alchemists helped develop many of
the apparatuses and procedures that are used in
laboratories today. Moreover, the results of their
experiments laid the basic conceptual framework
(15) of the modern science of chemistry.

7. The passage is mainly about the

   (A) early history of a scientific field.
   (B) manufacture of gold from other metals.
   (C) mystery surrounding the origins of chemistry.
   (D) links between chemistry, astrology and sociology.
   (E) specific results of alchemists' experiments.

8. According to the passage, alchemists are generally portrayed in history books as

   (A) wealthy businessmen.
   (B) rogues motivated by greed.
   (C) talented but misunderstood individuals.
   (D) the ancestors of today's chemists.
   (E) brilliant scientists.

9. It can be inferred from the passage that a "charlatan" (line 7)

   (A) existed only in the Middle Ages.
   (B) is not respected by historians.
   (C) practiced an early form of chemistry.
   (D) uses his research for criminal purposes.
   (E) understood the secret to making gold.

10. The style of the passage is most like that found in a

    (A) scientist's diary.
    (B) novel about alchemists.
    (C) history textbook.
    (D) newspaper article.
    (E) personal letter.

11. With which of the following statements would the author most likely agree?

    (A) Few alchemists ever became wealthy from their work.
    (B) Alchemy was a primitive, superstitious field of science.
    (C) Alchemy is becoming increasingly respectable among today's chemists.
    (D) Astrology and the occult also deserve consideration as legitimate sciences.
    (E) Alchemists helped pave the way for scientists today.

GO ON TO THE NEXT PAGE ⟩

Even such is time that takes in trust
Our youth, our joys, our all we have,
And pays us but with age and dust
Line Who in the dark and silent grave,
(5) When we have wandered all our ways,
Shut up the story of our days,
But from this earth, this grave this dust,
My God shall raise me up, I trust.   .

From the poem "Even Such is Time,"
by Sir Walter Raleigh

12. In this poem, time is described as doing which
of the following?

I. Causing pleasant experiences to end
II. Rewarding the author with immortality
III. Making people older

(A) I only
(B) II only
(C) I and III
(D) I and II only
(E) I, II and III

13. As used in line 6, the word "story" most likely
refers to

(A) a person's life.
(B) a narrative.
(C) a tale.
(D) an emotion.
(E) the human body.

14. The words "I trust" in line 8 primarily indicate
that the author

(A) has an unshakable belief in God.
(B) knows that all things come to an end.
(C) is unhappy at the prospect of dying.
(D) fears the process of growing older.
(E) hopes for some form of life after death.

15. With which of the following statements about
life would the author most likely agree?

(A) Time heals all wounds.
(B) Life must be enjoyed to its fullest extent.
(C) Time eventually takes back everything that
it gives.
(D) Material possessions are worthless.
(E) Time passes more quickly as we get older.

On May 18, 1980, in Washington State, the
volcano Mount Saint Helens erupted, sending a
cloud of dust 15 miles into the air. The explosion
Line was not unexpected; the earth's crust had shaken
(5) for weeks beforehand, providing people in the
surrounding area with plenty of advance warning.
In spite of these danger signals, no one was
prepared for the extent of the blast; over the course
of several weeks, the volcano's eruption ripped the
(10) top 1,300 feet off the mountain, resulting in a
landslide that was the largest in recorded history.
540 million tons of ash from the volcano were
spread over three states, altering the earth's
weather patterns for several years afterward. One
(15) thing missing from the initial eruption was fluid
lava usually identified with volcanic activity. Later
eruptions emitted a thick and oozing lava. Thick
lava is easily outrun because it moves extremely
slowly. In addition, thick lava creates taller
(20) volcanoes because it often cools and hardens
instead of flowing down the volcano's sides.

GO ON TO THE NEXT PAGE

16. This passage is primarily about

    (A) the geological history of Washington state.
    (B) the difficulty of predicting volcanic activity.
    (C) a contrast between different forms of lava.
    (D) a story of an unusual geological event.
    (E) the factors that cause landslides.

17. As used in line 6, the word "advance" means

    (A) ahead of time.
    (B) moving forward.
    (C) in the past.
    (D) undetected.
    (E) extremely urgent.

18. According to the passage, all of the following were caused by the Mt. St. Helens eruption EXCEPT

    (A) tidal waves.
    (B) streams of lava.
    (C) a massive landslide.
    (D) changes in the earth's climate.
    (E) the emission of clouds of ash.

19. It can be inferred from the passage that fluid lava (lines 15 and 16)

    (A) is very thick.
    (B) creates tall volcanoes.
    (C) is only found in the United States.
    (D) is not easily outrun.
    (E) destroyed many forests in Washington.

20. The author's style is best described as

    (A) surprised.
    (B) dramatic.
    (C) skeptical.
    (D) informative.
    (E) mysterious.

The cowboy of the American West is an enduring icon in popular culture, but Hawaiian cowboys predated their American counterparts by
Line several decades. In 1792, King Kamehameha the
(5) Great of Hawaii received gifts of beef cattle, goats, sheep, and horses from Captain George Vancouver. The introduction of these unfamiliar animals caused unrest among the native islanders, because the unruly animals often trampled the crops in
(10) their fields. Initially, the king protected his imports from wrathful Hawaiians under kapu laws. But in 1830, Kamehameha III decided to hire a few Spanish vaqueros from California to keep the animals under control. Soon the Hawaiians were
(15) riding, roping, and lassoing alongside the Spanish cowboys.

21. It can be inferred from the passage that the American cowboy

    (A) taught the Hawaiians how to ride and lasso.
    (B) accompanied the shipment of horses and cattle to Hawaii.
    (C) did not understand the Hawaiians' opposition to horses.
    (D) emerged in the West later than his counterpart in Hawaii.
    (E) was not able to lasso as well as the Hawaiian cowboy.

GO ON TO THE NEXT PAGE

22. According to the passage, all of the following are true about horses and cattle EXCEPT

    (A) they were unfamiliar to Hawaiians before 1792.
    (B) they were introduced to Hawaii in the 18th century.
    (C) they were protected by Hawaiian law.
    (D) they were found to be too expensive to import.
    (E) they were destructive to Hawaiian property.

23. According to the passage, the Hawaiian cowboys

    I. were taught to ride by the Spanish vaqueros.
    II. existed earlier than the American cowboys.
    III. proved better at roping and lassoing than their American counterparts.

    (A) I only
    (B) II only
    (C) I and II only
    (D) II and III only
    (E) I, II and III

24. This passage is primarily about

    (A) the roping of cattle.
    (B) the history of King Kamehameha.
    (C) the Spanish relationship with Hawaii.
    (D) the history of horses in Hawaii.
    (E) the introduction of cowboys to Hawaii.

25. The attitude of the writer toward the subject is

    (A) biased.
    (B) condescending.
    (C) neutral.
    (D) elated.
    (E) confused.

These are the times that try men's souls. The summer soldier and the sunshine patriot will, in this crisis, shrink from the service of their country;
Line but he that stands it now, deserves the love and
(5) thanks of man and woman. Tyranny, like hell is not easily conquered; yet we have this consolation with us, that the harder the conflict, the more glorious the triumph. What we obtain too cheap, we esteem too lightly; it is dearness only that gives
(10) everything its value. Heaven knows how to put a proper price upon its goods; and it would be strange indeed if so celestial an article as freedom should not be highly rated. Britain, with an army to enforce her tyranny, has declared that she has a
(15) right (not only to tax) but "to bind us in all cases whatsoever," and if being bound in that manner is not slavery, then is there not such a thing as slavery upon earth. Even the expression is impious; for so unlimited a power can belong only
(20) to God.

Excerpted from "The Crisis," by Thomas Paine

26. Which of the following best describes the main point of this speech?

    (A) The British Army presents a formidable opponent.
    (B) Governments cannot judge men's souls.
    (C) No task that is easy is worth undertaking.
    (D) Taxation is an inherently unjust system.
    (E) Rebellion against the British is justified.

27. As it is used in line 2, the word "summer" suggests

    (A) an affection for warmer climates.
    (B) a tendency to avoid difficult situations.
    (C) a willingness to fight for important causes.
    (D) a desire to fight in favorable conditions.
    (E) a fear of the changing seasons.

GO ON TO THE NEXT PAGE ⇒

28. According to the speech, the British

    (A) virtually enslaved their subjects.

    (B) rightfully increased taxation.

    (C) provided greater trade opportunities.

    (D) assembled a superior army.

    (E) sacrificed many of their soldiers.

29. With which of the following statements about war would the author most likely agree?

    (A) The greater the struggle, the more worthy the victory.

    (B) Success is attained by waiting for an opportune moment to strike.

    (C) It is wrong to fight against one's own country.

    (D) The odds of winning must always be carefully considered.

    (E) A true patriot would avoid participating in the brewing conflict.

        In recent years, scientific research has done
    much to alter long-held beliefs about history. This
    is particularly true of scholarship surrounding the
Line Silk Road. The Silk Road was a trans-Asian trading
 (5) route that extended across two continents, linking
    China with the center of European trade in the
    Mediterranean. Most famous for the transport of
    silk, this ancient highway was also the conduit for
    such items as roses, peaches, gunpowder, and
(10) paper. Systems of belief were also passed along the
    road: The spread of Christianity, Buddhism, and
    Islam was accelerated by the connection between
    East and West.
        Based on historical texts, historians have
(15) traditionally believed that the Silk Road was
    established in 115 B.C., yet the recent discovery of a
    much older piece of silk in Egypt suggests that the
    road was established at least a thousand years
    earlier. Through carbon dating, scientists dated the
(20) fabric of the newly discovered piece of silk to around
    1000 B.C. In that period, only the Chinese held the

secret to silk manufacturing; Mediterranean
countries would not develop the technology to
manufacture silk until the sixth century A.D. As a
(25) result, historians now believe that Asia and Europe
may have traded silk via the Silk Road as long ago as
the second century B.C.—though exactly how
traders navigated the plateaus, mountains and
deserts that lie along the route remains a mystery.

30. This passage is primarily about

    (A) the impact of a new discovery on a historical theory.

    (B) ancient trading routes between East and West.

    (C) the introduction of silk manufacturing to Europe.

    (D) conflict between Chinese and Mediterranean traders.

    (E) the spread of Christianity, Buddhism, and Islam.

31. As used in line 10, the phrase "systems of belief" most likely means

    (A) travel routes.

    (B) organizations.

    (C) languages.

    (D) religions.

    (E) military secrets.

32. According to the passage, all of the following were traded along the Silk Road EXCEPT

    (A) fabrics.

    (B) explosives.

    (C) fruit.

    (D) flowers.

    (E) jewels.

GO ON TO THE NEXT PAGE

33. It can be inferred from paragraph 2 that historians believe that

   (A) the silk fragment discovered in Egypt was a fake.
   (B) most ancient Egyptian garments were made of silk.
   (C) the ancient Egyptians were unable to cross plateaus, mountains or deserts.
   (D) carbon dating is not the most accurate method of dating artifacts.
   (E) the ancient silk fragment found in Egypt must have been imported from China.

34. The author's style is best described as

   (A) surprised.
   (B) dramatic.
   (C) poetic.
   (D) mysterious.
   (E) informative.

   During the 15th century, the Belgian city
   Bruges was the most important commercial city in
   the north of Europe. Like Florence in Italy, Bruges
Line derived its wealth from wool and banking. Ships
 (5) brought raw wool there from England and Spain,
   and carried away finished wool cloth, which was
   celebrated throughout Europe. Bankers came to
   Bruges on the heels of the wool merchants—
   among them, representatives of the House of
(10) Medici. Soon Bruges became the financial center
   for all of northern Europe. Merchants from Italy,
   the Near East, Russia, and Spain all congregated in
   Bruges. Even though nearby cities such as Ghent
   and Louvain also flourished, Bruges so outshone
(15) them in prosperity that the Duke of Burgundy
   made that city his capital and moved his court
   there in the early 15th century.

35. As it is used in line 4, the word "derived" most nearly means

   (A) created.
   (B) exchanged.
   (C) invested.
   (D) obtained.
   (E) traveled.

36. It can be inferred from the text that the arrival of representatives of the House of Medici in Bruges

   (A) improved the quality of life for all residents of Bruges.
   (B) increased the amount of raw wool brought to Bruges.
   (C) required the city to provide official translators.
   (D) secured the status of Bruges as an important financial center.
   (E) lowered the level of market activity in Bruges.

37. It can be inferred from the text that the wool brought to Bruges

   (A) was of the best quality available in northern Europe.
   (B) was not instrumental in Bruges' growth as a financial center.
   (C) was woven into cloth, and shipped throughout Europe.
   (D) was also sent to rival towns Ghent and Louvain.
   (E) was as valuable as gold and other precious metals.

GO ON TO THE NEXT PAGE

38. The author most likely mentions "merchants from Italy, the Near East, Russia, and Spain" in order to

   (A) illustrate the variety of merchants involved in the wool trade.

   (B) convey the excitement of Europe in the 15th century.

   (C) portray the peaceful cooperation of European countries.

   (D) indicate the poverty of trade in those countries.

   (E) demonstrate how successful Bruges became.

39. According to the text, why did the Duke of Burgundy choose Bruges over Ghent and Louvain as the site of his court?

   (A) Ghent was on the verge of a financial crisis.

   (B) Ghent and Louvain were too far away from Burgundy.

   (C) Bruges was unquestionably the most wealthy city.

   (D) Bruges produced a higher quality of wool fabric.

   (E) More painters and musicians lived in Bruges than in other cities.

40. Which of the following best states the main idea of the passage?

   (A) The growth of the wool trade transformed commerce in the Renaissance.

   (B) Tired of his court in France, the Duke of Burgundy moved to Bruges.

   (C) Wool and banking made Bruges the commercial center of northern Europe.

   (D) Bruges outshone Florence in prosperity and cultural diversity.

   (E) Most 15-century cities centered around banking and wool manufacture.

SECTION 3

Time—25 Minutes
25 Questions

In this section, there are five possible answer choices after each question. Choose which one is best. You may use the blank space at the right of the page for scratch work.

<u>Note</u>: Figures are drawn with the greatest possible accuracy, UNLESS stated "Not Drawn to Scale."

1. What is the reciprocal of $\frac{3}{4}$?

    (A) $\frac{1}{4}$

    (B) $\frac{3}{4}$

    (C) $\frac{4}{3}$

    (D) 3

    (E) 4

2. If $\frac{1}{4}N = 4$, then $\frac{1}{8}N =$

    (A) $\frac{1}{2}$

    (B) 1

    (C) 2

    (D) 8

    (E) 16

3. In Figure 1, the number of shaded triangles is what fractional part of the total number of triangles?

    (A) $\frac{1}{3}$

    (B) $\frac{2}{5}$

    (C) $\frac{2}{3}$

    (D) $\frac{4}{5}$

    (E) $\frac{3}{2}$

USE THIS SPACE FOR FIGURING.

Figure 1

GO ON TO THE NEXT PAGE

4. If the largest of five consecutive whole numbers is 10, then the average of these numbers is

   (A) 6
   (B) 7
   (C) 8
   (D) 9
   (E) 10

USE THIS SPACE FOR FIGURING.

5. $\dfrac{2}{3} \times \dfrac{3}{6} \times \dfrac{2}{4} =$

   (A) $\dfrac{1}{12}$

   (B) $\dfrac{1}{6}$

   (C) $\dfrac{3}{4}$

   (D) 1
   (E) 2

6. If the perimeter of the polygon in Figure 2 is 24, what is the value of $a + b$?

   (A) 5
   (B) 7
   (C) 9
   (D) 10
   (E) 15

Figure 2

7. Julie's grades for her three math tests were 75, 100, and 89. What is her average grade for these three tests?

   (A) 80
   (B) 82
   (C) 85
   (D) 88
   (E) 92

GO ON TO THE NEXT PAGE

8. What is the result when the product of 2 and 6 is subtracted from the sum of 10 and 14 ?

(A) 21

(B) 16

(C) 12

(D) 6

(E) 2

USE THIS SPACE FOR FIGURING.

9. N is a whole number between 3 and 6, and also a whole number between 4 and 8. What is the value of N?

(A) 7

(B) 6

(C) 5.5

(D) 5

(E) 4.5

10. All of the following are less than $\frac{3}{4}$ EXCEPT

(A) $\frac{2}{3}$

(B) $\frac{5}{8}$

(C) $\frac{14}{16}$

(D) $\frac{7}{12}$

(E) $\frac{4}{6}$

Questions 11–12 refer to the chart in Figure 3

11. How many more white cars than red cars were sold?

(A) 1

(B) 70

(C) 100

(D) 200

(E) 700

Popularity of Car Colors

Figure 3

GO ON TO THE NEXT PAGE

12. The number of black cars sold is how many times the number of green cars sold?

 (A) 4,000

 (B) 440

 (C) 400

 (D) 40

 (E) 4

USE THIS SPACE FOR FIGURING.

13. If $3 \times 4 \times N = 6 \times 2$, then $N =$

 (A) 0

 (B) 1

 (C) 2

 (D) 12

 (E) 24

14. If the perimeter of the rectangle in Figure 4 is 20, what is the value of m?

 (A) 2

 (B) 4

 (C) 5

 (D) 6

 (E) 8

Figure 4

15. A shirt sells for $40. If Cathy buys the shirt at a 15% discount, how much money does she save?

 (A) $4

 (B) $6

 (C) $10

 (D) $12

 (E) $15

16. If there are 14 blue socks and 21 red socks in a drawer, what is the ratio of blue socks to red socks?

 (A) 1:7

 (B) 3:2

 (C) 2:3

 (D) 2:5

 (E) 3:5

GO ON TO THE NEXT PAGE

17. A bucket is set on a table, as shown in Figure 5. Which of the following describes all of the points where the bucket touches the table?

USE THIS SPACE FOR FIGURING.

(A) ⌒

(B) ◖

(C) ◗

(D) ○

(E) ●

Figure 5

18. If two times a whole number is less than 5 and greater than 0, the number could be

(A) −2
(B) −1
(C) 0
(D) 2
(E) 4

19. If Cindy earns $20 per hour, how many hours must she work to earn $420 ?

(A) 42
(B) 24
(C) 21
(D) 12
(E) 16

20. If 0.73 is about $\frac{N}{8}$, then N is closest to

(A) 100
(B) 8
(C) 6
(D) 4
(E) 3

21. In a restaurant, 5 vegetarian meals are ordered for every 7 non vegetarian meals. What could be the total number of meals sold?

(A) 350
(B) 490
(C) 500
(D) 600
(E) 620

GO ON TO THE NEXT PAGE ⟹

22. If $N \blacklozenge 4 = \frac{1}{4}N$, for which of the following values of N is $N \blacklozenge 4$ *not* a whole number?

    (A) 4
    (B) 6
    (C) 8
    (D) 12
    (E) 16

USE THIS SPACE FOR FIGURING.

23. To which of the following is 1.01 closest?

    (A) 0.01
    (B) 0.1
    (C) 1
    (D) 1.1
    (E) 11

24. If $\frac{O}{3} = 75$, then O =

    (A) 75
    (B) 150
    (C) 225
    (D) 300
    (E) 450

25. When a number is tripled and the result is increased by 4, the number obtained is 25. What is the original number?

    (A) 21
    (B) 12
    (C) 7
    (D) 4
    (E) 3

IF YOU FINISH BEFORE TIME IS CALLED, YOU MAY CHECK YOUR WORK ON THIS SECTION ONLY. DO NOT TURN TO ANY OTHER SECTION IN THE TEST.

STOP

SECTION 4

Time—25 Minutes
60 Questions

This section consists of two different types of questions. There are directions and a sample question for each type.

Each of the following questions consists of one word followed by five words or phrases. You are to select the one word or phrase whose meaning is closest to the word in capital letters.

1. ALIAS:

   (A) formal relationship
   (B) assumed name
   (C) blatant falsehood
   (D) presumed location
   (E) deep emotion

2. PHOBIA:

   (A) illumination
   (B) retraction
   (C) anxiety
   (D) height
   (E) dismissal

3. PROPEL:

   (A) intend
   (B) belie
   (C) fly
   (D) project
   (E) repel

4. HEADSTRONG:

   (A) foreign
   (B) delicate
   (C) stubborn
   (D) useless
   (E) hysterical

5. CODDLE:

   (A) baby
   (B) waddle
   (C) carry
   (D) riddle
   (E) assume

6. KEEN:

   (A) sharp
   (B) nice
   (C) forgiving
   (D) dense
   (E) rotund

7. MURKY:

   (A) religious
   (B) musty
   (C) sentimental
   (D) gloomy
   (E) forgetful

8. TRYING:

   (A) impossible
   (B) strenuous
   (C) easy
   (D) weathered
   (E) morose

GO ON TO THE NEXT PAGE

9. ADHERE:

   (A) connect
   (B) alter
   (C) stick
   (D) listen
   (E) complete

10. ENIGMATIC:

   (A) attractive
   (B) confused
   (C) happy
   (D) mysterious
   (E) unfortunate

11. POMPOUS:

   (A) flat
   (B) concerned
   (C) arranged
   (D) colorful
   (E) pretentious

12. FATAL:

   (A) childish
   (B) painful
   (C) accidental
   (D) social
   (E) lethal

13. FREQUENT:

   (A) general
   (B) frail
   (C) locomotive
   (D) various
   (E) habitual

14. OSTENTATIOUS:

   (A) prevalent
   (B) confident
   (C) repetitive
   (D) flashy
   (E) elongated

15. DEARTH:

   (A) mortality
   (B) fear
   (C) lack
   (D) consumption
   (E) approval

16. BUFFET:

   (A) toss about
   (B) serenade to
   (C) place upon
   (D) start over
   (E) send back

17. WAIVE:

   (A) fold over
   (B) ride on
   (C) climb under
   (D) urge on
   (E) give up

18. INDUSTRY:

   (A) element
   (B) accusation
   (C) diligence
   (D) phobia
   (E) warehouse

GO ON TO THE NEXT PAGE

19. TREPIDATION:

   (A) fear
   (B) agriculture
   (C) masterpiece
   (D) scarcity
   (E) acumen

20. CONDONE:

   (A) respect
   (B) approve
   (C) give
   (D) stifle
   (E) elevate

21. HARBINGER:

   (A) messenger
   (B) entry
   (C) dock
   (D) lagoon
   (E) consequence

22. SENTRY:

   (A) watch
   (B) beginning
   (C) row
   (D) revolutionary
   (E) companion

23. ORBIT:

   (A) program
   (B) inertia
   (C) revolution
   (D) galaxy
   (E) project

24. PARADOX:

   (A) submission
   (B) contradiction
   (C) dislike
   (D) imperfection
   (E) curse

25. BUFFOON:

   (A) gas
   (B) median
   (C) sphere
   (D) fool
   (E) gift

26. IMMINENT:

   (A) impenetrable
   (B) impossible
   (C) immature
   (D) implicated
   (E) impending

27. TUMULT:

   (A) sustenance
   (B) disorder
   (C) juvenilia
   (D) dossier
   (E) philosophy

28. SPURN:

   (A) unearth
   (B) incinerate
   (C) twirl
   (D) reject
   (E) clash

GO ON TO THE NEXT PAGE

29. PLETHORA:

   (A) compassion
   (B) excess
   (C) waste
   (D) forewarning
   (E) myth

30. DISSEMINATE:

   (A) discourage
   (B) renovate
   (C) broadcast
   (D) clarify
   (E) subside

The following questions ask you to find relationships between words. For each question, select the choice that best completes the meaning of the sentence.

31. Scissors is to cut as pencil is to

   (A) snip
   (B) write
   (C) raze
   (D) turn
   (E) read

32. Pasta is to sauce as

   (A) noodle is to dough
   (B) tomato is to vine
   (C) napkin is to plate
   (D) toast is to jam
   (E) cheese is to milk

33. Bread is to crust as orange is to

   (A) butter
   (B) pudding
   (C) rind
   (D) tree
   (E) lemon

34. Team is to captain as

   (A) sport is to player
   (B) paper is to reporter
   (C) republic is to president
   (D) game to opponent
   (E) navy is to ensign

35. Olfactory is to smell as

   (A) sweet is to mouth
   (B) allergic is to nose
   (C) heavy is to strength
   (D) seasonal is to flower
   (E) tactile is to touch

36. Ruler is to measure as camera is to

   (A) piano
   (B) lung
   (C) soul
   (D) limb
   (E) photograph

37. Tiptoe is to walk as

   (A) whisper is to speech
   (B) dance is to rhythm
   (C) tumble is to tree
   (D) rasp is to throat
   (E) press is to wrinkle

GO ON TO THE NEXT PAGE

38. Kernel is to central as trivia is to

(A) controversial
(B) unimportant
(C) unleavened
(D) harvested
(E) productive

39. Fib is to liar as

(A) perform is to crew
(B) convict is to attorney
(C) flatter is to toady
(D) campaign is to politician
(E) tally is to banker

40. Nap is to sleep as snack is to

(A) rest
(B) meal
(C) biscuit
(D) part
(E) age

41. Fossil is to petrified as

(A) solution is to dissolved
(B) wood is to hard
(C) snowflake is wet
(D) fog is to dense
(E) gully is to craggy

42. Sphere is to round as

(A) rectangle is to shape
(B) protractor is to angle
(C) ball is to rubber
(D) triangle is to line
(E) honeycomb is to hexagonal

43. Careful is to picky as

(A) tired is to exhausted
(B) alert is to asleep
(C) concerned is to grateful
(D) forgiving is to peaceful
(E) fancy is to short

44. Cave is to rock as apse is to

(A) cliff
(B) plateau
(C) patio
(D) church
(E) stage

45. Wine is to grape as

(A) juice is to cherry
(B) berry is to stain
(C) glass is to ivory
(D) paper is to wood
(E) stone is to mud

46. Frog is to amphibian as bird is to

(A) mammal
(B) toad
(C) beak
(D) branch
(E) feather

47. Dentist is to drill as

(A) surgeon is to scalpel
(B) doctor is to stretcher
(C) farmer is to grain
(D) manager is to computer
(E) pilot is to wing

GO ON TO THE NEXT PAGE

48. Mosaic is to tile as

    (A) advertisement is to magazine
    (B) tapestry is to thread
    (C) billboard is to chart
    (D) sweater is to wool
    (E) poster is to frame

49. Pebble is to rock as drop is to

    (A) boulder
    (B) fountain
    (C) sand
    (D) liquid
    (E) grain

50. Levee is to river as

    (A) sail is to boat
    (B) bridge is to truck
    (C) train is to track
    (D) path is to forest
    (E) shoulder is to road

51. Redundant is to necessary as

    (A) desirable is to pretty
    (B) original is to needed
    (C) plain is to valuable
    (D) vague is to explicit
    (E) fake is to expensive

52. Coral is to pink as aquamarine is to

    (A) deep
    (B) rosy
    (C) shady
    (D) bland
    (E) blue

53. Fan is to air as heart is to

    (A) power
    (B) heat
    (C) lung
    (D) wind
    (E) blood

54. Palette is to colors as

    (A) kaleidoscope is to glass
    (B) collage is to images
    (C) paint is to canvases
    (D) brush is to pictures
    (E) side is to picture

55. Salutation is to letter as

    (A) postscript is to note
    (B) heading is to stationary
    (C) introduction is to book
    (D) postcard is to picture
    (E) handwriting is to analysis

56. Quill is to porcupine as

    (A) needle is to thread
    (B) wings is to duck
    (C) pouch is to kangaroo
    (D) tail is to pig
    (E) scent is to skunk

57. Caterpillar is to butterfly as

    (A) salmon is to fish
    (B) egg is to dinosaur
    (C) tadpole is to frog
    (D) nest is to chick
    (E) worm is to bait

GO ON TO THE NEXT PAGE

58. Budget is to cost as

(A) blueprint is to design
(B) ratio is to value
(C) demonstration is to argument
(D) definition is to vocabulary
(E) foundation is to concrete

59. Juror is to judge as soothsayer is to

(A) predict
(B) soften
(C) report
(D) punish
(E) deny

60. Buffer is to impact as

(A) median is to lane
(B) boundary is to design
(C) antiseptic is to infection
(D) bandage is to heal
(E) injury is to faul

IF YOU FINISH BEFORE TIME IS CALLED, YOU MAY CHECK YOUR WORK ON
THIS SECTION ONLY. DO NOT TURN TO ANY OTHER SECTION IN THE TEST.   STOP

PART FOUR: SSAT PRACTICE TESTS AND EXPLANATIONS

SECTION 5

Time—25 Minutes

Write an essay on the following prompt on the paper provided. Your essay should not exceed two pages and must be written in ink. Erasing is not allowed.

Prompt: <u>Capital punishment serves no purpose and should be ended.</u>

Do you agree or disagree with this statement? Use examples from history, literature, or your own personal experience to support your point of view.

_____

_____

_____

_____

_____

_____

_____

_____

_____

_____

_____

_____

_____

_____

_____

_____

_____

_____

_____

GO ON TO THE NEXT PAGE

ANSWERS AND EXPLANATIONS

SECTION 1: MATH

1. B

This question isn't as hard as it seems. Remember, a cube has six faces. Since you're asked which shape can be folded into a cube with no overlapping flap, the answer must contain exactly six faces. The only choice that does so is (B).

2. C

You know $19.95 is close to $20. Twenty percent of $20 would be $4, (C).

3. D

Five will divide evenly into numbers that end in five or zero. You are asked to divide 93 by 5. The largest number less than 93 that 5 divides into evenly is 90. This means that five will divide into 93 with a remainder of three.

4. E

This question is essentially an algebra question. Just isolate the □ and solve.

$$7{,}000 + \square - 500 = 9{,}500$$
$$7{,}000 + \square = 10{,}000$$
$$\square = 3{,}000$$

5. E

The perimeter of a rectangle is equal to $2(l + w)$, where l and w represent the length and width, respectively. The length of the rectangle is 12, so you need to find its width in order to solve. You're also told that the width of the rectangle is one third of its length, so $\frac{12}{3}$, or 4, is its width. Plugging in the formula, the perimeter is equal to: $2(12 + 4) = 2(16) = 32$, choice (E).

6. B

Angles about a point add up to 360°, so you can write the following equation to solve for a:

$$45 + 75 + a + 45 + 75 + a = 360$$
$$2a + 240 = 360$$
$$2a = 120$$
$$a = 60$$

7. C

The easiest way to solve is to compare each answer choice, looking for the largest digit in each place holder. The largest tenths' digit, for example, is 7. Eliminate (A) since its tenths' digit is 0. In the hundredths' place the largest digit is 9. (B) is out, too, since its hundredths' digit is 8. (E) doesn't have a thousandths', so it is understood to be 0, which is less than the 2 that appears in the thousandths places in (C) and (D). (D) doesn't have a digit in the ten-thousandths place, so it is understood to be 0. It can be eliminated since it is less than the 3 in the ten-thousandths' place. (C) is the largest.

8. D

Break this question down into parts, translating as you go. You're told that 4 added to 3 times a number N results in 36. Three times N can be represented algebraically as $3N$, and adding 4 to that can be written as $3N + 4$. The result is 36, so $3N + 4 = 36$, (D).

9. D.

You are looking for the choice that, when added to five, will result in an odd, whole number. Try each answer choice to see which does:

(A) $5 + 5 = 10$; not odd

(B) $3 + 5 = 8$; not odd

(C) $\frac{1}{2} + 5 = 5\frac{1}{2}$; not a whole number

(D) $0 + 5 = 5$; an odd, whole number!

(E) $-7 + 5 = -2$; not odd

10. B

Try drawing in the bull's leash to get a sense of how far it can graze. Since the length of the fence is 14 feet, and the length of the rope is seven feet, the bull will just be able to reach the center of each side, but not the corners. In other words, the bull will be able to graze in a circle with radius 7, as shown in (B). Though (D) also represents the region as a circle, it is too small.

11. D

A quick look at the answer choices tells you that your answer needs to be in decimal form. So, first convert to decimal form, then subtract. $0.875 - 0.625 = 0.25$. Another approach is to subract the fractions to get $\frac{7}{8} - \frac{5}{8} = \frac{2}{8}$. Since $\frac{2}{8} = \frac{1}{4}$, convert $\frac{1}{4}$ to 0.25.

12. A

The temperature was originally 20 degrees. It then dropped 32 degrees, so you need to subtract 32 from 20: $20 - 32 = -12$. So the temperature at midnight was -12, or 12 degrees below zero, (A).

13. D

According to the graph, the slice labeled "chocolate" represents $\frac{1}{4}$ of the entire pie. Since a total of 300 cones were sold, $\frac{1}{4} \times 300 = 75$ chocolate cones were sold.

14. C

First determine what the remainder is when 36 is divided by 5. Five goes into 36 seven times with a remainder of one. So you need to find which choice will divide into 65 and leave a remainder of one. Since $8 \times 8 = 64$, 65 will leave a remainder of one when divided by eight. The answer is (C).

15. C

The average formula is $\text{Average} = \frac{\text{Sum of the terms}}{\text{Number of terms}}$. Look at the graph to find the number of 911 calls made for each of the four days, and plug them into the formula:

$$\frac{500 + 1,000 + 500 + 1,500}{4} = \frac{3,500}{4} = 875$$

16. B

This is a straightforward symbolism problem. Plug in the values for y and z and solve.

$$y@z = y \times z - 2$$
$$3@7 = 3 \times 7 - 2$$
$$= 21 - 2$$
$$= 19$$

17. B

Plug the given information into the equation and solve for y.

$$y @ z = y \times z - 2$$
$$y @ 4 = 6$$
$$4y - 2 = 6$$

$$4y = 8$$
$$y = 2$$

18. D

Plug the given information into the equation and solve for z.

$$y @ z = y \times z - 2$$
$$\frac{1}{4} @ z = 0$$
$$\frac{1}{4} \times z \, 2 \, 2 = 0$$
$$\frac{1}{4}z = 2$$
$$z = 8$$

19. B

There are 25 girls and 15 boys in the class, a total of 40 students. One-fifth of the girls, or $\frac{25}{5} = 5$, and two-thirds of the boys, or $\frac{2}{3} \times 15 = 10$, ran the haunted house. So a total of $5 + 10 = 15$ students participated. Since the class has 40 students in all, $\frac{15}{50} = \frac{3}{8}$ of all the students participated.

20. E

Set up a proportion, letting N equal the number you are looking for:

$$\frac{7}{4} = \frac{28}{N}$$
$$4 \times 28 = 7N$$
$$112 = 7N$$
$$16 = N$$

21. E

Here is the rule for whether you can retrace a figure without having to lift your pencil: If exactly zero or two points have an odd number of intersecting line segments and/or curves, the figure can be drawn

without lifting. So, for example, if a figure has three places where an odd number of line segments intersect, you would have to lift your pencil to retrace it. Also, the number of points a figure has with an even number of intersecting line segments is irrelevant.

Count the number of line segments that meet at each point of intersection. Find all the points that bring together an odd number of line segments. If you find zero or two points that meet this condition, the diagram can be drawn without lifting your pencil.

So, in this question, the only figure that doesn't fit this criteria is (E). There are six points of intersection, four of which have an odd number of intersecting segments.

22. C

To find Jill's change, you need to know how much money she spent. Then subtract that amount from $10. Jill bought five sparkly stickers at $0.50 each and eight smelly stickers at $0.60 each:

$$(5)(0.50) + (8)(0.60) = \$7.30$$
$$\$10 - \$7.30 = \$2.70$$

23. D

Greg spent 45 minutes to finish one-third of the book. He still has two-thirds left to read, twice as much as he has already read. So he'll need to spend twice the time he already spent—an hour and a half. To finish by 11 P.M., he needs to start an hour and a half before 11 P.M., or 9:30 P.M.

24. C

Work systematically, checking one route at a time and keeping careful track of each path. There is a total of 4 paths from X to Y with a total length 7, as shown in the figures below:

25. D

You need the answer choice that is one more than a palindrome, so you should be able to subtract one from the correct answer choice and end up with a palindrome. (A) gives you the number 7,336. One less than 7,336 is 7,335, which is not a palindrome. Same thing for (B), (C), and (E). In (D), one less than the answer choice is 7,337, which is a palindrome.

SECTION 2: VERBAL

FICTION PASSAGE

First up is a narrative passage. The author is reminiscing about his childhood and some of the fantasies that he and his peers had about their future professions. As with all fiction passages, pay close attention to shifts in tone, and uses of simile, metaphor, and irony as you read.

1. C

This is a Main Idea question. You first need to summarize what the passage was about. The first two sentences contain the author's main idea: he and his peers wanted nothing more than to be steam-boatmen. This is essentially what (C) states.

(A) is tricky; it mentions a profession, but we were never told that the author chose to be a steam-boatman in adulthood.

2. D

We are asked to determine which profession the author did not consider. The easiest way to do this is to eliminate all choices that he did consider. By just looking back at the text, we can identify all choices except (D). Being a writer is never mentioned.

3. C

After the author uses the word "transient," he explains that while he and his friends had other professional aspirations, those desires went away. Only the desire to be a steam-boatman remained. In other words, the other desires were "short-lived" as in (C).

4. A

Immediately before line 6, we are told that the author and his friends had "short-lived ambitions." In other words, they had ambitions that disappeared very quickly. The phrase "all burning to become clowns" is an example of such a fleeting ambition.

5. B

This question is a little tricky. After the friends considered being clowns and minstrels, they dreamt of becoming pirates. The fact that the boys wanted to become pirates is in itself comical, but with the added reference about God permitting that if they were good, the lightheartedness and humor become evident. If you weren't sure about the answer, try the other choices. It couldn't be (E), because there is no rhyme here, and it couldn't be (D), because Twain isn't making fun of anyone. Pathos means sympathy, sorrow, so (A) is definitely out, too. (C) is wrong since nothing is being exaggerated.

6. A

The author is fondly looking back on his childhood days. Somber, cynical, and regretful are too negative; the author is not saying anything negative. Neither is he hopeful about the future or optimistic. So the only answer choice that makes sense is (A), nostalgic. Nostalgic means reminiscing about the old days.

ALCHEMY PASSAGE

Next up we have a science passage about alchemy. The first half describes alchemy and the unfavorable way in which it has been viewed by history. The second half of the passage explains the positive aspects of alchemy and how it paved the way for modern science.

7. A

Remember to summarize the main point to yourself before going to the questions. Here, the passage provides a brief history of alchemy. (A) best restates this idea. (B) is wrong because gold was never actually manufactured.

8. B

Lines 6–8 state that "the alchemist is generally portrayed by historians as a charlatan obsessed with dreams of impossible wealth." In other words, the historians feel that the alchemists were greedy. (B) restates this idea. Be careful of (D): It contains information stated in the passage, but this isn't the view of historians, which is what the question asks for.

9. B

Infer means to draw a conclusion. Read the surrounding lines: They tell you that a "charlatan" was portrayed as obsessively greedy by historians—so you can infer that historians did not respect "charlatans"—(B).

10. C

To determine where this passage most likely came from, you need to consider the author's tone and purpose. Does the passage sound positive, negative, or neutral? Does the author seem to be trying to convince us of something? In fact, the author's tone sounds very detached—as you do when you are explaining something. So a history book is the logical place to find this type of passage. The text doesn't sound like news, so (D) is out.

11. E

To answer this question you need to understand the author's point of view. The author makes it clear that while alchemy was viewed with disdain by historians, it did make a positive contribution to the sciences. (E) reflects this attitude. Watch out for choices that contain information not expressly stated in the passage—(A), (C), and (D). (B) is tricky: Even though the text says that historians felt alchemy was primitive and superstitious, we don't know if the author thinks this is the case.

POETRY PASSAGE

You are sure to see one poem on the SSAT, and when you do, be alert for tone and the use of metaphor. In the beginning of the passage, the poet describes the effects of time on one's life. The last part expresses the author's hope for an afterlife.

12. C

You are asked to determine what time does according to the poem. Roman numeral I is accurate: Lines 1–2 state that time "takes in trust our youth, our joys."

In other words, time does end joyous experiences. So right away we know (B) is out because it doesn't contain Roman numeral I. Roman numeral II is inaccurate: There's nothing in the poem to indicate that time bestows immortality. So (D) and (E) are now out as well. Roman numeral III is correct: It claims that time makes people older. In line 2, we're told that time takes away "our youth," which is another way of saying that we age as a result of time. We now see that while (A) is correct, it is too limiting and not sufficient, given the other options. (C) is the full and proper answer choice.

13. A

You need to make sure to pick the definition as it is used in the passage. Lines 5–6 read, "When we have wandered all our ways, shut up the story of our days, but from this earth, this grave this dust, my God shall raise me up, I trust." The idea here is that after we've lived out our lives, God will hopefully "raise" us up. The word "story" means "life," in other words, so (A) is correct. Watch out for (B): While story is most often defined as "narrative," that meaning doesn't make sense in the passage.

14. E

Lines 7–8 state "But from this earth, this grave this dust, My God shall raise me up, I trust." The author hopes that after having lived his life, he will be able to enter into some sort of afterlife." (E) restates this idea. (B) is tricky, since the text does state that all things come to an end, but that doesn't fit the context of these last two lines where the author is describing his hope for an afterlife.

15. C

This poem has two points: first, life takes away everything that we obtain, and second, the author

hopes for an afterlife. (C) restates point one. (A), (B), (D), and (E) are all conclusions that you could make, but they're not specifically stated within the poem.

MT. SAINT HELENS PASSAGE

This is a science passage describing the eruption of the volcano Mt. Saint Helens and its effects. The first part of the passage focuses on the physical results of the eruption, while the last part describes the kind of lava emitted.

16. D

As you were reading the passage, you should have tried to summarize the point. The text describes Mt. Saint Helens, its eruption, and what the eruption produced. (A) is far too broad, and (C) and (E) are too narrow and detailed. The information in (B) is not discussed.

17. A

Lines 4–7 state, "The explosion was not unexpected; the earth's crust had shaken for weeks beforehand, providing people in the surrounding area with plenty of advance warning." In other words, the shaking of the crust warned people of the impending volcano; "advance," therefore, means ahead of time. While "moving forward" (B) is one definition for advance, it is not the meaning that works in this context.

18. A

You need to identify the answer choice that contains information not mentioned in the passage. If something leaps out at you immediately, there's a good chance that it's the answer. If not, eliminate all answer choices that are mentioned in the passage until one remains. Only tidal waves isn't mentioned.

19. D

Fluid lava, in the question stem, is thin, flowing lava. The text states, "thick lava is easily outrun because it moves extremely slowly." Since thin and thick lava would naturally have opposite characteristics, we can assume that thin lava is not easily outrun—(D).

20. D

The author isn't speaking in praise of something, nor is he trying to persuade his readers of a certain point of view. His tone is informative and balanced. (C) is the best choice.

HAWAIIAN COWBOY PASSAGE

This humanities passage discusses how the cowboy came to Hawaii. The author explains that while the word *cowboy* conjures up an image of the American West, the Hawaiian cowboy actually emerged earlier than his Western counterpart.

21. D

The first sentence of the text tells us that American cowboys emerged later than Hawaiian ones. This is what (D) states. (A) contradicts the text, and (B), (C), and (E) present details not discussed in the text.

22. D

Here you have to research which answer choice was not mentioned in the passage. If something leaps out at you immediately, there's a good chance that that is the answer. If not, use process of elimination by looking back at the text. The only answer choice not mentioned is (D).

23. C

Evaluate each Roman numeral one at a time, eliminating answer choices as you go. Roman numeral I is supported directly by lines in the text,

so it is correct. We can now eliminate (B) and (D) because they do not contain Roman numeral I. Roman numeral II is also supported in the text, so it, too, is true. That means (A) can be eliminated. Finally, Roman numeral III is not supported by the passage, so it is not true. The answer must therefore be (C).

24. E

The passage discusses how the cowboy came to Hawaii, which is what (E) states. (A), (B), and (C) don't get the focus of the passage right, while (D) focuses too much on one detail. Even though the introduction of horses is mentioned in the text, it isn't the point of the entire passage.

25. C

The author isn't excited or confused, so (D) and (E) are out right away. Biased means prejudiced toward a point of view, and condescending means negative, and the tone was neither one of these things, so (A) and (B) are wrong, too. His tone is informative and balanced, so (C) is the answer.

"THE CRISIS" PASSAGE

This text comes from the famous writings of Thomas Paine. Paine was an American colonist who strongly supported the American Revolution and his opinions are clearly demonstrated here. He begins by trying to convince us that a struggle against the British will be difficult. He then goes on to justify the revolution, explaining that the British have enslaved the colonists.

26. E

(A) focuses on one detail, not on the overall point of the text. (B), (C), and (D) are similarly too detailed. While Paine makes the claim that only God can judge men's souls, and that taxation is unjust, these are only details. (E) sums up the entire passage: Rebellion against the British is justified.

27. B

The opening words of this passage, "These are the times that try men's souls," tells us that the current conditions are challenging. With the word "summer," Paine is making a contrast between the "summer" soldier and the soldier who can stand up to the brewing conflict. The "summer" soldier will not be able to meet the challenge—he has a "tendency to avoid difficult situations," (B). Watch out for (A): While it presents a valid definition of summer, it is not a definition that works in the context of the passage.

28. A

The author makes it clear that taxation by the British is not acceptable (lines 15–18), so (B) is wrong. (C), (D), and (E) present details not stated in the passage. (A) is supported by the passage: The author states ". . . and if being bound in that manner is not slavery, then is there not such a thing as slavery upon earth."

29. A

(C) and (E) are the opposite of what the first sentences state, so right away they can be ruled out. The author feels it is indeed acceptable to fight against one's own country, and that a true patriot would fight for a just cause. (B) and (D) present information that is never discussed. (A), however, is supported by the passage: "the harder the conflict, the more glorious the triumph."

SILK ROAD PASSAGE

This science passage tells us about the Silk Road, the ancient trading route that connected China to Rome. In the text, we learn about a piece of silk that was discovered in Egypt, and how that discovery affected our knowledge about the Silk Road.

30. A

The passage is about the Silk Road and how our knowledge of the Silk Road was affected by the discovery of a piece of silk. This is essentially what (A) states. (B) is wrong because it fails to mention the fragment of silk discussed in paragraph 2. (C) and (E) are wrong because they focus too much on details. And (D) introduces material which was never discussed.

31. D

Go to the reference lines and see if you can figure out what the term "systems of belief" means. We're told that "systems of belief" were passed along the road. Immediately after that, the spread of Christianity, Buddhism, and Islam are discussed. So we can assume that these three religions are examples of "systems of belief," making (D) the answer. No other choice fits the context.

32. E

We need to find which item was not traded along the Silk Road, so we can eliminate everything that is mentioned in the text. We can definitely eliminate (A), fabrics, since we know that silk was traded. (B) is wrong as well, since gunpowder is mentioned in the text. (C) and (D) are wrong as well, since peaches and roses are mentioned.

33. E

The best way to proceed here is to evaluate each answer choice and eliminate anything that doesn't agree with the information in the passage. (A) states that the silk fragment found in Egypt was a fake. But nothing in the passage indicates that this was the case. (B), too, brings up information that we don't know for certain; we aren't told that most Egyptian garments were made of silk. While we are told that it is difficult to know "exactly how traders navigated the plateaus," we are not told that the Egyptians were definitely "unable" to cross plateaus etc., so (C) is out. Neither is (D) supported by the text. Only (E) makes sense: We are told that only the Chinese knew how to make silk in 1000 B.C., so we can assume that the fragment found in Egypt dating back to 1000 B.C. must have been made in China.

34. E

As you read the text, ask yourself what the author's tone and purpose are. Does the passage sound positive or negative? Does the author seem to be making an emotional appeal or is she just presenting information? Since this is a science passage, the author is unlikely to be too biased. (A), (B), (C), and (D) are all wrong because they do not fit the tone or purpose here. Only (E) makes sense.

BRUGES PASSAGE

This passage discusses the city of Bruges in the 15 century. The first lines set up the author's main idea: "During the 15 century, the Belgian city Bruges was the most important commercial city in the north of Europe."

35. D

Immediately following the word "derived" is the phrase, "its wealth from wool and banking." The text then goes on to say that "ships brought raw wool… to Bruges." We can assume, then, that "derived" means obtained or got its wealth.

36. D

We're told that among those bankers who came to Bruges, "representatives of the House of Medici" also arrived. We are also told that "soon Bruges became the financial center for all of northern Europe." From this we can assume that the arrival of the Medicis influenced the status of Bruges—(D).

37. C

You need to go to the part of the passage that discusses wool. We do not know anything about the quality of the wool from the text, we only know that the finished cloth was famous in Europe. Nor is there anything to support the claims in (D) and (E). (B) contradicts the passage, as wool was very instrumental in the growth of Bruges. (C) is indeed supported by the text.

38. E

This is a purpose of detail question: You are asked to determine why a specific detail is mentioned. We are told that Bruges became "the financial center for all of northern Europe." Immediately afterward, we're told about the various merchants who came there, indicating how important a place it had become.

39. C

The text says that Bruges so outshone the other cities in prosperity that "the Duke of Burgundy made that city his capital." The Duke chose Bruges because of its prosperity—(C). (A) is totally incorrect, since the text says that Ghent was prosperous.

40. C

(A) is too broad; we are only dealing with Bruges, not the entire Renaissance world. (B) and (D) focus only on small details. (E) is out, too, as there's no evidence to support this statement. (C) is the best answer.

SECTION 3: MATH

1. C

Finding the reciprocal of a number involves flipping its numerator with its denominator. So the reciprocal of $\frac{3}{4}$ is simply $\frac{4}{3}$.

2. C

There are at least two ways to solve this problem. If you recognized that $\frac{1}{8}$ is half of $\frac{1}{4}$, $\frac{1}{8}N$ must be half of four, or two. Alternately, you could have solved the first equation for the value of N, and then plugged into the second expression.

$$\frac{1}{4}N = 4$$
$$\frac{1}{4} \qquad 4\left(N=4\right)$$
$$N = 16$$
$$\frac{1}{8}N = \frac{1}{8} \times 16 = 2$$

3. B

There are 10 triangles. Four of these are shaded. So $\frac{4}{10} = \frac{2}{5}$ of all the triangles are shaded.

4. C

The average of a group of consecutive integers is equal to the middle term. Since you're told that the largest of the five integers is 10, they must be six, seven, eight, nine, and 10. So the middle term and average is eight, (C).

5. B

The fastest way to solve this question is to simplify by canceling terms, and then to multiply.

$$\frac{2}{3} \times \frac{3}{6} \times \frac{2}{4} = \frac{2}{3} \times \frac{1}{2} \times \frac{1}{2}$$
$$= \frac{1}{3} \times \frac{1}{1} \times \frac{1}{2}$$
$$= \frac{1}{6}$$

6. C

The perimeter is the sum of all the sides of a figure. Set up an equation to solve for the sum of a and b.

$$a + b + 2 + 3 + 4 + 6 = 24$$
$$a + b + 15 = 24$$
$$a + b = 9$$

7. D

The average formula is:

$$\text{Average} = \frac{\text{Sum of terms}}{\text{Number of terms}}$$

Plug in Julie's three grades to find her average grade:

$$\frac{75 + 89 + 100}{3} = \frac{264}{3} = 88$$

8. C

You are first asked to find the product of two and six, or $2 \times 6 = 12$. You're then asked to subtract that product from the sum of 10 and 14, or $10 + 14 = 24$. So $24 - 12 = 12$, (C).

9. D

N is a whole number between three and six, so it could be four or five. N is also a whole number between four and eight, so it could be five, six, or seven. The only number that fits both these conditions is five.

10. C

Evaluate each answer choice and eliminate as you go. Since $\frac{2}{3} = \frac{8}{12}$ and $\frac{3}{4} = \frac{9}{12}$, (A) is less than $\frac{3}{4}$; eliminate. Since $\frac{3}{4} = \frac{6}{8}$, $\frac{5}{8}$ is less than $\frac{3}{4}$; eliminate (B). Since $\frac{14}{16} = \frac{7}{8}$ and $\frac{3}{4} = \frac{6}{8}$, (C) is not less than $\frac{3}{4}$ and it is the answer.

11. C

According to the chart, each car icon represents 100 cars. Since there are four icons in the white category, 400 white cars were sold. With three icons in the red category, 300 red cars were sold. So there were 400 − 300 = 100 more white than red cars sold.

12. E

According to the graph, there were 800 black cars sold, and only 200 green cars sold. In other words, the number of black cars sold is 800 divided by 200: four times the number of green cars sold.

13. B

Treat this question as a straightforward algebra problem. As you simplify, watch out for careless errors.

$$3 \times 4 \times N = 6 \times 2$$
$$12N = 12$$
$$N = 1$$

14. D

Perimeter of a rectangle is equal to $2(l + w)$, where l and w represent the length and width respectively. The width is four, the length is m, and the perimeter is 20, so plug into the formula.

$$20 = 2(m + 4)$$
$$20 = 2m + 8$$

$$12 = 2m$$
$$6 = m$$

15. B

The shirt is originally $40, but Cathy buys it at a 15 percent discount. You are asked to find out how much money Cathy saves, or 15 percent of $40.

$$15\% \times \$40 = (0.15)(\$40)$$
$$= \$6$$

16. C

Ratios can be expressed either with fractions or with a colon. A look at the answer choices reveals that the answer will be expressed with a colon. The ratio of 14 to 21 is therefore 14:21. You can reduce this ratio by a factor of 7, which simplifies to 2:3, (C).

17. E

You only need to be concerned with the bottom part of the bucket—the circular part. Since the entire circular bottom of the bucket touches the table, the figure that most accurately represents all the points where the bucket touches the table is (E).

18. D

Two times a whole number is less than 5 and greater than zero. So our end result must be 1, 2, 3, or 4. Therefore, the whole number could be $\frac{1}{2} = 1$ or $\frac{4}{2} = 2$ (half of 1 or 3 would not be a whole number). Of these, only 2 is listed as an answer choice so it's correct.

19. C

Think of this as a proportion problem. Cindy earns $20 for an hour of work. You want to figure out how many hours she needs to work to earn $420, so set up a proportion, letting x equal the number you're looking for:

$$\frac{20}{1} = \frac{420}{x}$$
$$20x = 420$$
$$x = 21$$

20. C

73 is close to 0.75, which can be expressed in fractional form as $\frac{3}{4}$. This also equals $\frac{6}{8}$. Of the choices, N is closest to 6, (C).

21. D

For every 5 vegetarian meals, 7 nonvegetarian meals are ordered. This means that the total number of meals ordered must be a multiple of 12 (since $7 + 5 = 12$). The only answer choice with a multiple of 12 is (D), 600.

22. B

You're asked to find which value of N will not result in a whole number. You can see that the symbol instructs you to take $\frac{1}{4}$ of N, so the number that is not a multiple of 4 will not produce a whole number value. The only number not divisible by 4 is (B), 6. Alternately, you could have plugged each answer choice into the expression to see which did not produce a whole number.

23. C

Because 0.1 is just 0.01 or one hundredth away from 1, it is the closest of the choices.

24. C

This is an algebra problem, where you need to treat the symbol as a variable, and isolate it on one side of the equation. Cross-multiplying shows that $3 \times 75 = O$, so $225 = O$, (C).

25. C

Let's set up an equation. Let N equal the original number. Translating, "when N is tripled" means $3 \times N$, or $3N$. "The result is increased by 4" means $+ 4$, or $3N + 4$. "The number obtained is 25" means $3N + 4 = 25$. Now simply isolate N to solve for it:

$$3N + 4 = 25$$
$$3N = 21$$
$$N = 7$$

SECTION 4: VERBAL

SYNONYMS

1. B

An alias is an assumed name. Superman's alias is Clark Kent.

2. C

To have a phobia is to have great fear or anxiety about something. To have a phobia of snakes is to have a fear of snakes.

3. D

To propel something is to thrust it forward, or to project it. A strong wind can propel a ship through the water. Note that project is used as a verb here, not as a noun. Your answer must always be the same word form as that of the stem word.

4. C

A headstrong person is stubborn and doesn't like to listen to anyone else. A headstrong horse may refuse to walk when you ask it to.

5. A

To coddle something is to treat it gently or to baby it. Too much coddling of a child, for example, may cause him to be insufficiently prepared to face the harsh realities of life.

6. A

To be keen is to be very smart or sharp. A keen mind is good at solving problems.

7. D

If something is murky, it is dark and mysterious, or gloomy. Murky water is hard to see through.

8. B

The word trying isn't used here as a verb as you might expect. It is used as an adjective. A trying situation is very demanding or strenuous. A trying hike, for example, will make you very tired. Always look at the root word to see what word form you need to use.

9. C

If you adhere to a decision, you stay with it, or stick to it. Adhesive tape is sticky tape—it adheres.

10. D

An enigmatic person is difficult to figure out—she is mysterious. Many people thought Howard Hughes was enigmatic because so little was known about him.

11. E

To be pompous is to be stuck up or pretentious. A pompous person feels and acts as though he is more important than he is.

12. E

Something that is fatal will kill you; it is lethal. A fatal blow is a blow that kills a person.

13. E

Something frequent happens regularly; it is habitual. A frequent flyer is a person who flies all the time.

14. D

An ostentatious person is a show-off; he is showy or flashy. An ostentatious outfit might include lots of jewelry and expensive-looking accessories.

15. C

A dearth of something is a lack of something. If an area has a dearth of water, then there's very little water in that area.

16. A

To be buffeted is to be tossed about. A small ship can be buffeted by large waves.

17. E

To waive something is to let it pass or to give it up. If you waive your right to vote, you give up your right to vote.

18. C

Industry is commonly thought of as manufacturing, but it also means hard work, or diligence. A person who possesses great industry is a person who is very diligent.

19. A

Trepidation is the same as fear. To watch a horror movie with great trepidation is to watch it with great fear.

20. B

To condone something is to approve of something or to support it. If one condones a certain type of behavior, then one approves of it.

21. A

A harbinger is a messenger. Dark clouds are often a harbinger of a rain storm.

22. A

A sentry is a group of people who look out for certain things—a watch. During war, the sentry looks out for the enemy.

23. C

An orbit occurs when one object circles around another object; it is a revolution. When the moon orbits the earth, it makes a revolution. Don't be tricked by the fact that revolution also means a war, as in the American Revolution. If a word has more than one meaning, make sure you consider them all before deciding that an answer choice is incorrect.

24. B

A paradox occurs when one thing is said, but another is meant—it's a confusion or a contradiction. The word "bittersweet" is a contradiction: How can something be bitter and sweet at the same time?

25. D

A buffoon is a person who everyone makes fun of—a fool. Clowns often pretend to be buffoons.

26. E

An imminent event is just about to happen—it is impending. For centuries, people have believed that the end of the world is imminent.

27. B

Tumult is havoc, or disorder. When a hurricane goes through towns, it can create a tumult.

28. D

To spurn someone is to scorn or reject someone. A spurned friend is a rejected friend.

29. B

Plethora is the opposite of dearth in question 15. A plethora is an abundance or an excess of something. If there's a plethora of corn, there's a great deal of corn.

30. C

To disseminate something is to spread it out or to broadcast it. To disseminate information is to broadcast it.

ANALOGIES

31. B

Scissors are specifically used to cut, just as a pencil is specifically used to write.

32. D

The specific topping for pasta is sauce; the specific topping for toast is jam. A noodle (A) is made out of dough, and tomato (B) grows on a vine.

33. C

The outer shell of bread is the crust. The outer shell of an orange is the rind.

34. C

A captain is the leader of a team, just as a president is the leader of a republic. Watch out for (A)—it mentions the word sports, which fits the subject matter of the stem pair, but does not match the bridge.

35. E

Olfactory refers to one's sense of smell, just as tactile refers to one's sense of touch.

36. E

A ruler is a tool used to measure something, just as a camera is a tool used to photograph something.

37. A

Tiptoe is a quiet kind of walk, as whisper is a quiet kind of speech. A rasp (D) is a harsh sound in one's throat.

38. B

A kernel is a central piece of information. Trivia is an unimportant piece of information.

39. C

A liar is a person who fibs, just as a toady is a person who flatters. A politician (D) by definition is not a person who campaigns, but rather, a person who engages in politics. To tally (E) is to count up: A banker may tally money, but he may also do other things like lend money.

40. B

A nap is a short sleep just as a snack is a short meal. A biscuit can be a type of snack, but we are looking for a word that fits the bridge "is a short."

41. A

A fossil is a substance which is petrified. A solution is a substance which is dissolved. Wood (B) is not necessarily hard, nor are snowflakes (C) necessarily wet.

42. E

A sphere is round in shape in the same way that a honeycomb is hexagonal in shape. A protractor (B) is used to measure an angle.

43. A

To be picky is to be extremely careful. Similarly, to be exhausted is to be extremely tired. To be alert (B) is to be awake.

44. D

A cave is the rounded, hollowed out part of a rock, just as an apse is the rounded, hollowed out part of a church. A plateau (B) is a large flat rock.

45. D

Wine is made from grapes, just as paper is made from wood. Juice (A) may or may not be made from cherries; it can be made from other ingredients as well.

46. A

A frog is a type of amphibian, as a bird is a type of mammal.

47. A

A dentist uses a drill in the way that a surgeon uses a scalpel. A doctor doesn't use a stretcher—his patients do. And though a farmer may harvest grain, he does not by definition use it.

48. B

A mosaic is a picture made up of individual tiles, the way a tapestry is a picture made up of individual threads. A sweater (D) may or may not be made out of wool.

49. D

A pebble is a tiny bit of rock, just as a drop is a tiny bit of liquid.

50. E

A levee is the border of a river, just as a shoulder is the border of a road. A path may or may not go through a forest.

51. D

Something that is redundant, by definition, is not necessary. Something that is vague, by definition, is not explicit. Something that is desirable (A) is not necessarily pretty.

52. E

Coral is a shade of pink, the way aquamarine is a shade of blue. Rosy (B) is another shade of pink, while bland (D) means plain.

53. E

A fan by definition circulates air, and a heart circulates blood.

54. B

A palette is an assortment of colors, and a collage is an assortment of images.

55. C

A salutation is an introductory greeting in a letter, as an introduction is an introductory greeting in a book. A postscript (A) occurs at the end of a letter.

56. E

A quill is a porcupine's means of defense just as a scent is a skunk's means of defense. Wings (B) are a duck's means of flight.

57. C

A caterpillar is an animal that turns into a butterfly. A tadpole is an animal that turns into a frog.

58. A

A budget is used to plan the cost of a project, the way a blueprint is used to plan the design of a project.

59. A

The job of a juror is to judge. The job of a soothsayer is to predict. A soothsayer predicts the future.

60. C

A buffer is used to prevent an impact, as an antiseptic is used to prevent an infection. A bandage (D) may help to heal a wound, but it will not prevent it, which is the bridge we need.

CHAPTER 19: SCORING YOUR SSAT PRACTICE TEST

Your SSAT score is calculated by using a formula that cannot be directly applied to your practice tests. Therefore, it is impossible to provide a completely accurate score for your practice tests. Nevertheless, you'll understandably want to get an idea of how well you have performed.

Follow the steps described below to obtain a rough approximation of what your score on the actual SSAT might be. First, add up the number of questions you got right and the number of questions you got wrong. Questions left blank are worth zero points. Then, do the math, based on the following:

	Verbal (60 questions total)	(Quantitative) Math (50 questions total)	Reading Comprehension (40 questions total)
+ 1 point for each right answer	_____	_____	_____
$-\frac{1}{4}$ point for each wrong answer	_____	_____	_____
TOTAL:	_____	_____	_____

This is called your **raw score.** Next, take your raw score and look at the following chart, which *approximates* a conversion to a **scaled score.** A scaled score takes into account the range in difficulty level of the various editions of the test.

Again, while the following scores and percentiles are close approximations, they do not reflect the official scores and percentiles used on the SSAT. Among other contributing factors, your actual test score will take into account the group of students to whom you will be compared on your test administration.

UPPER-LEVEL SCORES

Upper-level scores are based on a scale of 500–800. Once you have looked up your scaled score, refer to the 50th percentile score chart below: This will tell you the score at which equal numbers of students scored above and below you. With this information, you will be able to gauge how well you have done with respect to other students.

SCALED SCORES

Raw Score	Reading	Verbal	Math*
60		800	
55		800	
50		779	800
45		752	782
40	800	725	755
35	722	698	725
30	692	671	698
25	662	644	668
20	632	617	641
15	602	590	614
10	572	563	584
5	542	533	557
0	512	506	530
−5 and lower	500	500	500

* Both math sections have been combined. Add together both of your scores for those sections.

MEDIAN SCORE: 50TH PERCENTILE

Grade	Reading	Verbal	Quantitative
8	629	662	647
9	644	683	668
10	647	671	692
11	626	653	689

LOWER-LEVEL SCORES

Lower-level test scores are based on a scale of 440–710. Once you have looked up your scaled score, refer to the 50th percentile score chart below: That chart will tell you the score at which equal numbers of students scored above and below you. This way, you will be able to gauge how well you have done with respect to other students.

SCALED SCORES

Raw Score	Reading	Verbal	Math*
60		710	
55		710	
50		710	704
45		698	680
40	710	674	659
35	686	650	635
30	656	626	614
25	626	602	593
20	596	578	569
15	566	554	540
10	536	530	527
5	506	506	503
0	476	482	482
−5	446	458	458
−10 and lower	440	440	440

* Both math sections have been combined. Add together both of your scores for those sections.

MEDIAN SCORE: 50TH PERCENTILE

Grade	Reading	Verbal	Quantitative
5	569	584	563
6	593	614	593
7	611	638	614

ISEE PRACTICE TESTS AND EXPLANATIONS

ISEE TEST OVERVIEW

TOTAL TIME

Approximately 3 hours.

QUESTIONS

Aside from the essay, all questions are multiple-choice format, with all answer choices labeled (A)–(D).

CONTENT

The ISEE tests Math and Verbal skills. There are two scored Math sections, two scored Verbal sections, and one unscored Essay.

PACING

You are not expected to complete all items on the ISEE. This is particularly true if you are at the low end of the age range of test takers for your level. The best approach to pacing is to work as quickly as you can without losing accuracy. Further, if a question is giving you difficulty, circle it and move on. You can always come back to it later, but you shouldn't waste time on a question that is stumping you when you could be gaining valuable points elsewhere.

GUESSING

There is no guessing penalty on the ISEE. You receive 1 point for each question that you answer correctly. You don't lose any points for questions left blank or for questions answered incorrectly. As a result, it's always to your advantage to guess on questions you don't know. However, it's better to answer questions correctly, so only guess if you try to answer the question and can't figure it out, or if you are running out of time.

CHAPTER 20: ISEE PRACTICE TEST 1: UPPER- AND MIDDLE-LEVEL

HOW TO TAKE THIS PRACTICE TEST

Before taking this practice test, find a quiet room where you can work uninterrupted for three hours. Make sure you have a comfortable desk and several No. 2 pencils.

Use the answer sheet provided to record your answers. (You can cut it out or photocopy it.)

Once you start this practice test, don't stop until you have finished. Remember—you can review any questions within a section, but you may not go backward or forward a section.

You'll find an answer key and explanations following the test.

Note: There are no major differences between the Middle- and Upper-level ISEE tests, and most of the questions on both tests are appropriate to either the middle or upper levels.

The practice test here covers both levels. If you are taking this as a Middle-level test, a few of the questions will understandably be too difficult. Don't worry—just do the best you can—and know that on test day, you will see only those questions that are appropriate to your level. Remember, too, that your scores will be based on how you compare to others taking the Middle-level test.

Good luck.

ISEE Practice Test One: Upper- and Middle-Level Answer Sheet

Remove (or photocopy) the answer sheet and use it to complete the practice test.

Start with number 1 for each section. If a section has fewer questions than answer spaces, leave the extra spaces blank.

SECTION 1

1 (A)(B)(C)(D) 9 (A)(B)(C)(D) 17 (A)(B)(C)(D) 25 (A)(B)(C)(D) 33 (A)(B)(C)(D)
2 (A)(B)(C)(D) 10 (A)(B)(C)(D) 18 (A)(B)(C)(D) 26 (A)(B)(C)(D) 34 (A)(B)(C)(D)
3 (A)(B)(C)(D) 11 (A)(B)(C)(D) 19 (A)(B)(C)(D) 27 (A)(B)(C)(D) 35 (A)(B)(C)(D)
4 (A)(B)(C)(D) 12 (A)(B)(C)(D) 20 (A)(B)(C)(D) 28 (A)(B)(C)(D) 36 (A)(B)(C)(D)
5 (A)(B)(C)(D) 13 (A)(B)(C)(D) 21 (A)(B)(C)(D) 29 (A)(B)(C)(D) 37 (A)(B)(C)(D)
6 (A)(B)(C)(D) 14 (A)(B)(C)(D) 22 (A)(B)(C)(D) 30 (A)(B)(C)(D) 38 (A)(B)(C)(D)
7 (A)(B)(C)(D) 15 (A)(B)(C)(D) 23 (A)(B)(C)(D) 31 (A)(B)(C)(D) 39 (A)(B)(C)(D)
8 (A)(B)(C)(D) 16 (A)(B)(C)(D) 24 (A)(B)(C)(D) 32 (A)(B)(C)(D) 40 (A)(B)(C)(D)

right in section 1

wrong in section 1

SECTION 2

1 (A)(B)(C)(D) 9 (A)(B)(C)(D) 17 (A)(B)(C)(D) 25 (A)(B)(C)(D) 33 (A)(B)(C)(D)
2 (A)(B)(C)(D) 10 (A)(B)(C)(D) 18 (A)(B)(C)(D) 26 (A)(B)(C)(D) 34 (A)(B)(C)(D)
3 (A)(B)(C)(D) 11 (A)(B)(C)(D) 19 (A)(B)(C)(D) 27 (A)(B)(C)(D) 35 (A)(B)(C)(D)
4 (A)(B)(C)(D) 12 (A)(B)(C)(D) 20 (A)(B)(C)(D) 28 (A)(B)(C)(D) 36 (A)(B)(C)(D)
5 (A)(B)(C)(D) 13 (A)(B)(C)(D) 21 (A)(B)(C)(D) 29 (A)(B)(C)(D) 37 (A)(B)(C)(D)
6 (A)(B)(C)(D) 14 (A)(B)(C)(D) 22 (A)(B)(C)(D) 30 (A)(B)(C)(D) 38 (A)(B)(C)(D)
7 (A)(B)(C)(D) 15 (A)(B)(C)(D) 23 (A)(B)(C)(D) 31 (A)(B)(C)(D) 39 (A)(B)(C)(D)
8 (A)(B)(C)(D) 16 (A)(B)(C)(D) 24 (A)(B)(C)(D) 32 (A)(B)(C)(D) 40 (A)(B)(C)(D)

right in section 2

wrong in section 2

SECTION 3

1 (A)(B)(C)(D) 9 (A)(B)(C)(D) 17 (A)(B)(C)(D) 25 (A)(B)(C)(D) 33 (A)(B)(C)(D)
2 (A)(B)(C)(D) 10 (A)(B)(C)(D) 18 (A)(B)(C)(D) 26 (A)(B)(C)(D) 34 (A)(B)(C)(D)
3 (A)(B)(C)(D) 11 (A)(B)(C)(D) 19 (A)(B)(C)(D) 27 (A)(B)(C)(D) 35 (A)(B)(C)(D)
4 (A)(B)(C)(D) 12 (A)(B)(C)(D) 20 (A)(B)(C)(D) 28 (A)(B)(C)(D) 36 (A)(B)(C)(D)
5 (A)(B)(C)(D) 13 (A)(B)(C)(D) 21 (A)(B)(C)(D) 29 (A)(B)(C)(D) 37 (A)(B)(C)(D)
6 (A)(B)(C)(D) 14 (A)(B)(C)(D) 22 (A)(B)(C)(D) 30 (A)(B)(C)(D) 38 (A)(B)(C)(D)
7 (A)(B)(C)(D) 15 (A)(B)(C)(D) 23 (A)(B)(C)(D) 31 (A)(B)(C)(D) 39 (A)(B)(C)(D)
8 (A)(B)(C)(D) 16 (A)(B)(C)(D) 24 (A)(B)(C)(D) 32 (A)(B)(C)(D) 40 (A)(B)(C)(D)

right in section 3

wrong in section 3

SECTION 4

1 (A)(B)(C)(D) 11 (A)(B)(C)(D) 21 (A)(B)(C)(D) 31 (A)(B)(C)(D) 41 (A)(B)(C)(D)
2 (A)(B)(C)(D) 12 (A)(B)(C)(D) 22 (A)(B)(C)(D) 32 (A)(B)(C)(D) 42 (A)(B)(C)(D)
3 (A)(B)(C)(D) 13 (A)(B)(C)(D) 23 (A)(B)(C)(D) 33 (A)(B)(C)(D) 43 (A)(B)(C)(D)
4 (A)(B)(C)(D) 14 (A)(B)(C)(D) 24 (A)(B)(C)(D) 34 (A)(B)(C)(D) 44 (A)(B)(C)(D)
5 (A)(B)(C)(D) 15 (A)(B)(C)(D) 25 (A)(B)(C)(D) 35 (A)(B)(C)(D) 45 (A)(B)(C)(D)
6 (A)(B)(C)(D) 16 (A)(B)(C)(D) 26 (A)(B)(C)(D) 36 (A)(B)(C)(D) 46 (A)(B)(C)(D)
7 (A)(B)(C)(D) 17 (A)(B)(C)(D) 27 (A)(B)(C)(D) 37 (A)(B)(C)(D) 47 (A)(B)(C)(D)
8 (A)(B)(C)(D) 18 (A)(B)(C)(D) 28 (A)(B)(C)(D) 38 (A)(B)(C)(D) 48 (A)(B)(C)(D)
9 (A)(B)(C)(D) 19 (A)(B)(C)(D) 29 (A)(B)(C)(D) 39 (A)(B)(C)(D) 49 (A)(B)(C)(D)
10 (A)(B)(C)(D) 20 (A)(B)(C)(D) 30 (A)(B)(C)(D) 40 (A)(B)(C)(D) 50 (A)(B)(C)(D)

right in section 4

wrong in section 4

SECTION 1

Time—20 Minutes
40 Questions

This section consists of two different types of questions. There are directions and a sample question for each type.

Each of the following questions consists of one word followed by five words or phrases. Select the one word or phrase whose meaning is closest to the word in capital letters.

1. EXCESS:

   (A) exit
   (B) surplus
   (C) disorder
   (D) end

2. REIMBURSE:

   (A) punish
   (B) divert
   (C) compensate
   (D) recollect

3. ASTOUND:

   (A) stun
   (B) laugh
   (C) suspend
   (D) scold

4. MASSIVE:

   (A) high
   (B) inferior
   (C) huge
   (D) ancient

5. DIN:

   (A) departure
   (B) clamor
   (C) code
   (D) supper

6. SCARCE:

   (A) delicious
   (B) afraid
   (C) thin
   (D) rare

7. DECEIT:

   (A) civility
   (B) trickery
   (C) rudeness
   (D) despair

8. HALLOWED:

   (A) carved
   (B) distinguished
   (C) empty
   (D) sacred

GO ON TO THE NEXT PAGE

9. APPREHENSION:

   (A) appreciation

   (B) worry

   (C) aggravation

   (D) elevation

10. BLEAK:

   (A) charming

   (B) warm

   (C) drowsy

   (D) dreary

11. OFFEND:

   (A) divulge

   (B) betray

   (C) soothe

   (D) insult

12. VIGOROUS:

   (A) robust

   (B) hungry

   (C) destructive

   (D) lovely

13. DESPONDENT:

   (A) heightened

   (B) annoyed

   (C) relaxed

   (D) depressed

14. SATIATE:

   (A) prolong

   (B) elongate

   (C) seal

   (D) satisfy

15. SPONTANEOUS:

   (A) impulsive

   (B) excitable

   (C) ingenious

   (D) dazzling

16. WAN:

   (A) short

   (B) pale

   (C) foreign

   (D) insincere

17. ABHOR:

   (A) despise

   (B) horrify

   (C) avoid

   (D) deny

18. APPARITION:

   (A) clothing

   (B) ghost

   (C) guard

   (D) wall

19. BENEVOLENT:

   (A) disobedient

   (B) charitable

   (C) sensitive

   (D) widespread

20. TOLERANT:

   (A) open-minded

   (B) friendly

   (C) grave

   (D) ambitious

GO ON TO THE NEXT PAGE

Directions: Select the word(s) that best fit the meaning of each sentence.

21. The _____ writer was on her 12th novel.

    (A) myopic
    (B) prolific
    (C) nefarious
    (D) elusive

22. Though underfunded, the school made the best of its _____ resources.

    (A) meager
    (B) emphatic
    (C) acrid
    (D) belittled

23. The advent of the computer chip made Frank's job _____.

    (A) exuberant
    (B) eminent
    (C) belligerent
    (D) obsolete

24. All efforts to save the nature preserve proved _____.

    (A) inextricable
    (B) insular
    (C) glib
    (D) futile

25. Except for periods where they function as "loners," wolves are generally _____ animals, living in packs.

    (A) carnivorous
    (B) fearsome
    (C social
    (D) wild

26. The company employed many unproductive employees who had a(n) _____ approach to their work.

    (A) creative
    (B) discontented
    (C) independent
    (D) lackadaisical

27. The recent forest fire, which _____ the mountains of Indonesia, was the most severe _____ disaster the region has ever experienced.

    (A) destroyed .. inflammable
    (B) devastated .. environmental
    (C) singed .. intangible
    (D) burned .. scientific

28. Despite his _____ beginnings as the son of a minor tribal chieftain, the warrior became one of the greatest _____ in Asia.

    (A) humble .. rulers
    (B) luxurious .. leaders
    (C) innocent .. monarchs
    (D) regal .. kings

29. Although Angela was an interior decorator, her home was _____ decorated.

    (A) sufficiently
    (B) impressively
    (C) modestly
    (D) amply

30. Beneath the calm surface of the lake, marine creatures _____ continually for food.

    (A) qualified
    (B) survived
    (C) contested
    (D) gathered

GO ON TO THE NEXT PAGE

31. The captain demonstrated his _____ for the crew by bellowing his commands in a harsh voice.

    (A) admiration
    (B) contempt
    (C) reverence
    (D) affinity

32. The ballet dancers performed with a grace and _____ that left the audience breathless.

    (A) hilarity
    (B) ineptitude
    (C) elegance
    (D) reserve

33. Due to _____ weather, the school closed and _____ all classes.

    (A) cold .. continued
    (B) inclement .. canceled
    (C) humid .. alleviated
    (D) shoddy .. rescheduled

34. The volunteer association _____ people with a wide range of _____ to staff their offices.

    (A) recruited .. attributes
    (B) fired .. skills
    (C) rejected .. experiences
    (D) hired .. tendencies

35. In spite of her _____ work, Joanne did not receive a promotion.

    (A) tardy
    (B) industrious
    (C) irate
    (D) occasional

36. The sky jumper was _____ to survive after his parachute operated _____ .

    (A) unable .. perfectly
    (B) anxious .. instinctively
    (C) surprised .. adequately
    (D) fortunate .. improperly

37. The puppy was _____ to discipline, and whined when reprimanded by its new owner.

    (A) anxious
    (B) unaccustomed
    (C) jovial
    (D) used

38. The old _____ hated parties and refused to _____ in the festivities.

    (A) actor .. direct
    (B) curmudgeon .. partake
    (C) mediator .. take
    (D) surgeon .. place

39. Jeremy has a(n) _____ personality and is very uncomfortable in social situations.

    (A) jolly
    (B) introverted
    (C) outgoing
    (D) gregarious

40. The _____ agreement had never been written down but was understood and upheld by the governments of both countries.

    (A) tacit
    (B) public
    (C) distinguished
    (D) illegal

IF YOU FINISH BEFORE TIME IS CALLED, YOU MAY CHECK YOUR WORK ON THIS SECTION ONLY. DO NOT TURN TO ANY OTHER SECTION IN THE TEST.

STOP

SECTION 2

Time—35 Minutes

35 Questions

In this section there are four possible answers after each question. Choose which one is best. You may use the blank space at the right of the page for scratch work.

<u>Note</u>: Figures are drawn with the greatest possible accuracy, UNLESS stated "Not Drawn to Scale."

1. Two radii of a circle combine to form a diameter if they meet at an angle whose measure in degrees is

    (A)   90 degrees

    (B)   120 degrees

    (C)   180 degrees

    (D)   240 degrees

USE THIS SPACE FOR FIGURING.

2. The price of a stock doubled from Monday to Tuesday. What is the percent increase in the price of the stock from Monday to Tuesday?

    (A)   50%

    (B)   100%

    (C)   150%

    (D)   200%

3. Which of the following is true?

    (A) $0.2 \times 0.2 = 0.4$

    (B) $0.2 \times 2 = 0.04$

    (C) $\dfrac{0.2}{2} = 0.1$

    (D) $\dfrac{0.2}{0.1} = 0.01$

4. A square has a perimeter of 8. What is the length of one of its sides?

    (A)   2

    (B)   4

    (C)   8

    (D)   16

GO ON TO THE NEXT PAGE

USE THIS SPACE FOR FIGURING.

5. All of the following are equal to $\frac{1}{3}$ EXCEPT

   (A) $\frac{6}{18}$

   (B) $\frac{10}{30}$

   (C) $\frac{11}{33}$

   (D) $\frac{7}{24}$

6. If N is an integer, which of the following must be odd?

   (A) $2N$

   (B) $N + 1$

   (C) $2N + 1$

   (D) $3N + 1$

7. If $\frac{700}{x} = 35$, then $x =$

   (A) 2

   (B) 5

   (C) 20

   (D) 200

8. Which of the following is closest to 15%?

   (A) $\frac{1}{7}$

   (B) $\frac{1}{5}$

   (C) $\frac{1}{4}$

   (D) $\frac{1}{3}$

9. When A is divided by 5 it leaves a remainder of 3. What is the remainder when $A + 2$ is divided by 5?

   (A) 0

   (B) 1

   (C) 2

   (D) 3

GO ON TO THE NEXT PAGE

USE THIS SPACE FOR FIGURING.

10. The difference between 30% of 400 and 15% of 400 is

(A) 200

(B) 150

(C) 60

(D) 30

11. If $\dfrac{x}{3} = \dfrac{y}{6} = 3$, what is the value of $x + y$?

(A) 27

(B) 21

(C) 18

(D) 9

12. In the triangle in Figure 1, $x =$

(A) 50

(B) 60

(C) 80

(D) 100

Figure 1

13. In Figure 2, if triangle ABC and triangle CED are equilateral, then the measure in degrees of angle BCE is

(A) 60

(B) 90

(C) 120

(D) 180

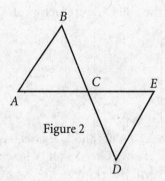

Figure 2

14. If 9 is added to the product of 12 and 4, the result is

(A) 17

(B) 25

(C) 57

(D) 84

GO ON TO THE NEXT PAGE

15. If 45 is divided by the product of 3 and 5, the result is

    (A) 3
    (B) 5
    (C) 9
    (D) 15

USE THIS SPACE FOR FIGURING.

16. Joe shoveled snow for $2\frac{1}{3}$ hours in the morning, and then for another $1\frac{3}{4}$ hours in the afternoon. How many hours did he shovel in total?

    (A) $3\frac{1}{6}$
    (B) $3\frac{5}{6}$
    (C) $4\frac{1}{12}$
    (D) 7

17. All of the following are factors of 27 EXCEPT

    (A) 1
    (B) 3
    (C) 7
    (D) 27

18. Greg has 50 cents and Margaret has $5. If Margaret gives Greg 75 cents, how much money will Greg have?

    (A) $1
    (B) $1.25
    (C) $1.50
    (D) $5.50

GO ON TO THE NEXT PAGE

19. $\dfrac{1}{2} + \dfrac{1}{6} =$

USE THIS SPACE FOR FIGURING.

(A) $\dfrac{1}{3}$

(B) $\dfrac{2}{3}$

(C) $\dfrac{5}{6}$

(D) $\dfrac{1}{12}$

20. How many integers are there from 1,960 to 1,980, inclusive?

(A) 10

(B) 20

(C) 21

(D) 30

GO ON TO THE NEXT PAGE

Directions: In questions 21–35, note the given information, if any, and then compare the quantity in Column A to the quantity in Column B. Next to the number of each question write

A   if the quantity in Column A is greater.

B   if the quantity in Column B is greater.

C   if the two quantities are equal.

D   if the relationship cannot be determined from the information given.

	Column A	Column B

21. $3 + 4$ | 3×4

22. $1{,}000 - 3.45002$ | $1{,}000 - 3.45601$

The ages of the 5 members of a certain family are
8, 12, 16, 20, and 24.

23. The average (arithmetic mean) age of the 5 family members | 16

The price of one grapefruit is $0.45 and the price of a bag of oranges is $2.45.

24. The price of a grapefruit | The price of an orange

25. Area of a triangle with a base of 6 and a height of 10 | Area of a triangle with a base of 12 and a height of 5

26. $\dfrac{1}{4}$ of 12,948 | 25% of 12,948

GO ON TO THE NEXT PAGE

Column A	Column B

27. n | n^2

28. $2(2x + 1)$ | $4x + 4$

29. $\dfrac{1}{4} + \dfrac{5}{8} + \dfrac{11}{12}$ | $\dfrac{3}{16} + \dfrac{3}{7} + \dfrac{2}{9}$

30. $9.9999 - 2$ | $0.99999 + 7$

$10M + 2 = 32$

31. 3 | M

32. 5% of 100 | 100% of 5

33. $\dfrac{1}{4}$ | $0.2569 - 0.007$

A sweater sells for $60.

34. The price of the sweater after a 10% discount | $50

35. 4.23×8 | 37.2×8

IF YOU FINISH BEFORE TIME IS CALLED, YOU MAY CHECK YOUR WORK ON
THIS SECTION ONLY. DO NOT TURN TO ANY OTHER SECTION IN THE TEST.

SECTION 3

Time—35 Minutes

40 Questions

> **Read each passage carefully and then answer the questions about it. For each question, decide on the basis of the passage which one of the choices best answers the question.**

The word "chocolate" is a generic term used to describe a variety of foods made from the seeds or beans of the cacao tree. The first people known to
Line have consumed chocolate were the Aztecs, who
(5) used cacao seeds to brew a bitter, aromatic drink. It was not until the Mexican expedition of Hernan Cortes in 1519, however, that Europeans first learned of cacao. Cortes came to the New World primarily in search of gold, but his interest was
(10) apparently also piqued by the Aztec's peculiar beverage, for when he returned to Spain, his ship's cargo included three chests of cacao beans. It was from these beans that Europe experienced its first taste of what seemed a very exotic beverage. The
(15) drink soon became popular among those wealthy enough to afford it, and over the next century cafes specializing in chocolate drinks began to spring up throughout Europe.

1. As used in line 1, the word "generic" means

    (A) scientific.

    (B) technical.

    (C) general.

    (D) obscure.

2. The passage suggests that chocolate foods can be

    (A) unhealthy if consumed in excessive quantities.

    (B) one of the staples of a society's diet.

    (C) made from various parts of the cacao tree.

    (D) made from ingredients other than the cacao tree.

3. It can be inferred from the passage that Cortes journeyed to Mexico mainly in order to

    (A) conquer the Aztecs.

    (B) increase his personal wealth.

    (C) claim new land for Spain.

    (D) gain personal glory.

4. The author implies in lines 9–14 that Cortes found the Aztecs' chocolate drink to be

    (A) sweet.

    (B) relaxing.

    (C) stimulating.

    (D) strange.

5. The passage suggests that most of the chocolate consumed by Europeans in the 1500s was

    (A) expensive.

    (B) candy.

    (C) made by Aztecs.

    (D) made by Cortes.

GO ON TO THE NEXT PAGE

It has been known for some time that wolves
live and hunt in hierarchically structured packs,
organized in a kind of "pecking order" similar to
Line that found in flocks of birds. At the top of the
(5) hierarchy in any wolf pack are the senior males,
dominating the others in all matters of privilege
and leadership. As many as three other distinct
subgroups may exist within a pack: mature wolves
with subordinate status in the hierarchy;
(10) immature wolves (who will not be treated as adults
until their second year); and outcast wolves
rejected by the rest of the pack. Each individual
wolf, moreover, occupies a specific position within
these subgroups, taking precedence over wolves of
(15) lower rank in the selection of food, mates, and
resting places, and holding a greater share of the
responsibility for protecting the pack from strange
wolves and other dangers.

6. According to the passage, wolves and birds are
similar in that they both

(A) mate for life.

(B) become adults at two years of age.

(C) defer to senior females.

(D) live in structured groups.

7. The passage suggests that our knowledge of the
social hierarchies of wolves is

(A) mostly theoretical.

(B) not a recent discovery.

(C) based on observations of individual
wolves.

(D) in need of long-range studies.

8. What is implied in the passage about outcast
wolves?

(A) They never share the pack's food.

(B) They sometimes kill the pack's young.

(C) Their status is lower than that of immature wolves.

(D) They are incapable of protecting the pack
from strange wolves.

9. According to the passage, the structure of a wolf
pack is determined by each wolf's share of all of
the following EXCEPT

(A) food.

(B) water.

(C) resting place.

(D) mate.

10. The author's attitude toward her subject may
best be described as

(A) admiring.

(B) critical.

(C) informative.

(D) indifferent.

GO ON TO THE NEXT PAGE

The Romantic poets in nineteenth-century Britain prided themselves on their rejection of many of the traditional practices of English poetry.
Line William Wordsworth, one of the leaders of the
(5) Romantic movement, wished to avoid what he considered the emotional insincerity and affectation characteristic of much earlier poetry; instead he attempted to achieve spontaneity and naturalness of expression in his verse. According
(10) to Wordsworth, a poet should be "a man speaking to men" rather than a detached observer delivering pronouncements from an ivory tower. John Keats, Wordsworth's younger contemporary, brought a similar attitude to his poetry. Keats tried to make
(15) even the structure of his sentences seem unpremeditated. "If poetry," he claimed, "comes not as naturally as the leaves to a tree, it had better not come at all."

11. The passage is primarily concerned with

    (A) describing an artistic movement.
    (B) detailing the achievements of William Wordsworth.
    (C) criticizing traditional English poetry.
    (D) providing information about John Keats.

12. As used in line 3, the word "traditional" means

    (A) conservative.
    (B) formal.
    (C) boring.
    (D) standard.

13. It is implied by the passage that

    (A) the Romantic poets wrote better poetry than their predecessors did.
    (B) Keats imitated Wordsworth's poetry.
    (C) Keats is considered a Romantic poet.
    (D) Keats only wrote poetry about nature.

14. By the statement that a poet should be "a man speaking to men," Wordsworth probably meant that poetry should

    (A) be written in the form of a dialogue.
    (B) always be read aloud to an audience.
    (C) not be written by women.
    (D) have the directness and spontaneity of real speech.

The Alps are becoming victims of their own grandeur. In a strange twist of fate, this vast and beautiful European mountain chain is being
Line destroyed by the very tourists it attracts. Every
(5) year, 20 million skiers visit the Alps. The Alpine roads are clogged by endless streams of vacationers in traffic jams 80 miles long. Off the roads, the Alpine terrain is threatened by the onslaught of ear-shattering dirt bikes, souped-up off-road
(10) vehicles, snowmobiles and helicopters. Snow cannons that create artificial surfaces for skiers smother the fragile Alpine flora and fauna, adding to the damage caused by factories belching out nitrous and sulfur dioxide and pouring PCBs,
(15) lead, and mercury into the rivers.

15. The primary focus of the passage is

    (A) the stunning beauty of the Alps.
    (B) the damage being done to the Alps each year by snowmobiles.
    (C) the irony of the Alps' gradual destruction by admiring visitors.
    (D) the fragile nature of the Alpine flora and fauna.

16. As used in line 2 , the word "grandeur" means

    (A) size.
    (B) location.
    (C) magnificence.
    (D) significance.

GO ON TO THE NEXT PAGE →

17. It can be inferred from the passage that snowmobiles and other vehicles

    (A) help to relieve congestion on Alpine roads.

    (B) damage the land they travel on.

    (C) kill more Alpine animals than predatory animals do.

    (D) should not be allowed anywhere in the Alps.

18. The passage implies that animals living in the Alps are threatened by

    (A) various forms of human transportation.

    (B) the construction of roads and houses.

    (C) an increase in noise levels.

    (D) the spread of industrial pollutants.

    Reconstructing extinct animals from their fossil bones is a challenging and exacting science. Fossil skeletons almost never survive intact. The
Line bones of one animal may be scattered far and
(5) wide by scavengers or by water. Fragments of several animals may come to rest in the same streambed or sandbar, and careful pains must be taken not to mismatch them. As a result, paleontologists must spend years studying the skeletons of living
(10) animals, documenting form and function and comparing anatomical details of related creatures before attempting to assemble a museum display. A collection of fossils, however fascinating, reveals its true worth only when assembled by an informed
(15) anatomist.

19. As used in line 3, the word "intact" means

    (A) indefinitely.

    (B) whole.

    (C) without impurities.

    (D) above ground.

20. The passage suggests that finding a complete fossil skeleton is

    (A) a rare occurrence.

    (B) easier in arid climates.

    (C) dependent on skill rather than luck.

    (D) possible only if the animal died of natural causes.

21. The passage suggests that a fossil skeleton may be incorrectly assembled if

    (A) the bones are recovered by an informed anatomist.

    (B) the assembly is done over a long period of time.

    (C) the animal's carcass was attacked by a scavenger.

    (D) the species is not yet extinct.

22. It can be inferred from the passage that scientists who work with fossils

    (A) are employed only by museums.

    (B) frequently make mistakes.

    (C) also study geology.

    (D) learn their craft from living species.

23. The author's attitude toward paleontologists who assemble fossil collections can best be described as

    (A) skeptical.

    (B) courteous.

    (C) respectful.

    (D) uninterested.

GO ON TO THE NEXT PAGE

Edward Stratmeyer, the creator of the Hardy
Boys, Nancy Drew, and the Bobbsey Twins, did not
gain enormous commercial success through luck
Line alone. His books, in which young amateur
(5) detectives had fantastic adventures and always
saved the day, had a particular appeal in the time
they were written. When Stratmeyer himself was a
boy, the harsh economics of an industrializing
America quickly forced children to become adults.
(10) By 1900, however, prosperity began to prolong
childhood, creating a new stage of life—
adolescence. From 1900 to 1930, the heyday of
Stratmeyer's career, adolescence came of age. Child
labor laws made schooling compulsory until
(15) the age of sixteen. Young Americans, with more
free time than the working youth of the previous
century, looked to fiction and fantasy for
adventure. Stratmeyer, writing under a variety of
pseudonyms, responded to the needs of his readers
(20) with a slew of heroic super-teens.

24. The passage primarily serves to explain

(A) the universal appeal of Stratmeyer's
characters.

(B) the benefits of mandatory schooling for
teenagers.

(C) the underlying reason for a writer's
popularity.

(D) the economic boom created by child
labor laws.

25. The passage suggests that the appeal of
Stratmeyer's fictional heroes lay partly in the
fact that

(A) they worked long hours in industrial jobs.

(B) their activities were not restricted by
fictional parents.

(C) they were the same age as his readers.

(D) they were based on young people
Stratmeyer actually knew.

26. According to the passage children under sixteen
during the 1930s

(A) led lives of fun and adventure.

(B) were better off financially than ever before.

(C) began to lose interest in Stratmeyer's
books.

(D) were legally required to attend school.

27. According to the passage, Stratmeyer wrote his
books

(A) in a single thirty-year span.

(B) using a series of pseudonyms.

(C) to pay off family debts.

(D) without ever gaining commercial success.

GO ON TO THE NEXT PAGE

The ventriloquist's "dummy," the wooden figure that a ventriloquist uses to create the illusion of "throwing" his or her voice, was first
Line developed in the 1880s. On the outside, the first
(5) dummies looked very much like those used today—with much the same exaggerated mouth and range of movement. On the inside, however, the best of these wooden figures were a curious fusion of engineering feats and sculpture.
(10) Underneath the wig, the back of the dummy's head opened up, revealing tangled innards of metal and wire, screws, and levers. Arguably the most mechanically complex figures were made by the McElroy brothers, who together created one
(15) hundred figures in the ten years prior to the Second World War. The mechanical brain of the McElroy dummy was assembled from some 300 different springs, pieces of metal, typewriter keys, and bicycle spokes—a synergistic effort comparable to
(20) the work of the Wright Brothers.

28. The primary purpose of the passage is to

    (A) compare the achievements of two different families of inventors.

    (B) relate the history of the ventriloquist's art.

    (C) compare the ventriloquists' dummies of the 19th century with those produced today.

    (D) describe the complex craftsmanship behind early ventriloquists' dummies.

29. It can be inferred from the passage that the outward appearance of ventriloquists' dummies

    (A) is meant to seem as lifelike as possible.

    (B) has not changed much since they were invented.

    (C) depends on what mechanical devices are inside them.

    (D) changed after the work of the McElroy brothers.

30. The passage suggests that the most complex dummies are

    (A) created using scientific and artistic craftsmanship.

    (B) able to fool the most discerning observer.

    (C) those with the widest range of movement.

    (D) those made since the end of the Second World War.

31. The author probably argues that the McElroy brothers' dummies were "a synergistic effort" (line 19) because

    (A) the McElroys were related to the Wright Brothers.

    (B) the McElroys borrowed design concepts from other inventors.

    (C) the McElroys worked together on the design.

    (D) their dummies required so much energy to operate.

32. The author's attitude toward the McElroy brothers can best be described as

    (A) skeptical.

    (B) puzzled.

    (C) elated.

    (D) appreciative.

GO ON TO THE NEXT PAGE

A jellyfish is only two thin layers of cells, covering the inner and outer surfaces of a saucer-shaped mass of nonliving gelatinous material.
Line Equipped with an arsenal of viciously stinging
(5) tentacles, the jellyfish, though considered primitive, is one of the few species that continue to hold the human predator at bay. Every attempt to control jellyfish on swimming beaches—nets, jellyfish-specific poisons, even biological controls—
(10) has failed. The Chrysaora, or stinging nettle, for example, appears to thrive in waters overenriched by sewage pollution, so much that stinging nettle congregations have clogged the intake pipes and the cooling systems of power plants. Another
(15) nuisance is Cassiopea, the mangrove jellyfish, a stinger whose population has exploded in the polluted canals of the Florida Keys, to the detriment of the tourist industry there.

33. The main focus of the passage is on

    (A) the physical structure of the jellyfish.
    (B) the ability of the jellyfish to foil its predator.
    (C) problems in Florida tourism caused by the jellyfish.
    (D) the positive effects of pollution on the jellyfish.

34. It can be inferred from the passage that the jellyfish is considered "primitive" because of its

    (A) simple physical structure.
    (B) stinging tentacles.
    (C) lack of mobility.
    (D) preference for warm water.

35. Which of the following can be inferred from the passage about the stinging nettle?

    (A) It is an especially primitive form of jellyfish.
    (B) It generally avoids swimming beaches and canals.
    (C) It survives conditions that might kill other marine species.
    (D) It is rarely found in the Florida Keys.

36. As used in line 18, the word "detriment" means

    (A) delight.
    (B) harm.
    (C) fault.
    (D) cause.

GO ON TO THE NEXT PAGE ⇒

In 1916, James VanDerZee opened a photography studio in New York City's Harlem. It was the eve of the Harlem Renaissance—the
Line decade-long flowering of art and culture that
(5) established Harlem as the most artistically vigorous African-American community in the nation. For some 40 years, VanDerZee captured the life and spirit of that burgeoning community, producing thousands of portraits, not only of
(10) notables, but of ordinary citizens—parents and children, brides and grooms, church groups, and women's clubs. Critics consider these images important today not only for their record of Harlem life, but for their reflection of their
(15) subjects' keen sense of the importance of their culture. VanDerZee's carefully staged photographs spotlighted his subjects' pride and self-assurance. His unique vision recorded a time, place and culture that might otherwise have slipped away.

37. This passage focuses primarily on

    (A) the cultural achievements of the Harlem Renaissance.

    (B) the history of African-American photography.

    (C) the creative influences that shaped one photographer's career.

    (D) the cultural record left by a Harlem photographer.

38. It can be inferred from the passage that VanDerZee opened his studio

    (A) just before the Harlem Renaissance began.

    (B) in order to photograph African-American celebrities.

    (C) without having previous photographic experience.

    (D) with financial support from his community.

39. The passage most likely describes the subjects of VanDerZee's photographs (lines 7–13) in order to

    (A) demonstrate the artist's flair for composition.

    (B) show that his work represented the whole community.

    (C) highlight the self-assurance of Harlem residents.

    (D) reflect upon the nature of photography.

40. The author's attitude toward VanDerZee can best be described as

    (A) neutral.

    (B) condescending.

    (C) admiring.

    (D) generous.

IF YOU FINISH BEFORE TIME IS CALLED, YOU MAY CHECK YOUR WORK ON THIS SECTION ONLY. DO NOT TURN TO ANY OTHER SECTION IN THE TEST.

STOP

SECTION 4

Time—40 Minutes

45 Questions

In this section there are four possible answers after each question. Choose which one is best. You may use the blank space at the right of the page for scratchwork.

Note: Figures are drawn with the greatest possible accuracy, UNLESS stated "Not Drawn to Scale."

1. Ralph is twice as old as Howie. If Ralph is x years old, how many years old is Howie, in terms of x?

   (A) $0.5x$

   (B) $2x$

   (C) $x + 2$

   (D) $x - 2$

USE THIS SPACE FOR FIGURING.

2. A bag contains only blue and red marbles. If there are three blue marbles for every red marble, what fraction of all the marbles is red?

   (A) $\dfrac{1}{4}$

   (B) $\dfrac{1}{3}$

   (C) $\dfrac{1}{2}$

   (D) $\dfrac{3}{4}$

3. On Monday the temperatures of four different cities were 55°, −18°, 25°, and −15°. What was the average (arithmetic mean) temperature on Monday for these four cities?

   (A) 103°

   (B) 20°

   (C) 12°

   (D) 11.75°

Questions 4–5 refer to the graph in Figure 1.

4. Approximately how many medium-sized shirts were sold?

   (A) 300

   (B) 400

   (C) 500

   (D) 600

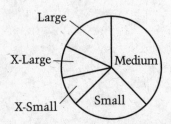

September Sales
for Ace T-Shirt Co.

Total Sales: 1,200 shirts

Figure 1

GO ON TO THE NEXT PAGE

5. If each shirt sells for $5.95, approximately how much was spent on small-sized shirts?

   (A) $300
   (B) $900
   (C) $1,800
   (D) $3,600

6. How many seconds are there in $\frac{1}{20}$ of a minute?

   (A) 2
   (B) 3
   (C) 20
   (D) 30

7. What is the greatest number of squares, each measuring two centimeters by two centimeters, that can be cut from a rectangle with a length of eight centimeters and a width of six centimeters?

   (A) 48
   (B) 12
   (C) 8
   (D) 6

8. Five percent of the guests at a Halloween party were dressed as witches. If there were eight witches at the party, how many guests were at the party?

   (A) 40
   (B) 80
   (C) 160
   (D) 200

USE THIS SPACE FOR FIGURING.

GO ON TO THE NEXT PAGE

Questions 9–10 refer to the following definition.

For all real numbers a and b, a@b = $(a \times b) - (a + b)$

Example: 6 @ 5 = $(6 \times 5) - (6 + 5) = 30 - 11 = 19$

USE THIS SPACE FOR FIGURING.

9. 9@8 =

(A) 73

(B) 72

(C) 71

(D) 55

10. If 10@$N = -1$, then $N =$

(A) 0

(B) 1

(C) 9

(D) 11

11. A record collection was divided among six people so that each received the same number of records. Which of the following could be the number of records in the collection?

(A) 10

(B) 15

(C) 21

(D) 24

12. At which of the following times is the smaller angle formed by the minute hand and the hour hand of a clock less than 90 degrees?

(A) 1:30

(B) 3:00

(C) 4:30

(D) 6:00

GO ON TO THE NEXT PAGE

13. Carol spent $\frac{1}{2}$ of her day at work, and $\frac{2}{3}$ of her time at work in meetings. What fraction of her entire day did Carol spend in meetings?

   (A) $\frac{1}{2}$

   (B) $\frac{1}{3}$

   (C) $\frac{1}{5}$

   (D) $\frac{1}{6}$

14. If $\frac{1}{2} \times S = 0.2$, then $S =$

   (A) $\frac{2}{5}$

   (B) $\frac{1}{4}$

   (C) $\frac{1}{5}$

   (D) $\frac{1}{10}$

15. If 50% of a number equals 75, then 10% of the number equals

   (A)   15

   (B)   30

   (C)   60

   (D) 150

16. If $\frac{1}{2} + \frac{1}{3} = \frac{M}{12}$, then $M =$

   (A)   8

   (B)   9

   (C) 10

   (D) 11

USE THIS SPACE FOR FIGURING.

GO ON TO THE NEXT PAGE

17. The perimeter of a rectangle is 32. If its length is three times as long as its width, what is its width?

(A) 12

(B) 8

(C) 6

(D) 4

$$2{,}955 \times A = 35{,}460$$
$$11{,}820 \times B = 35{,}460$$
$$3{,}940 \times C = 35{,}460$$
$$7{,}092 \times D = 35{,}460$$

18. If each of the above equations is correctly solved, which of the following has the greatest value?

(A) A

(B) B

(C) C

(D) D

19. In a certain garage, 3 out of every 10 cars are foreign. If there are 180 cars at the garage, how many of them are foreign?

(A) 27

(B) 45

(C) 54

(D) 60

20. If $N_¿ = N \times 10$, then $30_¿ + 2_¿ =$

(A) 32

(B) 302

(C) 320

(D) 3,200

USE THIS SPACE FOR FIGURING.

GO ON TO THE NEXT PAGE

21. Patricia began reading from the beginning of page 42 of a book, and stopped at the end of page 83. How many pages did she read?

   (A) 40
   (B) 41
   (C) 42
   (D) 43

22. In Figure 2, if $AB = 8$ and $AC = 14$, how far is the midpoint of AB from the midpoint of BC?

   (A) 3
   (B) 4
   (C) 7
   (D) 8

23. Judy has six more baseball cards than her brother. How many would she have to give him so that they would have an equal number of cards?

   (A) 6
   (B) 4
   (C) 3
   (D) 2

24. Fred averaged 168 on the first three games he bowled. What must he score on his fourth game in order to raise his average 5 points?

   (A) 158
   (B) 163
   (C) 178
   (D) 188

25. Which of the following equations could NEVER be true?

   (A) $N \times 0 = N$
   (B) $1 \times N = N$
   (C) $N \times N = N$
   (D) $N - 1 = N$

USE THIS SPACE FOR FIGURING.

$A \qquad B \qquad C$

Figure 2

GO ON TO THE NEXT PAGE

26. If X is the set of numbers greater than 6 and Y is the set of numbers less than 11, how many whole numbers exist that are in both sets?

    (A) 4
    (B) 5
    (C) 6
    (D) Infinitely many

27. Mary has 30% more money than June has. If June has $65, how much money does Mary have?

    (A) $84.50
    (B) $80
    (C) $50
    (D) $45.50

28. If 9 is x percent of 90, what is 50 percent of x?

    (A) 5
    (B) 10
    (C) 15
    (D) 18

29. A certain machine caps 5 bottles every 2 seconds. At this rate, how many bottles will be capped in 1 minute?

    (A) 75
    (B) 150
    (C) 225
    (D) 300

30. What is five percent of twenty percent of one hundred?

    (A) 1
    (B) 5
    (C) 20
    (D) 25

USE THIS SPACE FOR FIGURING.

GO ON TO THE NEXT PAGE

31. If an exam had 10 questions and Keith answered 2 questions incorrectly, what percent of the questions did he answer incorrectly?

    (A) 2%

    (B) 10%

    (C) 12%

    (D) 20%

32. The difference between 6,985 and 3,001 is approximately

    (A) 3,000

    (B) 3,500

    (C) 4,000

    (D) 4,500

33. One and one-third minus five-sixths equals

    (A) $\dfrac{1}{4}$

    (B) $\dfrac{1}{3}$

    (C) $\dfrac{1}{2}$

    (D) $\dfrac{3}{4}$

34. Patty and Liza went out for lunch. Patty paid $3.30 for a drink and two hot dogs. Liza paid $2.15 for a drink and one hot dog. How much did a hot dog cost?

    (A) $0.90

    (B) $1.15

    (C) $1.30

    (D) $1.65

USE THIS SPACE FOR FIGURING.

GO ON TO THE NEXT PAGE

35. If one-fourth of a number is 3, what is one-third of the same number?

   (A) 1
   (B) 2
   (C) 3
   (D) 4

USE THIS SPACE FOR FIGURING.

36. $2 \times 4 \times 7 \times 9$ is equal to the product of 18 and

   (A) 8
   (B) 14
   (C) 28
   (D) 36

37. If $12 + P = 20 - 2 \times 3$, then $P =$

   (A) 2
   (B) 14
   (C) 36
   (D) 42

38. One-tenth of 99 is

   (A) 0.99
   (B) 9.9
   (C) 99
   (D) 99.9

39. Twenty percent of 30 is

   (A) 6
   (B) 8
   (C) 10
   (D 12.5

40. $\dfrac{64}{2 \times 4} =$

   (A) 8
   (B) 24
   (C) 42
   (D) 128

GO ON TO THE NEXT PAGE

USE THIS SPACE FOR FIGURING.

41. $\dfrac{81}{9} + 2 =$

(A) 3

(B) 6

(C) 8

(D) 11

42. In a certain class, there are 6 girls for every 2 boys. What is the ratio of the number of girls to the entire class?

(A) 12:1

(B) 8:6

(C) 6:2

(D) 3:4

43. If $\dfrac{28}{a} = \dfrac{48}{12}$, then $a =$

(A) 7

(B) 8

(C) 9

(D) 10

44. If Set A contains all integers greater than 8, and Set B contains all integers less than 30, which of the following numbers could be in both sets?

(A) 0

(B) 2

(C) 4

(D) 9

45. $\dfrac{18 + 16}{4}$ equals

(A) 8

(B) 8.5

(C) 9

(D) 22

IF YOU FINISH BEFORE TIME IS CALLED, YOU MAY CHECK YOUR WORK ON THIS SECTION ONLY. DO NOT TURN TO ANY OTHER SECTION IN THE TEST.

 STOP

SECTION 5

Time—30 Minutes

DIRECTIONS: Write an essay on the following prompt on the paper provided. Your essay should NOT exceed two pages and must be written in ink. Erasing is not allowed.

Prompt: <u>You can't teach an old dog new tricks.</u>

Do you agree or disagree with this statement? Use examples from history, literature, or your own personal experience to support your point of view.

_____

_____

_____

_____

_____

_____

_____

_____

_____

_____

_____

_____

_____

_____

_____

_____

GO ON TO THE NEXT PAGE ⟩

_____

_____

_____

_____

_____

_____

_____

_____

_____

_____

_____

_____

_____

_____

_____

_____

_____

_____

_____

_____

_____

ANSWERS AND EXPLANATIONS

SECTION 1: VERBAL

SYNONYMS

1. B

An excess is an extra amount of something—a surplus.

2. C

To reimburse someone is to pay him back or to compensate him.

3. A

When you astound someone, you greatly surprise or stun him.

4. C

Something that is massive is extremely large or huge.

5. B

Din refers to a large and distracting sound or a clamor.

6. D

When something is scarce there is not a lot of it; it is very rare.

7. B

If you accuse someone of deceit, you are accusing him of being untruthful or of trickery.

8. D

You often hear the expression "hallowed ground," which means sacred ground.

9. B

If you have apprehension about something, you have an acute concern or worry about it.

10. D

When something is bleak, like the weather, it is very harsh or dreary.

11. D

To offend someone is to be extremely rude to them or to insult them.

12. A

Someone who is vigorous is very lively and healthy—robust.

13. D

A despondent person feels very hopeless and depressed.

14. D

If you are very hungry, and then eat a large meal, you can say that your appetite has been satiated or satisfied.

15. A

Spontaneous actions or behavior occur with no apparent reason or cause—they are impulsive.

16. B

Someone whose face is very wan is sickly and pale.

17. A

If you abhor liver or brussel sprouts, you dislike them immensely—you despise them.

18. B

If you see an apparition on Halloween, you are seeing something resembling a ghost.

19. B

A person who is benevolent is kind and giving—charitable.

20. A

A tolerant person does not become angry or intimidated by new and strange ideas because he is open-minded.

SENTENCE COMPLETIONS

21. B

This author has written a lot of novels, so we need a word that describes an author who writes a great deal. Prolific means producing abundant works.

22. A

The school has managed in this situation in spite of a lack of funds. Meager means deficient in quantity or scant. Don't be misled by (D), belittled. True, it has to do with little, but in an emotional sense. One feels belittled by public criticism.

23. D

With the advent, or arrival, of the computer chip, Frank's job became "something." Common sense tells us that his job became outdated or extinct. Obsolete means just that: no longer useful.

24. D

There were efforts to do something to the nature preserve. Whatever those efforts were, we can infer from the word "proved" that they were unsuccessful. Inextricable, (A), looks tempting, as it means incapable of being disentangled (think of extricating yourself from something), but it doesn't make sense here. Futile, (D), means having no useful result or ineffective.

25. C

The clue "except for" indicates that you're looking for the opposite of "loners"—social, (C).

26. D

"Unproductive" is the clue here—it suggests that the company employs people who don't work hard. In other words, they have a lackadaisical approach to their work.

27. B

(B) environmental is the only word that fits the second blank—a forest fire "devastated the region" fits the first blank.

28. A

"Despite" is a clue that indicates contrast—in spite of his humble beginnings, the chieftain became one of the greatest rulers.

29. C

Another contrast question—in spite of Angela's job as an interior decorator, her home might be modestly decorated.

30. C

Contested is the only word that fits the context here—you can't gather, qualify, or survive for food if you're a marine creature.

31. B

You're looking for a negative word here—(B)'s contempt fits the captain's attitude best.

32. C

Which word goes best with grace? Grace and (C), elegance, are the two words that best describe a ballet dancer.

33. B

A logical structure here—predict words like "bad" and "closed" for the two blanks here—(B)'s inclement and canceled work best.

34. A

The word "staff" indicates that the volunteer association is either (A), recruiting, or (D), hiring. (A)'s attributes is the word that best fits the idea of job qualifications.

35. B

The phrase "in spite of" indicates a contrast or paradox—you can tell that Joanne didn't get the promotion even though she worked hard. (B), industrious, is the only word that works.

36. D

The sky diver's reaction has to be consistent with his parachute—if it opened improperly, then he would be fortunate to survive.

37. B

The logic of the sentence suggests that the puppy would only whine if unaccustomed or unused to discipline.

38. B

Only (B), take, and (C), partake, make sense in the second blank; only curmudgeon meaning grumpy old man fits blank number one.

39. B

Another word for "uncomfortable in social situations" is (B), introverted.

40. A

If something is not written down, but understood, it is described as tacit, (A).

SECTION 2: MATH

1. C

A diameter is a chord that runs straight through the center of a circle. Two radii will form a diameter if they form a straight line, as shown in the figure below. A straight angle has 180°, so (C) is correct.

2. B

If the price of the stock doubled, it increased by its full price, or 100%, (B). If this isn't clear, pick a number for the original price of the stock, say $100. On Tuesday it would be twice this, or $200. So the increase is $200 − $100 = $100; $100 is 100% of $100, so again (B) is correct.

3. C

Evaluate each choice to see which is true:

(A) $0.2 \times 0.2 = 0.04$, not 0.4, so (A) is false

(B) $0.2 \times 2 = 0.4$, not 0.04, so (B) is false

(C) $0.2 \div 2 = 0.1$, so (C) is true

(D) $0.2 \div 0.1 = 2$, not 0.01, so (D) is false

4. A

A square has 4 equal sides, so its perimeter is equal to $4s$, where s represents the length of one of its sides. So $4s = 8$, and a side of the square has length 2.

5. D

Evaluate each choice to see which is not equal to $\frac{1}{3}$:

(A) $\frac{6}{18} = \frac{1}{3}$ (when you factor out a 6)

(B) $\frac{10}{30} = \frac{1}{3}$ (when you factor out a 10)

(C) $\frac{11}{33} = \frac{1}{3}$ (when you factor out an 11)

(D) $\frac{7}{24} \neq \frac{1}{3}$

6. C

Pick numbers for N and see which of the choices must be odd. The question says must, not can, so the correct choice will be the one that is odd no matter what number you pick. Start with $N = 1$:

(A) $2N = 2$; even so eliminate (A). Any integer multiplied by 2 will be even.

(B) $N + 1 = 2$; even so eliminate B)

(C) $2N + 1 = 3$; odd. To see if this is always the case, try $N = 2$: $2N + 1 = 5$; odd, so (C) is correct. Since any integer multiplied by 2 will be even, $2N + 1$ will always be odd.

(D) If $N = 1$, $3N + 1 = 4$; even so eliminate (D).

7. C

You know $\dfrac{700}{x} = 35$ so $35x = 700$ and $700 \div 35 = 20$. Thus, $x = 20$.

8. A

Fifteen percent $= \dfrac{15}{100} = 0.15$. Convert each choice to a decimal to see which comes closest to 0.15.

(A) $\dfrac{1}{7} = 0.142...$

(B) $\dfrac{1}{5} = 0.2$

(C) $\dfrac{1}{4} = 0.25$

(D) $\dfrac{1}{3} = 0.0\overline{33}$

Of the choices, 0.142 is closest to 0.15, so (A) is correct.

9. A

Pick a number for A. Since A leaves a remainder of 3 when divided by 5, let $A = 5 + 3 = 8$. You're asked for the remainder when $A + 2$, or 10 is divided by 5. 10 is divisible by 5, so it leaves a remainder of 0.

10. C

You could figure out 30% of 400, then figure out 15% of 400, and then find their difference, but it's not necessary. The difference between 30% of a number and 15% of that same number is $30\% - 15\% = 15\%$ of that number. 15% of 400 is 60, so (C) is correct.

11. A

Since $\dfrac{x}{3}$ and $\dfrac{y}{6}$ both equal 3, $\dfrac{x}{3} = 3$, and $x = 3 \times 3 = 9$ and $\dfrac{y}{6} = 3$, so $y = 3 \times 6 = 18$. So $x + y = 9 + 18 = 27$.

12. C

The triangle in Figure 1 is isosceles, since it has two sides of length 2. Therefore, the angles opposite these sides are also equal, and the unidentified base angle must equal 50°. The interior angles of a triangle sum to 180°, so $50 + 50 + x = 180$, $100 + x = 180$, and $x = 80$.

13. C

Since triangle ABC is equilateral, it has three 60° angles. Therefore, $\angle BCA$ is 60°. $\angle BCE$ is supplementary to $\angle BCA$, so $60 + \angle BCE = 180$ and $\angle BCE = 120$.

14. C

The product of two numbers is the result of multiplying them together, so the product of 12 and 4 is $12 \times 4 = 48$. Adding 9 to 48 gives you 57, (C).

15. A

The product of 3 and 5 is equal to $3 \times 5 = 15$. $45 \div 15 = 3$, (A).

16. C

Joe shoveled for a total of $2\dfrac{1}{3} + 1\dfrac{3}{4}$ hours. To add, first convert to improper fractions: $\dfrac{7}{3} + \dfrac{7}{4}$. Then find a common denominator: $\dfrac{28}{12} + \dfrac{21}{12} = \dfrac{49}{12}$. Lastly, convert to a mixed number: $= 4$.

17. C

Evaluate each choice to see whether it is a factor of 27:

(A) $1 \times 27 = 27$, so 1 is a factor

(B) $3 \times 9 = 27$, so 3 is a factor

(C) 7 is *not* a factor of 27

(D) $27 \times 1 = 27$, so 27 is a factor

18. B

Greg has $0.50 and is given $0.75, for a total of $1.25, (B).

19. B

$\frac{1}{2} + \frac{1}{6} = \frac{3}{6} + \frac{1}{6} = \frac{4}{6} = \frac{2}{3}$, (B)

20. C

To find the number of integers in an inclusive range, subtract the first integer from the last integer, and then add 1: $1,980 - 1,960 = 20$; $20 + 1 = 21$, choice (C).

21. B

In Column A, $3 + 4 = 7$. In Column B, $3 \times 4 = 12$. Since Column B is greater, (B) is correct.

22. A

You don't need to figure out the differences to answer this QC. In both cases you're subtracting some number from 1,000. Since you're subtracting more from 1,000 in Column B, the difference in Column B will be smaller than the difference in Column A.

23. C

$$\text{Average} = \frac{\text{Sum of terms}}{\text{Number of terms}}, \text{ so here:}$$

$$\text{average age} = \frac{8 + 12 + 16 + 20 + 24}{5}$$

$$= \frac{80}{5}$$

$$= 16$$

You could have saved time if you remembered that the average of a group of consecutive integers is equal to the middle value. The ages of the family happen to be consecutive multiples of 4, so their average is the middle value, or 16.

24. D

You're told that a grapefruit costs $0.45, so that's the value in Column A. You're told that a bag of oranges costs $2.45, but you're given no information about the number of oranges in the bag. If there were 2 oranges in the bag, each would cost about $1.25 and Column B would be greater. But if there were 10 oranges in the bag, each would cost about $0.25, and Column A would be greater. As it stands, you are not given enough information to determine which column is larger, so (D) is correct.

25. C

Area of a triangle is equal to $\frac{1}{2}$(base)(height). In Column A you have $\frac{1}{2}(6)(10) = 30$. In Column B you have $\frac{1}{2}(12)(5) = 30$. The columns are equal, so (C) is correct.

26. C

In Column A you have $\frac{1}{4}$ of 12,948 and in Column B you have 25% of 12,948. Since $\frac{1}{4} = 25\%$, the columns will be equal. Notice that you didn't need to do any calculation to solve this problem—in fact doing so would be wasting time you could use to answer other questions.

27. D

Pick numbers for *n*. If $n = 1$, Column A is 1 and Column B is $1^2 = 1$, and the columns are equal. But if $n = 2$, Column A is 2, and Column B is $2^2 = 4$, and Column B is greater. Since there is more than one possible relationship between the columns, (D) is correct.

28. B

Multiplying through Column A gives you $4x + 2$. Comparing piece by piece, while you may not know the value of $4x$, it will be the same in both columns. Looking at the second piece in each column, 4 is greater than 2, so Column B is greater.

29. A

It's not necessary—and is actually a waste of time— to find common denominators and calculate the sum in each column. Compare piece by piece. The first piece in Column A is $\frac{1}{4}$ and the first piece in Column B is $\frac{3}{16}$; $\frac{1}{4} = \frac{4}{16}$, so the first piece in A is bigger. The second piece in A is $\frac{5}{8}$, which is a little more than $\frac{1}{2}$, and the second piece in B is $\frac{3}{7}$, which is a little less than $\frac{1}{2}$. Therefore the second piece in A is greater. The third piece in A is $\frac{11}{12}$, which is greater than $\frac{1}{2}$, and the third piece in B is $\frac{2}{9}$, which is less than $\frac{1}{2}$. So the third piece in A is also greater, and Column A is greater.

30. B

The value in Column A is 7.9999, and the value in Column B is 7.99999. Column A only shows four places to the right of the decimal place, so any other places are understood to be zeros. Therefore Column A is actually 7.99990. So Column B is 0.00009 greater than Column A.

31. C

$10M + 2 = 32$, so $10M = 30$ and $M = 3$. Therefore the columns are equal.

32. C

This question is a breeze if you remember that a% of $b = b$% of a. If not, work it out. In Column A, 5% of 100 is 5. In Column B, 100% of 5 is 5. The columns are equal, so (C) is correct.

33. A

Put the columns in the same form so that they're easier to compare. In Column A, $\frac{1}{4} = 0.25$. In Column B, $0.2569 - 0.007 = 0.2499$, but it's enough to just see that it will be less than 0.25 in Column A.

34. A

A 10 percent discount on a price of $60 is $6, so the sale price is $60 − $6 = $54. This is greater than $50 in Column B.

35. B

Comparing piece by piece you see that the second pieces in both columns, namely 8, are equal. Since $4.23 < 37.2$, the first piece in B, 37.2, is greater, so Column B is greater.

SECTION 3: READING COMPREHENSION

CHOCOLATE PASSAGE

The first passage is about chocolate, which comes from the seed or beans of the cacao tree. You're told that chocolate was first known to have been consumed (in drink form) by the Aztec people of Mexico, that the Spanish explorer Cortes learned of chocolate in 1519, on his expedition among the Aztec, and that he brought three chests of cacao beans back to Spain. Over the next century, the passage concludes, the chocolate drink became popular with the wealthy throughout Europe.

1. C

Chocolate, we learn, is a "generic" term that describes "a variety of foods." Generic means general or relating to a whole group.

2. C

The passage's first sentence says that chocolate can be "made from the seeds or beans of the cacao tree." Since seeds and beans are two different parts of the tree, (C) is correct. The healthiness of chocolate (A) is not mentioned; we don't know whether it's a main food or staple of any society, (B); and we don't know what other ingredients, if any, go into making chocolate, (D).

3. B

Stick to what the passage actually says. "Cortes came to the New World primarily in search of gold..." Therefore, (B) is correct: he came to amass wealth—i.e., to get rich.

4. D

We learn that Cortes' "interest was...piqued by the Aztec's peculiar beverage." The word "peculiar" suggests that Cortes found the Aztec's chocolate drinks strange, (D). Several lines earlier, we learn that the drink was bitter, so (A) is incorrect. And the passage doesn't say whether the drink was relaxing, (B), or stimulating, (C).

5. A

This question points you to the passage's final sentence. It says there that, in the century after its introduction to Europe, the chocolate drink "became popular among those wealthy enough to afford it," which implies that chocolate was very expensive in Europe at that time, (A). This early European chocolate was a drink, not a candy (B). As far as we

know, Aztecs were not imported to make the drink, (C), only the cacao beans were. And the passage never suggests that Cortes himself made most of the chocolate consumed in Europe during the entire 16th century, (D).

Wolves Passage

The next passage is about the structured packs that wolves live in. These packs are described as hierarchies similar to the "pecking order" of birds. Senior male wolves are at the top of the hierarchy, followed by mature wolves, young or immature wolves, and outcast wolves. We learn that a wolf's place in the hierarchy determines its selection of "food, mates, and resting places," and how much responsibility each wolf is given in terms of protecting the pack from danger.

6. D

Wolves are compared with birds only in the first sentence, where the wolf pack structure is compared to the pecking order of a bird flock. So both species live in structured groups, and (D) is correct. We don't learn whether birds or wolves mate for life (A), when birds become "adults" (B), or whether either species defers to senior females (C).

7. B

The passage's opening sentence notes that "it has been known for some time" that wolves live in structured packs; therefore, our knowledge of such packs is not a recent discovery (B). (A) is wrong because the information given is not theoretical. (C) is presumably wrong because information about wolf packs must come from observations of the packs themselves, not individual wolves. And (D) is never suggested.

8. C

Outcast wolves are only mentioned in the third sentence, where we learn that they are fourth in order of importance, behind senior males, mature wolves, and immature wolves. So (C) is correct: the status of outcast wolves is lower than that of immature wolves. (A), (B), and (D) are all plausible statements, but none of them is implied in the passage.

9. B

The passage's final sentence says that the order of the pack determines the selection of "food, mates, and resting places," which eliminates choices (A), (C), and (D). It's plausible that a wolf's share of water (B) would also be determined by the pack structure, but this is never mentioned, so (B) is correct.

10. C

The author's attitude toward wolf packs may best be described as informative, (C).

ROMANTICS PASSAGE

The third passage is about the Romantic poets, a group of writers in 19th-century England who "prided themselves on their rejection of" earlier English poetry. In other words, the Romantic poets tried to write differently than their predecessors. In support of this thesis, you're told about how two major Romantic poets, Wordsworth and Keats, rejected pre-Romantic poems as insincere and affected, and tried to write more spontaneous-seeming poems.

11. A

The best choice is (A): the passage describes an artistic movement, the Romantic movement in British poetry. (B) and (D) are equally wrong as each focuses on only one Romantic poet. And while (C) describes how the Romantics felt about earlier

English poetry—they were critical of it—it doesn't sum up the passage, which also describes the kind of poetry the Romantics themselves tried to write.

12. D

The word "traditional" is used here to describe earlier British poetry. The Romantics rebelled against what they saw as the usual or standard practices of earlier poets, so (D) is correct. (A), (B), and (C) are all fairly plausible in context, but don't have the equivalent meaning of "traditional."

13. C

Which of these statements is implied in the passage? (C): since Keats was Wordsworth's contemporary, and brought a similar attitude to his poetry as this leader of the Romantic movement did, Keats must also be a Romantic poet. (A) isn't implied; all we know about Romantic poetry is that it was different than earlier poetry, not that it was better (even if the Romantics themselves thought it was). Similarly, (B) is wrong because we only know that Keats brought an attitude to his writing that was similar to Wordsworth's—we don't know if the younger man actually imitated his older contemporary or not. And while Keats said that poetry should be written "as naturally as the leaves to a tree," this is a comment about spontaneity—it doesn't imply that Keats's poems are actually about nature (D).

14. D

In the sentence just before the quoted one, we learn that Wordsworth "attempted to achieve spontaneity and naturalness of expression" in his poems. Therefore, (D) is correct. (A), (B), and (C) all interpret Wordsworth's statement too literally. Wordsworth meant that poetry should SEEM like spontaneous speech, not that it should actually be written in dialogue form, or always read aloud, or only be written by men.

ALPS PASSAGE

The next passage is about the Alps, a European mountain chain that is "being destroyed by the very tourists it attracts." After stating this thesis, the author goes on to describe some of the factors involved in the destruction: millions of visitors, traffic jams, off-road vehicles, and the artificial snow for skiers and chemical pollution from factories that harm plants and animals alike.

15. C

The primary focus of the passage is on the destruction of the Alps by tourists, making (C) correct. (C) also nicely points out the irony ("a strange twist of fate" in the author's words) of this destruction coming at the hands of the very people who admire the Alps. (A) leaves out the main point, that the beautiful Alps are being damaged. (B) and (D) each focus too narrowly on one element of the problem.

16. C

"Grandeur" is the quality of being grand or magnificent.

17. B

The fifth sentence says that snowmobiles and other off-road vehicles threaten the Alpine terrain. So these vehicles damage the land they travel on, and (B) is correct. (A) and (C) are never suggested. And while (D) may sound like a pretty good idea, the author never calls for an outright ban on such vehicles.

18. D

The phrase "flora and fauna" in the passage's final sentence is another way of saying "plants and animals." So the sentence says that plants and animals alike are threatened by artificial snowmakers, and by damage from factories "belching" pollutants "into the rivers." If the pollutants are going into the rivers, then at least one major element of the animals' water supply is being destroyed, which makes (D) correct. Tricky choice (A)'s phrase "forms of transportation" refers to the vehicles jamming the roads and threatening the terrain. "Terrain" refers to the land, which includes plants, but not animals—they aren't of the land, they just live on it.

FOSSILS PASSAGE

The fifth passage is about reconstructing extinct animals from their fossil bones. Basically, the author says it's a tough job, best done by experts. In the first place, it's difficult to find good fossil specimens. Experts who do so must then spend years studying the anatomy of living and/or extinct related creatures, if they want to succeed in assembling the fossils correctly.

19. B

Sentence 2 says that fossil skeletons are rarely found "intact," and sentence 3 goes on to explain why: one animal's bones may be "scattered far and wide." So "intact," is the opposite of "scattered"; something intact is together, complete, or whole, (B).

20. A

If fossil skeletons almost never survive intact—that is, in one piece—then to find a complete one is probably a rare occurrence, (A). The author does not cite climate, (B), or how the animal died, (D), as determining factors in finding a complete skeleton. And the opposite of (C) is the case: even for experts, finding a complete fossil skeleton is more a matter of luck than skill.

21. C

The third sentence indicates that the attack of a scavenger makes fossil bones hard to match. (A) contradicts the last line of the passage. (B) also contradicts the passage, which suggests that it takes a long time to correctly—not incorrectly—assemble a skeleton. As for (D), there's no reason to incorrectly assemble the skeleton of a living species, because the assembly can be checked against other members of the species.

22. D

The passage says that paleontologists "must spend years studying" the skeletons and anatomy of living animals. You can infer, then, that scientists who work with fossils learn from living species, (D). (B) is tricky, since the entire passage seems a warning that scientists can make mistakes if they're not careful. But this doesn't imply that they frequently do make mistakes. (C) is plausible—since you get fossils from the earth, it helps to know something about that earth, which is the subject of geology—but it's never suggested in the passage.

23. C

The author calls fossil reconstruction "challenging and exacting" work, requiring "careful pains" and years of study. It's safe to say, then, that the author has respect for paleontologists, and (C) is correct. Skeptical, (A), means doubtful of, as in: "I'm skeptical that you really did your homework." Courteous, (B), means polite; it's close to but not as good as respectful. Indifferent, (D), means having little feeling one way or the other—neither positive nor negative.

STRATMEYER PASSAGE

The sixth passage is about Edward Stratmeyer, a writer who created those fictional teen heroes and heroines the Hardy Boys, Nancy Drew, and the Bobbsey Twins. The author gives some biographical information about Stratmeyer, but the passage's main thrust is that he was so successful because his career coincided with the growth of a new population segment—adolescents. Labor laws passed early in this century required children to stay in school until the age of 16, which gave them more free time than they'd ever had before. Wanting adventure, they read Stratmeyer's books.

24. C

As noted above, the main thrust of the passage is not the universal appeal of Stratmeyer's characters, (A), how mandatory schooling benefited teenagers, (B), or the boom created by labor laws, (D). Instead, the author is interested in telling us why Stratmeyer was so popular.

25. C

The second sentence describes the adventurous young heroes of Stratmeyer's books as having particular appeal; the final sentence notes that Stratmeyer satisfied his readers' needs with a "slew of heroic super-teens." Since Stratmeyer's readers were mostly teenagers, you can infer that his fictional heroes appealed to them at least partly because readers and heroes were the same age, (C). (A), (B), and (D) are not mentioned in the passage.

26. D

The passage states that, by 1930, adolescence had come of age, because labor laws required children to be in school until the age of sixteen, which makes (D) correct. (A) distorts the passage: By 1930, adolescents had more free time, but it was Stratmeyer's heroes who led lives of fun and adventure. (B) distorts the fourth sentence, which notes that, by 1900, the nation was more prosperous—not that teens themselves were. (C) is tricky. 1930 is described as the end of the heyday of Stratmeyer's career, but that doesn't necessarily mean his reading audience started to drop. It may just as well mean he stopped writing so many books.

27. B

(A) is wrong because the 30-year span was the heyday, or best part, of Stratmeyer's career. This doesn't mean he wrote all his books within that span. The passage doesn't mention that his family was in debt, (C), and we know from the first sentence that, contrary to (D), he enjoyed enormous commercial success. This leaves correct choice (B): as the final sentence describes in passing, Stratmeyer wrote his books "under a variety of pseudonyms," or false names.

DUMMIES PASSAGE

The seventh passage is about ventriloquist's dummies. The author tells you when dummies were first developed, and that early dummies looked much like those of today on the outside, but on the inside were a complicated mixture of "engineering feats and sculpture." The passage goes on to describe the inside of early dummy heads, especially the dummies made by the McElroy brothers, whose creations are said to have rivaled those of the Wright Brothers—inventors of the airplane—in complexity.

28. D

The author's primary purpose here is to describe early ventriloquists' dummies—the care and craft that went into making them. This point is restated in correct choice (D). The two inventing families mentioned in (A)—the McElroy and Wright Brothers—are only compared briefly in the passage's last sentence, making this a poor choice for a primary purpose question. (B) is too general, and as for (C), the passage

compares early dummies with today's dummies only to tell us that both had similar exteriors. But the bulk of the passage is about the interiors of early dummies, and we learn nothing about the insides of today's dummies, so (D) remains best.

29. B

As described in the last question, the outsides of dummies are only mentioned in sentence 2: the outsides of early ones "looked very much like those used today." So you can infer (B), that outwardly, dummies haven't changed much since they were invented. (A) is not indicated, since at least one feature, the mouth, has always been "exaggerated." (C) is wrong because the outward appearance has remained the same even though the insides have changed over the years.

30. A

Correct choice (A) restates sentence 3: the interiors of the best dummies "were a curious fusion of engineering feats and sculpture"—that is, a mix of science and art. With their exaggerated features, even the best-made dummies aren't meant to fool the observer, (B); it's the "throwing" of the ventriloquist's voice that does the fooling. (C) distorts the point, in sentence 2, that dummies from all eras have similar range of movement. And the McElroy brothers' dummies, arguably the best ever made, were constructed before World War II, not after (D).

31. C

A "synergistic effort" describes two things working together so that the effect of the whole is more than the effect of the parts working separately. We know that the McElroy brothers worked together on their puppets, making (C) the correct answer. There's no evidence for (A). (B) and (D) are never mentioned.

32. D

The author clearly admires the work of the McElroy brothers, so (A) and (B) are easily eliminated. Elated, (C), means extremely happy, which doesn't seem fitting in the context of what is essentially a dry, expository passage.

JELLYFISH PASSAGE

The eighth passage is about jellyfish. The opening sentence describes the physical make-up of jellyfish, but the rest of the passage is about something else: how all our efforts to control jellyfish have been unsuccessful. Even human pollution, it turns out, creates aquatic environments that jellyfish thrive in. The author ends with examples of two species of jellyfish whose populations have continued to grow despite the presence of sewage or pollution in their water supply.

33. B

As pointed out above, the author spends only a sentence and a half on the physical structure of the jellyfish. The rest of the passage, its main focus, is on how jellyfish defeat our attempts to control them. This is what correct choice (B) says—"foil" means to defeat, and humans are, of course, the jellyfish's "predator." (C) and (D) are only mentioned at the end of the passage, as examples of the larger premise accurately described in (B).

34. A

Sentence 1 describes the jellyfish as only "two thin layers of cells" covering a mass of "nonliving" material. Sounds primitive, doesn't it? So the jellyfish is primitive because of its simple physical structure, and (A) is correct. The tentacles of the jellyfish (B) are only one aspect of its physical structure, so (A) remains the better, more comprehensive choice. (C) suggests that

jellyfish are primitive because they lack mobility, a claim the passage never makes and, indeed, seems to contradict (since some jellyfish can infiltrate power plants and canals). We're also never told that jellyfish prefer water of a particular temperature (D).

35. C

Sentence 4 discusses the stinging nettle jellyfish, so hardy that it thrives in sewage-polluted waters and has even clogged up power plants. We can infer, then, that such waters would be harmful, perhaps even fatal, to other, less durable species of marine life, and (C) is correct. The author calls all jellyfish primitive just once, way back in sentence 2. You can't infer from this lone statement that the stinging nettle is an especially primitive species (A). The passage neither states or suggests that any species of jellyfish avoids swimming beaches or canals (B). Similarly, just because one species, the mangrove jellyfish, is known to thrive in the Florida Keys, you can't infer that other species such as the stinging nettle are rarely found there (D).

36. B

Re-read the final sentence for a sense of context. The exploding population of mangrove jellyfish is a nuisance and a detriment to the local tourist industry. So "detriment" probably means something bad, which means you're looking for a word that sounds negative. Cross off "delight," (A), as too positive; "cause," (D), is too neutral, and besides, it doesn't make sense in context. The mangrove jellyfish is the "cause" of the tourist industry? We doubt it. Plugging (C) into the sentence doesn't make sense either. So (B) is correct: the exploding mangrove population has harmed the tourist industry.

PHOTOGRAPHY PASSAGE

The ninth and last passage on this test is about James VanDerZee, a photographer who worked in Harlem. We learn that VanDerZee's career started in 1916, just before an African-American cultural boom known as the Harlem Renaissance, and that, in a career spanning 40 years, he took thousands of photographs of Harlem residents. The passage states that these photographs—of celebrities and unknown citizens alike—are now considered an important cultural record of a proud community.

37. D

The main focus of this passage is clearly on the work of VanDerZee, how he created an important cultural record. (D), which restates this idea, is thus the correct answer. (A) is too broad in scope and too narrow in time frame: VanDerZee was just one artist among many who made up the Harlem Renaissance, and that "decade-long flowering" spanned only one-fourth of his productive career. (B) is similarly too broad, since VanDerZee is the only African-American photographer mentioned in the passage. And (C) is wrong because we're never told what creative influences shaped VanDerZee's career.

38. A

The passage states that VanDerZee opened his studio in 1916, on "the eve of the Harlem Renaissance." As it does in "Christmas Eve," the word "eve" means, literally or figuratively, the night before. So we can infer that 1916 was, figuratively, the night before or just before the beginning of the Harlem Renaissance, and (A) is correct. (B) is unlikely, since the passage states that VanDerZee photographed thousands of non-celebrities. In fact, we really know nothing (and so can infer nothing) of his original intentions, of his experience prior to opening the studio, (C), or of who bankrolled his studio, (D).

39. B

Sentence 3 describes VanDerZee's Harlem subjects as representing "the life and spirit of that burgeoning community." It also notes that they were not only "notables," or celebrities, but also "ordinary citizens." In other words, VanDerZee's subjects represented the entire Harlem community, and (B) is correct. The artist's flair for photographic composition, (A), and the self-assurance of his subjects, (C), are described further down in the passage, not in the lines in question. And (D) is too abstract and theoretical; the author wants to tell you whose pictures VanDerZee took, not to expound on the nature of photography in general.

40. C

The author describes VanDerZee as capturing the life of a community, as an artist respected by critics who had a "unique vision." In other words, the author admires VanDerZee, and (C) is correct. Neutral, (A), implies that the author doesn't feel one way or the other about VanDerZee, which clearly isn't the case. Condescending, (B), is a negative word that means "looking down on," and it's also inappropriate. "Generous," (D), seems to imply that the author is somehow giving VanDerZee the benefit of the doubt, looking kindly on a career that really wasn't as great as the author says it was. No such attitude is hinted at in the passage, so (C) is best.

SECTION 4: MATH

1. A

Ralph's age is represented by x. Since Ralph is twice as old as Howie, Howie is half as old as Ralph, or $0.5x$.

2. A

If there are three blue marbles for every red marble, one out of every 4 marbles is red. Therefore, red marbles represent $\frac{1}{4}$ of all the marbles.

3. D

Average = $\dfrac{\text{Sum of terms}}{\text{Number of terms}}$, so the average temperature on Monday was

$$\text{Average} = \frac{55° + (-18°) + 25° + (-15°)}{4}$$
$$= \frac{80° + (-30°)}{4}$$
$$= 11\frac{3}{4}° = 11.75°$$

4. B

Looking at the pie chart, you can see that the slice that represents medium shirts represents about $\frac{1}{3}$ of the pie. The entire pie represents 1,200 shirts, so $\frac{1}{3}$ represents 400 shirts, (B).

5. C

The slice that represents small shirts represents about $\frac{1}{4}$ of the pie. Since the whole pie is 1,200 shirts, there were 300 small shirts sold. Each shirt sold for $5.95. The question asks approximately how much was spent on the small shirts, so estimate the price of a shirt to be $6 to make the calculation easier. The choices are pretty far apart, so it's O.K. to do this. 300 × $6 = $1,800, so (C) is correct.

6. B

There are 60 seconds in a minute, so in $\frac{1}{20}$ of a minute there are $60 \times \frac{1}{20} = \frac{60}{20} = 3$ seconds.

7. B

Sketch yourself a diagram:

The 8-inch length can be divided into 4 2-inch segments and the 6-inch width can be divided into 32-inch segments, which gives you a total of 4 × 3 = 12 squares.

8. C

Five percent of the guests at the party were witches. There were 8 witches, so 8 represents five percent = $\frac{5}{100} = \frac{1}{20}$ of the guests. The total number of guests is 20 × 8 = 160.

9. D

Just plug into the formula: 9@8 = (9 × 8) – (9 + 8) = 72 – 17 = 55

10. B

Plug into the formula and solve for N:
$$10@N = -1$$
$$(10 \times N) - (10 + N) = -1$$
$$10N - 10 - N = -1$$
$$9N - 10 = -1$$
$$9N = 9$$
$$N = 1$$

11. D

If a record collection can be evenly divided among 6 people, the number of records must be a multiple of 6. Only (D), 24, is a multiple of 6, since 6 × 4 = 24.

12. C

Make yourself a few quick sketches:

Only at 4:30 is the smaller angle less than 90°, so (C) is correct.

13. B

Carol spent $\frac{1}{2}$ of her day at work, and $\frac{2}{3}$ of that time in meetings. So the amount of time she spent in meetings was $\frac{1}{2} \times \frac{2}{3} = \frac{2}{6} = \frac{1}{3}$ of her day.

14. A

If $\frac{1}{2} S = 0.2$, S is twice that, or $2 \times 0.2 = 0.4$. The answer choices are all given as fractions, so convert 0.4 to a fraction. 0.4 is four-tenths, or $\frac{4}{10}$, which reduces to $\frac{2}{5}$, (A).

15. A

Ten percent is one-fifth of 50%, so if 50% of a number is 75, 10% of that same number is $\frac{1}{5} \times 75 = 15$.

16. C

$$\frac{1}{2} + \frac{1}{3} = \frac{M}{12}$$
$$\frac{6}{12} + \frac{4}{12} = \frac{10}{12}$$

So $M = 10$.

17. D

Let w = the width of the rectangle. Its length is three times its width, or $3w$. Perimeter is equal to $2(l + w)$, where l and w represent length and width respectively. The perimeter is 32, so $2(l + w) = 32$. Plug in $3w$ for l: $2(3w + w) = 32$, $8w = 32$, $w = 4$.

18. A

It is possible to solve for each of the four variables, but it is really a waste of time. Note that each of the equations is equal to 35,460. Therefore, the largest variable will be the one with the smallest coefficient, because it takes fewer of a larger number to come up with the same product. Looking at the equations, you see that since 2,955 is the smallest coefficient, A must have the greatest value.

19. C

Let x = the number of foreign cars, and set up a proportion. $\frac{3}{10} = \frac{x}{180}$

$$(3)(180) = 10x$$
$$540 = 10x$$
$$54 = x$$

20. C

Plug in and solve.
If $N_¿ = N \times 10$, $30_¿ + 2_¿ = 30 \times 10 + 2 \times 10$
$$= 300 + 20$$
$$= 320$$

21. C

To find the number of integers in an inclusive range, subtract the smaller integer from the larger and then add one: $83 - 42 = 41 + 1 = 42$, (C).

22. C

Looking at the figure you can see that $AB + BC = AC$. Therefore, $8 + BC = 14$, and $BC = 6$. The midpoint of AB divides it into two segments of length 4, and the midpoint of BC divides it into two segments of length 3. Therefore the distance between their midpoints is $4 + 3 = 7$.

23. C

Judy has 6 cards more than her brother. For each to have an equal number, she would have to split her 6 extra cards between them, that is, give him 3 while keeping 3 for herself. If this isn't clear, pick numbers. Say Judy's brother had 4 cards. That would mean Judy had $4 + 6 = 10$ cards. If she gave him 3 she'd have $10 - 3 = 7$, and he would have $4 + 3 = 7$.

24. D

Since Average = $\dfrac{\text{Sum of terms}}{\text{Number of terms}}$, Average × Number of terms = Sum of terms. If Fred averaged 168 for his first three games, that means he scored a total of $3 \times 168 = 504$ points. With his last game Fred wants to score enough to raise his average by 5 points, bringing it up to $168 + 5 = 173$. That means he needs to score a total of $173 \times 4 = 692$ for all four games. Since he scored 504 in the first three games, he'd need to score $692 - 504 = 188$ in his last game.

25. D

Evaluate each statement. If you can come up with even one value for N that makes the statement true, eliminate it.

A: If $N = 0$, $0 \times 0 = 0$, and the statement is true—eliminate.

B: If $N = 1$, $1 \times 1 = 1$, and the statement is true—eliminate.

C: If $N = 1$, $1 \times 1 = 1$, and the statement is true—eliminate.

D: $N - 1 = N$, so $N = N + 1$. There is no value of N for which adding 1 to it will result in a sum of N, so this statement can never be true.

26. A

To find the numbers that are in both sets, start listing the integers greater than 6, but stop before you hit 11: 7, 8, 9, 10. There are 4, so (A) is correct.

27. A

If June has \$65, Mary has $\$65 + 30\%(\$65) = \$65 + \$19.50$
$= \$84.50$

28. A

Nine is $\dfrac{1}{10}$, or 10%, of 90, so $x = 10$. 50%, or $\dfrac{1}{2}$, of $10 = 5$.

29. B

Let x = the number of bottles capped in 1 minute, and set up a proportion. Be sure to convert 1 minute into 60 seconds.

$$\frac{5}{2} = \frac{x}{60}$$
$$(5)(60) = 2x$$
$$300 = 2x$$
$$150 = x$$

30. A

Take this problem in steps: 20% of 100 is 20; 5% of 20 is $(0.05)(20) = 1$.

31. D

Keith answered 2 out of 10 questions, or $\frac{2}{10}$ incorrectly. $\frac{2}{10} = \frac{1}{5}$, or 20%, choice (D).

32. C

You know 6,985 is approximately 7,000 and 3,001 is approximately 3,000. Therefore the difference between 6,985 and 3,001 is approximately $7,000 - 3,000 = 4,000$, (C).

33. C

Convert to improper fractions: $1\frac{1}{3} - \frac{5}{6} = \frac{4}{3} - \frac{5}{6}$.

Find a common denominator: $\frac{16}{12} - \frac{10}{12} = \frac{6}{12} = \frac{1}{2}$

34. B

Patty bought 2 hot dogs and a soda, and Liza bought 1 hot dog and a soda. Therefore the difference in what they paid, or $3.30 - $2.15 = $1.15, is the price of one hot dog.

35. D

If one-fourth of a number is 3, the number is $4 \times 3 = 12$. One-third of 12 is 4, (D).

36. C

Rewrite $2 \times 4 \times 7 \times 9$ as $(2 \times 9)(4 \times 7)$ or 18×28. (C) is correct.

37. A

$12 + P = 20 - 2 \times 3$

$12 + P = 20 - 6$

$12 + P = 14$

$P = 2$

38. B

One-tenth or 0.1 of 99 is 9.9, (B).

39. A

Twenty percent or $\frac{1}{5}$ of 30 is 6, (A).

$\frac{64}{2 \times 4} = \frac{64}{8}$, $= 8$, (A).

41. D

$\frac{81}{9} + 2 = 9 + 2 = 11$, (D).

42. D

If there are 6 girls for every 2 boys, the ratio of girls to the entire class is 6:(6 + 2) or 6:8, which reduces to 3:4, (D).

43. A

So $\frac{48}{12} = \frac{4}{1}$, so $\frac{28}{a} = \frac{4}{1}$. Cross-multiply to get $28 = 4a$, and $a = 7$, (A).

44. D

For a number to be in both sets, it must be greater than 8 and less than 30. The only choice that falls in this range is 9, (D).

45. B

You can determine $\frac{18 + 16}{4} = \frac{34}{4} = 8\frac{1}{2} = 8.5$, (B).

Now that you have reviewed the answer explanations, turn to chapter 23 for information on how to score your ISEE practice test.

CHAPTER 21: ISEE PRACTICE TEST 2: UPPER- AND MIDDLE-LEVEL

HOW TO TAKE THIS PRACTICE TEST

Before taking this practice test, find a quiet room where you can work uninterrupted for two and a half hours. Make sure you have a comfortable desk and several No. 2 pencils.

Use the answer sheet provided to record your answers. (You can cut it out or photocopy it.)

Once you start this practice test, don't stop until you have finished. Remember—you can review any questions within a section, but you may not go backward or forward a section.

You'll find an answer key and explanations following the test.

Note: There are no major differences between the Middle- and Upper-level ISEE tests, and most of the questions on both tests are appropriate to either the middle or upper levels.

The practice test here covers both levels. If you are taking this as a Middle-level test, a few of the questions will understandably be too difficult. Don't worry—just do the best you can—and know that on test day, you will see only those questions that are appropriate to your level. Remember, too, that your scores will be based on how you compare to others taking the Middle-level test.

Good luck.

ISEE Practice Test Two: Upper- and Middle-Level Answer Sheet

Remove (or photocopy) the answer sheet and use it to complete the practice test.
Start with number 1 for each section. If a section has fewer questions than answer spaces, leave the extra spaces blank.

SECTION 1

#		#		#		#		#	
1	Ⓐ Ⓑ Ⓒ Ⓓ	9	Ⓐ Ⓑ Ⓒ Ⓓ	17	Ⓐ Ⓑ Ⓒ Ⓓ	25	Ⓐ Ⓑ Ⓒ Ⓓ	33	Ⓐ Ⓑ Ⓒ Ⓓ
2	Ⓐ Ⓑ Ⓒ Ⓓ	10	Ⓐ Ⓑ Ⓒ Ⓓ	18	Ⓐ Ⓑ Ⓒ Ⓓ	26	Ⓐ Ⓑ Ⓒ Ⓓ	34	Ⓐ Ⓑ Ⓒ Ⓓ
3	Ⓐ Ⓑ Ⓒ Ⓓ	11	Ⓐ Ⓑ Ⓒ Ⓓ	19	Ⓐ Ⓑ Ⓒ Ⓓ	27	Ⓐ Ⓑ Ⓒ Ⓓ	35	Ⓐ Ⓑ Ⓒ Ⓓ
4	Ⓐ Ⓑ Ⓒ Ⓓ	12	Ⓐ Ⓑ Ⓒ Ⓓ	20	Ⓐ Ⓑ Ⓒ Ⓓ	28	Ⓐ Ⓑ Ⓒ Ⓓ	36	Ⓐ Ⓑ Ⓒ Ⓓ
5	Ⓐ Ⓑ Ⓒ Ⓓ	13	Ⓐ Ⓑ Ⓒ Ⓓ	21	Ⓐ Ⓑ Ⓒ Ⓓ	29	Ⓐ Ⓑ Ⓒ Ⓓ	37	Ⓐ Ⓑ Ⓒ Ⓓ
6	Ⓐ Ⓑ Ⓒ Ⓓ	14	Ⓐ Ⓑ Ⓒ Ⓓ	22	Ⓐ Ⓑ Ⓒ Ⓓ	30	Ⓐ Ⓑ Ⓒ Ⓓ	38	Ⓐ Ⓑ Ⓒ Ⓓ
7	Ⓐ Ⓑ Ⓒ Ⓓ	15	Ⓐ Ⓑ Ⓒ Ⓓ	23	Ⓐ Ⓑ Ⓒ Ⓓ	31	Ⓐ Ⓑ Ⓒ Ⓓ	39	Ⓐ Ⓑ Ⓒ Ⓓ
8	Ⓐ Ⓑ Ⓒ Ⓓ	16	Ⓐ Ⓑ Ⓒ Ⓓ	24	Ⓐ Ⓑ Ⓒ Ⓓ	32	Ⓐ Ⓑ Ⓒ Ⓓ	40	Ⓐ Ⓑ Ⓒ Ⓓ

right in section 1

wrong in section 1

SECTION 2

#		#		#		#		#	
1	Ⓐ Ⓑ Ⓒ Ⓓ	9	Ⓐ Ⓑ Ⓒ Ⓓ	17	Ⓐ Ⓑ Ⓒ Ⓓ	25	Ⓐ Ⓑ Ⓒ Ⓓ	33	Ⓐ Ⓑ Ⓒ Ⓓ
2	Ⓐ Ⓑ Ⓒ Ⓓ	10	Ⓐ Ⓑ Ⓒ Ⓓ	18	Ⓐ Ⓑ Ⓒ Ⓓ	26	Ⓐ Ⓑ Ⓒ Ⓓ	34	Ⓐ Ⓑ Ⓒ Ⓓ
3	Ⓐ Ⓑ Ⓒ Ⓓ	11	Ⓐ Ⓑ Ⓒ Ⓓ	19	Ⓐ Ⓑ Ⓒ Ⓓ	27	Ⓐ Ⓑ Ⓒ Ⓓ	35	Ⓐ Ⓑ Ⓒ Ⓓ
4	Ⓐ Ⓑ Ⓒ Ⓓ	12	Ⓐ Ⓑ Ⓒ Ⓓ	20	Ⓐ Ⓑ Ⓒ Ⓓ	28	Ⓐ Ⓑ Ⓒ Ⓓ	36	Ⓐ Ⓑ Ⓒ Ⓓ
5	Ⓐ Ⓑ Ⓒ Ⓓ	13	Ⓐ Ⓑ Ⓒ Ⓓ	21	Ⓐ Ⓑ Ⓒ Ⓓ	29	Ⓐ Ⓑ Ⓒ Ⓓ	37	Ⓐ Ⓑ Ⓒ Ⓓ
6	Ⓐ Ⓑ Ⓒ Ⓓ	14	Ⓐ Ⓑ Ⓒ Ⓓ	22	Ⓐ Ⓑ Ⓒ Ⓓ	30	Ⓐ Ⓑ Ⓒ Ⓓ	38	Ⓐ Ⓑ Ⓒ Ⓓ
7	Ⓐ Ⓑ Ⓒ Ⓓ	15	Ⓐ Ⓑ Ⓒ Ⓓ	23	Ⓐ Ⓑ Ⓒ Ⓓ	31	Ⓐ Ⓑ Ⓒ Ⓓ	39	Ⓐ Ⓑ Ⓒ Ⓓ
8	Ⓐ Ⓑ Ⓒ Ⓓ	16	Ⓐ Ⓑ Ⓒ Ⓓ	24	Ⓐ Ⓑ Ⓒ Ⓓ	32	Ⓐ Ⓑ Ⓒ Ⓓ	40	Ⓐ Ⓑ Ⓒ Ⓓ

right in section 2

wrong in section 2

SECTION 3

#		#		#		#		#	
1	Ⓐ Ⓑ Ⓒ Ⓓ	9	Ⓐ Ⓑ Ⓒ Ⓓ	17	Ⓐ Ⓑ Ⓒ Ⓓ	25	Ⓐ Ⓑ Ⓒ Ⓓ	33	Ⓐ Ⓑ Ⓒ Ⓓ
2	Ⓐ Ⓑ Ⓒ Ⓓ	10	Ⓐ Ⓑ Ⓒ Ⓓ	18	Ⓐ Ⓑ Ⓒ Ⓓ	26	Ⓐ Ⓑ Ⓒ Ⓓ	34	Ⓐ Ⓑ Ⓒ Ⓓ
3	Ⓐ Ⓑ Ⓒ Ⓓ	11	Ⓐ Ⓑ Ⓒ Ⓓ	19	Ⓐ Ⓑ Ⓒ Ⓓ	27	Ⓐ Ⓑ Ⓒ Ⓓ	35	Ⓐ Ⓑ Ⓒ Ⓓ
4	Ⓐ Ⓑ Ⓒ Ⓓ	12	Ⓐ Ⓑ Ⓒ Ⓓ	20	Ⓐ Ⓑ Ⓒ Ⓓ	28	Ⓐ Ⓑ Ⓒ Ⓓ	36	Ⓐ Ⓑ Ⓒ Ⓓ
5	Ⓐ Ⓑ Ⓒ Ⓓ	13	Ⓐ Ⓑ Ⓒ Ⓓ	21	Ⓐ Ⓑ Ⓒ Ⓓ	29	Ⓐ Ⓑ Ⓒ Ⓓ	37	Ⓐ Ⓑ Ⓒ Ⓓ
6	Ⓐ Ⓑ Ⓒ Ⓓ	14	Ⓐ Ⓑ Ⓒ Ⓓ	22	Ⓐ Ⓑ Ⓒ Ⓓ	30	Ⓐ Ⓑ Ⓒ Ⓓ	38	Ⓐ Ⓑ Ⓒ Ⓓ
7	Ⓐ Ⓑ Ⓒ Ⓓ	15	Ⓐ Ⓑ Ⓒ Ⓓ	23	Ⓐ Ⓑ Ⓒ Ⓓ	31	Ⓐ Ⓑ Ⓒ Ⓓ	39	Ⓐ Ⓑ Ⓒ Ⓓ
8	Ⓐ Ⓑ Ⓒ Ⓓ	16	Ⓐ Ⓑ Ⓒ Ⓓ	24	Ⓐ Ⓑ Ⓒ Ⓓ	32	Ⓐ Ⓑ Ⓒ Ⓓ	40	Ⓐ Ⓑ Ⓒ Ⓓ

right in section 3

wrong in section 3

SECTION 4

#		#		#		#		#	
1	Ⓐ Ⓑ Ⓒ Ⓓ	11	Ⓐ Ⓑ Ⓒ Ⓓ	21	Ⓐ Ⓑ Ⓒ Ⓓ	31	Ⓐ Ⓑ Ⓒ Ⓓ	41	Ⓐ Ⓑ Ⓒ Ⓓ
2	Ⓐ Ⓑ Ⓒ Ⓓ	12	Ⓐ Ⓑ Ⓒ Ⓓ	22	Ⓐ Ⓑ Ⓒ Ⓓ	32	Ⓐ Ⓑ Ⓒ Ⓓ	42	Ⓐ Ⓑ Ⓒ Ⓓ
3	Ⓐ Ⓑ Ⓒ Ⓓ	13	Ⓐ Ⓑ Ⓒ Ⓓ	23	Ⓐ Ⓑ Ⓒ Ⓓ	33	Ⓐ Ⓑ Ⓒ Ⓓ	43	Ⓐ Ⓑ Ⓒ Ⓓ
4	Ⓐ Ⓑ Ⓒ Ⓓ	14	Ⓐ Ⓑ Ⓒ Ⓓ	24	Ⓐ Ⓑ Ⓒ Ⓓ	34	Ⓐ Ⓑ Ⓒ Ⓓ	44	Ⓐ Ⓑ Ⓒ Ⓓ
5	Ⓐ Ⓑ Ⓒ Ⓓ	15	Ⓐ Ⓑ Ⓒ Ⓓ	25	Ⓐ Ⓑ Ⓒ Ⓓ	35	Ⓐ Ⓑ Ⓒ Ⓓ	45	Ⓐ Ⓑ Ⓒ Ⓓ
6	Ⓐ Ⓑ Ⓒ Ⓓ	16	Ⓐ Ⓑ Ⓒ Ⓓ	26	Ⓐ Ⓑ Ⓒ Ⓓ	36	Ⓐ Ⓑ Ⓒ Ⓓ	46	Ⓐ Ⓑ Ⓒ Ⓓ
7	Ⓐ Ⓑ Ⓒ Ⓓ	17	Ⓐ Ⓑ Ⓒ Ⓓ	27	Ⓐ Ⓑ Ⓒ Ⓓ	37	Ⓐ Ⓑ Ⓒ Ⓓ	47	Ⓐ Ⓑ Ⓒ Ⓓ
8	Ⓐ Ⓑ Ⓒ Ⓓ	18	Ⓐ Ⓑ Ⓒ Ⓓ	28	Ⓐ Ⓑ Ⓒ Ⓓ	38	Ⓐ Ⓑ Ⓒ Ⓓ	48	Ⓐ Ⓑ Ⓒ Ⓓ
9	Ⓐ Ⓑ Ⓒ Ⓓ	19	Ⓐ Ⓑ Ⓒ Ⓓ	29	Ⓐ Ⓑ Ⓒ Ⓓ	39	Ⓐ Ⓑ Ⓒ Ⓓ	49	Ⓐ Ⓑ Ⓒ Ⓓ
10	Ⓐ Ⓑ Ⓒ Ⓓ	20	Ⓐ Ⓑ Ⓒ Ⓓ	30	Ⓐ Ⓑ Ⓒ Ⓓ	40	Ⓐ Ⓑ Ⓒ Ⓓ	50	Ⓐ Ⓑ Ⓒ Ⓓ

right in section 4

wrong in section 4

SECTION 1

Time—20 Minutes
40 Questions

Each of the following questions consists of one word followed by four words or phrases. You are to select the one word or phrase whose meaning is closest to the word in capital letters.

---

1. DESECRATE:

   (A) defend
   (B) deny
   (C) describe
   (D) defile

2. LAUD:

   (A) touch
   (B) praise
   (C) insult
   (D) hear

3. AVERT:

   (A) vindicate
   (B) prevent
   (C) explain
   (D) dislike

4. PIETY:

   (A) rarity
   (B) smell
   (C) faith
   (D) meal

5. AMORAL:

   (A) unethical
   (B) lovable
   (C) transparent
   (D) imaginary

6. CANDOR:

   (A) odor
   (B) honesty
   (C) ability
   (D) wealth

7. HAUGHTINESS:

   (A) heat
   (B) height
   (C) rudeness
   (D) arrogance

8. VERIFY:

   (A) complete
   (B) prove
   (C) violate
   (D) consume

9. DECEIVE:

   (A) trick
   (B) empty
   (C) dye
   (D) view

10. FICTION:

    (A) presumption
    (B) growth
    (C) falsehood
    (D) wound

GO ON TO THE NEXT PAGE

11. HARDY:

   (A) healthy
   (B) mysterious
   (C) firm
   (D) obese

12. LYRICAL:

   (A) mythical
   (B) bright
   (C) musical
   (D) wet

13. METAMORPHOSIS:

   (A) change
   (B) compliment
   (C) rejection
   (D) meeting

14. LAMENT:

   (A) support
   (B) decline
   (C) solidify
   (D) grieve

15. ARID:

   (A) light
   (B) clean
   (C) worried
   (D) dry

16. PERCEPTIVE:

   (A) confused
   (B) round
   (C) observant
   (D) imbued

17. ADAMANT:

   (A) thin
   (B) enlarged
   (C) admiring
   (D) stubborn

18. NEUTRAL:

   (A) inventive
   (B) foreign
   (C) unbiased
   (D) detailed

19. DOCILE:

   (A) old
   (B) tame
   (C) active
   (D) rare

20. WARINESS:

   (A) extremity
   (B) caution
   (C) superiority
   (D) mobility

21. RATIONAL:

   (A) logical
   (B) extraneous
   (C) spare
   (D) complete

22. DARING:

   (A) courageous
   (B) risky
   (C) impractical
   (D) inevitable

GO ON TO THE NEXT PAGE

23. DONATE:

    (A) contribute
    (B) control
    (C) teach
    (D) conduct

24. TRANQUILITY:

    (A) fatigue
    (B) calm
    (C) warmth
    (D) origin

Directions: Select the word(s) that best fits the meaning of each sentence.

25. Raccoons are _____ : they come out at night to look for food and sleep during the day.

    (A) nocturnal
    (B) friendly
    (C) precocious
    (D) monolithic

26. Normally _____ , Jenny lacked her usual _____ when I called her and invited her to a movie.

    (A) absurd .. severity
    (B) scornful .. predilection
    (C) amiable .. enthusiasm
    (D) distraught .. cheeriness

27. The soap opera regularly dwells on the _____ aspects of life; just last week two characters died.

    (A) morbid
    (B) presumptuous
    (C) exciting
    (D) expensive

28. Once a(n) _____ gathering, the Greek festival has, in recent times, become highly _____ .

    (A) urban .. contemporary
    (B) religious .. commercialized
    (C) mournful .. gloomy
    (D) parallel .. transformed

29. The candidate changed his positions on so many issues that people began to think he was _____.

    (A) reliable
    (B) dependent
    (C) aloof
    (D) flighty

30. Melanie danced with such _____, that no one could _____ her talent any longer.

    (A) speed.. ascertain
    (B) grace .. affirm
    (C) agility .. question
    (D) melancholy .. deny

31. Sandy showed genuine _____ when she was caught: she cried and promised never to hurt anyone again.

    (A) remorse
    (B) melodrama
    (C) wit
    (D) enthusiasm

32. The _____ journey _____ us all; even my dog sat down to take a rest.

    (A) panoramic .. exhausted
    (B) tortuous .. invigorated
    (C) strenuous .. fatigued
    (D) arduous .. rejuvenated

GO ON TO THE NEXT PAGE →

33. Relying on every conceivable gimmick and stereotype, the latest Hollywood movie is not only _____ but _____ .

    (A) dull .. ambivalent
    (B) predictable .. absurd
    (C) complete .. erudite
    (D) boring .. enlightening

34. Lara not only respected her grandfather, she _____ him.

    (A) feared
    (B) retired
    (C) resembled
    (D) revered

35. That Chinese pieces of silk dating over 1,500 years old have been found in Egypt is _____ since the landscape between these two countries includes arid deserts and several _____ mountain ranges.

    (A) known .. required
    (B) impressive .. reduced
    (C) predictable .. steep
    (D) incredible .. massive

36. At first the empty house seemed frightening with all its cobwebs and creaking shutters, but we soon realized that it was quite _____ .

    (A) benign
    (B) deceptive
    (C) affluent
    (D) obliterated

37. Once a _____ propagated only by science fiction movies, the possibility of life on Mars has recently become more _____ .

    (A) wish .. doubtful
    (B) myth .. plausible
    (C) story .. impossible
    (D) hypothesis .. empty

38. Many writers of the 20th century were influenced by Hemingway's _____ writing style and consequently discontinued the _____ language characteristic of the 19th century novel.

    (A) sparse .. verbose
    (B) dull .. insipid
    (C) peaceful .. descriptive
    (D) complete .. florid

39. Dave never failed to charm listeners with his _____ stories.

    (A) lethargic
    (B) wan
    (C) insufferable
    (D) engaging

40. Screaming and laughing, the students were _____ by their _____ experience on the white-water raft.

    (A) amused .. tepid
    (B) irritated .. continued
    (C) exhilarated .. first
    (D) frightened .. secure

IF YOU FINISH BEFORE TIME IS CALLED, YOU MAY CHECK YOUR WORK ON THIS SECTION ONLY. DO NOT TURN TO ANY OTHER SECTION IN THE TEST. STOP

SECTION 2
Time—35 Minutes
35 Questions

In this section there are four possible answers after each question. Choose which one is best. You may use the blank space at the right of the page for scratch work.

<u>Note:</u> Figures are drawn with the greatest possible accuracy, UNLESS stated "Not Drawn to Scale."

---

1. If $Q + 7 - 8 + 3 = 23$, what is the value of Q?

    (A) 19

    (B) 20

    (C) 21

    (D) 22

USE THIS SPACE FOR FIGURING.

2. A kilogram is equal to how many grams?

    (A) −1,000

    (B) −100

    (C) 100

    (D) 1,000

3. What is the value of $\frac{1}{9} + \frac{7}{12} + \frac{5}{6}$?

    (A) $\frac{9}{13}$

    (B) $1\frac{19}{36}$

    (C) $1\frac{2}{3}$

    (D) 2

4. What is 15% of 60?

    (A) 6

    (B) 9

    (C) 12

    (D) 15

GO ON TO THE NEXT PAGE

5. If $a + 2 > 5$ and $a - 4 < 1$, which of the following is a possible value for a ?

   (A) 2
   (B) 3
   (C) 4
   (D) 5

6. If $2x + 4 = 26$, then $x + 4 =$

   (A) 9
   (B) 11
   (C) 13
   (D) 15

7. If the perimeter of an equilateral hexagon is 42, what is the sum of the lengths of 2 sides?

   (A) 6
   (B) 7
   (C) 12
   (D) 14

8. If Angelo earns $2,000 per month and spends 30% of his monthly earnings on rent, how much does he pay for rent each month?

   (A) $510
   (B) $600
   (C) $610
   (D) $680

9. A farmer pays $58 for 6 new chickens. How many eggs must the farmer sell at 16 cents apiece in order to pay for the chickens?

   (A) 360
   (B) 361
   (C) 362
   (D) 363

USE THIS SPACE FOR FIGURING.

GO ON TO THE NEXT PAGE

10. A certain moped needs 12 gallons of fuel to go 48 miles. At this rate, how many gallons of fuel are needed to go 60 miles?

 (A) 4
 (B) 5
 (C) 15
 (D) 24

USE THIS SPACE FOR FIGURING.

11. $1\frac{6}{11} + 1\frac{7}{22}$

 (A) $2\frac{13}{33}$

 (B) $2\frac{19}{22}$

 (C) $2\frac{10}{11}$

 (D) $2\frac{21}{22}$

12. If the average of 6 numbers is 9, what is the sum of those numbers?

 (A) 15
 (B) 30
 (C) 54
 (D) 96

13. If $\frac{1}{2} > x > 0$ and $\frac{1}{3} > x > \frac{1}{10}$, which of the following is a possible value for x?

 (A) $\frac{2}{3}$

 (B) 0.47

 (C) $\frac{1}{5}$

 (D) $\frac{1}{20}$

GO ON TO THE NEXT PAGE

14. If $3a + 6a = 36$, what is the value of a?

(A) 1
(B) 2
(C) 3
(D) 4

15. What is $\frac{1}{4}$ of 0.72?

(A) 0.018
(B) 0.18
(C) 1.8
(D) 18

16. In Figure 1, what is the total area?

(A) 10
(B) 24
(C) 28
(D) 45

17. How many different prime factors are there of 48?

(A) 1
(B) 2
(C) 3
(D) 4

18. Which of the following is a factor of 36 but not of 48?

(A) 3
(B) 6
(C) 12
(D) 18

19. If Figure 2 is a cube, what is its volume?

(A) 125
(B) 100
(C) 50
(D) 25

USE THIS SPACE FOR FIGURING.

Figure 1

Figure 2

GO ON TO THE NEXT PAGE

20. While studying for a history test, it took Jake 1 hour 15 minutes to review the first 30 pages. If he continues to study at the same pace, how long will it take him to review the remaining 70 pages?

(A) 2 hours 30 minutes

(B) 2 hours 37 minutes

(C) 2 hours 45 minutes

(D) 2 hours 55 minutes

USE THIS SPACE FOR FIGURING.

Directions: In questions 21–35, note the given information, if any, and then compare the quantity in Column A to the quantity in Column B. Next to the number of each question write

A if the quantity in Column A is greater.

B if the quantity in Column B is greater.

C if the two quantities are equal.

D if the relationship cannot be determined from the information given.

Column A	Column B
21. $\dfrac{1}{2} + \dfrac{3}{4} + \dfrac{7}{8}$	$\dfrac{2}{5} + \dfrac{3}{4} + \dfrac{7}{9}$
22. $\dfrac{4}{5} \times \dfrac{15}{45} \times \dfrac{3}{16}$	0.05
23. $\dfrac{4}{9} \times \dfrac{18}{6} \times \dfrac{12}{20}$	$\dfrac{5}{4}$

$$3x - 12 = 3x - 6x$$

24. $x + 2$	2

$$x > 0$$
$$y > 0$$

GO ON TO THE NEXT PAGE

<u>Column A</u>	<u>Column B</u>

USE THIS SPACE FOR FIGURING.

25.

$x + 1$ y

26.

5% of $(3 + 4)$ 4% of (3×4)

27.

0.46 $\dfrac{9}{20}$

28.

The number of 32-cent stamps that can be purchased with $5   The number of 29-cent stamps that can be purchased with $5

$$\frac{8}{9} > x > \frac{1}{2}$$

29.

x $\dfrac{2}{3}$

$$x < 0$$

30.

$2x$ $(2x)(1x)$

31.

Perimeter of an octagon with sides of equal length 8

GO ON TO THE NEXT PAGE

Column A	Column B	USE THIS SPACE FOR FIGURING.

32.

The number of prime factors of 21	3

$$\frac{5}{7} \text{ of } x \text{ is } 35$$

33.

x	48

34.

98% of 51	51% of 98

35.

20% of $42	$9

IF YOU FINISH BEFORE TIME IS CALLED, YOU MAY CHECK YOUR WORK ON THIS SECTION ONLY. DO NOT TURN TO ANY OTHER SECTION IN THE TEST.

STOP

SECTION 3

Time—40 Minutes

40 Questions

Read each passage carefully and then answer the questions about it. For each question, decide on the basis of the passage which one of the choices best answers the question.

Porcupines have justifiable confidence in their defensive armament. Adult porcupines have upwards of 30,000 quills, spiny hairs strong and
Line sharp enough to pierce the hide of any predator.
(5) These quills have tiny barbs just below the tip, and are so loosely set in the skin that if they are touched with any force they pull out of the porcupine and stick into the porcupine's attacker. The longest quills, up to four inches long, are on
(10) the porcupine's back and flanks, but the shorter ones that stud its muscular tail often do the most damage. With a few well-timed lashes, a porcupine can drive so many quills so quickly into an attacker as to give the erroneous impression that it
(15) can throw the spines like darts.

1. According to the passage, porcupines use their quills to

   (A) capture food.

   (B) protect their young.

   (C) defend themselves.

   (D) retain heat.

2. As used in line 1, the word "justifiable" means

   (A) intellectual.

   (B) understandable.

   (C) unreasonable.

   (D) defiant.

3. Porcupine quills are most nearly comparable in function to

   (A) shark teeth.

   (B) bear claws.

   (C) a rhinocerous horn.

   (D) cactus needles.

4. The passage suggests that the porcupine's longest quills are

   (A) less important for protection than its tail quills.

   (B) too loosely set in the skin to harm potential predators.

   (C) less numerous than the quills on other parts of its body.

   (D) sharper than the quills on its stomach, legs and tail.

The heyday of the log cabin occurred between 1780 and 1850, when a great number of settlers forged westward. While early cabins were
Line primitive, with dirt floor and sod roofs, later
(5) settlers built fine, two-story, log-hewn farmhouses with rooms for entertaining. By the 1840s, though, the log cabin began fading out. Factors contributing to its decline included sawmills, nails, and the rising popularity of the Greek
(10) Revival-style house, with its democratic roots in ancient Greece and its templed front facing the street. Trains brought hardware, manufactured goods, and an end to geographic isolation. Climate and the proximity of the local forest no longer set

GO ON TO THE NEXT PAGE

(15) architectural limits. In hundreds of towns, log homes were gradually sheathed with clapboard or brick, or, in many instances, were simply burned. Logs continued to house livestock, but after the 1850s, fewer and fewer people.

5. As used in line 3, the word "forged" means

   (A) fled.
   (B) wandered.
   (C) moved.
   (D) returned.

6. The passage suggests that the origins of the Greek Revival style

   (A) arose out of a general desire to replace log cabins.
   (B) widely influenced contemporary Greek architects.
   (C) were popular with devoutly religious Americans.
   (D) appealed to democratic-minded Americans.

7. It can be inferred from the passage that, unlike Greek Revival homes, log cabins

   (A) did not always face the street.
   (B) lacked indoor plumbing.
   (C) could not have glass windows.
   (D) were built near lakes and rivers.

8. It can be inferred from the passage that a limiting factor in the construction of a settler's log cabin was often

   (A) the availability of nails.
   (B) the location of the nearest forest.
   (C) the opinions of other settlers.
   (D) the laws of the local government.

9. According to the passage, most log structures after 1850 were built

   (A) in wilderness areas.
   (B) in frontier towns.
   (C) as railroad depots.
   (D) to shelter animals.

The plague, or Black Death, struck Europe in a series of outbreaks in the 13th and 14th centuries, killing an estimated one-third of the continent's
Line population. The epidemic wrought enormous
(5) changes in European society, some of which, ironically, were beneficial. Reform in the medical profession, which had mostly failed to relieve the suffering, was one of the most immediate benefits. A great many doctors died or simply ran away
(10) during the plague. By the 1300s, many universities were lacking professors of medicine and surgery. Into this void rushed people with new ideas. In addition, ordinary people began acquiring medical guides and taking command of their own health.
(15) Gradually, more medical texts began to appear in everyday languages rather than in Latin, making medical knowledge more accessible.

10. The passage focuses primarily on

   (A) the enormous loss of life caused by the plague.
   (B) the lack of qualified doctors during the plague.
   (C) one positive result of a catastrophic event.
   (D) the translation of medical texts into everyday language.

GO ON TO THE NEXT PAGE ⇨

11. As used in line 4, the word "wrought" means

   (A) caused.
   (B) needed.
   (C) accelerated.
   (D) offered.

12. The passage suggests that, prior to the plague outbreaks, European medicine was

   (A) hampered by a shortage of doctors.
   (B) available only to university students.
   (C) in need of sweeping changes.
   (D) practiced mainly in Latin-speaking countries.

13. It can be inferred from the passage that after the 1300s, medical texts

   (A) included information on how to cure the plague.
   (B) were more easily available to the general population.
   (C) were no longer written in Latin.
   (D) were not written by university professors.

   In the sport of orienteering, competitors use a map and compass to navigate their way cross-country along an unfamiliar course. The novice
Line quickly finds, however, that the most important
(5) question in orienteering is not compass bearing but choice of route. There are almost always several different ways to get from one point to another, and the beeline on a direct compass bearing over a mountain is seldom the best.
(10) Indeed, orienteers tend to disdain beelining over obstacles as a crude approach; they aspire to intellectual finesse. If climbing 20 feet in elevation requires the time and energy it would take to travel 250 feet on level ground—the sort of quick
(15) calculation orienteers are always making—then it

may be better to follow a prominent contour along one flank of the mountain, or even to stick to the safety of a trail looping around the base.

14. The passage suggests that a hiker with a map and compass is NOT orienteering if she

   (A) climbs more than one mountain per route.
   (B) travels over a known, familiar route.
   (C) takes more than one route per day.
   (D) follows a direct path over an obstacle.

15. According to the passage, an orienteer places greatest importance on

   (A) maintaining a single compass bearing.
   (B) avoiding hazardous terrain.
   (C) overcoming obstacles as fast as possible.
   (D) choosing the best route available.

16. It can be inferred from the passage that most orienteers would consider a competitor who climbs a mountain in order to take the most direct route to be

   (A) gaining a major advantage.
   (B) lacking sophistication.
   (C) breaking the rules.
   (D) endangering other competitors.

17. The passage suggests that one skill orienteers require is the ability to

   (A) run while carrying a backpack.
   (B) swim long distances.
   (C) set up a campsite.
   (D) make rapid calculations.

GO ON TO THE NEXT PAGE

Researchers have identified two phenomena that in previous literature were confounded under the category of nightmares. On the one hand,
Line there is the true nightmare, which is an actual,
(5) detailed dream. On the other there is the "night terror," from which the sleeper, often a child, suddenly awakes in great fright with no memory of a dream, often screaming and sometimes going off in a sleepwalking trance. Night terrors are seldom
(10) of serious consequence, no matter how horrifying they may appear to anxious parents. Outside of taking commonsense precautions—such as making sure a sleepwalker does not go to bed near an open window or on a balcony—there is nothing
(15) much to do about them. A child's night terrors can be reduced somewhat with a consistent sleep schedule and by avoiding excessive fatigue. Excessive concern or medication should usually be avoided.

18. As used in line 2, the word "confounded" means

    (A) entitled.

    (B) confused.

    (C) written.

    (D) underappreciated.

19. The passage suggests that, until recently, sleep researchers

    (A) knew very little about the nature of dreams.

    (B) studied only adult sleeping habits, not those of children.

    (C) did not differentiate between nightmares and night terrors.

    (D) prescribed medication for children suffering from night terrors.

20. According to the passage, a nightmare is a

    (A) full-fledged dream.

    (B) dream fragment.

    (C) hallucination.

    (D) trancelike state.

21. The passage implies that parents of children who experience night terrors

    (A) tend to dismiss them as inconsequential.

    (B) also suffered night terrors when they were children.

    (C) find their occurrence nearly as frightening as the children themselves do.

    (D) should consult a doctor as soon as possible.

22. Which of the following questions is NOT answered in the passage?

    (A) What is the difference between nightmares and night terrors?

    (B) What are some precautions parents can take to ensure the safety of children who experience night terrors?

    (C) Does a child who is frightened upon waking from a night terror remember dreaming?

    (D) Why does a consistent sleep schedule reduce the incidence of night terrors?

GO ON TO THE NEXT PAGE

The Neanderthal was an early human that
flourished throughout Europe and western Asia
between 35,000 and 85,000 years ago. Physically,
Line Neanderthals differed from modern humans in
(5) many important ways. They had massive limb
bones, a barrel chest, thick brow ridges, a receding
forehead and a bunlike bulge on the back of the
skull. Yet despite Neanderthals' reputation for low
intelligence, there is nothing that clearly
(10) distinguishes a Neanderthal's brain from that of
modern humans—except for the fact that, on
average, Neanderthal versions were slightly larger.
Combining enormous physical strength with
manifest intelligence, Neanderthals appeared to
(15) be supremely well adapted. Nevertheless, around
35,000 years ago, they vanished from the face of
the earth. The question of what became of the
Neanderthals still baffles paleontologists, and is
perhaps the most talked-about issue in human
(20) origins research today.

23. It can be inferred from the passage that most
Neanderthals probably had

(A) big arms.

(B) wide-set eyes.

(C) bowed legs.

(D) narrow feet.

24. According to the passage, Neanderthals lived

(A) in caves and mud dwellings.

(B) by hunting in packs.

(C) in Europe and Asia.

(D) on all the continents.

25. Based on information in the passage, modern
humans, when compared with Neanderthals,
probably have

(A) superior eyesight.

(B) a better sense of smell.

(C) less physical strength.

(D) more body hair.

26. The passage suggests that modern humans
tend to think of Neanderthals as

(A) peaceful.

(B) skilled artists.

(C) farmers.

(D) unintelligent.

27. According to the passage, one question
paleontologists are still trying to solve is

(A) what constituted the basic Neanderthal
diet.

(B) what were the Neanderthals' migratory
patterns.

(C) why the Neanderthal species became
extinct.

(D) where the Neanderthals originally
came from.

GO ON TO THE NEXT PAGE

While the art of magic has always relied upon
certain mechanics—angled mirrors, carefully
concealed trapdoors—it is the art of deception that
Line ultimately creates the illusion. The most important
(5) skill in any conjurer's repertoire is misdirection, the
fine art of prompting an audience to look elsewhere
at a critical moment. Presentation and timing are
everything; when a magician makes an extravagant
gesture with one hand, he is generally trying to
(10) divert your attention from the other. Misdirection
is not always as subtle as snapping fingers or
waving. One performer, wishing to distract his
audience while he spirited an assistant offstage,
arranged for a gorilla to ride a unicycle across the
(15) stage at the crucial moment. Whatever the
gimmick, the mechanics of magic are almost
beside the point; most magical effects owe their
success to pure stagecraft.

28. It can be inferred from the passage that angled
mirrors and trapdoors are

(A) devices used by most magicians only in
recent years.

(B) always activated by the magician's assistant, not the magician himself.

(C) less important for a successful illusion
than presentation and timing.

(D) gimmicks that perceptive audience members can observe.

29. As used in line 6, the word "prompting" means

(A) telling.

(B) attending.

(C) entertaining.

(D) persuading.

30. The primary focus of the passage is on the

(A) various gimmicks used in magic shows.

(B) necessity of using mechanical effects to
create an illusion.

(C) different ways in which a magician
deceives an audience.

(D) ways in which an audience can figure out
a magician's tricks.

31. The passage suggests that, when a magician
waves his hand grandly, he is

(A) signaling an assistant to enter onstage.

(B) diverting attention from his other hand.

(C) announcing the start of a new illusion.

(D) warming up in order to perform a trick.

GO ON TO THE NEXT PAGE

The American colonists were no less infatuated with wigs than were their European contemporaries. While cheaper wigs made from horse hair, goat hair, or duck feathers were available, the wealthy chose

Line
(5) expensive wigs crafted from real human hair. Initially, most wigs worn in the New World were imported from England, although by the start of the Revolution numerous wigmakers were plying their trade in the Colonies. But the American War of

(10) Independence—and, even more so, the subsequent French Revolution—brought the wig's giddy heyday to an abrupt end. As the heads of bigwigs began to roll from the guillotines, extravagance, ostentation and anything that smacked of class

(15) distinction or the depredations of royalty fell quickly out of fashion.

32. The primary focus of this passage is on

   (A) the elaborate construction of wigs in the American colonies.

   (B) the importance of English imports to the American colonies.

   (C) the effect of historical events on a particular fashion.

   (D) the influence of the War of Independence on commerce between England and the New World.

33. The passage implies that wigs made of human hair were

   (A) more easily maintained than horse hair wigs.

   (B) considered fashionable in England but not in France.

   (C) made from the heads of guillotine victims.

   (D) rarely worn by poor people.

34. What is suggested in the passage about wigmakers who worked in the Colonies?

   (A) Their numbers had grown considerably by the start of the American Revolution.

   (B) They were specialists in goat hair and duck feather wigs.

   (C) They designed wigs that looked very different from European wigs.

   (D) They remained loyal to the British during the War of Independence.

35. As used in lines 1–2, the phrase "infatuated with" means

   (A) dependent on.

   (B) fond of.

   (C) critical of.

   (D) repelled by.

GO ON TO THE NEXT PAGE

Coyotes are one of the most primitive of living dogs. According to the fossil record, a close relative of the contemporary coyote existed here two to
Line three million years ago. It in turn seems to have
(5) descended from a group of small canids that was widely dispersed throughout the world and that also gave rise to the jackals of Eurasia and Africa. One to two million years ago, a division occurred in North America between the coyote and the
(10) wolf. Time passed, and glaciers advanced and receded. Mammoths, saber-toothed tigers, and dire wolves (canids with enormous heads) came and went. Native horses left the continent over land bridges, and others returned on galleons. Through
(15) it all, coyotes remained basically the same— primitive in evolutionary terms but marvelously flexible, always progressive and innovative— riding out, adjusting to and exploiting the changes.

36. The primary focus of the passage is on

    (A) the ability of the coyote species to survive unchanged.
    (B) the unfortunate extinction of many prehistoric life forms.
    (C) the changing nature of animal life in prehistoric times.
    (D) the evolutionary division between coyotes and wolves.

37. The passage suggests that modern dogs are

    (A) direct descendants of dire wolves.
    (B) native to North America but not to Eurasia.
    (C) genetically related to coyotes.
    (D) lacking in evolutionary flexibility.

38. According to the passage, a close relative of the coyote existed in North America

    (A) ten million years ago.
    (B) seven million years ago.
    (C) five million years ago.
    (D) two million years ago.

39. The author probably mentions mammoths and saber-toothed tigers in order to give examples of

    (A) the coyote's more distant relatives.
    (B) animals that did not leave North America by land bridge.
    (C) species that the jackal hunted into extinction.
    (D) species that failed to adapt as the coyote did.

40. When the passage states that "others returned on galleons" (line 14), it most probably means that

    (A) some species of horse became extinct, then others appeared.
    (B) horses were re-introduced to North America when Europeans brought them by ship.
    (C) some coyotes were introduced into Africa and Eurasia.
    (D) prehistoric horses and dire wolves became extinct at roughly the same time.

IF YOU FINISH BEFORE TIME IS CALLED, YOU MAY CHECK YOUR WORK ON THIS SECTION ONLY. DO NOT TURN TO ANY OTHER SECTION IN THE TEST.

SECTION 4
Time—40 Minutes
40 Questions

In this section there are four possible answers after each question. Choose which one is best. You may use the blank space at the right of the page for scratch work.

<u>Note:</u> Figures are drawn with the greatest possible accuracy, UNLESS stated "Not Drawn to Scale."

1. What are all the values of x for which $(x - 2)(x + 5) = 0$?

    (A) -5
    (B) -2
    (C) 2 and -5
    (D) -2 and -5

2. Patty uses 2 gallons of paint to cover 875 square feet of surface. At this rate, how many gallons will she need to cover 4,375 square feet of surface?

    (A) 4
    (B) 5
    (C) 8
    (D) 10

3. What is the area of a triangle with a base of 4 inches and a height of 6 inches?

    (A) 10
    (B) 12
    (C) 20
    (D) 24

4. An equilateral triangle has sides of lengths $3x + 1$ and $x + 7$. What is the length of one side?

    (A) 3
    (B) 5
    (C) 8
    (D) 10

USE THIS SPACE FOR FIGURING.

GO ON TO THE NEXT PAGE

5. $(65 \times 10^2) + (31 \times 10^3) + 12 =$

   (A) 375,120.00

   (B) 37,512.00

   (C)   3,751.20

   (D)   375.12

6. Mr. Richman purchased a boat for $120,000. If the boat loses 20% of its value when placed in the water, how much did Mr. Richman lose in the value of his boat on its first use?

   (A) $2,400

   (B) $9,600

   (C) $24,000

   (D) $96,000

7. A dog is chained by a flexible leash to a stake in the ground in the center of his yard. If the leash is 8 meters long, what is the area in square meters in which he is able to run?

   (A) 8

   (B) 16

   (C) 8π

   (D) 64π

8. If Megan needs to drive 328 miles in 4 hours, at what rate of speed must she drive?

   (A) 92 miles per hour

   (B) 82 miles per hour

   (C) 72 miles per hour

   (D) 67 miles per hour

USE THIS SPACE FOR FIGURING.

GO ON TO THE NEXT PAGE

9. If a jet travels at a constant rate of 270 miles per hour, approximately how many hours will it take to reach its destination 3,300 miles away?

   (A) 23.68
   (B) 18.91
   (C) 15.38
   (D) 12.22

10. If $a = 3$ and $b = 4$, what is the value of $a^2 + 2ab + b^2$?

    (A) 14
    (B) 24
    (C) 49
    (D) 144

11. If $x - y = 5$ and $4x + 6y = 20$, then $x + y =$

    (A) 3
    (B) 4
    (C) 5
    (D) 6

12. How many distinct prime factors are there of 726?

    (A) 2
    (B) 3
    (C) 4
    (D) 5

13. If n is an odd number, which of the following must be even?

    (A) $-2n - 1$
    (B) $2n + 1$
    (C) $2n - 1$
    (D) $4n$

USE THIS SPACE FOR FIGURING.

GO ON TO THE NEXT PAGE

14. If Jamie is in school for 6 hours per day, 5 days per week, how many seconds does Jamie spend in school in one week?

   (A) 1,108,000
   (B)   180,000
   (C)   108,000
   (D)   18,000

USE THIS SPACE FOR FIGURING.

15. If it is snowing at a rate of 3.5 inches per hour and the storm is expected to continue at the same rate for the next 4 days. How many inches of snow accumulation can be expected?

   (A) 84
   (B) 168
   (C) 226
   (D) 336

16. Nicholas is x years old and Billy is three times as old as Nicholas. What was the sum of their ages, in years, 5 years ago?

   (A) $x - 5$
   (B) $2x + 2$
   (C) $3x - 10$
   (D) $4x - 10$

17. In a certain class, there are twice as many boys as girls. If the total number of students in the class is 36, how many boys are there?

   (A) 24
   (B) 18
   (C) 12
   (D) 9

GO ON TO THE NEXT PAGE

18. At a party, $\frac{1}{3}$ of the guests drank only soda and $\frac{2}{5}$ of the guests drank only juice. If the remaining 16 guests had nothing to drink, then how many guests were at the party?

    (A) 60
    (B) 50
    (C) 45
    (D) 30

19. If x and y are consecutive integers such that $xy = 6$ and y is greater than x, which of the following statements must be true?

    I. $x + y = 5$
    II. x is less than 6
    III. $\frac{x}{y} = \frac{2}{3}$

    (A) I only
    (B) II only
    (C) I and II only
    (D) I and III only

20. Jenny has y baseball cards. She gives 5 cards to each of three different friends, and in return receives 2 cards from each friend. How many cards does Jenny have after the exchange?

    (A) $y - 9$
    (B) $y - 5$
    (C) $y + 3$
    (D) $y + 5$

USE THIS SPACE FOR FIGURING.

GO ON TO THE NEXT PAGE

21. If two fair coins are tossed simultaneously, what is the probability that two tails are thrown?

    (A) 1

    (B) $\dfrac{1}{2}$

    (C) $\dfrac{1}{4}$

    (D) $\dfrac{1}{8}$

22. A duplicating machine makes copies at a constant rate of 15 copies per minute. A certain copy job requires 600 copies. What fraction of the job will the machine finish in 5 minutes?

    (A) $\dfrac{1}{200}$

    (B) $\dfrac{1}{40}$

    (C) $\dfrac{1}{8}$

    (D) $\dfrac{1}{5}$

23. Which of the following is a possible value of z if $2(z-3) > 6$ and $z + 4 < 15$?

    (A) 3

    (B) 6

    (C) 7

    (D) 11

USE THIS SPACE FOR FIGURING.

GO ON TO THE NEXT PAGE

24. In a certain library there are 3 fiction books for every 8 nonfiction books. If the library has 600 nonfiction books, how many books does it have?

    (A) 2,200

    (B) 1,400

    (C)   825

    (D)   800

25. If $x + y$ equals an odd number and $x + z$ equals an even number, each of the following could be true EXCEPT

    (A) x is even and y is odd.

    (B) y is even and z is odd.

    (C) x and z are even and y is odd.

    (D) x and y are even and z is odd.

26. On the first test, Ted scored 7 percentage points above the passing grade. On the second test he scored 12 percentage points lower than he did on his first test. His score on the second test was

    (A) 19 percentage points below the passing grade

    (B) 12 percentage points below the passing grade

    (C) 5 percentage points below the passing grade

    (D) 2 percentage points above the passing grade

27. In a class, 70 percent of the students are right-handed, and the rest are left handed. If 70 percent of the left-handed students have brown eyes, then left handed students with brown eyes make up what percent of the entire class?

    (A) 14%

    (B) 21%

    (C) 30%

    (D) 49%

USE THIS SPACE FOR FIGURING.

GO ON TO THE NEXT PAGE

Questions 28 and 29 refer to the following definition: For all real numbers q and r, let $q//r = (qr) - (q - r)$.

USE THIS SPACE FOR FIGURING.

28. $8//2 =$

(A) 6

(B) 8

(C) 10

(D) 16

29. If $P//3 = 11$, then $P =$

(A) 3

(B) 4

(C) 6

(D) 7

30. If the product of integers a and b is 16 and a is greater than 4, then which of the following must be true?

 I. $b = 2$

 II. The sum of a and b is greater than zero

III. a is greater than b

(A) II only

(B) III only

(C) I and II only

(D) II and III only

31. In Figure 1, what is the value of x ?

(A) 20

(B) 30

(C) 45

(D) 90

Figure 1

GO ON TO THE NEXT PAGE

32. In Figure 2, the distance from B to C is twice the distance from A to B and the distance from C to D is equal to half the distance from A to C. If the distance from B to C is 12, what is the distance from A to D?

    (A) 18
    (B) 24
    (C) 27
    (D) 32

33. What is the greatest number of squares with sides of 2 centimeters that can be cut from a square with an area of 36 square centimeters?

    (A) 4
    (B) 9
    (C) 18
    (D) 36

34. If $x = 4y + 3$, then what does $x - 5$ equal?

    (A) $4y - 8$
    (B) $4y - 2$
    (C) $4y + 5$
    (D) $5y - 8$

35. A grocer buys oranges at a price of 4 for $1 and then sells them in his store for 40 cents each. How many oranges must he sell to earn a profit of $3?

    (A) 2
    (B) 10
    (C) 15
    (D) 20

USE THIS SPACE FOR FIGURING.

Figure 2

GO ON TO THE NEXT PAGE

36. A wool sweater is on sale for $63 and a cotton sweater is on sale for $45. If the sale price for each sweater is 10% less than the original price, how much less did the cotton sweater cost than the wool sweater before either went on sale?

(A) $23.50

(B) $20

(C) $19.80

(D) $18

USE THIS SPACE FOR FIGURING.

37. John finished $\frac{1}{3}$ of his homework assignment between 6:00 P.M. and 7:30 P.M. He needs to finish the assignment by 11:00 P.M. If he works at the same rate, what is the latest time that he can return to his homework?

(A) 7:45 P.M.

(B) 8:00 P.M.

(C) 8:30 P.M.

(D) 9:30 P.M.

38. There are twice as many men as women on a track team. Medals were given to $\frac{1}{3}$ of the women. If there are 45 men and women on the team, how many women received medals?

(A) 5

(B) 6

(C) 10

(D) 11

GO ON TO THE NEXT PAGE

39. If m is greater than n, and n is greater than 4, which of the following is LEAST?

(A) $\dfrac{1}{4m}$

(B) $\dfrac{1}{4n}$

(C) $\dfrac{1}{4 + m}$

(D) $\dfrac{1}{4 + n}$

40. If $\dfrac{1}{5}$ of a number is less than 20, the number must be

(A) less than 4

(B) equal to 4

(C) greater than 4

(D) less than 100

41. A 6-story apartment building has x apartments on each of its lower 3 floors and y apartments on each of its upper 3 floors. If 3 people live in each apartment, how many people live in the building?

(A) $3x + 3y$

(B) $3x + 3y + 3$

(C) $9x + 9y$

(D) $3x + 3y + 18$

42. Joe spent 20% of his allowance on tapes. Then he spent 10% of what was left on a movie. After the movie, he was left with what percent of his original allowance?

(A) 65%

(B) 70%

(C) 72%

(D) 75%

USE THIS SPACE FOR FIGURING.

GO ON TO THE NEXT PAGE

43. Each of the *n* members in an organization may invite up to 3 guests to a conference. What is the maximum number of members and guests who might attend the conference?

    (A) $n + 3$

    (B) $3n$

    (C) $3n + 4$

    (D) $4n$

44. A square rug with each side 4 meters long is placed on a square floor. If each side of the rug is one third the length of one side of the floor, what is the area, in square meters, of the floor?

    (A) 144

    (B) 96

    (C) 64

    (D) 16

45. Figure 3 is composed of six squares. How many rectangles are there in the figure?

    (A) 20

    (B) 18

    (C) 15

    (D) 12

USE THIS SPACE FOR FIGURING.

Figure 3

IF YOU FINISH BEFORE TIME IS CALLED, YOU MAY CHECK YOUR WORK ON THIS SECTION ONLY. DO NOT TURN TO ANY OTHER SECTION IN THE TEST.

STOP

SECTION 5
Time—30 Minutes

> Directions: Write an essay on the following prompt on the paper provided. Your essay should NOT exceed two pages and must be written in ink. Erasing is not allowed.

Prompt: <u>Technology makes the world smaller every day.</u>

Do you agree or disagree with this statement? Use examples from history, literature, or your own personal experience to support your point of view.

GO ON TO THE NEXT PAGE

ANSWERS AND EXPLANATIONS

SECTION 1: VERBAL

SYNONYMS

1. D

To desecrate is to commit a sacrilegious act—to defile.

2. B

To laud is to praise in a lavish manner, e.g. "the spectators lauded the efforts of the competing athletes."

3. B

To avert is to prevent something from occurring, e.g, "the disaster was averted by the air-traffic controller."

4. C

Piety is another word for religious faith.

5. A

Amoral means without "without moral code." Ethics are a kind of moral code, so unethical is the best choice here.

6. B

Candor means honesty—a "candid camera," for example, is one that shows real-life events.

7. D

Haughtiness means excessive pride—arrogance. (C), rudeness, was a tempting wrong answer choice, but haughty people aren't necessarily rude.

8. B

To verify means to prove something, e.g., "the existence of UFOs has never been verified."

9. A

To deceive means to trick.

10. C

Look for secondary definitions—a fiction is a story that is untrue, so one possible meaning for fiction is falsehood, e.g. "his reputation was largely based on the fiction that he had fought in World War II."

11. A

Something that's hardy is healthy, e.g., "a hardy troop of soldiers."

12. C

Something that's lyrical is like a singing voice—it's musical.

13. A

Use roots here—*meta* means change, and *morph* means shape. So the closest synonym is change.

14. D

To lament for someone or something is to grieve.

15. D

Something that's arid is dry, e.g. an arid desert. Word association could have worked here, if you'd thought of *arrid* the deodorant.

16. C

A perceptive person is observant—he or she is able to see perceive things quickly and understand them.

17. D

An adamant person is convinced, resolute—stubborn, e.g,. "Dave was adamant about his decision to buy a Range Rover™."

18. C

Neutral people or parties are impartial. They don't take sides—they're unbiased.

19. B

Docile means tame, e.g., "the aggressive dog became docile in later life."

20. B

Wariness means caution—if you're wary, you're apprehensive about a situation.

21. A

Rational thinking means using the mind in a systematic manner—it's being logical, in other words.

22. A

Daring is a word used to describe a courageous person or activity, e.g., "the daring scheme went disastrously wrong."

23. A

To donate means to contribute money or possessions.

24. B

Tranquillity is a state of calm.

SENTENCE COMPLETIONS

25. A

The clue words "come out at night" indicate that raccoons are nocturnal.

26. C

The two clue words "normally" and "usual" suggest that both blanks mean more or less the same—(C) amiable .. enthusiasm works best here.

27. A

Death is a morbid subject—making (A) the best choice here.

28. B

You're looking for a contrast here; once a religious festival (B), the event is now commercialized.

29. D

A person who is constantly changing his views, is described as flighty.

30. C

You're looking for a positive word for the first blank, and a word meaning "deny" or "criticize" for the second blank. (C) agility .. question fits this description.

31. A

Predict a synonym for "guilt" here—(A) remorse is the correct answer.

32. C

The first blank should mean "tiring," so rule out (A). The only choice that means "tired" for the second blank is (C), fatigued. So strenuous .. fatigued is the correct answer.

33. B

The phrase "not only..but.." indicates that the second word is slightly more extreme than the first. Since you're looking for negative-sounding words, (B), predictable .. absurd, fits best.

34. D

Predict a more extreme version of "respect" for the blank here; revered works best in this context.

35. D

The first blank here should express the writer's incredulity—after all, it's pretty amazing that Chinese silk showed up in Egypt. (D)'s incredible .. massive best explains why this fact is so amazing.

36. A

"At first" should have clued you into the contrast here—the house seemed frightening, but later proved benign, or friendly.

37. B

You're looking for a contrast—once just a myth, UFO stories are now thought plausible or believable.

38. A

Again, should be a contrast here—(A) sparse means terse, brief, minimal, and verbose means excessively wordy.

39. D

The clues "charm his listeners" suggest a positive word here, such as (D), engaging.

40. C

Exhilarated best captures the mixture of fear and enjoyment suggested by the sentence—consistent with a first trip on a raft.

SECTION 2: Math

1. C

$$Q + 7 - 8 + 3 = 23$$
$$Q + 2 = 23$$
$$Q = 21$$

2. D

A kilogram is equal to 1,000 grams. Remember, "kilo" means 1,000. So a kilometer, for example, equals 1,000 meters.

3. B

To solve this problem, you need to find a common denominator. In this case, the lowest common denominator is 36.

$$\frac{1}{9} + \frac{7}{12} + \frac{5}{6} = \frac{4}{36} + \frac{21}{36} + \frac{30}{36}$$
$$= \frac{55}{36}$$
$$= 1\frac{19}{36}$$

4. B

$$15\% \text{ of } 60 = (15\%)(60)$$
$$= (0.15)(60)$$
$$= 9$$

5. C

To solve this problem, you first need to determine the limits of possible values for a:

$$a + 2 > 5$$
$$a > 3$$
$$a - 4 < 1$$
$$a < 5$$

So a is between 3 and 5. The only value from the answer choices that fits in the limits is (C), 4.

6. D

To solve this equation, we first need to find the value of x.

$$2x + 4 = 26$$
$$2x = 22, \text{ so } x = 11. \text{ So } 11 + 4 = 15.$$

7. D

The key to solving this problem is to take in the information one piece at a time. We're told that we have an equilateral hexagon. Equilateral means that all sides are equal: a hexagon has 6 sides. If we divide 6 into 42, we have the measure of one side: 7, so two sides would total 14.

8. B

Angelo earns $2,000. Of this money, he spends 30% on rent. We can easily turn this information into an equation.

$$\text{rent} = 30\% \text{ of } \$2,000$$
$$= (0.30)(\$2,000)$$
$$= \$600$$

9. D

The eggs cost 16 cents apiece. We need to figure out how many eggs can make up for the cost of 6 new chickens or 58 dollars. In other words, how many times does 16 cents divide into 58. Set this problem up as you would any division problem, paying attention to decimal places.

$$0.16\overline{)58.00}$$

$$16\overline{)5800.0}^{362.5}$$

Since the famer cannot sell half of an egg, he must sell 363 eggs.

10. C

Notice the use of the word "rate" in this problem. Don't be fooled by the terms "fuel" and "miles"—this is a straightforward rate problem and you want to set it up as such. Twelve gallons of fuel for 48 miles is the same as how many gallons for 60 miles?

$$\frac{12}{48} = \frac{x}{60}$$
$$48x = 12 \times 60$$
$$x = \frac{720}{48} = 15$$

11. B

To add mixed numbers, add the whole number parts and add the fraction parts. (Sometimes the sum of the fraction parts will be greater than 1, in which case you would need to make some adjustments.) To add the fraction parts, find a common denominator.

$$1\frac{6}{11} + 1\frac{7}{22} = 2 + \frac{6}{11} + \frac{7}{22}$$
$$= 2 + \frac{12}{22} + \frac{7}{22}$$
$$= 2\frac{19}{22}$$

12. C

Use the average formula:

$$\text{Average} = \frac{\text{Sum of the items}}{\text{Number of items}}$$
$$9 = \frac{\text{Sum}}{6}$$
$$\text{Sum} = 9 \times 6 = 54$$

13. C

Let's consider each answer choice. (A) gives us the value $\frac{2}{3}$. But we know that x must be smaller than $\frac{1}{2}$, and since $\frac{2}{3}$ is not, we can eliminate it. (B) proposes 0.47, but x must be smaller than $\frac{1}{3}$, and 0.47 is not. (C) gives us $\frac{1}{5}$, which is smaller than $\frac{1}{3}$, but larger than $\frac{1}{10}$—it fits the given criteria. Since there can only be one correct answer there is no reason to check the last answer choice. Choice (D) is wrong because $\frac{1}{20}$ is less than $\frac{1}{10}$ and x can not be less than $\frac{1}{10}$.

14. D

The best way to solve this problem is to solve for a.

$$3a + 6a = 36$$
$$9a = 36$$
$$a = 4$$

15. B

The easiest way to solve this problem is to convert $\frac{1}{4}$ to a decimal, 0.25, and then multiply. Again, make sure that you remember to count your decimal places.

$$(0.72) \times (0.25) = 0.18$$

16. C

The easiest way to solve this problem is to break the diagram on the right into two rectangles. Then solve for each area and add them together.

The area of the rectangle on top is $3 \times 6 = 18$. The area of the rectangle on bottom is $5 \times 2 = 10$. The total area is $18 + 10 = 28$.

17. B

First you need to break down 48 into its prime factors, and then determine how may *different* ones there are.

$$48 = 2 \times 24$$
$$= 2 \times 2 \times 12$$
$$= 2 \times 2 \times 2 \times 6$$
$$= 2 \times 2 \times 2 \times 2 \times 3$$

There are only two different prime factors for 48; 2 and 3.

18. D

Remember as you do this problem that a factor is a number that divides evenly into another number. Again, the easiest way to solve this problem is to consider each factor individually. (A) cannot be the answer because 3 is a factor of 36 and also 48. Ditto for (B), 6, and (C), 12. The answer must be (D), 18.

19. A

The formula for the volume of a cube is the length of a side cubed. We are told that the length of one side is 5. Five cubed equals 125, (A).

20. D

Doubling the rate that we are given, we have 2 hours and 30 minutes for Jake to review 60 pages. We know that the answer cannot be letter (A). But, we need to figure out how long it will take Jack to review those final 10 pages. To do that, we can divide the rate it takes Jake to review 30 pages by 3; that should give us the rate it takes to read 10 pages. 1 hour and 15 minutes is the same as 75 minutes. A third of 75 is 25—we know it will take Jake 25 minutes to read ten pages. Put it all together: 2 hours and 30 minutes plus 25 minutes, and we have 2 hours and 55 minutes for Jack to read his history book.

21. A

Remember to compare, not calculate: There is no reason to look for common denominators and solve here. The $\frac{1}{2}$ in column A is just slightly larger than the $\frac{2}{5}$ in Column B. Both columns contain $\frac{3}{4}$, and are therefore equal. The $\frac{7}{8}$ in column A is also larger than the $\frac{7}{9}$ in Column B, so overall, whatever the total value, Column A is larger than Column B.

22. C

Put the expressions in Column A and Column B in the same form so they are easy to compare. First, simplify the value under Column A. It's easy to multiply these fractions together because they cancel easily, giving us a final value of $\frac{1}{20}$, which in decimal form is 0.05. The columns are equal.

23. B

This problem is similar to the one above. First simplify the value under Column A, making sure that you cancel whenever possible. Under Column A we end up with the value $\frac{4}{5}$ which is less than 1. The value under Column B is $\frac{5}{4}$ which is greater than 1. So, the answer is (B).

24. A

The fastest way to solve this problem is to determine the value of x.

$$3x - 12 = 3x - 6x$$
$$-12 = -6x$$
$$2 = x$$

So x equals 2. If you add 2 to x, you get 4, a value larger the 2 in Column B. So Column A is larger.

25. D

The answer to this problem is (D). All we know about x and y, is that both are positive. But we don't know their relative values: we don't know if x is greater than y or visa versa. Consequently, we can't determine if adding the number 1 to the value of x would make Column A greater, less than or equal to the value under Column B. The answer here must therefore be (D).

26. B

Find the value of each column:

$$5\% \text{ of } (3 + 4) = 5\% \text{ of } 7$$
$$= (0.05)(7)$$
$$= 0.35$$
$$4\% \text{ of } (3 \times 4) = 4\% \text{ of } 12$$
$$= (0.04)(12)$$
$$= 0.48$$

27. A

The easiest way to solve this problem is to change the value under Column B, a fraction, into a decimal. $\frac{9}{20}$ is the same as $\frac{45}{100}$ or 0.45. Clearly Column A, with a value of 0.46, is larger than Column B.

28. B

This problem requires no math at all. You are given a certain amount of money—5 dollars. Can you buy more expensive items (32-cent stamps) or more cheaper items (29-cent stamps) with this money? You can buy more of the cheaper items, so the answer must be Column B.

29. D

You're given that x is between $\frac{8}{9}$ and $\frac{1}{2}$, and you're asked to compare x to $\frac{2}{3}$. $\frac{2}{3}$ is between $\frac{8}{9}$ and $\frac{1}{2}$, but so are lots of other fractions, some less than $\frac{2}{3}$ and others greater than $\frac{2}{3}$. Column A could be greater than, equal to, or less than Column B, so the answer is (D).

30. B

This is another problem that takes no math at all. We are told that x is negative. Before you start plugging in values for x, you should take a look at the expression under Column B; $(2x)(1x)$. If you multiply these xs together, whatever the value, the result would be positive. the value under Column A, however, would remain negative. Since a positive is always greater than a negative, the answer has to be (B).

31. D

Don't be fooled by the number 8 under Column B. Column A asks you to find the perimeter of an octagon with sides of equal length. The problem is, we don't know what those lengths are. One side could equal 1, in which case the answer would be (C). One side could be 2, in which case the answer would be (A). We already have two possibilities, which tells us that the correct answer must be (D).

32. B

The factors of 21 are 1, 3, 7, and 21. Of these only two are prime. Compare that to the value under Column B, 3, and the answer is clearly (B).

33. A

Translate the expression into an equation. $\frac{5}{7}$ of x is 35.

$$\frac{5}{7}x = 35$$
$$x = 35 \times \frac{7}{5}$$
$$x = 49$$

34. C

Remember the saying "A percent of B is equal to B percent of A"? If you do, then this question is a breeze. If not, you want to commit that rule to memory. In this case, 98% of 51 is $0.98 \times 51 = 49.98$, and 51% of 98 is $0.51 \times 98 = 49.98$. The columns are equal.

35. B

There are a few ways to solve this problem. The first is to actually calculate the math. Twenty percent of 42 is the same as $(0.20)(42)$ or 8.4. The other way to do this problem is to realize that 20% of 42 is the same as taking $\frac{1}{5}$ of 42. We know that $\frac{1}{5}$ of 45 is 9, the value under Column B. But we want $\frac{1}{5}$ of 42 which will be less than 9. In either case, the answer must be (B).

SECTION 3: READING COMPREHENSION

PORCUPINES PASSAGE

The first passage on this test is about the porcupine, an animal whose fur consists of thousands of tough, sharp quills. The author gives several facts about the quills—that they're barbed, how long they are, and what kind of damage they can do. The passage ends with a description of how the porcupine uses its tail as a defensive weapon, lashing out at attackers in a way that makes it seem as if the quills have been thrown like darts, even though they haven't been.

1. C

The passage's first sentence calls a porcupine's quills its "defensive armament." The last sentence talks about how the porcupine uses its tail to fight off attackers. So porcupines use their quills to defend themselves, and (C) is correct. (A) and (B) are plausible reasons why a porcupine would attack another animal, but the passage only describes the porcupine as taking defensive action. The heat-conserving properties, if any, of the porcupine's quills, (D), are never mentioned.

2. B

The passage opens with the statement that porcupines have "justifiable confidence" in the defensive capabilities of their quills. Another word for justifiable is understandable, (B), the correct answer. "Intellectual," (A), implies that porcupines have mental powers comparable to humans, which we know isn't true. "Unreasonable," (C), and "defiant," (D), suggest the opposite of "understandable," implying that porcupines have no reason to be so confident—when, as we see, they do have good reason.

3. D

Porcupine quills are long, sharp spines that, when touched, stick in the attacker. In the same way, cactus needles are long sharp spines that, when touched, stick in the attacker, so (D) is correct here. Teeth, claws, and horns choices (A), (B), and (C) are not outward coverings; they're also shaped differently than quills and needles, and can be used for other things than for defense. So (D) remains the best answer.

4. A

Sentence 4 says that the porcupine's longest quills are on its back and flank, but that the shorter quills on its tail "do the most damage." You can infer, then, that the longest quills aren't as important for defense as the shorter quills on the porcupine's tail; (A), which restates this idea, is correct. (B) implies that the longest quills are incapable of harming attackers.

But this contradicts the previous sentence, which says that the quills are so loosely set in the skin that any forceful touch will cause them to stick into the attacker. The passage says that each porcupine has up to 30,000 quills, but not that quills of a certain length are less numerous, (C), or sharper, (D), than quills of any other length.

LOG CABINS PASSAGE

The second passage is about log cabins, and the era of their greatest popularity—a period from 1780 to 1850. The author describes early simple cabins and grand later ones, and then discusses the factors that led to a decline in the log cabin's popularity, factors like the greater availability of hardware and building materials, the rising popularity of the Greek Revival style of house, and the spread of the railroads. The passage ends with a brief description of what happened to most log cabins as their heyday ended.

5. C

The first sentence says that "a great number of settlers forged westward." What word plugs in best for "forged"? (C)'s "moved." "Fled," (A), incorrectly implies that the settlers were running away from something, "wandered," (B), that their movements were aimless, without purpose. "Returned," (D), suggests that the settlers had already been out west, which makes little sense in context.

6. D

This is a tough question. The Greek Revival style is described as becoming increasingly popular, "with [i.e., because of] its democratic roots in ancient Greece..." So the origins of the new style lay in the ancient democracy of Greece —a fact that might well have appealed to the citizens of a young democratic nation like the United States—and (D) is the best answer. The passage never suggests that there had been a general desire to replace log cabins, (A), and never mentions contemporary Greek architects, (B), or devoutly religious Americans, (C).

7. A

The author indicates that Greek Revival houses became more popular than log cabins for two reasons: the democratic roots of the Greek Revival style, and the templed fronts of these houses, which faced the street. This last feature—that the fronts of Greek Revival houses faced the street—suggests that log cabins became less popular because they didn't always face the street, which makes (A) correct. The passage doesn't suggest that either style of house had indoor plumbing, (B), or that log cabins could not have glass windows, (C). And while log cabins may well have been built near lakes and rivers, (D), there's no suggestion that Greek Revival homes were not. So (A) is best here.

8. B

The question stem's reference to limiting factors in the architecture of log cabins recalls sentence 6: "Climate and the proximity of the local forest no longer set architectural limits." What does this mean? It means that, with the new railroads bringing lumber and hardware to formerly isolated regions, a settler's choice of which house to build was no longer dictated by local weather and the distance to the nearest forest. (B) restates this latter point, and it's correct. (A) is wrong because, unlike logs from the local forest, nails were not widely available. (C) and (D) bring up issues that aren't mentioned at all in the passage, and so cannot be inferred.

9. D

The passage's final sentence notes that, after the 1850's, log structures housed livestock but "fewer and fewer people." So most log structures built after 1850 housed animals, (D).

Plague Passage

Next up is a passage about the plague, an epidemic which killed one-third of the people in Europe in 13th and 14th centuries. The author says that, ironically, the plague created some beneficial changes in European society. One of these changes—the focal point of the passage—was in the medical profession. The plague created a shortage of doctors, allowing people with new ideas to enter the profession. In addition, having been failed by the old doctors with their Latin medical texts, ordinary people began clamoring for medical texts printed in everyday languages. These were eventually published, making medical knowledge more accessible to everyone.

10. C

As noted above, the primary focus of the passage is how at least one good thing came out of the terrible tragedy of the plague. (C) correctly restates this idea. (A) and (B) focus too narrowly on details mentioned in sentences 1 and 4. (D) is closer to the mark, but it too is a detail in the larger focus of the passage.

11. A

Plug the choices into the sentence in question, and (A) is clearly best: the epidemic caused enormous changes in European society. The changes were needed, (B), but needed by the society, not by the plague itself. "Accelerated," (C), means moved faster, which implies that the changes were already occurring before the plague. But the passage never suggests that this was so. "Offered," (D), doesn't work at all.

12. C

Sentence 6 says that, when the plague created a shortage of doctors, "people with new ideas" rushed in to fill the void, bringing needed reform (sentence 3) to the medical profession. This suggests that, prior to the plague, the medical profession was in need of new ideas—sweeping changes—which makes (C) correct. The shortage of doctors, (A), occurred during and after the plague, not before it. As for (B), while sentence 5 says that universities were short on medical professors, there's no evidence that medical care was available only to students in the pre-plague years. And (D) distorts the final sentence, which says that people demanded medical texts printed in their own languages, not the language of Latin. This doesn't mean that, before the plague, medicine was only practiced in Latin-speaking countries. (Latin is, in fact, and was even then, a "dead" language, the language of the long-vanquished Roman Empire.)

13. B

Take another look at the last sentence of the passage. It says that medical texts gradually began to be published in everyday languages instead of in Latin, "making medical knowledge more accessible." You can infer from this that, after the 1300s, easy-to-read medical texts were probably more available to the general public, an idea restated in correct choice (B). The passage never indicates that a cure for the plague, (A), would soon be found (in fact, it would not be found for several centuries). As for (C), just because more medical texts were published in everyday languages after the plague doesn't mean that, a hundred years later, none were written in

Latin. Finally, (D) is completely unsupported by the passage.

ORIENTEERING PASSAGE

The fourth passage is about the sport of orienteering, in which competitors make their way across unfamiliar terrain using only a map and a compass. The author focuses on the notion that the most important element of orienteering is choosing a good route. Why? Because the shortest route from point A to point B is rarely the fastest or easiest way.

14. B

What defines orienteering, if not having a compass and a map? Orienteers have to "navigate their way cross-country along an unfamiliar course." Therefore, a hiker with a map and compass is NOT orienteering if she travels over a known, familiar route, and (B) is correct. (A) and (B) propose rules that are never mentioned in the passage. (D) describes an orienteer who takes the "crude" approach.

15. D

As sentence 2 puts it, "the most important question in orienteering is not compass bearing but choice of route," which eliminates (A) and makes (D) correct. While it is no doubt important to avoid hazardous terrain, (B), and to overcome obstacles quickly, (C), the passage places the highest priority on the choice of route.

16. B

The competitor in question climbs a mountain to take the most direct route, but sentences 3 and 4 say that this is "seldom the best," and that orienteers "tend to disdain" competitors who do so as crude and lacking intellectual finesse, or sophistication, (B). (A) is wrong because the competitor's beeline approach will probably put him at a disadvantage in terms of both time and energy. The beeline approach may be stupid, but the author never says it's against the rules, (C), or that it can endanger other competitors, (D). So (B) is best.

17. D

The passage never mentions running or backpacks, (A), swimming, (B), or setting up campsites, (C). So (D) must be correct. And in fact, the final sentence of the passage notes that orienteers "are always making" quick calculations of the times and distances involved in various possible routes.

NIGHT TERRORS PASSAGE

Next up is a passage about two psychological phenomena: first, nightmares, and second, something called night terrors, where the sleeper, usually a child, wakes up in great fright with no memory of having dreamed. The passage begins with the statement that, while nightmares and night terrors used to be confused one with the other, researchers now know they are two different phenomena. The rest of the passage focuses on night terrors, noting that they're not really dangerous, that parents should use common sense, taking precautions and not worrying unduly.

18. B

Two phenomena, long "confounded" under one heading, are now known to be separate things. The word in question, then, should mean confused, or mixed-up, (B). None of the other words means anything remotely similar to "confounded."

19. C

The correct answer, (C), restates the first sentence of the passage. None of the other choices is suggested, even (D), which is a distorted echo of the passage's final sentence. The author says there that children suffering from night terrors should usually not be medicated. This is a far cry from saying that sleep researchers used to prescribe medication for such children, but have recently stopped.

20. A

Sentence 2 says that a nightmare "is an actual, detailed dream." (A) correctly restates this fact. No mention is made of dream fragments, (B), hallucinations, (C), or trances, (D).

21. C

What do we know about the parents of children who suffer from night terrors? That these parents themselves sometimes find their child's experience "horrifying." That a child suffering from night terrors can make a parent "anxious." We can infer, then, that the parents find night terrors nearly as frightening as the children do, and (C) is correct. (A) is the opposite of what the author says. (B) makes a hereditary leap; the passage never suggests that these parents also suffered night terrors when they were children. And the last sentence of the passage implies, if anything, that a doctor usually should not be consulted at all, rather than as soon as possible, (D).

22. D

The difference between nightmares and night terrors, (A), is defined in sentences 2 and 3. The question in (B) is answered in the second-to-last sentence of the passage. Sentence 3 notes that the child waking from a night terror does not remember dreaming, (C). This leaves (D) as correct, and indeed, the author merely advises a sleep schedule, never explaining why a sleep schedule helps reduce night terrors.

NEANDERTHALS PASSAGE

This passage is about the Neanderthal, an early human that lived in Europe and Asia until about 35,000 years ago. The passage puts forth two ideas: first, that Neanderthals were physically very different from modern humans and second, that despite their reputation to the contrary, Neanderthals were probably quite intelligent. The passage concludes with a teaser: the disappearance of this capable creature mystifies and fascinates scientists, and is "perhaps the most talked-about issue in human origins research today."

23. A

All four choices are physical attributes of the Neanderthal. In the author's description of Neanderthals, found in sentence 3, "massive limb bones" are the first item on the list. A "limb" is an arm or a leg, so you can infer from this that most Neanderthals had big arms, (A). You can't infer, however, that their legs were bowed, (C), because "bowed" implies shape, not size. The set of Neanderthal eyes, (A), and the breadth of their feet, (D), are never mentioned.

24. C

The opening sentence says that Neanderthals lived "throughout Europe and western Asia," which makes (C) correct. The passage never says what kind of dwellings they lived in, (A), how they hunted, (B), or whether they lived on all the continents, (D), and not just the two mentioned in the correct answer.

25. C

The author says that Neanderthals, unlike modern humans, had "massive limb bones," and "enormous physical strength." Modern humans, then probably have less physical strength than their Neanderthal cousins, and (C) is correct. No information is given on either species' eyesight, (A), sense of smell, (B), or amount of body hair, (D).

26. D

The only reference to what modern humans think of Neanderthals comes at the beginning of sentence 4: "yet despite the Neanderthals' reputation for low intelligence..." (D) is thus the correct inference.

27. C

The word "question" appears only once in the passage, in the final sentence. We know from the previous sentence that Neanderthals vanished or died out around 35,000 years ago. "The question of what became of the Neanderthals..." Therefore, (C) is correct. The questions of the Neanderthals' diet, (A), migratory patterns, (B), and origins, (D), are never raised in the passage.

MAGIC PASSAGE

The seventh passage is about magic. The author's big point is that, for a magician, the art of deception is more important than mechanical gimmicks such as trapdoors or mirrors. Magicians depend above all else on timing and misdirecting the audience's attention. The author gives one example of how misdirection need not be small and subtle: a gorilla riding across the stage on a unicycle to distract the audience from noticing his assistant being whisked offstage. That's it: deception, or stagecraft, is more important than the mechanics of magic.

28. C

The question stem takes you back to the first sentence of the passage, where the author says that mirrors and trapdoors are less important than the art of deception. Two sentences later, the author, expanding on this point, says that "presentation and timing are everything." You can infer, then, that mirrors and trapdoors are less important than presentation and timing, (C). More recent devices, (A), are not mentioned in the passage. (B) is never suggested, either. And (D) misses the point: a successful magician tries to conceal all such gimmicks from even the most perceptive audience members.

29. D

The quoted word appears in sentence 2, which says a magician must be skilled in misdirection, "the fine art of prompting an audience to look elsewhere at the crucial moment." Plugging in the words in the choices, (D) works best: a magician must persuade an audience to look elsewhere at the crucial moment. (A) is wrong, since if the audience is told to look elsewhere, they will of course do nothing of the sort. (B) doesn't make sense in context. (C) is a little tempting, since a gorilla riding across the stage would no doubt be entertaining. But "entertaining" does not mean the same thing as "prompting," so (D) is best here.

30. C

The main idea question. As previously noted, the author's focus is on magic—specifically, the idea that misdirection is more important to a magician's success than mechanical gimmicks such as mirrors - trapdoors. This eliminates (A) and (B), which ᵃ the gimmicks, and points to (C) as correct. ᵃᵃ narrowly on sentence 3, where the

author tries to educate you about how a magician practices deception. But the deception, and not an audience's perception of it, is the point here, so (C) is best.

31. B

Again, back to sentence 3. As the author says, when a magician waves his hand grandly, "he is generally trying to divert your attention from the other [hand]." Thus, (B) is correct.

WIGS PASSAGE

The eighth passage is about wigs, the wigs worn by American colonists in the years before the American Revolution. The author details what kinds of wigs were available, noting that those made of human hair were the most desirable and expensive. The passage ends with the point that, when the American and French Revolutions occurred, anything that seemed overly extravagant or status-conscious became very unpopular, and so wigs fell out of fashion.

32. C

Let's take the choices one by one. (A) doesn't sound right; the author doesn't go into the "elaborate construction" of American wigs. (B) is too general. The passage focuses on one particular English import: wigs. Furthermore, as sentence 3 notes, by the time of the Revolution, most American colonies had their own wigmakers. Skipping to choice (D), we find it has the same problem as (B): too general. That of course leaves (C) as correct. And it's true: the author focuses primarily on a particular fashion—the wearing of wigs—and the effect that historical events such as the American and French Revolutions had on this fashion.

33. D

Human-hair wigs are mentioned in sentence 2, which says that cheaper wigs were made of horse or goat hair or duck feathers, while "the wealthy chose expensive wigs" made of human hair. If these human-hair wigs were so expensive, then you can infer that poor people rarely wore them, making (D) correct. The relative ease of maintenance of human and horsehair wigs, (A), is never discussed in the passage. Nor does the author mention which wigs were fashionable in France, (B). And (C) is a particularly gruesome piece of fiction.

34. A

The first half of sentence 3 says that, in the beginning of the wig craze, most Americans wore wigs imported from England. This means that there probably weren't a lot of wigmakers in the Colonies. The second half of sentence 3 says that, by the start of the Revolutionary War, "numerous wigmakers were plying their trade in the Colonies." So you can infer that the number of wigmakers living in the Colonies must have increased considerably by the time of the Revolution, and (A) is correct. Sentence 3 is the only information we get about Colonial wigmakers, so statements (B), (C), and (D) are never suggested in the passage.

35. B

"Infatuated with" means having a crush on, being in love with or fond of someone or something. Therefore, (B) is correct. None of the phrases in choices (A), (C), and (D) has a meaning similar to "infatuated with."

COYOTES PASSAGE

The final passage is about coyotes. The author's main focus is not on the behavioral habits of living coyotes, but rather on the evolution of the coyote as found in the fossil record. Both the coyote and the wolf, we learn, had a common ancestor living in North America as long as three million years ago. One or two million years ago, the coyote and the wolf became separate species. As time passed, other species such as the mammoth and the saber-tooth tiger lived and became extinct, but the coyote endured—basically the same primitive animal, but still marvelously adaptable to its environment.

36. A

In most passages, the main idea is stated in the first or second sentence. Here the main idea becomes clear only at the end: that the coyote has endured for millions of years without evolving into a more advanced species—a point restated in correct choice (A). (B) focuses on a detail, how other species came and went. But these species are described in order to provide a contrast with the coyote, which not only avoided extinction, but did so without evolving. (C) has the same problem: the author's point is that, unlike other animals, the coyote did not change—it survived by staying the same. And (D) is a passing detail found in sentence 4—not significant enough to be the primary focus.

37. C

"Modern" dogs are mentioned only in the first sentence, which says that coyotes are "one of the most primitive of living dogs." This suggests that modern dogs are relatives of coyotes, as stated in (C). Dire wolves are extinct "canids"; we don't know from the passage whether they're related to modern dogs or not, but it's a pretty safe bet that modern dogs are not "direct descendants of dire wolves, as (A) suggests. Where modern dogs live, (B), is not mentioned, but again, common sense suggests they're found everywhere, not just in North America.

The evolutionary flexibility of modern dogs (D) is not discussed in the passage.

38. D

A fairly easy detail question. Sentence 2 says that "a close relative of the contemporary coyote existed here two to three million years ago." The choice closest to this estimate is (D), and it's correct.

39. D

Why does the author mention mammoths and saber-tooth tigers? Because they lived and became extinct, while the ever-adaptable coyote endured. In other words, these species died out because they failed to adapt as the coyote did, and (D) is correct. Neither animal in question is described as a relative of the coyote (A). Unlike wild horses, mammoths and tigers are not described as having left North America by land bridge (C), but that's beside the point. These species died out because they couldn't adapt—as the coyote did. And the author never says that jackals hunted any species into extinction, (D).

40. B

Here's a word-in-context question that really requires you to know the meaning of the word —the word, in this case, being "galleon." Maybe you've come across it in pirate stories; a galleon is a kind of ship. So the idea that other horses "returned on galleons" means that horses, who had left North America by land bridge, returned to the continent when brought by ship, making (B) correct. None of the other choices picks up on the proper meaning of "galleon."

SECTION 4: MATH

1. C

$(x-2)(x+5)$ will equal 0 when either factor $(x-2)$ or $(x+5)$ is 0. That's when x is 2 or –5.

2. D

Set up a proportion. 2 gallons for 875 square feet is the same as x gallons for 4,375 square feet:

$$\frac{2}{875} = \frac{x}{4,375}$$
$$875x = 2 \times 4,375$$
$$875x = 8,750$$
$$x = \frac{8,750}{875} = 10$$

3. B

Use the formula for the area of a triangle:

$$\text{Area} = \frac{1}{2}(\text{base})(\text{height})$$
$$= \frac{1}{2}(4 \text{ in.})(6 \text{ in.}) = 12 \text{ sq. in.}$$

4. D

The sides of an equilateral triangle are equal in length, so $3x+1$ and $x+7$ are equal:

$$3x + 1 = x + 7$$
$$3x - x = 7 - 1$$
$$2x = 6$$
$$x = 3$$

Plug $x = 3$ back into either of the expressions and you'll find that the length of each side is 10.

5. B

65 times 10^2 means 65 times 100, or 6,500. 31 times 10^3 means 31 times 1,000, or 31,000. Add 6,500 and 31,000 and 12 and you get 37,512.

6. C

He lost 20% of $120,000, which is 0.20 times $120,000, or $24,000.

7. D

The dog can run in a circular area with radius of 8 meters. Use the formula for the area of a circle:

$$\text{Area} = \pi \, (\text{radius})2$$
$$= \pi \, (8 \text{ meters})2$$
$$= 64\pi \text{ square meters}$$

8. B

Rate is distance divided by time. So 328 miles divided by 4 hours is $\frac{328}{4} = 82$ miles per hour.

9. D

If distance equals rate times time, then time equals distance divided by rate. Here the distance is 3,300 miles and the rate is 270 miles per hour. And 3,300 miles divided by 270 miles per hour is $\frac{3.300}{270} \approx 12.22$ hours.

10. C

Plug $a = 3$ and $b = 4$ into the expression:

$$a^2 + 2ab + b^2 = 3^2 + 2(3)(4) + 4^2$$
$$= 9 + 24 + 16$$
$$= 49$$

11. C

Look what happens when you just add the equations as presented:

$$x - y = 5$$
$$\underline{4x + 6y = 20}$$
$$5x + 5y = 25$$

Now just divide both sides by 5 and you get $x + y = 5$.

12. B

Break 726 down to its prime factorization by factoring out any prime factor you see one at a time:

$$726 = 2 \times 363$$
$$= 2 \times 3 \times 121$$
$$= 2 \times 3 \times 11 \times 11$$

The distinct prime factors are 2, 3, and 11. That's 3 distinct prime factors.

13. D

Plug any odd number in for n and evaluate the answer choices. If you take $n = 3$, you'll find that (A) is $-2(3) - 1 = -7$; (B) is $2(3) + 1 = 7$; (C) is $2(3) - 1 = 5$; and (D) is $4(3) = 12$. Only (D) is even.

14. C

6 hours a day for 5 days is 30 hours. 30 hours is $30 \times 60 = 1,800$ minutes, and 1,800 minutes is $1,800 \times 60 = 108,000$ seconds.

15. D

There are $4 \times 24 = 96$ hours in 4 days. 96 hours of snow at 3.5 inches per hour is $96 \times 3.5 = 336$ inches.

16. D

Today Nicholas is x years old and Billy is $3x$ years old. Five years ago Nicholas was $x - 5$ years old and Nicholas was $3x - 5$, so the sum of their ages was $(x - 5) + (3x - 5) = 4x - 10$.

17. A

If there are twice as many boys as girls, then $\frac{2}{5}$ of them are boys and $\frac{1}{3}$ are girls. Two-thirds of 36 is 24.

18. A

The $\frac{1}{3}$ who drank soda only and the $\frac{2}{5}$ who drank juice only account for $\frac{1}{3} + \frac{2}{5} = \frac{5}{15} + \frac{6}{15} = \frac{11}{15}$ of the guests. The 16 who drank nothing therefore account for the other $\frac{4}{15}$. So you want to find out what number multiplied by $\frac{4}{15}$ will give you 16: $\frac{4}{15}x =$ 16; $x = 16 \times \frac{15}{4} = 4 \times 15 = 60$.

19. B

You might think that x has to be 2 and y has to be 3, but in fact there's another pair of consecutive integers that have a product of 6: –3 and –2. So what you know is that either $x = 2$ and $y = 3$, or $x = -3$ and $y = -2$. All three statements are true in the first case (when x and y are positive), but only statement II is true in the second case (when x and y are negative).

20. A

She starts with y cards. Giving away 5 to each of 3 friends means giving away $3 \times 5 = 15$, leaving her with $y - 15$. Receiving 2 from each of 3 friends means receiving $3 \times 2 = 6$, leaving her with $y - 15 + 6 = y - 9$.

21. C

For each coin the probability of tails is $\frac{1}{2}$. The combined probability is the product of the separate probabilities: $\frac{1}{2} \times \frac{1}{2} = \frac{1}{4}$.

22. C

Five minutes at 15 copies per minute is $5 \times 15 = 75$ copies. 75 out of 600 is: $\frac{75}{600} = \frac{1}{8}$.

23. C

Simplify each inequality:

$$2(z - 3) > 6$$
$$2z - 6 > 6$$
$$2z > 6 + 6$$
$$2z > 12$$
$$z > 6$$
$$z + 4 < 15$$
$$z < 15 - 4$$
$$z < 11$$

So z is between 6 and 11. The only answer choice that qualifies is (C), 7.

24. C

Three fiction books for every 8 nonfiction books means that 8 out of 3 + 8, or $\frac{8}{11}$ of all the books are nonfiction. The 600 nonfiction books are $\frac{8}{11}$ of the number you're looking for, so:

$$\frac{8}{11}x = 600$$
$$x = 600 \times \frac{11}{8} = \frac{6,600}{8} = 825$$

25. D

(D) is impossible because if x and y were even and z were odd, then $x + y$ would be even and $x + z$ would be odd.

26. C

If you call the passing grade x, then his second score was $x + 7$, and his third score was $x + 7 - 12 = x - 5$, which is 5 less than x.

27. B

If 70 percent are right-handed and the rest are left-handed, then $100 - 70 = 30$ percent are left-handed. Of that 30 percent, 70 percent have brown hair.

Seventy percent of 30 percent is $(0.70)(0.30) = 0.21$, or 21 percent.

28. C

Plug $q = 8$ and $r = 2$ into the definition:

$$q//r = (qr) - (q - r)$$
$$8//2 = (8 \times 2) - (8 - 2)$$
$$= 16 - 6 = 10$$

29. B

Plug $q = P$ and $r = 3$ into the definition:

$$q//r = (qr) - (q - r)$$
$$P//3 = (P \times 3) - (P - 3)$$
$$= 3P - P + 3$$
$$= 2P + 3$$

Set that equal to 11, and solve for P:

$$2P + 3 = 11$$
$$2P = 11 - 3$$
$$2P = 8$$
$$P = 4$$

30. D

Since a is anything greater than 4, a can be 8 or 16, so b doesn't have to be 2—which eliminates statement I. But you do know that b has to be positive, because a is positive (it's greater than 4) and the product of a and b is positive (it's 16). Therefore the sum of a and b is positive, and statement II is true. And lastly, when $a = 8$, $b = 2$; and when $a = 16$, $b = 1$; a is greater than b, and statement III is true.

31. B

The three angles have to add up to 180°, so:

$$x + 2x + 3x = 180$$
$$6x = 180$$
$$x = 30$$

32. C

AB is half of BC, which is given as 12, so $AB = 6$, and $AC = 6 + 12 = 18$. CD is half of AC, so $CD = 9$, and thus $AD = AB + BC + CD = 6 + 12 + 9 = 27$.

33. B

A square with an area of 36 square centimeters has sides of length 6 centimeters. Thus each side of the large square gets cut into thirds, and the whole large square gets divided into $3 \times 3 = 9$ smaller squares:

34. B

Just subtract 5 from both sides of the given equation:

$$x = 4y + 3$$
$$x - 5 = 4y + 3 - 5$$
$$= 4y - 2$$

35. D

Four for a dollar means 25 cents each. Selling them for 40 cents each means a profit of 15 cents on every orange sold. To get a total profit of $3.00, he must sell $\dfrac{\$3.00}{\$0.15} = \dfrac{300}{15} = 20$ oranges.

36. B

Each sale price is 90% of the original price. Sixty-three dollar is 90% of what?

$$0.90x = \$63$$

$$x = \$\frac{63}{0.90} = \$70$$

The original price of the wool sweater was $70. And $45 is 90% of what?

$$0.90\,y = \$45$$

$$y = \$\frac{45}{0.90} = \$50$$

The original price of the cotton sweater was $20. The difference was $20.

37. B

It took him a hour and a half to do the first one-third, so it will take him twice that long—or 3 hours—to do the remaining two-thirds. To finish by 11:00 P.M., he must resume by 8:00 P.M.

38. A

If there are twice as many men as women on the team, then two-thirds of the team members are men and one-third are women. One-third of 45 is 15, so there are 15 women. One-third of those 15 women received medals, so that's 5 women medal-winners.

39. A

The four fractions you're comparing all have the same numerator (1) and they all have positive denominators, so the fraction with the least value must be the one with the greatest denominator. m is greater than n, so $4m$ is greater than $4n$, and $4 + m$ is greater than $4 + n$. That eliminates (B) and (D). And since m is greater than 4, $4m$ is greater than $4 + m$. Thus (A) has the greatest denominator, and therefore the least value.

40. D

Translate into algebra. If one-fifth of a number is less than 20, then:

$$\frac{1}{5}x < 20$$

$$x < 20 \times \frac{5}{1}$$

$$x < 100$$

41. C

The lower three floors have a total of $3x$ apartments. The upper three floors have a total of $3y$ apartments. That's a total of $3x + 3y$ apartments in the building. If there are 3 people in each apartment, then the total number of people is 3 times $(3x + 3y)$, or $9x + 9y$.

42. C

After spending 20% on tapes, Joe had 80% left. He then spent 10% of that, or 8%, leaving 100% − (20% + 8%) = 72%.

43. D

If every one of the n members invited 3 guests, that would be a total of $3n$ guests. n members plus $3n$ guests adds up to $n + 3n = 4n$ attendees.

44. A

If each side of the 4-by-4 rug is one-third of the sides of the floor, then it's a 12-by-12 floor, which would have an area of 144 square meters.

45. B

Each of the 6 squares is a rectangle.

Plus there are these 2 rectangles:

And these 2:

And these 2:

Plus this one:

And this one:

And lastly this one:

That's a total of 6 + 3 + 2 + 2 + 2 + 1 + 1 + 1 = 18

Now that you have reviewed the answer explanations, turn to chapter 23 for information on how to score your ISEE practice test.

CHAPTER 22: ISEE PRACTICE TEST 3: LOWER-LEVEL

HOW TO TAKE THIS PRACTICE TEST

Before taking this practice test, find a quiet room where you can work uninterrupted for three hours. Make sure you have a comfortable desk and several No. 2 pencils.

Use the answer sheet provided to record your answers. (You can cut it out or photocopy it.)

Once you start this practice test, don't stop until you've finished. Remember—you can review any questions within a section, but you may not go backward or forward a section.

You'll find an answer key, and explanations following the test.

Good luck.

ISEE Practice Test Three: Lower-Level Answer Sheet

Remove (or photocopy) the answer sheet and use it to complete the practice test.

Start with number 1 for each section. If a section has fewer questions than answer spaces, leave the extra spaces blank.

SECTION 1

1 (A)(B)(C)(D)	9 (A)(B)(C)(D)	17 (A)(B)(C)(D)	25 (A)(B)(C)(D)	33 (A)(B)(C)(D)
2 (A)(B)(C)(D)	10 (A)(B)(C)(D)	18 (A)(B)(C)(D)	26 (A)(B)(C)(D)	34 (A)(B)(C)(D)
3 (A)(B)(C)(D)	11 (A)(B)(C)(D)	19 (A)(B)(C)(D)	27 (A)(B)(C)(D)	35 (A)(B)(C)(D)
4 (A)(B)(C)(D)	12 (A)(B)(C)(D)	20 (A)(B)(C)(D)	28 (A)(B)(C)(D)	36 (A)(B)(C)(D)
5 (A)(B)(C)(D)	13 (A)(B)(C)(D)	21 (A)(B)(C)(D)	29 (A)(B)(C)(D)	37 (A)(B)(C)(D)
6 (A)(B)(C)(D)	14 (A)(B)(C)(D)	22 (A)(B)(C)(D)	30 (A)(B)(C)(D)	38 (A)(B)(C)(D)
7 (A)(B)(C)(D)	15 (A)(B)(C)(D)	23 (A)(B)(C)(D)	31 (A)(B)(C)(D)	39 (A)(B)(C)(D)
8 (A)(B)(C)(D)	16 (A)(B)(C)(D)	24 (A)(B)(C)(D)	32 (A)(B)(C)(D)	40 (A)(B)(C)(D)

right in section 1

wrong in section 1

SECTION 2

1 (A)(B)(C)(D)	9 (A)(B)(C)(D)	17 (A)(B)(C)(D)	25 (A)(B)(C)(D)	33 (A)(B)(C)(D)
2 (A)(B)(C)(D)	10 (A)(B)(C)(D)	18 (A)(B)(C)(D)	26 (A)(B)(C)(D)	34 (A)(B)(C)(D)
3 (A)(B)(C)(D)	11 (A)(B)(C)(D)	19 (A)(B)(C)(D)	27 (A)(B)(C)(D)	35 (A)(B)(C)(D)
4 (A)(B)(C)(D)	12 (A)(B)(C)(D)	20 (A)(B)(C)(D)	28 (A)(B)(C)(D)	36 (A)(B)(C)(D)
5 (A)(B)(C)(D)	13 (A)(B)(C)(D)	21 (A)(B)(C)(D)	29 (A)(B)(C)(D)	37 (A)(B)(C)(D)
6 (A)(B)(C)(D)	14 (A)(B)(C)(D)	22 (A)(B)(C)(D)	30 (A)(B)(C)(D)	38 (A)(B)(C)(D)
7 (A)(B)(C)(D)	15 (A)(B)(C)(D)	23 (A)(B)(C)(D)	31 (A)(B)(C)(D)	39 (A)(B)(C)(D)
8 (A)(B)(C)(D)	16 (A)(B)(C)(D)	24 (A)(B)(C)(D)	32 (A)(B)(C)(D)	40 (A)(B)(C)(D)

right in section 2

wrong in section 2

SECTION 3

1 (A)(B)(C)(D)	9 (A)(B)(C)(D)	17 (A)(B)(C)(D)	25 (A)(B)(C)(D)	33 (A)(B)(C)(D)
2 (A)(B)(C)(D)	10 (A)(B)(C)(D)	18 (A)(B)(C)(D)	26 (A)(B)(C)(D)	34 (A)(B)(C)(D)
3 (A)(B)(C)(D)	11 (A)(B)(C)(D)	19 (A)(B)(C)(D)	27 (A)(B)(C)(D)	35 (A)(B)(C)(D)
4 (A)(B)(C)(D)	12 (A)(B)(C)(D)	20 (A)(B)(C)(D)	28 (A)(B)(C)(D)	36 (A)(B)(C)(D)
5 (A)(B)(C)(D)	13 (A)(B)(C)(D)	21 (A)(B)(C)(D)	29 (A)(B)(C)(D)	37 (A)(B)(C)(D)
6 (A)(B)(C)(D)	14 (A)(B)(C)(D)	22 (A)(B)(C)(D)	30 (A)(B)(C)(D)	38 (A)(B)(C)(D)
7 (A)(B)(C)(D)	15 (A)(B)(C)(D)	23 (A)(B)(C)(D)	31 (A)(B)(C)(D)	39 (A)(B)(C)(D)
8 (A)(B)(C)(D)	16 (A)(B)(C)(D)	24 (A)(B)(C)(D)	32 (A)(B)(C)(D)	40 (A)(B)(C)(D)

right in section 3

wrong in section 3

SECTION 4

1 (A)(B)(C)(D)	9 (A)(B)(C)(D)	17 (A)(B)(C)(D)	25 (A)(B)(C)(D)	33 (A)(B)(C)(D)
2 (A)(B)(C)(D)	10 (A)(B)(C)(D)	18 (A)(B)(C)(D)	26 (A)(B)(C)(D)	34 (A)(B)(C)(D)
3 (A)(B)(C)(D)	11 (A)(B)(C)(D)	19 (A)(B)(C)(D)	27 (A)(B)(C)(D)	35 (A)(B)(C)(D)
4 (A)(B)(C)(D)	12 (A)(B)(C)(D)	20 (A)(B)(C)(D)	28 (A)(B)(C)(D)	36 (A)(B)(C)(D)
5 (A)(B)(C)(D)	13 (A)(B)(C)(D)	21 (A)(B)(C)(D)	29 (A)(B)(C)(D)	37 (A)(B)(C)(D)
6 (A)(B)(C)(D)	14 (A)(B)(C)(D)	22 (A)(B)(C)(D)	30 (A)(B)(C)(D)	38 (A)(B)(C)(D)
7 (A)(B)(C)(D)	15 (A)(B)(C)(D)	23 (A)(B)(C)(D)	31 (A)(B)(C)(D)	39 (A)(B)(C)(D)
8 (A)(B)(C)(D)	16 (A)(B)(C)(D)	24 (A)(B)(C)(D)	32 (A)(B)(C)(D)	40 (A)(B)(C)(D)

right in section 4

wrong in section 4

SECTION 1
Time—25 Minutes
40 Questions

Each of the following questions consists of one word followed by four words or phrases. You are to select the one word or phrase whose meaning is closest to the word in capital letters.

1. DECLINE:

   (A) decrease
   (B) promote
   (C) delete
   (D) agree

2. DELICATE:

   (A) strong
   (B) fragile
   (C) low
   (D) delicious

3. JUBILEE:

   (A) confidence
   (B) chaos
   (C) design
   (D) festival

4. LIBERATE:

   (A) release
   (B) work
   (C) chase
   (D) hope

5. TRANSFORM:

   (A) open
   (B) submit
   (C) change
   (D) keep

6. COLLIDE:

   (A) forget
   (B) crash
   (C) amplify
   (D) plan

7. PROCLAIM:

   (A) behave
   (B) preclude
   (C) submit
   (D) announce

8. CLAMOR:

   (A) own
   (B) shout
   (C) search
   (D) investigate

9. SYMPATHY:

   (A) understanding
   (B) harmony
   (C) affection
   (D) responsibility

10. INVENTION:

   (A) interpretation
   (B) party
   (C) delegation
   (D) creation

GO ON TO THE NEXT PAGE

11. AUTHORITY:

   (A) expert
   (B) respect
   (C) bravery
   (D) rivalry

12. ILLUSTRATE:

   (A) cover
   (B) draw
   (C) simulate
   (D) waste

13. COMMOTION:

   (A) happiness
   (B) trick
   (C) uproar
   (D) collaboration

14. EXHAUSTED:

   (A) clumsy
   (B) tired
   (C) accountable
   (D) excited

15. TREAD:

   (A) scatter
   (B) help
   (C) alarm
   (D) walk

16. DIGNITY:

   (A) pride
   (B) sorrow
   (C) brilliance
   (D) strength

17. MENTOR:

   (A) symbol
   (B) artist
   (C) collector
   (D) counselor

18. REACTION:

   (A) selection
   (B) response
   (C) care
   (D) achievement

19. ARTIFICIAL:

   (A) uncommon
   (B) similar
   (C) fake
   (D) decorate

20. DWINDLE:

   (A) ridicule
   (B) thwart
   (C) shrink
   (D) tarnish

Directions: Select the word(s) that best fit the meaning of each sentence.

21. Although Mrs. Brown had taught long division to her students numerous times, she decided to take the time to _____ it once more.

   (A) admonish
   (B) request
   (C) explain
   (D) employ

GO ON TO THE NEXT PAGE

22. Keesha's _____ nature would not allow her to ignore others who were feeling sad or lonely.

    (A) terse
    (B) intellectual
    (C) secure
    (D) compassionate

23. The toddler was so _____ that he often hid behind his mother's legs when introduced to strangers.

    (A) hyper
    (B) timid
    (C) young
    (D) disobedient

24. Alex often felt _____ after earning a high score on a test.

    (A) distressed
    (B) proud
    (C) helpless
    (D) intimidated

25. The low, gray clouds made the sky look _____.

    (A) trite
    (B) ominous
    (C) intentional
    (D) luminous

26. Judy noticed that the native vegetation created a _____ over the swamp.

    (A) canopy
    (B) hazard
    (C) reef
    (D) lagoon

27. Ling needed to win one more match in order to be the _____ of the tournament.

    (A) creator
    (B) center
    (C) choice
    (D) champion

28. Phoebe was _____ after she finished running the Boston Marathon.

    (A) conservative
    (B) fortunate
    (C) jubilant
    (D) confused

29. Jeff spilled grape juice on his essay, but it wasn't a big deal since he could just print out a _____ copy.

    (A) duplicate
    (B) creative
    (C) symbolic
    (D) previous

30. A _____ summer day for the young mother and her son included a two-mile walk around the neighborhood.

    (A) naïve
    (B) typical
    (C) confidential
    (D) dire

31. Even though Mischa was guilty, she tried to _____ it.

    (A) tell
    (B) shout
    (C) propose
    (D) deny

GO ON TO THE NEXT PAGE ⟹

32. Highway traffic was _____ due to the accident up ahead.

   (A) tight
   (B) stalled
   (C) reinforced
   (D) fatigued

33. The policeman told Clay he needed to_____ his speed on the road.

   (A) simplify
   (B) join
   (C) reduce
   (D) practice

34. In order to do well in school, the football player had to _____ his time between his practice and his studies.

   (A) balance
   (B) entertain
   (C) connect
   (D) perform

35. Allison left a note on the counter to _____ her father to buy more milk.

   (A) confront
   (B) urge
   (C) taunt
   (D) remind

36. The puppy looked _____ when he realized he was going to be left behind.

   (A) relieved
   (B) dejected
   (C) hungry
   (D) excited

37. The _____ solution to a problem takes both sides into account.

   (A) incredible
   (B) malicious
   (C) ideal
   (D) unexpected

38. The flight attendant instructed all passengers to _____ their seatbelts before takeoff.

   (A) maximize
   (B) fasten
   (C) cement
   (D) expedite

39. His _____effort at making up with Mary, complete with an insincere apology, did nothing to impress her.

   (A) gallant
   (B) half-hearted
   (C) refined
   (D) blunt

40. _____ she had limited access to the supply room, she always found a way to get what she needed.

   (A) Although
   (B) Since
   (C) Because
   (D) When

IF YOU FINISH BEFORE TIME IS CALLED, YOU MAY CHECK YOUR WORK ON THIS SECTION ONLY. DO NOT TURN TO ANY OTHER SECTION IN THE TEST.

SECTION 2

Time—35 Minutes

35 Questions

In this section there are four possible answers after each question. Choose which one is best. You may use the blank space at the right of the page for scratch work.

<u>Note</u>: Figures are drawn with the greatest possible accuracy, UNLESS stated "Not Drawn to Scale."

---

1. If $8 - x = 4$, and $10 + y = 12$, then $x - y =$

    (A) 2

    (B) 3

    (C) 4

    (D) 5

USE THIS SPACE FOR FIGURING.

2. Twenty students brought animals to school for pet day. Eight students brought dogs, four students brought birds, two brought cats, and the rest brought other animals. What fraction of the students brought other animals?

    (A) $\dfrac{3}{10}$

    (B) $\dfrac{6}{14}$

    (C) $\dfrac{10}{12}$

    (D) $\dfrac{3}{20}$

3. $8 \times 2 \times 6 \times 2$ is equal to the product of 16 and

    (A) 4

    (B) 8

    (C) 12

    (D) 16

4. Jennifer and José each swam five laps in 15 minutes. At the same rate of speed, how long would they need in order to swim 35 laps?

    (A) 35 minutes

    (B) 75 minutes

    (C) 105 minutes

    (D) 175 minutes

GO ON TO THE NEXT PAGE

5. A square has a perimeter of 16. What is the length of one side?

   (A) 2
   (B) 4
   (C) 6
   (D) 8

6. Which of the following is the smallest?

   (A) 0.0005
   (B) 0.005
   (C) 0.05
   (D) 0.5

7. Which of the following is equal to two-thirds?

   (A) $\frac{4}{12}$
   (B) $\frac{6}{12}$
   (C) $\frac{10}{15}$
   (D) $\frac{12}{15}$

8. Which fruit is included in the shaded section of Figure 1?

   (A) Apples
   (B) Peaches
   (C) Grapes
   (D) Bananas

9. Which of the following numbers is NOT a prime factor of 90?

   (A) 2
   (B) 3
   (C) 5
   (D) 9

USE THIS SPACE FOR FIGURING.

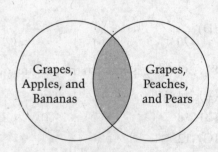

Figure 1

GO ON TO THE NEXT PAGE

10. In a semester of 40 school days, Mrs. Alvarez was out sick twice. What percent of the time was she out sick?

    (A)   3 percent
    (B)   4 percent
    (C)   5 percent
    (D) 10 percent

11. To which number is the arrow pointing in Figure 2?

    (A) $\dfrac{3}{8}$

    (B) $3\dfrac{3}{8}$

    (C) $3\dfrac{2}{4}$

    (D) $3\dfrac{5}{8}$

12. In the Venn diagram in Figure 3, the shaded region shows people who drive

    (A) cars and trucks.
    (B) trucks and motorcycles.
    (C) cars and motorcycles.
    (D) cars, trucks, and motorcycles.

13. The record for the 100-yard dash was 13.71 seconds. Andrew beat the record by a tenth of a second. What was Andrew's time?

    (A) 13.61 seconds
    (B) 13.72 seconds
    (C) 13.82 seconds
    (D) 14.71 seconds

USE THIS SPACE FOR FIGURING

Figure 2

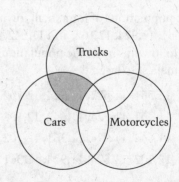

Figure 3

GO ON TO THE NEXT PAGE

14. During a 24-hour day, Shannon's cat sleeps $\frac{5}{6}$ of the time. How many hours does the cat sleep?

   (A) 16 hours
   (B) 18 hours
   (C) 20 hours
   (D) 22 hours

15. Kurt has four boxes. He wants to use the box with the smallest volume. Which box should Kurt use?

   (A) 2" high × 3" wide × 4" long
   (B) 2" high × 4" wide × 5" long
   (C) 3" high × 4" wide × 5" long
   (D) 4" high × 5" wide × 6" long

16. The populations of four small towns are 11,361, 11,924, 12,102, and 11,642. Which of the following shows the populations in order of smallest to largest?

   (A) 11,361, 11,642, 11,924, 12,102
   (B) 11,361, 11,924, 11,642, 12,102
   (C) 11,642, 11,924, 11,361, 12,102
   (D) 12,102, 11,624, 11,924, 11,361

17. Which of these numbers is equal to $\frac{65}{100}$?
   (A) 0.065
   (B) 0.65
   (C) 6.5
   (D) 65

18. Look at this series: 1, 3, 7, 15, 31, 63, ...What number comes next?

   (A) 64
   (B) 126
   (C) 127
   (D) 133

USE THIS SPACE FOR FIGURING.

GO ON TO THE NEXT PAGE

19. Christopher is nine times the age of his twin 4-year-old sons. How old is Christopher?

    (A) 30 years old
    (B) 32 years old
    (C) 34 years old
    (D) 36 years old

USE THIS SPACE FOR FIGURING.

20. Darby was making a fruit smoothie. The ingredients included 15 percent yogurt, 40 percent ice, and 10 percent bananas. The only other thing she put in was frozen strawberries. What fractional part of the smoothie was made up of strawberries?

    (A) $\dfrac{7}{20}$
    (B) $\dfrac{55}{100}$
    (C) $\dfrac{13}{20}$
    (D) $\dfrac{65}{100}$

21. What place does the 5 take in 23.654?

    (A) Tenths
    (B) Hundredths
    (C) Thousandths
    (D) Ten-thousandths

22. Mrs. Campton's classroom is 15 feet long and 22 feet wide. What is the area of her classroom?

    (A) 37 square feet
    (B) 74 square feet
    (C) 300 square feet
    (D) 330 square feet

GO ON TO THE NEXT PAGE

23. The O'Malleys have a rectangular pool that is 16' long and 8' wide. Their next-door neighbors want to build a congruent pool. What measurements will the neighbors' pool have?

   (A) 8' × 8'
   (B) 8' × 16'
   (C) 24' × 2'
   (D) 16' × 16'

24. Casey makes a 30 percent profit for every sale she makes selling cosmetics. If she sells $300 worth of cosmetics, how much money will she make?

   (A) $30
   (B) $90
   (C) $100
   (D) $200

25. Which of the following does NOT equal $\frac{1}{4}$?

   (A) $\frac{2}{8}$
   (B) $\frac{3}{12}$
   (C) $\frac{4}{16}$
   (D) $\frac{8}{20}$

26. Approximately how long is the drive from point A to point B in Figure 4?

   (A) 12 miles
   (B) 14 miles
   (C) 16 miles
   (D) 20 miles

USE THIS SPACE FOR FIGURING.

Figure 4

GO ON TO THE NEXT PAGE

27. Cecile received $10 as an allowance. She spent $1.15 on ice cream and $3.49 on a magazine. How much does Cecile have left?

    (A) $4.64

    (B) $5.36

    (C) $6.51

    (D) $8.85

28. The school bus can hold 50 children. Which two classes can use the school bus for their field trip?

    (A) A class of 14 and a class of 32

    (B) A class of 15 and a class of 36

    (C) A class of 25 and a class of 26

    (D) A class of 30 and a class of 25

29. Rover's dog food costs $19.85 for a 20-pound bag. Trixie's cat food costs $9.24 for a 10-pound bag. Which costs more?

    (A) One bag of dog food

    (B) Two bags of cat food

    (C) The quantities are the same

    (D) The answer cannot be determined from the information given

30. In a grocery cart, there is an equal number of vegetables, fruits, and breads. How many items could be in the cart?

    (A) 14

    (B) 38

    (C) 42

    (D) 56

31. Which transformation has been applied to the shape in Figure 5?

    (A) A reflection

    (B) A slide

    (C) A turn

    (D) A slide followed by a turn

USE THIS SPACE FOR FIGURING.

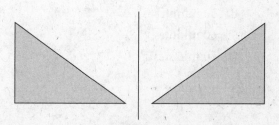

Figure 5

GO ON TO THE NEXT PAGE

32. Libby types 75 words per minute. How many words does she type per second?

   (A) 0.75

   (B) 1.25

   (C) 2

   (D) 7.5

33. In a geography class of 24 students, each student had to select a state on which to give a three-minute report. How long did the presentations last in total?

   (A) 1 hour, 6 minutes

   (B) 1 hour, 12 minutes

   (C) 1 hour, 15 minutes

   (D) 1 hour, 30 minutes

34. If the shaded section of the circle in Figure 6 signifies 850 types of flowers, how many flowers could the unshaded section represent?

   (A) 750

   (B) 800

   (C) 850

   (D) 900

35. Rebecca, Ian, and Clare were driving at the same speed. It took Rebecca 20 minutes to drive 15 miles. How long did it take Ian to drive 30 miles?

   (A) 40 minutes

   (B) 50 minutes

   (C) 60 minutes

   (D) 70 minutes

USE THIS SPACE FOR FIGURING.

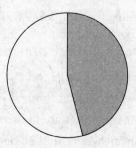

Figure 6

IF YOU FINISH BEFORE TIME IS CALLED, YOU MAY CHECK YOUR WORK ON THIS SECTION ONLY. DO NOT TURN TO ANY OTHER SECTION IN THE TEST.

STOP

SECTION 3

Time—40 Minutes
36 Questions

Read each passage carefully and then answer the questions about it. For each question, decide on the basis of the passage which one of the choices best answers the question.

Whale sharks (*Rhincodon typus*) are not whales and they are not mammals. They are the largest fish in the world. An average whale shark is around
Line 25 feet long, but they can reach up to 40 feet long.
(5) As with most sharks, the females are larger than the males.

You would think that with such a massive body this shark would be a fierce predator, but this mammoth fish is quite mild-mannered. It likes its
(10) solitude. Its mouth, which looks quite threatening, can open up to four-feet wide and has about 310 rows of teeth, or about 3,000 teeth in all. The interesting thing is, this gentle giant doesn't even really use the teeth. Instead, it filters plankton and
(15) krill through its gills for nourishment by simply opening its enormous mouth to take in a large amount of water. The plankton stay in the mouth for nourishment while the water strains through gills in the side of the mouth. Even though a whale
(20) shark has a huge body, its gullet is relatively small. So while a whale shark could actually fit larger food into its mouth, it would not be able to swallow it.

Whale sharks are quite beautiful. Their back and
(25) sides are a reddish or greenish-brown. The top of the body has white or yellowish spots and stripes of varying sizes, and the underside is whitish or yellowish-white. A diver looking for such beauty has nothing to fear: Whale sharks are harmless to
(30) people, and if met by a diver, would probably ignore him completely. They live in the open seas all over the world, preferring to stay in areas close to the equator for the mild temperatures. They reach adulthood at 25 to 30 years of age, and they could
(35) live to be 100 years old.

1. The purpose of this passage is to
   (A) explain why whale sharks are harmless to people.
   (B) explain why whale sharks are fish instead of mammals.
   (C) describe whale sharks.
   (D) explain how divers should deal with whale sharks.

2. Most female sharks are
   (A) larger than the males.
   (B) more beautiful than the males.
   (C) more dangerous than the males.
   (D) smaller than the males.

3. What is a predator?
   (A) A fish
   (B) A hunter
   (C) A mammal
   (D) A gentle giant

4. Which of the following is NOT true about whale sharks?
   (A) They use all 3,000 teeth.
   (B) They have mouths that can open up to four-feet wide.
   (C) They cannot swallow a large amount of food.
   (D) They eat mostly plankton and krill.

GO ON TO THE NEXT PAGE ⟶

5. If a scuba diver came across a whale shark, the whale shark would probably

    (A) swim away.
    (B) open its enormous mouth.
    (C) keep its eye on the diver.
    (D) pay no heed to the diver.

6. Whale sharks live

    (A) in open seas all over the world.
    (B) in colder parts of oceans.
    (C) in the Pacific Ocean only.
    (D) in extreme temperatures.

        There is nothing I like so well on a summer day
    as to hear the ding-ding song of the ice cream truck
Line as it's coming around the corner. That tune of "Do
 (5) Your Ears Hang Low" makes my heart jump. I race
    out the door to catch the truck before I miss it, but
    not before grabbing some change from the kitchen
    counter that my parents have left. It's something to
    do—something to cool me off—and it's the
(10) highlight of a typical lazy day.
        Once I catch the truck, I've got all the time in
    the world to hem and haw about what to get. I like
    to read through the entire side-of-the-truck menu,
    chatting with the girl behind the counter. I usually
(15) like an orange push-up, though occasionally I'll get
    an ice cream sandwich. I have to eat it slowly
    enough to enjoy it, but fast enough so that it
    doesn't drip down my arm. Finding this balance is
    tricky, and sometimes depends on whether the sky
(20) is cloudy or clear.
        Lots of my neighbors race out of their houses
    the way I do, hoping to get there in time. I'm
    usually first since my house is the closest to the
    corner, and if I can catch the truck, then they are
(25) usually all safe. Often, though, if I miss it, they
    miss it too. If that's the case, imagine how
    disappointed I am. If there's no change to grab from
    the counter or if the truck is going too fast, I get
    outside just in time to see its taillights turn off my

(30) street. On those days, I'm not allowed to go down
    that far to catch it. But when I do make it in time,
    that ice cream song stays with me for the rest of
    the day.

7. The purpose of the passage is to

    (A) challenge the reader to run to the ice cream truck.
    (B) prove that ice cream is the best treat on a summer day.
    (C) describe a summer treat.
    (D) teach the reader a new song.

8. What does it mean to "hem and haw"?

    (A) To take one's time in choosing.
    (B) To buy more than one thing.
    (C) To halt.
    (D) To choose quickly.

9. This passage is written in the

    (A) first person.
    (B) second person.
    (C) third person.
    (D) fourth person.

10. All of the following are true EXCEPT

    (A) the ice cream truck makes this person feel happy.
    (B) this person is not allowed to leave the street where she lives.
    (C) this person always gets an orange push-up.
    (D) other people in the neighborhood enjoy the ice cream truck too.

GO ON TO THE NEXT PAGE

11. The main character is probably a

   (A) baby.

   (B) toddler.

   (C) parent.

   (D) child.

12. This passage could be best described as

   (A) a memory.

   (B) a narrative.

   (C) a reflection.

   (D) an exposition.

In May, Bailey moved into a new house. His
large, fenced-in yard had potential, but the grass
needed to be weeded and some flowers needed to be
Line planted. Bailey invited some friends to his house to
(5) help. He provided good music, plenty of snacks,
and cold drinks. Everyone was amazed how much
they were able to accomplish in that one day!
   Bailey and Nolan started by weeding the front
yard. Then they planted ferns and marigolds
(10) underneath the olive tree. They planted a bleeding
heart vine and some red impatiens along the front
of the fence. Bailey left plenty of room between the
impatiens for the roses he would plant in the fall.
   Janet focused on the side of the back porch. She
(15) filled some holes with dirt, and then she hoed the
ground to make it level. She alternated planting
gardenias and black-eyed Susans. She knew that
gardenia blooms would smell lovely, and the bright
yellow flowers would be pleasing to the eye.
(20) Together these plants made an attractive garden bed.
   Meanwhile, Christina and Akiko worked along
the back of the porch. They laid 10 large stepping
stones in even spaces, and in between each stone,
planted red, orange, yellow, and pink purslane
(25) ground cover. They knew that the plants would
grow all around the stones to create a charming
walkway.
   Lilia and Nathan cleared weeds along the
whole right-side fence. This was back-breaking

(30) work, but the weeds had to go! Then they planted
red bougainvillea and blue plumbago bushes.
There was still space to plant some smaller
annuals, but Bailey would have to do that
another day.
(35)   After hours of work in the hot sun, the friends
were exhausted. They spent the rest of the
afternoon resting, talking, and laughing on the
porch, surrounded by the results of their hard
work. Thanks to the help of so many friends,
(40) Bailey's new house looks loved.

13. In paragraph one, what does it mean that the
   yard had potential?

   (A) There was the possibility that the yard
       would look good.

   (B) The yard was full of weeds and needed
       work.

   (C) The yard had no flowers.

   (D) Someone had been taking care of the yard.

14. Bailey wants his yard to look

   (A) unusual.

   (B) busy.

   (C) charming.

   (D) exhausting.

15. Bailey and Nolan

   (A) weeded the back yard.

   (B) planted an olive tree.

   (C) planted roses.

   (D) planted ferns and marigolds.

16. What did Janet do first?

   (A) She planted gardenias.

   (B) She planted black-eyed Susans.

   (C) She smoothed the ground.

   (D) She filled in some holes.

GO ON TO THE NEXT PAGE

17. Lilia and Nathan did all of the following EXCEPT

    (A) plant some small annuals.

    (B) plant bougainvillea.

    (C) plant plumbago bushes.

    (D) pull out weeds.

18. In the afternoon, the friends

    (A) admired their work.

    (B) continued working in the yard.

    (C) enjoyed going indoors.

    (D) sat quietly on the porch.

"Come on, come on," you think. "I can see the top!" You're almost there. The top. The summit. Your goal. The sun is beating down on your back
Line and you are there, in the moment, looking upward.
(5) Whatever you do, you cannot look down. Leg muscles shaking, fingertips clutching their hold, you think, "I can do this!"

This is rock climbing at its best. There's the challenge to face, the fear to overcome, the
(10) muscles to test, and finally, the exhilaration to feel. But would you rather ride horses? Hike? Do gymnastics? Do you stick your toe in the water first before jumping in? Or do you dive headfirst? Cautious, careful, or crazy, one week at an
(15) adventure camp could change your whole attitude about yourself and level of confidence.

Maybe you're thinking that "real kids" don't get to do these things. You're wrong. You don't even have to be an athlete. Today there are thousands of
(20) adventure camps across the country. So what are you waiting for? Sign up and go! What you do with your experience will be up to you.

19. What is the purpose of this passage?

    (A) To teach you about backpacking

    (B) To challenge you to change your lifestyle

    (C) To excite you about going to adventure camp

    (D) To encourage you have a better attitude

20. What is "exhilaration" (paragraph 2)?

    (A) Fear

    (B) Heat

    (C) Understanding

    (D) Excitement

21. Which of the following statements is NOT listed as a part of rock climbing?

    (A) The challenge of reaching the summit

    (B) Overcoming your fear

    (C) Testing your muscles

    (D) Spending time with friends

22. Why would someone choose to go to an adventure camp?

    (A) To challenge himself

    (B) To climb a mountain

    (C) To do gymnastics

    (D) To go hiking

23. What kind of person sticks his toe in the water before going in?

    (A) A risk-taker

    (B) An adventurous person

    (C) A cautious person

    (D) A mountain climber

24. In order to go to adventure camp, you must

    (A) be an athlete.

    (B) travel across the United States.

    (C) have a good attitude.

    (D) sign up.

GO ON TO THE NEXT PAGE ⇨

Here's what to do for the dogs while we're out of town:

Fido likes to go out first thing in the morning
Line and then before bed. There's no need to go out with
(5) her, just open the door and she'll go right into the
yard. If she needs to go in the middle of the day,
she'll stare at you intently and grunt. Both dogs
like a little walk in the morning and again at
around 4:30. After the morning walk, you can give
(10) them some bread as a treat.

Samson has to take arthritis pills: two in the
morning and one in the evening. Use peanut butter
or bread to hide the pills so that he'll eat them.
Fido gets two vitamins in the morning, which she
(15) loves, so you don't have to camouflage her pills.

I'm leaving peanut butter treats, chew sticks,
bacon, and sausages in the fridge. Use anything
you want! If you need more food, that's in the
garage. We leave the food bowl filled up all day so
(20) the dogs can eat whenever they are hungry. Please
make sure they always have cold water in their
bowls.

Thanks for all of your help! See you on
Saturday!
(25) Oh, one last thing: If you decide to take the
dogs to your house, don't forget to take the dog bed,
along with a blanket, so you can cover up Samson
if it starts to thunder.

25. What is the purpose of this passage?

    (A) To give directions for feeding two dogs
    (B) To give directions for taking care of two
        dogs
    (C) To give directions for walking two dogs
    (D) To give directions for giving medicine to
        two dogs

26. When do the dogs eat?

    (A) Whenever they are hungry
    (B) After their morning walk
    (C) In the afternoon
    (D) After their afternoon walk

27. Why do Samson's pills have to be hidden in
peanut butter or bread?

    (A) He will spit them out otherwise.
    (B) He might otherwise try to eat Fido's
        vitamins.
    (C) He likes peanut butter or bread as a
        breakfast treat.
    (D) He is spoiled.

28. How does Fido let you know if she needs to
go out?

    (A) She barks.
    (B) She only needs to go out during her
        regular walks.
    (C) She paces around the room.
    (D) She stares and grunts.

29. After their morning walk, the dogs get
what treat?

    (A) Sausages
    (B) A piece of bread
    (C) Dog food
    (D) A peanut butter treat

30. It can be inferred from the final sentence of the
passage that

    (A) Fido needs a blanket to keep warm.
    (B) the sound of thunder frightens Samson.
    (C) the sound of rain helps to calm the dogs.
    (D) Fido needs a blanket to fall asleep.

GO ON TO THE NEXT PAGE

Two years ago, Mrs. Pavlovic and her husband moved to the United States from Serbia with their two children. Today, their daughter, Andrijana, is
Line in the second grade.
(5)   The Pavlovic children speak English in public, but not at home. They are much more comfortable speaking Serbo-Croat at home. After two years here, Mrs. Pavlovic is still having a hard time learning English, and she depends on her children
(10) to translate. She was a teacher in Serbia, but in this country she is too shy even to volunteer in her daughter's classroom.

Unlike her mother, Andrijana speaks nearly perfect English. Learning English came easily for
(15) her since she is quite young. Her older brother's command of the language is pretty good, too, but not as good as Andrijana's. As for Mrs. Pavlovic, since she isn't yet comfortable with the language herself, it is hard for her to gauge how much
(20) English Andrijana really knows.

School was very different in Serbia. The teachers were much stricter, and punishments were harsh. Mrs. Pavlovic has told her daughter that if she does not try her best in school or
(25) misbehaves, they will move back to Serbia. Her concern is that American schools are too relaxed, and that her children may not learn anything here. In many ways, life is much better for the Pavlovic family in America, but in other ways it is harder.

31. The main idea of this passage is to

(A) explain how schools are different in Serbia and America.

(B) describe one family's move from Serbia to America.

(C) describe a mother's difficulty in learning English.

(D) relay the experience of a Serbian family in America.

32. Why is Andrijana's English better than her brother's?

(A) Her brother has not tried as hard to learn English.

(B) Andrijana's second-grade class helped her learn.

(C) Andrijana is younger than he, so learning English was probably easier for her.

(D) Her mother helped her more than she helped her brother.

33. In paragraph three, what does the word "gauge" most probably mean?

(A) Estimate

(B) Gather

(C) Reject

(D) Protect

34. Why won't Mrs. Pavlovic volunteer in her daughter's classroom?

(A) She is shy in front of children.

(B) She thinks the classroom is too relaxed.

(C) She doesn't have any skills.

(D) Her broken English makes her shy.

GO ON TO THE NEXT PAGE

35. According to Mrs. Pavlovic, what is the difference between American and Serbian schools?

    (A) Her daughter misbehaves more in American schools.
    (B) Serbian schools are stricter.
    (C) American schools are more academic.
    (D) Serbian schools are more lenient.

36. From the tone of the passage, why is life hard in America for the Pavlovic family?

    (A) The change in culture and language makes it difficult.
    (B) Andrijana has learned more English than the other family members.
    (C) Mrs. Pavlovic has become too shy in America.
    (D) The children have to translate for their parents in America.

IF YOU FINISH BEFORE TIME IS CALLED, YOU MAY CHECK YOUR WORK ON THIS SECTION ONLY. DO NOT TURN TO ANY OTHER SECTION IN THE TEST. STOP

SECTION 4

Time—40 Minutes

35 Questions

In this section there are four possible answers after each question. Choose which one is best.

Note: Figures are drawn with the greatest possible accuracy, UNLESS stated "Not Drawn to Scale."

1. Which is fifty-three thousand, nine hundred fourteen?

   (A) 53,914

   (B) 503,914

   (C) 530,914

   (D) 539,014

USE THIS SPACE FOR FIGURING.

2. Which is the largest fraction?

   (A) $\dfrac{6}{18}$

   (B) $\dfrac{1}{2}$

   (C) $\dfrac{5}{6}$

   (D) $\dfrac{9}{10}$

3. $\dfrac{1}{5} + \dfrac{2}{3} =$

   (A) $\dfrac{3}{15}$

   (B) $\dfrac{2}{8}$

   (C) $\dfrac{3}{8}$

   (D) $\dfrac{13}{15}$

4. $400 + 950 =$

   (A) 990

   (B) 1,350

   (C) 4,950

   (D) 9,450

GO ON TO THE NEXT PAGE

5. What is the product of 11 and 3?

    (A)   0.273

    (B)   3.66

    (C) 14

    (D) 33

USE THIS SPACE FOR FIGURING.

6. What is 5,772 divided by 6?

    (A)   662

    (B)   912

    (C)   962

    (D) 1,012

7. ___ $+ 8 - 19 = 50$

    (A) 11

    (B) 31

    (C) 39

    (D) 61

8. $15 \times 300 =$

    (A)   45

    (B)   450

    (C)   4,500

    (D) 45,000

9. $53.09 - 9.34 =$

    (A) 40.31

    (B) 42.25

    (C) 43.25

    (D) 43.75

10. $\frac{?}{15} = \frac{2}{3}$

    (A) 2

    (B) 4

    (C) 5

    (D) 10

GO ON TO THE NEXT PAGE

11. Marla twirls her hair once every six seconds. How many times does she twirl her hair in a minute?

    (A) 6
    (B) 8
    (C) 10
    (D) 12

12. $\underline{} + 16 - 5 = 40$

    What is the missing number?

    (A) 24
    (B) 29
    (C) 31
    (D) 33

13. A puppy weighed four pounds when he was six weeks old. Now that he is six months old, he has gained 80 percent more weight. How much does the puppy weigh now?

    (A) 7 pounds
    (B) 7.2 pounds
    (C) 12.8 pounds
    (D) 32 pounds

14. If $x = 5$, which of these statements is true?

    (A) $x + 8 = 11 + 3$
    (B) $x + 9 = 6 + 8$
    (C) $x + 10 = 15 - 5$
    (D) $x + 11 = 14 + 5$

15. What is the missing number in the pattern in Figure 1

    (A) 16
    (B) 17
    (C) 18
    (D) 19

USE THIS SPACE FOR FIGURING.

2	9
3	12
4	15
5	?

Figure 1

GO ON TO THE NEXT PAGE

16. If $n = 9$, which of these number sentences is true?

 (A) $2n - 6 = 14$
 (B) $3(n - 3) = 18$
 (C) $4(n + 5) = 18$
 (D) $5n + 8 = 22$

USE THIS SPACE FOR FIGURING.

17. What is the sum of 25 and 30?

 (A)   5
 (B)   55
 (C)   75
 (D) 750

18. Devon bought $8.96 worth of gas. He paid with a 20-dollar bill. How much change did he receive?

 (A) $11.04
 (B) $11.96
 (C) $12.14
 (D) $12.96

19. $500 - 409 = $ ___

 (A)   91
 (B) 109
 (C) 101
 (D) 191

20. What is the product of 5 and 20?

 (A)   4
 (B)   25
 (C)   75
 (D) 100

GO ON TO THE NEXT PAGE

21. If $8 + a = 15$ and $6 + b = 14$, then what is $a + b$?

    (A) 12
    (B) 13
    (C) 14
    (D) 15

USE THIS SPACE FOR FIGURING.

22. If $a = b$ and $b = c$, then

    (A) $a + b = c$
    (B) $a = c$
    (C) $bc = a$
    (D) $c + b = a$

23. The diameter of the circle in Figure 2 is 8 cm. What is the radius? NOTE: The radius is the length halfway across the circle.

    (A) 4 cm
    (B) 8 cm
    (C) 10 cm
    (D) 16 cm

Figure 2

24. What is the perimeter of the rectangle in Figure 3?

    (A) 18 in.
    (B) 30 in.
    (C) 36 in.
    (D) 72 in.

12 in.

6 in.

Figure 3

25. When folded on the lines, what will the shape in Figure 4 become?

    (A) Cylinder
    (B) Cube
    (C) Square pyramid
    (D) Sphere

Figure 4

GO ON TO THE NEXT PAGE

26. What is the volume of the box in Figure 5?

    (A) 12 cubic feet
    (B) 24 cubic feet
    (C) 48 cubic feet
    (D) 60 cubic feet

27. $5.123 + 2.627 =$

    (A) 7.65
    (B) 7.743
    (C) 7.749
    (D) 7.75

28. $10,000 - 45n =$

    (A) $955n$
    (B) $9,955n$
    (C) $99,955n$
    (D) The answer cannot be determined from
        the information given.

29. In a survey done of 45 students, twice as many
    students preferred dogs to cats. If all students
    preferred either a dog or a cat, how many
    people preferred dogs?

    (A) 15
    (B) 20
    (C) 25
    (D) 30

30. Which of the following is closest to 100.11?

    (A)   99.11
    (B) 101
    (C) 100.1
    (D) 100

USE THIS SPACE FOR FIGURING.

Figure 5

GO ON TO THE NEXT PAGE

USE THIS SPACE FOR FIGURING.

31. $\dfrac{1}{4} + \dfrac{5}{8} =$

    (A) $\dfrac{1}{2}$

    (B) $\dfrac{3}{4}$

    (C) $\dfrac{5}{6}$

    (D) $\dfrac{7}{8}$

32. What is the difference between 895 and 679?

    (A) 154

    (B) 200

    (C) 216

    (D) 1,574

33. In a jar, there are equal numbers of red, green, and yellow marbles. Which of the following could be the number of marbles in the jar?

    (A) 35

    (B) 47

    (C) 58

    (D) 72

34. What is the quotient of 66 and 22?

    (A) 3

    (B) 22

    (C) 33

    (D) 66

35. Which of these is a whole number greater than 15?

    (A) 14

    (B) 15.5

    (C) $16\dfrac{1}{2}$

    (D) 18

IF YOU FINISH BEFORE TIME IS CALLED, YOU MAY CHECK YOUR WORK ON THIS SECTION ONLY. DO NOT TURN TO ANY OTHER SECTION IN THE TEST.   STOP

SECTION 5
Time—30 Minutes

Write an essay on the following prompt on the paper provided. Your essay should not exceed two pages and must be written in ink. You must use a black or blue pen. Erasing is not allowed.

Prompt: Write about a time when you made a mistake.

_____

_____

_____

_____

_____

_____

_____

_____

_____

_____

_____

_____

_____

_____

_____

_____

_____

GO ON TO THE NEXT PAGE

ANSWER EXPLANATIONS

SECTION 1: VERBAL

SYNONYMS

1. A

To decline is to deteriorate or decrease.

2. B

Something delicate is also fragile, as in a delicate glass vase. Do not be misled by (D), just because the beginning letters are similar to that of the original word.

3. D

A jubilee is a celebration, such as an anniversary or festival.

4. A

To liberate is to set free or release from captivity.

5. C

When you transform your life, you change it.

6. B

When two items collide, they crash into each other.

7. D

To proclaim something means to announce it.

8. B

When you clamor for attention, you might shout so that you are noticed.

9. A

To show sympathy for another is to express sorrow and understanding of his feelings.

10. D

An invention is a new idea or creation.

11. A

An authority is an expert.

12. B

To illustrate is to draw.

13. C

To cause a commotion is to create a fuss or uproar. A collaboration is something that has involved the participation of several people.

14. B

When you feel exhausted, you are extremely tired.

15. D

Tread is another word for walk.

16. A

Dignity is a word describing the pride you feel in yourself.

17. D

A mentor is a tutor or coach. (D), counselor, is the closest in meaning.

18. B

A reaction is a response.

19. C

Something artificial, such as an artificial flower, is fake or unnatural.

20. C

To dwindle means to shrink or become steadily less, such as a dwindling bank account.

ANALOGIES

21. C

The sentence implies that the students need long division to be explained again. "Although" is a key word here: It suggests that you will need to repeat an idea again in the second clause. The verb "had taught" is closely related to explain. Numerous means many, so she had taught them many times before. Admonish means to caution, which does not make sense. Request means to ask for and employ means to use.

22. D

The blank requires you to fill in a word with the same meaning as not ignoring others who are feeling sad or lonely. A compassionate person is concerned for others. A terse person is dismissive or brief, an intellectual person thinks academically, and an insecure person lacks confidence, which has nothing to do with being concerned for others.

23. B

Hiding behind your mother's legs would suggest you are timid or shy. A toddler would probably be young as well, but being young does not explain why he would hide when meeting strangers. He might also be disobedient, but that, too, does not explain why he would hide.

24. B

Earning a high score is something one would be proud of. Feeling distressed (upset) would be the opposite of how you would feel under these circumstances. Neither would you feel helpless (defenseless). Intimidated means nervous or anxious so that answer choice is wrong as well.

25. B

Low, gray clouds are a sign of something—probably something bad or negative. Ominous means threatening and it is the correct answer. Trite means commonplace and unoriginal. Intentional means on purpose.

26. A

A canopy is a covering. From the other words in the sentence, we know we need something "created" by the vegetation. No other choice fits.

27. D

Ling is winning "in order to be" something. The only answer choice that makes sense is (D). A champion is a winner in a competition.

28. C

We know that Phoebe finished running the marathon, so she must be very happy. Jubilant means filled with joy, and it is the right answer. She might feel also fortunate (lucky), but between the two answer choices (B) and (C), jubilant is the better choice: We do not know for certain that she would feel lucky, but we can be fairly certain that she would feel happy.

29. A

Jeff needs to print out a new copy of his essay. (A), duplicate (double or identical) copy is what he would need to print. Don't be misled by (D), a previous copy: Previous means earlier or prior, and it is not quite right here. You wouldn't print out an earlier copy, you would print out an identical copy.

30. B

It seems as though a walk around the neighborhood is something the mother and son do on a daily basis—in other words, a typical day or a regular day. Naïve means inexperienced or innocent, confidential means private, and dire means terrible.

31. D

"Even though" tells us there must be a contrast here. We are told that Mischa is guilty, so the contrast is probably something that has to do with denying the truth—declaring it untrue.

32. B

An accident on the highway would stall traffic, or make it come to a standstill. That's another way of saying stalled traffic, (B). You might suspect (A) is correct, but it is not appropriate to say tight traffic. Fatigued means tired, and traffic cannot be tired.

33. C

A policeman would want Clay to lower, or reduce, his speed.

34. A

The football player would have to balance, or divide fairly, his time between practice and studying if he wants to do well in school. Entertain makes no sense here, nor does connect or perform.

35. D

The note is intended to remind her father. Don't be tricked by (B): It seems like it might be acceptable to say that she urged her father to get more milk, but then when you see (D) as an option, you see *remind* is the best possible answer choice.

36. B

Since the puppy was going to be left behind, we probably need a word that means unhappy. Dejected means unhappy. The puppy would not be relieved or excited if he were left behind, so (A) and (D) are clearly wrong.

37. C

The ideal solution would be the best solution. It means the perfect solution.

38. B

Because the flight is going to take off, the passengers must fasten, or close, their seatbelts. They would not need to maximize, cement, or speed up (expedite) their seat belts.

39. B

The word we are looking for has something to do with an insincere apology. Half-hearted means without interest or enthusiasm, and it is the only answer choice that makes sense.

40. A

We know that the two clauses here must be connected. The second clause tells us that this person could always get what she needed/ But then we see the phrase "limited access" in the first clause. That means the *opposite* of getting everything you need. Since we have a contrast here, "although" is the only word that makes sense. (B), since, suggests a "because" or "then" relationship (*since* this, *then* that). So (C) is out, too. This is a tricky question since all four answer choices seem to work at first glance.

SECTION 2: MATH

1. A

$8 - x = 4$, so $x = 4$. $10 + y = 12$, so $y = 2$. That means $x - y$ is the same as $4 - 2$.

2. A

First, figure out how many students brought other pets. Fourteen students brought dogs, birds, and cats, so that means six students brought other pets. The fraction is $\dfrac{6}{20}$, which reduces to $\dfrac{3}{10}$. You might have incorrectly chosen (B) since it has the number six in it.

3. C

$8 \times 2 = 16$ and $6 \times 2 = 12$. So $8 \times 2 \times 6 \times 2$ equals 16 times 12, (C).

4. C

Five laps in 15 minutes means three minutes per lap. If Jennifer and José want to swim 35 laps at three minutes each, that would take 105 minutes.

5. B

A square has four equal sides. Sixteen divided by four is 4. If you divided by two, you might have gotten an incorrect answer of 8, (D).

6. A

So, 0.0005 is equivalent to 5/10,000, which is the smallest number given. The farther away a digit is to the right of the decimal point, the smaller the place that digit is in.

7. C

Two-thirds is equal to $\dfrac{10}{15}$ because $2 \times 5 = 10$ and $3 \times 5 = 15$.

8. C

Grapes are the only fruit included in both circles.

9. D

A prime number is a number greater than one that can be divided evenly only by itself and by one. Nine is not a prime number because it can be divided by three. You might have suspected (D) was wrong because 90 is divisible by 9, but 9 is not prime.

10. C

Divide two by 40 to get 0.05, which is the same as five percent. You might have guessed four percent since the original number was 40, but that would be incorrect.

11. B

The interval from 3 to 4 is divided into 8 equal segments, so each segment has a length of $\dfrac{3}{8}$. Since there are 3 segments to where the arrow is pointing, the arrow is pointing to $3\dfrac{1}{8}$.

12. A

The shaded region shows people who drive cars and trucks. You might have guessed (D), since cars, trucks, and motorcycles are all included in the diagram, but the question asks you to look at the shaded region.

13. A

Since this is a race time, for Andrew to beat the record means his time is 0.1 second less than the record. Line up the decimal points to solve:

$$\begin{array}{r} 13.71 \\ -\ 0.1 \\ \hline 13.61 \end{array}$$

14. C

$\frac{5}{6}$ of 24 is $\frac{5}{6} \times 24 = 20$ hours.

15. A

Volume is length × width × height. The box with the smallest volume is the one in (A), $2 \times 3 \times 4 = 24$ cubic inches.

16. A

(A) shows the numbers from smallest to largest.

17. B

So $0.65 = \frac{65}{100}$ (sixty-five hundredths). (D), 65, is tempting, but you must remember to change your fraction to a decimal.

18. C

The pattern is doubling the difference of adjacent terms: +2, +4, +8, +16, +32, +64, and so on. 63 + 64 = 127.

19. D

To find Christopher's age, multiply the twins' age (4) by 9.

20. A

15 + 40 + 10 = 65 percent. Subtract that number from 100 percent and you get 35 percent. $\frac{35}{100}$ reduces to $\frac{7}{20}$. If you forgot to subtract from 100, you might have gotten wrong answer (C).

21. B

The 5 is in the hundredths place. From the decimal, moving right, the places are as follows: tenths, hundredths, thousandths.

22. D

Area equals length × width. If you had added instead of multiplied, except for the unit square feet, you would have gotten an incorrect answer of (A).

23. B

A congruent pool is a pool that will have the same measurements. A congruent figure is the same shape and size as the original figure.

24. B

The decimal equivalent of 30% is 0.3. So 0.3 × 300 = $90

25. D

$\frac{8}{20}$ reduces to $\frac{2}{5}$, not $\frac{1}{4}$. You can use the process of elimination to solve this question.

26. C

Let's approximate. Four miles plus four miles plus eight miles. The drive is about 16 miles.

27. B

Cecile spent a total of $1.15 + $3.49 = $4.64. From $10.00, that means $5.36 is left. Make sure to line up the decimal points.

28. A

The number of students cannot exceed 50. (A) is the only combination of classes that is less than or equal to 50.

29. A

One bag of dog food costs $19.85; 2 bags of cat food would cost $18.48.

30. C

The number of items in the cart must be a multiple of 3. Forty-two is divisible by 3 without a remainder, so 42 is a multiple of 3.

31. A

The shape has been reflected (flipped).

32. B

Divide 75 by 60 to find the answer. (A) and (D) are tricky because you might think you should be dividing by 10 or 100, but they are incorrect.

33. B

Multiply 24 times three to get 72 minutes. Since there are 60 minutes in an hour, that's the same as 1 hour, 12 minutes.

34. D

More of the circle is unshaded, so the number has to be higher than 850.

35. A

Fifteen miles divided by 20 minutes = 0.75 miles per minute. Thirty miles divided by 0.75 miles per minute = 40 minutes. You could also have realized that if Rebecca and Ian are driving at the same speed, it will take Ian twice as long to drive twice as far. 2 × 20 = 40 minutes. If you had added Rebecca's 20 minutes to her 30 miles, you would have gotten the number in incorrect answer (B).

SECTION 3: READING COMPREHENSION

WHALE SHARKS PASSAGE

1. C

This is a descriptive passage. The other three answer choices are details included in the passage, but none gives the purpose or main idea of the passage.

2. A

The passage states that most female sharks are larger than the males. As for (B), the passage does state how beautiful whale sharks are, though it doesn't say anything about their being more beautiful than the males.

3. B

A predator is a hunter—one that preys or destroys. The meaning is implied from the text, "You would think that with such a massive body this shark would be a fierce predator, but this mammoth fish is quite docile. It likes its solitude." The other three answer choices are words used in the passage, but none of them mean the same thing as predator.

4. A

The whale shark's teeth are largely useless. Since you are asked which answer choice is not true, you can go back to the passage to find the three that are true. Then, use the process of elimination.

5. D

To pay no heed means to pay no attention to something, to ignore. You can reread the last paragraph of the passage to find out that whale sharks will probably ignore divers.

6. A

The last paragraph of the passage states that whale sharks live in open seas all over the world.

Ice Cream Truck Passage

7. C

The function of the passage is to describe a summer treat. It does not challenge, prove, or teach anything.

8. A

To "hem and haw" means to take one's time in choosing. Read the context of the words surrounding this phrase, and you will see that it suggests taking one's time.

9. A

When a passage uses the author's own voice, and when it uses pronouns *I* and *me*, it is written in first person. That means the story is told from the author's perspective.

10. C

You must find the answer choice that is not true here. (C) is not true: Though the author usually gets an orange push-up, that's not always the case. The other three answer choices are indeed stated in the passage.

11. D

Since the writer needs permission to grab change and run to catch the truck but is not allowed off of the street, she is probably a child. A baby or toddler would not be able to run out to the ice cream truck, and a parent would not need permission to go to the ice cream truck.

12. C

The passage is one person's reflection of what makes up an enjoyable summer day. You might have thought (A) was correct: This passage seems to be someone's memory, but it isn't about one specific event. A narrative is a story and an exposition explains.

Yard Work Passage

13. A

"The yard had potential," means the yard could look good if some work was done to it. You may have chosen (B) because the yard was indeed full of weeds and it did need work, but as that's not what the question asked, it is wrong.

14. C

Bailey wanted the yard to look charming. He and his friends were busy all day, but that is not how the yard looked.

15. D

Bailey and Nolan planted ferns and marigolds under an olive tree that was already there. You might have chosen the incorrect answer of (A). Bailey and Nolan did some weeding, but they weeded in the front yard, not the back.

16. D

Janet had to fill in the holes before she could do the rest of her work.

17. A

Lilia and Nathan left room to plant annuals at a later time, but they did not actually do it that day.

18. A

The friends were on the porch "surrounded by their work," which implies that they were also admiring their work. You may have chosen (D) because the friends were sitting on the porch, but they were talking and laughing rather than sitting quietly.

ADVENTURE CAMPS PASSAGE

19. C

The purpose of the passage is to excite you about going to adventure camp. It does not challenge you to change your life, only to try something new.

20. D

The meaning of exhilaration is implied in the sentence. It means excitement or stimulation.

21. D

Use the process of elimination to see that being with friends is not mentioned.

22. A

One might do yoga or climb a mountain or go backpacking while there, but no matter what activity you choose, adventure camp would challenge a kid.

23. C

A cautious person would test the water before jumping into it.

24. D

There is no special skill needed to go to adventure camp. You just need to sign up to go. You might think that traveling across the United States would be required, but since there are camps all over the country, you could visit one in your area.

DOG CARE PASSAGE

25. B

The passage is intended to give directions for taking care of Samson and Fido. Feeding, walking, and giving medicine are mentioned, but those answers are all details that are part of the overall care. The main idea of the passage is reflected in (B).

26. A

Since the dog food bowl is left full all day, the dogs can eat whenever they are hungry.

27. A

Since the pills have to be hidden in bread or peanut butter, Samson must not like the taste of them. He would probably spit them out if given them plain. Chances are, he likes the taste of peanut butter or bread. He may also be spoiled, but that doesn't explain why he needs his pills hidden in something sweet.

28. D

Fido stares and grunts when she needs to go out. The other three choices are not mentioned in the text.

29. B

The dogs get a piece of bread as a breakfast treat. Though the text does mention the other choices, you are asked to identify the treat the dogs get after their morning walk.

30. B

Samson needs to be covered up with a blanket if it starts to thunder, so the sound of thunder must scare him.

SERBIANS IN AMERICA PASSAGE

31. D

The passage describes the Pavlovic family since they moved from Serbia to America. The other three choices are true and incorporated into the passage, but (D) best sums up the main idea.

32. C

As explained in paragraph three, "Learning English came easily for Andrijana since she was quite young." Being younger, she would have an advantage over her family in learning English. We have no evidence at all from the text that the other answer choices are true.

33. A

To gauge means to estimate, to judge. From the context (meaning) of the sentence, since Mrs. Pavlovic does not yet understand English, there is no way for her to determine how much English her daughter truly speaks.

34. D

Mrs. Pavlovic used to be a teacher, so it isn't the classroom that makes her shy. It must be her broken English. And while she does think American schools are too relaxed, that does not explain her reluctance to volunteer.

35. B

In Mrs. Pavlovic's opinion, Serbian schools are strict, while American schools are too relaxed.

36. A

Language barriers and cultural differences make it hard for the family to adjust. The schools are different, but that is not the reason life is hard.

SECTION 4: MATH

1. A

To solve, read each answer choice individually:

(A) fifty-three thousand, nine hundred fourteen—YES

(B) five hundred three thousand, nine hundred fourteen—NO

(C) five hundred thirty thousand, nine hundred fourteen—NO

(D) five hundred thirty-nine thousand, fourteen—NO

2. D

$\frac{6}{18}$ is less than $\frac{1}{2}$ because the numerator 6 of $\frac{6}{18}$ is less than half of the denominator 18. $\frac{1}{2}$ is less than each of $\frac{5}{6}$ and $\frac{9}{10}$ because the numerator of each of those two fractions is greater than half of the denominator. So we must compare $\frac{5}{6}$ with $\frac{9}{10}$ to find the greatest fraction. The easiest way to compare these fractions is to convert them to decimals. $\frac{5}{6} = 0.8\bar{3}$ and $\frac{9}{10} = 0.9$. So $\frac{9}{10}$ is the largest fraction.

3. D

$\frac{1}{5} + \frac{2}{3} = \frac{3}{15} + \frac{10}{15} = \frac{13}{15}$ You might have chosen (C) if you had simply added the numerators and denominators together, but that is not the correct way to solve.

4. B

$400 + 950 = 1,350$

5. D

The product is the answer when you multiply: $11 \times 3 = 33$. If you didn't know that product means to multiply, you might have added and gotten (C), which was 14.

6. C

5,772 ÷ 6 = 962

7. D

To solve, turn the question around: 50 + 19 − 8 = __. If you forgot to change your signs, you would get 39, which is (C). You have to change + to − when you move the numbers across the equals sign. The answer is 61.

8. C

15 × 300 = 4,500. A good rule of thumb is that there are the same number of zeros at the end of a number in the question as in the answer.

9. D

Line up the decimal points before you subtract. You have to borrow in order to find the answer.

$$
\begin{array}{r}
12 \\
4\,\cancel{2}. \\
\cancel{5}\,\cancel{3}.\cancel{0}\,9 \\
9.3\,4 \\
\hline
4\,3.7\,5
\end{array}
$$

10. D

Convert $\frac{2}{3}$ to a fraction with a denominator of 15. Since $3 \times 5 = 15$, then $\frac{2}{3} = \frac{2 \times 5}{3 \times 15} = \frac{10}{15}$ So ? is 10.

11. C

There are 60 seconds in a minute. Sixty divided by 6 = 10. She twirls her hair 10 times in a minute.

12. B

This question would be an easy one to backsolve. Plug in the answer choices and see which one works. You could also move the numbers across the equals signs. You have to change + to − and you have to change − to + . So ___ = 40 − 16 + 5. The answer is 29.

13. B

Eighty percent is the same as 0.80. To find out how much weight the puppy has gained, multiply: 4 × 0.80 = 3.2. Add the original weight (4 pounds) to the gained weight (3.2). Then 4 + 3.2 = 7.2.

14. B

Substitute in 5 for *x* and see which answer choice results in a true statement. When you solve, choice (B) becomes 14 = 14, which is the only true statement here.

15. C

The numbers on the right-hand column skip by three: 9, 12, 15. Fifteen plus three is 18, so that must be the missing number.

16. B

Plug 9 into each answer choice. For (B), after you have substituted, you must find the value of what is in parenthesis first, then multiply by three. If you tried to multiply before you subtracted, you would have gotten an incorrect value.

17. B

The sum is the result of addition. So 25 + 30 = 55. If you multiplied the numbers, you would have gotten (D), which is incorrect.

18. A

$20 – $8.96 = $11.04. You must line up the decimal points and borrow.

19. A

You must borrow to solve this subtraction question.

$$
\begin{array}{r}
10 \\
\cancel{5}\;\cancel{0}\;\cancel{0} \\
4\;0\;9 \\
\hline
9\;1
\end{array}
$$

20. D

The product is the result of multiplication. Here, $5 \times 20 = 100$. If you added you might have come up with (B), which is incorrect.

21. D

If $8 + a = 15$, then $a = 15 – 8 = 7$. If $6 + b = 14$, then $b = 14 – 6 = 8$. $a = 7$ and $b = 8$, so $a + b$ is the same as $7 + 8$.

22. B

If $a = b$ and $b = c$ then it follows logically that $a = c$.

23. A

The diameter is the full length across the circle. The radius is the length halfway across. If we're given that the diameter is 8 cm, the radius is half of that: 4 cm. If you doubled the length of 8 cm, you would have gotten 16, which would have been incorrect.

24. C

To find the perimeter, add the lengths of all four sides: 12 + 6 + 12 + 6 = 36 inches.

25. B

A cube is made up of six squares. The six squares in the figure can be folded into a cube.

26. D

Volume = Length × Width × Height. The volume in cubic feet is $5 \times 4 \times 3 = 60$.

27. D

Line up the decimal points to add.

28. D

Since n is unknown, the answer cannot be determined.

29. D

Solve this problem by thinking of three groups: One group that likes cats, and two groups that like dogs. Divide 45 by 3 to see that there are 15 students in each group. There are 2 dog groups, so multiply 15×2 to get 30.

30. C

There is only 0.01 difference between 100.11 and 100.1. If you weren't sure, you could subtract for each to solve.

31. D

Find a common denominator. The lowest common denominator is 8. Convert $\frac{1}{4}$ to $\frac{2}{8}$.
Then add: $\frac{2}{8} + \frac{5}{8} = \frac{7}{8}$.

32. C

The difference is the answer when you subtract. If you added, you would have arrived at incorrect (D).

33. D

The number must be divisible by three with no remainder.

34. A

The quotient is the result of division, so the answer is 66 divided by 22, which is 3. You might have suspected (C) was correct since you were looking at two other double-digit numbers, but (C) is not correct.

35. D

A whole number has no fraction or decimal point. Also, the number has to be greater than 15, so (D) is the only possible answer.

See chapter 23 on how to score your ISEE practice test.

CHAPTER 23: SCORING YOUR ISEE PRACTICE TEST

The ISEE calculates scores through a formula that compares each student's score against the scores of other students of the same grade level. The governing board of the ISEE does not release any information about how scores are actually calculated, so we are unable to provide you with a scaled score on your practice tests.

So, rather than worrying over what the numbers mean, just concentrate on improving your performance. Look over all the answers and explanations we have provided. Since you won't know how hard the actual test will be on Test Day, or how other students will do, simply focusing on performing your best in your practice will put you in the right frame of mind to do just that on Test Day.

| Part Six |

LEARNING RESOURCES

CHAPTER 24: VOCABULARY REFERENCE

ROOT LIST

ROOT	MEANING	EXAMPLES
A, AN	*not, without*	amoral, atrophy, asymmetrical, anarchy, anesthetic, anonymity, anomaly, annul
AB, A	*from, away, apart*	abnegate, abortive, abrogate, abscond, absolve, abstemious, abstruse, avert, aversion, abnormal, abdicate, aberration, abhor, abject, abjure, ablution
AC, ACR	*sharp, sour*	acid, acerbic, exacerbate, acute, acuity, acumen, acrid, acrimony
AD, A	*to, toward*	adhere, adjacent, adjunct, admonish, adroit, adumbrate, advent, abeyance, abet, accede, accretion, acquiesce, affluent, aggrandize, aggregate, alleviate, alliteration, allude, allure, ascribe, aspersion, aspire, assail, assonance, attest
ALI, ALTR	*another*	alias, alienate, inalienable, altruism
AM, AMI	*love*	amorous, amicable, amiable, amity
AMBI, AMPHI	*both*	ambiguous, ambivalent, ambidextrous, amphibious
AMBL, AMBUL	*walk*	amble, ambulatory, perambulator, somnambulist
ANIM	*mind, spirit, breath*	animal, animosity, unanimous, magnanimous
ANN, ENN	*year*	annual, annuity, superannuated, biennial, perennial
ANTE, ANT	*before*	antecedent, antediluvian, antebellum, antepenultimate, anterior, antiquity, antiquated, anticipate
ANTHROP	*human*	anthropology, anthropomorphic, misanthrope, philanthropy
ANTI, ANT	*against, opposite*	antidote, antipathy, antithesis, antacid, antagonist, antonym

ROOT	MEANING	EXAMPLES
AUD	*hear*	audio, audience, audition, auditory, audible
AUTO	*self*	autobiography, autocrat, autonomous
BELLI, BELL	*war*	belligerent, bellicose, antebellum, rebellion
BENE, BEN	*good*	benevolent, benefactor, beneficent, benign
BI	*two*	bicycle, bisect, bilateral, bilingual, biped
BIBLIO	*book*	Bible, bibliography, bibliophile
BIO	*life*	biography, biology, amphibious, symbiotic, macrobiotics
BURS	*money, purse*	reimburse, disburse, bursar
CAD, CAS, CID	*happen, fall*	accident, cadence, cascade, deciduous
CAP, CIP	*head*	captain, decapitate, capitulate, precipitous, precipitate, recapitulate
CARN	*flesh*	carnal, carnage, carnival, carnivorous, incarnate, incarnadine
CAP, CAPT, CEPT, CIP	*take, hold, seize*	capable, capacious, captivate, deception, intercept, precept, inception, anticipate, emancipate, incipient, percipient
CED, CESS	*yield, go*	cede, precede, accede, recede, antecedent, intercede, secede, cession, cease, cessation, incessant
CHROM	*color*	chrome, chromatic, monochrome
CHRON	*time*	chronology, chronic, anachronism
CIDE	*murder*	suicide, homicide, regicide, patricide
CIRCUM	*around*	circumference, circumlocution, circumnavigate, circumscribe, circumspect, circumvent
CLIN, CLIV	*slope*	incline, declivity, proclivity
CLUD, CLUS, CLAUS, CLOIS	*shut, close*	conclude, reclusive, claustrophobia, cloister, preclude, occlude
CO, COM, CON	*with, together*	coeducation, coagulate, coalesce, coerce, cogent, cognate, collateral, colloquial, colloquy, commensurate, commodious, compassion, compatriot, complacent, compliant, complicity, compunction, concerto, conciliatory, concord, concur, condone, conflagration, congeal, congenial, congenital, conglomerate, conjure, conjugal, conscientious, consecrate, consensus, consonant, constrained, contentious, contrite, contusion, convalescence, convene, convivial, convoke, convoluted, congress

ROOT	MEANING	EXAMPLES
COGN, GNO	*know*	recognize, cognition, cognizance, incognito, diagnosis, agnostic, prognosis, gnostic, ignorant
CONTRA	*against*	controversy, incontrovertible, contravene, contradict
CORP	*body*	corpse, corporeal, corpulence
COSMO, COSM	*world*	cosmopolitan, cosmos, microcosm, macrocosm
CRAC, CRAT	*rule, power*	democracy, bureaucracy, theocracy, autocrat, aristocrat, technocrat
CRED	*trust, believe*	incredible, credulous, credence
CRESC, CRET	*grow*	crescent, crescendo, accretion
CULP	*blame, fault*	culprit, culpable, inculpate, exculpate
CURR, CURS	*run*	current, concur, cursory, precursor, incursion
DE	*down, out, apart*	depart, debase, debilitate, declivity, decry, deface, defamatory, defunct, delegate, demarcation, demean, demur, deplete, deplore, depravity, deprecate, deride, derivative, desist, detest
DEC	*ten, tenth*	decade, decimal, decathlon, decimate
DEMO, DEM	*people*	democrat, demographics, demagogue, epidemic, pandemic, endemic
DI, DIURN	*day*	diary, diurnal, quotidian
DIA	*across*	diagonal, diatribe, diaphanous
DIC, DICT	*speak*	diction, interdict, predict, abdicate, indict, verdict, dictum
DIS, DIF, DI	*not, apart, away*	disaffected, disband, disbar, disburse, discern, discordant, discredit, discursive, disheveled, disparage, disparate, dispassionate, dispirit, dissemble, disseminate, dissension, dissipate, dissonant, dissuade, distend, differentiate, diffidence, diffuse, digress, divert
DOC, DOCT	*teach*	doctrine, docile, doctrinaire
DOL	*pain*	condolence, doleful, dolorous, indolent
DUC, DUCT	*lead*	seduce, induce, conduct, viaduct, induct
EGO	*self*	ego, egoist, egocentric
EN, EM	*in, into*	enter, entice, encumber, endemic, ensconce, enthrall, entreat, embellish, embezzle, embroil, empathy
ERR	*wander*	erratic, aberration, errant

ROOT	MEANING	EXAMPLES
EU	*well, good*	eulogy, euphemism, euphony, euphoria, eurythmics, euthanasia
EX, E	*out, out of*	exit, exacerbate, excerpt, excommunicate, exculpate, execrable, exhume, exonerate, exorbitant, exorcise, expatriate, expedient, expiate, expunge, expurgate, extenuate, extort, extremity, extricate, extrinsic, exult, evoke, evict, evince, elicit, egress, egregious
FAC, FIC, FECT, FY, FEA	*make, do*	factory, facility, benefactor, malefactor, fiction, fictive, beneficent, affect, confection, refectory, magnify, unify, rectify, vilify, feasible
FAL, FALS	*deceive*	false, infallible, fallacious
FERV	*boil*	fervent, fervid, effervescent
FID	*faith, trust*	confident, diffidence, perfidious, fidelity
FLU, FLUX	*flow*	fluent, flux, affluent, confluence, effluvia, superfluous
FORE	*before*	forecast, foreboding, forestall
FRAG, FRAC	*break*	fragment, fracture, diffract, fractious, refract
FUS	*pour*	profuse, infusion, effusive, diffuse
GEN	*birth, class, kin*	generation, congenital, homogeneous, heterogeneous, ingenious, engender, progenitor, progeny
GRAD, GRESS	*step*	graduate, gradual, retrograde, centigrade, degrade, gradation, gradient, progress, congress, digress, transgress, ingress, egress
GRAPH, GRAM	*writing*	biography, bibliography, epigraph, grammar, epigram
GRAT	*pleasing*	grateful, gratitude, gratis, ingrate, congratulate, gratuitous, gratuity
GRAV, GRIEV	*heavy*	grave, gravity, aggravate, grieve, aggrieve, grievous
GREG	*crowd, flock*	segregate, gregarious, egregious, congregate, aggregate
HABIT, HIBIT	*have, hold*	habit, inhibit, cohabit, habitat
HAP	*by chance*	happen, haphazard, hapless, mishap
HELIO, HELI	*sun*	heliocentric, helium, heliotrope, aphelion, perihelion
HETERO	*other*	heterosexual, heterogeneous, heterodox
HOL	*whole*	holocaust, catholic, holistic

ROOT	MEANING	EXAMPLES
HOMO	*same*	homosexual, homogenize, homogeneous, homonym
HOMO	*man*	Homo sapiens, homicide, bonhomie
HYDR	*water*	hydrant, hydrate, dehydration
HYPER	*too much, excess*	hyperactive, hyperbole, hyperventilate
HYPO	*too little, under*	hypodermic, hypothermia, hypochondria, hypothesis, hypothetical
IN, IG, IL, IM, IR	*not*	incorrigible, indefatigable, indelible, indubitable, inept, inert, inexorable, insatiable, insentient, insolvent, insomnia, interminable, intractable, incessant, inextricable, infallible, infamy, innumerable, inoperable, insipid, intemperate, intrepid, inviolable, ignorant, ignominious, ignoble, illicit, illimitable, immaculate, immutable, impasse, impeccable, impecunious, impertinent, implacable, impotent, impregnable, improvident, impassioned, impervious, irregular
IN, IL, IM, IR	*in, on, into*	invade, inaugurate, incandescent, incarcerate, incense, indenture, induct, ingratiate, introvert, incarnate, inception, incisive, infer, infusion, ingress, innate, inquest, inscribe, insinuate, inter, illustrate, imbue, immerse, implicate, irrigate, irritate
INTER	*between, among*	intercede, intercept, interdiction, interject, interlocutor, interloper, intermediary, intermittent, interpolate, interpose, interregnum, interrogate, intersect, intervene
INTRA, INTR	*within*	intrastate, intravenous, intramural, intrinsic
IT, ITER	*between, among*	transit, itinerant, reiterate, transitory
JECT, JET	*throw*	eject, interject, abject, trajectory, jettison
JOUR	*day*	journal, adjourn, sojourn
JUD	*judge*	judge, judicious, prejudice, adjudicate
JUNCT, JUG	*join*	junction, adjunct, injunction, conjugal, subjugate
JUR	*swear, law*	jury, abjure, adjure, conjure, perjure, jurisprudence
LAT	*side*	lateral, collateral, unilateral, bilateral, quadrilateral
LAV, LAU, LU	*wash*	lavatory, laundry, ablution, antediluvian
LEG, LEC, LEX	*read, speak*	legible, lecture, lexicon
LEV	*light*	elevate, levitate, levity, alleviate

ROOT	MEANING	EXAMPLES
LIBER	*free*	liberty, liberal, libertarian, libertine
LIG, LECT	*choose, gather*	eligible, elect, select
LIG, LI, LY	*bind*	ligament, oblige, religion, liable, liaison, lien, ally
LING, LANG	*tongue*	lingo, language, linguistics, bilingual
LITER	*letter*	literate, alliteration, literal
LITH	*stone*	monolith, lithograph, megalith
LOQU, LOC, LOG	*speech, thought*	eloquent, loquacious, colloquial, colloquy, soliloquy, circumlocution, interlocutor, monologue, dialogue, eulogy, philology, neologism
LUC, LUM	*light*	lucid, illuminate, elucidate, pellucid, translucent
LUD, LUS	*play*	ludicrous, allude, delusion, allusion, illusory
MACRO	*great*	macrocosm, macrobiotics
MAG, MAJ, MAS, MAX	*great*	magnify, majesty, master, maximum, magnanimous, magnate, magnitude
MAL	*bad*	malady, maladroit, malevolent, malodorous
MAN	*hand*	manual, manuscript, emancipate, manifest
MAR	*sea*	submarine, marine, maritime
MATER, MATR	*mother*	maternal, matron, matrilineal
MEDI	*middle*	intermediary, medieval, mediate
MEGA	*great*	megaphone, megalomania, megaton, megalith
MEMOR, MEMEN	*remember*	memory, memento, memorabilia, memoir
METER, METR, MENS	*measure*	meter, thermometer, perimeter, metronome, commensurate
MICRO	*small*	microscope, microorganism, microcosm, microbe
MIS	*wrong, bad, hate*	misunderstand, misanthrope, misapprehension, misconstrue, misnomer, mishap
MIT, MISS	*send*	transmit, emit, missive
MOLL	*soft*	mollify, emollient, mollusk
MON, MONIT	*warn*	admonish, monitor, premonition
MONO	*one*	monologue, monotonous, monogamy, monolith, monochrome
MOR	*custom, manner*	moral, mores, morose
MOR, MORT	*dead*	morbid, moribund, mortal, amortize
MORPH	*shape*	amorphous, anthropomorphic, metamorphosis, morphology

ROOT	MEANING	EXAMPLES
MOV, MOT, MOB, MOM	*move*	remove, motion, mobile, momentum, momentous
MUT	*change*	mutate, mutability, immutable, commute
NAT, NASC	*born*	native, nativity, natal, neonate, innate, cognate, nascent, renascent, renaissance
NAU, NAV	*ship, sailor*	nautical, nauseous, navy, circumnavigate
NEG	*not, deny*	negative, abnegate, renege
NEO	*new*	neoclassical, neophyte, neologism, neonate
NIHIL	*none, nothing*	annihilation, nihilism
NOM, NYM	*name*	nominate, nomenclature, nominal, cognomen, misnomer, ignominious, antonym, homonym, pseudonym, synonym, anonymity
NOX, NIC, NEC, NOC	*harm*	obnoxious, noxious, pernicious, internecine, innocuous
NOV	*new*	novelty, innovation, novitiate
NUMER	*number*	numeral, numerous, innumerable, enumerate
OB	*against*	obstruct, obdurate, obfuscate, obnoxious, obsequious, obstinate, obstreperous, obtrusive
OMNI	*all*	omnipresent, omnipotent, omniscient, omnivorous
ONER	*burden*	onerous, onus, exonerate
OPER	*work*	operate, cooperate, inoperable
PAC	*peace*	pacify, pacifist, pacific
PALP	*feel*	palpable, palpitation
PAN	*all*	panorama, panacea, panegyric, pandemic, panoply
PATER, PATR	*father*	paternal, paternity, patriot, compatriot, expatriate, patrimony, patricide, patrician
PATH, PASS	*feel, suffer*	sympathy, antipathy, empathy, apathy, pathos, impassioned
PEC	*money*	pecuniary, impecunious, peculation
PED, POD	*foot*	pedestrian, pediment, expedient, biped, quadruped, tripod
PEL, PULS	*drive*	compel, compelling, expel, propel, compulsion
PEN	*almost*	peninsula, penultimate, penumbra
PEND, PENS	*hang*	pendant, pendulous, compendium, suspense, propensity

ROOT	MEANING	EXAMPLES
PER	*through, by, for, throughout*	perambulator, percipient, perfunctory, permeable, perspicacious, pertinacious, perturbation, perusal, perennial, peregrinate
PER	*against, destruction*	perfidious, pernicious, perjure
PERI	*around*	perimeter, periphery, perihelion, peripatetic
PET	*seek, go toward*	petition, impetus, impetuous, petulant, centripetal
PHIL	*love*	philosopher, philanderer, philanthropy, bibliophile, philology
PHOB	*fear*	phobia, claustrophobia, xenophobia
PHON	*sound*	phonograph, megaphone, euphony, phonetics, phonics
PLAC	*calm, please*	placate, implacable, placid, complacent
PON, POS	*put, place*	postpone, proponent, exponent, preposition, posit, interpose, juxtaposition, depose
PORT	*carry*	portable, deportment, rapport
POT	*drink*	potion, potable
POT	*power*	potential, potent, impotent, potentate, omnipotence
PRE	*before*	precede, precipitate, preclude, precocious, precursor, predilection, predisposition, preponderance, prepossessing, presage, prescient, prejudice, predict, premonition, preposition
PRIM, PRI	*first*	prime, primary, primal, primeval, primordial, pristine
PRO	*ahead, forth*	proceed, proclivity, procrastinator, profane, profuse, progenitor, progeny, prognosis, prologue, promontory, propel, proponent, propose, proscribe, protestation, provoke
PROTO	*first*	prototype, protagonist, protocol
PROX, PROP	*near*	approximate, propinquity, proximity
PSEUDO	*false*	pseudoscientific, pseudonym
PYR	*fire*	pyre, pyrotechnics, pyromania
QUAD, QUAR, QUAT	*four*	quadrilateral, quadrant, quadruped, quarter, quarantine, quaternary
QUES, QUER, QUIS, QUIR	*question*	quest, inquest, query, querulous, inquisitive, inquiry
QUIE	*quiet*	disquiet, acquiesce, quiescent, requiem
QUINT, QUIN	*five*	quintuplets, quintessence

ROOT	MEANING	EXAMPLES
RADI, RAMI	*branch*	radius, radiate, radiant, eradicate, ramification
RECT, REG	*straight, rule*	rectangle, rectitude, rectify, regular
REG	*king, rule*	regal, regent, interregnum
RETRO	*backward*	retrospective, retroactive, retrograde
RID, RIS	*laugh*	ridiculous, deride, derision
ROG	*ask*	interrogate, derogatory, abrogate, arrogate, arrogant
RUD	*rough, crude*	rude, erudite, rudimentary
RUPT	*break*	disrupt, interrupt, rupture, erupt
SACR, SANCT	*holy*	sacred, sacrilege, consecrate, sanctify, sanction, sacrosanct
SCRIB, SCRIPT, SCRIV	*write*	scribe, ascribe, circumscribe, inscribe, proscribe, script, manuscript, scrivener
SE	*apart, away*	separate, segregate, secede, sedition
SEC, SECT, SEG	*cut*	sector, dissect, bisect, intersect, segment, secant
SED, SID	*sit*	sedate, sedentary, supersede, reside, residence, assiduous, insidious
SEM	*seed, sow*	seminar, seminal, disseminate
SEN	*old*	senior, senile, senescent
SENT, SENS	*feel, think*	sentiment, nonsense, assent, sentient, consensus, sensual
SEQU, SECU	*follow*	sequence, sequel, subsequent, obsequious, obsequy, non sequitur, consecutive
SIM, SEM	*similar, same*	similar, semblance, dissemble, verisimilitude
SIGN	*mark, sign*	signal, designation, assignation
SIN	*curve*	sine curve, sinuous, insinuate
SOL	*sun*	solar, parasol, solarium, solstice
SOL	*alone*	solo, solitude, soliloquy, solipsism
SOMN	*sleep*	insomnia, somnolent, somnambulist
SON	*sound*	sonic, consonance, dissonance, assonance, sonorous, resonate
SOPH	*wisdom*	philosopher, sophistry, sophisticated, sophomoric
SPEC, SPIC	*see, look*	spectator, circumspect, retrospective, perspective, perspicacious
SPER	*hope*	prosper, prosperous, despair, desperate
SPERS, SPAR	*scatter*	disperse, sparse, aspersion, disparate
SPIR	*breathe*	respire, inspire, spiritual, aspire, transpire

ROOT	MEANING	EXAMPLES
STRICT, STRING	*bind*	strict, stricture, constrict, stringent, astringent
STRUCT, STRU	*build*	structure, construe, obstruct
SUB	*under*	subconscious, subjugate, subliminal, subpoena, subsequent, subterranean, subvert
SUMM	*highest*	summit, summary, consummate
SUPER, SUR	*above*	supervise, supercilious, supersede, superannuated, superfluous, insurmountable, surfeit
SURGE, SURRECT	*rise*	surge, resurgent, insurgent, insurrection
SYN, SYM	*together*	synthesis, sympathy, synonym, syncopation, synopsis, symposium, symbiosis
TACIT, TIC	*silent*	tacit, taciturn, reticent
TACT, TAG, TANG	*touch*	tact, tactile, contagious, tangent, tangential, tangible
TEN, TIN, TAIN	*hold, twist*	detention, tenable, tenacious, pertinacious, retinue, retain
TEND, TENS, TENT	*stretch*	intend, distend, tension, tensile, ostensible, contentious
TERM	*end*	terminal, terminus, terminate, interminable
TERR	*earth, land*	terrain, terrestrial, extraterrestrial, subterranean
TEST	*witness*	testify, attest, testimonial, testament, detest, protestation
THE	*god*	atheist, theology, apotheosis, theocracy
THERM	*heat*	thermometer, thermal, thermonuclear, hypothermia
TIM	*fear, frightened*	timid, intimidate, timorous
TOP	*place*	topic, topography, utopia
TORT	*twist*	distort, extort, tortuous
TORP	*stiff, numb*	torpedo, torpid, torpor
TOX	*poison*	toxic, toxin, intoxication
TRACT	*draw*	tractor, intractable, protract
TRANS	*across, over, through, beyond*	transport, transgress, transient, transitory, translucent, transmutation, transpire, intransigent
TREM, TREP	*shake*	tremble, tremor, tremulous, trepidation, intrepid
TURB	*shake*	disturb, turbulent, perturbation
UMBR	*shadow*	umbrella, umbrage, adumbrate, penumbra
UNI, UN	*one*	unify, unilateral, unanimous
URB	*city*	urban, suburban, urbane
VAC	*empty*	vacant, evacuate, vacuous

ROOT	MEANING	EXAMPLES
VAL, VAIL	*value, strength*	valid, valor, ambivalent, convalescence, avail, prevail, countervail
VEN, VENT	*come*	convene, contravene, intervene, venue, convention, circumvent, advent, adventitious
VER	*true*	verify, verity, verisimilitude, veracious, aver, verdict
VERB	*word*	verbal, verbose, verbiage, verbatim
VERT, VERS	*turn*	avert, convert, revert, incontrovertible, divert, subvert, versatile, aversion
VICT, VINC	*conquer*	victory, conviction, evict, evince, invincible
VID, VIS	*see*	evident, vision, visage, supervise
VIL	*base, mean*	vile, vilify, revile
VIV, VIT	*life*	vivid, vital, convivial, vivacious
VOC, VOK, VOW	*call, voice*	vocal, equivocate, vociferous, convoke, evoke, invoke, avow
VOL	*wish*	voluntary, malevolent, benevolent, volition
VOLV, VOLUT	*turn, roll*	revolve, evolve, convoluted
VOR	*eat*	devour, carnivorous, omnivorous, voracious

VOCABULARY LIST

WORD	DEFINITION, CONTEXT, SYNONYMS
ABDICATE	to give up a position, right, or power *With the angry mob clamoring outside the palace, the king abdicated his throne and fled with his mistress.* Synonyms: **quit, resign, renounce, step down**
ABDUCT	forcefully and wrongfully to carry, take, or lead away *The kidnappers planned to abduct the child and hold her for ransom.* Synonyms: **kidnap, carry off**
ABHOR	to hate, to view with repugnance, to detest *After repeated failure to learn the Pythagorean theorem, Susan began to abhor geometry.* Synonyms: **hate, loathe, abominate**
ABSURD	ridiculously unreasonable, lacking logic *Ironing one's underwear is absurd.* Synonyms: **ridiculous, ludicrous, preposterous, bizarre**
ABYSS	deep hole; deep immeasurable space, gulf or cavity *Looking down into the abyss was terrifying, for I could not see the bottom.* Synonyms: **chasm, pit**
ACCELERATE	to increase in speed, cause to move faster *The new disease has spread like wildfire, causing researchers to accelerate their search for a cure.* Synonyms: **speed up, hasten, expedite**
ACCLAIM	(n) praise, enthusiastic approval *The artist won international acclaim; critics and viewers all over the world were intrigued by the works.* Synonyms: **praise, approval** (v) to approve, to welcome with applause and praise *The critic was eager to acclaim the actress for her performance.* Synonyms: **cheer, applaud, praise, honor**
ACUTE	sharp in some way (as in an acute angle) or sharp in intellect; crucial *There is an acute shortage of food, which will ultimately result in a famine if something is not done soon to increase the food supply.* Synonyms: **perceptive, sharp, keen, shrewd; crucial**
ADAGE	old saying, proverb *"A penny saved is a penny earned" is a popular adage.* Synonyms: **proverb, maxim**

WORD	DEFINITION, CONTEXT, SYNONYMS
ADHERE	to stick fast; to hold to *After we put glue on his pants, John adhered to the chair. He was a strict Catholic who adhered to all the teachings of the Church.* Synonyms: **stick to** (like glue or adhesive tape); **follow**
ADJOURN	to postpone; to suspend (a meeting) for a period of time *Since it was late in the day, the prosecutor moved that the court adjourn for the day.* Synonyms: **suspend, recess, postpone**
ADJUNCT	something or someone associated with another but in a defendant or secondary position *An adjunct professor is one not given the same full-time status as other faculty members.* Synonyms: **additional, supporting, assisting, accessory**
ADMONISH	to scold (sometimes in a good natured way); to urge to duty, remind; to advise against something *My mother began to admonish me about my poor grades.* Synonyms: **warn, caution, scold**
ADORN	to decorate or add beauty to, for instance with ornaments: to make pleasing, more attractive *She adorned her hair with flowers.* Synonyms: **decorate, ornament, embellish**
ADVERSARY	opponent or enemy *Democrats and Republicans are usually adversaries in the political world.* Synonyms: **enemy, foe, opponent**
AERONAUTIC	relating to aircraft *The Air Force's Stealth plane is reported to be a masterpiece of aeronautic design.*
AFFABLE	pleasantly easy to get along with; friendly and warm *He was an affable host and made us feel right at home.* Synonyms: **agreeable, amiable**
AFFECTATION	attempt to appear to be what one is not for the purpose of impressing others (for instance, pretending to have a pretentiously cultured accent) *Justin once spent three months in France and has now acquired the silly affectation of using French phrases in casual conversation.* Synonyms: **pretension, unnaturalness, artificiality, mannerism, pretense, airs, sham, facade, pose, posture**

WORD	DEFINITION, CONTEXT, SYNONYMS
AGHAST	overcome by surprise, disgust, or amazement; seized with terror; shocked *The investigator was* aghast *at the horrible conditions in the nursing home.* Synonyms: **astounded, dismayed, appalled, astonished, shocked**
AGILITY	condition of being able to move quickly and easily or being mentally alert *Strength and agility are important for an athlete.* Synonyms: **skillfulness, dexterity, nimbleness**
AGITATE	to shake or grow excited; to move around a lot, to disturb or excite emotionally *The bat's flight into the classroom managed to* agitate *the teacher so much that he went home early.* Synonyms: **disturb, upset, stir up** (like a washing machine)
AIMLESS	lacking purpose or goals *After its engine died, the boat drifted* aimlessly *for days.* Synonyms: **purposeless, haphazard, accidental**
ALLEVIATE	to make easier to bear, lessen *This medicine will help to* alleviate *the pain.* Synonyms: **relieve, allay, assuage, ease, decrease, lessen, mitigate**
ALLURE	fascination, appeal *Video games have an* allure *that some people find impossible to resist.* Synonyms: **temptation, attraction, fascination**
ALOOF	distant in relations with other people *The newcomer remained* aloof *from all our activities and therefore made no new friends.* Synonyms: **detached, cool, blase, remote**
ALTRUISTIC	concerned for the welfare of others *The* altruistic *woman gave out money to all who seemed needy.* Synonyms: **benevolent, charitable, compassionate, humane**
AMATEUR	someone not paid to engage in a hobby, sport, art, etc. *Since professionals couldn't play, only* amateur *athletes were allowed to participate in the Olympics.* Synonyms: **devotee, dabbler, enthusiast, buff, nonprofessional** (adj) like an amateur *The brilliant author James Joyce was an* amateur *singer.*

WORD	DEFINITION, CONTEXT, SYNONYMS
AMEND	to improve; to alter, to add to, or subtract from by formal procedure *Congress will* amend *the bill so that the President will sign it.* Synonyms: **alter, improve, repair, mend, make better, ameliorate**
AMOROUS	having to do with love *The love-sick young poet wrote many* amorous *poems about his girlfriend.* Synonyms: **romantic, erotic**
AMORPHOUS	lacking a specific shape *In the movie, "The Blob," the creature was an* amorphous *one that was constantly changing shape.* Synonyms: **shapeless, vague**
AMPHIBIAN	animal at home on both land and in the water *A frog, which lives both on land and in the water, is an* amphibian.
ANGULAR	having clear angles or thin and bony facial features. *The figures on the left side of the painting are very* angular, *whereas the figures on the right are rounded.* Synonyms: **lanky, gaunt. bony**
ANIMOSITY	feeling of ill will, intense dislike for someone or something *The deep-rooted* animosity *between them made it difficult for the brothers to work together.* Synonyms: **ill will, ill feeling, bitterness, rancor, acrimony**
ANNIHILATE	to destroy completely *The first troops to land on the beach during the invasion were* annihilated *by the powerful artillery of the enemy.* Synonyms: **destroy, devastate, demolish**
ANTIDOTE	remedy to relieve the effects of poison *The first aid kit included an* antidote *for snake bite.* Synonyms: **remedy, counteragent, neutralizer**
APERTURE	opening *The* aperture *of a camera lens is a circular opening of variable diameter that regulates the amount of light entering the lens.* Synonyms: **hole, gap, space, opening, crack**
AQUEOUS	similar to, or composed of water *The inside of an eyeball is filled with an* aqueous *substance.* Synonyms: **watery, aquatic, hydrous, liquid**

WORD	DEFINITION, CONTEXT, SYNONYMS
ARDENT	characterized by passion or desire *After a 25 game losing streak, even the Mets' most* ardent *fans realized the team wouldn't finish first.* Synonyms: **passionate, enthusiastic, fervent**
ARID	very dry, lacking moisture; unproductive, unimaginative *The* arid *farmland produced no crops.* Synonyms: **dry, parched, barren; dull, uninteresting, insipid**
AROMA	pleasing fragrance; any odor or smell *The* aroma *in the bakery made her mouth water.* Synonyms: **smell, fragrance, odor**
ARTICULATE	(adj) well-spoken, lucidly presented *Joe's* articulate *argument was so persuasive that we all agreed with him.* Synonyms: **eloquent, glib** (v) to pronounce clearly *The great actor* articulated *every word so clearly it was easy to understand him.* Synonyms: **enunciate**
ARTIFICE	(1) trickery, clever ruse *Ralph's use of rubber masks proved to be a brilliant* artifice. Synonyms: **stratagem, trick, ploy, deception, ruse, maneuver** (2) ability to create or imagine *Many question the meaningfulness of Jamie's science fiction novel, but its fantastic images and ingenious plot cannot fail to impress one with his sheer* artifice. Synonyms: **creativity, inventiveness, innovation, resourcefulness, imagination, ingenuity**
ASCERTAIN	to find out or discover by examination *Try though he did, the archaeologist couldn't* ascertain *the correct age of the Piltdown man's skeleton.* Synonyms: **determine, discover, unearth, find out**
ASSAILABLE	able to be attacked or assaulted by blows or words *Carcassonne was widely thought to be an* unassailable *fortress after it resisted a siege by Charlemagne.* Synonyms: **vulnerable, exposed, unprotected**

WORD	DEFINITION, CONTEXT, SYNONYMS
ASTOUND	to overwhelm with amazement *The extent of his great knowledge never ceases to* astound *me.* Synonyms: **amaze, stupefy, stun**
ASTUTE	shrewd and perceptive; able to understand clearly and quickly *The novelist Judy Blume is an* astute *judge of human character.* Synonyms: **keen, discerning, penetrating, incisive, perceptive; crafty, foxy, wily, shrewd**
ATROCITY	horrible, usually brutal, act *During the Indian bid for freedom from British colonial rule, a British officer committed the* atrocity *of slaughtering a large congregation of peaceful Indian demonstrators.* Synonyms: **horror, barbarity, outrage**
AUDACITY	boldness or daring, especially with disregard for personal safety *He had the* audacity *to insult the President to his face.* Synonyms: **a lot of nerve: boldness, daring, impudence**
AUTHORITATIVE	having great authority *J. R. R. Tolkien, who had written many books about Old English poetry, was widely considered to be the most* authoritative *scholar in the field.* Synonyms: **masterful**
BANAL	boringly predictable *A boring conversation is likely to be full of* banal *statements like "Have a nice day."* Synonyms: **boring, dull, bland, insipid**
BANISH	to send away, condemn to exile; drive or put away *After the incident with the Jello, Arthur was* banished *from the lunchroom.* Synonyms: **send away, get rid of, expel, exile, deport**
BARRIER	anything that makes progress harder or impossible; a limit or boundary *The Pythagorean theorem has been a* barrier *to Donald's complete understanding of geometry. To discourage visitors, Janet built a* barrier *in front of the entrance to her room.* Synonyms: **something that blocks or limits: obstacle**
BEGUILE	to delude, deceive by trickery *Beguiled by the supernatural songs of the Sirens, Odysseus wanted to abandon all his men and forget his family.* Synonyms: **charm, allure, bewitch, captivate**

WORD	DEFINITION, CONTEXT, SYNONYMS
BELLIGERENCE	aggressive hostility *A soldier can be shocked by the* belligerence *of his enemy.* Synonyms: **aggressiveness, combativeness**
BENEFACTOR	someone giving financial or general assistance *A wealthy alumnus who gives 5 million to his old college would be considered a great* benefactor. Synonyms: **patron, backer, donor**
BENEFICIAL	advantageous, helpful, conferring benefit *Eating vegetables and getting 8 hours of sleep is* beneficial *to your health, but it sure isn't much fun.* Synonyms: **has a good effect; advantageous, favorable**
BENEVOLENCE	inclination to do good deeds *The* benevolence *of the generous donor was recognized by a plaque.* Synonyms: **largess**
BEWILDERED	completely confused or puzzled, perplexed *I was* bewildered *by the complex algebra problem.* Synonyms: **confused, puzzled, perplexed**
BIAS	(n) prejudice, particular tendency *Racial* bias *in employment is illegal in the United States.* Synonyms: **partiality** (v) to cause prejudice in (a person); to influence unfairly *The article is not completely accurate, and may* bias *some readers.* Synonyms: **show favor or prejudice**
BILE	ill temper, irritability *Mr. Watkins is very harsh when he grades essays; his comments reveal his* bile *and sharp tongue.* Synonyms: **bitterness, bad temper**
BLISS	supreme happiness, utter joy or contentment; heaven, paradise *For lovers of ice cream, this new flavor is absolute* bliss. Synonyms: **joy, delight, ecstasy**
BOISTEROUS	loud and unrestrained *The* boisterous *party make so much noise last night that I got no sleep.* Synonyms: **loud, noisy, raucous**
BOTANIST	scientist specializing in study of plants *A* botanist *is a scientist who studies plants.*

WORD	DEFINITION, CONTEXT, SYNONYMS
BOUNTY	generosity in giving; reward *In the Old West,* bounty *hunters often pursued outlaws in hopes of reward.* Synonyms: **abundance, cornucopia, reward, loot**
BRAVADO	showy and pretentious display of courage *The coward's* bravado *quickly vanished when his captors threatened to hit him; he began to whine for mercy.* Synonyms: **bluster, bombast, swagger**
BREVITY	state of being brief, of not lasting a long time *The* brevity *of your visit to my home implied that you did not enjoy my family's company.* Synonyms: **shortness, fleetness, swiftness**
BRIG	ship's prison *Captain Bligh had the rebellious sailor thrown into the* brig. Synonyms: **jail, prison**
BURNISH	(n) to make shine by rubbing, as with a cloth *Mr. Jin loved to stand in the sun and* burnish *his luxury car until it gleamed.* Synonyms: **shine, polish, buff, varnish** (n) shininess produced by burnishing *They all admired the* burnish *on the car.* Synonyms: **shine, luster, gleam, brilliance**
CACHE	hiding place for treasures, etc.; anything in such a hiding place *The secret panel hid a* cache *of jewels.* [It sounds like cash.] Synonyms: **stash**
CAJOLE	to wheedle, persuade with promises or flattery, coax *The spoiled girl could* cajole *her father into buying her anything.* Synonyms: **coax, wheedle**
CAMOUFLAGE	(n) disguise worn in order to deceive an enemy; for instance, uniforms the color of trees and dirt *The soldiers wore* camouflage *on their helmets.* Synonyms: **disguise** (v) to deceive by means of camouflage *They have* camouflaged *the missile silo in order to deceive enemy bombers.* Synonyms: **disguise, obscure, cloud, hide**

WORD	DEFINITION, CONTEXT, SYNONYMS
CANDOR	frankness and sincerity; fairness *The* candor *of his confession impressed his parents, and they gave him a light punishment as a result.* Synonyms: **honesty, sincerity**
CANINE	relating to dogs Canine *relates to dogs in the same way as feline relates to cats.*
CANTANKEROUS	quarrelsome and grouchy *The old grouch was always in a* cantankerous *mood.* Synonyms: **grouchy, argumentative, ill-tempered**
CAPRICE	sudden, unpredictable change *With the* caprice *of an irrational man, he often went from rage to laughter.* Synonyms: **impulse, whim, fancy**
CASCADE	(n) waterfall, as in a type of fireworks resembling a waterfall Synonyms: **waterfall, torrent** (v) to fall like a cascade *The stream flowed over the cliff and* cascaded *down into the valley below.*
CATASTROPHE	disastrous event *The eruption was truly a* catastrophe; *lava and ash buried several towns on the slopes of the volcano.* Synonyms: **disaster, ruin, devastation**
CELESTIAL	relating to the heavens *Venus is a* celestial *body sometimes visible form Earth.* Synonyms: **heavenly, divine, spiritual**
CENSOR	to remove material from books, plays, magazines, etc. for moral, political, or religious reasons *After they* censored *the "dirty" parts out of the book, all that was left was the dedication and half of the cover.* Synonyms: **suppress, delete**
CHASM	gorge or deep canyon *If you look down from the top floor of a New York City skyscraper, it seems as though you're looking into a deep* chasm. Synonyms: **ravine, canyon, abyss**
CHOLERIC	bad-tempered *The grumpy old man was* choleric *whenever he didn't get his morning coffee.* Synonyms: **bad-tempered**

WORD	DEFINITION, CONTEXT, SYNONYMS
CHOREOGRAPHER	person creating and arranging dances for stage performances *After being an innovative dancer, Martha Graham became a* choreographer *and arranged many innovative dance performances for her company.*
CHORUS	group acting together *The* chorus *of over fifty people harmonized as one.* Synonyms: **group, band**
CHRONIC	continuing over a long period of time, long-standing *Joshua suffered from* chronic *tiredness; most days he slept straight through geometry class.* Synonyms: **continuous, constant, persistent, confirmed, settled**
CIRCUMSCRIBE	to encircle with a line; to limit in any way *The Howards' country estate is* circumscribed *by rolling hills.* Synonyms: **limit, outline, bound, define, encompass**
COLLISION	crash, clash, or conflict *The* collision *of the two cars made a terrible sound and tied up traffic for hours.* Synonyms: **crash, clash, impact**
COMMUNICATIVE	talkative and likely to communicate Synonyms: **talkative, articulate, vocal, expressive**
COMPASSION	deep feeling of pity or sympathy for others *The jury decided that the cold-hearted killer felt no* compassion *for his victims.* Synonyms: **pity, sympathy, mercy**
COMPEL	to force someone or something to act *Chinese water-torture couldn't* compel *the spy to reveal his secrets.* Synonyms: **force, coerce, goad, motivate**
COMPETENT	having enough skill for some purpose; adequate but not exceptional *He was not the most qualified candidate, but at least he was* competent. Synonyms: **qualified, capable, fit**
CONCISE	brief and compact *Barry gave a* concise *speech: he said everything he needed to and was finished in five minutes.* Synonyms: **brief, terse, succinct, compact**

WORD	DEFINITION, CONTEXT, SYNONYMS
CONDONE	to pardon, to forgive, or overlook *"We cannot* condone *your behavior," said Ben's parents after he missed his curfew. "You are grounded for two weeks."* Synonyms: **pardon, excuse, forgive, absolve, overlook, accept, tolerate, allow, permit, suffer, endure, bear, stomach**
CONFIDENTIAL	done secretly or in confidence *The* confidential *memorandum listed everyone's salary.* Synonyms: **secret, covert, off-the-record**
CONSTRICT	to squeeze, make tighter *As my chest became* constricted, *I found it difficult to breathe.* Synonyms: **choke, stifle, contract, smother**
CONTEMPLATION	thoughtful observation *When the philosopher studied complicated issues, he often became so lost in* contemplation *that he forget to eat or sleep.* Synonyms: **thought, deliberation, meditation, reflection**
CONTEND	to fight or struggle against; to debate *Some people* contend *that no boxer past or present would have been able to contend with Muhammad Ali for boxing's World Heavyweight Championship.* Synonyms: **combat, compete; argue, assert**
CONTENTIOUS	eager to quarrel *The* contentious *gentleman in the bar angrily ridiculed whatever anyone said* Synonyms: **quarrelsome, cantankerous, feisty, combative, irascible, pugnacious**
CONVENE	to assemble or meet *The members of the board* convene *at least once a week.* Synonyms: **gather, assemble, meet**
CONVENTIONAL	established or approved by general usage Conventional *wisdom today says that a good job requires a college education.* Synonyms: **customary, well-established, habitual**
COPIOUS	abundant, large in number or quantity, plentiful *The hostess had prepared* copious *amounts of food.* Synonyms: **abundant, plentiful, profuse**

WORD	DEFINITION, CONTEXT, SYNONYMS
COUNTENANCE	(n) face or facial expression, or the general appearance or behavior of something or someone *Jeremy felt quite unsettled about the new Music Appreciation instructor; she seemed to have such an evil* countenance. Synonyms: **face, aspect, appearance, bearing, demeanor, air, visage** (v) to approve or support *When Dorothy and Irene started their nightly pillow fight, the babysitter warned them, "I will not* countenance *such behavior."* Synonyms: **sanction, approve, endorse, bless, favor, encourage, condone**
COUPLET	unit of poetry with two rhyming lines *Rub a dub, dub/Three men in a tub is an example of a* couplet.
COURIER	person who carries messages, news, or information *The* courier *will deliver the document.* Synonyms: **messenger, runner, carrier**
CUE	hint or guiding suggestion *My mother cleared her throat loudly, which was my* cue *to be quiet and let her speak.* Synonyms: **hint, prompt, signal**
CURVATURE	state of being curved *Someone with* curvature *of the spine usually doesn't stand up straight.* Synonyms: **arc, arch. bow**
DAWDLE	to waste time with idle lingering *If you* dawdle *on your way to school, you'll be late.* Synonyms: **delay, linger, dally**
DEADLOCK	standoff caused by opposition of two conflicting forces *Despite days of debate, the legislature remained* deadlocked *at 50 votes "yea" and 50 votes "nay."* Synonyms: **stalemate, standoff, standstill**
DEARTH	scarcity, lack *The* dearth *of supplies in our city made it difficult to hold out for long against the attack of the aliens.* Synonyms: **shortage, lack, scarcity**
DEBRIS	charred or spoiled remains of something that has been destroyed *Scavengers searched for valuables amid the* debris. Synonyms: **trash, rubbish, wreckage, remains**

WORD	DEFINITION, CONTEXT, SYNONYMS
DECADE	period of ten years *The 60's are known as the* decade *of protest.* Synonyms: **ten years**
DECEIT	deception or tricky falseness *Morgan Le Fay, the sorceress, used spells and* deceit *to lure Merlin away from Camelot.* Synonyms: **dishonesty, fraudulence, deception, trickery**
DECEIVE	to delude or mislead *A liar often will try to* deceive *you by not telling the truth.* Synonyms: **mislead, delude, trick, dupe, lie**
DECLAMATION	exercise in speech-giving; attack or protest *The candidate made a* declamation *against the new tax law.* Synonyms: **long speech, harangue**
DEFICIENT	defective, insufficient, or inadequate *Failing to study will make you* deficient *in your readiness for the test.* Synonyms: **inadequate, defective, insufficient, failing, lacking**
DEHYDRATE	to remove water from *Too much time in the sun will* dehydrate *you.* Synonyms: **remove water from, dry out, parch**
DEJECT	to depress or make sad *He was too ambitious to become* dejected *by a temporary setback.* Synonyms: **sadden, depress, discourage, dishearten**
DELUDE	to deceive, to mislead *After three hours of pouring rain, we stopped* deluding *ourselves that the picnic could go on.* Synonyms: **deceive, dupe, hoax, trick**
DELUGE	(n) flood, large overflowing of water. Or too much of anything *The president's veto of the housing bill brought a* deluge *of angry calls and letters from people all over America.* Synonyms: **flood, overflow, inundation, torrent** (v) to overflow, to inundate, to flood *The actor was* deluged *with fan mail.* Synonyms: **inundate, engulf, flood, overwhelm**

WORD	DEFINITION, CONTEXT, SYNONYMS
DEMOTE	to reduce to a lower grade or class *The army will* demote *any soldier who disobeys orders.* Synonyms: **downgrade**
DEPLORE	to regard as deeply regrettable and hateful *"I simply* deplore *your table manners," she told him, as he stuck his head into the bowl to lick the last of the oatmeal.* Synonyms: **regret, lament, bemoan, bewail, mourn, grieve for, denounce, condemn, protest, oppose, despise, loathe, abominate**
DESOLATION	condition of being deserted and destroyed *The terrible flood, which destroyed all the buildings and caused everyone to flee, left only* desolation *in its path.* Synonyms: **barrenness, desertion, bleakness**
DESPICABLE	deserving contempt *Stealing from poor people is* despicable. *In fact, stealing from anyone is* despicable. Synonyms: **hateful, contemptible, base, mean, vile, detestable, depraved**
DESPONDENT	in a state of depression *Mrs. Baker was* despondent *after her husband's death.* Synonyms: **depressed, morose, gloomy, sad, brooding, desolate, forlorn, woeful, mournful, dejected**
DESTITUTE	bereft (of something), without or left without (something); poor Destitute *of friends, Charlotte wandered the streets alone. "I have no money," Jerome said; "I am* destitute." Synonyms: **bereft, devoid, lacking; poor, impoverished**
DEVASTATE	to lay waste, make desolate; to overwhelm *News of the death of his beloved wife will* devastate *him.* Synonyms: **ruin, wreck**
DEVOTEE	someone passionately devoted *The opera* devotee *didn't mind standing on line for hours to get a ticket.* Synonym: **enthusiast, fan, admirer**
DEVOUT	deeply religious *Priests and nuns are known to be* devout *people.* Synonyms: **pious, religious, reverent**

WORD	DEFINITION, CONTEXT, SYNONYMS
DEXTERITY	skill in using the hands or body, agility; cleverness *The gymnast who won the contest demonstrated the highest level of* dexterity *of all the competitors. She was the only one who didn't fall off the balance beam.* Synonyms: **skill, agility**
DIMINISH	to become or to make smaller in size, number, or degree *He was once such a beautiful actor, but now his beauty has greatly* diminished! *As has his bank account.* Synonyms: **decrease, lessen, dwindle, shrink, contract, decline, subside, wane, fade, recede, weaken, moderate**
DIN	loud, confused noise *The* din *in the cafeteria made conversation difficult.* Synonyms: **noise, uproar, clamor**
DINGY	dark or drab in color; dirty, shabby, squalid *He lived alone in a depressing,* dingy *apartment.* Synonyms: **dirty, filthy, shabby, dark**
DIPLOMATIC	tactful; skilled in the art of conducting negotiations and other relations between nations *Our host had a very* diplomatic *nature which enabled her to bring together people who disagreed strongly on many points.* Synonyms: **polite, tactful**
DISCLAIM	to deny ownership of or association with *Francine's statement was so silly that she later* disclaimed *it, pretending that it had been made by someone who looked exactly like her.* Synonyms: **repudiate, reject, disown, disavow, renounce**
DISCURSIVE	covering a wide area or digressing from a topic *The professor, who was known for his* discursive *speaking style, covered everything from armadillos to zebras in his zoology lecture.* Synonyms: **digressive, rambling**
DISMAL	causing gloom; cheerless *Our team made a* dismal *showing in the play-offs; we lost every game.* Synonyms: **miserable, dreary**
DISPUTE	(n) argument or quarrel *The* dispute *between the United States and the Soviet Union arose in part as a result of disagreement over the occupation of Berlin.* (v) to argue or quarrel. Synonyms: **argue, disagree with**

WORD	DEFINITION, CONTEXT, SYNONYMS
DISSEMINATE	to scatter or spread widely *The news wire service* disseminates *information rapidly, so that events get reported all over the world shortly after they happen.* Synonyms: **spread (an idea or a message), broadcast, disperse**
DIVERT	(1) to change the course of *Emergency crews tried to* divert *the flood waters by building a wall of sandbags across the road.* Synonyms: **deflect, reroute, turn, detour** (2) to draw someone's attention by amusing them. *While their mother napped, Dad* diverted *the twins by playing hide and seek.* Synonyms: **amuse, entertain, distract**
DOFF	to remove or take off, as clothing *Baseball players usually* doff *their hats during the National Anthem.* Synonyms: **take a piece of clothing off**
DOGGED	persistent in effort; stubbornly tenacious *He worked steadily with a* dogged *determination to finish the difficult task.* Synonyms: **stubborn (as a bulldog), obstinate**
DOGMATIC	asserting without proof; stating opinion as if it were fact in a definite and forceful manner *The* dogmatic *professor would not listen to the students' views; she did not allow debate in class.* Synonyms: **absolute, opinionated, dictatorial, authoritative, arrogant**
DOZE	to nap or sleep lightly *I was so tired from working all night that I kept* dozing *off during the next day.* Synonyms: **nap, sleep**
DUNGEON	underground room in fortress often used to keep prisoners *Henry VIII ordered that Anne Boleyn be kept in the* dungeon *of the Tower of London until she was beheaded.* Synonyms: **vault, cellar**
EBULLIENT	overflowing with fervor, enthusiasm, or excitement; high-spirited *The* ebullient *child exhausted the baby-sitter, who lacked the energy needed to keep up with her.* Synonyms: **bubbling, enthusiastic, exuberant**

WORD	DEFINITION, CONTEXT, SYNONYMS
ECCENTRIC	(n) person who differs from the accepted norms in an odd way *The old* eccentric *was given to burning hundred-dollar bills.* Synonyms: **freak, oddball, weirdo, nonconformist** (adj) *deviating from accepted conduct.* *Her* eccentric *behavior began to worry her close friends.* Synonyms: **odd, unorthodox, unconventional, offbeat**
ECSTATIC	deliriously overjoyed *Mortimer was* ecstatic *when he learned of his 1600 SAT scores.* Synonyms: **delighted, overjoyed, euphoric**
EDDY	small whirlpool or any similar current Eddies *can be in the air or water. When water gets pulled down a drain, it forms a small whirlpool, or an* eddy. Synonyms: **swirling water, whirlpool**
EFFECT	(n) result, impression *The* effect *of the new policy will not be known for some time, as it often takes several years for new programs to have a noticeable impact.* Synonyms: **result, impression** (v) *to produce, make or bring about* *We are willing to make any sacrifice in order to* effect *lasting change for the better.* Synonyms: **produce, cause, bring about**
ELUSIVE	hard to find or express *The* elusive *nature of the platypus makes it difficult to sight platypus in the wild. Their ugliness makes it unpleasant.* Synonyms: **hard to catch; slippery, evasive**
EMBELLISH	to add detail, make more complicated *Sanjev's short story is too short: it needs to be* embellished *with more details about life among penguins.* Synonyms: **elaborate, expand, ornament**
EMINENT	distinguished, high in rank or station *They were amazed that such an* eminent *scholar could have made such an obvious error.* Synonyms: **prominent, well-known, famous, distinguished, noteworthy**
EMULATE	to imitate or copy *Hundreds of writers have* emulated *Stephen King, but the result is usually a poor imitation.* Synonyms: **imitate, simulate, copy, follow**

WORD	DEFINITION, CONTEXT, SYNONYMS
ENACT	to make into law *The government wishes to* enact *the new law in January.* Synonyms: **pass** (a law), **decree; act out**
ENCOMPASS	to form a circle or a ring around *In New York City, Manhattan is an island so it is completely* encompassed *by water.* Synonyms: **encircle, circumscribe**
ENDORSE	to approve, sustain, support *The principal refused to* endorse *the plan to put a video arcade in the cafeteria.* Synonyms: **accept, approve, authorize, accredit, encourage, advocate, favor, support**
ENIGMA	mystery or riddle *The source of the mysterious hole remained an* enigma. Synonyms: **mystery, riddle, puzzle**
ENIGMATIC	unexplainable, mysterious *The students found the new history teacher to be* enigmatic; *none of them could figure out what he was thinking.* Synonyms: **mysterious, unexplainable, inexplicable, incomprehensible, strange, puzzling, baffling, bewildering, perplexing, cryptic**
ENSNARE	to capture in, or involve, as in a snare *The investigators managed to* ensnare *the corrupt official when they offered him a bribe that he accepted.* Synonyms: **trap**
ENTICE	to lure or attract by feeding desires *Millions of dollars couldn't* entice *Michael Jordan to play basketball in Europe.* Synonyms: **tempt, lure, attract**
ENTOURAGE	group of followers, attendants or assistants *The movie star was always followed around by an* entourage *of flunkies and assistants.* Synonyms: **group, retinue, coterie**
ERA	period of time *The invention of the atomic bomb marked the beginning of a new* era *in warfare.* Synonyms: **period of time, age, epoch**

WORD	DEFINITION, CONTEXT, SYNONYMS
ERR	to make a mistake (as in error) *To err is human; we have all made mistakes.* Synonyms: **make a mistake or error; go wrong, sin**
ERUDITE	knowledgeable and learned *We were not surprised to read the praises of Mario's history of ancient Greece, for we had expected an* erudite *work from him.* Synonyms: **wise, learned, knowledgeable, informed**
ESSENTIAL	of the innermost nature of something; basic, fundamental; of great importance *Eating vegetables is* essential *to your well-being.* Synonyms: **basic, central, fundamental, important, crucial, necessary, urgent**
ETIQUETTE	code of social behavior *Some people think that* etiquette *forbids eating with your elbows on the table.* Synonyms: **manners, propriety, decorum**
EVACUATE	to empty out, remove, or withdraw *The National Guard had to* evacuate *thousands of people following the catastrophe.* Synonyms: **expel, empty, vacate, remove**
EXOTIC	of foreign origin or character: strange, exciting *The atmosphere of the restaurant was* exotic, *but the food was pedestrian.* Synonyms: **foreign, alien, unfamiliar**
EXPAND	to make greater, broader, larger, or more detailed *Friedrich now sells only scary plastic fangs, but he plans to* expand *his business to include rubber vampire bats with glowing eyes.* Synonyms: **enlarge, increase, augment, extend, broaden, widen, stretch, spread, swell, inflate, dilate, bloat**
EXPUNGE	to delete or omit completely *The censor wanted to* expunge *all parts of Joyce's Ulysses he thought were obscene.* Synonyms: **erase, obliterate, strike out**
EXTRACTION	process of removal or something removed *My toothache meant I had to undergo the* extraction *of my wisdom teeth.* Synonyms: **removal**

WORD	DEFINITION, CONTEXT, SYNONYMS
EXTRICATE	to release from difficulty or an entanglement *The fly was unable to* extricate *itself from the flypaper.* Synonyms: **disengage, release, withdraw**
EXTROVERTED	outgoing or interested in people *An* extrovert *wouldn't think twice about going to a party of strangers.* Synonyms: **outgoing, gregarious**
FANATIC	someone with excessive enthusiasm, especially in politics or religion *Unable to listen to differing opinions, the* fanatic *politician screamed at his opponent and ran out of the debate.* Synonyms: **zealous**
FATAL	causing, or capable of causing, death or ruin *The racer driver suffered a* fatal *accident when his car hit a patch of oil on the roadway.* Synonyms: **lethal, deadly, killing, mortal, malignant**
FATIGUE	(v) to exhaust the strength of *The energetic baby* fatigued *me.* Synonyms: **tire out, weary, enervate** (n) weariness, tiredness from exertion *The recruits suffered from* fatigue *after the twenty-mile march.* Synonyms: **exhaustion, weariness**
FAUNA	animals of a given area *Darwin studied the* fauna *of the Galapagos Islands.* Synonyms: **animals, creatures, beasts**
FELICITY	happiness, bliss *She was so good, she deserved nothing but* felicity *her whole life.* Synonyms: **happiness, contentment, bliss**
FEROCIOUS	savage and fierce Ferocious *Arctic wolves will hunt and kill much larger animals in pursuit of food.* Synonyms: **fierce**
FERVENT	showing great warmth, intensity, feeling, enthusiasm; hot, burning, glowing *I am a* fervent *admirer of that author's works; I think she is a genius.* Synonyms: **warm, eager, enthusiastic**
FICKLE	easily changeable, especially in emotions *My uncle is a very* fidile *bachelor who dates someone new every week.* Synonyms: **inconstant**

WORD	DEFINITION, CONTEXT, SYNONYMS
FIDELITY	faithfulness to duties; truthfulness *A traitor is someone whose* fidelity *is questioned.* Synonyms: **loyalty, allegiance, faithfulness, devotion, truthfulness, accuracy**
FINALE	the final part of some entertainment, often music *The* finale *of the 1812 Overture is often accompanied by fireworks.* Synonyms: **end, finish, conclusion, wind-up**
FLAGRANT	outrageously glaring, noticeable or evident; notorious, scandalous *His* flagrant *disregard for the rules has resulted in his dismissal from the job.* Synonyms: **obvious, glaring**
FLIPPANT	not serious, playful; irreverent *John was* flippant *to the teacher, so she sent him to the principal's office* Synonyms: **frivolous, flip, playful**
FLOW	to move along in a stream or like a stream; to proceed continuously (As in a computer flowchart, which shows how a program flows.) *People* flowed *out of the crowded department store through the main doors.* Synonyms: **run, stream** (like water)
FORETELL	to predict the future *Some prophets claim to* foretell *the future.* Synonyms: **forecast, prophesy, auger**
FORMIDABLE	able to inspire awe or wonder because of outstanding power, size, etc *The steep face of rock we were directed to climb was indeed* formidable. Synonyms: **impressive, awe-inspiring, impregnable, invincible**
FOUNDATION	basis or groundwork of anything: whether a building or idea *The claim that the sun revolves around the earth has no* foundation, *because scientific evidence disproves this claim.* Synonyms: **bottom, groundwork, basis**
FRAGILE	easily broken, or damaged *The Ming dynasty porcelain vase was* fragile *and needed to be handled carefully* Synonyms: **breakable, frail, brittle, delicate**

WORD	DEFINITION, CONTEXT, SYNONYMS
FREQUENT	(adj) happening or occurring at short intervals *He travels so much he's a member of five* frequent *flyer plans.* Synonyms: **repeated, regular, habitual, common** (v) to visit often *My friend loves antique-hunting and* frequents *the local antique shops.*
FUTILE	ineffective, useless: unimportant *Our attempt to reach the shore before the storm was* futile; *the wind blew us back into the middle of the lake.* Synonyms: **useless, hopeless, pointless**
GARRULOUS	talkative and likely to chatter *My* garrulous *friend often talks on the telephone for hours at a time.* Synonyms: **talkative, loquacious**
GERMINATE	to bud or sprout *Three weeks after planting, the seeds will* germinate. Synonyms: **sprout, grow**
GLEE	joy, pleasure, happiness *The child was filled with* glee *at the sight of so many presents.* Synonyms: **joy, elation**
GLIB	able to speak profusely; having a ready flow of words. It often implies <u>lying</u> or <u>deceit</u> *The politician was a* glib *speaker.* Synonyms: **flip, fluent, verbose, smooth, smug**
GREGARIOUS	fond of company *For the* gregarious *person, dormitory life is a pleasure.* Synonyms: **sociable, companionable, amiable, convivial**
GROTESQUE	odd or unnatural in some way *The minotaur is a* grotesque *creature out of mythology: part man and part bull.* Synonyms: **bizarre, outlandish, ugly**
GROVEL	to humble oneself, to beg *The dog* groveled *at his owner's feet.* Synonyms: **crawl, beg**
GRUESOME	grisly, horrible *The horror film was filled with* gruesome *scenes.* Synonyms: **frightful, shocking, ghastly**
HALLOWED	regarded as holy; sacred *The Constitution is a* hallowed *document in the United States.* Synonyms: **holy, sacred**

WORD	DEFINITION, CONTEXT, SYNONYMS
HARBINGER	omen, precursor, forerunner *The groundhog's appearance on February 2 is a* harbinger *of spring.* Synonyms: **precursor, forerunner, omen, messenger**
HARSH	stern or cruel; physically uncomfortable; unpleasant to the ear Harsh *words were exchanged during their argument. They barely survived the* harsh *winter nights.* Synonyms: **rough, strict, severe**
HASTY	done quickly (often too quickly); rushed, sloppy *Henry was too* hasty *in completing his research paper, and forgot to put his name on it.* Synonyms: **rushed, sloppy, shoddy, careless**
HEED	(n) careful attention, notice, observation *Pay* heed *to his warnings about that place; he's been there enough times to know the dangers.* (v) to listen to and obey Synonyms: **listen to, obey**
HERBIVOROUS	feeding on plants *A cow is a* herbivorous *animal.* Synonyms: **plant-eating**
HETEROGENEOUS	not uniform; made up of different parts that remain separate. (Its opposite is homogeneous) *The United Nations is a* heterogeneous *body.* Synonyms: **mixed, unlike, diverse, dissimilar, various**
HEXAGON	polygon having six sides *A* hexagon *has six sides and an octagon has eight.*
HIBERNATE	to spend the winter in a sleep-like, dormant state *During winter, bears* hibernate *in caves.* Synonyms: **sleep**
HIVE	structure where bees live *My friend, Les, is so interested in bees that he'll watch them going into and out of one of their* hives *for hours.*
HORRID	something that causes horror, or is at least pretty bad *The weather has been just* horrid; *we've had three storms in a week.* Synonyms: **dreadful, horrible, shocking**
HOVEL	small, miserable shack. *In Charles Dickens's novels poor people often live in terrible, dirty* hovels. Synonyms: **shack, shanty**

WORD	DEFINITION, CONTEXT, SYNONYMS
HUMID	moist or damp *It is so humid in the jungle that it is advisable to wear light, loose clothing.* Synonyms: **moist, damp, sultry**
IGNITE	(literally) to set on fire; (figuratively) to stir emotionally, (light a fire under someone) *If you ignite that match, you might burn the whole house down.* *Through his speaking ability, the speaker was able to ignite the people who attended his speeches.* Synonyms: **light, kindle, inflame; rouse, excite, agitate, stir, provoke, prod, inspire**
ILLITERACY	inability to read and write *If everyone learned how to read and write, illiteracy wouldn't be a problem.*
IMMACULATE	spotless; free from error *After I cleaned my apartment for hours, it was finally immaculate.* Synonyms: **errorless, faultless; unblemished, impeccable**
IMMINENT	about to happen, on the verge of occurring *Joan was becoming nervous about her imminent wedding.* Synonyms: **impending, approaching, near**
IMMORTAL	never-dying *Someone who never grows old and never dies is immortal.* Synonyms: **undying, eternal**
IMPASSE	road having no exit or a dilemma with no solution *A rock slide produced an impasse so we could proceed no further on the road.* Synonyms: **deadlock, standoff, stalemate, standstill**
IMPERVIOUS	incapable of being penetrated; unable to be influenced *Superman was impervious to bullets.* Synonyms: **impenetrable**
IMPIOUS	lacking piety or respect for religion Synonyms: **irreverent, sacrilegious**
IMPLY	to suggest without stating directly *Although Jane did not state that she loved Mr. Rochester, it was clearly implied in her look.* Synonyms: **hint, suggest, intimate**

WORD	DEFINITION, CONTEXT, SYNONYMS
INADVERTENT	unintentional *I wrote my paper in such a hurry that I made many* inadvertent *errors.* Synonyms: **accidental, unintentional**
INCENTIVE	motivation or drive to do a particular task or to go in a given direction *His father's encouragement gave him the* incentive *to try again.* Synonyms: **motive, inducement, stimulus**
INCREDULOUS	not believing *I was* incredulous *about Ismael's wild fishing story about 'the one that got away.'* Synonyms: **skeptical, disbelieving**
INDICATE	to point out or make known with a good degree of certainty *Recent polls* indicate *that the Democrats will probably be victorious.* Synonyms: **disclose, show, reveal, imply, signify**
INERT	having no power to move or act; resisting motion or action *In the heat of the desert afternoon, lizards are* inert. Synonyms: **sluggish, passive, inactive, dormant, lethargic, lifeless**
INFECTIOUS	able to be passed from one person to another (such as an infection); contagious *Her laughter was* infectious, *and soon we were all laughing.* Synonyms: **catching, contagious**
INGENIOUS	possessing or displaying great creativity and resourcefulness *Luther found an* ingenious *way to solve the math problem.* Synonyms: **brilliant, inspired, imaginative, shrewd, crafty, cunning, resourceful**
INGENUITY	inventive skill or cleverness *Use your* ingenuity *to come up with a new solution to the problem.* Synonyms: **creativity, cleverness, inventiveness**
INHABIT	to reside or live in *Arboreal creatures, such as monkeys,* inhabit *the trees.* Synonyms: **live, occupy, reside, dwell, stay**
INNATE	present at birth *The plan was doomed from the start; there was an* innate *problem in it.* Synonyms: **natural, inborn, inherent, instinctive**

WORD	DEFINITION, CONTEXT, SYNONYMS
INNOCENT	pure, not guilty, someone with the simplicity of a baby *Those accused of practicing witchcraft in Salem were clearly* innocent *of any such act.* Synonyms: **pure, harmless, guiltless, naïve, chaste**
INSINUATION	devious hint or sly suggestion made to cause suspicion or doubts *During the last election, the* insinuation *that the Congressman had taken kickbacks cost him thousands of votes.* Synonyms: **hint, suggestion, reference, implication**
INSOMNIA	inability to fall sleep *No matter how tired I am, I continue to suffer from* insomnia. Synonyms: **sleeplessness**
INSURGENT	(n) rebel, (adj) rising in revolt, starting a revolution *The* insurgent *crew staged a mutiny and threw the captain overboard.* Synonyms: **rebellious**
IRATE	full of anger, wrathful, incensed *He was* irate *at being wrongly accused of the crime.* Synonyms: **angry, indignant, infuriated, enraged**
JEER	to mock in an abusive way; taunting remark *As the foolish political candidate stumbled through his poorly written speech, the crowd began to* jeer. Synonyms: **ridicule, mock, scoff; gibe, taunt**
JUBILANT	feeling joy or happiness *We were* jubilant *after our victory in the state championships.* Synonyms: **very happy, exultant, gleeful, joyful, ecstatic**
JUDICIOUS	having wise judgment *The wise and distinguished judge was well-known for having a* judicious *temperament.* Synonyms: **wise, sage, sagacious**
KINETIC	relating to motion *A* kinetic *sculpture is one that moves.* Synonyms: **animated, energetic, spirited, moving**
LAGOON	shallow body of water connected to a much larger one, as a lake or sea *The pirates anchored their ship offshore and rowed into the* lagoon, *where they went ashore.* Synonyms: **inlet, pool**

WORD	DEFINITION, CONTEXT, SYNONYMS
LENIENT	merciful, not strict *When the Commissioner only fined the pitcher fifty dollars for throwing a baseball at a batter, many fans thought the punishment was too lenient.* Synonyms: **merciful, indulgent**
LETHARGY	drowsiness, tiredness, inability to do anything much *A feeling of* lethargy *came over me, and I wanted nothing more than a nice long nap.* Synonyms: **sluggishness, fatigue**
LIMBER	bending and moving easily *The gymnast warmed up for thirty minutes so that she would be* limber *before her routine.* Synonyms: **agile, supple**
LUNGE	(n) sudden forward movement, plunge (v) to thrust something forward *The toboggan* lunged *forward at the point where the slope became quite steep.* Synonyms: **thrust, plunge**
MAGNANIMOUS	having a great or noble spirit, acting generously, patiently, or kindly *Although at first he seemed cold, Uncle Frank turned out to be a very* magnanimous *fellow.* Synonyms: **big-hearted, generous, noble, princely, forgiving, patient, tolerant, indulgent, ungrudging, unresentful**
MALFUNCTION	to fail to function; an instance of failing to function *The* malfunction *of the main booster rocket meant that the space capsule wasn't launched on schedule.* Synonyms: **failure**
MALLEABLE	can be molded or shaped *Gold is so* malleable *that it can be beaten into a thin foil.* Synonyms: **soft, flexible, yielding**
MAR	to damage something and make it imperfect *Telephone poles* mar *the beauty of the countryside.* Synonyms: **deform, impair, spoil, disfigure, damage**

WORD	DEFINITION, CONTEXT, SYNONYMS
MARVEL	(n) amazing thing; something astonishing or marvelous *It was a* marvel *that they survived the crash.* Synonyms: **miracle, prodigy, wonder** (v) to be surprised or full of wonder *I* marvel *at your ability to remain calm.* Synonyms: **wonder**
MEAGER	very small or insufficient *He rented an expensive apartment and dined at fine restaurants, but he earned a* meager *wage and soon ran out of money.* Synonyms: **slight, trifling, skimpy, puny, scant, inadequate, insufficient, insubstantial**
MEEK	humble and submissive *People who are too* meek *won't stand up for themselves.* Synonyms: **passive, unassertive, docile, compliant**
MELANCHOLY	very sad or depressing *The rainy weather made James feel* melancholy. Synonyms: **gloomy, mournful, somber**
METEOROLOGIST	scientist dealing with weather and weather conditions *Although the* meteorologist *predicted a heat wave, the temperature remained below freezing.*
MIMIC	imitate, copy not always in a complimentary way *Mary got in trouble for* mimicking *the teacher.* Synonyms: **mock, impersonate, simulate, counterfeit**
MINUSCULE	tiny, miniature *Dave needed a magnifying glass to read the* minuscule *print on the lease.* Synonyms: **microscopic, minute**
MISBEGOTTEN	poorly conceived, poorly planned, based on false assumptions or false reasoning *It came as no surprise when Fred's* misbegotten *scheme proved an utter failure.* Synonyms: **illegitimate, ill-conceived**
MOURN	feel sad for, regret *The family gathered to* mourn *for the dead.* Synonyms: **lament, grieve**

WORD	DEFINITION, CONTEXT, SYNONYMS
MURKY	dark, dim *Jill groped her way down the* murky *hallway.* Synonyms: **obscure, gloomy**
NAUSEOUS	sickening, makes you feel sick, or turns your stomach *The cook mixed skim milk with green eels, and produced a concoction that was truly* nauseous. Synonyms: **revolting, disgusting, nauseating**
NEBULOUS	hazy, not well-defined *During the campaign, the candidate promised to fight crime. But when reporters asked for details, his plan was* nebulous—*he could not say whether he would hire more police or support longer jail sentences.* Synonyms: **hazy, cloudy, ill-defined, unclear, shapeless, vague, unspecific**
NIMBLE	quick and agile in movement or thought *A* nimble *athlete is a well-coordinated one.* Synonyms: **agile, active, quick, clever, cunning**
NOMAD	someone who has no permanent home and wanders *The Berbers are a tribe of* nomads *who travel from place to place searching for grassland for their herds.* Synonyms: **wanderer, vagrant**
NOTIFY	to tell, let know, give notice *The landlord failed to* notify *the tenants of the planned demolition of the building.* Synonyms: **tell, inform, apprise**
OBESE	very fat *Some* obese *people suffer from anxiety-induced overeating.* Synonyms: **fat, corpulent, portly**
OBNOXIOUS	offensive and very disagreeable *The last time I went to the movies, an* obnoxious *person sitting beside me talked loudly during the entire movie.* Synonyms: **offensive, repugnant, repellant**
OBSCURE	(v) to hide or make difficult to find (adj) *hard to see; unknown, uncertain* *The speaker's style was so confusing that it* obscured *his main point rather than clarified it.* Synonyms: **confuse, becloud; vague, unclear, dubious**

WORD	DEFINITION, CONTEXT, SYNONYMS
OBSERVATION	(1) examination *Close observation of Arnold led Anne to believe that he was hiding something.* Synonyms: **attention, watching** (2) remark, comment *Damon amused the class with his witty observation about the teacher's methods.* Synonyms: **pronouncement, opinion**
OBSOLETE	no longer in use; discarded or outmoded *It's as obsolete as black-and-white television.* Synonyms: **outdated, passé, old-fashioned**
OBSTINATE	stubborn *Hal's mother tried to get him to eat his spinach, but he remained obstinate.* Synonyms: **mulish, dogged**
OBSTRUCT	to get in the way of; to block; to hamper *He removed his hat so as not to obstruct another's view of the stage.* Synonyms: **block, check, clog, impede**
OBTUSE	not acute; someone who is not smart; thick, dull *Alfred was too obtuse to realize that the sum of the angles of a triangle is 180 degrees.* Synonyms: **slow, stupid**
OLFACTORY	relating to the sense of smell *In human beings, olfactory sensations are perceived with the nose.*
OMINOUS	threatening, menacing, having the character of an evil omen *The sky filled with ominous dark clouds before the storm.* Synonyms: **foreboding**
OPPORTUNE	appropriate to time or circumstances: timely, lucky *Dalbert's investment in plastics, made just before the demand for plastics began to rise, was opportune.* Synonyms: **timely, appropriate, lucky**
OPTION	choice, selection, preference *Donna carefully considered every option before making her final decision.* Synonyms: **alternative, election**

540 OF LEARNING RESOURCES

WORD	DEFINITION, CONTEXT, SYNONYMS
ORBIT	to move around some object, as a planet; to circle *The moon* orbits *the earth, which in turn* orbits *the sun.* Synonyms: **circle, revolve, circuit** (n) the actual route the thing takes when it goes around the other thing, as in the orbit of the moon around the earth *The German shepherd dog approached the intruder cautiously, circled him and sniffed, made two more* orbits, *and then walked away.* Synonyms: **circuit, revolution**
ORCHID	purple (as in the flower) *The vice-principal turned* orchid *with rage.* Synonyms: **lavender**
OSTENTATIOUS	pretentious and flashy *Some think Donald Trump's Taj Mahal casino, which he proudly calls the Eighth Wonder of the World, is really an* ostentatious *display of wealth and poor taste.* Synonyms: **conspicuous, flashy, flamboyant, showy**
PALATABLE	good tasting *Her cooking is quite* palatable. Synonyms: **savory, agreeable, appetizing, delicious, acceptable**
PARADOX	contradiction, something that doesn't fit: something that shouldn't be true because it seems to offend common sense, yet is true anyway *The* paradox *of government is that the person who most desires power is the person who least deserves it.* Synonyms: **contradiction**
PASSIVE	not active; someone who lets things happen rather than himself taking action *Ned portrayed himself as the* passive *victim of external forces.* Synonyms: **submissive**
PEDDLE	sell (although usually used in a somewhat bad way. *People* peddle *rags or junk; not Tiffany jewelry or Gucci luggage.)* *Bill got a job going door to door to* peddle *vacuum cleaners.* Synonyms: **hawk, vend**

WORD	DEFINITION, CONTEXT, SYNONYMS
PEDESTRIAN	(adj) common, everyday, usual *The critics called the new restaurant's food* pedestrian; *it never had many customers, and eventually closed.* Synonyms: **plodding, prosaic, commonplace, ordinary, plain, mundane, humdrum, trite, banal, drab, colorless, boring, barren, unimaginative, uninspired, undistinguished, unremarkable, unexceptional** (n) one who does not ride but walks *With the way the taxis speed, it can be dangerous to be a* pedestrian *in New York. Of course, it's dangerous to be in the cab too, which leaves little choice but to stay home in bed.* Synonyms: **walker, hiker, stroller**
PERJURY	making deliberately false statements when under oath *Mr. Mason accused the witness of* perjury. Synonyms: **falsehood, fraud, lies**
PERSEVERE	to continue in some course of action despite setbacks and opposition *Although at first the problems looked difficult, Wendy* persevered, *and found that she could answer almost all of them.* Synonyms: **continue, struggle, endure, persist**
PETRIFY	literally, to turn to stone; figuratively, to paralyze with fear or with surprise *The movie is so frightening that it would* petrify *even the bravest viewer.* Synonyms: **shock, stun, stiffen, paralyze, fossilize**
PIOUS	religiously devout or moral *Saul, a* pious *man, walks, to the synagogue on the Sabbath and prays daily.* Synonyms: **devout, religious, God-fearing, reverent, moral, upstanding, scrupulous**
PLAGIARISM	copying of someone else's work and claiming it as your own *The notable scientist lost his job when his* plagiarism *was revealed; years before, he had copied a research paper from a magazine.* Synonyms: **copying, stealing**

WORD	DEFINITION, CONTEXT, SYNONYMS
PLAUSIBLE	seeming to be true
	Joachim's excuse for lateness to class sounded plausible *at the time, but I later learned that it had been a lie.*
	Synonyms: **credible, believable, likely, probable, conceivable**
POMPOUS	characterized by stiff, unnatural formality
	Gerald began his speech to the class with a pompous *quote from Julius Caesar.*
	Synonyms: **stuffy, stiff, affected, mannered, unnatural, pretentious, self-important, conceited**
PROCRASTINATE	to postpone; to put something off to a later time
	Don't procrastinate; *do your homework now.*
	Synonyms: **delay, postpone, defer**
PROFOUND	deep, wise, serious
	Both the Book of Ecclesiastes and the Tao Te Ching contain profound *observations about human life.*
	Synonyms: **wise, deep, sagacious**
PROLIFIC	producing great amounts; fertile
	Stephen King, a prolific *writer, seems to write new books as fast as they are published.*
	Synonyms: **productive, fertile**
PROPEL	to move, make something go forward
	An ill-timed push on the gas pedal propelled *the car through the plate glass window of the dealership.*
	Synonyms: **compel, project, drive**
PROPHESY	to predict the future using divine guidance
	The ancient Greek oracles at Delphi were supposed to be able to prophesy *the future.*
	Synonyms: **predict. foretell, forecast, auger**
PUNGENT	sharp, flavorful (sometimes too flavorful)
	The soup was so pungent *that it brought tears to Alice's eyes.*
	Synonyms: **peppery, hot, piquant, biting, acrid**
PURSUE	to chase, go after
	The cat pursued *the squirrel up the tree.*
	Synonyms: **trail, tail, dog, follow**

WORD	DEFINITION, CONTEXT, SYNONYMS
QUELL	to quiet something raucous (often a rebellion); crush, defeat, conquer *The dictator dispatched troops to* quell *the rebellion.* Synonyms: **quash, overpower, overcome, quench, suppress**
QUENCH	to satisfy a need or desire *After coming in from the desert, Ezra needed gallons of water to* quench *his thirst.* Synonyms: **satisfy, extinguish, subdue, sate**
RABBLE	large, disorderly, and easily excited mob *The* rabble *waited anxiously below the king's window for news of the tax decree.* Synonyms: **crowd, mob, multitude, horde**
RABID	(literally) afflicted with rabies, a disease of the nervous system that causes convulsions and wildly irrational behavior (figuratively) acting fanatically or madly, as if afflicted by rabies. Rabid *animals can sometimes be identified by saliva dripping from their jaws and by frantic behavior. [Sounds pleasant, doesn't it?]* *The first speaker was calm, but the second—a wild-eyed man advocating the destruction of all tractors—was positively* rabid. Synonyms: **fanatical, mad, crazy, irrational, wild-eyed, maniacal, lunatic, incoherent**
RANCOR	bad feeling, bitterness *Herbert was so filled with* rancor *that he could think of nothing but taking revenge on those who had humiliated him.* Synonyms: **animosity, resentment, hatred, malice, spite**
RANDOM	lacking order, free from order or bias *She conducted a* random *survey of garage mechanics by drawing their names from a hat.* Synonyms: **chance, haphazard, unordered, unbiased**
RANSACK	to search thoroughly and messily *Did the burglars* ransack *your entire house?* Synonyms: **plunder, pillage, search, loot, pilfer, steal**
RATIFY	to approve formally *The Senate* ratified *treaty after only a brief debate.* Synonyms: **confirm, affirm, endorse, approve, sanction**

WORD	DEFINITION, CONTEXT, SYNONYMS
RAVENOUS	(literally) wildly eager to eat; (figuratively) hungry for anything *The homeless man had not had a bite of food in two days and was* ravenous. *The abandoned puppy was* ravenous *for affection and tenderness.* Synonyms: **hungry, famished, voracious, starved**
RAZE	to destroy (a building, city, etc.) utterly *The house had been* razed: *where once it had stood there was nothing but splinters and bricks.* Synonyms: **demolish, destroy, wreck, level, flatten**
RECLUSE	someone who lives far away from other people *Anthony left the city and lived as a* recluse *in the desert.* Synonyms: **hermit, loner**
RECUR	to return; to occur again *The problem is bound to* recur *if you don't solve it now.* Synonyms: **return, repeat**
REEK	(literally) giving off a strong, offensive odor; strong smell *Boy! Something really* reeks *in here. Did you bring a dead skunk with you or something?* Synonyms: **stink** (figuratively) to be pervaded by something unpleasant The city government reeks of corruption.
REFRAIN	to stop or avoid doing something, quit *The librarian insisted that everyone* refrain *from making any noise.* Synonyms: **abstain, cease, desist**
REGAL	royal, splendid *Prince Charles was married with full* regal *ceremony.* Synonyms: **kingly, majestic**
REIGN	rule over, govern, dominate [Pronounced like rain.] *The British monarch used to* reign *over the entire British Empire.* Synonyms: **rule, prevail**
REIMBURSE	to repay someone for their expenses *If you buy me lunch today, I'll* reimburse *you tomorrow.* Synonyms: **repay, compensate**
REINFORCE	strengthen, add to *The purpose of the homework is to* reinforce *what's taught in class.* Synonyms: **support**

WORD	DEFINITION, CONTEXT, SYNONYMS
REMINISCENCE	memory or act of recalling the past *The old timer's* reminiscence *of his childhood was of a time when there were no cars.* Synonyms: **collection, recall, memory, nostalgia**
RENOWNED	well-known, famous, celebrated *Having spent her whole childhood banging on things, Jane grew up to be a* renowned *drummer.* Synonyms: **famed, distinguished, notable**
REPARTEE	witty conversation, retort *As a master of* repartee, *Bob was the hit of every party he attended.* Synonyms: **banter**
REPUDIATE	to reject what one was once associated with *After Grace discovered that her friends had been spreading false rumors about her, she* repudiated *them and made new friends.* Synonyms: **disown, reject, renounce**
REPUGNANT	something gross, repulsive, or revolting *Bill liked his macaroni and cheese with jelly, a combination that many of his friends found* repugnant. Synonyms: **distasteful, objectionable, offensive**
RESIDUE	something that remains after a part is taken *The fire burned everything leaving only a* residue *of ash and charred debris.* Synonyms: **remainder, remnant, leftover**
REVEAL	show, divulge, expose *Wendy cut through the frog's abdominal wall to* reveal *the internal organs.* Synonyms: **unveil, disclose**
REVEL	celebrate noisily, have a party *The whole school got together to* revel *in the football team's victory.* Synonyms: **celebrate, indulge, enjoy**
ROUT	conquer, defeat, and chase off *The renewed onslaught* routed *the enemy.* Synonyms: **overwhelm, overcome, subdue, scatter**

WORD	DEFINITION, CONTEXT, SYNONYMS
SATELLITE	moon, a small thing going around a bigger thing [Well, you try to define it!] *A spy* satellite *can take pictures of the people and things that it passes above as it circles the globe.* Synonyms: **moon**
SATURATE	to fill something to the point where it can hold no more *Reading the entire encyclopedia will* saturate *your mind with facts.* Synonyms: **soak, fill, drench, permeate**
SAUCY	impudent, impertinent, flippant *She always got in trouble with her parents for her* saucy *remarks.* Synonyms: **pert, lively, rude, insolent**
SAVOR	to enjoy something with relish or delight *I* savored *every bite of my father's chocolate cream pie.* Synonyms: **taste, relish, enjoy, appreciate**
SCALD	burn with hot liquid or steam *Sharon was* scalded *when she bumped into a pot of boiling water.* Synonyms: **burn, scorch, boil**
SCARCE	rare, uncommon *Water is* scarce *in the Sahara Desert.* Synonyms: **sparse, infrequent**
SCATHING	overly critical *Walter was depressed by the* scathing *reviews that his play received.* Synonyms: **searing, crushing, harmful**
SCHISM	division or separation between groups of members within an organization *Because half of the student council wanted the jukebox in the cafeteria, and the other half wanted it in the library, the council suffered a* schism. Synonyms: **disunity, break, division, conflict, clash**
SCRUPULOUS	acting in accordance with a strict moral code; thorough in the performance of a task *David could not have stolen Sheila's money; he was too* scrupulous *to carry out the threat. Roger is a* scrupulous *editor who checks every word his reporters write.* Synonyms: **moral, upstanding, virtuous, principled, ethical, careful, conscientious, thorough, diligent**

WORD	DEFINITION, CONTEXT, SYNONYMS
SECURE	(v) to fasten, make secure *I had secured my suitcase in the overhead luggage rack at the beginning of the journey.* Synonyms: **fasten, bind, clamp** (adj) well-fastened, not likely to fall or come loose *My suitcase seemed secure in the luggage rack. But then it fell on me.* Synonyms: **fastened, fixed, bound, safe, stable**
SEETHE	to heave or bubble from great inner turmoil, as a volcano; to boil *Immediately after learning of Roger's gossip about me, I began to boil with anger, and by the time I reached his house I was seething.* Synonyms: **boil, bubble, steam, foam, surge, heave, swell**
SENTRY	guard, sentinel, watchman *Mitchell stood as sentry while the other boys were in the boys room smoking.* Synonyms: **watch, lookout**
SEQUEL	addition or result; story that continues a previous one *I hear they're making another sequel to the Friday the 13th movies.* Synonyms: **aftermath, outcome, continuation, consequence**
SHREWD	clever, keen-witted, cunning, sharp in practical affairs *He was a shrewd businessman and soon parlayed his meager savings into a fortune.* Synonyms: **clever, keen, astute, cunning, wily, sharp, discerning**
SIGNIFICANT	meaningful, important, relevant *A good detective knows that something that hardly seems worth noticing may be highly significant.* Synonyms: **consequential, momentous, weighty**
SINISTER	threatening, evil, menacing *His friendly manner concealed sinister designs.* Synonyms: **ominous, wicked**

WORD	DEFINITION, CONTEXT, SYNONYMS
SLACK	(n) lack of tautness or tension; a time of little activity or dullness
	There was no wind; the sails hung slack *and the boat was motionless.*
	Synonyms: **lull, relaxation**
	(adj) sluggish, idle, barely moving, loose, relaxed
	The slack *atmosphere made it unlikely that anyone would work efficiently.*
	Synonyms: **lax, negligent, remiss, careless, inactive, slow, loose, relaxed**
SOCIABLE	friendly, companionable
	Although they maintain their independence, cats are sociable *creatures.*
	Synonyms: **gregarious, companionable, friendly, affable, amiable**
SOLICIT	to seek (something) from another; to make a request of someone
	The tennis player disagreed with the first judge's decision, so he solicited *the opinion of the second judge. I* solicited *my parents for money. But they said no.*
	Synonyms: **request, seek, petition, beg**
SPECIFY	to mention, name or require specifically or exactly
	The report specified *the steps to be taken in an emergency.*
	Synonyms: **detail, identify, stipulate, itemize, define, state**
SPLICE	to join, bind, attach; in film editing, to join two pieces of film
	The editor removed all the scenes with the troublesome actress and spliced *the remainder together.*
	Synonyms: **join, bind, connect, attach, link, unite**
SPURN	reject with scorn, turn away
	When Harvey proposed to Harriet, she spurned *him; she loved another man.*
	Synonyms: **refuse, snub**
SQUALID	very dirty or foul; wretched
	The squalid *living conditions in the tenement building outraged the new tenants.*
	Synonyms: **filthy, sordid, poor, foul**
SQUANDER	to waste (often money) on some worthless purchase or practice
	While I have carefully saved money to buy the piano I have always wanted, my friend Sean has squandered *his earnings on thousands of lottery tickets.*
	Synonyms: **waste, fritter away, consume, exhaust**

WORD	DEFINITION, CONTEXT, SYNONYMS
STAUNCH	steady, loyal *A dog is a* staunch *friend.* Synonyms: **firm, sturdy, stable, solid, established, substantial, steadfast, faithful, unfailing**
STEALTHY	sneaky, secret *The children made a* stealthy *raid on the refrigerator during the night.* Synonyms: **sneaky, furtive, clandestine**
STRESS	emphasize, point out *Vanessa wrote on the blackboard the main points that she was going to* stress *in her lecture.* Synonyms: **highlight**
SUAVE	smooth, graceful, and confident in speech and behavior (sometimes insincerely) *Nina was a* suave *young woman who knew exactly how to act in any situation.* Synonyms: **smooth, gracious, courtly, worldly, sophisticated, urbane, cosmopolitan, cultivated, cultured, refined**
SUBDUE	to bring under control; to decrease the intensity of (as in the adjective subdued) *The king's army attempted to* subdue *the rebellious peasants, who were threatening to storm the castle.* Synonyms: **control, vanquish, suppress, repress, master, overcome, tame**
SUCCEED	(1) to follow, come after *George Bush* succeeded *Ronald Reagan as President.* Synonyms: **follow, replace** (2) to prosper, do well *Valerie was resolved to* succeed *in her new school.* Synonyms: **flourish, thrive**
SUCCUMB	to give in, to submit *Don't* succumb *to temptation.* Synonyms: **yield, surrender, give in, submit, die, expire**
SUFFICE	to be adequate or enough *"A light dinner should* suffice *the average person," said the thin man, eating his lettuce sandwich.* Synonyms: **satisfy**

WORD	DEFINITION, CONTEXT, SYNONYMS
SUMMIT	highest level or point *The first people to reach the summit of Mt. Everest were Tenzing Norgay and Edmund Hillary.* Synonyms: **apex, peak, top, pinnacle**
SUPERB	wonderful, superior, excellent *The main course was merely adequate, but the dessert was superb.* Synonyms: **splendid, magnificent, grand**
SUPPRESS	crush, hold in, hide *The students could hardly suppress their excitement on the last day of school.* Synonyms: **quell, contain**
SURFEIT	overly abundant supply, an excess *There certainly is no surfeit of gasoline this year.* Synonyms: **excess, glut, overabundance**
SURMISE	(v) to guess, to infer *From his torn pants and bloody nose I surmised that he had been in a fight.* Synonyms: **guess, conjecture, speculate, hypothesize, infer** (n) instance of surmising *My surmise was correct; he had been in a fight.*
SURROGATE	person or thing substituted for another *When I was ill, my friend agreed to act as my surrogate and give my speech for me.* Synonyms: **proxy, substitute, alternate**
SUSCEPTIBLE	vulnerable, liable to be affected by something *Because of her weakened state, Valerie was susceptible to infection.* Synonyms: **vulnerable, open, exposed**
SUSPENSE	fear or anticipation of waiting for something; something having to do with fear or mystery, as in a suspense novel *Joe was in an agony of suspense waiting to find out if he'd gotten the lead part in the school play.* Synonyms: **apprehension, anxiety**
SYNOPSIS	short summary, outline *Oren wrote a one-page synopsis of a 55-page book.* Synonyms: **summary, outline**

WORD	DEFINITION, CONTEXT, SYNONYMS
TACITURN	quiet, tending not to speak *Lyle is a* taciturn *boy who plays by himself and rarely says a word.* Synonyms: **quiet, shy, reserved, guarded**
TACTFUL	acting with sensitivity to others' feelings *I sent Eva to explain our sudden departure to our smelly hosts, for she is the most* tactful *person I know.* Synonyms: **diplomatic, discreet, judicious, sensitive, considerate, thoughtful, politic, delicate**
TAINT	to poison, as a drink; to corrupt, as a person *"I have* tainted *the princess's wine with a potion that will age her horribly in a few short weeks!" the witch proclaimed gleefully.* Synonyms: **poison, contaminate, infect, spoil; corrupt, debase, pervert, stain, blemish**
TAMPER	bother, interfere, meddle *Dan* tampered *with the thermostat and raised the temperature in the room to 85 degrees* Synonyms: **tinker, manipulate**
TANGIBLE	can be felt by touching; having actual substance *The storming of the castle didn't bring the soldiers* tangible *rewards, but it brought them great honor. They would have preferred the rewards.* Synonyms: **material, real, touchable, palpable, concrete, perceptible**
TAUT	stretched tightly; tense *The tightrope was* taut. Synonyms: **tight, stretched, tense, strained**
TEMPERATE	denying oneself too much pleasure; avoiding extreme positions; moderate, sensible; a mild climate *Lloyd is the most* temperate *student I have ever met; even on Friday night he goes to bed early. The* temperate *weather of California is a welcome change from the harsh winters and muggy summers of New York.* Synonyms: **self-denying; sensible, level-headed, rational, moderate, restrained, mild**
TENACIOUS	steadily pursuing a goal, unwilling to give up; stubborn *For years, against all odds, women* tenaciously *fought for the right to vote.* Synonyms: **persistent, persevering, untiring, tireless**

WORD	DEFINITION, CONTEXT, SYNONYMS
TEPID	neither hot nor cold, lukewarm; lacking character or spirit, bland *Roxanne refused to take a bath in the* tepid *water, fearing that she would catch a cold. Neither liking nor disliking Finnegan's film, the critics gave it* tepid *reviews.* Synonyms: **lukewarm, mild, temperate; unenthusiastic, halfhearted, indifferent**
TERMINATE	to stop, end *Amy and Zoe* terminated *their friendship, and never spoke to each other again.* Synonyms: **cease, finish, conclude**
TERSE	concise, brief, using few words *Kate was noted for her* terse *replies, rarely going beyond "yes" or "no."* Synonyms: **concise, succinct, compact**
TETHER	(n) chain or rope tied to an animal to keep it within specific bounds *The cheetah chewed through its* tether *and wandered off.* Synonyms: **rope, chain** (v) to fasten or confine I have to tether my dog to the fence to keep it out of the neighbor's yard. Synonyms: **tie, fasten**
TOKEN	(n) sign or symbol *I offered him a chocolate bar as a* token *of my gratitude for his help.* Synonyms: **symbol, expression, representation** (adj) existing in name or appearance only, without depth, or significance *He offered me a* token *handshake, but I knew that we were in fact still enemies.* Synonyms: **nominal, superficial, meaningless**
TORRID	extremely hot, scorching *The* torrid *weather destroyed the crops.* Synonyms: **hot, parched, sizzling**
TREPIDATION	fear, apprehension *Mike approached the door of the principal's office with* trepidation. Synonyms: **fright, anxiety, trembling, hesitation**
TRITE	lacking originality, inspiration, and interest *Lindsay's graduation speech was the same* trite *nonsense we've heard a hundred times in the past.* Synonyms: **tired, banal, unoriginal, common, stale, stock**

WORD	DEFINITION, CONTEXT, SYNONYMS
TUMULT	noise and confusion *The tumult of the No Nukes demonstrators drowned out the president's speech.* Synonyms: **racket, disorder**
TYRANNY	harsh exercise of absolute power, as in the deadly dinosaur *Tyrannosaurus Rex* *The students accused Mrs. Morgenstern of tyranny when she assigned them seats instead of letting them choose their own.* Synonyms: **oppression, repression**
ULTIMATE	marking the highest point; cannot be improved upon; final *The new fashions from Paris are the ultimate in chic.* Synonyms: **maximum, remotest, final, conclusive, last, elemental, primary, fundamental**
UNANIMOUS	approved by everyone concerned *The Student Council voted unanimously; not one person opposed the plan.* Synonyms: **unchallenged, uncontested, unopposed, united, harmonious**
UNKEMPT	messy, sloppily maintained *Sam's long hair and wrinkled shirt seemed unkempt to his grandmother; she told him he looked like a bum.* Synonyms: **sloppy, slovenly, ruffled, disheveled, messy, untidy, ragged**
USURP	to seize, take by force (most often used of abstract nouns like "power" rather than concrete nouns like "bathrobe"). *The vice principal was power-hungry, and tended to usurp the principal's power.* Synonyms: **seize, grab, steal, snatch**
VACATE	leave as in a vacation *The police ordered the demonstrators to vacate the park.* Synonyms: **depart, go**
VACUOUS	silly, empty-headed, not serious *The book that Victor loved when he was six struck him as utterly vacuous when he was twenty. But he still liked the pictures.* Synonyms: **shallow, vapid**

WORD	DEFINITION, CONTEXT, SYNONYMS
VAGUE	not clear or certain *It took us a while to find John's house because the directions were vague.* Synonyms: **nebulous, imprecise**
VEHEMENT	with deep feeling *Susanne responded to the accusation of cheating with a* vehement *denial* Synonyms: **passionate, earnest, fervent**
VEND	to sell goods *Every Saturday in the summer, craftsmen* vend *their products in the park.* Synonyms: **sell, peddle, merchandise**
VEX	to irritate to a great degree, to annoy *Your constant sniveling is beginning to* vex *me.* Synonyms: **tease, irritate, provoke, torment, pester, harass, bother, annoy**
VITALIZE	make something come alive *The government's flagrant acts of injustice* vitalized *the opposition.* Synonyms: **animate, vivify**
VIVACIOUS	lively, full of spirit *Quiet and withdrawn at first, Joan became increasingly* vivacious. Synonyms: **animated, sprightly, spirited**
WAN	unnaturally pale, lacking color *The sick child had a* wan *face.* Synonyms: **pale, ashen, bloodless**
WANTONLY	without a reason *Instead of singling out appropriate targets for his anger, the crazed robot struck out* wantonly. Synonyms: **randomly, indiscriminately**
WRATH	extreme anger *He denounced the criminals in a speech filled with righteous* wrath. Synonyms: **ire, fury, rage**
WRETCHED	miserable, pathetic *Steve felt* wretched *when he failed the test.* Synonyms: **dejected, woebegone, forlorn**

WORD	DEFINITION, CONTEXT, SYNONYMS
WRITHE	to squirm or twist as if in pain *After the being hit by a car, the pedestrian was* writhing *in pain.* Synonyms: **squirm, twitch, twist**
ZEALOUS	enthusiastic, eager *Serge was a* zealous *supporter of the cause who never missed a rally.* Synonyms: **fervent, fervid, intense, passionate**

CHAPTER 25: MATH REFERENCE

NUMBER PROPERTIES

1. **Number Categories: Integers**

   Integers are **whole numbers**; they include negative or positive whole numbers and zero.

2. **Adding/Subtracting Signed Numbers**

   To **add a positive and a negative,** first ignore the signs and find the positive difference between the number parts. Then attach the sign of the original number with the larger number part. For example, to add 23 and –34, first ignore the minus sign and find the positive difference between 23 and 34—that's 11. Then attach the sign of the number with the larger number part—in this case it's the negative sign from the –34. So, 23 + (–34) = –11.

   Make **subtraction** situations simpler by turning them into addition. Think of –17 – (–21) as –17 + (+21).

   To **add or subtract a string of positives and negatives,** first turn everything into addition. Then combine the positives and negatives so that the string is reduced to the sum of a single positive number and a single negative number.

3. **Multiplying/Dividing Signed Numbers**

   To multiply and/or divide positives and negatives, treat the number parts as usual and **attach a minus sign if there were originally an odd number of negatives.** To multiply –2, –3, and –5, first multiply the number parts: $2 \times 3 \times 5 = 30$. Then go back and note that there were three—an odd number—negatives, so the product is negative: $(-2) \times (-3) \times (-5) = -30$.

4. **Prime Numbers**

   A prime number is an integer greater than 1 that has no positive factor other than one and itself. Two is the only even prime number.

5. **Counting Consecutive Integers**

   To count consecutive integers, **subtract the smallest from the largest and add 1.** To count the integers from 13 through 31, subtract: $31 - 13 = 18$. Then add 1: $18 + 1 = 19$.

6. **PEMDAS**

   When performing multiple operations, remember to perform them in the right order of operations: **PEMDAS.** That means **Parentheses** first, then **Exponents,** then **Multiplication and Division** (left to right), and lastly, **Addition and**

Subtraction (left to right). In the expression $9 - 2 \times (5 - 3)^2 + 6 \div 3$, begin with the parentheses: $(5 - 3) = 2$. Then do the exponent: $2^2 = 4$. Now the expression is: $9 - 2 \times 4 + 6 \div 3$. Next do the multiplication and division to get: $9 - 8 + 2$, which equals 3. If you have difficulty remembering PEMDAS, try this sentence: **P**lease **E**xcuse **M**y **D**ear **A**unt **S**ally.

7. **Rounding**

Look at the number to the right of the digit in question. If it is 4 or less, leave the digit in question as it is and replace all the digits to the right with zeros. If it is 5 or more, increase the digit in question by 1 and replace all the digits to its right with zeros. To round 654,321 to the nearest hundred, look at the digit in the hundreds' place: 3. Since the number to its right is 2, the 3 remains: 654,300.

DIVISIBILITY

8. **Factor/Multiple**

The **factors** of integer n are the positive integers that divide into n with no remainder. The **multiples** of n are the integers that n divides into with no remainder. For example, 6 is a factor of 12, and 24 is a multiple of 12. 12 is both a factor and a multiple of itself, since $12 \div 12 = 1$ and $12 \times 1 = 12$.

9. **Common Multiple**

A common multiple is a number that is a multiple of two or more integers. You can always get a common multiple of two integers by **multiplying** them, but unless the two numbers are relative primes, the product will not be the *least* common multiple. For example, to find

a common multiple for 12 and 15, you could just multiply: $12 \times 15 = 180$.

10. **Least Common Multiple (LCM)**

To find the least common multiple, check out the **multiples of the larger integer** until you find one that's **also a multiple of the smaller.** To find the LCM of 12 and 15, begin by taking the multiples of 15: 15 is not divisible by 12; 30 is not; nor is 45. But the next multiple of 15, 60, *is* divisible by 12, so it's the LCM.

11. **Greatest Common Factor (GCF)**

To find the greatest common factor, break down both integers into their prime factorizations and multiply **all the prime factors they have in common.** For example $36 = 2 \times 2 \times 3 \times 3$, and $48 = 2 \times 2 \times 2 \times 2 \times 3$. What they have in common is two 2s and one 3, so the GCF is $2 \times 2 \times 3 = 12$.

12. **Even/Odd**

To predict whether a sum, difference, or product will be even or odd, just **take simple numbers such as 1 and 2 and see what happens.** There are rules—"odd times even is even," for example—but there's no need to memorize them. What happens with one set of numbers generally happens with all similar sets.

13. **Multiples of 2 and 4**

An integer is divisible by 2 (which is even) if the **last digit is even.** An integer is divisible by 4 if the **last two digits form a multiple of 4.** The last digit of 562 is 2, which is even, so 562 is a multiple of 2. The last two digits form 62, which is *not* divisible by 4, so 562 is not a multiple of 4. The integer 512, however, is divisible by 4 because the last two digits form 12, which is a multiple of 4.

14. Multiples of 3 and 9

An integer is divisible by 3 if the **sum of its digits is divisible by 3.** An integer is divisible by 9 if the **sum of its digits is divisible by 9.** The sum of the digits in 957 is 21, which is divisible by 3 but not by 9, so 957 is divisible by 3 but not by 9.

15. Multiples of 6

An integer is divisible by 6 if it meets the divisibility requirements of 2 and 3, that is, if its last digit is even and the sum of its digits is divisible by 3. The last digit of 456 is even, and the sum of its digits is 15, which is divisible by 3, so 456 is divisible by 6.

16. Multiples of 5 and 10

An integer is divisible by 5 if the **last digit is 5 or 0.** An integer is divisible by 10 if the **last digit is 0.** The last digit of 665 is 5, so 665 is a multiple of 5 but *not* a multiple of 10.

17. Remainders

The remainder is the **whole number left over after division.** For example, 487 is 2 more than 485, which is a multiple of 5, so when 487 is divided by 5, the remainder will be 2.

FRACTIONS AND DECIMALS

18. Reducing Fractions

To reduce a fraction to lowest terms, **factor out and cancel** all factors the numerator and denominator have in common.

$$\frac{28}{36} = \frac{4 \times 7}{4 \times 9} = \frac{7}{9}$$

19. Adding/Subtracting Fractions

To add or subtract fractions, first find a **common denominator,** then add or subtract the numerators.

$$\frac{2}{15} + \frac{3}{10} = \frac{4}{30} + \frac{9}{30} = \frac{4+9}{30} = \frac{13}{30}$$

20. Multiplying Fractions

To multiply fractions, **multiply** the numerators and **multiply** the denominators.

$$\frac{5}{7} \times \frac{3}{4} = \frac{5 \times 3}{7 \times 4} = \frac{15}{28}$$

21. Dividing Fractions

To divide fractions, **invert** the second one and **multiply.**

$$\frac{1}{2} \div \frac{3}{5} = \frac{1}{2} \times \frac{5}{3} = \frac{1 \times 5}{2 \times 3} = \frac{5}{6}$$

22. Converting a Mixed Number to an Improper Fraction

To convert a mixed number to an improper fraction, **multiply** the whole number part by the denominator, then **add** the numerator. The result is the new numerator (over the same denominator). To convert $7\frac{1}{3}$, first multiply 7 by 3, then add 1, to get the new numerator of 22. Put that over the same denominator, 3, to get $\frac{22}{3}$.

23. Converting an Improper Fraction to a Mixed Number

To convert an improper fraction to a mixed number, divide the denominator into the numerator to get a **whole number quotient with a remainder.** The quotient becomes the whole number part of the mixed number, and the remainder becomes the new numerator—with the same denominator. To convert $\frac{108}{5}$, divide 5 into 108, which yields 21 with a remainder of 3. Therefore, $\frac{108}{5} = 21\frac{3}{5}$.

24. Reciprocal

To find the reciprocal of a fraction, **switch the numerator and the denominator.** The reciprocal of $\frac{3}{7}$ is $\frac{7}{3}$. The reciprocal of 5 is $\frac{1}{5}$. The product of reciprocals is 1.

25. Comparing Fractions

One way to compare fractions is to **re-express them with a common denominator.** For example, $\frac{3}{4} = \frac{21}{28}$ and $\frac{5}{7} = \frac{20}{28}$. $\frac{21}{28}$ is greater than $\frac{20}{28}$, so $\frac{3}{4}$ is greater than $\frac{5}{7}$. Another way to compare fractions is to **convert them both to decimals.** For example, $\frac{3}{4}$ converts to 0.75, and $\frac{5}{7}$ converts to approximately 0.714.

26. Converting Fractions to Decimals

To convert a fraction to a decimal, **divide the bottom into the top.** To convert $\frac{5}{8}$, divide 8 into 5, yielding 0.625.

27. Converting Decimals to Fractions

To convert a decimal to a fraction, set the decimal over 1 and **multiply the numerator and denominator by 10 raised to the number of digits to the right of the decimal point.** To convert 0.625 to a fraction: $\frac{0.625}{1} \times \frac{10^3}{10^3}$, or $\frac{1,000}{1,000}$.

Then simplify: $\frac{625}{1,000} = \frac{5 \times 125}{8 \times 125} = \frac{5}{8}$.

28. Repeating Decimal

To find a particular digit in a repeating decimal, note the **number of digits in the cluster that repeats.** If there are two digits in that cluster, then every second digit is the same. If there are three digits in that cluster, then every third digit is the same. And so on. For example, the decimal equivalent of $\frac{1}{27}$ is 0.037037037..., which is best written $0.\overline{037}$. There are three digits in the repeating cluster, so every third digit is the same: 7. To find the 50th digit, look for the multiple of three just less than 50—that's 48. The 48th digit is 7, and with the 49th digit the pattern repeats with 0. The 50th digit is 3.

29. Identifying the Parts and the Whole

The key to solving most fractions and percents story problems is to identify the part and the whole. Usually you'll find the **part** associated with the verb *is/are* and the **whole** associated with the word *of.* In the sentence, "Half of the boys are blonds," the whole is the boys ("*of* the boys"), and the part is the blonds ("*are* blonds").

PERCENTS

30. Percent Formula

Whether you need to find the part, the whole, or the percent, use the same formula:

$$\textbf{Part} = \textbf{Percent} \times \textbf{Whole}$$

Example: What is 12% of 25?
Setup: Part = 0.12 × 25
(Answer: 3)

Example: Fifteen is 3% of what number?
Setup: $15 = 0.03 \times$ Whole
(Answer: 500)

Example: Forty-five is what percent of 9?
Setup: $45 = \text{Percent} \times 9$
(Answer: 500%)

31. Percent Increase and Decrease

To increase a number by a percent, **add the percent to 100 percent,** convert to a decimal, and multiply. To increase 40 by 25 percent, add 25 percent to 100 percent, convert 125 percent to 1.25, and multiply by 40. $1.25 \times 40 = 50$.

32. Finding the Original Whole

To find the **original whole before a percent increase or decrease, set up an equation.** Think of the result of a 15 percent increase over x as $1.15x$.

Example: After a 5 percent increase, the population was 59,346. What was the population before the increase?
Setup: $1.05x = 59{,}346$

33. Combined Percent Increase and Decrease

To determine the combined effect of multiple percent increases and/or decreases, **start with 100 and see what happens.**

Example: A price went up 10 percent one year, and the new price went up 20 percent the next year. What was the combined percent increase?
Setup: Year 1: $100 + (10$ percent of $100) = 110$. Year 2: $110 + (20$ percent of $110) = 132$. That's a combined 32 percent increase.

AVERAGE, MEDIAN, AND MODE

34. Average Formula

To find the average of a set of numbers, **add them up and divide by the number of numbers.**

$$\text{Average} = \frac{\text{Sum of the terms}}{\text{Number of terms}}$$

To find the average of the five numbers 12, 15, 23, 40, and 40, first add them: $12 + 15 + 23 + 40 + 40 = 130$. Then divide the sum by 5: $130 \div 5 = 26$.

35. Average of Consecutive Numbers

The average of a group of consecutive numbers is always the middle value. The average of 21, 22, 23, 24, and 25 is 23. You can also find the average of consecutive numbers by averaging the smallest and the largest.

So the average of the group of numbers above is the same as the average of 21 and 25:

$$\frac{21 + 25}{2} = \frac{46}{2} = 23$$

36. Using the Average to Find the Sum

Sum = (Average) × (Number of terms)

If the average of ten numbers is 50, then they add up to 50×10, or 500.

37. Finding the Missing Number

To find a missing number when you're given the average, **use the sum.** If the average of four numbers is 7, then the sum of those four numbers is 7×4, or 28. Suppose that three of the numbers are 3, 5, and 8. These three numbers add up to 16 of that 28, which leaves 12 for the fourth number.

38. Median

The median of a set of numbers is the **value that falls in the middle of the set.** If you have five test scores, and they are 88, 86, 57, 94, and 73, you must first list the scores in increasing or decreasing order:

$$57, 73, 86, 88, 94$$

The median is the middle number, or 86. If there is an even number of values in a set (six test scores, for instance), simply take the average of the two middle numbers.

39. Mode

The mode of a set of numbers is the **value that appears most often.** If your test scores were 88, 57, 68, 85, 99, 93, 93, 84, and 81, the mode of the scores would be 93 because it appears more often than any other score. If there is a tie for the most common value in a set, the set has more than one mode.

RATIOS, PROPORTIONS, AND RATES

40. Setting up a Ratio

To find a ratio, put the number associated with the word *of* **on top** and the quantity associated with the word *to* **on the bottom** and reduce. The ratio of 20 oranges to 12 apples is $\frac{20}{12}$, which reduces to $\frac{5}{3}$.

41. Part-to-Part Ratios and Part-to-Whole Ratios

If the parts add up to the whole, a part-to-part ratio can be turned into two part-to-whole ratios by putting **each number in the original ratio over the sum of the numbers.** If the ratio of males to females is 1 to 2, then the males-to-people ratio is $\frac{1}{1+2} = \frac{1}{3}$ and the females-to-people ratio is $\frac{2}{1+2} = \frac{2}{3}$. In other words, $\frac{2}{3}$ of all the people are female.

42. Solving a Proportion

To solve a proportion, **cross-multiply**:

$$\frac{x}{5} = \frac{3}{4}$$
$$4x = 3 \times 5$$
$$x = \frac{15}{4} = 3.75$$

43. Rate

To solve a rates problem, set up a proportion:

Example: A certain machine produces 50 pencils in 30 minutes. How many pencils will this machine produce in 75 minutes?

Set-up: $\frac{50 \text{ pencils}}{30 \text{ minutes}} = \frac{x \text{ pencils}}{75 \text{ minutes}}$

$$30x = 50 \times 75$$
$$x = 125$$

Sometimes you'll need to **use the units** to keep things straight.

Example: If snow is falling at the rate of one foot every four hours, how many inches of snow will fall in seven hours?

Setup:

$$\frac{1 \text{ foot}}{4 \text{ hours}} = \frac{x \text{ inches}}{7 \text{ hours}}$$

$$\frac{12 \text{ inches}}{4 \text{ hours}} = \frac{x \text{ inches}}{7 \text{ hours}}$$

$$4x = 12 \times 7$$

$$x = 21$$

POSSIBILITIES AND PROBABILITY

44. Counting the Possibilities

The fundamental counting principle: If there are **m ways** one event can happen and **n ways** a second event can happen, then there are **m × n ways** for the two events to happen. For example, with five shirts and seven pairs of pants to choose from, you can put together 5 × 7 = 35 different outfits.

45. Probability

$$\text{Probability} = \frac{\textbf{Favorable outcomes}}{\textbf{Total possible outcomes}}$$

If you have 12 shirts in a drawer and 9 of them are white, the probability of picking a white shirt at random is $\frac{9}{12} = \frac{3}{4}$. This probability can also be expressed as 0.75 or 75%.

EXPONENTS AND RADICALS

46. Multiplying and Dividing Powers

To multiply powers with the same base, **add the exponents and keep the same base**:

$$x^3 \times x^4 = x^{3+4} = x^7$$

To divide powers with the same base, **subtract the exponents and keep the same base**:

$$y^{13} \div y^8 = y^{13-8} = y^5$$

47. Raising Powers to Powers

To raise a power to a power, **multiply the exponents**:

$$(x^3)^4 = x^{3 \times 4} = x^{12}$$

48. Simplifying Square Roots

To simplify a square root, **factor out the perfect squares** under the radical, unsquare them and put the result in front.

$$\sqrt{12} = \sqrt{4 \times 3} = \sqrt{4} \times \sqrt{3} = 2\sqrt{3}$$

49. Adding and Subtracting Roots

You can add or subtract radical expressions **when the part under the radicals is the same:**

$$2\sqrt{3} + 3\sqrt{3} = 5\sqrt{3}$$

Don't try to add or subtract when the radical parts are different. There's not much you can do with an expression like:

$$3\sqrt{5} + 3\sqrt{7}$$

50. Multiplying and Dividing Roots

The product of square roots is equal to the **square root of the product**:

$$\sqrt{3} \times \sqrt{5} = \sqrt{3 \times 5} = \sqrt{15}$$

The quotient of square roots is equal to the **square root of the quotient**:

$$\frac{\sqrt{6}}{\sqrt{3}} = \sqrt{\frac{6}{3}} = \sqrt{2}$$

ALGEBRAIC EXPRESSIONS

51. Substitution

Replace the variables with the given values and follow the order of operations (PEMDAS)—Parentheses, Exponents, Multiplication and Division from left to right, Addition and Subtraction from left to right. To find the value of $5x - 6$ when $x = -2$, plug in -2 for x:

$$5(-2) - 6 = -10 - 6 = -16.$$

52. Adding and Subtracting Monomials

To combine like terms, **keep the variable part unchanged while adding or subtracting the coefficients:**

$$2a + 3a = (2 + 3)a = 5a$$

53. Adding and Subtracting Polynomials

To add or subtract polynomials, **combine like terms.**

$$(3x^2 + 5x - 7) - (x^2 + 12) =$$
$$(3x^2 - x^2) + 5x + (-7 - 12) =$$
$$2x^2 + 5x - 19$$

54. Multiplying Monomials

To multiply monomials, **multiply the coefficients and the variables separately:**

$$2a \times 3a = (2 \times 3)(a \times a) = 6a^2$$

SOLVING EQUATIONS

55. Solving a Linear Equation

To solve an equation, do whatever is necessary to both sides to **isolate the variable.** To solve the equation $5x - 12 = -2x + 9$, first get all the xs on one side by adding $2x$ to both sides: $7x - 12 = 9$. Then add 12 to both sides: $7x = 21$. Then divide both sides by 7: $x = 3$.

56. Solving "in Terms of"

To solve an equation for one variable **in terms of** another means to **isolate the one variable on one side of the equation,** leaving an expression containing the other variable on the other side of the equation. To solve the equation $3x - 10y = -5x + 6y$ for x in terms of y, isolate x:

$$3x - 10y = -5x + 6y$$
$$3x + 5x = 6y + 10y$$
$$8x = 16y$$
$$x = 2y$$

57. Translating from English into Algebra

To translate from English into algebra, **look for the key words and systematically turn phrases into algebraic expressions and sentences into equations.** Be careful about order, especially when subtraction is called for.

Example: The charge for a phone call is r cents for the first three minutes and s cents for each minute thereafter. What is the cost, in cents, of a phone call lasting exactly t minutes? ($t > 3$)

Setup: The charge begins with r, and then something more is added, depending on the length of the call. The amount added is s times the number of minutes past three minutes. If the total number of minutes is t, then the number of minutes past three is $t - 3$. So the charge is $r + s(t - 3)$.

58. Solving an Inequality

To solve an inequality, do whatever is necessary to both sides to **isolate the variable.** Just remember that when you **multiply or divide both sides by a negative number,** you must

reverse the sign. To solve $-5x + 7 < -3$, subtract 7 from both sides to get: $-5x < -10$. Now divide both sides by -5, remembering to reverse the sign: $x > 2$.

59. Symbolism

When a problem supplies you with an unfamiliar symbol, it will always define this symbol and indicate the operation you are to perform. Simply plug in to the prescribed definition and solve.

Example: Let $a\spadesuit$ be defined for all positive integers a by the equation $a\spadesuit = \dfrac{a}{4} - \dfrac{a}{6}$. What is $12\spadesuit$?

Setup: Just plug in and solve.
$$12\spadesuit = \frac{12}{4} - \frac{12}{6} = 3 - 2 = 1.$$

LINES AND ANGLES

60. Line Segments

A line segment is a piece of a line and has an exact measurable length. That length is the distance between the two endpoints. The midpoint is the point exactly in the middle of the line segment. The midpoint divides the line segment into two equal parts.

61. Supplementary Angles

Two angles that add up to 180 degrees are supplementary. When two lines intersect, the adjacent angles are supplementary.

In the figure above, angles x and y are adjacent and supplementary.

62. Perpendicular Lines

Lines that intersect to form right angles are said to be perpendicular. When two lines are perpendicular, they intersect to form four right angles.

Right angles are generally indicated by small boxes, as shown in the figure above.

63. Intersecting Lines

When two lines intersect, **adjacent angles are supplementary and vertical angles are equal.**

In the figure above, the angles marked $a°$ and $b°$ are adjacent and supplementary, so $a + b = 180$. Furthermore, the angles marked $a°$ and $60°$ are vertical and equal, so $a = 60$.

64. Complementary Angles

Two angles whose measure sum to 90 degrees are said to be complementary. A $30°$ angle and a $60°$ angle are complementary.

65. Right Angles

A right angle is an angle that **measures 90 degrees.** In right triangle ABC below, angle BAC is a right angle.

As shown in the figure above, a right angle is usually indicated by a small box.

TRIANGLES—GENERAL

66. Interior Angles of a Triangle

The three angles of any triangle add up to 180°.

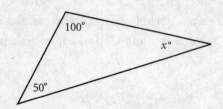

In the figure above, $x + 50 + 100 = 180$, so $x = 30$.

67. Exterior Angles of a Triangle

An exterior angle of a triangle is equal to the **sum of the remote interior angles.**

In the figure above, the exterior angle labeled $x°$ is equal to the sum of the remote interior angles: $x = 50 + 100 = 150$.

The three exterior angles of a triangle add up to 360°.

In the figure above, $a + b + c = 360$.

68. Area of a Triangle

$$\text{Area of Triangle} = \frac{1}{2}\,(\text{base})(\text{height})$$

The height is the perpendicular distance between the side that's chosen as the base and the opposite vertex.

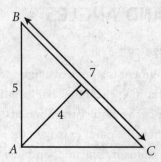

In the triangle above, 4 is the height when the 7 is chosen as the base.

$$\text{Area} = \frac{1}{2}bh = \frac{1}{2}(7)(4) = 14$$

69. Similar Triangles

Similar triangles have the same shape; **corresponding angles are equal and corresponding sides are proportional.**

The triangles above are similar because they have the same angles. The 3 corresponds to the 4 and the 6 corresponds to the s.

$$\frac{3}{4} = \frac{6}{s}$$
$$3s = 24$$
$$s = 8$$

70. Isosceles Triangles

An isosceles triangle is a triangle that has **two equal sides.** Not only are two sides equal, but the angles opposite the equal sides, called base angles, are also equal.

71. Equilateral Triangles

Equilateral triangles are triangles in which **all three sides are equal.** Since all the sides are equal, all the angles are also equal. All three angles in an equilateral triangle measure 60 degrees, regardless of the lengths of sides.

RIGHT TRIANGLES

72. Pythagorean Theorem

For all right triangles:

$$(\text{leg}_1)^2 + (\text{leg}_2)^2 = (\text{hypotenuse})^2$$

If one leg is 2 and the other leg is 3, then:

$$2^2 + 3^2 = c^2$$
$$c^2 = 4 + 9$$
$$c = \sqrt{13}$$

73. The 3-4-5 Triangle

If a right triangle's leg-to-leg ratio is 3:4, or if the leg-to-hypotenuse ratio is 3:5 or 4:5, it's a 3-4-5 triangle and you don't need to use the Pythagorean theorem to find the third side. Just figure out what multiple of 3-4-5 it is.

In the right triangle shown, one leg is 30 and the hypotenuse is 50. This is 10 times 3-4-5. The other leg is 40.

74. The 5-12-13 Triangle

If a right triangle's leg-to-leg ratio is 5:12, or if the leg-to-hypotenuse ratio is 5:13 or 12:13, then it's a 5-12-13 triangle. You don't need to use the Pythagorean theorem to find the third side. Just figure out what multiple of 5-12-13 it is.

Here one leg is 36 and the hypotenuse is 39. This is 3 times 5-12-13. The other leg is 15.

75. The 30-60-90 Triangle

The sides of a 30-60-90 triangle are in a ratio of $x : x\sqrt{3} : 2x$; the Pythagorean theorem is not necessary.

If the hypotenuse is 6, then the shorter leg is half that, or 3; and then the longer leg is equal to the short leg times $\sqrt{3}$, or $3\sqrt{3}$.

76. The Isosceles Right Triangle

An isosceles right triangle has a right angle and two 45-degree angles. The legs of an isosceles right triangle are equal. The sides of a 45-45-90 triangle are in a ratio of $x : x : x\sqrt{2}$.

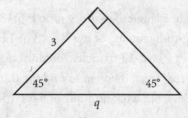

If one leg is 3, then the other leg is also 3, and the hypotenuse is equal to a leg times $\sqrt{2}$, or $3\sqrt{2}$.

QUADRILATERALS

77. Characteristics of a Rectangle

A rectangle is a **four-sided figure with four right angles.** Opposite sides are equal. Diagonals are equal.

Quadrilateral *ABCD* above is shown to have three right angles. The fourth angle therefore also measures 90°, and *ABCD* is a rectangle. The perimeter of a rectangle is equal to the sum of the lengths of the four sides, which is equivalent to 2(length + width).

78. Area of a Rectangle

Area of a Rectangle = Length × Width

The area of a 7-by-3 rectangle is 7 × 3 = 21.

79. Characteristics of a Parallelogram

A parallelogram has **two pairs of parallel sides.** Opposite sides are equal. Opposite angles are equal. Consecutive angles add up to 180°.

In the figure above, s is the length of the side opposite the 3, so $s = 3$.

The square above, with sides of length 5, has an area of $5^2 = 25$.

80. Area of a Parallelogram

Area of a Parallelogram = base × height

In parallelogram $KLMN$ above, 4 is the height when LM or KN is used as the base. Base × height = $6 \times 4 = 24$.

81. Characteristics of a Square

A square is a **rectangle with four equal sides.**

If $PQRS$ is a square, all sides are the same length as QR. The perimeter of a square is equal to four times the length of one side.

82. Area of a Square

Area of a Square = (Side)^2

CIRCLES

83. Circumference of a Circle

Circumference = $2\pi r$

In the circle above, the radius is 3, and so the circumference is $2\pi(3) = 6\pi$.

84. Area of a Circle

Area of a Circle = πr^2

The area of the circle above is $\pi(4)^2 = 16\pi$.

CHAPTER 26: WRITING SKILLS

PUNCTUATION REVIEW

COMMAS

1. USE COMMAS TO SEPARATE ITEMS IN A SERIES

If more than two items are listed in a series, they should be separated by commas. The final comma—the one that precedes the word "and"—may be omitted. An omitted final comma would not be considered an error on the PSAT.

> Example: My recipe for buttermilk biscuits includes flour, baking soda, salt, shortening, and buttermilk.

> ALSO RIGHT: My recipe for buttermilk biscuits includes flour, baking soda, salt, shortening and buttermilk.

Be watchful for commas placed **before** the first element of a series **or after** the last element.

> WRONG: My recipe for chocolate cake includes, flour, baking soda, sugar, eggs, milk and chocolate.

> WRONG: Flour, baking soda, sugar, eggs, milk and chocolate, are the ingredients in my chocolate cake.

2. USE COMMAS TO SEPARATE TWO OR MORE ADJECTIVES BEFORE A NOUN

> Example: I can't believe you sat through that long, dull movie three times in a row.

It is **incorrect** to place a comma **after** the last adjective in a series.

> WRONG: The manatee is a blubbery, bewhiskered, creature.

3. USE COMMAS TO SET OFF PARENTHETICAL CLAUSES AND PHRASES

If a phrase or clause is not necessary to the main idea expressed by a sentence, it should be set off by commas.

> Example: Phillip, who never had any formal chef's training, bakes excellent cheesecake.

The main idea here is that Phillip bakes an excellent cheesecake. The intervening clause merely serves to further describe Phillip; it should therefore be enclosed in commas.

4. USE COMMAS AFTER INTRODUCTORY PHRASES

Example: Having watered his petunias every day during the drought, Harold was disappointed when his garden was destroyed by aphids.

Example: After the banquet, Harold and Melissa went dancing.

5. USE COMMAS TO SEPARATE INDEPENDENT CLAUSES

Use a comma before a conjunction (*and, but, nor, yet*, etc.) that connects two independent clauses.

Example: Marta is good at basketball, but she's better at soccer.

SEMICOLONS

Like commas, semicolons can be used to separate independent clauses. As we saw above, two related independent clauses that are connected by a conjunction such as *and, but, nor,* or *yet* should be punctuated by a comma. If the words *and, but, nor,* or *yet* aren't used, the clauses should be separated by a semicolon.

Example: Whooping cranes are an endangered species; there are only fifty of them alive today.

Example: Whooping cranes are an endangered species, and they are unlikely to survive if we continue to pollute their habitat.

Semicolons may also be used between independent clauses connected by words like *therefore, nevertheless,* and *moreover.* For more on this topic, see the section on "Sentence Structure" in this Appendix.

COLONS

In Standard Written English, the colon is used only as a means of signaling that what follows is a list, definition, explanation, or restatement of what has gone before. A word or phrase such as *like the following, as follows, namely,* or *this* is often used along with the colon to make it clear that a list, summary, or explanation is coming up.

Example: This is what I found in her refrigerator: a moldy lime and a jar of peanut butter.

Example: Your instructions are as follows: Read the passage carefully, answer the questions, and turn over your answer sheet.

THE DASH

The dash has two uses. One is to indicate an abrupt break in thought.

Example: The alligator, unlike the crocodile, will usually not attack humans—unless, that is, she feels that her young are in danger.

The dash can also be used to set off a parenthetical expression from the rest of the sentence.

Example: At 32° Fahrenheit—which is zero on the Celsius scale—water will freeze.

THE APOSTROPHE

The apostrophe has two distinct functions. It is used with contracted verb forms to indicate that one or more letters have been eliminated:

Example: The **boy's** an expert at chess. (The boy is an expert at chess.)

Example: The **boy's** left for the day. (The boy has left for the day.)

The apostrophe is also used to indicate the possessive form of a noun.

> Example: The **boy's** face was covered with mosquito bites after a day in the swamp.

GRAMMAR REVIEW

SUBJECT-VERB AGREEMENT

The form of a verb must match, or agree with, its subject in two ways: person and number.

1. AGREEMENT OF PERSON

When we talk about "person," we're talking about whether the subject and verb of a sentence show that the author is making a statement about himself (first person), the person he is speaking to (second person), or some other person, place, or thing (third person).

First Person Subjects: **I,** we.

> Example: **I am** going to Paris. **We are** going to Rome.

Second Person Subject: you.

> Example: **Are you** sure you weren't imagining that flying saucer?

Third Person Subjects: he, she, they, it, *and names of people, places, and things.*

> Example: **He is driving** me crazy.

2. AGREEMENT OF NUMBER

When we talk about number, we're talking about whether the subject and verb show that one thing is being discussed (singular) or that more than one thing is being discussed (plural).

> HINT: Subjects and verbs must agree in number. Subjects and verbs that don't agree in number appear very frequently on the PSAT.

> WRONG: The **children catches** the school bus every morning.

> RIGHT: The **children catch** the school bus every morning.

Be especially careful of subject-verb agreement when the subject and verb are separated by a long string of words.

> WRONG: **Wild animals** in jungles all over the world **is endangered**.

> RIGHT: **Wild animals** in jungles all over the world **are endangered**.

PRONOUNS

A pronoun is a word that is used in place of a noun. The antecedent of a pronoun is the word to which the pronoun refers.

> Example: <u>Mary</u> was late for work because <u>she</u>
>   ANTECEDENT   PRONOUN
> forgot to set the alarm.

Occasionally, an antecedent will appear in a sentence *after* the pronoun.

> Example: Because <u>he</u> sneezes so often, <u>Arthur</u>
>   PRONOUN   ANTECEDENT
> always thinks <u>he</u> might have the flu.
>   PRONOUN

1. PRONOUNS AND AGREEMENT

In clear, grammatical writing, a pronoun must clearly refer to, and agree with, its antecedent.

Number agreement of pronouns is more frequently tested on the PSAT than person agreement, although you may see a question that tests person agreement.

NUMBER AND PERSON

	Singular	Plural
First Person	I, me	we, us
	my, mine	our, ours
Second Person	you	you
	your, yours	your, yours
Third Person	he, him	they, them
	she, her	
	it	
	one	
	his	their, theirs
	her, hers	
	its	
	one's	

Number Agreement

Pronouns must agree in number with their antecedents. A singular pronoun should stand in for a singular antecedent. A plural pronoun should stand in for a plural antecedent. Here's a typical PSAT pronoun error.

> WRONG: The bank turned Harry down when he applied for a loan because **their** credit department discovered that he didn't have a job.

What does the plural possessive *their* refer to? The singular noun *bank*. The singular possessive its is what we need here.

> RIGHT: The bank turned Harry down for a loan because **its** credit department discovered that he didn't have a job.

Person Agreement

Pronouns must agree with their antecedents in person too. A first-person pronoun should stand in for a first-person antecedent, and so on. One more thing to remember about which pronoun to use with which antecedent: Never use the relative pronoun *which* to refer to a human being. Use *who* or *whom* or *that*.

> WRONG: The woman **which** is standing at the piano is my sister.

> RIGHT: The woman **who** is standing at the piano is my sister.

2. PRONOUNS AND CASE

A more subtle type of pronoun problem is one in which the pronoun is in the wrong case. Look at the following chart:

CASE

	Subjective	Objective
First Person	I	me
	we	us
Second Person	you	you
Third Person	he	him
	she	her
	it	it
	they	them
	one	one
Relative Pronouns	who	whom
	that	that
	which	which

When to Use Subjective Case Pronouns

Use the subjective case for the subject of a sentence.

Example: **She** is falling asleep.

WRONG: Nancy, Claire, and **me** are going to the ballet.

RIGHT: Nancy, Claire, and **I** are going to the ballet.

Use the subjective case after a linking verb like *to be*.

Example: It is **I.**

Use the subjective case in comparisons between the subject of verbs that are not stated, but understood.

Example: Gary is taller than **they** (are).

When to Use Objective Case Pronouns

Use the objective case for the object of a verb.

Example: I called **her.**

Use the objective case for the object of a preposition.

Example: I laughed at **him.**

Use the objective case after infinitives and gerunds.

Example: Asking **him** to go was a big mistake.

Example: To give **him** the scare of his life, we all jumped out of his closet.

Use the objective case in comparisons between objects of verbs that are not stated but understood.

Example: She calls you more than (she calls) **me.**

3. WHO AND WHOM

Another thing you'll need to know is when to use the relative pronoun *who* (subjective case) and when to use the relative pronoun *whom* (objective case: *whom* goes with *him* and *them*). The following method is very helpful when you're deciding which one to use.

Example: Sylvester, (*who* or *whom*?) is afraid of the dark, sleeps with a Donald Duck night-light on.

Look only at the relative pronoun in its clause. Ignore the rest of the sentence.

(Who or whom?) is afraid of the dark.

Turn the clause into a question. Ask yourself:

Who or whom is afraid of the dark?

Answer the question with an ordinary personal pronoun.

He is.

If you've answered the question with a subjective case pronoun (as you have here), you need the subjective case who in the relative clause.

Sylvester, **who** is afraid of the dark, sleeps with a Donald Duck night-light on.

If you answer the question with an objective case pronoun, you need the objective case *whom* in the relative clause.

HINT: Try answering the question with he or him. Who goes with he (subjective case) and whom goes with him (objective case).

SENTENCE STRUCTURE

A **sentence** is a group of words that can stand alone because it expresses a complete thought. To express a complete thought, it must contain a subject, about which something is said, and a verb, which says something about the subject.

> Example: Dogs bark.
>
> Example: The explorers slept in yak-hide tents.
>
> Example: Looking out of the window, John saw a flying saucer.

Every sentence consists of at least one clause. Many sentences contain more than one clause (and phrases, too).

A **clause** is a group of words that contains a subject and a verb. "Dogs bark," "The explorers slept in a yak-hide tent," and "John saw a flying saucer" are all clauses.

A **phrase** is a group of words that does not have both a subject and a verb. "Looking out of the window" is a phrase.

1. SENTENCE FRAGMENTS

On the PSAT, some of those innocent-looking groups of words beginning with capital letters and ending with periods are only masquerading as sentences. In reality, they're sentence fragments.

A sentence fragment is a group of words that seems to be a sentence but which is *grammatically* incomplete because it lacks a subject or a verb, **or** which is *logically* incomplete because other elements necessary for it to express a complete thought are missing.

> WRONG: Eggs and fresh vegetables on sale at the farmers' market.

This is not a complete sentence because there's no verb to say something about the subject, *eggs and fresh vegetables*.

> WRONG: Because Richard likes hippopotamuses.

Even though this contains a subject (Richard) and a verb (likes), it's not a complete sentence because it doesn't express a complete thought. We don't know what's true "*because* Richard likes hippopotamuses."

> WRONG: Martha dreams about dinosaurs although.

This isn't a complete sentence because it doesn't express a complete thought. What makes Martha's dreaming about dinosaurs in need of qualification or explanation?

2. RUN-ON SENTENCES

Just as unacceptable as an incomplete sentence is a "too-complete" sentence, a run-on sentence.

A run-on sentence is actually two complete sentences stuck together either with just a comma or with no punctuation at all.

> WRONG: The children had been playing in the park, they were covered with mud.
>
> WRONG: The children had been playing in the park they were covered with mud.

There are a number of ways to fix this kind of problem. They all involve a punctuation mark or a connecting word that can properly connect two clauses.

Join the clauses with a semicolon.

> RIGHT: The children had been playing in the park; they were covered with mud.

Join the clauses with a coordinating conjunction (*and, but, for, nor, or, so, yet*) and a comma.

> RIGHT: The children had been playing in the park, and they were covered with mud.

Join the clauses with a subordinating conjunction (*after, although, if, since, while*).

> RIGHT: Because the children had been playing in the park, they were covered with mud.
>
> OR
>
> RIGHT: The children were covered with mud because they had been playing in the park.

And, of course, the two halves of a run-on sentence can be written as two separate, complete sentences.

> RIGHT: The children had been playing in the park. They were covered with mud.

VERBS

On the PSAT you'll find items that are wrong because a verb is in the wrong tense. To spot this kind of problem, you need to be familiar both with the way each tense is used **and** with the ways the tenses are used together. English has six tenses, and each has a simple form and a progressive form.

	Simple	**Progressive**
Present	I work	I am working
Past	I worked	I was working
Future	I will work	I will be working

Present Perfect	I have worked	I have been working
Past Perfect	I had worked	I had been working
Future Perfect	I will have worked	I will have been working

1. USING THE PRESENT TENSE

Use the present tense to describe a state or action occurring in the present time.

> Example: I **am** a student.
>
> Example: They **are studying** the Holy Roman Empire.

Use the present tense to describe habitual action.

> Example: They **eat** at Joe's Diner every night.
>
> Example: My father never **drinks** coffee.

Use the present tense to describe things that are always true.

> Example: The earth **is** round.
>
> Example: Grass **is** green.

2. USING THE PAST TENSE

Use the simple past tense to describe an event or state that took place at a specific time in the past and is now over and done with.

> Example: Norman **broke** his toe when he tripped over his son's tricycle.

3. USING THE FUTURE TENSE

Use the future tense for actions expected in the future.

> Example: I **will call** you on Wednesday.

We often express future actions with the expression *to be going to*.

> Example: I **am going to move** to another apartment soon.

4. USING THE PRESENT PERFECT TENSE

Use the present perfect tense for actions and states that started in the past and continue up to and into the present time.

> Example: I **have been living** here for the last two years.

Use the present perfect for actions and states that happened a number of times in the past and may happen again in the future.

> Example: I **have heard** that song several times on the radio.

Use the present perfect for something that happened at an unspecified time in the past.

> Example: Anna **has seen** that movie already.

5. USING THE PAST PERFECT TENSE

The past perfect tense is used to represent past actions or states that were completed before other past actions or states. The more recent past event is expressed in the simple past, and the earlier past event is expressed in the past perfect.

Example: When I turned my computer on this morning, I realized that I **had exited** the program yesterday without saving my work.

6. USING THE FUTURE PERFECT TENSE

Use the future perfect tense for a future state or event that will take place before another future event.

> Example: By the end of the week, I **will have worked** four hours of overtime.

7. USING THE PROPER PAST PARTICIPLE FORM

If you use the present, past, or future perfect tense, make sure that you use the past participle and not the simple past tense.

> WRONG: I have **swam** in that pool every day this week.

> RIGHT: I have **swum** in that pool every day this week.

Irregular verbs have two different forms for simple past and past participle tenses. The following are some of the most common irregular verbs.

IRREGULAR VERBS

Infinitive	Simple Past	Past Participle
arise	arose	arisen
become	became	become
begin	began	begun
blow	blew	blown
break	broke	broken
come	came	come
do	did	done
draw	drew	drawn
drink	drank	drunk

Infinitive	Simple Past	Past Participle
drive	drove	driven
eat	ate	eaten
fall	fell	fallen
fly	flew	flown
freeze	froze	frozen
give	gave	given
grow	grew	grown
know	knew	known
ride	rode	ridden
rise	rose	risen
run	ran	run
see	saw	seen
shake	shook	shaken
shrink	shrank	shrunk
sing	sang	sung
speak	spoke	spoken
take	took	taken
throw	threw	thrown

ADJECTIVES AND ADVERBS

On the PSAT, you may find an occasional item that's wrong because it uses an adjective where an adverb is called for, or vice versa.

An adjective modifies, or describes, a noun or pronoun.

> Example: A woman in a **white** dress stood next to the **old** tree.

> Example: The boat, **leaky** and **dirty**, hadn't been used in years.

An adverb modifies a verb, an adjective, or another adverb. Most, but not all, adverbs end in -*ly*. (Don't forget that some **adjectives**—*friendly, lovely*—also end in -*ly*.)

> Example: The interviewer looked *approvingly* at the *neatly* dressed applicant.

PARALLEL STRUCTURE

On the PSAT, matching constructions must be expressed in parallel form. Make sure that when a sentence contains a **list** or makes a **comparison**, the items being listed or compared exhibit parallel structure.

1. *Items in a List*

   WRONG: I love **skipping**, **jumping**, and **to play** tiddlywinks.

   WRONG: I love **to skip**, **jump**, and **to play** tiddlywinks.

   RIGHT: I love to **skip**, **jump**, and **play** tiddlywinks.

   ALSO RIGHT: I love **to skip**, **to jump**, and **to play** tiddlywinks.

   ALSO RIGHT: I love **skipping**, **jumping**, and **playing** tiddlywinks.

2. *Items in a Comparison*

   Comparisons must do more than just exhibit parallel structure. Most faulty comparisons relate to the notion that you can't compare apples and oranges. You don't merely want comparisons to be grammatically similar; they must be logically similar as well.

   WRONG: **To visualize** success is not the same as **achieving** it.

   RIGHT: **To visualize** success is not the same as **to achieve** it.

   ALSO RIGHT: **Visualizing** success is not the same as **achieving** it.

WRONG: **The rules of chess** are more complex than **checkers**.

RIGHT: **The rules of chess** are more complex than **those of checkers**.

ALSO RIGHT: **Chess** is more complex than **checkers**.

STYLE REVIEW

PRONOUNS AND REFERENCE

When we talk about pronouns and their antecedents, we say pronouns refer to or refer back to their antecedents. We noted earlier that pronouns must agree in person and number with their antecedents. But a different kind of pronoun reference problem exists when a pronoun either doesn't refer to any antecedent at all or doesn't refer clearly to one, and only one, antecedent.

Sometimes an incorrectly used pronoun has no antecedent.

POOR: Joe doesn't like what **they play** on this radio station.

Who are *they*? We can't tell, because there is no antecedent for *they*. On the PSAT, this sort of usage is an error.

RIGHT: Joe doesn't like what **the disc jockeys play** on this radio station.

Don't use pronouns without antecedents when doing so makes a sentence unclear. Sometimes a pronoun seems to have an antecedent until you look closely and see that the word that appears to be the antecedent is not a noun, but an adjective,

a possessive form, or a verb. The antecedent of a pronoun must be a noun.

WRONG: When you are painting, make sure you don't get **it** on the floor.

RIGHT: When you are painting, make sure you don't get **paint** on the floor.

Other examples of pronoun reference problems:

WRONG: I've always been interested in astronomy and finally have decided to become **one**.

RIGHT: I've always been interested in astronomy and finally have decided to become an **astronomer**.

Don't use pronouns with remote references. A pronoun that is too far away from what it refers to is said to have a remote antecedent.

WRONG: Jane quit smoking and, as a result, temporarily put on a lot of weight. **It** was very bad for her health.

RIGHT: Jane quit smoking because **it** was very bad for her health, and, as a result, she temporarily gained a lot of weight.

Don't use pronouns with faulty broad reference. A pronoun with broad reference is one that refers to a whole idea instead of to a single noun.

WRONG: He built a fence to stop people from looking into his backyard. **That's** not easy.

RIGHT: He built a fence to stop people from looking into his backyard. **The fence was not easy to build**.

REDUNDANCY

This type of style error is frequently tested on the PSAT. Words or phrases are redundant when they have basically the same meaning as something already stated in the sentence. Don't use two phrases when one is sufficient.

> WRONG: The school was **established and founded** in 1906.

> RIGHT: The school was **established** in 1906.

RELEVANCE

Irrelevant asides, even when set off in parentheses, are to be avoided on the PSAT. Everything in the sentence should serve to get across the point in question. Something unrelated to that point should be cut.

> POOR: No one can say for sure just how successful the new law will be in the fight against crime (just as no one can be sure whether he or she will ever be a victim of a crime).

> BETTER: No one can say for sure just how successful the new law will be in the fight against crime.

VERBOSITY

Sometimes having extra words in a sentence results in a style problem. Conciseness is something that is valued on the PSAT.

> WORDY: The supply of **musical instruments that are antique** is limited, so they become more valuable each year.

> BETTER: The supply of **antique musical instruments** is limited, so they become more valuable each year.

> WORDY: We **were in agreement with each other** that Max was an unsuspecting old fool.

> BETTER: We **agreed** that Max was an unsuspecting old fool.

COMMONLY MISUSED WORDS

accept/except

Don't confuse the two. To *accept* means to receive or agree to something, whereas *except* is usually a preposition meaning excluding, although it can also mean to leave out.

> WRONG: Can you **except** my apology?

> RIGHT: Can you **accept** my apology?

affect/effect

These are easy to confuse. To *affect* means to have an *effect* on something. When the word is being used as a verb, the proper word to use is almost always *affect*; when it's being used as a noun, the proper word to use is almost always *effect*. (It should be noted that *effect* can also be a verb, meaning to bring about or cause to happen.)

> WRONG: His affectations **effected** me to no good **affect**.

> RIGHT: His affectations **affected** me to no good **effect**.

among/between

In most cases, you should use *between* for two items and *among* for more than two.

> Example: The competition **between** Anne and Michael has grown more intense.

> Example: He is always at his best **among** strangers.

But use common sense. Sometimes *among* is not appropriate.

> Example: Plant the trees in the area **between** the road, the wall, and the fence.

amount/number

Amount should be used to refer to a uncountable quantity. *Number* should refer to a countable quantity.

> Example: The **amount** of food he threw away would feed a substantial **number** of people.

as/like

Like is a preposition; it takes a noun object. *As*, when functioning as a conjunction, introduces a subordinate clause. Remember, a clause is a part of a sentence containing a subject and verb.

> Example: He sings **like** an angel.

> Example: He sings **as** an angel sings.

as . . . as . . .

The idiom is *as . . . as . . .* , **not** *as . . . than . . .*

> WRONG: That suit is as expensive than this one.

> RIGHT: That suit is as expensive as this one.

fewer/less

Use *fewer* before a plural noun; use less before a singular one.

> Example: There are **fewer** apples on this tree than there were last year.

> Example: He makes **less** money than she does.

neither . . . nor . . .

The correlative conjunction is *neither . . . nor . . .* , **not** *neither . . . or . . .*

> Example: He is **neither** strong **nor** flexible.

> Avoid the redundancy caused by using *nor* following a negative.

> WRONG: Alice's departure was **not** noticed by Debby **nor** Sue.

> RIGHT: Alice's departure was **not** noticed by Debby **or** Sue.

its/it's

Many people confuse *its* and *it's*. *Its* is possessive; *it's* is a contraction of *it is*:

> Example: The cat licked **its** paws.

> Example: **It's** raining cats and dogs.

their/they're/there

Many people confuse *their*, *there*, and *they're*. *Their* is possessive; *they're* is a contraction of *they are*:

> Example: The girls rode **their** bikes home.

> Example: **They're** training for the big race.

There has two uses: It can indicate place and it can be used as an expletive—a word that doesn't do anything in a sentence except delay the subject.

> Example: Put the book over **there**.

> Example: **There** will be fifteen runners competing for the prize.

COMMONLY TESTED IDIOMS

Some phrases are wrong simply because that's just not the way we say it in English. This is especially true of preposition-verb word combinations. For instance,

> WRONG: The fashion police **frowns at** wearing hats adorned with flowers.

> RIGHT: The fashion police **frowns upon** wearing hats adorned with flowers.

The first sentence is only wrong because *frowns at* is not the correct idiomatic expression. Either your ear will recognize the correct idiom or it won't. Can you trust your ear on the following commonly tested idioms?

Commonly Tested Idioms

associate *with*	different *from*
accuse *of*	discriminate *against*
apologize *for*	distinguish *from*
arrive *at*	dream *about/of*
believe *in*	forbid *to*
believe *to be*	frown *upon*
apologize *for*	object *to*
attribute *to*	prohibit *from*
continue *to*	substitute *for*
contrast *with*	target *at*
credit *with*	use *as*
decide *to*	view *as*
define *as*	worry *about*